The Editor

DAVID S. REYNOLDS is Distinguished Professor of English and American Studies at the Graduate Center of the City University of New York. His books include *Walt Whitman's America: A Cultural Biography*; *John Brown, Abolitionist*; *Beneath the American Renaissance: The Subversive Imagination in the Age of Emerson and Melville*; *Mightier than the Sword: "Uncle Tom's Cabin" and the Battle for America*; *Waking Giant: America in the Age of Jackson*; *Walt Whitman*; *George Lippard*; and *Faith in Fiction: The Emergence of Religious Literature in America*. Reynolds is the editor or co-editor of seven books, including Walt Whitman's *Leaves of Grass: The 150th Anniversary Edition*, *A Historical Guide to Walt Whitman*, Harriet Beecher Stowe's *Uncle Tom's Cabin: The Splendid Edition*, and George Lippard's *The Quaker City; or, The Monks of Monk Hall*. He is the winner of the Bancroft Prize, the Christian Gauss Award, the Ambassador Book Award, the Gustavus Myers Outstanding Book Prize, the John Hope Franklin Publication Prize (Honorable Mention), and finalist for the National Book Critics Circle Award. He is a regular contributor to the *New York Times Book Review*.

A NORTON CRITICAL EDITION

LINCOLN'S SELECTED WRITINGS

AUTHORITATIVE TEXTS

LINCOLN IN HIS ERA

MODERN VIEWS

Edited by

DAVID S. REYNOLDS
THE GRADUATE CENTER
OF THE
CITY UNIVERSITY OF NEW YORK

W · W · NORTON & COMPANY · *New York* · *London*

W. W. Norton & Company has been independent since its founding in 1923, when William Warder Norton and Mary D. Herter Norton first published lectures delivered at the People's Institute, the adult education division of New York City's Cooper Union. The firm soon expanded its program beyond the Institute, publishing books by celebrated academics from America and abroad. By midcentury, the two major pillars of Norton's publishing program—trade books and college texts—were firmly established. In the 1950s, the Norton family transferred control of the company to its employees, and today—with a staff of four hundred and a comparable number of trade, college, and professional titles published each year—W. W. Norton & Company stands as the largest and oldest publishing house owned wholly by its employees.

Copyright © 2015 by W. W. Norton & Company, Inc.

Library of Congress Cataloging-in-Publication Data

Lincoln, Abraham, 1809–1865
  [Works. Selections]
  Lincoln's selected writings : authoritative texts : Lincoln in his era : commentary and contexts : modern views / edited by David S. Reynolds, the Graduate Center of the City University of New York. — First edition.
      pages cm. — (A Norton critical edition)
  Includes bibliographical references and index.
  ISBN 978-0-393-92179-3 (pbk.)
  1. Lincoln, Abraham, 1809–1865.   2. Presidents—United States—Biography.   3. United States—Politics and government—1861–1865.
4. United States—Politics and government—1815–1861.   I. Reynolds, David S., 1948– editor.   II. Title.
  E457.92 2014
  973.7092—dc23

                                                                    2014005853

W. W. Norton & Company, Inc., 500 Fifth Avenue, New York, NY 10110
wwnorton.com

W. W. Norton & Company Ltd., Castle House, 75/76 Wells Street,
London W1T 3QT

1 2 3 4 5 6 7 8 9 0

Contents

Lincoln in His Era

Illustrations

Preface

"Of all the great national heroes and statesmen of history Lincoln is the only real giant."[1] This statement by Leo Tolstoy is hard to dispute. Abraham Lincoln (1809–1865) is generally recognized as America's greatest president and its central historical figure.

Lincoln embodied many American ideals and qualities. The archetypal self-made man, he was born in a one-room Kentucky log cabin, had a hardscrabble frontier childhood, and rose through various occupations to become an Illinois lawyer, a Whig congressman, and the sixteenth president of the United States. An autodidact, he had less than one year of formal education and yet could recite Shakespeare from memory, and he enjoyed a variety of writings, including *Aesop's Fables*, newspapers, Robert Burns's poetry, William Ellery Channing's sermons, ancient history, popular humor columns, and volumes of Daniel Webster's and Henry Clay's speeches. Inquisitive and curious, he rejected his parents' Calvinistic Baptist religion and passed through a skeptical, freethinking phase before reaching a panreligious outlook that took into account both divine providence and human effort, fate and action. Folksy and funny, he was given to storytelling and telling bawdy jokes; yet he had a melancholy side that, some say, yielded periods of depression.

He excelled in different roles. As a lawyer, he handled some five thousand cases over twenty-four years. As a politician, he skillfully built the Whig Party in Illinois before navigating his way to the Republican nomination for president in 1860. As president, he developed a firm-handed style that involved making highly difficult but ultimately effective decisions that led to the emancipation of America's four million enslaved blacks. As commander-in-chief, he helped guide battlefield strategy and made a succession of military appointments that ended with the brutal, victorious Hammer and Anvil campaign of Sherman and Grant.

Lincoln was hardly alone in combining his hatred of slavery with a deep commitment to the Union, the Constitution, and the Declaration of Independence. His antislavery reading of the Declaration had appeared at least as early as the congressional debates during the Missouri crisis in 1819. Thereafter, it had shaped almost every variety of abolitionism and then influenced the Liberty and Free Soil Parties in the 1840s. But he was the first to bring it to national prominence—in his 1858 debates with Senator Stephen Douglas—and then to capitalize on it fully in politics, with his successful runs for the presidency in 1860 and 1864. His initial public pronouncements on slavery were not nearly as radical as those of abolitionists like William Lloyd Garrison or Wendell Phillips, whom he

---

1. Leo Tolstoy, interview with Count S. Stakeberg, in *The Lincoln Anthology: Great Writers on His Life and Legacy from 1860 to Now*, edited by Harold Holzer (New York, 2009), p. 386.

opposed because of their dismissal of the Constitution (which they regarded as a proslavery document) and their demand for the separation of the North from the South. But radicalism is not itself a measure of sincerity or devotion to the antislavery cause. Lincoln loathed slavery to his core. He rebuilt his political career in the 1850s on his unswerving belief that slavery had to be placed on the road to extinction, and he is justly remembered as the Great Emancipator.

This moniker, of course, is questioned by those who take note of his conservative streak. Through much of his career he accepted the hidebound racial views that were prevalent in his era. He once said that there is "a physical difference" between whites and blacks[2] that might prevent the races from living on equal terms in America, which helps explain his initial support of so-called colonization, the plan to deport emancipated blacks to Liberia, Central America, or elsewhere. Critics of Lincoln focus on such views and on the fact that the Emancipation Proclamation, which freed enslaved people living in states disloyal to the Union, was a partial gesture made under military necessity. But we must recognize that the Emancipation Proclamation was an enormously important document, greeted with wild celebration among many Americans and with bitter hostility by others. It's utterly mistaken to say that Lincoln was a reluctant emancipator and that "racism was the center and circumference of his being," as one historian writes.[3] There's no reason to doubt declarations by Lincoln such as "I have always hated slavery, I think as much as any Abolitionist," or "I hate it because of the monstrous injustice of slavery itself. I hate it because it deprives our republican example of its just influence in the world."[4] Lincoln's respect for African Americans grew measurably during the Civil War as he witnessed the courage of black Union soldiers and became close to black leaders like Frederick Douglass, who said, "In all my interviews with Mr. Lincoln, I was impressed with his entire freedom from popular prejudice against the colored race."[5] He also abandoned the idea of deporting blacks and revised his position from simply trying to stop slavery's spread to advocating its extinction by force and by constitutional amendment. Toward the end of the war he proposed that the vote should be granted to blacks who were, in his phrase, "very intelligent" or who had served in the Union Army[6]—a significant step toward the Fifteenth Amendment, which in 1870 awarded suffrage to African American males.

The driving quest of Lincoln's political life was to hasten slavery's destruction without violating the Constitution or destroying the existing political system, as disunionists on both sides of the slavery divide felt impelled to do. He wanted to end slavery while preserving the United States, which he considered the world's greatest hope for democracy. His choice was to aim toward emancipation while keeping within the nation's established governmental structures and respecting the Union and the electoral process, which he defended in the firmest military manner.

2. First Lincoln-Douglas Debate, Ottawa, Illinois, August 21, 1858 (see p. 149).
3. Lerone Bennett, *Forced into Glory: Abraham Lincoln's White Dream* (Chicago, 2000), p. 66.
4. Speech at Chicago, Illinois, July 10, 1858 (see p. 139) and speech on the Kansas-Nebraska Act, October 16, 1854 (see p. 86).
5. *Reminiscences of Abraham Lincoln by Distinguished Men of His Time*, edited by Allen T. Rice (New York, 1886), p. 193.
6. To Michael Hahn, March 13, 1864 (see p. 338).

He bolstered the antislavery cause by presenting the Founding Fathers in the best light possible. That was a delicate task, for the Founders had left slavery intact, even though some of them—particularly Hamilton, Franklin, and Paine—publicly denounced it. Lincoln's argument, advanced in several speeches, was that Founders had put slavery on a path to extinction and that the nation had swerved from that path. Besides presenting a forcefully egalitarian reading of the Declaration, he pointed to the Founders' plan to abolish the slave trade by 1808 and their passage of the Northwest Ordinance, which barred slavery in territories northwest of the Ohio River. He insisted that this original antislavery impulse had been betrayed over the years as result of several proslavery measures, most notably the Kansas-Nebraska Act of 1854, which opened up the western territories for slavery, and the Dred Scott decision of 1857, which denied citizenship to blacks.

But Lincoln did more than just bring attention to antislavery ideals intrinsic in the Founders' vision; he positively reshaped these ideals through his speeches. Some of these speeches—such as his arguments in the debates with Douglas or the address at Cooper Union in New York— were notable for their lawyerly logic and historical acuity. Others, particularly the Gettysburg Address and the Second Inaugural, were pithy and inspirational. Several of his speeches contain resonant images—the House Divided, the better angels of our nature, the mystic chords of memory, a new birth of freedom, malice toward none—that have attained timelessness and universality.

The present volume shows many sides of Lincoln. Among the thousands of books on Lincoln, this is the only one to date that brings together three types of Lincoln-related writings: a broad sampling of his own works, a range of comments on him—from the laudatory to the harshly critical—in his own era, and modern views of him. Any such volume is, by nature, selective, and there are many fine writings on Lincoln that I've had to omit. From a multitude of possibilities, I've selected writings by and about Lincoln that I feel are representative, stimulating, and informative. My choice of texts accords with my view that so a colossal figure as Lincoln can be best approached from a multidimensional, interdisciplinary perspective.

The historian and activist W. E. B. Du Bois remarked that Lincoln was "big enough to be inconsistent. . . . He was a man—a big, inconsistent, brave man."[7] But Lincoln was actually far bigger than that. He was able to own and even overcome many of his inconsistencies, and despite some severe personal setbacks, he maintained a firm moral purpose that steered America through the worst crisis of its history.

This book tries to capture his unmatched amplitude of spirit.

7. W. E. B. Du Bois, from *The Crisis* (May 1922), in *The Lincoln Anthology*, p. 435.

A Note on the Texts
and Acknowledgments

Almost all the Lincoln writings in this volume are from the Abraham Lincoln Association's *The Collected Works of Abraham Lincoln*, 8 vols. (New Brunswick, N.J., 1953–55), edited by Roy P. Basler, with the assistance of Marion Dolores Pratt and Lloyd A. Dunlap.* "Verse on Lee's Invasion of the North, July 19, 1863," is taken from the *Supplement* (1974) to *The Collected Works*. One text, "To Erastus Corning and Others," is reprinted from the June 15, 1863, *New York Tribune*. Draft of the Emancipation Proclamation, July 22, 1862, is transcribed from *Abraham Lincoln Papers at the Library of Congress*, Manuscript Division (Washington, D.C.: American Memory Project, 2000–02).

In this volume, I retain Lincoln's original spelling, grammar, and usage, but I silently suppress the brackets that Roy B. Basler put around his conjectural insertions as result of damaged or unreadable manuscripts. Take, for example, the following passage in Lincoln's "Fragments on the Tariff," which appears in Basler with bracketed additions:

> While the uselessness of the carrying labour is [equally true] of all the articles mentioned, and of many others not men[tioned,] it is, perhaps, more glaringly obvious in relation to the cotten [goods we] purchase from abroad. The raw cotten, from which they are made, itself grows in our own country; is carried by land and by water to England, [is] there spun, wove, dyed, stamped &c; and then carried back [again] and worn in the very country where it grew, and partly by the very persons who grew it.

In reproducing these sentences, I keep Lincoln's errors (e.g., "cotten") while discarding Basler's brackets. The passage thus becomes:

> While the uselessness of the carrying labour is equally true of all the articles mentioned, and of many others not mentioned, it is, perhaps, more glaringly obvious in relation to the cotten goods we purchase from abroad. The raw cotten, from which they are made, itself grows in our own country; is carried by land and by water to England, is there spun, wove, dyed, stamped &c; and then carried back again and worn in the very country where it grew, and partly by the very persons who grew it.

Many of Lincoln's writings, especially his letters, appear in their original form signed by him ("A. Lincoln" was his preferred signature). For most of the documents in this book, I have dropped the signature.

---

* These appear by permission of the American Lincoln Association.

I'm grateful to Sean Wilentz and Eric Foner for their input into this volume. I'm indebted to Ryan Everitt, who tirelessly helped reproduce and format documents, and to Christina Katopodis and Aline Reynolds, who gave me invaluable assistance in the proofing phase. Special thanks go to Carol Bemis, Rivka Genesen, and Thea Goodrich at Norton, who have been wonderful to work with.

Abbreviations

ALP *Abraham Lincoln Papers at the Library of Congress*, Manuscript Division. Washington, D.C.: American Memory Project, 2000–02.

CP *The Salmon P. Chase Papers*. Edited by John Niven. 5 vols. Kent, OH: Kent State University Press, 1993–98.

CW *The Collected Works of Abraham Lincoln*. 8 vols. Edited by Roy P. Basler. New Brunswick, NJ, Rutgers University Press, 1953–55.

HI *Herndon's Informants: Letters, Interviews, and Statements about Abraham Lincoln*. Edited by Douglas L. Wilson, et al. Urbana: University of Illinois Press, 1998.

HW William H. Herndon and Jesse W. Weik. *Abraham Lincoln: The True Story of a Great Life*. 2 vols. New York: D. Appleton, 1892.

JAH *Journal of American History*.

JALA *Journal of the Illinois State Historical Society*.

OR *The War of the Rebellion: A Compilation of the Official Records of the Union and Confederate Armies*. Edited by Robert N. Scott, et al. 70 vols. Washington, D.C.: Government Printing Office, 1880–1901.

PW Walt Whitman. *Prose Works, 1892*. Edited by Floyd Stovall. 2 vols. New York: New York University Press, 1963. Vol. 1: *Specimen Days* (1963). Vol. 2: *Collected and Other Prose* (1964).

WD *Diary of Gideon Welles*. Edited by Howard K. Beale. 3 vols. New York: Norton, 1960.

LINCOLN'S
SELECTED WRITINGS

To the People of Sangamo County[1]

To the People of Sangamo County
Fellow-citizens: Having become a candidate for the honorable office of one of your representatives in the next General Assembly of this state, in accordance with an established custom, and the principles of true republicanism, it becomes my duty to make known to you—the people whom I propose to represent—my sentiments with regard to local affairs.

Time and experience have verified to a demonstration, the public utility of internal improvements. That the poorest and most thinly populated countries would be greatly benefitted by the opening of good roads, and in the clearing of navigable streams within their limits, is what no person will deny. But yet it is folly to undertake works of this or any other kind, without first knowing that we are able to finish them—as half finished work generally proves to be labor lost. There cannot justly be any objection to having rail roads and canals, any more than to other good things, provided they cost nothing. The only objection is to paying for them; and the objection to paying arises from the want of ability to pay.

With respect to the county of Sangamo, some more easy means of communication than we now possess, for the purpose of facilitating the task of exporting the surplus products of its fertile soil, and importing necessary articles from abroad, are indispensably necessary. A meeting has been held of the citizens of Jacksonville, and the adjacent country, for the purpose of deliberating and enquiring into the expediency of constructing a rail road from some eligible point on the Illinois river, through the town of Jacksonville, in Morgan county, to the town of Springfield, in Sangamo county. This is, indeed, a very desirable object. No other improvement that reason will justify us in hoping for, can equal in utility the rail road. It is a never failing source of communication, between places of business remotely situated from each other. Upon the rail road the regular progress of commercial intercourse is not interrupted by either high or low water, or freezing weather, which are the principal difficulties that render our future hopes of water communication precarious and uncertain. Yet, however desirable an object the construction of a rail road through our country may be; however high our imaginations may be heated at thoughts of it—there is always a heart appalling shock accompanying the account of its cost, which forces us to shrink from our pleasing anticipations. The probable cost of this contemplated rail road is estimated at $290,000;—the bare statement of which, in my opinion, is sufficient to justify the belief, that the improvement of Sangamo river is an object much better suited to our infant resources.

Respecting this view, I think I may say, without the fear of being contradicted, that its navigation may be rendered completely practicable, as high as the mouth of the South Fork, or probably higher, to vessels of from 25 to 30 tons burthen, for at least one half of all common years, and to vessels of much greater burthen a part of that time. From my peculiar circumstances, it is probable that for the last twelve months I have given

---

1. Or Sangamon, the county in central Illinois where the Kentucky-born Lincoln lived, first in New Salem (1831–37) and then in the state capital of Springfield (1837–61).

as particular attention to the stage of the water in this river, as any other person in the country. In the month of March, 1831, in company with others, I commenced the building of a flat boat on the Sangamo, and finished and took her out in the course of the spring. Since that time, I have been concerned in the mill at New Salem. These circumstances are sufficient evidence, that I have not been very inattentive to the stages of the water. The time at which we crossed the mill dam, being in the last days of April, the water was lower than it had been since the breaking of winter in February, or than it was for several weeks after. The principal difficulties we encountered in descending the river, were from the drifted timber, which obstructions all know is not difficult to be removed. Knowing almost precisely the height of water at that time, I believe I am safe in saying that it has as often been higher as lower since.

From this view of the subject, it appears that my calculations with regard to the navigation of the Sangamo, cannot be unfounded in reason; but whatever may be its natural advantages, certain it is, that it never can be practically useful to any great extent, without being greatly improved by art. The drifted timber, as I have before mentioned, is the most formidable barrier to this object. Of all parts of this river, none will require so much labor in proportion, to make it navigable, as the last thirty or thirty-five miles; and going with the meanderings of the channel, when we are this distance above its mouth, we are only between twelve and eighteen miles above Beardstown, in something near a straight direction; and this route is upon such low ground as to retain water in many places during the season, and in all parts such as to draw two-thirds or three-fourths of the river water at all high stages.

This route is upon prairie land the whole distance;—so that it appears to me, by removing the turf, a sufficient width and damming up the old channel, the whole river in a short time would wash its way through, thereby curtailing the distance, and increasing the velocity of the current very considerably, while there would be no timber upon the banks to obstruct its navigation in future; and being nearly straight, the timber which might float in at the head, would be apt to go clear through. There are also many places above this where the river, in its zig zag course, forms such complete peninsulas, as to be easier cut through at the necks than to remove the obstructions from the bends—which if done, would also lessen the distance.

What the cost of this work would be, I am unable to say. It is probable, however, it would not be greater than is common to streams of the same length. Finally, I believe the improvement of the Sangamo river, to be vastly important and highly desirable to the people of this county; and if elected, any measure in the legislature having this for its object, which may appear judicious, will meet my approbation, and shall receive my support.

It appears that the practice of loaning money at exorbitant rates of interest, has already been opened as a field for discussion; so I suppose I may enter upon it without claiming the honor, or risking the danger, which may await its first explorer. It seems as though we are never to have an end to this baneful and corroding system, acting almost as prejudicial to the general interests of the community as a direct tax of several thousand dollars annually laid on each county, for the benefit of a few individuals only, unless there be a law made setting a limit to the rates of usury. A law for this purpose, I am of opinion, may be made, without materially injuring any class of people. In cases of extreme necessity there could always be means found to cheat the law, while in all other cases it would have its intended effect. I would not favor the passage of a law upon this subject, which might be very easily evaded. Let it be such that the labor and difficulty of evading it, could only be justified in cases of the greatest necessity.

Upon the subject of education, not presuming to dictate any plan or system respecting it, I can only say that I view it as the most important subject which we as a people can be engaged in. That every man may receive at least, a moderate education, and thereby be enabled to read the histories of his own and other countries, by which he may duly appreciate the value of our free institutions, appears to be an object of vital importance, even on this account alone, to say nothing of the advantages and satisfaction to be derived from all being able to read the scriptures and other works, both of a religious and moral nature, for themselves. For my part, I desire to see the time when education, and by its means, morality, sobriety, enterprise and industry, shall become much more general than at present, and should be gratified to have it in my power to contribute something to the advancement of any measure which might have a tendency to accelerate the happy period.

With regard to existing laws, some alterations are thought to be necessary. Many respectable men have suggested that our estray laws—the law respecting the issuing of executions, the road law, and some others, are deficient in their present form, and require alterations. But considering the great probability that the framers of those laws were wiser than myself, I should prefer not meddling with them, unless they were first attacked by others, in which case I should feel it both a privilege and a duty to take that stand, which in my view, might tend most to the advancement of justice.

But, Fellow-Citizens, I shall conclude. Considering the great degree of modesty which should always attend youth, it is probable I have already been more presuming than becomes me. However, upon the subjects of which I have treated, I have spoken as I thought. I may be wrong in regard to any or all of them; but holding it a sound maxim, that it is better to be only sometimes right, than at all times wrong, so soon as I discover my opinions to be erroneous, I shall be ready to renounce them.

Every man is said to have his peculiar ambition. Whether it be true or not, I can say for one that I have no other so great as that of being truly esteemed of my fellow men, by rendering myself worthy of their esteem. How far I shall succeed in gratifying this ambition, is yet to be developed. I am young and unknown to many of you. I was born and have ever remained in the most humble walks of life. I have no wealthy or popular relations to recommend me. My case is thrown exclusively upon the independent voters of this county, and if elected they will have conferred a favor upon me, for which I shall be unremitting in my labors to compensate. But if the good people in their wisdom shall see fit to keep me in the background, I have been too familiar with disappointments to be very much chagrined. Your friend and fellow-citizen,

New Salem, March 9, 1832

To the Editor of the Sangamo Journal

To the Editor of the Journal: New Salem, June 13, 1836.
In your paper of last Saturday, I see a communication over the signature
of "Many Voters," in which the candidates who are announced in the
Journal, are called upon to "show their hands." Agreed. Here's mine!

I go for all sharing the privileges of the government, who assist in bearing its burthens. Consequently I go for admitting all whites to the right of
suffrage, who pay taxes or bear arms, (by no means excluding females.)

If elected, I shall consider the whole people of Sangamon my constituents, as well those that oppose, as those that support me.[1]

While acting as their representative, I shall be governed by their will,
on all subjects upon which I have the means of knowing what their will
is; and upon all others, I shall do what my own judgment teaches me
will best advance their interests. Whether elected or not, I go for distrib-
uting the proceeds of the sales of the public lands to the several states, to
enable our state, in common with others, to dig canals and construct rail
roads, without borrowing money and paying interest on it.

If alive on the first Monday in November, I shall vote for Hugh L. White
for President.[2] Very respectfully,

Protest in the Illinois Legislature on Slavery

The following protest was presented to the House, which was read and
ordered to be spread on the journals, to wit:

"Resolutions upon the subject of domestic slavery having passed both
branches of the General Assembly at its present session, the undersigned
hereby protest against the passage of the same.

They believe that the institution of slavery is founded on both injustice
and bad policy; but that the promulgation of abolition doctrines tends
rather to increase than to abate its evils.

They believe that the Congress of the United States has no power,
under the constitution, to interfere with the institution of slavery in the
different States.

They believe that the Congress of the United States has the power,
under the constitution, to abolish slavery in the District of Columbia; but
that that power ought not to be exercised unless at the request of the
people of said District.

The difference between these opinions and those contained in the said
resolutions, is their reason for entering this protest."

DAN STONE,

A. LINCOLN,

Representatives from the county of Sangamon.

March 3, 1837

1. In the August 11 election for the Illinois House of Representatives, Lincoln received the highest number of votes among seventeen candidates from Sangamon County. All seven members
   of the legislature elected from the country were Whigs.
2. U.S. Senator White of Tennessee won Sangamon County but lost Illinois to Martin Van Buren,
   who won all but two states that year.

To Mary S. Owens[1]

Friend Mary   Springfield, May 7. 1837

I have commenced two letters to send you before this, both of which displeased me before I got half done, and so I tore them up. The first I thought wasn't serious enough, and the second was on the other extreme. I shall send this, turn out as it may.

This thing of living in Springfield is rather a dull business after all, at least it is so to me. I am quite as lonesome here as I ever was anywhere in my life. I have been spoken to by but one woman since I've been here, and should not have been by her, if she could have avoided it. I've never been to church yet, nor probably shall not be soon. I stay away because I am conscious I should not know how to behave myself.

I am often thinking about what we said of your coming to live at Springfield. I am afraid you would not be satisfied. There is a great deal of flourishing about in carriages here, which it would be your doom to see without shareing in it. You would have to be poor without the means of hiding your poverty. Do you believe you could bear that patiently? Whatever woman may cast her lot with mine, should any ever do so, it is my intention to do all in my power to make her happy and contented; and there is nothing I can imagine, that would make me more unhappy than to fail in the effort. I know I should be much happier with you than the way I am, provided I saw no signs of discontent in you. What you have said to me may have been in jest, or I may have misunderstood it. If so, then let it be forgotten; if otherwise, I much wish you would think seriously before you decide. For my part I have already decided. What I have said I will most positively abide by, provided you wish it. My opinion is that you had better not do it. You have not been accustomed to hardship, and it may be more severe than you now immagine. I know you are capable of thinking correctly on any subject; and if you deliberate maturely upon this, before you decide, then I am willing to abide your decision.

You must write me a good long letter after you get this. You have nothing else to do, and though it might not seem interesting to you, after you had written it, it would be a good deal of company to me in this "busy wilderness." Tell your sister I dont want to hear any more about selling out and moving. That gives me the hypo[2] whenever I think of it. Yours, &c.

To Mary S. Owens

Friend Mary.   Springfield Aug. 16th 1837

You will, no doubt, think it rather strange, that I should write you a letter on the same day on which we parted; and I can only account for it by supposing, that seeing you lately makes me think of you more than usual,

---

1. A twenty-six-year-old Kentucky woman staying in New Salem with her sister, Mrs. Bennett Abell, who tried to arrange a match between Lincoln and Mary. The couple reached some kind of understanding that apparently proved mutually unsatisfactory.
2. I.e., hypochondria; the blues.

while at our late meeting we had but few expressions of thoughts. You must know that I can not see you, or think of you, with entire indifference; and yet it may be, that you, are mistaken in regard to what my real feelings towards you are. If I knew you were not, I should not trouble you with this letter. Perhaps any other man would know enough without further information; but I consider it my peculiar right to plead ignorance, and your bounden duty to allow the plea. I want in all cases to do right, and most particularly so, in all cases with women. I want, at this particular time, more than any thing else, to do right with you, and if I knew it would be doing right, as I rather suspect it would, to let you alone, I would do it. And for the purpose of making the matter as plain as possible, I now say, that you can now drop the subject, dismiss your thoughts (if you ever had any) from me forever, and leave this letter unanswered, without calling forth one accusing murmer from me. And I will even go further, and say, that if it will add any thing to your comfort, or peace of mind, to do so, it is my sincere wish that you should. Do not understand by this, that I wish to cut your acquaintance. I mean no such thing. What I do wish is, that our further acquaintance shall depend upon yourself. If such further acquaintance would contribute nothing to your happiness, I am sure it would not to mine. If you feel yourself in any degree bound to me, I am now willing to release you, provided you wish it; while, on the other hand, I am willing, and even anxious to bind you faster, if I can be convinced that it will, in any considerable degree, add to your happiness. This, indeed, is the whole question with me. Nothing would make me more miserable than to believe you miserable—nothing more happy, than to know you were so.

In what I have now said, I think I can not be misunderstood; and to make myself understood, is the only object of this letter.

If it suits you best to not answer this—farewell—a long life and a merry one attend you. But if you conclude to write back, speak as plainly as I do. There can be neither harm nor danger, in saying, to me, any thing you think, just in the manner you think it.

My respects to your sister. Your friend

Address to the Young Men's Lyceum of Springfield, Illinois

The Perpetuation of Our Political Institutions

As a subject for the remarks of the evening, *the perpetuation of our political institutions*, is selected.

In the great journal of things happening under the sun, we, the American People, find our account running, under date of the nineteenth century of the Christian era. We find ourselves in the peaceful possession, of the fairest portion of the earth, as regards extent of territory, fertility of soil, and salubrity of climate. We find ourselves under the government of a system of political institutions, conducing more essentially to the ends of civil and religious liberty, than any of which the history of former times tells us. We, when mounting the stage of existence, found ourselves the legal inheritors of these fundamental blessings. We toiled not in the acquirement or establishment of them—they are a legacy bequeathed us, by a *once* hardy, brave, and patriotic, but *now* lamented and departed race of ancestors. Their's was the task (and nobly they performed it) to possess themselves, and through themselves, us, of this goodly land; and to uprear upon its hills and its valleys, a political edifice of liberty, and equal rights; 'tis ours only, to transmit these, the former, unprofaned by the foot of an invader; the latter, undecayed by the lapse of time, and untorn by usurpation—to the latest generation that fate shall permit the world to know. This task of gratitude to our fathers, justice to ourselves, duty to posterity, and love for our species in general, all imperatively require us faithfully to perform.

How, then, shall we perform it? At what point shall we expect the approach of danger? By what means shall we fortify against it? Shall we expect some transatlantic military giant, to step the Ocean, and crush us at a blow? Never! All the armies of Europe, Asia and Africa combined, with all the treasure of the earth (our own excepted) in their military chest; with a Buonaparte for a commander, could not by force, take a drink from the Ohio, or make a track on the Blue Ridge, in a trial of a thousand years.

At what point then is the approach of danger to be expected? I answer, if it ever reach us, it must spring up amongst us. It cannot come from abroad. If destruction be our lot, we must ourselves be its author and finisher. As a nation of freemen, we must live through all time, or die by suicide.

I hope I am over wary; but if I am not, there is, even now, something of ill-omen amongst us. I mean the increasing disregard for law which pervades the country; the growing disposition to substitute the wild and furious passions, in lieu of the sober judgement of Courts; and the worse than savage mobs, for the executive ministers of justice. This disposition is awfully fearful in any community; and that it now exists in ours, though grating to our feelings to admit, it would be a violation of truth, and an insult to our intelligence, to deny. Accounts of outrages committed by mobs, form the every-day news of the times. They have pervaded the country, from New England to Louisiana;—they are neither peculiar to the eternal snows of the former, nor the burning suns of the latter;—they are not the creature of climate—neither are they confined to the slaveholding, or the non-slaveholding States. Alike, they spring up among the pleasure hunting masters of Southern slaves, and the order loving citizens of the land of steady habits. Whatever, then, their cause may be, it is common to the whole country.

It would be tedious, as well as useless, to recount the horrors of all of them. Those happening in the State of Mississippi, and at St. Louis,[1] are, perhaps, the most dangerous in example, and revolting to humanity. In the Mississippi case, they first commenced by hanging the regular gamblers:[2] a set of men, certainly not following for a livelihood, a very useful, or very

1. The lynching on April 28, 1836, of the black St. Louis boat worker Francis L. McIntosh, which occurred after he had killed a policeman who had tried to arrest him, was strongly denounced by the antislavery journalist Elijah Lovejoy (1802–1837), who was himself murdered the next year by a mob.
2. In the summer of 1835, a mob of vigilantes captured and hanged five gamblers in Vicksburg, Mississippi. Also that summer, a rumored slave revolt led to the rounding up of enslaved blacks, who were summarily hanged, as were two whites implicated in the plot. Panic spread, and more executions followed in other Mississippi towns. In the end, twelve whites and a far larger number of blacks supposedly linked to the plot were killed.

honest occupation; but one which, so far from being forbidden by the laws, was actually licensed by an act of the Legislature, passed but a single year before. Next, negroes, suspected of conspiring to raise an insurrection, were caught up and hanged in all parts of the State: then, white men, supposed to be leagued with the negroes; and finally, strangers, from neighboring States, going thither on business, were, in many instances, subjected to the same fate. Thus went on this process of hanging, from gamblers to negroes, from negroes to white citizens, and from these to strangers; till, dead men were seen literally dangling from the boughs of trees upon every road side; and in numbers almost sufficient, to rival the native Spanish moss of the country, as a drapery of the forest.

Turn, then, to that horror-striking scene at St. Louis. A single victim was only sacrificed there. His story is very short; and is, perhaps, the most highly tragic, of any thing of its length, that has ever been witnessed in real life. A mulatto man, by the name of McIntosh, was seized in the street, dragged to the suburbs of the city, chained to a tree, and actually burned to death; and all within a single hour from the time he had been a freeman, attending to his own business, and at peace with the world.

Such are the effects of mob law; and such are the scenes, becoming more and more frequent in this land so lately famed for love of law and order; and the stories of which, have even now grown too familiar, to attract any thing more, than an idle remark.

But you are, perhaps, ready to ask, "What has this to do with the perpetuation of our political institutions?" I answer, it has much to do with it. Its direct consequences are, comparatively speaking, but a small evil; and much of its danger consists, in the proneness of our minds, to regard its direct, as its only consequences. Abstractly considered, the hanging of the gamblers at Vicksburg, was of but little consequence. They constitute a portion of population, that is worse than useless in any community; and their death, if no pernicious example be set by it, is never matter of reasonable regret with any one. If they were annually swept, from the stage of existence, by the plague or small pox, honest men would, perhaps, be much profited, by the operation. Similar too, is the correct reasoning, in regard to the burning of the negro at St. Louis. He had forfeited his life, by the perpetration of an outrageous murder, upon one of the most worthy and respectable citizens of the city; and had he not died as he did, he must have died by the sentence of the law, in a very short time afterwards. As to him alone, it was as well the way it was, as it could otherwise have been. But the example in either case, was fearful. When men take it in their heads to day, to hang gamblers, or burn murderers, they should recollect, that, in the confusion usually attending such transactions, they will be as likely to hang or burn some one, who is neither a gambler nor a murderer as one who is; and that, acting upon the example they set, the mob of to-morrow, may, and probably will, hang or burn some of them, by the very same mistake. And not only so; the innocent, those who have ever set their faces against violations of law in every shape, alike with the guilty, fall victims to the ravages of mob law; and thus it goes on, step by step, till all the walls erected for the defence of the persons and property of individuals, are trodden down, and disregarded. But all this even, is not the full extent of the evil. By such examples, by instances of the perpetrators of such acts going unpunished, the lawless in spirit, are encouraged to become lawless in practice; and having been used to no restraint, but dread of punishment, they thus become, absolutely unrestrained. Having ever regarded Government as their deadliest bane, they make a jubilee of the suspension of its operations; and pray for nothing so much, as its total annihilation. While, on the other hand, good men, men who love tranquility, who desire to abide by the laws, and enjoy their benefits, who would gladly spill their blood in the defence of their country; seeing their property destroyed; their families insulted, and their lives endangered; their persons injured; and seeing nothing in prospect that forebodes a change for the better; become tired of, and disgusted with, a Government that offers them no protection; and are not much averse to a change in which they imagine they have nothing to lose. Thus, then, by the operation of this mobocratic spirit, which all must admit, is now abroad in the land, the strongest bulwark of any Government, and particularly of those constituted like ours, may effectually be broken down and destroyed—I mean the *attachment* of the People. Whenever this effect shall be produced among us; whenever the vicious portion of population shall be permitted to gather in bands of hundreds and thousands, and burn churches, ravage and rob provision stores, throw printing presses into rivers, shoot editors, and hang and burn obnoxious persons at pleasure, and with impunity; depend on it, this Government cannot last. By such things, the feelings of the best citizens will become more or less alienated from it; and thus it will be left without friends, or with too few, and those few too weak, to make their friendship effectual. At such a time and under such circumstances, men of sufficient talent and ambition will not be wanting to seize the opportunity, strike the blow, and overturn that fair fabric, which for the last half century, has been the fondest hope, of the lovers of freedom, throughout the world.

I know the American People are *much* attached to their Government;—I know they would suffer *much* for its sake;—I know they would endure evils long and patiently, before they would ever think of exchanging it for another. Yet, notwithstanding all this, if the laws be continually despised and disregarded, if their rights to be secure in their persons and property, are held by no better tenure than the caprice of a mob, the alienation of their affections from the Government is the natural consequence; and to that, sooner or later, it must come.

Here then, is one point at which danger may be expected.

The question recurs "how shall we fortify against it?" The answer is simple. Let every American, every lover of liberty, every well wisher to his posterity, swear by the blood of the Revolution, never to violate in the least particular, the laws of the country; and never to tolerate their violation by others. As the patriots of seventy-six did to the support of the Declaration of Independence, so to the support of the Constitution and Laws, let every American pledge his life, his property, and his sacred honor;—let every man remember that to violate the law, is to trample on the blood of his father, and to tear the character of his own, and his children's liberty. Let reverence for the laws, be breathed by every American mother, to the lisping babe, that prattles on her lap—let it be taught in schools, in seminaries, and in colleges;—let it be written in Primmers, spelling books, and in Almanacs;—let it be preached from the pulpit, proclaimed in legislative halls, and enforced in courts of justice. And, in short, let it become the *political religion* of the nation; and let the old and the young, the rich and the poor, the grave and the gay, of all sexes and tongues, and colors and conditions, sacrifice unceasingly upon its altars.

While ever a state of feeling, such as this, shall universally, or even, very generally prevail throughout the nation, vain will be every effort, and fruitless every attempt, to subvert our national freedom.

When I so pressingly urge a strict observance of all the laws, let me not be understood as saying there are no bad laws, nor that grievances may not arise, for the redress of which, no legal provisions have been made. I mean to say no such thing. But I do mean to say, that, although bad laws, if they exist, should be repealed as soon as possible, still while they continue in force, for the sake of example, they should be religiously observed. So also in unprovided cases. If such arise, let proper legal provisions be made for them with the least possible delay; but, till then, let them if not too intolerable, be borne with.

There is no grievance that is a fit object of redress by mob law. In any case that arises, as for instance, the promulgation of abolitionism, one of two positions is necessarily true; that is, the thing is right within itself, and therefore deserves the protection of all law and all good citizens; or, it is wrong, and therefore proper to be prohibited by legal enactments; and in neither case, is the interposition of mob law, either necessary, justifiable, or excusable.

But, it may be asked, why suppose danger to our political institutions? Have we not preserved them for more than fifty years? And why may we not for fifty times as long?

We hope there is no *sufficient* reason. We hope all dangers may be overcome; but to conclude that no danger may ever arise, would itself be extremely dangerous. There are now, and will hereafter be, many causes, dangerous in their tendency, which have not existed heretofore; and which are not too insignificant to merit attention. That our government should have been maintained in its original form from its establishment until now, is not much to be wondered at. It had many props to support it through that period, which now are decayed, and crumbled away. Through that period, it was felt by all, to be an undecided experiment; now, it is understood to be a successful one. Then, all that sought celebrity and fame, and distinction, expected to find them in the success of that experiment. Their *all* was staked upon it:—their destiny was *inseparably* linked with it. Their ambition aspired to display before an admiring world, a practical demonstration of the truth of a proposition, which had hitherto been considered, at best no better, than problematical; namely, *the capability of a people to govern themselves*. If they succeeded, they were to be immortalized; their names were to be transferred to counties and cities, and rivers and mountains; and to be revered and sung, and toasted through all time. If they failed, they were to be called knaves and fools, and fanatics for a fleeting hour; then to sink and be forgotten. They succeeded. The experiment is successful; and thousands have won their deathless names in making it so. But the game is caught; and I believe it is true, that with the catching, end the pleasures of the chase. This field of glory is harvested, and the crop is already appropriated. But new reapers will arise, and *they*, too, will seek a field. It is to deny, what the history of the world tells us is true, to suppose that men of ambition and talents will not continue to spring up amongst us. And, when they do, they will as naturally seek the gratification of their ruling passion, as others have *so* done before them. The question then, is, can that gratification be found in supporting and maintaining an edifice that has been erected by others? Most certainly it cannot. Many great and good men sufficiently qualified for any task they should undertake, may ever be found, whose ambition would aspire to nothing beyond a seat in Congress, a gubernatorial or a presidential chair; *but such belong not to the family of the lion, or the tribe of the eagle.* What! think you these places would satisfy an Alexander, a Caesar, or a Napoleon?[3] Never! Towering genius disdains a beaten path. It seeks regions hitherto unexplored. It sees *no distinction* in adding story to story, upon the monuments of fame, erected to the memory of others. It *denies* that it is glory enough to serve under any chief. It *scorns* to tread in the footsteps of *any* predecessor, however illustrious. It thirsts and burns for distinction; and, if possible, it will have it, whether at the expense of emancipating slaves, or enslaving freemen. Is it unreasonable then to expect, that some man possessed of the loftiest genius, coupled with ambition sufficient to push it to its utmost stretch, will at some time, spring up among us? And when such a one does, it will require the people to be united with each other, attached to the government and laws, and generally intelligent, to successfully frustrate his designs.

Distinction will be his paramount object; and although he would as willingly, perhaps more so, acquire it by doing good as harm; yet, that opportunity being past, and nothing left to be done in the way of building up, he would set boldly to the task of pulling down.

Here then, is a probable case, highly dangerous, and such a one as could not have well existed heretofore.

Another reason which *once was*; but which, to the same extent, is *now no more*, has done much in maintaining our institutions thus far. I mean the powerful influence which the interesting scenes of the revolution had upon the *passions* of the people as distinguished from their judgment. By this influence, the jealousy, envy, and avarice, incident to our nature, and so common to a state of peace, prosperity, and conscious strength, were, for the time, in a great measure smothered and rendered inactive; while the deep rooted principles of *hate*, and the powerful motive of *revenge*, instead of being turned against each other, were directed exclusively against the British nation. And thus, from the force of circumstances, the basest principles of our nature, were either made to lie dormant, or to become the active agents in the advancement of the noblest of cause— that of establishing and maintaining civil and religious liberty.

But this state of feeling *must fade, is fading, has faded*, with the circumstances that produced it.

I do not mean to say, that the scenes of the revolution *are now* or *ever will be* entirely forgotten; but that like every thing else, they must fade upon the memory of the world, and grow more and more dim by the lapse of time. In history, we hope, they will be read of, and recounted, so long as the bible shall be read;—but even granting that they will, their influence

---

3. Napoleon Bonaparte (1769–1821), French military and political leader. Alexander the Great (356–323 B.C.E.), king of Macedon, Greece. Julius Caesar (100–44 B.C.E.) Roman general and statesman.

cannot be what it heretofore has been. Even then, they *cannot be* so universally known, nor so vividly felt, as they were by the generation just gone to rest. At the close of that struggle, nearly every adult male had been a participator in some of its scenes. The consequence was, that of those scenes, in the form of a husband, a father, a son or a brother, a *living history was* to be found in every family—a history bearing the indubitable testimonies of its own authenticity, in the limbs mangled, in the scars of wounds received, in the midst of the very scenes related—a history, too, that could be read and understood alike by all, the wise and the ignorant, the learned and the unlearned. But *those* histories are gone. They *can* be read no more forever. They *were* a fortress of strength; but, what invading foemen could *never do*, the silent artillery of time *has done*; the levelling of its walls. They are gone. They *were* a forest of giant oaks; but the all resistless hurricane has swept over them, and left only, here and there, a lonely trunk, despoiled of its verdure, shorn of its foliage; unshading and unshaded, to murmur in a few more gentle breezes, and to combat with its mutilated limbs, a few more ruder storms, then to sink, and be no more.

They *were* the pillars of the temple of liberty; and now, that they have crumbled away, that temple must fall, unless we, their descendants, supply their places with other pillars, hewn from the solid quarry of sober reason. Passion has helped us; but can do so no more. It will in future be our enemy. Reason, cold, calculating, unimpassioned reason, must furnish all the materials for our future support and defence. Let those materials be moulded into *general intelligence, sound morality* and, in particular, *a reverence for the constitution and laws*; and, that we improved to the last; that we remained free to the last; that we revered his name to the last; that, during his long sleep, we permitted no hostile foot to pass over or desecrate his resting place; shall be that which to learn the last trump shall awaken our WASHINGTON.

Upon these let the proud fabric of freedom rest, as the rock of its basis; and as truly as has been said of the only greater institution, *"the gates of hell shall not prevail against it."*[4]

January 27, 1838

To Mrs. Orville H. Browning[1]

Dear Madam: Springfield, April 1. 1838.
Without appologising for being egotistical, I shall make the history of so much of my own life, as has elapsed since I saw you, the subject of this letter. And by the way I now discover, that, in order to give a full and inteligible account of the things I have done and suffered *since* I saw you, I shall necessarily have to relate some that happened *before*.

It was, then, in the autumn of 1836, that a married lady of my acquaintance, and who was a great friend of mine, being about to pay a visit to

---

4. In the Bible, Jesus tells his disciple Peter, "Upon this rock I will build my church; and the gates of hell shall not prevail against it" (Matthew 16:18).
1. Née Eliza Caldwell, the wife of Lincoln's friend Orville H. Browning (1806–1881), a Whig politician of Quincy, Illinois, who later became a Republican U.S. representative (and eventually senator) from Illinois.

her father and other relatives residing in Kentucky, proposed to me, that on her return she would bring a sister of hers[2] with her, upon condition that I would engage to become her brother-in-law with all convenient dispach. I, of course, accepted the proposal; for you know I could not have done otherwise, had I really been averse to it; but privately between you and me, I was most confoundedly well pleased with the project. I had seen the said sister some three years before, thought her inteligent and agreeable, and saw no good objection to plodding life through hand in hand with her. Time passed on, the lady took her journey and in due time returned, sister in company sure enough. This stomached[3] me a little; for it appeared to me, that her coming so readily showed that she was a trifle too willing; but on reflection it occured to me, that she might have been prevailed on by her married sister to come, without any thing concerning me ever having been mentioned to her; and so I concluded that if no other objection presented itself, I would consent to wave this. All this occured upon my hearing of her arrival in the neighbourhood; for, be it remembered, I had not yet *seen* her, except about three years previous, as before mentioned.

In a few days we had an interview, and although I had seen her before, she did not look as my immagination had pictured her. I knew she was over-size, but she now appeared a fair match for Falstaff;[4] I knew she was called an "old maid", and I felt no doubt of the truth of at least half of the appelation; but now, when I beheld her, I could not for my life avoid thinking of my mother; and this, not from withered features, for her skin was too full of fat, to permit its contracting in to wrinkles; but from her want of teeth, weather-beaten appearance in general, and from a kind of notion that ran in my head, that *nothing* could have commenced at the size of infancy, and reached her present bulk in less than thirtyfive or forty years; and, in short, I was not all pleased with her. But what could I do? I had told her sister that I would take her for better or for worse; and I made a point of honor and conscience in all things, to stick to my word, especially if others had been induced to act on it, which in this case, I doubted not they had, for I was now fairly convinced, that no other man on earth would have her, and hence the conclusion that they were bent on holding me to my bargain. Well, thought I, I have said it, and, be consequences what they may, it shall not be my fault if I fail to do it. At once I determined to consider her my wife; and this done, all my powers of discovery were put to the rack, in search of perfections in her, which might be fairly set-off against her defects. I tried to immagine she was handsome, which, but for her unfortunate corpulency, was actually true. Exclusive of this, no woman that I have seen, has a finer face. I also tried to convince myself, that the mind was much more to be valued than the person; and in this, she was not inferior, as I could discover, to any with whom I had been acquainted.

Shortly after this, without attempting to come to any positive understanding with her, I set out for Vandalia, where and when you first saw me. During my stay there, I had letters from her, which did not change my opinion of either her intelect or intention; but on the contrary, confirmed it in both.

2. Mary S. Owens.
3. Disturbed.
4. A rotund, boastful character who appears in three plays by Shakespeare.

All this while, although I was fixed "firm as the surge repelling rock" in my resolution, I found I was continually repenting the rashness, which had led me to make it. Through life I have been in no bondage, either real or immaginary from the thraldom of which I so much desired to be free.

After my return home, I saw nothing to change my opinion of her in any particular. She was the same and so was I. I now spent my time between planing how I might get along through life after my contemplated change of circumstances should have taken place; and how I might procrastinate the evil day for a time, which I really dreaded as much—perhaps more, than an irishman does the halter.

After all my suffering upon this deeply interesting subject, here I am, wholly unexpectedly, completely out of the "scrape"; and I now want to know, if you can guess how I got out of it. Out clear in every sense of the term; no violation of word, honor or conscience. I dont believe you can guess, and so I may as well tell you at once. As the lawyers say, it was done in the manner following, towit. After I had delayed the matter as long as I thought I could in honor do, which by the way had brought me round into the last fall, I concluded I might as well bring it to a consumation without further delay; and so I mustered my resolution, and made the proposal to her direct; but, shocking to relate, she answered, No. At first I supposed she did it through an affectation of modesty, which I thought but ill-become her, under the peculiar circumstances of her case; but on my renewal of the charge, I found she repeled it with greater firmness than before. I tried it again and again, but with the same success, or rather with the same want of success. I finally was forced to give it up, at which I verry unexpectedly found myself mortified almost beyond endurance. I was mortified, it seemed to me, in a hundred different ways. My vanity was deeply wounded by the reflection, that I had so long been too stupid to discover her intentions, and at the same time never doubting that I understood them perfectly; and also, that she whom I had taught myself to believe no body else would have, had actually rejected me with all my fancied greatness; and to cap the whole, I then, for the first time, began to suspect that I was really a little in love with her. But let it all go. I'll try and out live it. Others have been made fools of by the girls; but this can never be with truth said of me. I most emphatically, in this instance, made a fool of myself. I have now come to the conclusion never again to think of marrying; and for this reason; I can never be satisfied with any one who would be block-head enough to have me.

When you receive this, write me a long yarn about something to amuse me. Give my respects to Mr. Browning. Your sincere friend

From Speech on the Sub-Treasury[1] at Springfield, Illinois

Fellow citizens:—It is peculiarly embarrassing to me to attempt a continuance of the discussion, on this evening, which has been conducted in

1. A banking system proposed by Democratic President Martin Van Buren (1782–1873) that was intended to be a substitute for both the bygone national Second Bank of the United States (1817–36) and the state "pet banks" that had been implemented by President Andrew Jackson in 1837. In the subtreasury plan, national funds were deposited in government vaults (or subtreasuries) around the nation. After fierce debate, Van Buren's system went into effect in July 1840. Lincoln here expresses the Whig Party's hostile viewpoint.

this Hall on several preceding ones. It is so, because on each of those evenings, there was a much fuller attendance than now, without any reason for its being so, except the greater *interest* the community feel in the Speakers who addressed them *then*, than they do in *him* who is to do so now. I am, indeed, apprehensive, that the few who have attended, have done so, more to spare me of mortification, than in the hope of being interested in any thing I may be able to say. This circumstance casts a damp upon my spirits, which I am sure I shall be unable to overcome during the evening. But enough of preface.

The subject heretofore, and now to be discussed, is the Sub-Treasury scheme of the present Administration, as a means of collecting, safe-keeping, transferring and disbursing the revenues of the Nation, as contrasted with a National Bank for the same purposes. Mr. Douglass has said that we (the Whigs), have not dared to meet them (the Locos),[2] in argument on this question. I protest against this assertion. I assert that we have again and again, during this discussion, urged facts and arguments against the Sub-Treasury, which they have neither dared to deny nor attempted to answer. But lest some may be led to believe that we really wish to avoid the question, I now propose, in my humble way, to urge those arguments again; at the same time, begging the audience to mark well the positions I shall take, and the proof I shall offer to sustain them, and that they will not again permit Mr. Douglass or his friends, to escape the force of them, by a round and groundless assertion, that we "dare not meet them in argument."

Of the Sub-Treasury then, as contrasted with a National Bank, for the before enumerated purposes, I lay down the following propositions, to wit:

1st. It will injuriously affect the community by its operation on the circulating medium.

2d. It will be a more expensive fiscal agent.

3d. It will be a less secure depository of the public money.

* * *

I now come to the proposition, that [the subtreasury system] would be less secure than a National Bank, as a depository of the public money. The experience of the past, I think, proves the truth of this. And here, inasmuch as I rely chiefly upon experience to establish it, let me ask, how is it that we know any thing—that any event will occur, that any combination of circumstances will produce a certain result—except by the analogies of past experience? What has once happened, will invariably happen again, when the same circumstances which combined to produce it, shall again combine in the same way. We all feel that we know that a blast of wind would extinguish the flame of the candle that stands by me. How do we know it? We have never seen this flame thus extinguished. We know it, because we have seen through all our lives, that a blast of wind extinguishes the flame of a candle whenever it is thrown fully upon it. Again, we all feel to *know* that we have to die. How? We have never died yet. We

2. Nickname for the Democratic Party, derived from matches called *locofocos* (Spanish for "crazy lights") that were lit at a Democratic rally in 1835. Stephen A. Douglas (1813–1861), an Illinois Democrat and Lincoln's long-time political opponent on many issues.

know it, because we know, or at least think we know, that of all the beings, just like ourselves, who have been coming into the world for six thousand years, not one is now living who was here two hundred years ago.

I repeat then, that we know nothing of what will happen in future, but by the analogy of experience, and that the fair analogy of past experience fully proves that the Sub-Treasury would be a less safe depository of the public money than a National Bank. Examine it. By the Sub-Treasury scheme, the public money is to be kept, between the times of its collection and disbursement, by Treasurers of the Mint, Custom-house officers, Land officers, and some new officers to be appointed in the same way that those first enumerated are. Has a year passed since the organization of the Government, that numerous defalcations have not occurred among this class of officers? Look at Swartwout with his $1,200,000, Price with his $75,000, Harris with his $109,000, Hawkins with his $100,000, Linn[3] with his $55,000, together with some twenty-five hundred lesser lights. Place the public money again in these same hands, and will it not again go the same way? Most assuredly it will. But turn to the history of the National Bank in this country, and we shall there see, that those Banks performed the fiscal operations of the Government thro' a period of 40 years, received, safely kept, transferred, disbursed, an aggregate of nearly five hundred millions of dollars; and that, in all that time, and with all that money, not one dollar, nor one cent, did the Government lose by them. Place the public money again in a similar depository, and will it not again be safe?

But, conclusive as the experience of fifty years is, that individuals are unsafe depositories of the public money, and of forty years that National Banks are safe depositories, we are not left to rely solely upon that experience for the truth of those propositions. If experience were silent upon the subject, conclusive reasons could be shown for the truth of them.

It is often urged, that to say the public money will be more secure in a National Bank, than in the hands of individuals, as proposed in the Sub-Treasury, is to say, that Bank directors and Bank officers are more honest than sworn officers of the Government. Not so. We insist on no such thing. We say that public officers, selected with reference to their capacity and honesty, (which by the way, we deny is the practice in these days,) stand an equal chance, precisely, of being capable and honest, with Bank officers selected by the same rule. We further say, that with however much care selections may be made, there will be some unfaithful and dishonest in both classes. The experience of the whole world, in all by-gone times, proves this true. The Saviour of the world chose twelve disciples, and even one of that small number, selected by superhuman wisdom, turned out a traitor and a devil. And, it may not be improper here to add, that Judas carried the bag—was the Sub-Treasurer of the Saviour and his disciples.

We then, do not say, nor need we say, to maintain our proposition, that Bank officers are more honest than Government officers, selected by the same rule. What we do say, is, that the *interest* of the Sub-Treasurer is

---

3. William J. Linn, an Illinois bank commissioner. Samuel Swartwout, a collector of the Port of New York. William M. Price of New York. W. P. Harris of Columbus, Missisippi. L. Hawkins of Helena, Arkansas.

against his duty—while the *interest* of the Bank is *on the side of its duty*. Take instances—a Sub-Treasurer has in his hands one hundred thousand dollars of public money; his *duty* says—"You ought to pay this money over"—but his *interest* says, "You ought to run away with this sum, and be a nabob the balance of your life." And who that knows anything of human nature, doubts that, in many instances, interest will prevail over duty, and that the Sub-Treasurer will prefer opulent knavery in a foreign land, to honest poverty at home? But how different is it with a Bank. Besides the Government money deposited with it, it is doing business upon a large capital of its own. If it proves faithful to the Government, it continues its business; if unfaithful, it forfeits its charter, breaks up its business, and thereby loses more than all it can make by seizing upon the Government funds in its possession. Its *interest*, therefore, is on the side of its duty—is to be faithful to the Government, and consequently, even the dishonest amongst its managers, have no temptation to be faithless to it. Even if robberies happen in the Bank, the losses are borne by the Bank, and the Government loses nothing. It is for this reason then, that we say a Bank is the more secure. It is because of that admirable feature in the Bank system, which places the *interest* and the *duty* of the depository both on one side; whereas that feature can never enter into the Sub-Treasury system. By the latter, the *interest* of the individuals keeping the public money, will wage an eternal war with their *duty*, and in very many instances must be victorious. In answer to the argument drawn from the fact that individual depositories of public money, have always proved unsafe, it is urged that even if we had a National Bank, the money has to *pass through* the same individual hands, that it will under the Sub-Treasury. This is only partially true in fact, and wholly fallacious in argument.

It is only partially true, in fact, because by the Sub-Treasury, four Receivers General are to be appointed by the President and Senate. These are new officers, and consequently, it cannot be true that the money, or any portion of it, has heretofore passed thro' their hands. These four new officers are to be located at New York, Boston, Charleston and St. Louis, and consequently are to be the depositories of all the money collected at or near those points; so that more than three-fourths of the public money will fall into the keeping of these four new officers, which did not exist as officers under the National Bank system. It is only partially true, then, that the money passes through the same hands, under a National Bank, as it would do under the Sub-Treasury.

It is true, that under either system, individuals must be employed as Collectors of the Customs, Receivers at the Land Offices, &c. &c. but the difference is, that under the Bank system, the receivers of all sorts, receive the money and pay it over to the Bank once a week when the collections are large, and once a month when they are small, whereas, by the Sub-Treasury system, individuals are not only to collect the money, but they are to *keep* it also, or pay it over to other individuals equally unsafe as themselves, to be by them kept, until it is wanted for disbursement. It is during the time that it is thus lying idle in their hands, that opportunity is afforded, and temptation held out to them to embezzle and escape with it. By the Bank system, each Collector or Receiver, is to deposite in Bank all the money in his hands at the end of each month at most, and to send the Bank certificates of deposite to the Secretary of the Treasury.

Whenever that certificate of deposite fails to arrive at the proper time, the Secretary *knows* that the officer thus failing, is acting the knave; and if he is himself disposed to do his duty, he has him immediately removed from office, and thereby cuts him off from the possibility of embezzling but little more than the receipts of a single month. But by the Sub-Treasury System, the money is to lie month after month in the hands of individuals; larger amounts are to accumulate in the hands of the Receivers General, and some others, by perhaps ten to one, than ever accumulated in the hands of individuals before; yet during all this time, in relation to this great stake, the Secretary of the Treasury can comparatively know nothing. Reports, to be sure, he will have, but reports are often false, and always false when made by a knave to cloak his knavery. Long experience has shown, that nothing short of an actual demand of the money will expose an adroit peculator. Ask him for reports and he will give them to your heart's content; send agents to examine and count the money in his hands, and he will borrow of a friend, merely to be counted and then returned, a sufficient sum to make the sum square. Try what you will, it will all fail till you demand the money—then, and not till then, the truth will come.

The sum of the whole matter, I take to be this: Under the Bank system, while sums of money, by the law, were permitted to lie in the hands of individuals, *for very short periods only*, many and very large defalcations occurred by those individuals. Under the Sub-Treasury system, *much larger sums* are to lie in the hands of individuals *for much longer periods*, thereby multiplying temptation in proportion as the sums *are larger*; and multiplying *opportunity* in proportion as the periods *are longer* to, and for, those individuals to embezzle and escape with the public treasure; and, therefore, just in the proportion, that the *temptation* and the *opportunity* are greater under the Sub-Treasury than the Bank system, will the peculations and defalcations be greater under the former than they have been under the latter. The truth of this, independent of actual experience, is but little less than self-evident. I therefore, leave it.

But it is said, and truly too, that there is to be a *Penitentiary Department* to the Sub-Treasury. This, the advocates of the system will have it, will be a "*king-cure-all*." Before I go farther, may I not ask if the Penitentiary Department, is not itself an admission that they expect the public money to be stolen? Why build the cage if they expect to catch no birds? But to the question how effectual the Penitentiary will be in preventing defalcations. How effectual have Penitentiaries heretofore been in preventing the crimes they were established to suppress? Has not confinement in them long been the legal penalty of larceny, forgery, robbery, and many other crimes, in almost all the States? And yet, are not those crimes committed weekly, daily, nay, and even hourly, in every one of those States? Again, the gallows has long been the penalty of murder, and yet we scarcely open a newspaper, that does not relate a new case of that crime. If then, the Penitentiary has ever *heretofore* failed to prevent larceny, forgery and robbery, and the gallows and halter have likewise failed to prevent murder, by what process of reasoning, I ask, is it that we are to conclude the Penitentiary will *hereafter* prevent the stealing of the public money? But our opponents seem to think they answer the charge, that the money will be stolen, fully, if they can show that they will bring the offenders to punishment. Not so. Will the punishment of the thief bring back the stolen money? No more so than the hanging of a murderer restores his victim to life. What is the object desired? Certainly not the greatest number of thieves we can catch, but that the money may not be stolen. If, then, any plan can be devised for depositing the public treasure, where it will be never stolen, never embezzled, is not that the plan to be adopted? Turn, then, to a National Bank, and you have that plan, fully and completely successful, as tested by the experience of forty years.

I have now done with the three propositions that the Sub-Treasury would injuriously affect the currency, and would be more *expensive* and *less secure* as a depository of the public money than a National Bank. How far I have succeeded in establishing their truth is for others to judge.

Omitting, for want of time, what I had intended to say as to the effect of the Sub-Treasury, to bring the public money under the more immediate control of the President, than it has ever heretofore been, I now only ask the audience, when Mr. Calhoun[4] shall answer me, *to hold him to the questions*. Permit him not to escape them. Require him *either* to show, that the Sub-Treasury *would not* injuriously affect the *currency*, or that we should in some way, receive an equivalent for that injurious effect. Require him either to show that the Sub-Treasury *would not be more expensive* as a fiscal agent, than a Bank, or that we should, in some way be compensated for that additional expense. And particularly require him to show, that the public money *would be as secure* in the Sub-Treasury as in a National Bank, or that the additional *insecurity* would be over-balanced by some good result of the proposed change.

No one of them, in my humble judgment, will he be able to do; and I venture the prediction, and ask that it may be especially noted, *that he will not attempt to answer the proposition, that the Sub-Treasury would be more expensive than a National Bank as a fiscal agent of the Government.*

As a sweeping objection to a National Bank, and consequently an argument in favor of the Sub-Treasury as a substitute for it, it often has been urged, and doubtless will be again, that such a bank is unconstitutional. We have often heretofore shown, and therefore need not in detail do so again, that a majority of the Revolutionary patriarchs, whoever acted officially upon the question, commencing with Gen. Washington and embracing Gen. Jackson, the larger number of the signers of the Declaration, and of the framers of the Constitution, who were in the Congress of 1791, have decided upon their oaths that such a bank is constitutional. We have also shown that the votes of Congress have more often been in favor of than against its constitutionality. In addition to all this we have shown that the Supreme Court—that tribunal which the Constitution has itself established to decide Constitutional questions—has solemnly decided that such a bank is constitutional. Protesting that these authorities ought to settle the question—ought to be conclusive, I will not urge them further now. I now propose to take a view of the question which I have not known to be taken by anyone before. It is, that whatever objection ever has or ever can be made to the constitutionality of a bank, will apply with equal force in its whole length, breadth and proportions to the

4. John Calhoun, Democratic politician of Sangamon County, who was to give a speech in reply to Lincoln on December 28.

Sub-Treasury. Our opponents say, there is no *express* authority in the Constitution to establish a Bank, and therefore a Bank is unconstitutional; but we, with equal truth, may say, there is no *express* authority in the Constitution to establish a Sub-Treasury, and therefore a Sub-Treasury is unconstitutional. Who then, has the advantage of this *"express authority"* argument? Does it not cut equally both ways? Does it not wound them as deeply and as deadly as it does us?

Our position is that both are constitutional. The Constitution enumerates expressly several powers which Congress may exercise, superadded to which is a general authority "to make all laws necessary and proper," for carrying into effect all the powers vested by the Constitution of the Government of the United States. One of the express powers given Congress, is "To lay and collect taxes; duties, imposts, and excises; to pay the debts, and provide for the common defence and general welfare of the United States." Now, Congress is expressly authorized to make all laws necessary and proper for carrying this power into execution. To carry it into execution, it is indispensably necessary to collect, safely keep, transfer, and disburse a revenue. To do this, a Bank is "necessary and proper." But, say our opponents, to authorize the making of a Bank, the *necessity* must be so great, that the power just recited, would be nugatory without it; and that that *necessity* is expressly negatived by the fact, that they have got along *ten* whole years without such a *Bank.* Immediately we turn on them, and say, that that sort of *necessity* for a Sub-Treasury does not exist, because we have got along *forty* whole years without one. And this time, it may be observed, that we are not merely equal with them in the argument, but we beat them *forty* to *ten,* or which is the same thing, *four* to *one.* On examination, it will be found, that the absurd rule, which prescribes that before we can constitutionally adopt a National Bank as a fiscal agent, we must show an *indispensable necessity* for it, will exclude every sort of fiscal agent that the mind of man can conceive. A *Bank* is not *indispensable,* because we can take the *Sub-Treasury;* the *Sub-Treasury* is not indispensable because we can take the *Bank.* The rule is too absurd to need further comment. Upon the phrase *"necessary and proper,"* in the Constitution, it seems to me more reasonable to say, that *some* fiscal agent is *indispensably necessary;* but, inasmuch as no *particular sort* of agent is thus *indispensable,* because some *other* sort might be adopted, we are left to choose that sort of agent, which may be most *"proper"* on grounds of expediency.

But it is said the Constitution gives no power to Congress to pass acts of incorporation. Indeed! What is the passing of an act of incorporation, but the *making of a law?* Is any one wise enough to tell? The Constitution expressly gives Congress power *"to pass all laws necessary and proper,"* &c. If, then, the passing of a Bank charter, be the *"making a law necessary and proper,"* is it not clearly within the constitutional power of Congress to do so?

I now leave the Bank and the Sub-Treasury to try to answer, in a brief way, some of the arguments which, on previous evenings here, have been urged by Messrs. Lamborn[5] and Douglass. Mr. Lamborn admits that *"errors,"* as he charitably calls them, have occurred under the present and

---

5. Josiah Lamborn (1809–1847), Democratic politician and lawyer who served as attorney general of Illinois from 1840 to 1843.

late administrations, but he insists that as great "errors" have occurred under all administrations. This we respectfully deny. We admit that errors may have occurred under all administrations; but we insist that there is *no parallel* between them and those of the two last.[6] If they can show that their errors are no greater in number and magnitude, than those of former times, we call off the dogs.

But they can do no such thing. To be brief, I will now attempt a contrast of the "errors" of the two latter, with those of former administrations, in relation to the public expenditures only. What I am now about to say, as to the expenditures, will be, in all cases, exclusive of payments on the National debt. By an examination of authentic public documents, consisting of the regular series of annual reports, made by all the Secretaries of the Treasury from the establishment of the Government down to the close of the year 1838, the following contrasts will be presented.

1st. The last *ten* years under Gen. Jackson and Mr. Van Buren, cost more money than the first *twenty-seven* did, (including the heavy expenses of the late British war;)[7] under Washington, Adams, Jefferson, and Madison.

2d. The last year of J. Q. Adams' administration cost, in round numbers, *thirteen* millions, being about *one* dollar to each soul in the nation; the last (1838) of Mr. Van Buren's cost *forty* millions, being about *two dollars and fifty cents* to each soul; and being larger than the expenditure of Mr. Adams in the proportion of *five* to *two*.

3d. The highest annual expenditure during the late British war, being in 1814, and while we had in actual service rising 188,000 militia, together with the whole regular army, swelling the number to greatly over 200,000, and they to be clad, fed and transported from point to point, with great rapidity and corresponding expense, and to be furnished with arms and ammunition, and they to be transported in like manner, and at like expense, was no more in round numbers than *thirty* millions; whereas, the annual expenditure of 1838, under Mr. Van Buren, and while we were at peace with every government in the world, was *forty* millions; being over the highest year of the late and very expensive war, in the proportion of *four* to *three*.

4th. Gen. Washington administered the Government *eight* years for *sixteen* millions. Mr. Van Buren administered it *one* year (1838) for *forty* millions; so that Mr. Van Buren expended *twice and a half* as much in *one* year, as Gen. Washington did in *eight*, and being in the proportion of *twenty* to *one*—or, in other words, had Gen. Washington administered the Government *twenty* years, at the same average expense that he did for *eight*, he would have carried us through the whole *twenty*, for no more money than Mr. Van Buren has expended in getting us through the single *one* of 1838.

Other facts, equally astounding, might be presented from the same authentic document; but I deem the foregoing abundantly sufficient to establish the proposition, that there is no parallel between the *"errors"* of the present and late administrations, and those of former times, and that Mr. Van Buren is wholly out of the line of all precedents.

6. Reference to the administrations of Democrats Andrew Jackson (who held office from 1829 to 1837) and Martin Van Buren, who succeeded Jackson in 1837.
7. The War of 1812.

But, Mr. Douglass, seeing that the enormous expenditure of 1838, has no parallel in the olden times, comes in with a long list of excuses for it. This list of excuses I will rapidly examine, and show, as I think, that the few of them which are true, prove nothing; and that the majority of them are wholly untrue in fact. He first says, that the expenditures of that year were made under the appropriations of Congress—*one branch of which was a Whig body*. It is true that those expenditures were made under the appropriations of Congress; but it is *untrue* that either branch of Congress was a *Whig* body. The Senate had fallen into the hands of the administration, more than a year before, as proven by the passage of the Expunging Resolution;[8] and at the time those appropriations were made, there were too few Whigs in that body, to make a respectable struggle, in point of numbers, upon any question. This is notorious to all. The House of Representatives that voted those appropriations, was the same that first assembled at the called session of September, 1838. Although it refused to pass the Sub-Treasury Bill, a majority of its members were elected as friends of the administration, and proved their adherence to it, by the election of a Van Buren Speaker, and two Van Buren clerks. It is clear then, that both branches of the Congress that passed those appropriations were in the hands of Mr. Van Buren's friends, so that the Whigs had no power to arrest them, as Mr. Douglass would insist. And is not the charge of extravagant expenditures, equally well sustained, if shown to have been made by a Van Buren Congress, as if shown to have been made in any other way? A Van Buren Congress passed the bill; and Mr. Van Buren himself approved them, and consequently the party are wholly responsible for them.

Mr. Douglass next says that a portion of the expenditures of that year was made for the purchase of public lands from the Indians. Now it happens that no such purchase was made during that year. It is true that some money was paid that year in pursuance of Indian treaties; but no more, or rather not as much as had been paid on the same account in each of several preceding years.

Next he says that the Florida war[9] created many millions of this year's expenditure. This is true, and it is also true that during that and every other year that that war has existed, it has cost three or four times as much as it would have done under an honest and judicious administration of the Government. The large sums foolishly, not to say corruptly, thrown away in that war constitute one of the just causes of complaint against the administration. Take a single instance. The agents of the Government in connection with that war needed a certain Steamboat; the owner proposed to sell it for ten thousand dollars; the agents refused to give that sum, but hired the boat at one hundred dollars per day, and kept it at that hire till it amounted to ninety-two thousand dollars. This fact is not found in the public reports, but depends with me, on the verbal statement of an officer of the navy, who says he knows it to be true. That the administration ought to be credited for the *reasonable* expenses of the Florida war, we have never denied. Those *reasonable* charges, we say,

---

8. A resolution approved by the Senate in 1837 that erased from the official record an 1834 censure of Andrew Jackson for his having removed deposits from the Bank of the United States.
9. The ongoing war against the Seminole Indians in Florida, which had begun in 1814 and flared up periodically, including the four years from 1835 onward.

could not exceed one or two millions a year. Deduct such a sum from the forty-million expenditure of 1838, and the remainder will still be without a parallel as an annual expenditure.

Again, Mr. Douglass says that the removal of the Indians to the country west of the Mississippi created much of the expenditure of 1838. I have examined the public documents in relation to this matter, and find that less was paid for the removal of Indians in that than in some former years. The whole sum expended on that account in that year did not much exceed one-quarter of a million. For this small sum, altho' we do not think the administration entitled to credit, because large sums have been expended in the same way in former years, we consent it may take one and make the most of it.

Next, Mr. Douglass says that five millions of the expenditures of 1838 consisted of the payment of the French indemnity money to its individual claimants. I have carefully examined the public documents, and thereby find this statement to be wholly untrue. Of the forty millions of dollars expended in 1838, I am enabled to say positively that not one dollar consisted of payments on the French indemnities. So much for that excuse.

Next comes the Post-office. He says that five millions were expended during that year to sustain that department. By a like examination of public documents, I find this also wholly untrue. Of the so often mentioned forty millions, not one dollar went to the Post-office. I am glad, however, that the Post-office has been referred to, because it warrants me in digressing a little to inquire how it is that that department of the Government has become a *charge* upon the Treasury, whereas under Mr. Adams and the Presidents before him it not only, to use a homely phrase, cut its own fodder, but actually threw a surplus into the Treasury. Although nothing of the forty millions was paid on that account in 1838, it is true that five millions are appropriated *to be so expended* in 1839; showing clearly that the department has become a *charge* upon the Treasury. How has this happened? I account for it in this way. The chief expense of the Post-office Department consists of the payments of Contractors for carrying the mail. Contracts for carrying the mails are by law let to the lowest bidders, after advertisement. This plan introduces competition, and insures the transportation of the mails at fair prices, so long as it is faithfully adhered to. It has ever been adhered to until Mr. Barry[1] was made Postmaster-General. When he came into office, he formed the purpose of throwing the mail contracts into the hands of his friends, to the exclusion of his opponents. To effect this, the plan of letting to the lowest bidder must be evaded, and it must be done in this way: the favorite bid less by perhaps three or four hundred per cent, than the contract could be performed for, and consequently shutting out all honest competition, became the contractor. The Postmaster-General would immediately add some slight additional duty to the contract, and under the pretense of extra allowance for extra services run the contract to double, triple, and often quadruple what honest and fair bidders had proposed to take it at. In 1834 the finances of the department had become so deranged that total concealment was no longer possible, and consequently a committee of the Senate were directed to make a

---

1. William Taylor Barry (1784–1835), a Kentucky politician and U.S. postmaster general under President Andrew Jackson from 1829 to 1835.

thorough investigation of its affairs. Their report is found in the Senate Documents of 1833–34, Vol. 5, Doc. 422; which documents may be seen at the Secretary's office, and I presume elsewhere in the State. The report shows numerous cases of similar import, of one of which I give the substance. The contract for carrying the mail upon a certain route had expired, and of course was to be let again. The old contractor offered to take it for $300 a year, the mail to be transported thereon three times a week, or for $600 transported daily. One James Reeside bid $40 for three times a week, or $99 daily, and of course received the contract. On the examination of the committee, it was discovered that Reeside had received for the service on this route, which he had contracted to render for less than $100, the enormous sum of $1,999! This is but a single case. Many similar ones, covering some ten or twenty pages of a large volume, are given in that report. The department was found to be insolvent to the amount of half a million, and to have been so grossly mismanaged, or rather so corruptly managed, in almost every particular, that the best friends of the Post Master General made no defence of his administration of it. They admitted that he was wholly unqualified for that office; but still he was retained in it by the President, until he resigned voluntarily about a year afterwards. And when he resigned it what do you think became of him? Why, he sunk into obscurity and disgrace, to be sure, you will say. No such thing. Well, then, what did become of him? Why the President immediately expressed his high disapprobation of his almost unequalled incapacity and corruption, by appointing him to a foreign mission, with a salary and outfit of $18,000 a year. The party now attempt to throw Barry off, and to avoid the responsibility of his sins. Did not the President endorse those sins, when on the very heel of their commission, he appointed their author to the very highest and most honorable office in his gift, and which is but a single step behind the very goal of American political ambition.

I return to another of Mr. Douglass' excuses for the expenditures of 1838, at the same time announcing the pleasing intelligence, that this is the last one. He says that ten millions of that years expenditure, was a contingent appropriation, to prosecute an anticipated war with Great Britain, on the Maine boundary question. Few words will settle this. First: that the ten millions appropriated was not *made* till 1839, and consequently could not have been expended in 1838; and, second: although it was appropriated, it has never been expended at all. Those who heard Mr. Douglass, recollect that he indulged himself in a contemptuous expression of pity for me. "Now he's got me," thought I. But when he went on to say that five millions of the expenditure of 1838, were payments of the French indemnities, *which I knew to be untrue*; that five millions had been for the Post Office, *which I knew to be untrue*; that ten millions had been for the Maine boundary war, *which I not only knew to be untrue, but supremely ridiculous also*; and when I saw that he was stupid enough to hope, that I would permit such groundless and audacious assertions to go unexposed, I readily consented, that on the score both of veracity and sagacity, the audience should judge whether he or I were the more deserving of the world's contempt.

Mr. Lamborn insists that the difference between the Van Buren party, and the Whigs is, that although, the former sometimes err in *practice*, they are always correct in *principle*—whereas the latter are wrong in *principle*—and the better to impress this proposition, he uses a figurative expression in these words: *"The Democrats are vulnerable in the heel, but they are sound in the head and the heart."* The first branch of the figure, that is that the Democrats are vulnerable in the heel, I admit is not merely figuratively, but literally true. Who that looks but for a moment at their Swartwouts, their Prices, their Harringtons, and their hundreds of others, scampering away with the public money to Texas, to Europe, and to every spot of the earth where a villain may hope to find refuge from justice, can at all doubt that they are most distressingly affected in their *heels* with a species of *"running itch."* It seems that this malady of their heels, operates on these *sound-headed* and *honest-hearted* creatures, very much like the cork-leg, in the comic song, did on its owner: which, when he had once got started on it, the more he tried to stop it, the more it would run away. At the hazard of wearing this point thread bare, I will relate an anecdote, which seems too strikingly in point to be omitted. A witty Irish soldier, who was always boasting of his bravery, when no danger was near, but who invariably retreated without orders at the first charge of an engagement, being asked by his Captain why he did so, replied: "Captain, I have as brave a *heart* as Julius Caesar ever had; but some how or other, whenever danger approaches, my *cowardly* legs will run away with it." So with Mr. Lamborn's party. They take the public money into their hand for the most laudable purpose, that *wise heads* and *honest hearts* can dictate; but before they can possibly get it out again their rascally *"vulnerable heels"* will run away with them.

Seriously: this proposition of Mr. Lamborn is nothing more or less, than a request that his party may be tried by their *professions* instead of their *practices*. Perhaps no position that the party assumes is more liable to, or more deserving of exposure, than this very modest request; and nothing but the unwarrantable length, to which I have already extended these remarks, forbids me now attempting to expose it. For the reason given, I pass it by.

I shall advert to but one more point.

Mr. Lamborn refers to the late elections in the States, and from their results, confidently predicts, that every State in the Union will vote for Mr. Van Buren at the next Presidential election. Address *that* argument to *cowards* and to *knaves*; with the *free* and the *brave* it will effect nothing. It *may* be true, if it *must*, let it. Many free countries have lost their liberty; and *ours may* lose hers; but if she shall, be it my proudest plume, not that I was the *last* to desert, but that I *never* deserted her. I know that the great volcano at Washington, aroused and directed by the evil spirit that reigns there, is belching forth the lava of political corruption, in a current broad and deep, which is sweeping with frightful velocity over the whole length and breadth of the land, bidding fair to leave unscathed no green spot or living thing, while on its bosom are riding like demons on the waves of Hell, the imps of that evil spirit, and fiendishly taunting all those who dare resist its destroying course, with the hopelessness of their effort; and knowing this, I cannot deny that all may be swept away. Broken by it, I, too, may be; bow to it I never will. The *probability* that we may fall in the struggle *ought not* to deter us from the support of a cause we believe to be just; it *shall not* deter me. If ever I feel the soul within me elevate and expand to those dimensions not wholly unworthy of its Almighty Architect, it is when I contemplate the cause of my country, deserted by all the world beside, and I standing up boldly and alone and hurling defiance at her victorious oppressors. Here, without contemplating consequences, before High Heaven, and in the face of the world, I swear eternal fidelity to the just cause, as I deem it, of the land of my life, my liberty and my love. And who, that thinks with me, will not fearlessly adopt the oath that I take. Let none faulter, who thinks he is right, and we may succeed. But, if after all, we shall fail, be it so. We still shall have the proud consolation of saying to our consciences, and to the departed shade of our country's freedom, that the cause approved of our judgment, and adored of our hearts, in disaster, in chains, in torture, in death, we NEVER faultered in defending.

December 26, 1839

Lincoln's Plan of Campaign in 1840

1st. Appoint one person in each county as county captain, and take his pledge to perform promptly all the duties assigned him.

Duties of the County Captain

1st. To procure from the poll-books a separate list for each Precinct of all the names of all those persons who voted the Whig ticket in August.

2nd. To appoint one person in each Precinct as Precinct Captain, and, by a personal interview with him, procure his pledge, to perform promptly all the duties assigned him.

3rd. To deliver to each Precinct Captain the list of names as above, belonging to his Precinct; and also a written list of his duties.

Duties of the Precinct Captain

1st. To divide the list of names delivered him by the county Captain, into Sections of ten who reside most convenient to each other.

2nd. To appoint one person of each Section as Section Captain, and by a personal interview with him, procure his pledge to perform promptly all the duties assigned him.

3rd. To deliver to each Section Captain the list of names belonging to his Section and also a written list of his duties.

Duties of the Section Captain

1st. To see each man of his Section face to face, and procure his pledge that he will for no consideration (impossibilities excepted) stay from the polls on the first monday in November; and that he will record his vote as early on the day as possible.

2nd. To add to his Section the name of every person in his vicinity who did not vote with us in August, but who will vote with us in the fall, and take the same pledge of him, as from the others.

3rd. To task himself to procure at least such additional names to his Section.

ca. January 1840

To John T. Stuart[1]

Dear Stuart: Jany. 23rd. 1841– Springfield, Ills.
Yours of the 3rd. Inst. is reed. & I proceed to answer it as well as I can, tho' from the deplorable state of my mind at this time, I fear I shall give you but little satisfaction. About the matter of the congressional election, I can only tell you, that there is a bill now before the Senate adopting the General Ticket system;[2] but whether the party have fully determined on it's adoption is yet uncertain. There is no sign of opposition to you among our friends, and none that I can learn among our enemies; tho', of course, there will be, if the Genl. Ticket be adopted. The Chicago American, Peoria Register, & Sangamo Journal, have already hoisted your flag upon their own responsibility; & the other whig papers of the District are expected to follow immediately. On last evening there was a meeting of our friends at Butler's; and I submitted the question to them & found them unanamously in favour of having you announced as a candidate. A few of us this morning, however, concluded, that as you were already being announced in the papers, we would delay announcing you, *as by your own authority* for a week or two. We thought that to appear too keen about it might spur our opponents on about their Genl. Ticket project. Upon the whole, I think I may say with certainty, that your reelection is sure, if it be in the power of the whigs to make it so.

For not giving you a general summary of news, you *must* pardon me; it is not in my power to do so. I am now the most miserable man living. If what I feel were equally distributed to the whole human family, there would not be one cheerful face on the earth. Whether I shall ever be better I can not tell; I awfully forebode I shall not. To remain as I am is impossible; I must die or be better, it appears to me. The matter you speak of on my account, you may attend to as you say, unless you shall hear of my condition forbidding it. I say this, because I fear I shall be unable to attend to any business here, and a change of scene might help me. If I could be myself, I would rather remain at home with Judge Logan.[3] I can write no more. Your friend, as ever—

From To Mary Speed[1]

Miss Mary Speed,   Bloomington, Illinois,
Louisville, Ky.   Sept. 27th. 1841

*   *   *

We got on board the Steam Boat Lebanon, in the locks of the Canal about 12. o'clock. M. of the day we left, and reached St. Louis the next

---

1. John Todd Stuart (1807–85), Whig politician and lawyer who, during the Black Hawk War, had been a major in the battalion in which Lincoln was the captain of a company. From 1837 to 1841, he and Lincoln were law partners in Springfield.
2. Illinois Whigs were discussing a system, already in use among Democrats, whereby a political convention would be held to outline general party policies to bring focus to the campaign and reduce the number of candidates. Stuart won reelection to Congress in June.
3. Stephen T. Logan (1800–1880), attorney and former circuit judge, was Lincoln's law partner in Springfield from 1841 to 1844.
1. The half-sister of Lincoln's Springfield friend Joshua F. Speed (1814–1882).

monday at 8 P.M. Nothing of interest happened during the passage, except the vexatious delays occasioned by the sand bars be thought interesting. By the way, a fine example was presented on board the boat for contemplating the effect of *condition* upon human happiness. A gentleman had purchased twelve negroes in diferent parts of Kentucky and was taking them to a farm in the South. They were chained six and six together. A small iron clevis was around the left wrist of each, and this fastened to the main chain by a shorter one at a convenient distance from, the others; so that the negroes were strung together precisely like so many fish upon a trot-line. In this condition they were being separated forever from the scenes of their childhood, their friends, their fathers and mothers, and brothers and sisters, and many of them, from their wives and children, and going into perpetual slavery where the lash of the master is proverbially more ruthless and unrelenting than any other where; and yet amid all these distressing circumstances, as we would think them, they were the most cheerful and apparantly happy creatures on board. One, whose offence for which he had been sold was an over-fondness for his wife, played the fiddle almost continually; and the others danced, sung, cracked jokes, and played various games with cards from day to day. How true it is that "God tempers the wind to the shorn lamb," or in other words, that He renders the worst of human conditions tolerable, while He permits the best, to be nothing better than tolerable.

*   *   *

Address to the Washington Temperance Society[1] of Springfield, Illinois

Although the Temperance cause has been in progress for near twenty years, it is apparent to all, that it is, *just now*, being crowned with a degree of success, hitherto unparalleled.

The list of its friends is daily swelled by the additions of fifties, of hundreds, and of thousands. The cause itself seems suddenly transformed from a cold abstract theory, to a living, breathing, active, and powerful chieftain, going forth "conquering and to conquer."[2] The citadels of his great adversary are daily being stormed and dismantled; his temples and his altars, where the rites of his idolatrous worship have long been performed, and where human sacrifices have long been wont to be made, are daily desecrated and deserted. The trump of the conqueror's fame is sounding from hill to hill, from sea to sea, and from land to land, and calling millions to his standard at a blast.

For this new and splendid success, we heartily rejoice. That that success is so much greater *now* than *heretofore*, is doubtless owing to rational causes; and if we would have it to continue, we shall do well to enquire what those causes are. The warfare heretofore waged against the demon of Intemperance, has, some how or other, been erroneous. Either the

1. A nationwide temperance organization, with many local branches, founded in 1840. The Washingtonians had a distinctly working-class character and consisted largely of reformed drunkards.
2. From Revelation 6:2.

champions engaged, or the tactics they adopted, have not been the most proper. These champions for the most part, have been Preachers, Lawyers, and hired agents. Between these and the mass of mankind, there is a want of *approachability*, if the term be admissible, partially at least, fatal to their success. They are supposed to have no sympathy of feeling or interest, with those very persons whom it is their object to convince and persuade.

And again, it is so easy and so common to ascribe motives to men of these classes, other than those they profess to act upon. The *preacher*, it is said, advocates temperance because he is a fanatic, and desires a union of Church and State; the *lawyer*, from his pride and vanity of hearing himself speak; and the *hired agent*, for his salary. But when one, who has long been known as a victim of intemperance, bursts the fetters that have bound him, and appears before his neighbors "clothed, and in his right mind,"[3] a redeemed specimen of long lost humanity, and stands up with tears of joy trembling in eyes, to tell of the miseries *once* endured, *now* to be endured no more forever; of his once naked and starving children, now clad and fed comfortably; of a wife long weighed down with woe, weeping, and a broken heart, now restored to health, happiness, and renewed affection; and how easily it all is done, once it is resolved to be done; however simple his language, there is a logic, and an eloquence in it, that few, with human feelings, can resist. They cannot say that *he* desires a union of church and state, for he is not a church member; they can not say *he* is vain of hearing himself speak, for his whole demeanor shows, he would gladly avoid speaking at all; they cannot say *he* speaks for pay for he receives none, and asks for none. Nor can his sincerity in any way be doubted; or his sympathy for those he would persuade to imitate his example, be denied.

In my judgment, it is to the battles of this new class of champions that our late success is greatly, perhaps chiefly, owing. But, had the old school champions themselves, been of the most wise selecting, was their *system* of tactics, the most judicious? It seems to me, it was not. Too much denunciation against dram sellers and dram-drinkers was indulged in. This, I think, was both impolitic and unjust. It was *impolitic*, because, it is not much in the nature of man to be driven to any thing; still less to be driven about that which is exclusively his own business; and least of all, where such driving is to be submitted to, at the expense of pecuniary interest, or burning appetite. When the dram-seller and drinker, were incessantly told, not in the accents of entreaty and persuasion, diffidently addressed by erring man to an erring brother; but in the thundering tones of anathema and denunciation, with which the lordly Judge often groups together all the crimes of the felon's life, and thrusts them in his face just ere he passes sentence of death upon him, that *they* were the authors of all the vice and misery and crime in the land; that *they* were the manufacturers and material of all the thieves and robbers and murderers that infested the earth; that *their* houses were the workshops of the devil; and that *their persons* should be shunned by all the good and virtuous, as moral pestilences—I say, when they were told all this, and in this way, it is not

3. From Luke 8:35.

wonderful that they were slow, *very slow*, to acknowledge the truth of such denunciations, and to join the ranks of their denouncers, in a hue and cry against themselves.

To have expected them to do otherwise than as they did—to have expected them not to meet denunciation with denunciation, crimination with crimination, and anathema with anathema, was to expect a reversal of human nature, which is God's decree, and never can be reversed. When the conduct of men is designed to be influenced, *persuasion*, kind, unassuming persuasion, should ever be adopted. It is an old and a true maxim, that a "drop of honey catches more flies than a gallon of gall." So with men. If you would win a man to your cause, *first* convince him that you are his sincere friend. Therein is a drop of honey that catches his heart, which, say what he will, is the great high road to his reason, and which, when once gained, you will find but little trouble in convincing his judgment of the justice of your cause, if indeed that cause really be a just one. On the contrary, assume to dictate to his judgment, or to command his action, or to mark him as one to be shunned and despised, and he will retreat within himself, close all the avenues to his head and his heart; and tho' your cause be naked truth itself, transformed to the heaviest lance, harder than steel, and sharper than steel can be made, and tho' you throw it with more than Herculean force and precision, you shall no more be able to pierce him, than to penetrate the hard shell of a tortoise with a rye straw.

Such is man, and so *must* he be understood by those who would lead him, even to his own best interest.

On this point, the Washingtonians greatly excel the temperance advocates of former times. Those whom *they* desire to convince and persuade, are their old friends and companions. They know they are not demons, nor even the worst of men. *They* know that generally, they are kind, generous and charitable, even beyond the example of their more staid and sober neighbors. *They* are practical philanthropists; and *they* glow with a generous and brotherly zeal, that mere theorizers are incapable of feeling. Benevolence and charity possess *their* hearts entirely; and out of the abundance of their hearts, their tongues give utterance. "Love through all their actions runs, and all their words are mild."[4] In this spirit they speak and act, and in the same, they are heard and regarded. And when such is the temper of the advocate, and such of the audience, no good cause can be unsuccessful.

But I have said that denunciations against dram-sellers and dram-drinkers, are *unjust* as well as impolitic. Let us see.

I have not enquired at what period of time the use of intoxicating drinks commenced; nor is it important to know. It is sufficient that to all of us who now inhabit the world, the practice of drinking them, is just as old as the world itself,—that is, we have seen the one, just as long as we have seen the other. When all such of us, as have now reached the years of maturity, first opened our eyes upon the stage of existence, we found intoxicating liquor, recognized by every body, used by every body, and repudiated by nobody. It commonly entered into the first draught of the

---

4. From "Let Dogs Delight to Bark and Bite" (1715) by the English hymn writer Isaac Watts (1674–1748).

infant, and the last draught of the dying man. From the sideboard of the parson, down to the ragged pocket of the houseless loafer, it was constantly found. Physicians prescribed it in this, that, and the other disease. Government provided it for its soldiers and sailors; and to have a rolling or raising, a husking or hoe-down, any where without it, was *positively insufferable*.

So too, it was every where a respectable article of manufacture and of merchandize. The making of it was regarded as an honorable livelihood; and he who could make most, was the most enterprising and respectable. Large and small manufactories of it were every where erected, in which all the earthly goods of their owners were invested. Wagons drew it from town to town—boats bore it from clime to clime, and the winds wafted it from nation to nation; and merchants bought and sold it, by wholesale and by retail, with precisely the same feelings, on the part of seller, buyer, and bystander, as are felt at the selling and buying of flour, beef, bacon, or any other of the real necessaries of life. Universal public opinion not only tolerated, but recognized and adopted its use.

It is true, that even *then*, it was known and acknowledged, that many were greatly injured by it; but none seemed to think the injury arose from the *use* of a *bad thing*, but from the *abuse* of a *very good thing*. The victims to it were pitied, and compassionated, just as now are, the heirs of consumptions, and other hereditary diseases. Their failing was treated as a *misfortune*, and not as a *crime*, or even as a *disgrace*.

If, then, what I have been saying be true, is it wonderful, that *some* should think and act *now*, as *all* thought and acted *twenty years ago*? And is it *just* to assail, *contemn*, or despise them, for doing so? The universal *sense* of mankind, on any subject, is an argument, or at least an *influence* not easily overcome. The success of the argument in favor of the existence of an over-ruling Providence, mainly depends upon that sense; and men ought not, in justice, to be denounced for yielding to it, in any case, or for giving it up slowly, *especially*, where they are backed by interest, fixed habits, or burning appetites.

Another error, as it seems to me, into which the old reformers fell, was, the position that all habitual drunkards were utterly incorrigible, and therefore, must be turned adrift, and damned without remedy, in order that the grace of temperance might abound to the temperate *then*, and to all mankind some hundred years *thereafter*. There is in this something so repugnant to humanity, so uncharitable, so cold-blooded and feelingless, that it never did, nor ever can enlist the enthusiasm of a popular cause. We could not love the man who taught it—we could not hear him with patience. The heart could not throw open its portals to it. The generous man could not adopt it. It could not mix with his blood. It looked so fiendishly selfish, so like throwing fathers and brothers overboard, to lighten the boat for our security—that the noble minded shrank from the manifest meanness of the thing.

And besides this, the benefits of a reformation to be effected by such a system, were too remote in point of time, to warmly engage many in its behalf. Few can be induced to labor exclusively for posterity; and none will do it enthusiastically. Posterity has done nothing for us; and theorise on it as we may, practically we shall do very little for it, unless we are made to think, we are, at the same time, doing something for ourselves.

What an ignorance of human nature does it exhibit, to ask or expect a whole community to rise up and labor for the *temporal* happiness of *others* after *themselves* shall be consigned to the dust, a majority of which community take no pains whatever to secure their own eternal welfare, at a no greater distant day? Great distance, in either time or space, has wonderful power to lull and render quiescent the human mind. Pleasures to be enjoyed, or pains to be endured, *after* we shall be dead and gone, are but little regarded, even in our *own* cases, and much less in the cases of others.

Still, in addition to this, there is something so ludicrous in *promises* of good, or *threats* of evil, a great way off, as to render the whole subject with which they are connected, easily turned into ridicule. "Better lay down that spade you're stealing, Paddy,—if you don't you'll pay for it at the day of judgment." "By the powers, if ye'll credit me so long, I'll take another, jist."

By the Washingtonians, this system of consigning the habitual drunkard to hopeless ruin, is repudiated. *They* adopt a more enlarged philanthropy. *They* go for present as well as future good. *They* labor for all *now* living, as well as all *hereafter* to live. *They* teach *hope* to all—*despair* to none. As applying to *their* cause, *they* deny the doctrine of unpardonable sin. As in Christianity it is taught, so in this *they* teach, that

> "While the lamp holds out to burn,
> The vilest sinner may return."[5]

And, what is matter of the most profound gratulation, they, by experiment upon experiment, and example upon example, prove the maxim to be no less true in the one case than in the other. On every hand we behold those, who but yesterday, were the chief of sinners, now the chief apostles of the cause. Drunken devils are cast out by ones, by sevens, and by legions; and their unfortunate victims, like the poor possessed, who was redeemed from his long and lonely wanderings in the tombs, are publishing to the ends of the earth, how great things have been done for them.

To these *new champions*, and this *new* system of tactics, our late success is mainly owing; and to *them* we must chiefly look for the final consummation. The ball is now rolling gloriously on, and none are so able as *they* to increase its speed, and its bulk—to add to its momentum, and its magnitude. Even though unlearned in letters, for this task, none others are so well educated. To fit them for this work, they have been taught in the true school. *They* have been in *that* gulf, from which they would teach others the means of escape. *They* have passed that prison wall, which others have long declared impassable; and who that has not, shall dare to weigh opinions with *them*, as to the mode of passing.

But if it be true, as I have insisted, that those who have suffered by intemperance *personally*, and have reformed, are the most powerful and efficient instruments to push the reformation to ultimate success, it does not follow, that those who have not suffered, have no part left them to perform. Whether or not the world would be vastly benefitted by a total and final banishment from it of all intoxicating drinks, seems to me not *now* to be an open question. Three-fourths of mankind confess the affirmative with their *tongues*, and, I believe, all the rest acknowledge it in their *hearts*.

---

5. From the hymn "Life, the Day of Grace and Hope" (1707).

Ought *any*, then, to refuse their aid in doing what the good of the *whole* demands? Shall he, who cannot do *much*, be, for that reason, excused if he do *nothing*? "But," says one, "what good can I do by signing the pledge? I never drink even without signing."[6] This question has already been asked and answered more than millions of times. Let it be answered once more. For the man to suddenly, or in any other way, to break off from the use of drams, who has indulged in them for a long course of years, and until his appetite for them has become ten or a hundred fold stronger, and more craving, than any natural appetite can be, requires a most powerful moral effort. In such an undertaking, he needs every moral support and influence, that can possibly be brought to his aid, and thrown around him. And not only so; but every moral prop, should be taken *from* whatever argument might rise in his mind to lure him to his backsliding. When he casts his eyes around him, he should be able to see, all that he respects, all that he admires, and all that he loves, kindly and anxiously pointing him onward; and none beckoning him back, to his former miserable "wallowing in the mire."

But it is said by some, that men will *think* and *act* for themselves; that none will disuse spirits or any thing else, merely because his neighbors do; and that *moral influence* is not that powerful engine contended for. Let us examine this. Let me ask the man who would maintain this position most stiffly, what compensation he will accept to go to church some Sunday and sit during the sermon with his wife's bonnet upon his head? Not a trifle, I'll venture. And why not? There would be nothing irreligious in it: nothing immoral, nothing uncomfortable. Then why not? Is it not because there would be something egregiously unfashionable in it? Then it is the influence of *fashion*; and what is the influence of fashion, but the influence that *other* people's actions have on our own actions, the strong inclination each of us feels to do as we see all our neighbors do? Nor is the influence of fashion confined to any particular thing or class of things. It is just as strong on one subject as another. Let us make it as unfashionable to withhold our names from the temperance pledge as for husbands to wear their wives bonnets to church, and instances will be just as rare in the one case as the other.

"But," say some, "we are no drunkards; and we shall not acknowledge ourselves such by joining a reformed drunkard's society, whatever our influence might be." Surely no Christian will adhere to this objection. If they believe, as they profess, that Omnipotence condescended to take on himself the form of sinful man, and, as such, to die an ignominious death for their sakes, surely they will not refuse submission to the infinitely lesser condescension, for the temporal, and perhaps eternal salvation, of a large, erring, and unfortunate class of their own fellow creatures. Nor is the condescension very great.

In my judgment, such of us as have never fallen victims, have been spared more from the absence of appetite, than from any mental or moral superiority over those who have. Indeed, I believe, if we take habitual drunkards as a class, their heads and their hearts will bear an advantageous comparison with those of any other class. There seems ever to have

---

6. A reference to the well-known fact that a large percentage of Americans who signed pledges of total abstinence soon took up drinking again.

been a proneness in the brilliant, and the warm-blooded, to fall into this vice. The demon of intemperance ever seems to have delighted in sucking the blood of genius and of generosity. What one of us but can call to mind some dear relative, more promising in youth than all his fellows, who has fallen a sacrifice to his rapacity? He ever seems to have gone forth, like the Egyptian angel of death, commissioned to slay if not the first, the fairest born of every family. Shall he now be arrested in his desolating career? In that arrest, all can give aid that will; and who shall be excused that *can*, and will not? Far around as human breath has ever blown, he keeps our fathers, our brothers, our sons, and our friends, prostrate in the chains of moral death. To all the living every where, we cry, "come sound the moral resurrection trump, that these may rise and stand up, an exceeding great army"—"Come from the four winds, O breath! and breathe upon these slain, that they may live."[7]

If the relative grandeur of revolutions shall be estimated by the great amount of human misery they alleviate, and the small amount they inflict, then, indeed, will this be the grandest the world shall ever have seen. Of our political revolution of '76, we all are justly proud. It has given us a degree of political freedom, far exceeding that of any other of the nations of the earth. In it the world has found a solution of that long mooted problem, as to the capability of man to govern himself. In it was the germ which has vegetated, and still is to grow and expand into the universal liberty of mankind.

But with all these glorious results, past, present, and to come, it had its evils too. It breathed forth famine, swam in blood and rode on fire; and long, long after, the orphan's cry, and the widow's wail, continued to break the sad silence that ensued. These were the price, the inevitable price, paid for the blessings it bought.

Turn now, to the temperance revolution. In *it*, we shall find a stronger bondage broken; a viler slavery, manumitted; a greater tyrant deposed. In *it*, more of want supplied, more disease healed, more sorrow assuaged. By *it* no orphans starving, no widows weeping. By *it*, none wounded in feeling, none injured in interest. Even the dram-maker, and dram seller, will have glided into other occupations so gradually, as never to have felt the shock of change; and will stand ready to join all others in the universal song of gladness.

And what a noble ally this, to the cause of political freedom. With such an aid, its march cannot fail to be on and on, till every son of earth shall drink in rich fruition, the sorrow quenching draughts of perfect liberty. Happy day, when, all appetites controled, all passions subdued, all matters subjected, *mind*, all conquering *mind*, shall live and move the monarch of the world. Glorious consummation! Hail fall of Fury! Reign of Reason, all hail!

And when the victory shall be complete—when there shall be neither a slave nor a drunkard on the earth—how proud the title of that *Land*, which may truly claim to be the birthplace and the cradle of both those revolutions, that shall have ended in that victory. How nobly distinguished

---

7. Ezekiel 37:9–10: "Then he said unto me, Prophesy unto the wind, prophesy, son of man, and say to the wind, Thus saith the Lord God; Come from the four winds, O breath, and breathe upon these slain, that they may live. So I prophesied as he commanded me, and the breath came into them, and they lived, and stood up upon their feet, an exceeding great army."

that People, who shall have planted, and nurtured to maturity, both the political and moral freedom of their species.

This is the one hundred and tenth anniversary of the birthday of Washington. We are met to celebrate this day. Washington is the mightiest name of earth—*long since* mightiest in the cause of civil liberty; *still* mightiest in moral reformation. On that name, an eulogy is expected. It cannot be. To add brightness to the sun, or glory to the name of Washington, is alike impossible. Let none attempt it. In solemn awe pronounce the name, and in its naked deathless splendor, leave it shining on.

February 22, 1842

Duel Instructions to Elias H. Merryman[1]

In case Whitesides[2] shall signify a wish to adjust this affair without further difficulty, let him know that if the present papers be withdrawn, & a note from Mr. Shields asking to know if I am the author of the articles of which he complains, and asking that I shall make him gentlemanly satisfaction, if I am the author, and this without menace, or dictation as to what that satisfaction shall be, a pledge is made, that the following answer shall be given—

"I did write the 'Lost Township' letter which appeared in the Journal of the 2nd. Inst. but had no participation, in any form, in any other article alluding to you. I wrote that, wholly for political effect. I had no intention of injuring your personal or private character or standing as a man or a gentleman; and I did not then think, and do not now think that that article, could produce or has produced that effect against you, and had I anticipated such an effect I would have forborne to write it. And I will add, that your conduct towards me, so far as I knew, had always been gentlemanly; and that I had no personal pique against you, and no cause for any."

If this should be done, I leave it with you to arrange what shall & what shall not be published.

If nothing like this is done—the preliminaries of the fight are to be—

1st. Weapons—Cavalry broad swords of the largest size, precisely equal in all respects—and such as now used by the cavalry company at Jacksonville.

2nd. Position—A plank ten feet long, & from nine to twelve inches broad to be firmly fixed on edge, on the ground, as the line between us which neither is to pass his foot over upon forfeit of his life. Next a line drawn on the ground on either side of said plank & paralel with it, each at the distance of the whole length of the sword and three feet additional from the plank; and the passing of his own such line by either party during the fight shall be deemed a surrender of the contest.

3. Time—On thursday evening at five o'clock if you can get it so; but in no case to be at a greater distance of time than friday evening at five o'clock.

1. Lincoln's second in a duel that had been arranged with Democrat James Shields (1810–1879), the Illinois state auditor who had challenged Lincoln because of the latter's anonymously published criticism of him. The duel was averted through the intervention of mutual friends and Lincoln's assurances that the criticism was political, not personal. Shields went on to serve as a U.S. senator from Illinois and, later, from Minnesota and Missouri.
2. John D. Whiteside (1794–1850), Democrat and state politician in Illinois.

4th. Place—Within three miles of Alton on the opposite side of the river, the particular spot to be agreed on by you.

Any preliminary details coming within the above rules, you are at liberty to make at your discretion; but you are in no case to swerve from these rules, or to pass beyond their limits.

September 19, 1842

From To Martin S. Morris[1]

Friend Morris: Springfield March 26th. 1843
Your letter of the 23rd. was received on yesterday morning, and for which (instead of an excuse which you thought proper to ask).

I tender you my sincere thanks. It is truly gratifying to me to learn that while the people of Sangamon have cast me off, my old friends of Menard who have known me longest and best of any, still retain their confidence in me. It would astonish if not amuse, the older citizens of your County who twelve years ago knew me a stranger, friendless, uneducated, penniless boy, working on a flat boat—at ten dollars per month to learn that I have been put down here as the candidate of pride, wealth, and aristocratic family distinction. Yet so chiefly it was. There was too the strangest combination of church influence against me. Baker is a Campbellite,[2] and therefore as I suppose, with few exceptions got all that church. My wife has some relatives in the Presbyterian and some in the Episcopal Churches, and therefore, wherever it would tell, I was set down as either the one or the other, whilst it was every where contended that no christian ought to go for me, because I belonged to no church, was suspected of being a deist,[3] and had talked about fighting a duel. With all these things Baker, of course had nothing to do. Nor do I complain of them. As to his own church going for him, I think that was right enough, and as to the influences I have spoken of in the other, though they were very strong, it would be grossly untrue and unjust to charge that they acted upon them in a body or even very nearly so. I only mean that those influences levied a tax of a considerable per cent upon my strength throughout the religious community.

＊   ＊   ＊

---

1. Martin Sims Morris of Petersburg was one of two delegates from Menard County in the Illinois race for Congress. In preliminary jockeying for the Whig candidacy, Lincoln competed with his Springfield friend, lawyer Edward D. Baker (1811–1861), who won the endorsement of Sangamon County, partly because of charges against Lincoln on religious grounds and his supposed privileged status (the aristocracy mentioned in the letter probably refers to Lincoln's marriage into the wealthy Todd family). As it turned out, neither Baker nor Lincoln won the Whig nomination at Pekin in May 1843.
2. A follower of Thomas and Alexander Campbell, leaders of the Disciples of Christ, which in 1832 merged with the Christians to form the American Restoration Movement.
3. A skeptical rationalist; one who disbelieves in revealed religion.

To Williamson Durley[1]

Friend Durley: Springfield, Octr. 3. 1845

When I saw you at home, it was agreed that I should write to you and your
brother Madison. Until I then saw you, I was not aware of your being what
is generally called an abolitionist, or, as you call yourself, a Liberty-man;
though I well knew there were many such in your county. I was glad to hear
you say that you intend to attempt to bring about, at the next election in
Putnam, a union of the whigs proper, and such of the liberty men, as are
whigs in principle on all questions save only that of slavery. So far as I can
perceive, by such union, neither party need yield any thing, on the point in
difference between them. If the whig abolitionists of New York had voted
with us last fall, Mr. Clay[2] would now be president, whig principles in the
ascendent, and Texas not annexed; whereas by the division, all that either
had at stake in the contest, was lost. And, indeed, it was extremely probable, beforehand, that such would be the result. As I always understood, the
Liberty-men deprecated the annexation of Texas extremely; and, this being
so, why they should refuse to so cast their votes as to prevent it, even to me,
seemed wonderful. What was their process of reasoning, I can only judge
from what a single one of them told me. It was this: "We are not to do evil
that good may come." This general, proposition is doubtless correct; but
did it apply? If by your votes you could have prevented the extention, &c. of
slavery, would it not have been good and not evil so to have used your votes,
even though it involved the casting of them for a slaveholder? By the fruit
the tree is to be known. An evil tree can not bring forth good fruit. If the
fruit of electing Mr. Clay would have been to prevent the extension of slavery, could the act of electing have been evil?

But I will not argue farther, I perhaps ought to say that individually I
never was much interested in the Texas question. I never could see much
good to come of annexation; inasmuch, as they were already a free republican people on our own model; on the other hand, I never could very
clearly see how the annexation would augment the evil of slavery. It
always seemed to me that slaves would be taken there in about equal
numbers, with or without annexation. And if more were taken because of
annexation, still there would be just so many the fewer left, where they
were taken from. It is possibly true, to some extent, that with annexation,
some slaves may be sent to Texas and continued in slavery, that otherwise
might have been liberated. To whatever extent this may be true, I think
annexation an evil. I hold it to be a paramount duty of us in the free
states, due to the Union of the states, and perhaps to liberty itself (paradox though it may seem) to let the slavery of the other states alone; while,
on the other hand, I hold it to be equally clear, that we should never
knowingly lend ourselves directly or indirectly, to prevent that slavery
from dying a natural death—to find new places for it to live in, when it

1. A Hennepin, Illinois, farmer (1810–1901) and county commissioner of Putnam County. He
   and his brother Madison were supporters of Lincoln.
2. Henry Clay (1777–1852), Kentucky Whig and Lincoln's ideal statesman, served ten terms in
   the Senate and seven in the House of Representatives and was known as the Great Pacificator
   because he helped devise several compromises over the slavery issue. Though a slave owner, he
   advocated the gradual abolition of slavery and colonization (the deportation of blacks to Liberia or elsewhere). In the presidential race of 1844, Clay was defeated by Democrat John Tyler.

can no longer exist in the old. Of course I am not now considering what would be our duty, in cases of insurrection among the slaves.

To recur to the Texas question, I understand the Liberty men to have viewed annexation as a much greater evil than I ever did; and I, would like to convince you if I could, that they could have prevented it, without violation of principle, if they had chosen.

I intend this letter for you and Madison together; and if you and he or either shall think fit to drop me a line, I shall be pleased. Yours with respect

My Childhood-Home I See Again[1]

My childhood-home I see again,
    And gladden with the view;
And still as mem'ries crowd my brain,
    There's sadness in it too.

5 O memory! thou mid-way world
    'Twixt Earth and Paradise;
Where things decayed, and loved ones lost
    In dreamy shadows rise.

And freed from all that's gross or vile,
10   Seem hallowed, pure, and bright,
Like scenes in some enchanted isle,
    All bathed in liquid light.

As distant mountains please the eye,
    When twilight chases day—
15 As bugle-tones, that, passing by,
    In distance die away—

As leaving some grand water-fall
    We ling'ring, list it's roar,
So memory will hallow all
20   We've known, but know no more.

Now twenty years have passed away,
    Since here I bid farewell
To woods, and fields, and scenes of play
    And school-mates loved so well.

25 Where many were, how few remain
    Of old familiar things!
But seeing these to mind again
    The lost and absent brings.

The friends I left that parting day—
30   How changed, as time has sped!

---

1. Lincoln was inspired by an 1844 visit to his childhood home in southwestern Indiana, where he had lived from 1816 to 1830.

Young childhood grown, strong manhood grey,
 And half of all are dead.

I hear the lone survivors tell
 How nought from death could save,
35 Till every sound appears a knell,
 And every spot a grave.

I range the fields with pensive tread,
 And pace the hollow rooms;
And feel (companions of the dead)
40 I'm living in the tombs.

And here's an object more of dread,
 Than ought the grave contains—
A human-form, with reason fled,
 While wretched life remains.

45 Poor Matthew![2] Once of genius bright,—
 A fortune-favored child—
Now locked for aye, in mental night,
 A haggard mad-man wild.

Poor Matthew! I have ne'er forgot
50 When first with maddened will,
Yourself you maimed, your father fought,
 And mother strove to kill;

And terror spread, and neighbours ran,
 Your dang'rous strength to bind;
55 And soon a howling crazy man,
 Your limbs were fast confined.

How then you writhed and shrieked aloud,
 Your bones and sinnews bared;
And fiendish on the gaping crowd,
60 With burning eye-balls glared.

And begged, and swore, and wept, and prayed,
 With maniac laughter joined—
How fearful are the signs displayed,
 By pangs that kill the mind!

65 And when at length, tho' drear and long,
 Time soothed your fiercer woes—
How plaintively your mournful song,
 Upon the still night rose.

---

2. Matthew Gentry, Lincoln's boyhood friend, who became mentally ill and at nineteen tried to kill his parents.

I've heard it oft, as if I dreamed,
70   Far-distant, sweet, and lone;
The funeral dirge it ever seemed
    Of reason dead and gone.

To drink it's strains, I've stole away,
    All silently and still,
75 Ere yet the rising god of day
    Had streaked the Eastern hill.

Air held his breath; the trees all still
    Seemed sorr'wing angels round.
Their swelling tears in dew-drops fell
80   Upon the list'ning ground.

But this is past, and nought remains
    That raised you o'er the brute.
Your mad'ning shrieks and soothing strains
    Are like forever mute.

85 Now fare thee well: more thou the cause
    Than subject now of woe.
All mental pangs, but time's kind laws,
    Hast lost the power to know.

And now away to seek some scene
90   Less painful than the last—
With less of horror mingled in
    The present and the past.

The very spot where grew the bread
    That formed my bones, I see.
95 How strange, old field, on thee to tread,
    And feel I'm part of thee!

ca. April 1846

Handbill Replying to Charges of Infidelity

To the Voters of the Seventh Congressional District.

Fellow citizens:

A charge having got into circulation in some of the neighborhoods of this District, in substance that I am an open scoffer at Christianity, I have by the advice of some friends concluded to notice the subject in this form. That I am not a member of any Christian Church, is true; but I have never denied the truth of the Scriptures; and I have never spoken with intentional disrespect of religion in general, or of any denomination of Christians in particular. It is true that in early life I was inclined to believe in what I understand is called the "Doctrine of Necessity"—that is, that the human mind is impelled to action, or held in rest by some power, over which the mind itself has no control; and I have sometimes (with one, two or three, but never publicly) tried to maintain this opinion in argument. The habit of arguing thus however, I have, entirely left off for more than five years. And I add here, I have always understood this same opinion to be held by several of the Christian denominations. The foregoing, is the whole truth, briefly stated, in relation to myself, upon this subject.

I do not think I could myself, be brought to support a man for office, whom I knew to be an open enemy of, and scoffer at, religion. Leaving the higher matter of eternal consequences, between him and his Maker, I still do not think any man has the right thus to insult the feelings, and injure the morals, of the community in which he may live. If, then, I was guilty of such conduct, I should blame no man who should condemn me for it; but I do blame those, whoever they may be, who falsely put such a charge in circulation against me.

July 31, 1846.

The Bear Hunt

A wild-bear chace, didst never see?
    Then hast thou lived in vain.
Thy richest bump of glorious glee,
    Lies desert in thy brain.

5 When first my father settled here,
    'Twas then the frontier line:
The panther's scream, filled night with fear
    And bears preyed on the swine.

But wo for Bruin's short lived fun,
10   When rose the squealing cry;
Now man and horse, with dog and gun,
    For vengeance, at him fly.

A sound of danger strikes his ear;
    He gives the breeze a snuff:
15 Away he bounds, with little fear,
    And seeks the tangled *rough*.

On press his foes, and reach the ground,
    Where's left his half munched meal;
The dogs, in circles, scent around,
20   And find his fresh made trail.

With instant cry, away they dash,
    And men as fast pursue;
O'er logs they leap, through water splash,
    And shout the brisk halloo.

25 Now to elude the eager pack,
       Bear shuns the open ground;
    Through matted vines, he shapes his track
       And runs it, round and round.

    The tall fleet cur, with deep-mouthed voice,
30   Now speeds him, as the wind;
    While half-grown pup, and short-legged fice,[1]
       Are yelping far behind.

    And fresh recruits are dropping in
       To join the merry *corps*:
35 With yelp and yell,—a mingled din—
       The woods are in a roar.

    And round, and round the chace now goes,
       The world's alive with fun;
    Nick Carter's horse, his rider throws,
40   And more, Hill drops his gun.

    Now sorely pressed, bear glances back,
       And lolls his tired tongue;
    When as, to force him from his track,
       An ambush on him sprung.

45 Across the glade he sweeps for flight,
       And fully is in view.
    The dogs, new-fired, by the sight,
       Their cry, and speed, renew.

    The foremost ones, now reach his rear,
50   He turns, they dash away;
    And circling now, the wrathful bear,
       They have him full at bay.

    At top of speed, the horse-men come,
       All screaming in a row.
55 "Whoop! Take him Tiger. Seize him Drum."
       Bang,—bang—the rifles go.

    And furious now, the dogs he tears,
       And crushes in his ire.
    Wheels right and left, and upward rears,
60   With eyes of burning fire.

    But leaden death is at his heart,
       Vain all the strength he plies.
    And, spouting blood from every part,
       He reels, and sinks, and dies.

1. Mongrel dog.

65 And now a dinsome clamor rose,
   'Bout who should have his skin;
   Who first draws blood, each hunter knows,
   This prize must always win.

   But who did this, and how to trace
70   What's true from what's a lie,
   Like lawyers, in a murder case
   They stoutly *argufy*.

   Aforesaid fice, of blustering mood,
   Behind, and quite forgot,
75 Just now emerging from the wood,
   Arrives upon the spot.

   With grinning teeth, and up-turned hair—
   Brim full of spunk and wrath,
   He growls, and seizes on dead bear,
80   And shakes for life and death.

   And swells as if his skin would tear,
   And growls and shakes again;
   And swears, as plain as dog can swear,
   That he has won the skin.

85 Conceited whelp![2] we laugh at thee—
   Nor mind, that not a few
   Of pompous, two-legged dogs there be,
   Conceited quite as you.

before February 25, 1847

From Fragments on the Tariff

*   *   *

In the early days of the world, the Almighty said to the first of our race
"In the sweat of thy face shalt thou eat bread";[1] and since then, if we except
the *light* and the *air* of heaven, no good thing has been, or can be enjoyed
by us, without having first cost labour. And, inasmuch as most good things
are produced by labour, it follows that all such things of right belong to
those whose labour has produced them. But it has so happened in all ages
of the world, that *some* have laboured, and *others* have, without labour,
enjoyed a large proportion of the fruits. This is wrong, and should not
continue. To secure to each labourer the whole product of his labour, or as
nearly as possible, is a most worthy object of any good government. But
then the question arises, how can a government best, effect this? In our
own country, in it's present condition, will the protective principle *advance*

2. Puppy.
1. Genesis 3:19.

or *retard* this object? Upon this subject, the habits of our whole species fall into three great classes—*useful* labour, *useless* labour and *idleness*. Of these the first only is meritorious; and to it all the products of labour rightfully belong; but the two latter, while they exist, are heavy pensioners upon the first, robbing it of a large portion of it's just rights. The only remedy for this is to, as far as possible, drive *useless* labour and *idleness* out of existence. And, first, as to useles labour. Before making war upon this, we must learn to distinguish it from the useful. It appears to me, then, that all labour done *directly* and *incidentally* in *carrying* articles to their place of consumption, which could have been produced in sufficient abundance, *with as little labour, at the place of consumption*, as at the place they were carried from, is useless labour. Let us take a few examples of the application of this principle to our own country. Iron & every thing made of iron, can be produced, in sufficient abundance, and with as little labour, in the United States, as any where else in the world; therefore, all labour done in bringing iron & it's fabrics from a foreign country to the United States, is useless labour. The same precisely may be said of cotten, wool, and of their fabrics respectively, as well as many other articles. While the uselessness of the carrying labour is equally true of all the articles mentioned, and of many others not mentioned, it is, perhaps, more glaringly obvious in relation to the cotten goods we purchase from abroad. The raw cotten, from which they are made, itself grows in our own country; is carried by land and by water to England, is there spun, wove, dyed, stamped &c; and then carried back again and worn in the very country where it grew, and partly by the very persons who grew it. Why should it not be spun, wove &c. in the very neighbourhood where it both grows and is consumed, and the carrying about thereby dispensed with? Has nature interposed any obstacle? Are not as good and as abundant here as elsewhere? Will not as small an amount of human labour answer here as elsewhere? We may easily see that the cost of this useless labour is very heavy. It includes, not only the cost of the actual carriage, but also the insurances of every kind, and the profits the merchants through whose hands it passes. All these create a heavy burthen necessarily falling upon the useful labour connected with such articles, either *depressing* the price to the *producer*, or enhancing it to the *consumer*, or, what is more probable, doing both in part. A supposed case, will serve to illustrate several points now to the purpose. A, in the interior of South Carolina, has one hundred pounds of cotten, which we suppose to be the precise product of one mans labour for twenty days; B, in Manchester, England, has one hundred yards of cotten cloth, the precise product of the same amount of labour. This lot of cotten, and lot of cloth are precisely equal to each other in their intrinsic value. But A. wishes to part with his cotten for the largest quantity of cloth he can get; B, also wishes to part with his cloth for the greatest quantity of cotten he can get. An exchange is therefore necessary; but before this can be effected, the cotten must be carried to Manchester, and the cloth to South Carolina. The cotten starts to Manchester; the man that hauls it to Charleston in his waggon, takes a little of it out to pay him for his trouble; the merchant, who stores it a while before the ship is ready to sail, takes a little out, for his trouble; the shipowner, who carries it across the water, takes a little out for his trouble, still before it gets to Manchester, it is tolled two or three times more for drayage, storage, commission, and so on; so that when it reaches B's hands there are but seventyfive pounds of it left. The cloth, too, in it's transit from Manchester to South Carolina goes through the same process of tolling, so that when it reaches A there are but seventyfive yards of it. Now, in this case, A. and B. have each parted with twenty days labour; and each received but fifteen in return. But now let us suppose that B. has removed to the side of A's farm, in South Carolina, and has there made his lot of cloth. Is it not clear that he and A. can then exchange their cloth & cotten, each getting the *whole* of what the other parts with?

This supposed case shows the utter uselessness of the carrying labour in all similar cases, and also the direct burthen it imposes upon useful labour. And whoever will take up the train of reflection suggested by this case, and run it out to the full extent of it's just application, will be astonished, at the amount of useless labour he will thus discover to be done in this very way. I am mistaken, if it is not in fact many times over equal to all the real want in the world. This useless labour I would have discontinued, and those engaged in it, added to the class of useful labourers. If I be asked whether I would destroy all commerce, I answer "Certainly not"—I would continue it where it is *necessary*, and *discontinue* it, where it is not. An instance: I would continue commerce so far as it is employed in bringing us coffee, and I would discontinue it so far as it is employed in bringing us cotten goods.

But let us yield the point, and admit that, by abandoning to protective policy, our farmers can purchase their supplies of manufactured articles *cheaper* than before; and then let us see whether, even at that, the farmers will, upon the whole, be gainers by the change. To simplify this question, let us suppose our whole population to consist of but twenty men. Under the prevalence of the protective policy, fifteen of these are farmers, one is a miller, one manufactures iron, one, implements from iron, one cotten goods, and one woolen goods. The farmers discover, that, owing to labour only costing one quarter as much in Europe as here, they can buy iron, iron implements, cotten goods, & woolen goods cheaper, when brought from Europe, than when made by their neighbours. They are the majority, and therefore have both the legal and moral right to have their interest first consulted. They throw off the protective policy, and cease buying these articles of their neighbours. But they soon discover that to buy, and at the cheaper rate, requires something to buy with. Falling short in this particular, one of these farmers, takes a load of wheat to the miller, and gets it made into flour, and starts, as had been his custom, to the iron furnace; he approaches the well known spot, but, strange to say, all is cold and still as death—no smoke rises, no furnace roars, no anvil rings. After some search he finds the owner of the desolate place, and calls out to him, "Come, Vulcan,[2] dont you want to buy a load of flour?" "Why" says Vulcan "I am hungry enough, to be sure—have'nt tasted bread for a week—but then you see my works are stopped, and I have nothing to give for your flour." "But, Vulcan, why dont you go to work and get something?" "I am ready to do so; will you hire me, farmer?" "Oh, no; I could only set you to raising wheat, and you see I have more of that already than I can get any thing for." "But give me employment, and send your flour to Europe for a

2. Ancient Roman god of fire, often portrayed as a blacksmith.

market." "Why, Vulcan, how silly you talk. Dont you know they raise wheat in Europe as well as here, and that *labour* is so cheap there as to fix the price of flour there so low as scarcely to pay the long carriage of it from here, leaving nothing whatever to me." "But, farmer, could'nt you pay to raise and prepare garden stuffs, and fruits, such as radishes, cabages, irish and sweet potatoes, cucumbers, water-melons and musk-melons, plumbs, pears, peaches, apples, and the like; all these are good things and used to sell well." "So they did use to sell well, but it was to you we sold them, and now you tell us you have nothing to buy with. Of course I can not sell such things to the other farmers, because each of them raises enough for himself, and, in fact, rather wishes to sell than to buy. Neither can I send them to Europe for a market; because, to say nothing of European markets being stocked with such articles at lower prices than I can afford, they are of such a nature as to rot before they could reach there. The truth is, Vulcan, I am compelled to quit raising these things altogether, except a few for my own use, and this leaves part of my own time idle on my hands, instead of my finding employment for you."

If at any time all labour should cease, and all existing provisions be equally divided among the people, at the end of a single year there could scarcely be one human being left alive—all would have perished by want of subsistence.

So again, if upon such division, all that sort of labour, which produces provisions, should cease, and each individual should take up so much of his share as he could, and carry it continually around his habitation, although in this carrying, the amount of labour going on might be as great as ever, so long as it could last, at the end of the year the result would be precisely the same—that is, none would be left living.

The first of these propositions shows, that universal *idleness* would speedily result in universal *ruin*; and the second shows, that *useless labour* is, in this respect, the same as idleness.

I submit, then, whether it does not follow, that *partial* idleness, and partial *useless labour*, would, in the proportion of their extent, in like manner result, in partial ruin—whether, if *all* should subsist upon the labour the *one half* should perform, it would not result in very scanty allowance to the whole.

Believing that these propositions, and the conclusions I draw from them can not be successfully controverted, I, for the present, assume their correctness, and proceed to try to show, that the abandonment of the protective policy by the American Government, must result in the increase of both useless labour, and idleness; and so, in proportion, must produce want and ruin among our people.

August 1846–December 1847

"Spot" Resolutions in the United States House of Representatives

Whereas the President of the United States, in his message of May 11th. 1846, has declared that "The Mexican Government not only refused to receive him" (the envoy of the U.S.) "or listen to his propositions, but, after a long continued series of menaces, have at last invaded *our teritory*, and shed the blood of our fellow *citizens* on *our own soil*"

And again, in his message of December 8, 1846 that "We had ample cause of war against Mexico, long before the breaking out of hostilities. But even then we forbore to take redress into our own hands, until Mexico herself became the aggressor by invading our soil in hostile array, and shedding the blood of our *citizens*'"

And yet again, in his message of December 7- 1847 that "The Mexican Government refused even to hear the terms of adjustment which he" (our minister of peace) "was authorized to propose; and finally, under wholly unjustifiable pretexts, involved the two countries in war, by invading the teritory of the State of Texas, striking the first blow, and shedding the blood of our *citizens* on *our own soil*"

And whereas this House desires to obtain a full knowledge of all the facts which go to establish whether the particular spot of soil on which the blood of our *citizens* was so shed, was, or was not, *our own soil*, at that time; therefore

Resolved by the House of Representatives, that the President of the United States be respectfully requested to inform this House—

First: Whether the spot of soil on which the blood of our *citizens* was shed, as in his messages declared, was, or was not, within the teritories of Spain, at least from the treaty of 1819 until the Mexican revolution

Second: Whether that spot is, or is not, within the teritory which was wrested from Spain, by the Mexican revolution.

Third: Whether that spot is, or is not, within a settlement of people, which settlement had existed ever since long before the Texas revolution, until it's inhabitants fled from the approach of the U.S. Army.

Fourth: Whether that settlement is, or is not, isolated from any and all other settlements, by the Gulf of Mexico, and the Rio Grande, on the South and West, and by wide uninhabited regions on the North and East.

Fifth: Whether the *People* of that settlement, or a *majority* of them, or *any* of them, had ever, previous to the bloodshed, mentioned in his messages, submitted themselves to the government or laws of Texas, or of the United States, by *consent*, or by *compulsion*, either by accepting office, or voting at elections, or paying taxes, or serving on juries, or having process served upon them, or in *any other way*.

Sixth: Whether the People of that settlement, did, or did not, flee from the approach of the United States Army, leaving unprotected their homes and their growing crops, *before* the blood was shed, as in his messages stated; and whether the first blood so shed, was, or was not shed, within the *inclosure* of the People, or some of them, who had thus fled from it.

Seventh: Whether our citizens, whose blood was shed, as in his messages declared, were, or were not, at that time, armed officers, and soldiers, sent into that settlement, by the military order of the President through the Secretary of War—and

Eighth: Whether the military force of the United States, including those *citizens*, was, or was not, so sent into that settlement, after Genl. Taylor had, more than once, intimated to the War Department that, in his opinion, no such movement was necessary to the defence or protection of Texas.

December 22, 1847

To William H. Herndon[1]

Dear William: Washington, Feb. 15. 1848
Your letter of the 29th. Jany. was received last night. Being exclusively a constitutional argument, I wish to submit some reflections upon it in the same spirit of kindness that I know actuates you. Let me first state what I understand to be your position. It is, that if it shall become *necessary, to repel invasion,* the President may, without violation of the Constitution, cross the line, and *invade* the teritory of another country; and that whether such *necessity* exists in any given case, the President is to be the *sole* judge.

Before going further, consider well whether this is, or is not your position. If it is, it is a position that neither the President himself, nor any friend of his, so far as I know, has ever taken. Their only positions are first, that the soil was *ours* where hostilities commenced, and second, that whether it was rightfully ours or not, *Congress had annexed it,* and the President, for that reason was bound to defend it, both of which are as clearly proved to be false in fact, as you can prove that your house is not mine. That soil was not ours; and Congress did not annex or attempt to annex it. But to return to your position: Allow the President to invade a neighboring nation, whenever *he* shall deem it necessary to repel an invasion, and you allow him to do so, *whenever he may choose* to say he deems it necessary for such purpose—and you allow him to make war at pleasure. Study to see if you can fix *any limit* to his power in this respect, after you have given him so much as you propose. If, to-day, he should choose to say he thinks it necessary to invade Canada, to prevent the British from invading us, how could you stop him? You may say to him, "I see no probability of the British invading us" but he will say to you "be silent; I see it, if you dont."

The provision of the Constitution giving the war-making power to Congress, was dictated, as I understand it, by the following reasons. Kings had always been involving and impoverishing their people in wars, pretending generally, if not always, that the good of the people was the object. This, our Convention understood to be the most oppressive of all Kingly oppressions; and they resolved to so frame the Constitution that *no one man* should hold the power of bringing this oppression upon us. But your view destroys the whole matter, and places our President where kings have always stood. Write soon again. Yours truly,

To Mary Todd Lincoln[1]

Dear Mary: Washington, April 16, 1848-
In this troublesomeworld, we are never quite satisfied. When you were here, I thought you hindered me some in attending to business; but now, having nothing but business—no variety—it has grown exceedingly

---

1. Lincoln's law partner in Springfield (1818–1891) who later wrote a biography of the president.
1. A member of a wealthy Kentucky family (1818–1882) who married Lincoln in November 1842.

tasteless to me. I hate to sit down and direct documents, and I hate to stay in this old room by myself. You know I told you in last Sunday's letter, I was going to make a little speech during the week; but the week has passed away without my getting a chance to do so; and now my interest in the subject has passed away too. Your second and third letters have been received since I wrote before. Dear Eddy[2] thinks father is *"gone tapila."* Has any further discovery been made as to the breaking into your grandmother's house? If I were she, I would not remain there alone. You mention that your uncle John Parker is likely to be at Lexington. Dont forget to present him my very kindest regards.

I went yesterday to hunt the little plaid stockings, as you wished; but found that McKnight has quit business, and Allen had not a single pair of the description you give, and only one plaid pair of any sort that I thought would fit "Eddy's dear little feet." I have a notion to make another trial to-morrow morning. If I could get them, I have an excellent chance of sending them. Mr. Warrick Tunstall, of St. Louis is here. He is to leave early this week, and to go by Lexington. He says he knows you, and will call to see you; and he voluntarily asked, if I had not some package to send to you.

I wish you to enjoy yourself in every possible way; but is there no danger of wounding the feelings of your good father, by being so openly intimate with the Wickliffe family?[3]

Mrs. Broome[4] has not removed yet; but she thinks of doing so tomorrow. All the house—or rather, all with whom you were on decided good terms—send their love to you. The others say nothing.

Very soon after you went away, I got what I think a very pretty set of shirt-bosom studs[5]—modest little ones, jet, set in gold, only costing 50 cents a piece, or 1.50 for the whole.

Suppose you do not prefix the "Hon" to the address on your letters to me any more. I like the letters very much, but I would rather they should not have that upon them. It is not necessary, as I suppose you have thought, to have them to come free.

And you are entirely free from head-ache? That is good—good—considering it is the first spring you have been free from it since we were acquainted. I am afraid you will get so well, and fat, and young, as to be wanting to marry again. Tell Louisa[6] I want her to watch you a little for me. Get weighed, and write me how much you weigh.

I did not get rid of the impression of that foolish dream about dear Bobby till I got your letter written the same day. What did he and Eddy think of the little letters father sent them? Dont let the blessed fellows forget father.

A day or two ago Mr. Strong,[7] here in Congress, said to me that Matilda would visit here within two or three weeks. Suppose you write her a letter,

2. Edward Baker Lincoln (1846–1850), Lincoln's second son. *gonetapila*: i.e. gone to the capital.
3. A reference to a bitter dispute, resulting in a lawsuit, between Lincoln's father-in-law, Robert S. Todd, and Robert Wickliffe, who had married Mary Todd Russell, a cousin of Todd's.
4. Evidently a boarder at the boarding house on Capitol Hill where Lincoln was living.
5. Decorative shirt fasteners.
6. Louisa Withers Dresser (1810–1891), wife of the prominent Springfield, Ill. Minister, Rev. Charles Dresser (1800–1865).
7. William Strong, Pennsylvania Democrat, married to Matilda Edwards of Alton, Illinois.

and enclose it in one of mine; and if she comes I will deliver it to her, and if she does not, I will send it to her. Most affectionately

To William H. Herndon

Dear William   Washington, June 12, 1848
On my return from Philadelphia, where I had been attending the nomination of "Old Rough"[1]—I found your letter in a mass of others, which had accumulated in my absence. By many, and often, it had been said they would not abide the nomination of Taylor; but since the deed has been done, they are fast falling in, and in my opinion we shall have a most overwhelming, glorious, triumph. One unmistakable sign is, that all the odds and ends are with us—Barnburners, Native Americans, Tyler men, disappointed office seeking locofocos,[2] and the Lord knows what. This is important, if in nothing else, in showing which way the wind blows. Some of the sanguine men here, set down all the states as certain for Taylor, but Illinois, and it as doubtful. Can not something be done, even in Illinois? Taylor's nomination takes the locos on the blind side. It turns the war thunder against them. The war is now to them, the gallows of Haman,[3] which they built for us, and on which they are doomed to be hanged themselves.

Excuse this short letter. I have so many to write, that I can not devote much time to any one. Yours as ever

From Speech in the U.S. House of Representatives on the Presidential Question

Gen: Taylor and the Veto[1]

Mr. Speaker
Our democratic friends seem to be in great distress because they think our candidate for the Presidency dont suit *us*. Most of them can not find out that Gen: Taylor has any principles at all; some, however, have discovered that he has *one*, but that that one is entirely wrong. This one principle, is his position on the veto power. The gentleman from Tennessee (Mr. Stanton)[2] who has just taken his seat, indeed, has said there is

---

1. I.e., Zachary Taylor (1784–1850), the Whig candidate for the presidency in 1848, known as Old Rough and Ready, who was also a general in the Mexican War.
2. Regular Democrats. "Barnburners": antislavery Democrats, so-called because they were compared to a farmer who burned down a barn to kill a few rats. "Native Americans": nativists who resisted the tide of newly arriving immigrants. "Tylermen": supporters of outgoing President John Tyler (1790–1862).
3. In the Old Testament, Haman is a Persian officer of the court who is hanged on the same gallows he had designed for an enemy (see Esther 7: 9–10).
1. At issue was a statement on the presidential veto power made by Zachary Taylor. In an April 22, 1848, letter to his brother-in-law, J. S. Allison, Taylor had said that the veto power should be used conservatively—a controversial position, given Congress's ongoing consideration of the Wilmot Proviso, a bill that, if signed into law, would have banned the extension of slavery into the western territories. Most Democrats, who favored the spread of slavery, feared that Taylor would not veto such a bill. Whigs were divided over the issue, according to their views of slavery.
2. Frederick P. Stanton (1814–1894), Democratic congressman who represented Tennessee's Tenth Congressional District from 1845 to 1854.

very little if any difference on this question between Gen: Taylor and all the Presidents; and he seems to think it sufficient detraction from Gen: Taylor's position on it, that it has nothing new in it. But all others, whom I have heard speak, assail it furiously. A new member from Kentucky (Mr. Clark)[3] of very considerable ability, was in particular concern about it. He thought it altogether novel, and unprecedented, for a President, or a Presidential candidate to think of approving bills whose constitutionality may not be entirely clear to his own mind. He thinks the ark of our safety is gone, unless Presidents shall always veto such bills, as in their judgment, may be of *doubtful* constitutionality. However clear congress may be of their authority to pass any particular act, the gentleman from Kentucky thinks the President must veto it if *he* has *doubts* about it. Now I have neither time nor inclination to argue with the gentleman on the veto power as an original question; but I wish to show that Gen: Taylor, and not he, agrees with the earlier statesmen on this question. When the bill chartering the first bank of the United States passed Congress, it's constitutionality was questioned. Mr. Madison,[4] then in the House of Representatives, as well as others, had opposed it on that ground. Gen: Washington, as President, was called on to approve or reject it. He sought and obtained on the constitutional question the separate written opinions of Jefferson, Hamilton, and Edmund Randolph;[5] they then being respectively Secretary of State, Secretary of the Treasury, and Attorney General. Hamilton's opinion was for the power; while Randolph's and Jefferson's were both against it. Mr. Jefferson, after giving his opinion decidedly against the constitutionality of that bill, closes his letter with the paragraph which I now read:

"It must be admitted, however, that, unless the President's mind, on a view of every thing, which is urged for and against this bill, is tollerably clear that it is unauthorized by the constitution; if the *pro* and the *con* hang so even as to ballance his judgment, a just respect for the wisdom of the legislature, would naturally decide the ballance in favor of their opinion: it is chiefly for cases, where they are clearly misled by error, ambition, or interest, that the constitution has placed a check in the negative of the President.

February 15— 1791—   Thomas Jefferson—"

Gen: Taylor's opinion, as expressed in his Allison letter, is as I now read:

"The power given by the veto, is a high conservative power; but in my opinion, should never be exercised except in cases of clear violation of the constitution, or manifest haste, and want of consideration by congress."

It is here seen that, in Mr. Jefferson's opinion, if on the constitutionality of any given bill, the President *doubts*, he is not to veto it, as the gentleman from Kentucky would have him to do, but is to defer to congress,

---

3. Beverly L. Clarke (1809–1860), Democratic U.S. Representative from Kentucky who served in Congress from 1847 to 1849.
4. James Madison (1751–1836) of Virginia stood opposed to strong veto power for the president, which for him, as for other antifederalists, gave excessive power to the national government.
5. An antifederalist (1753–1813) who was hostile to the idea, as was Thomas Jefferson (1743–1826). Alexander Hamilton (1755–1804), a federalist from New York, supported a powerful central government.

and approve it. And if we compare the opinions of Jefferson and Taylor, as expressed in these paragraphs, we shall find them more exactly alike, than we can often find any two expressions, having any litteral difference. None but interested fault-finders, I think, can discover any substantial variation.

Taylor on Measures of Policy

But gentlemen on the other side are unanamously agreed that Gen: Taylor has no other principles. They are in utter darkness as to his opinions on any of the questions of policy which occupy the public attention. But is there any doubt as to what he will *do* on the prominent questions, if elected? Not the least. It is not possible to know what he will, or would do, in every immaginable case; because many questions have passed away, and others doubtless will arise which none of us have yet thought of; but on the prominent questions of Currency, Tariff, internal improvements, and Wilmot Proviso, Gen: Taylor's course is at least as well defined as is Gen: Cass'.[6] Why, in their eagerness to get at Gen: Taylor, several democratic members here, have desired to know whether, in case of his election, a bankrupt law is to be established. Can they tell us Gen: Cass' opinion on this question? (Some member answered "He is against it") Aye, how do you know he is? There is nothing about it in the Platform, nor elsewhere that I have seen. If the gentleman knows of any thing, which I do not, he can show it. But to return: Gen: Taylor, in his Allison letter, says

"Upon the subject of the tariff, the currency, the improvements of our great high-ways, rivers, lakes, and harbors, the will of the people, as expressed through their representatives in congress, ought to be respected and carried out by the executive."

Now this is the whole matter. In substance, it is this: The people say to Gen: Taylor "If you are elected, shall we have a national bank?" He answers "*Your* will, gentlemen, not *mine*" "What about the Tariff?" "Say yourselves." "Shall our rivers and harbours be improved?" "Just as you please" "If you desire a bank, an alteration of the tariff, internal improvements, any, or all, I will not hinder you; if you do not desire them, I will not attempt to force them on you" "Send up your members of congress from the various districts, with opinions according to your own; and if they are for these measures, or any of them, I shall have nothing to oppose; if they are not for them, I shall not, by any appliances whatever, attempt to dragoon them into their adoption." Now, can there be any difficulty in understanding this? To you democrats, it may not seem like principle; but surely you can not fail to perceive the position plainly enough. The distinction between it, and the position of your candidate is broad and obvious; and I admit, you have a clear right to show it is wrong if you can; but you have no right to pretend you can not see it at all. We see it; and to us it appears

---

6. Lewis Cass (1782–1866), 1848 Democratic presidential candidate from Michigan, running against Taylor. In general, Democrats opposed a protective tariff, federal funding of internal improvements, and an overreliance of paper money (as opposed to specie, or hard currency). Most Whigs disagreed with the Democrats on these issues. There was conflict within both parties over the Wilmot Proviso, which was passed by the House but not by the Senate.

like principle, and the best sort of principle at that—the principle of
allowing the people to do as they please with their own business. My
friend from Indiana (C. B. Smith)[7] has aptly asked "Are you willing to
trust the people?" Some of you answered, substantially "We are willing to
trust the people; but the President is as much the representative of the
people as Congress." In a certain sense, and to a certain extent, he is the
representative of the people. He is elected by them, as well as congress is.
But can he, in the nature of things, know the wants of the people, as well
as three hundred other men, coming from all the various localities of the
nation? If so, where is the propriety of having a congress? That the constitution gives the President a negative on legislation, all know; but that this
negative should be so combined with platforms, and other appliances, as
to enable him, and, in fact, almost compel him, to take the whole of legislation into his own hands, is what we object to, is what Gen: Taylor objects
to, and is what constitutes the broad distinction between you and us. To
thus transfer legislation, is clearly to take it from those who understand,
with minuteness, the interests of the people, and give it to one who does
not, and can not so well understand it. I understand your idea, that if a
Presidential candidate avow his opinion upon a given question, or rather,
upon all questions, and the people, with full knowledge of this, elect
him, they thereby distinctly approve all those opinions. This, though plaus-
able, is a most pernicious deception. By means of it, measures are adopted
or rejected, contrary to the wishes of the whole of one party, and often
nearly half of the other. The process is this. Three, four, or half a dozen
questions are prominent at a given time; the party selects it's candidate,
and he takes his position on each of these questions. On all but one, his
positions have already been endorsed at former elections, and his party
fully committed to them; but that one is new, and a large portion of them
are against it. But what are they to do? The whole are strung together; and
they must take all, or reject all. They can not take what they like, and
leave the rest. What they are already committed to, being the majority,
they shut their eyes, and gulp the whole. Next election, still another is
introduced in the same way. If we run our eyes along the line of the past,
we shall see that almost, if not quite all the articles of the present democratic creed, have been at first forced upon the party in this very way. And
just now, and just so, opposition to internal improvements is to be established, if Gen: Cass shall be elected. Almost half the democrats here, are
for improvements; but they will vote for Cass, and if he succeeds, their
votes will have aided in closing the doors against improvements. Now this
is a process which we think is wrong. We prefer a candidate, who, like
Gen: Taylor, will allow the people to have their own way, regardless of his
private opinions; and I should think the internal improvement democrats,
at least, ought to prefer such a candidate. He would force nothing on them
which they dont want, and he would allow them to have improvements,
which their own candidate, if elected, will not.

Mr. Speaker, I have said Gen: Taylors position is as well defined, as is
that of Gen: Cass. In saying this I admit I do not certainly know what he
would do on the Wilmot Proviso. I am a Northern man, or rather, a West-

7. Caleb Blood Smith (1808–1864), a Whig from Indiana, served in the U.S. Congress from 1843
    to 1849. During the first two years of the Civil War, he was Lincoln's secretary of the interior.

ern free state man, with a constituency I believe to be, and with personal feelings I know to be, against the extension of slavery. As such, and with what information I have, I hope and *believe*, Gen: Taylor, if elected, would not veto the Proviso. *But* I do not *know* it. Yet, if I knew he would, I still would vote for him. I should do so, because, in my judgment, his election alone, can defeat Gen: Cass; and because, *should* slavery thereby go to the teritory we now have, just so much will certainly happen by the election of Cass; and, in addition, a course of policy, leading to new wars, new acquisitions of teritory and still further extensions of slavery. One of the two is to be President; which is preferable?

✻ ✻ ✻

Old Horses and Military Coat Tails

But I suppose I can not reasonably hope to convince you that we have any principles. The most I can expect, is to assure you that we think we have, and are quite contented with them. The other day, one of the gentlemen from Georgia (Mr. Iverson)[8] an eloquent man, and a man of learning, so far as I could judge, not being learned, myself, came down upon us astonishingly. He spoke in what the Baltimore American calls the "scathing and withering style." At the end of his second severe flash, I was struck blind, and found myself feeling with my fingers for an assurance of my continued physical existence. A little of the bone was left, and I gradually revived. He eulogised Mr. Clay in high and beautiful terms, and then declared that we had deserted all our principles, and had turned Henry Clay out, like an old horse to root. This is terribly severe. It can not be answered by argument; at least, I can not so answer it. I merely wish to ask the gentleman if the whigs are the only party he can think of, who some times turn old horses out to root. Is not a certain Martin Van Buren, an old horses which your own party have turned out to root? and is he not rooting a little to your discomfort about now?[9] But in not nominating Mr. Clay, we deserted our principles, you say. Ah! in what? Tell us, ye men of principles, what principle we violated. We say you did violate principle in discarding Van Buren, and we can tell you how. You violated the primary, the cardinal, the one great living principle of all Democratic representative government—the principle, that the representative is bound to carry out the known will of his constituents. A large majority of the Baltimore Convention of 1844,[1] were, by their constituents, instructed to procure Van Buren's nomination if they could. In violation, in utter, glaring contempt of this, you rejected him—rejected him, as the gentleman from New-York (Mr. Birdsall)[2] the other day, expressly admitted, for *availability*— that same "General availability" which you charge upon us, and daily chew

8. Alfred Iverson (1798–1873), a Georgia Democrat who served in the U.S. House of Representatives from 1847 to 1849 and in the U. S. Senate from 1855 to 1861.
9. Van Buren, the New York Democrat who served as the U.S. president from 1837 to 1841, was the presidential candidate of the antislavery Free Soil Party in the 1848 election.
1. At the Democratic convention in Baltimore in May 1844, Van Buren came close to winning the party's nomination for the presidency but lost to the dark horse candidate James K. Polk (1795–1849) because of enthusiasm for the annexation of Texas on the part of proslavery members of the party.
2. Democratic congressman Ausburn Birdsall (1814–1903).

over here, as something exceedingly odious and unprincipled. But the gentleman from Georgia (Mr. Iverson) gave us a second speech yesterday, all well considered, and put down in writing, in which Van Buren was scathed and withered a "few" for his present position and movements. I can not remember the gentlemans precise language; but I do remember he put Van Buren down, down, till he got him where he was finally to "stink" and "rot."

Mr. Speaker, it is no business, or inclination of mine, to defend Martin Van Buren. In the war of extermination now waging between him and his old admirers, I say, devil take the hindmost—and the foremost. But there is no mistaking the origin of the breach; and if the curse of "stinking" and "rotting" is to fall on the first and greatest violators of principle in the matter, I disinterestedly suggest, that the gentleman from Georgia, and his present co-workers, are bound to take it upon themselves.

But the gentleman from Georgia further says we have deserted all our principles, and taken shelter under Gen: Taylor's military coat-tail; and he seems to think this is exceedingly degrading. Well, as his faith is, so be it unto him. But can he remember no other military coat tail under which a certain other party have been sheltering for near a quarter of a century? Has he no acquaintance with the ample military coat tail of Gen: Jackson?[3] Does he not know that his own party have run the five last Presidential races under that coat-tail? and that they are now running the sixth, under the same cover? Yes sir, that coat tail was used, not only for Gen: Jackson himself; but has been clung to, with the gripe of death, by every democratic candidate since. You have never ventured, and dare not now venture, from under it. Your campaign papers have constantly been "Old Hickories" with rude likenesses of the old general upon them; hickory poles, and hickory brooms, your never-ending emblems; Mr. Polk himself was "Young Hickory" "Little Hickory" or something so; and even now, your campaign paper here, is proclaiming that Cass and Butler[4] are of the true "Hickory stripe." No sir, you dare not give it up.

Like a horde of hungry ticks you have stuck to the tail of the Hermitage[5] lion to the end of his life; and you are still sticking to it, and drawing a loathsome sustenance from it, after he is dead. A fellow once advertised that he had made a discovery by which he could make a new man out of an old one, and have enough of the stuff left to make a little yellow dog. Just such a discovery has Gen: Jackson's popularity been to you. You not only twice made President of him out of it, but you have had enough of the stuff left, to make Presidents of several comparatively small men since; and it is your chief reliance now to make still another.

Mr. Speaker, old horses, and military coat-tails, or tails of any sort, are not figures of speech, such as I would be the first to introduce into discussions here; but as the gentleman from Georgia has thought fit to introduce

3. Andrew Jackson, U.S. president from 1829 to 1837, was revered as a military hero, largely because of his victory against the British at the Battle of New Orleans in the War of 1812. He was known as Old Hickory because of his toughness, like that of hickory wood.
4. William Orlando Butler (1791–1880) of Kentucky was the Democratic nominee for vice president under Lewis Cass of Michigan in the 1848 presidential race.
5. The plantation home of Andrew Jackson, near Nashville, Tennessee.

them, he, and you, are welcome to all you have made, or can make, by them. If you have any more old horses, trot them out; any more tails, just cock them, and come at us.

I repeat, I would not introduce this mode of discussion here; but I wish gentlemen on the other side to understand, that the use of degrading figures is a game at which they may not find themselves able to take all the winnings. (We give it up). Aye, you give it up, and well you may; but for a very different reason from that which you would have us understand. The point—the power to hurt—of all figures, consists in the *truthfulness* of their application; and, understanding this, you may well give it up. They are weapons which hit you, but miss us.

Military Tail of the Great Michigander

But in my hurry I was very near closing on the subject of military tails before I was done with it. There is one entire article of the sort I have not discussed yet; I mean the military tail you democrats are now engaged in dovetailing onto the great Michigander.[6] Yes sir, all his biographers (and they are legion) have him in hand, tying him to a military tail, like so many mischievous boys tying a dog to a bladder of beans. True, the material they have is very limited; but they drive at it, might and main. He *in*vaded Canada without resistance, and he *out*vaded it without pursuit. As he did both under orders, I suppose there was, to him, neither credit or discredit in them; but they are made to constitute a large part of the tail. He was not at Hull's surrender, but he was close by; he was volunteer aid to Gen: Harrison on the day of the battle of the Thames; and, as you said in 1840, Harrison was picking huckleberries two miles off while the battle was fought, I suppose it is a just conclusion with you, to say Cass was aiding Harrison to pick huckleberries. This is about all, except the mooted question of the broken sword.[7] Some authors say he broke it, some say he threw it away, and some others, who ought to know, say nothing about it. Perhaps it would be a fair historical compromise to say, if he did not break it, he did n't do any thing else with it.

By the way, Mr. Speaker, did you know I am a military hero?[8] Yes sir; in the days of the Black Hawk war, I fought, bled, and came away. Speaking of Gen: Cass' career, reminds me of my own. I was not at Stillman's defeat, but I was about as near it, as Cass was to Hulls surrender; and, like him, I saw the place very soon afterwards. It is quite certain I did not break my sword, for I had none to break; but I bent a musket pretty badly on one occasion. If Cass broke his sword, the idea is, he broke it in desperation; I bent the musket by accident. If Gen: Cass went in advance of me in

---

6. Lincoln makes fun here of the mixed military record of Lewis Cass, who during the War of 1812 had served under General William Hull (1753–1825), whose foray into Canada was followed by retreat and the surrender of Detroit, and then under General William Henry Harrison, who defeated the Indian leader Tecumseh in the Battle of the Thames.

7. According to some reports, Cass, angry over Hull's surrender of Detroit to the British, broke his sword so that it would not fall into enemy hands.

8. Lincoln in this paragraph gives a mock-heroic account of his brief service in the Black Hawk War in 1832. Lincoln, who never saw combat, spent weeks with three successive militia companies wandering through woods and swamps before his eighty-day enlistment ended. For a time, Lincoln was stationed near the place where disorganized troops under Major Isaiah Stillman (1793–1861) fled after a losing encounter with a band of Indians.

picking huckleberries, I guess I surpassed him in charges upon the wild onions. If he saw any live, fighting indians, it was more than I did; but I had a good many bloody struggles with the musquetoes; and, although I never fainted from loss of blood, I can truly say I was often very hungry. Mr. Speaker, if I should ever conclude to doff whatever our democratic friends may suppose there is of black cockade federalism about me, and thereupon, they shall take me up as their candidate for the Presidency, I protest they shall not make fun of me, as they have of Gen: Cass, by attempting to write me into a military hero.

⁕ ⁕ ⁕

The Whigs and the War

But, as Gen: Taylor is, par excellence, the hero of the Mexican war;[9] and, as you democrats say we whigs have always opposed the war, you think it must be very awkward and embarrassing for us to go for Gen: Taylor. The declaration that we have always opposed the war, is true or false, accordingly as one may understand the term "opposing the war." If to say "the war was unnecessarily and unconstitutionally commenced by the President" be opposing the war, then the whigs have very generally opposed it. Whenever they have spoken at all, they have said this; and they have said it on what has appeared good reason to them. The marching an army into the midst of a peaceful Mexican settlement, frightening the inhabitants away, leaving their growing crops, and other property to destruction, to *you* may appear a perfectly amiable, peaceful, unprovoking procedure; but it does not appear so to *us*. So to call such an act, to us appears no other than a naked, impudent absurdity, and we speak of it accordingly. But if, when the war had begun, and had become the cause of the country, the giving of our money and our blood, in common with yours, was support of the war, then it is not true that we have always opposed the war. With few individual exceptions, you have constantly had our votes here for all the necessary supplies. And, more than this, you have had the services, the blood, and the lives of our political bretheren in every trial, and on every field. The beardless boy, and the mature man—the humble and the distinguished, you have had them. Through suffering and death, by disease, and in battle, they have endured, and fought, and fell with you. Clay and Webster each gave a son, never to be returned. From the state of my own residence, besides other worthy but less known whig names, we sent Marshall, Morrison, Baker, and Hardin;[1] they all fought, and one fell; and in the fall of that one, we lost our best whig man. Nor were the whigs few in number, or

---

9. Fought (1846–48) because Mexico and the United States failed to settle peacefully their dispute over the location of the border of Texas. President James K. Polk wanted to take control of Mexican-occupied territories that stretched westward to the Pacific. Congress approved Polk's declaration of war in May 1846. Democrats, motivated by a spirit of Manifest Destiny, generally supported the war, whereas many Whigs, especially in the North, opposed it. Antislavery Whigs like Lincoln considered the war a Southern effort to promote the western spread of slavery.

1. John J. Hardin (1810–1847), Whig congressman from Illinois who was killed at Buena Vista. Thomas Francis Marshall (1801–1864), Whig congressman from Kentucky who served as a captain in the Mexican War. J. L. D. "Don" Morrison (1816–1888), Illinois Whig who served as a lieutenant colonel under Taylor in many battles during the Mexican War. Edward D. Baker, Lincoln's former law partner in Illinois (1811–1861) who served as a U.S. Army colonel in both the Mexican War and the Civil War; he was killed in the Battle of Ball's Bluff.

laggard in the day of danger. In that fearful, bloody, breathless struggle at Buena Vista, where each man's hard task was to beat back five foes or die himself, of the five high officers who perished, four were whigs.

In speaking of this, I mean no odious comparison between the lion-hearted whigs and democrats who fought there. On other occasions, and among the lower officers and privates on *that* occasion, I doubt not the proportion was different. I wish to do justice to all. I think of all those brave men as Americans, in whose proud fame, as an American, I too have a share. Many of them, whigs and democrats, are my constituents and personal friends; and I thank them—more than thank them—one and all, for the high, imperishable honor they have confered on our common state.

But the distinction between the cause of the *President* in beginning the war, and the cause of the *country* after it was begun, is a distinction which you can not perceive. To you the President, and the country, seems to be all one. You are interested to see no distinction between them; and I venture to suggest that possibly your interest blinds you a little. We see the distinction, as we think, clearly enough; and our friends who have fought in the war have no difficulty in seeing it also. What those who have fallen would say were they alive and here, of course we can never know; but with those who have returned there is no difficulty. Col: Haskell, and Major Gaines,[2] members here, both fought in the war; and one of them underwent extraordinary perils and hardships; still they, like all other whigs here, vote, on the record, that the war was unnecessarily and unconstitutionally commenced by the President. And even Gen: Taylor himself, the noblest Roman of them all, has declared that as a citizen, and particularly as a soldier, it is sufficient for him to know that his country is at war with a foreign nation, to do all in his power to bring it to a speedy and honorable termination, by the most vigorous and energetic opperations, without enquiring about it's justice, or any thing else connected with it.

Mr. Speaker, let our democratic friends be comforted with the assurance, that we are content with our position, content with our company, and content with our candidate; and that although they, in their generous sympathy, think we ought to be miserable, we really are not, and that they may dismiss the great anxiety they have on *our* account.

Divided Gangs of Hogs

Mr. Speaker, I see I have but three minutes left, and this forces me to throw out one whole branch of my subject. A single word on still another. The democrats are kind enough to frequently remind us that we have some dissensions in our ranks. Our good, friend from Baltimore, immediately before me (Mr. McLane)[3] expressed some doubt the other day as to which branch of our party, Gen: Taylor would ultimately fall into the hands of. That was a new idea to me. I knew we had dissenters, but I did

---

2. John Pollard Gaines (1795–1857), elected as a Whig to the Thirtieth Congress (1847–49) while he was a war prisoner in Mexico City. William T. Haskell (1818–1859), Democrat representative from Tennessee who fought in the war and served in Congress from 1847 to 1849.
3. Robert Milligan McLane (1815–1898), Democrat who served as a U.S. representative from Maryland from 1847 to 1851.

not know they were trying to get our candidate away from us. I would like to say a word to our dissenters, but I have not the time. Some such *we* certainly have; have *you* none, gentlemen democrats? Is it all union and harmony in *your* ranks?—no bickerings?—no divisions?[4] If there be doubt as to which of our divisions will get our candidate, is there no doubt as to which of your candidates will get your party? I have heard some things from New-York; and if they are true, one might well say of your party there, as a drunken fellow once said when he heard the reading of an indictment for hog-stealing. The clerk read on till he got to, and through the words "did steal, take, and carry away, ten boars, ten sows, ten shoats, and ten pigs" at which he exclaimed "Well, by golly, that is the most equally divided gang of hogs, I ever did hear of." If there is any *other* gang of hogs more equally divided than the democrats of New-York are about this time, I have not heard of it.

July 27, 1848

Fragment on Niagara Falls

Niagara-Falls! By what mysterious power is it that millions and millions, are drawn from all parts of the world, to gaze upon Niagara Falls? There is no mystery about the thing itself. Every effect is just such as any inteligent man knowing the causes, would anticipate, without it. If the water moving onward in a great river, reaches a point where there is a perpendicular jog, of a hundred feet in descent, in the bottom of the river,—it is plain the water will have a violent and continuous plunge at that point. It is also plain the water, thus plunging, will foam, and roar, and send up a mist, continuously, in which last, during sunshine, there will be perpetual rainbows. The mere physical of Niagara Falls is only this. Yet this is really a very small part of that world's wonder. It's power to excite reflection, and emotion, is it's great charm. The geologist will demonstrate that the plunge, or fall, was once at Lake Ontario, and has worn it's way back to it's present position; he will ascertain how *fast* it is wearing now, and so get a basis for determining how *long* it has been wearing back from Lake Ontario, and finally demonstrate by it that this world is at least fourteen thousand years old. A philosopher of a slightly different turn will say Niagara Falls is only the lip of the basin out of which pours all the surplus water which rains down on two or three hundred thousand square miles of the earth's surface. He will estimate with approximate accuracy, that five hundred thousand tons of water, falls with it's full weight, a distance of a hundred feet each minute—thus exerting a force equal to the lifting of the same weight, through the same space, in the same time. And then the further reflection comes that this vast amount of water, constantly pouring *down*, is supplied by an equal amount constantly *lifted up*, by the sun; and still he says, "If this much is lifted up, for *this one* space of two or three hundred thousand square miles, an equal amount must be lifted for every other equal space"; and he is overwhelmed in the contemplation of

---

4. Lincoln seems to refer especially to disputes between proslavery Democrats and antislavery ones, largely centered in New York.

the vast power the sun is constantly exerting in quiet, noiseless operation of lifting water *up* to be rained *down* again.

But still there is more. It calls up the indefinite past. When Columbus first sought this continent—when Christ suffered on the cross—when Moses led Israel through the Red-Sea—nay, even, when Adam first came from the hand of his Maker—then as now, Niagara was roaring here. The eyes of that species of extinct giants, whose bones fill the mounds of America, have gazed on Niagara, as ours do now. Cotemporary with the whole race of men, and older than the first man, Niagara is strong, and fresh to-day as ten thousand years ago. The Mammoth and Mastadon—now so long dead, that fragments of their monstrous bones, alone testify, that they ever lived, have gazed on Niagara. In that long—long time, never still for a single moment. Never dried, never froze, never slept, never rested,

ca. September 25–30, 1848

To Thomas Lincoln and John D. Johnston[1]

My dear father: Washington, Decr. 24th. 1848-
Your letter of the 7th. was received night before last. I very cheerfully send you the twenty dollars, which sum you say is necessary to save your land from sale. It is singular that you should have forgotten a judgment against you; and it is more singular that the plaintiff should have let you forget it so long, particularly as I suppose you have always had property enough to satisfy a judgment of that amount. Before you pay it, it would be well to be sure you have not paid it; or, at least, that you can not prove you have paid it. Give my love to Mother, and all the connections. Affectionately your Son

Dear Johnston:
Your request for eighty dollars, I do not think it best, to comply with now. At the various times when I have helped you a little, you have said to me "We can get along very well now" but in a very short time I find you in the same difficulty again. Now this can only happen by some defect in your *conduct*. What that defect is I think I know. You are not *lazy*, and still you *are* an *idler*. I doubt whether since I saw you, you have done a good whole day's work in any one day. You do not very much dislike to work; and still you do not work much, merely because it does not seem to you that you could get much for it. This habit of uselessly wasting time, is the whole difficulty; and it is vastly important to you, and still more so to your children that you should break this habit. It is more important to them, because they have longer to live, and can keep out of an idle habit before they are in it; easier than they can get out after they are in.

You are now in need of some ready money; and what I propose is, that you shall go to work, "tooth and nails" for some body who will give you money for it. Let father and your boys take charge of things at home—prepare for a crop, and make the crop; and you go to work for the best money wages, or in discharge of any debt you owe, that you can get. And to secure you a fair reward for your labor, I now promise you, that for

---

1. Lincoln's father and step-brother, respectively.

every dollar you will, between this and the first of next May, get for your own labor, either in money, or in your own indebtedness, I will then give you one other dollar. By this, if you hire yourself at ten dollars a month, from me you will get ten more, making twenty dollars a month for your work. In this, I do not mean you shall go off to St. Louis, or the lead mines, or the gold mines, in California, but I mean for you to go at it for the best wages you can get close to home in Coles county. Now if you will do this, you will soon be out of debt, and what is better, you will have a habit that will keep you from getting in debt again. But if I should now clear you out, next year you will be just as deep in as ever. You say you would almost give your place in Heaven for $70 or $80. Then you value your place in Heaven very cheaply for I am sure you can with the offer I make you get the seventy or eighty dollars for four or five months work. You say if I furnish you the money you will deed me the land, and, if you dont pay the money back, you will deliver possession. Nonsense! If you cant now live with the land, how will you then live without it? You have always been kind to me, and I do not now mean to be unkind to you. On the contrary, if you will but follow my advice, you will find it worth more than eight times eighty dollars to you. Affectionately Your brother

Proposal in the U.S. House of Representatives for Abolition of Slavery in the District of Columbia

Mr. Lincoln appealed to his colleague [Mr. Wentworth] to withdraw his motion, to enable him to read a proposition which he intended to submit, if the vote should be reconsidered.

Mr. Wentworth[1] again withdrew his motion for that purpose.

Mr. LINCOLN said, that by the courtesy of his colleague, he would say, that if the vote on the resolution was reconsidered, he should make an effort to introduce an amendment, which he should now read.

And Mr. L. read as follows:

Strike out all before and after the word "Resolved" and insert the following, towit: That the Committee on the District of Columbia be instructed to report a bill in substance as follows, towit:

Section 1   Be it enacted by the Senate and House of Representatives of the United States of America, in Congress assembled: That no person not now within the District of Columbia, nor now owned by any person or persons now resident within it, nor hereafter born within it, shall ever be held in slavery within said District.

Section 2.   That no person now within said District, or now owned by any person, or persons now resident within the same, or hereafter born within it, shall ever be held in slavery without the limits of said District: *Provided*, that officers of the government of the United States, being citizens of the slave-holding states, coming into said District on public business, and remaining only so long as may be reasonably necessary for that object, may be attended into, and out of, said District, and while there, by the necessary servants of themselves and their families, without their right to hold such servants in service, being thereby impaired.

1. John Wentworth (1815–1888), a Illinois Democrat who had successfully moved to table a December 1848 House resolution to draft legislation to abolish the slave trade in Washington, D.C.

Section 3. That all children born of slave mothers within said District on, or after the first day of January in the year of our Lord one thousand, eight hundred and fifty shall be free; but shall be reasonably supported and educated, by the respective owners of their mothers or by their heirs or representatives, and shall owe reasonable service, as apprentices, to such owners, heirs and representatives until they respectively arrive at the age of ———— years when they shall be entirely free; and the municipal authorities of Washington and Georgetown, within their respective jurisdictional limits, are hereby empowered and required to make all suitable and necessary provisions for enforcing obedience to this section, on the part of both masters and apprentices.

Section 4. That all persons now within said District lawfully held as slaves, or now owned by any person or persons now resident within said District, shall remain such, at the will of their respective owners, their heirs and legal representatives: *Provided* that any such owner, or his legal representative, may at any time receive from the treasury of the United States the full value of his or her slave, of the class in this section mentioned, upon which such slave shall be forthwith and forever free: and *provided further* that the President of the United States, the Secretary of State, and the Secretary of the Treasury shall be a board for determining the value of such slaves as their owners may desire to emancipate under this section; and whose duty it shall be to hold a session for the purpose, on the first monday of each calendar month; to receive all applications; and, on satisfactory evidence in each case, that the person presented for valuation, is a slave, and of the class in this section mentioned, and is owned by the applicant, shall value such slave at his or her full cash value, and give to the applicant an order on the treasury for the amount; and also to such slave a certificate of freedom.

Section 5 That the municipal authorities of Washington and Georgetown, within their respective jurisdictional limits, are hereby empowered and required to provide active and efficient means to arrest, and deliver up to their owners, all fugitive slaves escaping into said District.

Section 6 That the election officers within said District of Columbia, are hereby empowered and required to open polls at all the usual places of holding elections, on the first monday of April next, and receive the vote of every free white male citizen above the age of twentyone years, having resided within said District for the period of one year or more next preceding the time of such voting, for, or against this act; to proceed, in taking said votes, in all respects not herein specified, as at elections under the municipal laws; and, with as little delay as possible, to transmit correct statements of the votes so cast to the President of the United States. And it shall be the duty of the President to canvass said votes immediately, and, if a majority of them be found to be for this act, to forthwith issue his proclamation giving notice of the fact; and this act shall only be in full force and effect on, and after the day of such proclamation.

Section 7. That involuntary servitude for the punishment of crime, whereof the party shall have been duly convicted shall in no wise be prohibited by this act.

Section 8. That for all the purposes of this act the jurisdictional limits of Washington are extended to all parts of the District of Columbia not now included within the present limits of Georgetown.

Mr. Lincoln then said, that he was authorized to say, that of about fifteen of the leading citizens of the District of Columbia to whom this proposition had been submitted, there was not one but who approved of the adoption of such a proposition. He did not wish to be misunderstood. He did not know whether or not they would vote for this bill on the first Monday of April; but he repeated, that out of fifteen persons to whom it had been submitted, he had authority to say that every one of them desired that some proposition like this should pass.

January 10, 1849

Notes on the Practice of Law

I am not an accomplished lawyer. I find quite as much material for a lecture, in those points wherein I have failed, as in those wherein I have been moderately successful.

The leading rule for the lawyer, as for the man, of every calling, is *diligence*. Leave nothing for to-morrow, which can be done to-day. Never let your correspondence fall behind. Whatever piece of business you have in hand, before stopping, do all the labor pertaining to it which can *then* be done. When you bring a common-law suit, if you have the facts for doing so, write the declaration at once. If a law point be involved, examine the books, and note the authority you rely on, upon the declaration itself, where you are sure to find it when wanted. The same of defences and pleas. In business not likely to be litigated—ordinary collection cases, foreclosures, partitions, and the like,—make all examinations of titles, and note them, and even draft orders and decrees in advance. This course has a tripple advantage; it avoids omissions and neglect, *saves* your labor, when once done; performs the labor out of court when you *have* leisure, rather than in court, when you have not. Extemporaneous speaking should be practiced and cultivated. It is the lawyer's avenue to the public. However able and faithful he may be in other respects, people are slow to bring him business, if he cannot make a speech. And yet there is not a more fatal error to young lawyers, than relying too much on speech-making. If any one, upon his rare powers of speaking, shall claim exemption from the drudgery of the law, his case is a failure in advance.

Discourage litigation. Persuade your neighbors to compromise whenever you can. Point out to them how the *nominal* winner is often a *real* loser—in fees, and expenses, and waste of time. As a peace-maker the lawyer has a superior opertunity of being a good man. There will still be business enough.

Never stir up litigation. A worse man can scarcely be found than one who does this. Who can be more nearly a fiend than he who habitually overhauls the Register of deeds, in search of defects in titles, whereon to stir up strife, and put money in his pocket? A moral tone ought to be infused into the profession, which should drive such men out of it.

The matter of fees is important far beyond the mere question of bread and butter involved. Properly attended to fuller justice is done to both lawyer and client. An exorbitant fee should never be claimed. As a general rule, never take your whole fee in advance, nor any more than a small retainer. When fully paid before hand, you are more than a common mortal if you can feel the same interest in the case, as if something was still in prospect for you, as well as for your client. And when you lack interest in the case, the job will very likely lack skill and diligence in the performance. Settle the *amount* of fee, and take a note in advance. Then you will feel that you are working for something, and you are sure to do your work faithfully and well. Never sell a fee-note—at least, not before the consideration service is performed. It leads to negligence and dishonesty— negligence, by losing interest in the case, and dishonesty in refusing to refund, when you have allowed the consideration to fail.

There is a vague popular belief that lawyers are necessarily dishonest. I say *vague*, because when we consider to what extent *confidence*, and *honors* are reposed in, and conferred upon lawyers by the people, it appears improbable that their *impression* of dishonesty is very distinct and vivid. Yet the impression, is common—almost universal. Let no young man, choosing the law for a calling, for a moment yield to this pop- ular belief. Resolve to be honest at all events; and if, in your own judg- ment, you can not be an honest lawyer, resolve to be honest without being a lawyer. Choose some other occupation, rather than one in the choosing of which you do, in advance, consent to be a knave.

July 1, 1850?

From Eulogy on Zachary Taylor at Chicago, Illinois

*   *   *

It did not happen to Gen. Taylor once in his life, to fight a battle on equal terms, or on terms advantageous to himself—and yet he was never beaten, and never retreated. In *all*, the odds was greatly against him; in each, defeat seemed inevitable; and yet *in all*, he triumphed. Wherever he has led, while the battle still raged, the issue was painfully doubtful; yet in each and all, when the din had ceased, and the smoke had blown away, our country's flag was still seen, fluttering in the breeze.

Gen. Taylor's battles were not distinguished for brilliant military manoeuvers; but in all, he seems rather to have conquered by the exercise of a sober and steady judgment, coupled with a dogged incapacity to understand that defeat was possible. His rarest military trait, was a com- bination of negatives—absence of *excitement* and absence of *fear*. He could not be *flurried*, and he could not be *scared*.

In connection with Gen. Taylor's military character, may be men- tioned his relations with his brother officers, and his soldiers. Terrible as he was to his country's enemies, no man was so little disposed to have difficulty with his friends. During the period of his life, *duelling* was a practice not quite uncommon among gentlemen in the peaceful avoca- tions of life, and still more common, among the officers of the Army and Navy. Yet, so far as I can learn, a *duel* with Gen. Taylor, has never been talked of.

He was alike averse to *sudden*, and to *startling* quarrels; and he pur- sued no man with *revenge*. A notable, and a noble instance of this, is found in his conduct to the gallant and now lamented Gen. Worth.[1] A short while before the battles of the 8th and 9th of May, some questions of precedence arose between Worth, (then a colonel) and some other officer, which question it seems Gen. Taylor's duty to decide. He decided against Worth. Worth was greatly offended, left the Army, came to the United States, and tendered his resignation to the authorities at Washington. It is said, that in his passionate feeling, he hesitated not to speak harshly and disparagingly of Gen. Taylor. He was an officer of the highest character; and his word, on military subjects, and about military men, could not, with the country, pass for nothing. In this absence from the army of Col. Worth, the unexpected turn of things brought on the battles of the 8th and 9th. He was deeply mortified—in almost absolute desperation—at having lost the opportunity of being present, and taking part in those battles. The laurels won by his previous service, in his own eyes, seemed withering away. The Government, both *wisely* and *generously*, I think, declined accepting his resignation; and he returned to Gen. Taylor. Then came Gen. Taylor's *opportunity* for revenge. The battle of Monterey was approaching, and even at hand. Taylor *could* if he *would*, so place Worth in that battle, that his name would scarcely be noticed in the report. But no. He felt it was due to the service, to assign the real post of honor to some one of the best officers; he knew Worth was one of the best, and he felt that it was *generous* to allow him, then and there, to retrieve his secret loss. Accordingly he assigned to Col. Worth in that assault, what was *par excellence*, the post of honor; and, the duties of which, he executed so well, and so brilliantly, as to eclipse, in that battle, even Gen. Taylor himself.

As to Gen. Taylor's relations with his soldiers, details would be endless. It is perhaps enough to say—and it is far from the *least* of his honors that we can *truly* say—that of the many who served with him through the long course of forty years, all testify to the uniform kindness, and his constant care for, and hearty sympathy with, their every want and every suffering; while none can be found to declare, that he was ever a tyrant anywhere, in anything.

Going back a little in point of time, it is proper to say that so soon as the news of the battles of the 8th and 9th of May 1846, had fairly reached the United States, Gen. Taylor began to be named for the next Presidency, by letter writers, newspapers, public meetings and conventions in various parts of the country.

These nominations were generally put forth as being of a noparty character. Up to this time I think it highly probable—nay, almost certain, that Gen. Taylor had never thought of the Presidency in connection with himself. And there is reason for believing that the first intelligence of these nominations rather *amused* than *seriously* interested him. Yet I should be insincere, were I not to confess, that in my opinion, the repeated, and steady manifestations in his favor, *did* beget in his mind a laudable ambition to reach the high distinction of the Presidential chair.

As the time for the Presidential canvass approached, it was seen that general nominations, combining anything near the number of votes necessary to an election, could not be made without some pretty strong and

---

1. William Jenkins Worth (1794–1849), a military officer during the War of 1812, the Second Seminole War, and the Mexican War.

decided reference to party politics. Accordingly, in the month of May, 1848, the great Democratic party nominated as their candidate, an able and distinguished member of their own party, on strictly party grounds. Almost immediately following this, the Whig party, in general convention, nominated Gen. Taylor as their candidate. The election came off in the November following; and though there was also a third candidate, the two former only, received any vote in the electoral college. Gen. Taylor, having the majority of them was duly elected; and he entered on the duties of that high and responsible office, March 5th, 1849.

The incidents of his administration up to the time of his death, are too familiar and too fresh to require any direct repetition.

The Presidency, even to the most experienced politicians, is no bed of roses; and Gen. Taylor like others, found thorns within it. No human being can fill that station and escape censure. Still I hope and believe when Gen. Taylor's official conduct shall come to be viewed in the calm light of history, he will be found to have *deserved* as little as any who have succeeded him.

Upon the death of Gen. Taylor, as it would in the case of the death of any President, we are naturally led to consider what will be its effect, politically, upon the country. I will not pretend to believe that all the wisdom, or all the patriotism of the country, died with Gen. Taylor. But we know that *wisdom* and *patriotism*, in a public office, under institutions like ours, are wholly inefficient and worthless, unless they are sustained by the confidence and devotion of the people. And I confess my apprehensions, that in the death of the late President, we have lost a degree of that confidence and devotion, which will not soon again pertain to any successor. Between public measures regarded as antagonistic, there is often less real difference in its bearing on the public weal, than there is between the dispute being *kept up*, or being *settled* either way. I fear the one great question of the day, is not now so likely to be partially acquiesced in by the different sections of the Union, as it would have been, could Gen. Taylor have been spared to us. Yet, under all circumstances, trusting to our Maker, and through his wisdom and beneficence, to the great body of our people, we will not despair, nor despond.

In Gen. Taylor's general public relation to his country, what will strongly impress a close observer, was his unostentatious, self-sacrificing, long enduring devotion to his *duty*. He indulged in no recreations, he visited no public places, seeking applause; but quietly, as the earth in its orbit, he was always at his post. Along our whole Indian frontier, thro' summer and winter, in sunshine and storm, like a sleepless sentinel, *he* has *watched*, while *we* have *slept* for forty long years. How well might the dying hero say at last, "I have done my duty, I am ready to go."

Nor can I help thinking that the American people, in electing Gen. Taylor to the presidency, thereby showing their high appreciation, of his sterling, but unobtrusive qualities, did their *country* a service, and *themselves* an imperishable honor. It is *much* for the young to know, that treading the hard path of duty, as he trod it, *will* be noticed, and *will* lead to high places.

But he is gone. The conqueror at last is conquered. The fruits of his labor, his name, his memory and example, are all that is left us—his example, verifying the great truth, that "he that humbleth himself, shall be exalted"[2] teaching, that to serve one's country with a singleness of purpose, gives assurance of that country's gratitude, secures its best honors, and makes "a dying bed, soft as downy pillows are."[3]

The death of the late President may not be without its use, in reminding us, that *we*, too, must die. Death, abstractly considered, is the same with the high as with the low; but practically, we are not so much aroused to the contemplation of our own mortal natures, by the fall of *many* undistinguished, as that of *one* great, and well known, name. By the latter, we are forced to muse, and ponder, sadly.

"Oh, why should the spirit of mortal be proud"

So the multitude goes, like the flower or the weed,
That withers away to let others succeed;
So the multitude comes, even those we behold,
To repeat every tale that has often been told.

5 For we are the same, our fathers have been,
We see the same sights our fathers have seen;
We drink the same streams and see the same sun
And run the same course our fathers have run.

They loved; but the story we cannot unfold;
10 They scorned, but the heart of the haughty is cold;
They grieved, but no wail from their slumbers will come,
They joyed, but the tongue of their gladness is dumb.

They died! Aye, they died; we things that are now;
That work on the turf that lies on their brow,
15 And make in their dwellings a transient abode,
Meet the things that they met on their pilgrimage road.

Yea! hope and despondency, pleasure and pain,
Are mingled together in sun-shine and rain;
And the smile and the tear, and the song and the dirge,
20 Still follow each other, like surge upon surge.

'Tis the wink of an eye, 'tis the draught of a breath,
From the blossoms of health, to the paleness of death.
From the gilded saloon, to the bier and the shroud.
Oh, why should the spirit of mortal be proud![4]

July 25, 1850

---

2. Luke 14:11.
3. Cf. "Jesus can make a dying bed / Feel soft as down pillows are," "Hymn 31" by Isaac Watts.
4. From William Knox's "Mortality," one of Lincoln's favorite poems.

Eulogy on Henry Clay at Springfield, Illinois

On the fourth day of July, 1776, the people of a few feeble and oppressed colonies of Great Britain, inhabiting a portion of the Atlantic coast of North America, publicly declared their national independence, and made their appeal to the justice of their cause, and to the God of battles, for the maintainance of that declaration. That people were few in numbers, and without resources, save only their own wise heads and stout hearts. Within the first year of that declared independence, and while its maintainance was yet problematical—while the bloody struggle between those resolute rebels, and their haughty would-be masters, was still waging, of undistinguished parents, and in an obscure district of one of those colonies, Henry Clay was born. The infant nation, and the infant child began the race of life together. For three quarters of a century they have travelled hand in hand. They have been companions ever. The nation has passed its perils, and is free, prosperous, and powerful. The child has reached his manhood, his middle age, his old age, and is dead. In all that has concerned the nation the man ever sympathised; and now the nation mourns for the man.

The day after his death, one of the public Journals, opposed to him politically, held the following pathetic and beautiful language, which I adopt, partly because such high and exclusive eulogy, originating with a political friend, might offend good taste, but chiefly, because I could not, in any language of my own, so well express my thoughts—

"Alas! who can realize that Henry Clay is dead! Who can realize that never again that majestic form shall rise in the council-chambers of his country to beat back the storms of anarchy which may threaten, or pour the oil of peace upon the troubled billows as they rage and menace around? Who can realize, that the workings of that mighty mind have ceased—that the throbbings of that gallant heart are stilled—that the mighty sweep of that graceful arm will be felt no more, and the magic of that eloquent tongue, which spake as spake no other tongue besides, is hushed—hushed forever! Who can realize that freedom's champion—the champion of a civilized world, and of all tongues and kindreds and people, has indeed fallen! Alas, in those dark hours, which, as they come in the history of all nations, must come in ours—those hours of peril and dread which our land has experienced, and which she may be called to experience again—to whom now may her people look up for that council and advice, which only wisdom and experience and patriotism can give, and which only the undoubting confidence of a nation will receive? Perchance, in the whole circle of the great and gifted of our land, there remains but one on whose shoulders the mighty mantle of the departed statesman may fall—one, while we now write, is doubtless pouring his tears over the bier of his brother and his friend—brother, friend ever, yet in political sentiment, as far apart as party could make them. Ah, it is at times like these, that the petty distinctions of mere party disappear. We see only the great, the grand, the noble features of the departed statesman; and we do not even beg permission to bow at his feet and mingle our tears with those who have ever been his political adherents—we do not beg this permission—we claim it as a right, though we feel it as a privilege.

Henry Clay belonged to his country—to the world, mere party cannot claim men like him. His career has been national—his fame has filled the earth—his memory will endure to 'the last syllable of recorded time.'

"Henry Clay is dead!—He breathed his last on yesterday at twenty minutes after eleven, in his chamber at Washington. To those who followed his lead in public affairs, it more appropriately belongs to pronounce his eulogy, and pay specific honors to the memory of the illustrious dead—but all Americans may show the grief which his death inspires, for, his character and fame are national property. As on a question of liberty, he knew no North, no South, no East, no West, but only the Union, which held them all in its sacred circle, so now his countrymen will know no grief, that is not as widespread as the bounds of the confederacy. The career of Henry Clay was a public career. From his youth he has been devoted to the public service, at a period too, in the world's history justly regarded as a remarkable era in human affairs. He witnessed in the beginning the throes of the French Revolution. He saw the rise and fall of Napoleon.[1] He was called upon to legislate for America, and direct her policy when all Europe was the battle-field of contending dynasties, and when the struggle for supremacy imperilled the rights of all neutral nations. His voice, spoke war and peace in the contest with Great Britain.

"When Greece rose against the Turks and struck for liberty, his name was mingled with the battle-cry of freedom. When South America threw off the thraldom of Spain, his speeches were read at the head of her armies by Bolivar.[2] His name has been, and will continue to be, hallowed in two hemispheres, for it is—

> 'One of the few the immortal names
> That were not born to die,'[3]

"To the ardent patriot and profound statesman, he added a quality possessed by few of the gifted on earth. His eloquence has not been surpassed. In the effective power to move the heart of man, Clay was without an equal, and the heaven born endowment, in the spirit of its origin, has been most conspicuously exhibited against intestine feud. On at least three important occasions, he has quelled our civil commotions, by a power and influence, which belonged to no other statesman of his age and times. And in our last internal discord,[4] when this Union trembled to its center—in old age, he left the shades of private life and gave the death blow to fraternal strife, with the vigor of his earlier years in a series of Senatorial efforts, which in themselves would bring immortality, by challenging comparison with the efforts of any statesman in any age. He exorcised the demon which possessed the body politic, and gave peace to a distracted land. Alas! the achievement cost him his life! He sank day by day to the tomb—his pale, but noble brow, bound with a triple wreath, put there by a grateful country. May his ashes rest in peace, while his

---

1. Napoleon Bonaparte (1769–1821), a prominent French military and political leader.
2. Simón Bolivar (1783–1830), a Venezuelan military and political leader who led several South American countries to independence from Spain.
3. Fitz-Greene Halleck's "Marco Bozzaris" (1825).
4. The bitter congressional debate that led to the Compromise of 1850.

spirit goes to take its station among the great and good men who preceded him!"

While it is customary, and proper, upon occasions like the present, to give a brief sketch of the life of the deceased; in the case of Mr. Clay, it is less necessary than most others; for his biography has been written and re-written, and read, and re-read, for the last twenty-five years; so that, with the exception of a few of the latest incidents of his life, all is as well known, as it can be. The short sketch which I give is, therefore merely to maintain the connection of this discourse.

Henry Clay was born on the 12th of April 1777, in Hanover county, Virginia. Of his father, who died in the fourth or fifth year of Henry's age, little seems to be known, except that he was a respectable man, and a preacher of the baptist persuasion. Mr. Clay's education, to the end of his life, was comparatively limited. I say *"to the end of his life,"* because I have understood that, from time to time, he added something to his education during the greater part of his whole life. Mr. Clay's lack of a more perfect early education, however it may be regretted generally, teaches at least one profitable lesson; it teaches that in this country, one can scarcely be so poor, but that, if he *will*, he *can* acquire sufficient education to get through the world respectably. In his twenty-third year Mr. Clay was licenced to practice law, and emigrated to Lexington, Kentucky. Here he commenced and continued the practice till the year 1803, when he was first elected to the Kentucky Legislature. By successive elections he was continued in the Legislature till the latter part of 1806, when he was elected to fill a vacancy, of a single session, in the United States Senate. In 1807 he was again elected to the Kentucky House of Representatives, and by that body, chosen its speaker. In 1808 he was re-elected to the same body. In 1809 he was again chosen to fill a vacancy of two years in the United States Senate. In 1811 he was elected to the United States House of Representatives, and on the first day of taking his seat in that body, he was chosen its speaker. In 1813 he was again elected Speaker. Early in 1814, being the period of our last British war,[5] Mr. Clay was sent as commissioner, with others, to negotiate a treaty of peace, which treaty was concluded in the latter part of the same year. On his return from Europe he was again elected to the lower branch of Congress, and on taking his seat in December 1815 was called to his old post—the speaker's chair, a position in which he was retained, by successive elections, with one brief intermission, till the inauguration of John Q. Adams[6] in March 1825. He was then appointed Secretary of State, and occupied that important station till the inauguration of Gen. Jackson in March 1829. After this he returned to Kentucky, resumed the practice of the law, and continued it till the Autumn of 1831, when he was by the Legislature of Kentucky, again placed in the United States Senate. By a re-election he was continued in the Senate till he resigned his seat, and retired, in March 1842. In December 1849 he again took his seat in the Senate, which he again resigned only a few months before his death.

By the foregoing it is perceived that the period from the beginning of Mr. Clay's official life, in 1803, to the end of it in 1852, is but one year

5. The War of 1812. Andrew Jackson (1767–1845) served two terms as president (1829–37).
6. John Quincy Adams (1767–1848), the sixth President of the United States (1825–1829).

short of half a century; and that the sum of all the intervals in it, will not amount to ten years. But mere duration of time in office, constitutes the smallest part of Mr. Clay's history. Throughout that long period, he has constantly been the most loved, and most implicitly followed by friends, and the most dreaded by opponents, of all living American politicians. In all the great questions which have agitated the country, and particularly in those great and fearful crises, the Missouri question—the Nullification question, and the late slavery question, as connected with the newly acquired territory,[7] involving and endangering the stability of the Union, his has been the leading and most conspicuous part. In 1824 he was first a candidate for the Presidency, and was defeated; and, although he was successively defeated for the same office in 1832, and in 1844, there has never been a moment since 1824 till after 1848 when a very large portion of the American people did not cling to him with an enthusiastic hope and purpose of still elevating him to the Presidency. With other men, to be defeated, was to be forgotten; but to him, defeat was but a trifling incident, neither changing him, or the world's estimate of him. Even those of both political parties, who have been preferred to him for the highest office, have run far briefer courses than he, and left him, still shining, high in the heavens of the political world. Jackson, Van Buren, Harrison, Polk, and Taylor,[8] all rose *after*, and set long before him. The spell—the long enduring spell—with which the souls of men were bound to him, is a miracle. Who can compass it? It is probably true he owed his pre-eminence to no one quality, but to a fortunate combination of several. He was surpassingly eloquent; but many eloquent men fail utterly; and they are not, as a class, generally successful. His judgment was excellent; but many men of good judgment, live and die unnoticed. His will was indomitable; but this quality often secures to its owner nothing better than a character for useless obstinacy. These then were Mr. Clay's leading qualities. No one of them is very uncommon; but all taken together are rarely combined in a single individual; and this is probably the reason why such men as Henry Clay are so rare in the world.

Mr. Clay's eloquence did not consist, as many fine specimens of eloquence does, of types and figures—of antithesis, and elegant arrangement of words and sentences; but rather of that deeply earnest and impassioned tone, and manner, which can proceed only from great sincerity and a thorough conviction, in the speaker of the justice and importance of his cause. This it is, that truly touches the chords of human sympathy; and those who heard Mr. Clay, never failed to be moved by it, or ever afterwards, forgot the impression. All his efforts were made for practical effect. He never spoke merely to be heard. He never delivered a Fourth of

7. Clay had played a key role in forging the three compromises mentioned here. "Missouri question": i.e., Missouri Compromise (1820), which admitted Missouri as a slave state and Maine as a free state and also prohibited slavery in all new states in the Louisiana Purchase north of latitude 36°30′. "Nullification question": of 1832, in which South Carolina threatened to leave the Union in protest against a high tariff, a situation that was resolved when Congress approved a new tariff, proposed by Clay, that gradually reduced rates over a decade. "Slavery question": i.e., Compromise of 1850, in which Clay advocated measures for both the North and the South that temporarily settled slavery-related disputes that had arisen in the wake of the acquisition of vast western territories.

8. All presidents of the United States. Martin Van Buren (1782–1862) served one term (1837–41). William Henry Harrison (1773–1841) died in office a month after he was elected. James K. Polk (1795–1849) served one term (1845–49). Zachary Taylor (1784–1850) served from 1849 until his death in office.

July Oration, or an eulogy on an occasion like this. As a politician or statesman, no one was so habitually careful to avoid all sectional ground. Whatever he did, he did for the whole country. In the construction of his measures he ever carefully surveyed every part of the field, and duly weighed every conflicting interest. Feeling, as he did, and as the truth surely is, that the world's best hope depended on the continued Union of these States, he was ever jealous of, and watchful for, whatever might have the slightest tendency to separate them.

Mr. Clay's predominant sentiment, from first to last, was a deep devotion to the cause of human liberty—a strong sympathy with the oppressed every where, and an ardent wish for their elevation. With him, this was a primary and all controlling passion. Subsidiary to this was the conduct of his whole life. He loved his country partly because it was his own country, but mostly because it was a free country; and he burned with a zeal for its advancement, prosperity and glory, because he saw in such, the advancement, prosperity and glory, of human liberty, human right and human nature. He desired the prosperity of his countrymen partly because they were his countrymen, but chiefly to show to the world that freemen could be prosperous.

That his views and measures were always the wisest, needs not to be affirmed; nor should it be, on this occasion, where so many, thinking differently, join in doing honor to his memory. A free people, in times of peace and quiet—when pressed by no common danger—naturally divide into parties. At such times, the man who is of neither party, is not— cannot be, of any consequence. Mr. Clay, therefore, was of a party. Taking a prominent part, as he did, in all the great political questions of his country for the last half century, the wisdom of his course on many, is doubted and denied by a large portion of his countrymen; and of such it is not now proper to speak particularly. But there are many others, about his course upon which, there is little or no disagreement amongst intelligent and patriotic Americans. Of these last are the War of 1812, the Missouri question, Nullification, and the now recent compromise measures. In 1812 Mr. Clay, though not unknown, was still a young man. Whether we should go to war with Great Britain, being the question of the day, a minority opposed the declaration of war by Congress, while the majority, though apparently inclining to war, had, for years, wavered, and hesitated to act decisively. Meanwhile British aggressions multiplied, and grew more daring and aggravated. By Mr. Clay, more than any other man, the struggle was brought to a decision in Congress. The question, being now fully before congress, came up, in a variety of ways, in rapid succession, on most of which occasions Mr. Clay spoke. Adding to all the logic, of which the subject was susceptible, that noble inspiration, which came to him as it came to no other, he aroused, and nerved, and inspired his friends, and confounded and bore-down all opposition. Several of his speeches, on these occasions, were reported, and are still extant; but the best of these all never was. During its delivery the reporters forgot their vocations, dropped their pens, and sat enchanted from near the beginning to quite the close. The speech now lives only in the memory of a few old men; and the enthusiasm with which they cherish their recollection of it is absolutely astonishing. The precise language of this speech we shall never know; but we do know—we cannot help knowing, that, with deep pathos, it pleaded the cause of the injured sailor—that it invoked the genius of the revolution—that it apostrophised the names of Otis, of Henry and of Washington[9]—that it appealed to the interest, the pride, the honor and the glory of the nation—that it shamed and taunted the timidity of friends—that it scorned, and scouted, and withered the temerity of domestic foes—that it bearded and defied the British Lion—and rising, and swelling, and maddening in its course, it sounded the onset, till the charge, the shock, the steady struggle, and the glorious victory, all passed in vivid review before the entranced hearers.

Important and exciting as was the War question, of 1812, it never so alarmed the sagacious statesmen of the country for the safety of the republic, as afterwards did the Missouri question. This sprang from that unfortunate source of discord—negro slavery. When our Federal Constitution was adopted, we owned no territory beyond the limits or ownership of the states, except the territory North-West of the River Ohio, and East of the Mississippi. What has since been formed into the States of Maine, Kentucky, and Tennessee, was, I believe, within the limits of or owned by Massachusetts, Virginia, and North Carolina. As to the North Western Territory, provision had been made, even before the adoption of the Constitution, that slavery should never go there.[1] On the admission of the States into the Union carved from the territory we owned before the constitution, no question—or at most, no considerable question—arose about slavery—those which were within the limits of or owned by the old states, following, respectively, the condition of the parent state, and those within the North West territory, following the previously made provision. But in 1803 we purchased Louisiana of the French; and it included with much more, what has since been formed into the State of Missouri. With regard to it, nothing had been done to forestall the question of slavery. When, therefore, in 1819, Missouri, having formed a State constitution, without excluding slavery, and with slavery already actually existing within its limits, knocked at the door of the Union for admission, almost the entire representation of the non-slaveholding states, objected. A fearful and angry struggle instantly followed. This alarmed thinking men, more than any previous question, because, unlike all the former, it divided the country by geographical lines. Other questions had their opposing partizans in all localities of the country and in almost every family; so that no division of the Union could follow such, without a separation of friends, to quite as great an extent, as that of opponents. Not so with the Missouri question. On this a geographical line could be traced which, in the main, would separate opponents only. This was the danger. Mr. Jefferson, then in retirement wrote:

"I had for a long time ceased to read newspapers, or to pay any attention to public affairs, confident they were in good hands, and content to

---

9. George Washington (1732–1799), commander of the Continental Army in the Revolution, president of the convention that drafted the U.S. Constitution, and the first U.S. president. "Cause of the injured sailor": a leading member of the so-called War Hawks in Congress, Clay protested vehemently against the seizure of American ships by warring European powers and the British navy's practice of impressing (abducting) American sailors. James Otis Jr. (1725–1783), a patriot who during the American Revolution popularized the slogan "Taxation without representation is tyranny." Patrick Henry (1736–1799) who declared, "Give me liberty or give me death."
1. The Northwest Ordinance, passed by the Congress of the Confederation of the United States on July 13, 1787, prohibited slavery in territories northwest of the Ohio River.

be a passenger in our bark to the shore from which I am not distant. But this momentous question, like a fire bell in the night, awakened, and filled me with terror. I considered it at once as the knell of the Union. It is hushed, indeed, for the moment. But this is a reprieve only, not a final sentence. A geographical line, co-inciding with a marked principle, moral and political, once conceived, and held up to the angry passions of men, will never be obliterated; and every irritation will mark it deeper and deeper. I can say, with conscious truth, that there is not a man on earth who would sacrifice more than I would to relieve us from this heavy reproach, in any *practicable* way. The cession of that kind of property, for so it is misnamed, is a bagatelle which would not cost me a second thought, if, in that way, a general emancipation, and *expatriation* could be effected; and, gradually, and with due sacrifices I think it might be. But as it is, we have the wolf by the ears and we can neither hold him, nor safely let him go. Justice is in one scale, and self-preservation in the other."[2]

Mr. Clay was in congress, and, perceiving the danger, at once engaged his whole energies to avert it. It began, as I have said, in 1819; and it did not terminate till 1821. Missouri would not yield the point; and congress—that is, a majority in congress—by repeated votes, showed a determination to not admit the state unless it should yield. After several failures, and great labor on the part of Mr. Clay to so present the question that a majority could consent to the admission, it was, by a vote, rejected, and as all seemed to think, finally. A sullen gloom hung over the nation. All felt that the rejection of Missouri, was equivalent to a dissolution of the Union: because those states which already had, what Missouri was rejected for refusing to relinquish, would go with Missouri. All deprecated and deplored this, but none saw how to avert it. For the judgment of Members to be convinced of the necessity of yielding, was not the whole difficulty; each had a constituency to meet, and to answer to. Mr. Clay, though worn down, and exhausted, was appealed to by members, to renew his efforts at compromise. He did so, and by some judicious modifications of his plan, coupled with laborious efforts with individual members, and his own over-mastering eloquence upon the floor, he finally secured the admission of the State. Brightly, and captivating as it had previously shown, it was now perceived that his great eloquence, was a mere embellishment, or, at most, but a helping hand to his inventive genius, and his devotion to his country in the day of her extreme peril.

After the settlement of the Missouri question, although a portion of the American people have differed with Mr. Clay, and a majority even, appear generally to have been opposed to him on questions of ordinary administration, he seems constantly to have been regarded by all, as *the* man for a crisis. Accordingly, in the days of Nullification, and more recently in the re-appearance of the slavery question, connected with our territory newly acquired of Mexico, the task of devising a mode of adjustment, seems to have been cast upon Mr. Clay, by common consent—and his performance of the task, in each case, was little else than a literal fulfilment of the public expectation.

---

2. Jefferson in a letter to John Holmes, April 22, 1820.

Mr. Clay's efforts in behalf of the South Americans, and afterwards, in behalf of the Greeks, in the times of their respective struggles for civil liberty[3] are among the finest on record, upon the noblest of all themes; and bear ample corroboration of what I have said was his ruling passion—a love of liberty and right, unselfishly, and for their own sakes.

Having been led to allude to domestic slavery so frequently already, I am unwilling to close without referring more particularly to Mr. Clay's views and conduct in regard to it. He ever was, on principle and in feeling, opposed to slavery. The very earliest, and one of the latest public efforts of his life, separated by a period of more than fifty years, were both made in favor of gradual emancipation of the slaves in Kentucky. He did not perceive, that on a question of human right, the negroes were to be excepted from the human race. And yet Mr. Clay was the owner of slaves. Cast into life where slavery was already widely spread and deeply seated, he did not perceive, as I think no wise man has perceived, how it could be at *once* eradicated, without producing a greater evil, even to the cause of human liberty itself. His feeling and his judgment, therefore, ever led him to oppose both extremes of opinion on the subject. Those who would shiver into fragments the Union of these States; tear to tatters its now venerated constitution; and even burn the last copy of the Bible, rather than slavery should continue a single hour, together with all their more halting sympathisers, have received, and are receiving their just execration;[4] and the name, and opinions, and influence of Mr. Clay, are fully, and, as I trust, effectually and enduringly, arrayed against them. But I would also, if I could, array his name, opinions, and influence against the opposite extreme—against a few, but an increasing number of men, who, for the sake of perpetuating slavery, are beginning to assail and to ridicule the white-man's charter of freedom—the declaration that "all men are created free and equal." So far as I have learned, the first American, of any note, to do or attempt this, was the late John C. Calhoun;[5] and if I mistake not, it soon after found its way into some of the messages of the Governors of South Carolina. We, however, look for, and are not much shocked by, political eccentricities and heresies in South Carolina. But, only last year, I saw with astonishment, what purported to be a letter of a very distinguished and influential clergyman of Virginia, copied, with apparent approbation, into a St. Louis newspaper, containing the following, to me, very extraordinary language—

"I am fully aware that there is a text in some Bibles that is not in mine. Professional abolitionists have made more use of it, than of any passage in the Bible. It came, however, as I trace it, from Saint Voltaire,[6] and was

---

3. Clay was an ardent supporter of emerging South American nations, several of which owed their survival largely to his advocacy of their cause in the face of threatened European intervention. Clay also gave support to Greece in its revolution against Turkish rule.
4. Reference to radical abolitionists, such as William Lloyd Garrison (1805–1879), who were widely unpopular, even in the North, because of their extreme views. Garrison called for the separation of North from the South over the slavery issue and denounced the Constitution as "a covenant with death and an agreement with hell" because he believed it condoned slavery.
5. South Carolina senator (1782–1850) who in 1837 pronounced slavery "a good—a great good" because it placed "the Central African race" in a position that was "comfortable, . . . respectable, . . . civilized." Calhoun declared that the statement in the Declaration of Independence that all men are created equal is the "most false and dangerous of all political errors."
6. Pen name of François-Marie Arouet (1694–1778), an 18th-century French Enlightenment writer and philosopher who influenced several Founding Fathers with his ideas about civil liberties and human equality.

baptized by Thomas Jefferson, and since almost universally regarded as canonical authority 'All men are born free and equal.'

"This is a genuine coin in the political currency of our generation. I am sorry to say that I have never seen two men of whom it is true. But I must admit I never saw the Siamese twins, and therefore will not dogmatically say that no man ever saw a proof of this sage aphorism."

This sounds strangely in republican America. The like was not heard in the fresher days of the Republic. Let us contrast with it the language of that truly national man, whose life and death we now commemorate and lament. I quote from a speech of Mr. Clay delivered before the American Colonization Society[7] in 1827.

"We are reproached with doing mischief by the agitation of this question. The society goes into no household to disturb its domestic tranquility; it addresses itself to no slaves to weaken their obligations of obedience. It seeks to affect no man's property. It neither has the power nor the will to affect the property of any one contrary to his consent. The execution of its scheme would augment instead of diminishing the value of the property left behind. The society, composed of free men, concerns itself only with the free. Collateral consequences we are not responsible for. It is not this society which has produced the great moral revolution which the age exhibits. What would they, who thus reproach us, have done? If they would repress all tendencies towards liberty, and ultimate emancipation, they must do more than put down the benevolent efforts of this society. They must go back to the era of our liberty and independence, and muzzle the cannon which thunders its annual joyous return. They must renew the slave trade with all its train of atrocities. They must suppress the workings of British philanthropy, seeking to meliorate the condition of the unfortunate West Indian slave. They must arrest the career of South American deliverance from thraldom. They must blow out the moral lights around us, and extinguish that greatest torch of all which America presents to a benighted world—pointing the way to their rights, their liberties, and their happiness. And when they have achieved all those purposes their work will be yet incomplete. They must penetrate the human soul, and eradicate the light of reason, and the love of liberty. Then, and not till then, when universal darkness and despair prevail, can you perpetuate slavery, and repress all sympathy, and all humane, and benevolent efforts among free men, in behalf of the unhappy portion of our race doomed to bondage."

The American Colonization Society was organized in 1816. Mr. Clay, though not its projector, was one of its earliest members; and he died, as for the many preceding years he had been, its President. It was one of the most cherished objects of his direct care and consideration; and the association of his name with it has probably been its very greatest collateral support. He considered it no demerit in the society, that it tended to relieve slave-holders from the troublesome presence of the free negroes; but this was far from being its whole merit in his estimation. In the same speech from which I have quoted he says: "There is a moral fitness in the

7. Advocated the deportation of free blacks and emancipated slaves to Africa. Founded in December 1816, its early members included Clay, James Monroe (1758–1831), Andrew Jackson, and John Randolph. Although the society managed to deport only around thirteen thousand blacks by 1865, colonization was a popular idea, endorsed by notables such as Daniel Webster (1782–1852), Francis Scott Key (1779–1843), Catharine Beecher (1800–1878), and, until the middle of the Civil War, Lincoln.

idea of returning to Africa her children, whose ancestors have been torn from her by the ruthless hand of fraud and violence. Transplanted in a foreign land, they will carry back to their native soil the rich fruits of religion, civilization, law and liberty. May it not be one of the great designs of the Ruler of the universe, (whose ways are often inscrutable by shortsighted mortals,) thus to transform an original crime, into a signal blessing to that most unfortunate portion of the globe?" This suggestion of the possible ultimate redemption of the African race and African continent, was made twenty-five years ago. Every succeeding year has added strength to the hope of its realization. May it indeed be realized! Pharaoh's country was cursed with plagues, and his hosts were drowned in the Red Sea for striving to retain a captive people who had already served them more than four hundred years. May like disasters never befall us! If as the friends of colonization hope, the present and coming generations of our countrymen shall by any means, succeed in freeing our land from the dangerous presence of slavery; and, at the same time, in restoring a captive people to their long-lost father-land, with bright prospects for the future; and this too, so gradually, that neither races nor individuals shall have suffered by the change, it will indeed be a glorious consummation. And if, to such a consummation, the efforts of Mr. Clay shall have contributed, it will be what he most ardently wished, and none of his labors will have been more valuable to his country and his kind.

But Henry Clay is dead. His long and eventful life is closed. Our country is prosperous and powerful; but could it have been quite all it has been, and is, and is to be, without Henry Clay? Such a man the times have demanded, and such, in the providence of God was given us. But he is gone. Let us strive to deserve, as far as mortals may, the continued care of Divine Providence, trusting that, in future national emergencies, He will not fail to provide us the instruments of safety and security.

July 6, 1852

Fragments on Slavery

dent truth. Made so plain by our good Father in Heaven, that all *feel* and *understand* it, even down to brutes and creeping insects. The ant, who has toiled and dragged a crumb to his nest, will furiously defend the fruit of his labor, against whatever robber assails him. So plain, that the most dumb and stupid slave that ever toiled for a master, does constantly *know* that he is wronged. So plain that no one, high or low, ever does mistake it, except in a plainly *selfish* way; for although volume upon volume is written to prove slavery a very good thing, we never hear of the man who wishes to take the good of it, *by being a slave himself.*

Most governments have been based, practically, on the denial of equal rights of men, as I have, in part, stated them; *ours* began, by *affirming* those rights. *They* said, some men are too *ignorant*, and *vicious*, to share in government. Possibly so, said we; and, by your system, you would always keep them ignorant, and vicious. We proposed to give *all* a chance; and we expected the weak to grow stronger, the ignorant, wiser; and all better, and happier together.

We made the experiment; and the fruit is before us. Look at it—think of it. Look at it, in it's aggregate grandeur, of extent of country, and numbers of population—of ship, and steamboat, and rail-

----

If A. can prove, however conclusively, that he may, of right, enslave B.—why may not B. snatch the same argument, and prove equally, that he may enslave A?—

You say A. is white, and B. is black. It is *color*, then; the lighter, having the right to enslave the darker? Take care. By this rule, you are to be slave to the first man you meet, with a fairer skin than your own.

You do not mean *color* exactly?—You mean the whites are *intellectually* the superiors of the blacks, and, therefore have the right to enslave them? Take care again. By this rule, you are to be slave to the first man you meet, with an intellect superior to your own.

But, say you, it is a question of *interest*; and, if you can make it your *interest*, you have the right to enslave another. Very well. And if he can make it his interest, he has the right to enslave you.

April 1, 1854?

Fragments on Government

The legitimate object of government, is to do for a community of people, whatever they need to have done, but can not do, *at all*, or can not, *so well do*, for themselves—in their separate, and individual capacities.

In all that the people can individually do as well for themselves, government ought not to interfere.

The desirable things which the individuals of a people can not do, or can not well do, for themselves, fall into two classes: those which have relation to *wrongs*, and those which have not. Each of these branch off into an infinite variety of subdivisions.

The first—that in relation to wrongs—embraces all crimes, misdemeanors, and non-performance of contracts. The other embraces all which, in its nature, and without wrong, requires combined action, as public roads and highways, public schools, charities, pauperism, orphanage, estates of the deceased, and the machinery of government itself.

From this it appears that if all men were just, there still would be *some*, though not *so much*, need of government.

Government is a combination of the people of a country to effect certain objects by joint effort. The best framed and best administered governments are necessarily expensive; while by errors in frame and maladministration most of them are more onerous than they need be, and some of them very oppressive. Why, then, should we have government? Why not each individual take to himself the whole fruit of his labor, without having any of it taxed away, in services, corn, or money? Why not take just so much land as he can cultivate with his own hands, without buying it of any one?

The legitimate object of government is "to do for the people what needs to be done, but which they can not, by individual effort, do at all, or do so well, for themselves." There are many such things—some of them exist independently of the injustice in the world. Making and maintaining roads, bridges, and the like; providing for the helpless young and afflicted; common schools; and disposing of deceased men's property, are instances.

But a far larger class of objects springs from the injustice of men. If one people will make war upon another, it is a necessity with that other to unite and coöperate for defense. Hence the military department. If some men will kill, or beat, or constrain others, or despoil them of property, by force, fraud, or noncompliance with contracts, it is a common object with peaceful and just men to prevent it. Hence the criminal and civil departments.

July 1, 1854?

From Speech on the Kansas-Nebraska Act[1] at Peoria, Illinois

Mr. Lincoln's Speech

✳ ✳ ✳

The repeal of the Missouri Compromise, and the propriety of its restoration, constitute the subject of what I am about to say.

As I desire to present my own connected view of this subject, my remarks will not be, specifically, an answer to Judge Douglas; yet, as I proceed, the main points he has presented will arise, and will receive such respectful attention as I may be able to give them.

I wish further to say, that I do not propose to question the patriotism, or to assail the motives of any man, or class of men; but rather to strictly confine myself to the naked merits of the question.

I also wish to be no less than National in all the positions I may take; and whenever I take ground which others have thought, or may think, narrow, sectional and dangerous to the Union, I hope to give a reason, which will appear sufficient, at least to some, why I think differently.

And, as this subject is no other, than part and parcel of the larger general question of domestic-slavery, I wish to MAKE and to KEEP the distinction between the EXISTING institution, and the EXTENSION of it, so broad, and so clear, that no honest man can misunderstand me, and no dishonest one, successfully misrepresent me.[2]

In order to a clear understanding of what the Missouri Compromise is, a short history of the preceding kindred subjects will perhaps be proper. When we established our independence, we did not own, or claim, the

1. This act, passed in May 1854, created the new territories of Kansas and Nebraska. It stirred controversy because it repealed the Missouri Compromise by giving territorial settlers the right to vote to accept or reject slavery.
2. This principle of preventing the westward expansion of slavery became the bulwark of the Republican Party, which arose in anti-Nebraska meetings in 1854 and became a national organization in 1856.

country to which this compromise applies. Indeed, strictly speaking, the confederacy then owned no country at all; the States respectively owned the country within their limits; and some of them owned territory beyond their strict State limits. Virginia thus owned the North-Western territory—the country out of which the principal part of Ohio, all Indiana, all Illinois, all Michigan and all Wisconsin, have since been formed. She also owned (perhaps within her then limits) what has since been formed into the State of Kentucky. North Carolina thus owned what is now the State of Tennessee; and South Carolina and Georgia, in separate parts, owned what are now Mississippi and Alabama. Connecticut, I think, owned the little remaining part of Ohio—being the same where they now send Giddings to Congress, and beat all creation at making cheese. These territories, together with the States themselves, constituted all the country over which the confederacy then claimed any sort of jurisdiction. We were then living under the Articles of Confederation, which were superceded by the Constitution several years afterwards. The question of ceding these territories to the general government was set on foot. Mr. Jefferson, the author of the Declaration of Independence, and otherwise a chief actor in the revolution; then a delegate in Congress; afterwards twice President; who was, is, and perhaps will continue to be, the most distinguished politician of our history; a Virginian by birth and continued residence, and withal, a slave-holder; conceived the idea of taking that occasion, to prevent slavery ever going into the north-western territory. He prevailed on the Virginia Legislature to adopt his views, and to cede the territory, making the prohibition of slavery therein,[3] a condition of the deed. Congress accepted the cession, with the condition; and in the first Ordinance (which the acts of Congress were then called) for the government of the territory, provided that slavery should never be permitted therein. This is the famed ordinance of '87 so often spoken of. Thenceforward, for sixty-one years, and until in 1848, the last scrap of this territory came into the Union as the State of Wisconsin, all parties acted in quiet obedience to this ordinance. It is now what Jefferson foresaw and intended—the happy home of teeming millions of free, white, prosperous people, and no slave amongst them.

Thus, with the author of the declaration of Independence, the policy of prohibiting slavery in new territory originated. Thus, away back of the constitution, in the pure fresh, free breath of the revolution, the State of Virginia, and the National congress put that policy in practice. Thus through sixty odd of the best years of the republic did that policy steadily work to its great and beneficent end. And thus, in those five states, and five millions of free, enterprising people, we have before us the rich fruits of this policy. But *now* new light breaks upon us. Now congress declares this ought never to have been; and the like of it, must never be again. The sacred right of self government is grossly violated by it! We even find some men, who drew their first breath, and every other breath of their lives, under this very restriction, now live in dread of absolute suffoca-

---

3. A reference to the Northwest Ordinance (1787), which prohibited slavery in territories northwest of the Ohio River.

tion, if they should be restricted in the "sacred right" of taking slaves to Nebraska. That *perfect* liberty they sigh for—the liberty of making slaves of other people—Jefferson never thought of; their own father never thought of; they never thought of themselves, a year ago. How fortunate for them, they did not sooner become sensible of their great misery! Oh, how difficult it is to treat with respect, such assaults upon all we have ever really held sacred.

But to return to history. In 1803 we purchased what was then called Louisiana, of France. It included the now states of Louisiana, Arkansas, Missouri, and Iowa; also the territory of Minnesota, and the present bone of contention, Kansas and Nebraska. Slavery already existed among the French at New Orleans; and, to some extent, at St. Louis. In 1812 Louisiana came into the Union as a slave state, without controversy. In 1818 or '19, Missouri showed signs of a wish to come in with slavery. This was resisted by northern members of Congress; and thus began the first great slavery agitation in the nation. This controversy lasted several months, and became very angry and exciting; the House of Representatives voting steadily for the prohibition of slavery in Missouri, and the Senate voting as steadily against it. Threats of breaking up the Union were freely made; and the ablest public men of the day became seriously alarmed. At length a compromise was made, in which, like all compromises, both sides yielded something. It was a law passed on the 6th day of March, 1820, providing that Missouri might come into the Union *with* slavery, but that in all the remaining part of the territory purchased of France, which lies north of 36 degrees and 30 minutes north latitude, slavery should never be permitted. This provision of law, *is the Missouri Compromise*. In excluding slavery North of the line, the same language is employed as in the Ordinance of '87. It directly applied to Iowa, Minnesota, and to the present bone of contention, Kansas and Nebraska. Whether there should or should not, be slavery south of that line, nothing was said in the law; but Arkansas constituted the principal remaining part, south of the line; and it has since been admitted as a slave state without serious controversy. More recently, Iowa, north of the line, came in as a free state without controversy. Still later, Minnesota, north of the line, had a territorial organization without controversy. Texas principally south of the line, and West of Arkansas; though originally within the purchase from France, had, in 1819, been traded off to Spain, in our treaty for the acquisition of Florida. It had thus become a part of Mexico. Mexico revolutionized and became independent of Spain. American citizens began settling rapidly, with their slaves in the southern part of Texas. Soon they revolutionized against Mexico, and established an independent government of their own, adopting a constitution, with slavery, strongly resembling the constitutions of our slave states. By still another rapid move, Texas, claiming a boundary much further West, than when we parted with her in 1819, was brought back to the United States, and admitted into the Union as a slave state. There then was little or no settlement in the northern part of Texas, a considerable portion of which lay north of the Missouri line; and in the resolutions admitting her into the Union, the Missouri restriction was expressly extended westward across her territory. This was in 1845, only nine years ago.

Thus originated the Missouri Compromise; and thus has it been respected down to 1845. And even four years later, in 1849, our distinguished Senator;[4] in a public address, held the following language in relation to it:

"The Missouri Compromise had been in practical operation for about a quarter of a century, and had received the sanction and approbation of men of all parties in every section of the Union. It had allayed all sectional jealousies and irritations growing out of this vexed question, and harmonized and tranquilized the whole country. It had given to Henry Clay, as its prominent champion, the proud sobriquet of the "*Great Pacificator*" and by that title and for that service, his political friends had repeatedly appealed to the people to rally under his standard, as a presidential candidate, as the man who had exhibited the patriotism and the power to suppress, an unholy and treasonable agitation, and preserve the Union. He was not aware that any man or any party from any section of the Union, had ever urged as an objection to Mr. Clay, that he was the great champion of the Missouri Compromise. On the contrary, the effort was made by the opponents of Mr. Clay, to prove that he was not entitled to the exclusive merit of that great patriotic measure, and that the honor was equally due to others as well as to him, for securing its adoption— that it had its origin in the hearts of all patriotic men, who desired to preserve and perpetuate the blessings of our glorious Union—an origin akin that of the constitution of the United States, conceived in the same spirit of fraternal affection, and calculated to remove forever, the only danger, which seemed to threaten, at some distant day, to sever the social bond of union. All the evidences of public opinion at that day, seemed to indicate that this Compromise had been canonized in the hearts of the American people, as a sacred thing which no ruthless hand would ever be reckless enough to disturb."

I do not read this extract to involve Judge Douglas in an inconsistency. If he afterwards thought he had been wrong, it was right for him to change. I bring this forward merely to show the high estimate placed on the Missouri Compromise by all parties up to so late as the year 1849.

But, going back a little, in point of time, our war with Mexico broke out in 1846. When Congress was about adjourning that session, President Polk asked them to place two millions of dollars under his control, to be used by him in the recess, if found practicable and expedient, in negociating a treaty of peace with Mexico, and acquiring some part of her territory. A bill was duly got up, for the purpose, and was progressing swimmingly, in the House of Representatives, when a member by the name of David Wilmot, a democrat from Pennsylvania, moved as an amendment "Provided that in any territory thus acquired, there shall never be slavery."

This is the origin of the far-famed "Wilmot Proviso." It created a great flutter; but it stuck like wax, was voted into the bill, and the bill passed with it through the House. The Senate, however, adjourned without final action on it and so both appropriation and proviso were lost, for the time. The war continued, and at the next session, the president renewed his request for the appropriation, enlarging the amount, I think, to three million. Again came the proviso; and defeated the measure. Congress adjourned again, and the war went on. In Dec., 1847, the new congress

4. Stephen A. Douglas.

assembled. I was in the lower House that term. The "Wilmot Proviso" or the principle of it, was constantly coming up in some shape or other, and I think I may venture to say I voted for it at least forty times; during the short term I was there. The Senate, however, held it in check, and it never became law. In the spring of 1848 a treaty of peace was made with Mexico; by which we obtained that portion of her country which now constitutes the territories of New Mexico and Utah, and the now state of California. By this treaty the Wilmot Proviso was defeated, as so far as it was intended to be, a condition of the acquisition of territory. Its friends however, were still determined to find some way to restrain slavery from getting into the new country. This new acquisition lay directly West of our old purchase from France, and extended west to the Pacific ocean—and was so situated that if the Missouri line should be extended straight West, the new country would be divided by such extended line, leaving some North and some South of it. On Judge Douglas' motion a bill, or provision of a bill, passed the Senate to so extend the Missouri line. The Proviso men in the House, including myself, voted it down, because by implication, it gave up the Southern part to slavery, while we were bent on having it *all* free.

In the fall of 1848 the gold mines were discovered in California. This attracted people to it with unprecedented rapidity, so that on, or soon after, the meeting of the new congress in Dec., 1849, she already had a population of nearly a hundred thousand, had called a convention, formed a state constitution, excluding slavery, and was knocking for admission into the Union. The Proviso men, of course were for letting her in, but the Senate, always true to the other side would not consent to her admission. And there California stood, kept *out* of the Union, because she would not let slavery *into* her borders. Under all the circumstances perhaps this was not wrong. There were other points of dispute, connected with the general question of slavery, which equally needed adjustment. The South clamored for a more efficient fugitive slave law. The North clamored for the abolition of a peculiar species of slave trade in the District of Columbia, in connection with which, in view from the windows of the capitol, a sort of negro-livery stable, where droves of negroes were collected, temporarily kept, and finally taken to Southern markets, precisely like droves of horses, had been openly maintained for fifty years. Utah and New Mexico needed territorial governments; and whether slavery should or should not be prohibited within them, was another question. The indefinite Western boundary of Texas was to be settled. She was received a slave state; and consequently the farther West the slavery men could push her boundary, the more slave country they secured. And the farther East the slavery opponents could thrust the boundary back, the less slave ground was secured. Thus this was just as clearly a slavery question as any of the others.

These points all needed adjustment; and they were all held up, perhaps wisely to make them help to adjust one another. The Union, now, as in 1820, was thought to be in danger; and devotion to the Union rightfully inclined men to yield somewhat, in points where nothing else could have so inclined them. A compromise was finally effected. The south got their new fugitive-slave law; and the North got California, (the far best part of our acquisition from Mexico,) as a free State. The south got a provision that New Mexico and Utah, *when admitted as States*, may come in *with* or *without* slavery as they may then choose; and the north got the slave-trade abolished in the District of Columbia. The north got the western boundary of Texas, thence further back eastward than the south desired; but, in turn, they gave Texas ten millions of dollars, with which to pay her old debts. This is the Compromise of 1850.

Preceding the Presidential election of 1852, each of the great political parties, democrats and whigs, met in convention, and adopted resolutions endorsing the compromise of '50; as a "finality," a final settlement, so far as these parties could make it so, of all slavery agitation. Previous to this, in 1851, the Illinois Legislature had indorsed it.

During this long period of time Nebraska had remained, substantially an uninhabited country, but now emigration to, and settlement within it began to take place. It is about one third as large as the present United States, and its importance so long overlooked, begins to come into view. The restriction of slavery by the Missouri Compromise directly applies to it; in fact, was first made, and has since been maintained, expressly for it. In 1853, a bill to give it a territorial government passed the House of Representatives, and, in the hands of Judge Douglas, failed of passing the Senate only for want of time. This bill contained no repeal of the Missouri Compromise. Indeed, when it was assailed because it did not contain such repeal, Judge Douglas defended it in its existing form. On January 4th, 1854, Judge Douglas introduces a new bill to give Nebraska territorial government. He accompanies this bill with a report, in which last, he expressly recommends that the Missouri Compromise shall neither be affirmed nor repealed.

Before long the bill is so modified as to make two territories instead of one; calling the Southern one Kansas.

Also, about a month after the introduction of the bill, on the judge's own motion, it is so amended as to declare the Missouri Compromise inoperative and void; and, substantially, that the People who go and settle there may establish slavery, or exclude it, as they may see fit. In this shape the bill passed both branches of congress, and became a law.

This is the *repeal* of the Missouri Compromise. The foregoing history may not be precisely accurate in every particular; but I am sure it is sufficiently so, for all the uses I shall attempt to make of it, and in it, we have before us, the chief material enabling us to correctly judge whether the repeal of the Missouri Compromise is right or wrong.

I think, and shall try to show, that it is wrong; wrong in its direct effect, letting slavery into Kansas and Nebraska—and wrong in its prospective principle, allowing it to spread to every other part of the wide world, where men can be found inclined to take it.

This *declared* indifference, but as I must think, covert *real* zeal for the spread of slavery, I can not but hate. I hate it because of the monstrous injustice of slavery itself. I hate it because it deprives our republican example of its just influence in the world—enables the enemies of free institutions, with plausibility, to taunt us as hypocrites—causes the real friends of freedom to doubt our sincerity, and especially because it forces so many really good men amongst ourselves into an open war with the very fundamental principles of civil liberty—criticising the Declaration of Independence, and insisting that there is no right principle of action but *self-interest*.

Before proceeding, let me say I think I have no prejudice against the Southern people. They are just what we would be in their situation. If slavery did not now exist amongst them, they would not introduce it. If it did now exist amongst us, we should not instantly give it up. This I believe of the masses north and south. Doubtless there are individuals, on both sides, who would not hold slaves under any circumstances; and others who would gladly introduce slavery anew, if it were out of existence. We know that some southern men do free their slaves, go north, and become tip-top abolitionists; while some northern ones go south, and become most cruel slave-masters.

When southern people tell us they are no more responsible for the origin of slavery, than we; I acknowledge the fact. When it is said that the institution exists; and that it is very difficult to get rid of it, in any satisfactory way, I can understand and appreciate the saying. I surely will not blame them for not doing what I should not know how to do myself. If all earthly power were given me, I should not know what to do, as to the existing institution. My first impulse would be to free all the slaves, and send them to Liberia,[5]—to their own native land. But a moment's reflection would convince me, that whatever of high hope, (as I think there is) there may be in this, in the long run, its sudden execution is impossible. If they were all landed there in a day, they would all perish in the next ten days; and there are not surplus shipping and surplus money enough in the world to carry them there in many times ten days. What then? Free them all, and keep them among us as underlings? Is it quite certain that this betters their condition? I think I would not hold one in slavery, at any rate; yet the point is not clear enough for me to denounce people upon. What next? Free them, and make them politically and socially, our equals? My own feelings will not admit of this; and if mine would, we well know that those of the great mass of white people will not. Whether this feeling accords with justice and sound judgment, is not the sole question, if indeed, it is any part of it. A universal feeling, whether well or ill-founded, can not be safely disregarded. We can not, then, make them equals. It does seem to me that systems of gradual emancipation might be adopted; but for their tardiness in this, I will not undertake to judge our brethren of the south.

When they remind us of their constitutional rights, I acknowledge them, not grudgingly, but fully, and fairly; and I would give them any legislation for the reclaiming of their fugitives, which should not, in its stringency, be more likely to carry a free man into slavery, than our ordinary criminal laws are to hang an innocent one.

But all this, to my judgment, furnishes no more excuse for permitting slavery to go into our own free territory, than it would for reviving the African slave trade by law. The law which forbids the bringing of slaves *from* Africa; and that which has so long forbid the taking them *to* Nebraska, can hardly be distinguished on any moral principle; and the repeal of the former could find quite as plausible excuses as that of the latter.

---

5. On the west coast of Africa and settled by expatriated American blacks ever since 1820, when the American Colonization Society first shipped free blacks there. By 1867, the society had sent some thirteen hundred emigrants to Liberia.

* * *

Equal justice to the south, it is said, requires us to consent to the extending of slavery to new countries. That is to say, inasmuch as you do not object to my taking my hog to Nebraska, therefore I must not object to you taking your slave. Now, I admit this is perfectly logical, if there is no difference between hogs and negroes. But while you thus require me to deny the humanity of the negro, I wish to ask whether you of the south yourselves, have ever been willing to do as much? It is kindly provided that of all those who come into the world, only a small percentage are natural tyrants. That percentage is no larger in the slave States than in the free. The great majority, south as well as north, have human sympathies, of which they can no more divest themselves than they can of their sensibility to physical pain. These sympathies in the bosoms of the southern people, manifest in many ways, their sense of the wrong of slavery, and their consciousness that, after all, there is humanity in the negro. If they deny this, let me address them a few plain questions. In 1820 you joined the north, almost unanimously, in declaring the African slave trade piracy, and in annexing to it the punishment of death.[6] Why did you do this? If you did not feel that it was wrong, why did you join in providing that men should be hung for it? The practice was no more than bringing wild negroes from Africa, to sell to such as would buy them. But you never thought of hanging men for catching and selling wild horses, wild buffaloes or wild bears.

Again, you have amongst you, a sneaking individual, of the class of native tyrants, known as the "SLAVE-DEALER." He watches your necessities, and crawls up to buy your slave, at a speculating price. If you cannot help it, you sell to him; but if you can help it, you drive him from your door. You despise him utterly. You do not recognize him as a friend, or even as an honest man. Your children must not play with his; they may rollick freely with the little negroes, but not with the "slave-dealers" children. If you are obliged to deal with him, you try to get through the job without so much as touching him. It is common with you to join hands with the men you meet; but with the slave dealer you avoid the ceremony—instinctively shrinking from the snaky contact. If he grows rich and retires from business, you still remember him, and still keep up the ban of non-intercourse upon him and his family. Now why is this? You do not so treat the man who deals in corn, cattle or tobacco.

And yet again; there are in the United States and territories, including the District of Columbia, 433,643 free blacks. At $500 per head they are worth over two hundred millions of dollars. How comes this vast amount of property to be running about without owners? We do not see free horses or free cattle running at large. How is this? All these free blacks are the descendants of slaves, or have been slaves themselves, and they would be slaves now, but for SOMETHING which has operated on their white owners, inducing them, at vast pecuniary sacrifices, to liberate them. What is that SOMETHING? Is there any mistaking it? In all these cases it is your sense of justice, and human sympathy, continually telling you, that the poor negro has some natural right to himself—that those

6. According to the Act of 1820, anyone who participated in the African slave trade was subject to a conviction of piracy, which was punishable by death.

who deny it, and make mere merchandise of him, deserve kickings, contempt and death.

And now, why will you ask us to deny the humanity of the slave? and estimate him only as the equal of the hog? Why ask us to do what you will not do yourselves? Why ask us to do for *nothing*, what two hundred million of dollars could not induce you to do?

But one great argument in the support of the repeal of the Missouri Compromise, is still to come. That argument is "the sacred right of self government." It seems our distinguished Senator has found great difficulty in getting his antagonists, even in the Senate to meet him fairly on this argument—some poet has said

"Fools rush in where angels fear to tread."[7]

At the hazzard of being thought one of the fools of this quotation, I meet that argument—I rush in, I take that bull by the horns.

I trust I understand, and truly estimate the right of self-government. My faith in the proposition that each man should do precisely as he pleases with all which is exclusively his own, lies at the foundation of the sense of justice there is in me. I extend the principles to communities of men, as well as to individuals. I so extend it, because it is politically wise, as well as naturally just: politically wise, in saving us from broils about matters which do not concern us. Here, or at Washington, I would not trouble myself with the oyster laws of Virginia, or the cranberry laws of Indiana.

The doctrine of self government is right—absolutely and eternally right—but it has no just application, as here attempted. Or perhaps I should rather say that whether it has such just application depends upon whether a negro is *not* or *is* a man. If he is *not* a man, why in that case, he who *is* a man may, as a matter of self-government, do just as he pleases with him. But if the negro *is* a man, is it not to that extent, a total destruction of self-government, to say that he too shall not govern *himself*? When the white man governs himself that is self-government; but when he governs himself, and also governs *another* man, that is *more* than self-government—that is despotism. If the negro is a *man*, why then my ancient faith teaches me that "all men are created equal;" and that there can be no moral right in connection with one man's making a slave of another.

Judge Douglas frequently, with bitter irony and sarcasm, paraphrases our argument by saying "The white people of Nebraska are good enough to govern themselves, *but they are not good enough to govern a few miserable negroes!!*"

Well I doubt not that the people of Nebraska are, and will continue to be as good as the average of people elsewhere. I do not say the contrary. What I do say is, that no man is good enough to govern another man, *without that other's consent*. I say this is the leading principle—the sheet anchor of American republicanism. Our Declaration of Independence says:

"We hold these truths to be self evident: that all men are created equal; that they are endowed by their Creator with certain inalienable rights; that among these are life, liberty and the pursuit of happiness. That to

7. Alexander Pope's *An Essay on Criticism* (1711).

secure these rights, governments are instituted among men, DERIVING THEIR JUST POWERS FROM THE CONSENT OF THE GOVERNED."

I have quoted so much at this time merely to show that according to our ancient faith, the just powers of governments are derived from the consent of the governed. Now the relation of masters and slaves is, PRO TANTO,[8] a total violation of this principle. The master not only governs the slave without his consent; but he governs him by a set of rules altogether different from those which he prescribes for himself. Allow ALL the governed an equal voice in the government, and that, and that only is self government.

Let it not be said I am contending for the establishment of political and social equality between the whites and blacks. I have already said the contrary. I am not now combating the argument of NECESSITY, arising from the fact that the blacks are already amongst us; but I am combating what is set up as MORAL argument for allowing them to be taken where they have never yet been—arguing against the EXTENSION of a bad thing, which where it already exists, we must of necessity, manage as we best can.

In support of his application of the doctrine of self-government, Senator Douglas has sought to bring to his aid the opinions and examples of our revolutionary fathers. I am glad he has done this. I love the sentiments of those old-time men; and shall be most happy to abide by their opinions. He shows us that when it was in contemplation for the colonies to break off from Great Britain, and set up a new government for themselves, several of the states instructed their delegates to go for the measure PROVIDED EACH STATE SHOULD BE ALLOWED TO REGULATE ITS DOMESTIC CONCERNS IN ITS OWN WAY. I do not quote; but this in substance. This was right. I see nothing objectionable in it. I also think it probable that it had some reference to the existence of slavery amongst them. I will not deny that it had. But had it, in any reference to the carrying of slavery into NEW COUNTRIES? That is the question; and we will let the fathers themselves answer it.

This same generation of men, and mostly the same individuals of the generation, who declared this principle—who declared independence—who fought the war of the revolution through—who afterwards made the constitution under which we still live—these same men passed the ordinance of '87, declaring that slavery should never go to the north-west territory. I have no doubt Judge Douglas thinks they were very inconsistent in this. It is a question of discrimination between them and him. But there is not an inch of ground left for his claiming that their opinions—their example—their authority—are on his side in this controversy.

Again, is not Nebraska, while a territory, a part of us? Do we not own the country? And if we surrender the control of it, do we not surrender the right of self-government? It is part of ourselves. If you say we shall not control it because it is ONLY part, the same is true of every other part; and when all the parts are gone, what has become of the whole? What is then left of us? What use for the general government, when there is nothing left for it to govern?

---

8. To that extent (Latin).

But you say this question should be left to the people of Nebraska, because they are more particularly interested. If this be the rule, you must leave it to each individual to say for himself whether he will have slaves. What better moral right have thirty-one citizens of Nebraska to say, that the thirty-second shall not hold slaves, than the people of the thirty-one States have to say that slavery shall not go into the thirty-second State at all?

But if it is a sacred right for the people of Nebraska to take and hold slaves there, it is equally their sacred right to buy them where they can buy them cheapest; and that undoubtedly will be on the coast of Africa; provided you will consent to not hang them for going there to buy them. You must remove this restriction too, from the sacred right of self-government. I am aware you say that taking slaves from the States to Nebraska, does not make slaves of freemen; but the African slave-trader can say just as much. He does not catch free negroes and bring them here. He finds them already slaves in the hands of their black captors, and he honestly buys them at the rate of about a red cotton handkerchief a head. This is very cheap, and it is a great abridgement of the sacred right of self-government to hang men for engaging in this profitable trade!

Another important objection to this application of the right of self-government, is that it enables the first FEW, to deprive the succeeding MANY, of a free exercise of the right of self-government. The first few may get slavery IN, and the subsequent many cannot easily get it OUT. How common is the remark now in the slave States—"If we were only clear of our slaves, how much better it would be for us." They are actually deprived of the privilege of governing themselves as they would, by the action of a very few, in the beginning. The same thing was true of the whole nation at the time our constitution was formed.

Whether slavery shall go into Nebraska, or other new territories, is not a matter of exclusive concern to the people who may go there. The whole nation is interested that the best use shall be made of these territories. We want them for the homes of free white people. This they cannot be, to any considerable extent, if slavery shall be planted within them. Slave States are places for poor white people to remove FROM; not to remove TO. New free States are the places for poor people to go to and better their condition. For this use, the nation needs these territories.

Still further; there are constitutional relations between the slave and free States, which are degrading to the latter. We are under legal obligations to catch and return their runaway slaves to them[9]—a sort of dirty, disagreeable job, which I believe, as a general rule the slave-holders will not perform for one another. Then again, in the control of the government— the management of the partnership affairs—they have greatly the advantage of us. By the constitution, each State has two Senators—each has a number of Representatives; in proportion to the number of its people— and each has a number of presidential electors, equal to the whole number of its Senators and Representatives together. But in ascertaining the number of the people, for this purpose, five slaves are counted as being

---

9. The Fugitive Slave Act of 1850 imposed heavy penalties on northerners found guilty of aiding runaway slaves.

equal to three whites.[1] The slaves do not vote; they are only counted and so used, as to swell the influence of the white people's votes. The practical effect of this is more aptly shown by a comparison of the States of South Carolina and Maine. South Carolina has six representatives, and so has Maine; South Carolina has eight presidential electors, and so has Maine. This is precise equality so far; and, of course they are equal in Senators, each having two. Thus in the control of the government, the two States are equals precisely. But how are they in the number of their white people? Maine has 581,813—while South Carolina has 274,567. Maine has twice as many as South Carolina, and 32,679 over. Thus each white man in South Carolina is more than the double of any man in Maine. This is all because South Carolina, besides her free people, has 384,984 slaves. The South Carolinian has precisely the same advantage over the white man in every other free State, as well as in Maine. He is more than the double of any one of us in this crowd. The same advantage, but not to the same extent, is held by all the citizens of the slave States, over those of the free; and it is an absolute truth, without an exception, that there is no voter in any slave State, but who has more legal power in the government, than any voter in any free State. There is no instance of exact equality; and the disadvantage is against us the whole chapter through. This principle, in the aggregate, gives the slave States, in the present Congress, twenty additional representatives— being seven more than the whole majority by which they passed the Nebraska bill.

Now all this is manifestly unfair; yet I do not mention it to complain of it, in so far as it is already settled. It is in the constitution; and I do not, for that cause, or any other cause, propose to destroy, or alter, or disregard the constitution. I stand to it, fairly, fully, and firmly.

But when I am told I must leave it altogether to OTHER PEOPLE to say whether new partners are to be bred up and brought into the firm, on the same degrading terms against me, I respectfully demur. I insist, that whether I shall be a whole man, or only, the half of one, in comparison with others, is a question in which I am somewhat concerned; and one which no other man can have a sacred right of deciding for me. If I am wrong in this—if it really be a sacred right of self-government, in the man who shall go to Nebraska, to decide whether he will be the EQUAL of me or the DOUBLE of me, then after he shall have exercised that right, and thereby shall have reduced me to a still smaller fraction of a man than I already am, I should like for some gentleman deeply skilled in the mysteries of sacred rights, to provide himself with a microscope, and peep about, and find out, if he can, what has become of my sacred rights! They will surely be too small for detection with the naked eye.

Finally, I insist, that if there is ANY THING which it is the duty of the WHOLE PEOPLE to never entrust to any hands but their own, that thing is the preservation and perpetuity, of their own liberties, and institutions. And if they shall think, as I do, that the extension of slavery endangers them, more than any, or all other causes, how recreant to themselves, if they submit the question, and with it, the fate of their country, to a

---

1. This principle was established by the so-called Three-Fifths Compromise in the Constitution.

mere hand-full of men, bent only on temporary self-interest. If this question of slavery extension were an insignificant one—one having no power to do harm—it might be shuffled aside in this way. But being, as it is, the great Behemoth of danger, shall the strong gripe of the nation be loosened upon him, to entrust him to the hands of such feeble keepers?

I have done with this mighty argument, of self-government. Go, sacred thing! Go in peace.

But Nebraska is urged as a great Union-saving measure. Well I too, go for saving the Union. Much as I hate slavery, I would consent to the extension of it rather than see the Union dissolved, just as I would consent to any GREAT evil, to avoid a GREATER one. But when I go to Union saving, I must believe, at least, that the means I employ has some adaptation to the end. To my mind, Nebraska has no such adaptation.

"It hath no relish of salvation in it."[2]

It is an aggravation, rather, of the only one thing which ever endangers the Union. When it came upon us, all was peace and quiet. The nation was looking to the forming of new bonds of Union; and a long course of peace and prosperity seemed to lie before us. In the whole range of possibility, there scarcely appears to me to have been any thing, out of which the slavery agitation could have been revived, except the very project of repealing the Missouri compromise. Every inch of territory we owned, already had a definite settlement of the slavery question, and by which, all parties were pledged to abide. Indeed, there was no uninhabited country on the continent, which we could acquire; if we except some extreme northern regions, which are wholly out of the question. In this state of case, the genius of Discord himself, could scarcely have invented a way of again getting us by the ears, but by turning back and destroying the peace measures of the past. The councils of that genius seem to have prevailed, the Missouri compromise was repealed; and here we are, in the midst of a new slavery agitation, such, I think, as we have never seen before. Who is responsible for this? Is it those who resist the measure; or those who, causelessly, brought it forward, and pressed it through, having reason to know, and, in fact, knowing it must and would be so resisted? It could not but be expected by its author, that it would be looked upon as a measure for the extension of slavery, aggravated by a gross breach of faith. Argue as you will, and long as you will, this is the naked FRONT and ASPECT, of the measure. And in this aspect, it could not but produce agitation. Slavery is founded in the selfishness of man's nature—opposition to it, is his love of justice. These principles are an eternal antagonism; and when brought into collision so fiercely, as slavery extension brings them, shocks, and throes, and convulsions must ceaselessly follow. Repeal the Missouri compromise—repeal all compromises—repeal the declaration of independence—repeal all past history, you still can not repeal human nature. It still will be the abundance of man's heart, that slavery extension is wrong; and out of the abundance of his heart, his mouth will continue to speak.

The structure, too, of the Nebraska bill is very peculiar. The people are to decide the question of slavery for themselves; but WHEN they are to

2. Shakespeare's *Hamlet*, 3.3.92.

decide; or HOW they are to decide; or whether, when the question is once decided, it is to remain so, or is it to be subject to an indefinite succession of new trials, the law does not say, Is it to be decided by the first dozen settlers who arrive there? or is it to await the arrival of a hundred? Is it to be decided by a vote of the people? or a vote of the legislature? or, indeed by a vote of any sort? To these questions, the law gives no answer. There is a mystery about this; for when a member proposed to give the legislature express authority to exclude slavery, it was hooted down by the friends of the bill. This fact is worth remembering. Some yankees, in the east, are sending emigrants to Nebraska, to exclude slavery from it; and, so far as I can judge, they expect the question to be decided by voting, in some way or other. But the Missourians are awake too. They are within a stone's throw of the contested ground. They hold meetings, and pass resolutions, in which not the slightest allusion to voting is made. They resolve that slavery already exists in the territory; that more shall go there; that they, remaining in Missouri will protect it; and that abolitionists shall be hung, or driven away. Through all this, bowie-knives and six-shooters are seen plainly enough; but never a glimpse of the ballot-box. And, really, what is to be the result of this? Each party WITHIN, having numerous and determined backers WITHOUT, is it not probable that the contest will come to blows, and bloodshed? Could there be a more apt invention to bring about collision and violence, on the slavery question, than this Nebraska project is? I do not charge, or believe, that such was intended by Congress; but if they had literally formed a ring, and placed champions within it to fight out the controversy, the fight could be no more likely to come off, than it is. And if this fight should begin, is it likely to take a very peaceful, Union-saving turn? Will not the first drop of blood so shed, be the real knell of the Union?

The Missouri Compromise ought to be restored. For the sake of the Union, it ought to be restored. We ought to elect a House of Representatives which will vote its restoration. If by any means, we omit to do this, what follows? Slavery may or may not be established in Nebraska. But whether it be or not, we shall have repudiated—discarded from the councils of the Nation—the SPIRIT of COMPROMISE; for who after this will ever trust in a national compromise? The spirit of mutual concession—that spirit which first gave us the constitution, and which has thrice saved the Union—we shall have strangled and cast from us forever. And what shall we have in lieu of it? The South flushed with triumph and tempted to excesses; the North, betrayed, as they believe, brooding on wrong and burning for revenge. One side will provoke; the other resent. The one will taunt, the other defy; one aggresses, the other retaliates. Already a few in the North, defy all constitutional restraints, resist the execution of the fugitive slave law, and even menace the institution of slavery in the states where it exists.

Already a few in the South, claim the constitutional right to take to and hold slaves in the free states—demand the revival of the slave trade; and demand a treaty with Great Britain by which fugitive slaves may be reclaimed from Canada. As yet they are but few on either side. It is a grave question for the lovers of the Union, whether the final destruction of the Missouri Compromise, and with it the spirit of all compromise will or will not embolden and embitter each of these, and fatally increase the numbers of both.

But restore the compromise, and what then? We thereby restore the national faith, the national confidence, the national feeling of brotherhood. We thereby reinstate the spirit of concession and compromise— that spirit which has never failed us in past perils, and which may be safely trusted for all the future. The south ought to join in doing this. The peace of the nation is as dear to them as to us. In memories of the past and hopes of the future, they share as largely as we. It would be on their part, a great act—great in its spirit, and great in its effect. It would be worth to the nation a hundred years' purchase of peace and prosperity. And what of sacrifice would they make? They only surrender to us, what they gave us for a consideration long, long ago; what they have not now, asked for, struggled or cared for; what has been thrust upon them, not less to their own astonishment than to ours.

But it is said we cannot restore it; that though we elect every member of the lower house, the Senate is still against us. It is quite true, that of the Senators who passed the Nebraska bill, a majority of the whole Senate will retain their seats in spite of the elections of this and the next year. But if at these elections, their several constituencies shall clearly express their will against Nebraska, will these senators disregard their will? Will they neither obey, nor make room for those who will?

But even if we fail to technically restore the compromise, it is still a great point to carry a popular vote in favor of the restoration. The moral weight of such a vote can not be estimated too highly. The authors of Nebraska are not at all satisfied with the destruction of the compromise—an endorsement of this PRINCIPLE, they proclaim to be the great object. With them, Nebraska alone is a small matter—to establish a principle, for FUTURE USE, is what they particularly desire.

That future use is to be the planting of slavery wherever in the wide world, local and unorganized opposition can not prevent it. Now if you wish to give them this endorsement—if you wish to establish this principle—do so. I shall regret it; but it is your right. On the contrary if you are opposed to the principle—intend to give it no such endorsement—let no wheedling, no sophistry, divert you from throwing a direct vote against it.

Some men, mostly whigs, who condemn the repeal of the Missouri Compromise, nevertheless hesitate to go for its restoration, lest they be thrown in company with the abolitionist. Will they allow me as an old whig to tell them good humoredly, that I think this is very silly? Stand with anybody that stands RIGHT. Stand with him while he is right and PART with him when he goes wrong. Stand WITH the abolitionist in restoring the Missouri Compromise; and stand AGAINST him when he attempts to repeal the fugitive slave law. In the latter case you stand with the southern disunionist. What of that? you are still right. In both cases you are right. In both cases you oppose the dangerous extremes. In both you stand on middle ground and hold the ship level and steady. In both you are national and nothing less than national. This is good old whig ground. To desert such ground, because of any company, is to be less than a whig— less than a man—less than an American.

I particularly object to the new position which the avowed principle of this Nebraska law gives to slavery in the body politic. I object to it because it assumes that there CAN be MORAL RIGHT in the enslaving of one man by another. I object to it as a dangerous dalliance for a free people—a sad evidence that, feeling prosperity we forget right—that liberty, as a principle, we have ceased to revere. I object to it because the fathers of the republic eschewed, and rejected it. The argument of "Necessity" was the only argument they ever admitted in favor of slavery; and so far, and so far only as it carried them, did they ever go. They found the institution existing among us, which they could not help; and they cast blame upon the British King for having permitted its introduction. BEFORE the constitution, they prohibited its introduction into the north-western Territory—the only country we owned, then free from it. AT the framing and adoption of the constitution, they forbore to so much as mention the word "slave" or "slavery" in the whole instrument. In the provision for the recovery of fugitives, the slave is spoken of as a "PERSON HELD TO SERVICE OR LABOR."[3] In that prohibiting the abolition of the African slave trade for twenty years, that trade is spoken of as "The migration or importation of such persons as any of the States NOW EXISTING, shall think proper to admit," &c. These are the only provisions alluding to slavery. Thus, the thing is hid away, in the constitution, just as an afflicted man hides away a wen or a cancer, which he dares not cut out at once, lest he bleed to death; with the promise, nevertheless, that the cutting may begin at the end of a given time. Less than this our fathers COULD not do; and MORE they WOULD not do. Necessity drove them so far, and farther, they would not go. But this is not all. The earliest Congress, under the constitution, took the same view of slavery. They hedged and hemmed it in to the narrowest limits of necessity.

In 1794, they prohibited an out-going slave-trade—that is, the taking of slaves FROM the United States to sell.

In 1798, they prohibited the bringing of slaves from Africa, INTO the Mississippi Territory—this territory then comprising what are now the States of Mississippi and Alabama. This was TEN YEARS before they had the authority to do the same thing as to the States existing at the adoption of the constitution.

In 1800 they prohibited AMERICAN CITIZENS from trading in slaves between foreign countries—as, for instance, from Africa to Brazil.

In 1803 they passed a law in aid of one or two State laws, in restraint of the internal slave trade.

In 1807, in apparent hot haste, they passed the law, nearly a year in advance, to take effect the first day of 1808—the very first day the constitution would permit—prohibiting the African slave trade by heavy pecuniary and corporal penalties.

In 1820, finding these provisions ineffectual, they declared the trade piracy, and annexed to it, the extreme penalty of death. While all this was passing in the general government, five or six of the original slave States had adopted systems of gradual emancipation;[4] and by which the institution was rapidly becoming extinct within these limits.

---

3. Article IV, Section 2, Clause 3 of the Constitution stipulates that "No person held to service or labour in one state, under the laws thereof, escaping into another, shall, in consequence of any law or regulation therein, be discharged from such service or labour, but shall be delivered up on claim of the party to whom such service or labour may be due." This provision would be superseded in 1865 by the Thirteenth Amendment, which abolished slavery.
4. Vermont banned slavery in 1777, Massachusetts in 1783. Gradual emancipation bills were passed in Pennsylvania (1780), Connecticut (1784), Rhode Island (1784), New York (1799), and New Jersey (1804).

Thus we see, the plain unmistakable spirit of that age, towards slavery, was hostility to the PRINCIPLE, and toleration, ONLY BY NECESSITY.

But now it is to be transformed into a "sacred right." Nebraska brings it forth, places it on the high road to extension and perpetuity; and, with a pat on its back, says to it, "Go, and God speed you." Henceforth it is to be the chief jewel of the nation—the very figure-head of the ship of State. Little by little, but steadily as man's march to the grave, we have been giving up the OLD for the NEW faith. Near eighty years ago we began by declaring that all men are created equal; but now from that beginning we have run down to the other declaration, that for SOME men to enslave OTHERS is a "sacred right of self-government." These principles can not stand together. They are as opposite as God and mammon; and whoever holds to the one, must despise the other. When Pettit,[5] in connection with his support of the Nebraska bill, called the Declaration of Independence "a self-evident lie" he only did what consistency and candor require all other Nebraska men to do. Of the forty odd Nebraska Senators who sat present and heard him, no one rebuked him. Nor am I apprized that any Nebraska newspaper, or any Nebraska orator, in the whole nation, has ever yet rebuked him. If this had been said among Marion's[6] men, Southerners though they were, what would have become of the man who said it? If this had been said to the men who captured André,[7] the man who said it, would probably have been hung sooner than André was. If it had been said in old Independence Hall, seventy-eight years ago, the very door-keeper would have throttled the man, and thrust him into the street.

Let no one be deceived. The spirit of seventy-six and the spirit of Nebraska, are utter antagonisms; and the former is being rapidly displaced by the latter.

Fellow countrymen—Americans south, as well as north, shall we make no effort to arrest this? Already the liberal party throughout the world, express the apprehension "that the one retrograde institution in America, is undermining the principles of progress, and fatally violating the noblest political system the world ever saw." This is not the taunt of enemies, but the warning of friends. Is it quite safe to disregard it—to despise it? Is there no danger to liberty itself, in discarding the earliest practice, and first precept of our ancient faith? In our greedy chase to make profit of the negro, let us beware, lest we "cancel and tear to pieces" even the white man's charter of freedom.

Our republican robe is soiled, and trailed in the dust. Let us repurify it. Let us turn and wash it white, in the spirit, if not the blood, of the Revolution. Let us turn slavery from its claims of "moral right," back upon its existing legal rights, and its arguments of "necessity." Let us return it to the position our fathers gave it; and there let it rest in peace. Let us re-adopt the Declaration of Independence, and with it, the practices, and policy, which harmonize with it. Let north and south—let all

5. John Pettit (1807–1877), Indiana Democrat who served in the House (1843–49) and in the Senate (1853–55).
6. Francis Marion (1732–1795), Revolutionary War officer from South Carolina who was known as "The Swamp Fox" because of his successful use of guerilla tactics against the British.
7. John André (1750–1780), British spy who was executed during the Revolutionary War.

Americans—let all lovers of liberty everywhere—join in the great and good work. If we do this, we shall not only have saved the Union; but we shall have so saved it, as to make, and to keep it, forever worthy of the saving. We shall have so saved it, that the succeeding millions of free happy people, the world over, shall rise up, and call us blessed, to the latest generations.

*   *   *

October 16, 1854

To George Robertson[1]

Hon: Geo. Robertson   Springfield, Ills.
Lexington, Ky.   Aug. 15. 1855
My dear Sir: The volume[2] you left for me has been received. I am really grateful for the honor of your kind remembrance, as well as for the book. The partial reading I have already given it, has afforded me much of both pleasure and instruction. It was new to me that the exact question[3] which led to the Missouri compromise, had arisen before it arose in regard to Missouri; and that you had taken so prominent a part in it. Your short, but able and patriotic speech upon that occasion, has not been improved upon since, by those holding the same views; and, with all the lights you then had, the views you took appear to me as very reasonable.

You are not a friend of slavery in the abstract. In that speech you spoke of "*the peaceful extinction of slavery*" and used other expressions indicating your belief that the thing was, at some time, to have an end. Since then we have had thirty six years of experience; and this experience has demonstrated, I think, that there is no peaceful extinction of slavery in prospect for us. The signal failure of Henry Clay, and other good and great men, in 1849, to effect any thing in favor of gradual emancipation in Kentucky, together with a thousand other signs, extinguishes that hope utterly. On the question of liberty, as a principle, we are not what we have been. When we were the political slaves of King George, and wanted to be free, we called the maxim that "all men are created equal" a self evident truth; but now when we have grown fat, and have lost all dread of being slaves ourselves, we have become so greedy to be masters that we call the same maxim "a self-evident lie" The fourth of July has not quite dwindled away; it is still a great day—*for burning fire-crackers*!!!

That spirit which desired the peaceful extinction of slavery, has itself become extinct, with the *occasion*, and the men of the Revolution. Under the impulse of that occasion, nearly half the states adopted systems of emancipation at once; and it is a significant fact, that not a single state has done the like since. So far as peaceful, voluntary emancipation is concerned, the condition of the negro slave in America, scarcely less terrible to the contemplation of a free mind, is now as fixed, and hopeless of

---

1. A Kentucky attorney, politician, and law professor (1790–1874) who had represented Lincoln and the other Illinois heirs of Robert S. Todd in the suit against Robert Wickliffe in 1849.
2. Roberston's *Scrap Book on Law and Politics, Men and Times* (1855).
3. The effort, in 1819, to prohibit slavery from the newly formed Arkansas Territory, which Robertson, then a U.S. congressman, had opposed.

change for the better, as that of the lost souls of the finally impenitent. The Autocrat of all the Russias[4] will resign his crown, and proclaim his subjects free republicans sooner than will our American masters voluntarily give up their slaves.

Our political problem now is "Can we, as a nation, continue together *permanently—forever*—half slave, and half free?" The problem is too mighty for me. May God, in his mercy, superintend the solution. Your much obliged friend, and humble servant

To Joshua F. Speed[1]

Dear Speed: Springfield, Aug: 24, 1855
You know what a poor correspondent I am. Ever since I received your very agreeable letter of the 22nd. of May I have been intending to write you in answer to it. You suggest that in political action now, you and I would differ. I suppose we would; not quite as much, however, as you may think. You know I dislike slavery; and you fully admit the abstract wrong of it. So far there is no cause of difference. But you say that sooner than yield your legal right to the slave—especially at the bidding of those who are not themselves interested, you would see the Union dissolved. I am not aware that *any one* is bidding you to yield that right; very certainly *I* am not. I leave that matter entirely to yourself. I also acknowledge *your* rights and *my* obligations, under the constitution, in regard to your slaves. I confess I hate to see the poor creatures hunted down, and caught, and carried back to their stripes, and unrewarded toils; but I bite my lip and keep quiet. In 1841 you and I had together a tedious low-water trip, on a Steam Boat from Louisville to St. Louis. You may remember, as I well do, that from Louisville to the mouth of the Ohio there were, on board, ten or a dozen slaves, shackled together with irons. That sight was a continual torment to me; and I see something like it every time I touch the Ohio, or any other slave-border. It is hardly fair for you to assume, that I have no interest in a thing which has, and continually exercises, the power of making me miserable. You ought rather to appreciate how much the great body of the Northern people do crucify their feelings, in order to maintain their loyalty to the constitution and the Union.

I do oppose the extension of slavery, because my judgment and feelings so prompt me; and I am under no obligation to the contrary. If for this you and I must differ, differ we must. You say if you were President, you would send an army and hang the leaders of the Missouri outrages upon the Kansas elections;[2] still, if Kansas fairly votes herself a slave state, she must be admitted, or the Union must be dissolved. But how if she votes herself a slave state *unfairly*—that is, by the very means for which you say you would hang men? Must she still be admitted, or the Union be dis-

---

4. Alexander II (1818–1881), who became Emperor of Russia in March 1855.
1. Lincoln and Speed (1814–1882) had first met in Springfield in 1837 and lived together for four years. They remained close until Lincoln's death. Born into a slaveholding family in Kentucky, Speed remained in Springfield from 1835 to 1841 before returning to Kentucky to help manage his family's plantation.
2. In the territorial elections in Kansas, armed Missourians known as Border Ruffians crossed over into Kansas, where they forcibly took over polling booths in order to cast votes for the proslavery party there.

solved? That will be the phase of the question when it first becomes a practical one. In your assumption that there may be a *fair* decision of the slavery question in Kansas, I plainly see you and I would differ about the Nebraska-law. I look upon that enactment not as a *law*, but as *violence* from the beginning. It was conceived in violence, passed in violence, is maintained in violence, and is being executed in violence. I say it was *conceived* in violence, because the destruction of the Missouri Compromise, under the circumstances, was nothing less than violence. It was *passed* in violence, because it could not have passed at all but for the votes of many members, in violent disregard of the known will of their constituents. It is *maintained* in violence because the elections since, clearly demand it's repeal, and this demand is openly disregarded. *You* say men ought to be hung for the way they are executing that law; and *I* say the way it is being executed is quite as good as any of its antecedents. It is being executed in the precise way which was intended from the first; else why does no Nebraska man express astonishment or condemnation? Poor Reeder[3] is the only public man who has been silly enough to believe that any thing like fairness was ever intended; and he has been bravely undeceived.

That Kansas will form a Slave constitution, and, with it, will ask to be admitted into the Union, I take to be an already settled question; and so settled by the very means you so pointedly condemn. By every principle of law, ever held by any court, North or South, every negro taken to Kansas is free; yet in utter disregard of this—in the spirit of violence merely—that beautiful Legislature[4] gravely passes a law to hang men who shall venture to inform a negro of his legal rights. This is the substance, and real object of the law. If, like Haman, they should hang upon the gallows of their own building, I shall not be among the mourners for their fate.

In my humble sphere, I shall advocate the restoration of the Missouri Compromise, so long as Kansas remains a territory; and when, by all these foul means, it seeks to come into the Union as a Slave-state, I shall oppose it. I am very loth, in any case, to withhold my assent to the enjoyment of property *acquired*, or *located*, in good faith; but I do not admit that *good faith*, in taking a negro to Kansas, to be held in slavery, is a *possibility* with any man. Any man who has sense enough to be the controller of his own property, has too much sense to misunderstand the outrageous character of this whole Nebraska business. But I digress. In my opposition to the admission of Kansas I shall have some company; but we may be beaten. If we are, I shall not, on that account, attempt to dissolve the Union. On the contrary, if we succeed, there will be enough of us to take care of the Union. I think it probable, however, we shall be beaten. Standing as a unit among yourselves, you can, directly, and indirectly, bribe enough of our men to carry the day—as you could on an open proposition to establish monarchy. Get hold of some man in the North, whose position and ability is such, that he can make the support of your measure—whatever it may be—a *democratic party necessity*, and the thing is done. *Appropos* of this, let me tell you an anecdote. Douglas introduced the

3. Andrew H. Reeder (1807–1864), first governor of the Kansas Territory, supported the free-soil settlers there and was summarily removed by President Franklin Pierce (1804–1869).
4. After Governor Reeder's failed effort to establish fairness in Kansas politics, proslavery forces established a fraudulent legislature aimed at winning the territory for slavery.

Nebraska bill in January. In February afterwards, there was a call session of the Illinois Legislature. Of the one hundred members composing the two branches of that body, about seventy were democrats. These latter held a caucus, in which the Nebraska bill was talked of, if not formally discussed. It was thereby discovered that just three, and no more, were in favor of the measure. In a day or two Douglas' orders came on to have resolutions passed approving the bill; and they were passed by large majorities!!! The truth of this is vouched for by a bolting democratic member. The masses too, democratic as well as whig, were even, nearer unanamous against it; but as soon as the party necessity of supporting it, became apparent, the way the democracy began to see the *wisdom* and *justice* of it, was perfectly astonishing.

You say if Kansas fairly votes herself a free state, as a christian you will rather rejoice at it. All decent slave-holders *talk* that way; and I do not doubt their candor. But they never *vote* that way. Although in a private letter, or conversation, you will express your preference that Kansas shall be free, you would vote for no man for Congress who would say the same thing publicly. No such man could be elected from any district in any slave-state. You think Stringfellow & Co[5] ought to be hung; and yet, at the next presidential election you will vote for the exact type and representative of Stringfellow. The slave-breeders and slave-traders, are a small, odious and detested class, among you; and yet in politics, they dictate the course of all of you, and are as completely your masters, as you are the masters of your own negroes.

You enquire where I now stand. That is a disputed point. I think I am a whig; but others say there are no whigs, and that I am an abolitionist. When I was at Washington I voted for the Wilmot Proviso as good as forty times, and I never heard of any one attempting to unwhig me for that. I now do no more than oppose the *extension* of slavery.

I am not a Know-Nothing.[6] That is certain. How could I be? How can any one who abhors the oppression of negroes, be in favor of degrading classes of white people? Our progress in degeneracy appears to me to be pretty rapid. As a nation, we began by declaring that *"all men are created equal."* We now practically read it "all men are created equal, *except negroes.*" When the Know-Nothings get control, it will read "all men are created equal, except negroes, *and foreigners, and catholics.*" When it comes to this I should prefer emigrating to some country where they make no pretence of loving liberty—to Russia, for instance, where despotism can be taken pure, and without the base alloy of hypocracy.

Mary will probably pass a day or two in Louisville in October. My kindest regards to Mrs. Speed. On the leading subject of this letter, I have more of her sympathy than I have of yours.

And yet let say I am Your friend forever

5. Benjamin F. Stringfellow (1816–1891), a fiery Missouri politician, businessman, and writer who endorsed the proslavery Border Ruffians and excoriated free-soil Kansans.
6. Know Nothings, whose members maintained secrecy by claiming to outsiders that they knew nothing about the group, were a powerful nativist organization aimed at stopping the surge of Europeans—many of them Irish Catholics—who arrived in America during the 1850s.

Speech at Bloomington, Illinois[1]

Abraham Lincoln, of Sangamon, came upon the platform amid deafening applause. He enumerated the pressing reasons of the present movement. He was here ready to fuse with anyone who would unite with him to oppose slave power; spoke of the bugbear disunion which was so vaguely threatened. It was to be remembered that the *Union must be preserved in the purity of its principles as well as in the integrity of its territorial parts.* It must be "Liberty and Union, now and forever, one and inseparable." The sentiment in favor of white slavery now prevailed in all the slave state papers, except those of Kentucky, Tennessee and Missouri and Maryland. Such was the progress of the National Democracy. Douglas once claimed against him that Democracy favored more than his principles, the individual rights of man. Was it not strange that he must stand there now to defend those rights against their former eulogist? The Black Democracy were endeavoring to cite Henry Clay to reconcile old Whigs[2] to their doctrine, and repaid them with the very cheap compliment of National Whigs.

May 29, 1856

Fragment on Sectionalism

Sectionalism

It is constantly objected to Fremont & Dayton,[1] that they are supported by a sectional party, who, by their sectionalism, endanger the National Union. This objection, more than all others, causes men, really opposed to slavery extension, to hesitate. Practically, it is the most difficult objection we have to meet.

For this reason, I now propose to examine it, a little more carefully than I have heretofore done, or seen it done by others.

First, then, what is the question between the parties, respectively represented by Buchanan and Fremont?

Simply this: "*Shall slavery be allowed to extend into U.S. teritories, now legally free?*'" Buchanan says it *shall*; and Fremont says it shall *not*.

That is the *naked* issue, and the *whole* of it. Lay the respective platforms side by side; and the difference between them, will be found to amount to precisely that.

True, each party charges upon the other, *designs* much beyond what is involved in the issue, as stated; but as these charges can not be fully proved either way, it is probably better to reject them on both sides, and stick to the naked issue, as it is clearly made up on the record.

---

1. This report of a speech (known as the Lost Speech) at an antislavery convention appeared in the *Alton Weekly Courier,* June 5, 1856.
2. The Whig Party as it had existed under Henry Clay (1777–1852), who had forged compromises on slavery. "National Whigs": a short-lived political group that tried vainly to save the Whig Party by mollifying tensions between the North and the South.
1. John C. Frémont (1813–1890) of California and William L. Dayton (1807–1864) of New Jersey, the 1856 presidential and vice presidential candidates, respectively, of the nascent Republican Party. The Democratic ticket consisted of James Buchanan (1791–1868) of Pennsylvania and John C. Breckinridge (1821–1875) of Kentucky.

And now, to restate the question *"Shall slavery be allowed to extend into U.S. teritories, now legally free?"* I beg to know *how* one side of that question is more sectional than the other? Of course I expect to effect nothing with the man who makes this charge of sectionalism, without caring whether it is just or not. But of the *candid, fair*, man who has been puzzled with this charge, I do ask how is *one* side of this question, more *sectional*, than the other? I beg of him to consider well, and answer calmly.

If one side be as sectional as the other, nothing is gained, as to sectionalism, by changing sides; so that each must choose sides of the question on some other ground—as I should think, according, as the one side or the other, shall appear nearest right.

If he shall really think slavery *ought* to be extended, let him go to Buchanan; if he think it ought *not* let him go to Fremont.

But, Fremont and Dayton, are both residents of the free-states; and this fact has been vaunted, in high places, as excessive *sectionalism*.

While interested individuals become indignant and excited, against this manifestation of sectionalism, I am very happy to know, that the Constitution remains calm—keeps cool—upon the subject. It does say that President and Vice President shall be resident of different states; but it does not say one must live in a *slave*, and the other in a *free* state.

It has been a *custom* to take one from a slave, and the other from a free state; but the custom has not, at all been uniform. In 1828 Gen. Jackson and Mr. Calhoun, both from slave-states, were placed on the same ticket; and Mr. Adams and Dr. Rush[2] both from the free-states, were pitted against them. Gen: Jackson and Mr. Calhoun were elected; and qualified and served under the election; yet the whole thing never suggested the idea of sectionalism.

In 1841, the president, Gen. Harrison, died, by which Mr. Tyler,[3] the Vice-President, & a slave state man, became president. Mr. Mangum,[4] another slave-state man, was placed in the Vice Presidential chair, served out the term, and no fuss about it—no sectionalism thought of.

In 1853 the present president[5] came into office. He is a free-state man. Mr. King,[6] the new Vice President elect, was a slave state man; but he died without entering on the duties of his office. At first, his vacancy was filled by Atchison, another slave-state man; but he soon resigned, and the place was supplied by Bright,[7] a free-state man. So that right now, and for the year and a half last past, our president and vice-president are both actually free-state men.

But, it is said, the friends of Fremont, avow the purpose of electing him exclusively by free-state votes, and that this is unendurable *sectionalism*.

This statement of fact, is not exactly true. With the friends of Fremont, it is an *expected necessity*, but it is not an *"avowed purpose,"* to elect him, if at all, principally, by free state votes; but it is, with equal intensity, true

2. In 1828, Andrew Jackson of Tennessee and John C. Calhoun of South Carolina ran against John Quincy Adams (1767-1848) of Massachusetts and Richard Rush (1780–1859) of Pennsylvania.
3. John Tyler of Virginia.
4. Willie P. Mangum (1792–1861) of North Carolina.
5. Franklin Pierce of New Hampshire.
6. William R. King (1786–1853) of Alabama.
7. Jesse D. Bright (1812–1875) of Indiana. David R. Atchison (1807–1886) of Missouri.

that Buchanan's friends expect to elect him, if at all, chiefly by slave-state votes.

Here, again, the sectionalism, is just as much on one side as the other.

The thing which gives most color to the charge of Sectionalism, made against those who oppose the spread of slavery into free teritory, is the fact that *they* can get no votes in the slave-states, while their opponents get all, or nearly so, in the slave-states, and also, a large number in the free States. To state it in another way, the Extensionists, can get votes all over the Nation, while the Restrictionists can get them only in the free states.

This being the fact, *why* is it so? It is not because one *side* of the question dividing them, is more sectional than the *other*; nor because of any difference in the mental or moral structure of the people North and South. It is because, in that question, the people of the South have an immediate palpable and immensely great pecuniary interest; while, with the people of the North, it is merely an abstract question of moral right, with only *slight*, and *remote* pecuniary interest added.

The slaves of the South, at a moderate estimate, are worth a thousand millions of dollars. Let it be permanently settled that this property may extend to new teritory, without restraint, and it greatly *enhances*, perhaps quite *doubles*, its value at once. This immense, palpable pecuniary interest, on the question of extending slavery, unites the Southern people, as one man. But it can not be demonstrated that the *North* will gain a dollar by restricting it.

Moral principle is all, or nearly all, that unites us of the North. Pity 'tis, it is so, but this is a looser bond, than pecuniary interest. Right here is the plain cause of *their perfect* union and *our want* of it. And see how it works. If a Southern man aspires to be president, they choke him down instantly, in order that the glittering prize of the presidency, may be held up, on Southern terms, to the greedy eyes of Northern ambition. With this they tempt us, and break in upon us.

The democratic party, in 1844, elected a Southern president. Since then, they have neither had a Southern candidate for *election*, or *nomination*. Their Conventions of 1848–1852 and 1856, have been struggles exclusively among *Northern* men, each vieing to outbid the other for the Southern vote—the South standing calmly by to finally cry going, going, gone, to the highest bidder; and, at the same time, to make its power more distinctly seen, and thereby to secure a still higher bid at the next succeeding struggle.

"Actions speak louder than words" is the maxim; and, if true, the South now distinctly says to the North "Give us the *measures*, and you take the *men*"

The total withdrawal of Southern aspirants, for the presidency, multiplies the number of Northern ones. These last, in competing with each other, commit themselves to the utmost verge that, through their own greediness, they have the least hope their Northern supporters will bear. Having got committed, in a race of competetion, necessity drives them into union to sustain themselves. Each, at first secures all he can, on personal attachments to him, and through *hopes* resting on him personally. Next, they unite with one another, and with the perfectly banded South, to make the offensive position they have got into, "a party measure." This done, large additional numbers are secured.

When the repeal of the Missouri compromise was first proposed, at the North there was litterally *"nobody"* in favor of it. In February 1854 our Legislature met in call, or extra, session. From them Douglas sought an indorsement of his then pending measure of

Repeal. In our Legislature were about 70 democrats to 30 whigs. The former held a caucus, in which it was resolved to give Douglas the desired indorsement. Some of the members of that caucus bolted—would not stand it—and they now divulge the secrets. They say that the caucus fairly confessed that the Repeal was wrong; and they placed their determination to indorse it, solely on the ground that it was *necessary* to sustain Douglas. Here we have the direct evidence of how the Nebraska-bill obtained it's strength in Illinois. It was given, not in a sense of right, but in the teeth of a sense of wrong, to *sustain Douglas.* So Illinois was divided. So New England, for Pierce; Michigan for Cass, Pensylvania for Buchanan, and all for the Democratic party.

And when, by such means, they have got a large portion of the Northern people into a position contrary to their own honest impulses, and sense of right; they have the impudence to turn upon those who do stand firm, and call them sectional.

Were it not too serious a matter, this cool impudence would be laughable, to say the least.

Recurring to the question *"Shall slavery be allowed to extend into U.S. teritory now legally free?"*

This is a sectional question—that is to say, it is a question, in its nature calculated to divide the American people geographically. Who is to *blame* for that? *who* can help it? Either side *can* help it; but how? Simply by *yielding* to the other side. There is no other way. In the whole range of *possibility*, there is no other way. Then, which side shall yield? To this again, there can be but one answer—the side which is in the *wrong.* True, we differ, as to which side is wrong; and we boldly say, let all who really think slavery ought to spread into free teritory, openly go over against us. There is where they rightfully belong.

But why should any go, who really think slavery ought not to spread? Do they really think the *right* ought to yield to the *wrong?* Are they afraid to stand by the *right?* Do they fear that the constitution is too weak to sustain them in the right? Do they really think that by right surrendering to wrong, the hopes of our constitution, our Union, and our liberties, can possibly be bettered?

ca. July 23, 1856

Speech at Kalamazoo, Michigan

Fellow countrymen:—Under the Constitution of the U.S. another Presidential contest approaches us. All over this land—that portion at least, of which I know much—the people are assembling to consider the proper course to be adopted by them. One of the first considerations is to learn what the people differ about. If we ascertain what we differ about, we shall be better able to decide. The question of slavery, at the present day, should be not only the greatest question, but very nearly the sole question. Our opponents, however, prefer that this should not be the case. To get at this question, I will occupy your attention but a single moment. The question is simply this:—shall slavery be spread into the new Territories, or not? This is the naked question. If we should support Fremont successfully in this, it may be charged that we will not be content with restricting slavery in the new territories. If we should charge that James Buchanan,[1] by his platform, is bound to extend slavery into the territories, and that he is in favor of its being thus spread, we should be puzzled to prove it. We believe it, nevertheless. By taking the issue as I present it, whether it shall be permitted as an issue, is made up between the parties. Each takes his own stand. This is the question: Shall the Government of the United States prohibit slavery in the United States.

We have been in the habit of deploring the fact that slavery exists amongst us. We have ever deplored it. Our forefathers did, and they declared, as we have done in later years, the blame rested on the mother Government of Great Britain. We constantly condemn Great Britain for not preventing slavery from coming amongst us. She would not interfere to prevent it, and so individuals were enabled to introduce the institution without opposition. I have alluded to this, to ask you if this is not exactly the policy of Buchanan and his friends, to place this government in the attitude then occupied by the government of Great Britain—placing the nation in the position to authorize the territories to reproach it, for refusing to allow them to hold slaves. I would like to ask your attention, any gentleman to tell me when the people of Kansas are going to decide. When are they to do it? How are they to do it? I asked that question two years ago—when, and how are they to do it? Not many weeks ago, our new Senator from Illinois, (Mr. Trumbull)[2] asked Douglas how it could be done. Douglas is a great man—at keeping from answering questions he don't want to answer. He would not answer. He said it was a question for the Supreme Court to decide. In the North, his friends argue that the people can decide it at any time. The Southerners say there is no power in the people, whatever. We know that from the time that white people have been allowed in the territory, they have brought slaves with them. Suppose the people come up to vote as freely, and with as perfect protection as we could do it here. Will they be at liberty to vote their sentiments? If they can, then all that has ever been said about our provincial ancestors is untrue, and they could have done so, also. We know our Southern friends say that the General Government cannot interfere. The people, say they, have no right to interfere. They could as truly say,—"It is amongst us—we cannot get rid of it."

But I am afraid I waste too much time on this point. I take it as an illustration of the principle, that slaves are admitted into the territories. And, while I am speaking of Kansas, how will that operate? Can men vote truly? We will suppose that there are ten men who go into Kansas to settle. Nine of these are opposed to slavery. One has ten slaves. The slaveholder is a good man in other respects; he is a good neighbor, and being a wealthy man, he is enabled to do the others many neighborly kindnesses. They like the man, though they don't like the system by

---

1. The fifteenth president of the United States (1857–1861), the Democrat Buchanan (1791–1868) was morally opposed to slavery but believed it was protected by the Constitution.
2. Lyman Trumbull (1813–1896), Republican.

which he holds his fellow-men in bondage. And here let me say, that in intellectual and physical structure, our Southern brethren do not differ from us. They are, like us, subject to passions, and it is only their odious institution of slavery, that makes the breach between us. These ten men of whom I was speaking, live together three or four years; they inter-marry; their family ties are strengthened. And who wonders that in time, the people learn to look upon slavery with complacency? This is the way in which slavery is planted, and gains so firm a foothold. I think this is a strong card that the Nebraska party have played, and won upon, in this game.

I suppose that this crowd are opposed to the admission of slavery into Kansas, yet it is true that in all crowds there are some who differ from the majority. I want to ask the Buchanan men, who are against the spread of slavery, if there be any present, why not vote for the man who is against it? I understand that Mr. Fillmore's[3] position is precisely like Buchanan's. I understand that, by the Nebraska bill, a door has been opened for the spread of slavery in the Territories. Examine, if you please, and see if they have ever done any such thing as try to shut the door. It is true that Fill-more tickles a few of his friends with the notion that he is not the cause of the door being opened. Well; it brings him into this position: he tries to get both sides, one by denouncing those who opened the door, and the other by hinting that he doesn't care a fig for its being open. If he were Presi-dent, he would have one side or the other—he would either restrict slavery or not. Of course it would be so. There could be no middle way. You who hate slavery and love freedom, why not, as Fillmore and Buchanan are on the same ground, vote for Fremont? Why not vote for the man who takes your side of the question? "Well," says Buchanier, "it is none of our busi-ness." But is it not our business? There are several reasons why I think it is our business. But let us see how it is. Others have urged these reasons before, but they are still of use. By our Constitution we are represented in Congress in proportion to numbers, and in counting the numbers that give us our representatives, three slaves are counted as two people. The State of Maine has six representatives in the lower house of Congress. In strength South Carolina is equal to her. But stop! Maine has *twice as many* white people, and 32,000 to boot! And is that fair? I don't complain of it. This regulation was put in force when the exigencies of the times demanded it, and could not have been avoided. Now, one man in South Carolina is the same as two men here. Maine should have twice as many men in Congress as South Carolina. It is a fact that any man in South Carolina has more influence and power in Congress today than any two now before me. The same thing is true of all slave States, though it may not be in the same proportion. It is a truth that cannot be denied, that in all the free States no white man is the equal of the white man of the slave States. But this is in the Constitution, and we must stand up to it. The question, then, is, "Have we no interest as to whether the white man of the North shall be the equal of the white man of the South?" Once when I used this argument in the presence of Douglas,[4] he answered that in the

3. Millard Fillmore (1800–1874) of New York served as president from 1850 to 1853 and thereaf-ter remained politically active. He supported the Kansas Nebraska Act. During the Civil War, he was a critic of Lincoln.
4. Senator Stephen A. Douglas of Illinois.

North the black man was counted as a full man, and had an equal vote with the white, while at the South they were counted at but three-fifths. And Douglas, when he had made this reply, doubtless thought he had forever silenced the objection.

Have we no interest in the free Territories of the United States—that they should be kept open for the homes of free white people? As our Northern States are growing more and more in wealth and population, we are continually in want of an outlet, through which it may pass out to enrich our country. In this we have an interest—a deep and abiding interest. There is another thing, and that is the mature knowledge we have—the greatest interest of all. It is the doctrine, that the people are to be driven from the maxims of our free Government, that despises the spirit which for eighty years has celebrated the anniversary of our national independence.

We are a great empire. We are eighty years old. We stand at once the wonder and admiration of the whole world, and we must enquire what it is that has given us so much prosperity, and we shall understand that to give up that one thing, would be to give up all future prosperity. This cause is that every man can make himself. It has been said that such a race of prosperity has been run nowhere else. We find a people on the North-east, who have a different government from ours, being ruled by a Queen. Turning to the South, we see a people who, while they boast of being free, keep their fellow beings in bondage. Compare our Free States with either, shall we say here that we have no interest in keeping that principle alive? Shall we say—"Let it be." No—we have an interest in the maintenance of the principles of the Government, and without this interest, it is worth nothing. I have noticed in Southern newspapers, particularly the Richmond *Enquirer*, the Southern view of the Free States. They insist that slavery has a right to spread. They defend it upon principle. They insist that their slaves are far better off than Northern freemen. What a mistaken view do these men have of Northern laborers! They think that men are always to remain laborers here—but there is no such class. The man who labored for another last year, this year labors for himself, and next year he will hire others to labor for him. These men don't understand when they think in this manner of Northern free labor. When these reasons can be introduced, tell me not that we have no interest in keeping the Territories free for the settlement of free laborers.

I pass, then, from this question. I think we have an ever growing interest in maintaining the free institutions of our country.

It is said that our party is a sectional party. It has been said in high quarters that if Fremont and Dayton were elected the Union would be dissolved. The South do not think so. I believe it! I believe it! It is a shameful thing that the subject is talked of so much. Did we not have a Southern President and Vice-President at one time? And yet the Union has not yet been dissolved. Why, at this very moment, there is a Northern President and Vice-President. Pierce and King were elected, and King died without ever taking his seat. The Senate elected a Northern man[5] from their own numbers, to perform the duties of the Vice-President. He resigned his

---

5. David R. Atchison was elected president pro tempore of the Senate on March 3, 1853, and resigned the next December to devote his energies to winning the Kansas and Nebraska territories for slavery.

seat, however, as soon as he got the job of making a slave State out of Kansas. Was not that a great mistake?

(A voice.—"He didn't mean that!")

Then why didn't he speak what he did mean? Why did not he speak what he ought to have spoken? That was the very thing. He should have spoken manly, and we should then have known where to have found him. It is said we expect to elect Fremont[6] by Northern votes. Certainly we do not think the South will elect him. But let us ask the question differently. Does not Buchanan expect to be elected by Southern votes? Fillmore, however, will go out of this contest the most national man we have. He has no prospect of having a single vote on either side of Mason and Dixon's line,[7] to trouble his poor soul about. (Laughter and cheers.)

We believe that it is right that slavery should not be tolerated in the new territories, yet we cannot get support for this doctrine, except in one part of the country. Slavery is looked upon by men in the light of dollars and cents. The estimated worth of the slaves at the South is $1,000,000,000, and in a very few years, if the institution shall be admitted into the territories, they will have increased fifty per cent in value.

Our adversaries charge Fremont with being an abolitionist. When pressed to show proof, they frankly confess that they can show no such thing. They then run off upon the assertion that his supporters are abolitionists. But this they have never attempted to prove. I know of no word in the language that has been used so much as that one "abolitionist," having no definition. It has no meaning unless taken as designating a person who is abolishing something. If that be its signification, the supporters of Fremont are not abolitionists. In Kansas all who come there are perfectly free to regulate their own social relations. There has never been a man there who was an abolitionists—for what was there to be abolished? People there had perfect freedom to express what they wished on the subject, when the Nebraska bill was first passed. Our friends in the South, who support Buchanan, have five disunion men to one at the North. This disunion is a sectional question. Who is to blame for it? Are we? I don't care how you express it. This government is sought to be put on a new track. Slavery is to be made a ruling element in our government. The question can be avoided in but two ways. By the one, we must submit, and allow slavery to triumph, or, by the other, we must triumph over the black demon. We have chosen the latter manner. If you of the North wish to get rid of this question, you must decide between these two ways—submit and vote for Buchanan, submit and vote that slavery is a just and good thing and immediately get rid of the question; or unite with us, and help us to triumph. We would all like to have the question done away with, but we cannot submit.

They tell us that we are in company with men who have long been known as abolitionists. What care we how many may feel disposed to labor for our cause? Why do not you, Buchanan men, come in and use your influence to make our party respectable? (Laughter.) How is the dissolution of the Union to be consummated? They tell us that the Union is in danger. Who will divide it? Is it those who make the charge? Are they

6. John C. Frémont, the antislavery Republican who lost to Democrat James Buchanan in the 1856 presidential race.

7. A symbolic line separating the North and the South.

themselves the persons who wish to see this result? A majority will never dissolve the Union. Can a minority do it? When this Nebraska bill was first introduced into Congress, the sense of the Democratic party was outraged. That party has ever prided itself, that it was the friend of individual, universal freedom. It was that principle upon which they carried their measures. When the Kansas scheme was conceived, it was natural that this respect and sense should have been outraged. Now I make this appeal to the Democratic citizens here. Don't you find yourself making arguments in support of these measures, which you never would have made before? Did you ever do it before this Nebraska bill compelled you to do it? If you answer this in the affirmative, see how a whole party have been turned away from their love of liberty! And now, my Democratic friends, come forward. Throw off these things, and come to the rescue of this great principle of equality. Don't interfere with anything in the Constitution. That must be maintained, for it is the only safeguard of our liberties. And not to Democrats alone do I make this appeal, but to all who love these great and true principles. Come, and keep coming! Strike, and strike again! So sure as God lives, the victory shall be yours. (Great cheering.)

August 27, 1856

On Stephen Douglas

Twenty-two years ago Judge Douglas and I first became acquainted. We were both young then; he a trifle younger than I. Even then, we were both ambitious; I, perhaps, quite as much so as he. With *me*, the race of ambition has been a failure—a flat failure; with *him* it has been one of splendid success.[1] His name fills the nation; and is not unknown, even, in foreign lands. I affect no contempt for the high eminence he has reached. So reached, that the oppressed of my species, might have shared with me in the elevation, I would rather stand on that eminence, than wear the richest crown that ever pressed a monarch's brow.

ca. December 1856

Fragment on Formation of the Republican Party

Upon those men who are, in sentiment, opposed to the spread, and nationalization of slavery, rests the task of preventing it. The Republican organization is the embodyment of that sentiment; though, as yet, it by no means embraces all the individuals holding that sentiment. The party is newly formed; and in forming, old party ties had to be broken, and the attractions of party pride, and influential leaders were wholly wanting. In spite of old differences, prejudices, and animosities, it's members were drawn together by a paramount common danger. They formed and manouvered

---

1. The Illinois Democrat Stephen A. Douglas enjoyed a run of political prominence in the U.S. House of Representatives (1843–46) and then in the U.S. Senate (1845–61).

in the face of the deciplined enemy, and in the teeth of all his persistent misrepresentations. Of course, they fell far short of gathering in all of their own. And yet, a year ago, they stood up, an army over thirteen hundred thousand strong. That army is, to-day, the best hope of the nation, and of the world. Their work is before them; and from which they may not guiltlessly turn away.

ca. February 28, 1857

Speech on the *Dred Scott* Decision[1] at Springfield, Illinois

Fellow citizens:—I am here to-night, partly by the invitation of some of you and partly by my own inclination. Two weeks ago Judge Douglas spoke here on the several subjects of Kansas, the Dred Scott decision, and Utah.[2] I listened to the speech at the time, and have read the report of it since. It was intended to controvert opinions which I think just, and to assail (politically, not personally,) those men who, in common with me, entertain those opinions. For this reason I wished then, and still wish, to make some answer to it, which I now take the opportunity of doing.

I begin with Utah. If it prove to be true, as is probable, that the people of Utah are in open rebellion to the United States, then Judge Douglas is in favor of repealing their territorial organization, and attaching them to the adjoining States for judicial purposes. I say, too, if they are in rebellion, they ought to be somehow coerced to obedience; and I am not now prepared to admit or deny that the Judge's mode of coercing them is not as good as any. The Republicans can fall in with it without taking back anything they have ever said. To be sure, it would be a considerable backing down by Judge Douglas from his much vaunted doctrine of self-government for the territories; but this is only additional proof of what was very plain from the beginning, that that doctrine was a mere deceitful pretense for the benefit of slavery. Those who could not see that much in the Nebraska act itself, which forced Governors, and Secretaries, and Judges on the people of the territories, without their choice or consent, could not be made to see, though one should rise from the dead to testify.

But in all this, it is very plain the Judge evades the only question the Republicans have ever pressed upon the Democracy in regard to Utah. That question the Judge well knows to be this: "If the people of Utah shall peacefully form a State Constitution tolerating polygamy, will the Democracy admit them into the Union?" There is nothing in the United States

1. In the case of *Dred Scott v. Sanford*, decided in March 1857, the Supreme Court ruled 7–2 that American blacks had no citizenship rights and that the Missouri Compromise was unconstitutional. The case originated when an enslaved black man, Dred Scott (1795–1858), sued for the freedom of him, his wife, and their two daughters because their master had taken them to live in a free state and then in a northwest territory where slavery was prohibited by the Ordinance of 1787.
2. A reference to the controversy over the Territory of Utah, where Mormons had publicly announced the practice of polygamy in August 1852.

Constitution or law against polygamy; and why is it not a part of the Judge's "sacred right of self-government" for that people to have it, or rather to *keep* it, if they choose? These questions, so far as I know, the Judge never answers. It might involve the Democracy to answer them either way, and they go unanswered.

As to Kansas. The substance of the Judge's speech on Kansas is an effort to put the free State men in the wrong for not voting at the election of delegates to the Constitutional Convention. He says: *"There is every reason to hope and believe that the law will be fairly interpreted and impartially executed, so as to insure to every bona fide inhabitant the free and quiet exercise of the elective franchise."*

It appears extraordinary that Judge Douglas should make such a statement. He knows that, by the law, no one can vote who has not been registered; and he knows that the free State men place their refusal to vote on the ground that but few of them have been registered. It is *possible* this is not true, but Judge Douglas knows it is asserted to be true in letters, newspapers and public speeches, and borne by every mail, and blown by every breeze to the eyes and ears of the world. He knows it is boldly declared that the people of many whole counties, and many whole neighborhoods in others, are left unregistered; yet, he does not venture to contradict the declaration, nor to point out how they *can* vote without being registered; but he just slips along, not seeming to know there is any such question of fact, and complacently declares: "There is every reason to hope and believe that the law will be fairly and impartially executed, so as to insure to every *bona fide* inhabitant the free and quiet exercise of the elective franchise."

I readily agree that if all had a chance to vote, they ought to have voted. If, on the contrary, as they allege, and Judge Douglas ventures not to particularly contradict, few only of the free State men had a chance to vote, they were perfectly right in staying from the polls in a body.

By the way since the Judge spoke, the Kansas election has come off. The Judge expressed his confidence that all the Democrats in Kansas would do their duty—including "free state Democrats" of course. The returns received here as yet are very incomplete; but so far as they go, they indicate that only about one sixth of the registered voters, have really voted; and this too, when not more, perhaps, than one half of the rightful voters have been registered, thus showing the thing to have been altogether the most exquisite farce ever enacted. I am watching with considerable interest, to ascertain what figure "the free state Democrats" cut in the concern. Of course they voted—all democrats do their duty—and of course they did not vote for slave-state candidates. We soon shall know how many delegates *they* elected, how many candidates they had, pledged for a free state; and how many votes were cast for them.

Allow me to barely whisper my suspicion that there were no such things in Kansas "as free state Democrats"—that they were altogether mythical, good only to figure in newspapers and speeches in the free states. If there should prove to be one real living free state Democrat in Kansas, I suggest that it might be well to catch him, and stuff and preserve his skin, as an interesting specimen of that soon to be extinct variety of the genus, Democrat.

And now as to the Dred Scott decision. That decision declares two propositions—first, that a negro cannot sue in the U.S. Courts; and secondly, that Congress cannot prohibit slavery in the Territories. It was made by a divided court—dividing differently on the different points. Judge Douglas does not discuss the merits of the decision; and, in that respect, I shall follow his example, believing I could no more improve on McLean and Curtis, than he could on Taney.[3]

He denounces all who question the correctness of that decision, as offering violent resistance to it. But who resists it? Who has, in spite of the decision, declared Dred Scott free, and resisted the authority of his master over him?

Judicial decisions have two uses—first, to absolutely determine the case decided, and secondly, to indicate to the public how other similar cases will be decided when they arise. For the latter use, they are called "precedents" and "authorities."

We believe, as much as Judge Douglas, (perhaps more) in obedience to, and respect for the judicial department of government. We think its decisions on Constitutional questions, when fully settled, should control, not only the particular cases decided, but the general policy of the country, subject to be disturbed only by amendments of the Constitution as provided in that instrument itself. More than this would be revolution. But we think the Dred Scott decision is erroneous. We know the court that made it, has often overruled its own decisions, and we shall do what we can to have it to over-rule this. We offer no *resistance* to it.

Judicial decisions are of greater or less authority as precedents, according to circumstances. That this should be so, accords both with common sense, and the customary, understanding of the legal profession.

If this important decision had been made by the unanimous concurrence of the judges, and without any apparent partisan bias, and in accordance with legal public expectation, and with the steady practice of the departments throughout our history, and had been in no part, based on assumed historical facts which are not really true; or, if wanting in some of these, it had been before the court more than once, and had there been affirmed and re-affirmed through a course of years, it then might be, perhaps would be, factious, nay, even revolutionary, to not acquiesce in it as a precedent.

But when, as it is true we find it wanting in all these claims to the public confidence, it is not resistance, it is not factious, it is not even disrespectful, to treat it as not having yet quite established a settled doctrine for the country—But Judge Douglas considers this view awful. Hear him:

"The courts are the tribunals prescribed by the Constitution and created by the authority of the people to determine, expound and enforce the law. Hence, whoever resists the final decision of the highest judicial tribunal, aims a deadly blow to our whole Republican system of government—a blow, which if successful would place all our rights and liberties at the mercy of passion, anarchy and violence. I repeat, therefore, that if resistance to the decisions of the Supreme Court of the United States, in a matter like the points decided in the Dred Scott case, clearly within their jurisdiction as defined by the Constitution, shall be forced upon the country as a political issue, it will become a distinct and naked issue between

3. Roger B. Taney (1777–1864), chief justice who summarized the majority opinion by stating that black people were "so far inferior that they had no rights which the white man was bound to respect." Justices John McLean (1785–1861) and Benjamin R. Curtis (1809–1874) dissented.

the friends and the enemies of the Constitution—the friends and the enemies of the supremacy of the laws."

Why this same Supreme court once decided a national bank to be constitutional; but Gen. Jackson, as President of the United States, disregarded
the decision, and vetoed a bill for a re-charter, partly on constitutional
ground, declaring that each public functionary must support the Constitution, *as he understands it.*" But hear the General's own words. Here they
are, taken from his veto message:

"It is maintained by the advocates of the bank, that its constitutionality, in all its features, ought to be considered as settled by precedent, and
by the decision of the Supreme Court. To this conclusion I cannot assent.
Mere precedent is a dangerous source of authority, and should not be
regarded as deciding questions of constitutional power, except where the
acquiescence of the people and the States can be considered as well settled. So far from this being the case on this subject, an argument against
the bank might be based on precedent. One Congress in 1791, decided in
favor of a bank; another in 1811, decided against it. One Congress in 1815
decided against a bank; another in 1816 decided in its favor. Prior to the
present Congress, therefore the precedents drawn from that source were
equal. If we resort to the States, the expressions of legislative, judicial
and executive opinions against the bank have been probably to those in
its favor as four to one. There is nothing in precedent, therefore, which if
its authority were admitted, ought to weigh in favor of the act before me."

I drop the quotations merely to remark that all there ever was, in the
way of precedent up to the Dred Scott decision, on the points therein
decided, had been against that decision. But hear Gen. Jackson further—

"If the opinion of the Supreme court covered the whole ground of this
act, it ought not to control the co-ordinate authorities of this Government. The Congress, the executive and the court, must each for itself be
guided by its own opinion of the Constitution. Each public officer, who
takes an oath to support the Constitution, swears that he will support it
as he understands it, and not as it is understood by others."

Again and again have I heard Judge Douglas denounce that bank decision, and applaud Gen. Jackson for disregarding it. It would be interesting for him to look over his recent speech, and see how exactly his fierce
philippics against us for resisting Supreme Court decisions, fall upon his
own head. It will call to his mind a long and fierce political war in this country, upon an issue which, in his own language, and, of course, in his own
changeless estimation, was "a distinct and naked issue between the friends
and the enemies of the Constitution," and in which war he fought in the
ranks of the enemies of the Constitution.

I have said, in substance, that the Dred Scott decision was, in part,
based on assumed historical facts which were not really true; and I ought
not to leave the subject without giving some reasons for saying this; I therefore give an instance or two, which I think fully sustain me. Chief Justice
Taney, in delivering the opinion of the majority of the Court, insists at
great length that negroes were no part of the people who made, or for
whom was made, the Declaration of Independence, or the Constitution of
the United States.

On the contrary, Judge Curtis, in his dissenting opinion, shows that in
five of the then thirteen states, to wit, New Hampshire, Massachusetts,

New York, New Jersey and North Carolina, free negroes were voters, and, in proportion to their numbers, had the same part in making the Constitution that the white people had. He shows this with so much particularity as to leave no doubt of its truth; and, as a sort of conclusion on that point, holds the following language:

"The Constitution was ordained and established by the people of the United States, through the action, in each State, of those persons who were qualified by its laws to act thereon in behalf of themselves and all other citizens of the State. In some of the States, as we have seen, colored persons were among those qualified by law to act on the subject. These colored persons were not only included in the body of 'the people of the United States,' by whom the Constitution was ordained and established; but in at least five of the States they had the power to act, and, doubtless, did act, by their suffrages, upon the question of its adoption."

Again, Chief Justice Taney says: "It is difficult, at this day to realize the state of public opinion in relation to that unfortunate race, which prevailed in the civilized and enlightened portions of the world at the time of the Declaration of Independence, and when the Constitution of the United States was framed and adopted." And again, after quoting from the Declaration, he says: "The general words above quoted would seem to include the whole human family, and if they were used in a similar instrument at this day, would be so understood."

In these the Chief Justice does not directly assert, but plainly assumes, as a fact, that the public estimate of the black man is more favorable *now* than it was in the days of the Revolution. This assumption is a mistake. In some trifling particulars, the condition of that race has been ameliorated; but, as a whole, in this country, the change between then and now is decidedly the other way; and their ultimate destiny has never appeared so hopeless as in the last three or four years. In two of the five States— New Jersey and North Carolina—that then gave the free negro the right of voting, the right has since been taken away; and in a third—New York—it has been greatly abridged;[4] while it has not been extended, so far as I know, to a single additional State, though the number of the States has more than doubled. In those days, as I understand, masters could, at their own pleasure, emancipate their slaves; but since then, such legal restraints have been made upon emancipation, as to amount almost to prohibition. In those days, Legislatures held the unquestioned power to abolish slavery in their respective States; but now it is becoming quite fashionable for State Constitutions to withhold that power from the Legislatures. In those days, by common consent, the spread of the black man's bondage to new countries was prohibited; but now, Congress decides that it *will* not continue the prohibition, and the Supreme Court decides that it *could* not if it would. In those days, our Declaration of Independence was held sacred by all, and thought to include all; but now, to aid in making the bondage of the negro universal and eternal, it is assailed, and sneered at, and construed, and hawked at, and torn, till, if its framers could rise from their graves, they could not at all recognize it. All the powers of earth

---

4. Blacks lost the right to vote in New Jersey in 1807 and in North Carolina in 1835. In 1821, New York abolished property qualifications for whites while raising them from $150 to $250 for blacks, many of whom thereby lost the vote.

seem rapidly combining against him. Mammon is after him; ambition follows, and philosophy follows, and the Theology of the day is fast joining the cry. They have him in his prison house; they have searched his person, and left no prying instrument with him. One after another they have closed the heavy iron doors upon him, and now they have him, as it were, bolted in with a lock of a hundred keys, which can never be unlocked without the concurrence of every key; the keys in the hands of a hundred different men, and they scattered to a hundred different and distant places; and they stand musing as to what invention, in all the dominions of mind and matter, can be produced to make the impossibility of his escape more complete than it is.

It is grossly incorrect to say or assume, that the public estimate of the negro is more favorable now than it was at the origin of the government.

Three years and a half ago, Judge Douglas brought forward his famous Nebraska bill. The country was at once in a blaze. He scorned all opposition, and carried it through Congress. Since then he has seen himself superseded in a Presidential nomination, by one indorsing the general doctrine of his measure,[5] but at the same time standing clear of the odium of its untimely agitation, and its gross breach of national faith; and he has seen that successful rival Constitutionally elected, not by the strength of friends, but by the division of adversaries, being in a popular minority of nearly four hundred thousand votes. He has seen his chief aids in his own State, Shields and Richardson,[6] politically speaking, successively tried, convicted, and executed, for an offense not their own, but his. And now he sees his own case, standing next on the docket for trial.

There is a natural disgust in the minds of nearly all white people, to the idea of an indiscriminate amalgamation[7] of the white and black races; and Judge Douglas evidently is basing his chief hope, upon the chances of being able to appropriate the benefit of this disgust to himself. If he can, by much drumming and repeating, fasten the odium of that idea upon his adversaries, he thinks he can struggle through the storm. He therefore clings to this hope, as a drowning man to the last plank. He makes an occasion for lugging it in from the opposition to the Dred Scott decision. He finds the Republicans insisting that the Declaration of Independence includes ALL men, black as well as white; and forthwith he boldly denies that it includes negroes at all, and proceeds to argue gravely that all who contend it does, do so only because they want to vote, and eat, and sleep, and marry with negroes! He will have it that they cannot be consistent else. Now I protest against that counterfeit logic which concludes that, because I do not want a black woman for a *slave* I must necessarily want her for a *wife*. I need not have her for either, I can just leave her alone. In some respects she certainly is not my equal; but in her natural right to eat the bread she earns with her own hands without asking leave of any one else, she is my equal, and the equal of all others.

Chief Justice Taney, in his opinion in the Dred Scott case, admits that the language of the Declaration is broad enough to include the whole

5. I.e., James Buchanan.
6. James Shields (1810–1879) and William A. Richardson (1811–1875), Illinois Democrats who were widely attacked for their support of the Kansas-Nebraska Act when they ran for office in 1854.
7. Miscegenation.

human family, but he and Judge Douglas argue that the authors of that instrument did not intend to include negroes, by the fact that they did not at once, actually place them on an equality with the whites. Now this grave argument comes to just nothing at all, by the other fact, that they did not at once, *or ever afterwards*, actually place all white people on an equality with one or another. And this is the staple argument of both the Chief Justice and the Senator, for doing this obvious violence to the plain unmistakable language of the Declaration. I think the authors of that notable instrument intended to include *all* men, but they did not intend to declare all men equal *in all respects*. They did not mean to say all were equal in color, size, intellect, moral developments, or social capacity. They defined with tolerable distinctness, in what respects they did consider all men created equal—equal in "certain inalienable rights, among which are life, liberty, and the pursuit of happiness." This they said, and this meant. They did not mean to assert the obvious untruth, that all were then actually enjoying that equality, nor yet, that they were about to confer it immediately upon them. In fact they had no power to confer such a boon. They meant simply to declare the *right*, so that the *enforcement* of it might follow as fast as circumstances should permit. They meant to set up a standard maxim for free society, which should be familiar to all, and revered by all; constantly looked to, constantly labored for, and even though never perfectly attained, constantly approximated, and thereby constantly spreading and deepening its influence, and augmenting the happiness and value of life to all people of all colors everywhere. The assertion that "all men are created equal" was of no practical use in effecting our separation from Great Britain; and it was placed in the Declaration, not for that, but for future use. Its authors meant it to be, thank God, it is now proving itself, a stumbling block to those who in after times might seek to turn a free people back into the hateful paths of despotism. They knew the proneness of prosperity to breed tyrants, and they meant when such should re-appear in this fair land and commence their vocation they should find left for them at least one hard nut to crack.

I have now briefly expressed my view of the *meaning* and *objects* of that part of the Declaration of Independence which declares that "all men are created equal."

Now let us hear Judge Douglas' view of the same subject, as I find it in the printed report of his late speech. Here it is:

"No man can vindicate the character, motives and conduct of the signers of the Declaration of Independence, except upon the hypothesis that they referred to the white race alone, and not to the African, when they declared all men to have been created equal—that they were speaking of British subjects on this continent being equal to British subjects born and residing in Great Britain—that they were entitled to the same inalienable rights, and among them were enumerated life, liberty and the pursuit of happiness. The Declaration was adopted for the purpose of justifying the colonists in the eyes of the civilized world in withdrawing their allegiance from the British crown, and dissolving their connection with the mother country."

My good friends, read that carefully over some leisure hour, and ponder well upon it—see what a mere wreck—mangled ruin—it makes of our once glorious Declaration.

"They were speaking of British subjects on this continent being equal to British subjects born and residing in Great Britain!" Why, according to this, not only negroes but white people outside of Great Britain and America are not spoken of in that instrument. The English, Irish and Scotch, along with white Americans, were included to be sure, but the French, Germans and other white people of the world are all gone to pot along with the Judge's inferior races.

I had thought the Declaration promised something better than the condition of British subjects; but no, it only meant that we should be *equal* to them in their own oppressed and *unequal* condition. According to that, it gave no promise that having kicked off the King and Lords of Great Britain, we should not at once be saddled with a King and Lords of our own.

I had thought the Declaration contemplated the progressive improvement in the condition of all men everywhere; but no, it merely "was adopted for the purpose of justifying the colonists in the eyes of the civilized world in withdrawing their allegiance from the British crown, and dissolving their connection with the mother country." Why, that object having been effected some eighty years ago, the Declaration is of no practical use now—mere rubbish—old wadding left to rot on the battle-field after the victory is won.

I understand you are preparing to celebrate the "Fourth," to-morrow week. What for? The doings of that day had no reference to the present; and quite half of you are not even descendants of those who were referred to at that day. But I suppose you will celebrate; and will even go so far as to read the Declaration. Suppose after you read it once in the old fashioned way, you read it once more with Judge Douglas' version. It will then run thus: "We hold these truths to be self-evident that all British subjects who were on this continent eighty-one years ago, were created equal to all British subjects born and *then* residing in Great Britain."

And now I appeal to all—to Democrats as well as others,—are you really willing that the Declaration shall be thus frittered away?—thus left no more at most, than an interesting memorial of the dead past? thus shorn of its vitality, and practical value; and left without the *germ* or even the *suggestion* of the individual rights of man in it?

But Judge Douglas is especially horrified at the thought of the mixing blood by the white and black races: agreed for once—a thousand times agreed. There are white men enough to marry all the white women, and black men enough to marry all the black women; and so let them be married. On this point we fully agree with the Judge; and when he shall show that his policy is better adapted to prevent amalgamation than ours we shall drop ours, and adopt his. Let us see. In 1850 there were in the United States, 405,751, mulattoes. Very few of these are the offspring of whites and *free* blacks; nearly all have sprung from black *slaves* and white masters. A separation of the races is the only perfect preventive of amalgamation but as an immediate separation is impossible the next best thing is to *keep* them apart *where* they are not already together. If white and black people never get together in Kansas, they will never mix blood in Kansas. That is at least one self-evident truth. A few free colored persons may get into the free States, in any event; but their number is too insignificant to amount to much in the way of mixing blood. In 1850 there were in the free states, 56,649 mulattoes; but for the most part they were not born there—they came from the slave States, ready made up. In the same year the slave States had 348,874 mulattoes all of home production. The proportion of free mulattoes to free blacks—the only colored classes in the free states—is much greater in the slave than in the free states. It is worthy of note too, that among the free states those which make the colored man the nearest to equal the white, have, proportionably the fewest mulattoes the least of amalgamation. In New Hampshire, the State which goes farthest towards equality between the races, there are just 184 Mulattoes while there are in Virginia—how many do you think? 79,775, being 23,126 more than in all the free States together.

These statistics show that slavery is the greatest source of amalgamation; and next to it, not the elevation, but the degeneration of the free blacks. Yet Judge Douglas dreads the slightest restraints on the spread of slavery, and the slightest human recognition of the negro, as tending horribly to amalgamation.

This very Dred Scott case affords a strong test as to which party most favors amalgamation, the Republicans or the dear Union-saving Democracy. Dred Scott, his wife and two daughters were all involved in the suit. We desired the court to have held that they were citizens so far at least as to entitle them to a hearing as to whether they were free or not; and then, also, that they were in fact and in law really free. Could we have had our way, the chances of these black girls, ever mixing their blood with that of white people, would have been diminished at least to the extent that it could not have been without their consent. But Judge Douglas is delighted to have them decided to be slaves, and not human enough to have a hearing, even if they were free, and thus left subject to the forced concubinage of their masters, and liable to become the mothers of mulattoes in spite of themselves—the very state of case that produces nine tenths of all the mulattoes—all the mixing of blood in the nation.

Of course, I state this case as an illustration only, not meaning to say or intimate that the master of Dred Scott and his family, or any more than a per centage of masters generally, are inclined to exercise this particular power which they hold over their female slaves.

I have said that the separation of the races is the only perfect preventive of amalgamation. I have no right to say all the members of the Republican party are in favor of this, nor to say that as a party they are in favor of it. There is nothing in their platform directly on the subject. But I can say a very large proportion of its members are for it, and that the chief plank in their platform—opposition to the spread of slavery—is most favorable to that separation.

Such separation, if ever effected at all, must be effected by colonization; and no political party, as such, is now doing anything directly for colonization. Party operations at present only favor or retard colonization incidentally. The enterprise is a difficult one; but "when there is a will there is a way;" and what colonization needs most is a hearty will. Will springs from the two elements of moral sense and self-interest. Let us be brought to believe it is morally right, and, at the same time, favorable to, or, at least, not against, our interest, to transfer the African to his native clime, and

8. A coin.

we shall find a way to do it, however great the task may be. The children of Israel, to such numbers as to include four hundred thousand fighting men, went out of Egyptian bondage in a body.

How differently the respective courses of the Democratic and Republican parties incidentally bear on the question of forming a will—a public sentiment—for colonization, is easy to see. The Republicans inculcate, with whatever of ability they can, that the negro is a man; that his bondage is cruelly wrong, and that the field of his oppression ought not to be enlarged. The Democrats deny his manhood; deny, or dwarf to insignificance, the wrong of his bondage; so far as possible, crush all sympathy for him, and cultivate and excite hatred and disgust against him; compliment themselves as Union-savers for doing so; and call the indefinite outspreading of his bondage "a sacred right of self-government."

The plainest print cannot be read through a gold eagle;[8] and it will be ever hard to find many men who will send a slave to Liberia, and pay his passage while they can send him to a new country, Kansas for instance, and sell him for fifteen hundred dollars, and the rise.

June 26, 1857

Draft of a Speech

From time to time, ever since the Chicago "Times" and "Illinois State Register" declared their opposition to the Lecompton constitution,[1] and it began to be understood that Judge Douglas was also opposed to it, I have been accosted by friends of his with the question, "What do you think now?" Since the delivery of his speech in the Senate,[2] the question has been varied a little. "Have you read Douglas's speech?" "Yes." "Well, what do you think of it?" In every instance the question is accompanied with an anxious inquiring stare, which asks, quite as plainly as words could, "Can't you go for Douglas[3] now?" Like boys who have set a bird-trap, they are watching to see if the birds are picking at the bait and likely to go under.

I think, then, Judge Douglas knows that the Republicans wish Kansas to be a free State. He knows that they know, if the question be fairly submitted to a vote of the people of Kansas, it will be a free State; and he would not object at all if, by drawing their attention to this particular fact, and himself becoming vociferous for such fair vote, they should be induced to drop their own organization, fall into rank behind him, and form a great free-State Democratic party.

But before Republicans do this, I think they ought to require a few questions to be answered on the other side. If they so fall in with Judge Douglas, and Kansas shall be secured as a free State, there then remaining

---

1. A proslavery constitution, written in Lecompton, Kansas, (1855) in answer to an antislavery one that had been issued in Topeka. The Lecompton Constitution, endorsed on the federal level by President Buchanan and by many Southern Democrats, was widely attacked in the North. The two newspapers mentioned here editorialized against it in November 1857.
2. On December 9, 1857, the day after President Buchanan commended the Lecompton constitution, Senator Stephen A. Douglas denounced it, arguing that it was not fairly voted on by the settlers of Kansas and therefore violated the principle of popular sovereignty.
3. Senator Stephen A. Douglas.

no cause of difference between him and the regular Democracy, will not the Republicans stand ready, haltered and harnessed, to be handed over by him to the regular Democracy, to filibuster indefinitely for additional slave territory,—to carry slavery into all the States, as well as Territories, under the Dred Scott decision,[4] construed and enlarged from time to time, according to the demands of the regular slave Democracy,—and to assist in reviving the African slave-trade in order that all may buy negroes where they can be bought cheapest, as a clear incident of that "sacred right of property," now held in some quarters to be above all constitutions?

By so falling in, will we not be committed to or at least compromitted with, the Nebraska policy?

If so, we should remember that Kansas is saved, not by that policy or its authors, but in spite of both—by an effort that cannot be kept up in future cases.

Did Judge Douglas help any to get a free-State majority into Kansas? Not a bit of it—the exact contrary. Does he now express any wish that Kansas, or any other place, shall be free? Nothing like it. He tells us, in this very speech,[5] expected to be so palatable to Republicans, that he cares not whether slavery is voted down or voted up. His whole effort is devoted to clearing the ring, and giving slavery and freedom a fair fight. With one who considers slavery just as good as freedom, this is perfectly natural and consistent.

But have Republicans any sympathy with such a view? They think slavery is wrong; and that, like every other wrong which some men will commit if left alone, it ought to be prohibited by law. They consider it not only morally wrong, but a "deadly poison" in a government like ours, professedly based on the equality of men. Upon this radical difference of opinion with Judge Douglas, the Republican party was organized. There is all the difference between him and them now that there ever was. He will not say that he has changed; have you?

Again, we ought to be informed as to Judge Douglas's present opinion as to the inclination of Republicans to marry with negroes. By his Springfield speech we know what it was last June; and by his resolution[6] dropped at Jacksonville in September we know what it was then. Perhaps we have something even later in a Chicago speech, in which the danger of being "stunk out of church"[7] was descanted upon. But what is his opinion on the point now? There is, or will be, a sure sign to judge by. If this charge shall be silently dropped by the judge and his friends, if no more resolutions on the subject shall be passed in Douglas Democratic meetings and conventions, it will be safe to swear that he is courting. Our "witching

---

4. The Supreme Court decision (1857) that declared that blacks were not U.S. citizens.
5. See no. 2, p. 120.
6. A political document supporting the *Dred Scott* decision and opposing "Negro equality" that, according to a newspaper report, Douglas allegedly dropped in a railway station in Jacksonville, Illinois, in September. A Democratic newspaper, the *Jacksonville Sentinel*, on October 16, 1857, dismissed the supposed document as a Republican hoax but came out with its own version of a resolution supporting the inferiority of blacks as maintained by the *Dred Scott* ruling. "Springfield speech": Douglas's speech on June 12, 1857, which Lincoln answered on June 26, 1857 (see pp. 111–20.).
7. Douglas was reported as having said in a Chicago speech on November 11, 1857, that "Black Republicans . . . will allow the blacks to push us from our sidewalk (Oh!) and elbow us out of car seats (Oh? Oh!) and stink us out of our places of worship" (*Chicago Daily Democratic Press*, November 12, 1857).

smile" has "caught his youthful fancy"; and henceforth Cuffy[8] and he are rival beaux for our gushing affections.

We also ought to insist on knowing what the judge now thinks on "Sectionalism." Last year he thought it was a "clincher" against us on the question of Sectionalism, that we could get no support in the slave States, and could not be allowed to speak, or even breathe, south of the Ohio River.

In vain did we appeal to the justice of our principles. He would have it that the treatment we received was conclusive evidence that we deserved it. He and his friends would bring speakers from the slave States to their meetings and conventions in the free States, and parade about, arm in arm with them, breathing in every gesture and tone, "How we national apples do swim!" Let him cast about for this particular evidence of his own nationality now. Why, just now, he and Fremont[9] would make the closest race imaginable in the Southern States.

In the present aspect of affairs what ought the Republicans to do? I think they ought not to oppose any measure merely because Judge Douglas proposes it. Whether the Lecompton constitution should be accepted or rejected is a question upon which, in the minds of men not committed to any of its antecedents, and controlled only by the Federal Constitution, by republican principles, and by a sound morality, it seems to me there could not be two opinions. It should be throttled and killed as hastily and as heartily as a rabid dog. What those should do who are committed to all its antecedents is their business, not ours. If, therefore, Judge Douglas's bill[1] secures a fair vote to the people of Kansas, without contrivance to commit any one farther, I think Republican members of Congress ought to support it. They can do so without any inconsistency. They believe Congress ought to prohibit slavery wherever it can be done without violation of the Constitution or of good faith. And having seen the noses counted, and actually knowing that a majority of the people of Kansas are against slavery, passing an act to secure them a fair vote is little else than prohibiting slavery in Kansas by act of Congress.

Congress cannot dictate a constitution to a new State. All it can do at that point is to secure the people a fair chance to form one for themselves, and then to accept or reject it when they ask admission into the Union. As I understand, Republicans claim no more than this. But they do claim that Congress can and ought to keep slavery out of a Territory, up to the time of its people forming a State constitution; and they should now be careful to not stultify themselves to any extent on that point.

I am glad Judge Douglas has, at last, distinctly told us that he cares not whether slavery be voted down or voted up. Not so much that this is any news to me; nor yet that it may be slightly new to some of that class of his friends who delight to say that they "are as much opposed to slavery as anybody."

I am glad because it affords such a true and excellent definition of the Nebraska policy itself. That policy, honestly administered, is exactly that.

---

8. A black person (colloquial); a version of *kofi*, an African word for a male born on a Friday. The quotations are from Robert Burns's poem "The Soldier's Return" (1793).
9. John C. Frémont.
1. Proposed on December 18, 1857, authorizing the people of Kansas to form a constitution. The measure was dropped in favor of a Buchanan administration bill and later the so-called English Bill, which offered Kansans public land on the condition that they adopt the Lecompton Constitution.

It seeks to bring the people of the nation to not care anything about slavery. This is Nebraskaism in its abstract purity—in its very best dress.

Now, I take it, nearly everybody does care something about slavery—is either for it or against it; and that the statesmanship of a measure which conforms to the sentiments of nobody might well be doubted in advance.

But Nebraskaism did not originate as a piece of statesmanship. General Cass,[2] in 1848, invented it, as a political manoeuver, to secure himself the Democratic nomination for the presidency. It served its purpose then, and sunk out of sight. Six years later Judge Douglas fished it up, and glozed it over with what he called, and still persists in calling, "sacred rights of self-government."

Well, I, too, believe in self-government as I understand it; but I do not understand that the privilege one man takes of making a slave of another, or holding him as such, is any part of "self-government." To call it so is, to my mind, simply absurd and ridiculous. I am for the people of the whole nation doing just as they please in all matters which concern the whole nation; for those of each part doing just as they choose in all matters which concern no other part; and for each individual doing just as he chooses in all matters which concern nobody else. This is the principle. Of course I am content with any exception which the Constitution, or the actually existing state of things, makes a necessity. But neither the principle nor the exception will admit the indefinite spread and perpetuity of human slavery.

I think the true magnitude of the slavery element in this nation is scarcely appreciated by any one. Four years ago the Nebraska policy was adopted, professedly, to drive the agitation of the subject into the Territories, and out of every other place, and especially out of Congress.

When Mr. Buchanan accepted the presidential nomination, he felicitated himself with the belief that the whole thing would be quieted and forgotten in about six weeks. In his inaugural, and in his Silliman letter,[3] at their respective dates, he was just not quite in reach of the same happy consummation. And now, in his first annual message, he urges the acceptance of the Lecompton constitution (not quite satisfactory to him) on the sole ground of getting this little unimportant matter out of the way.

Meanwhile, in those four years, there has really been more angry agitation of this subject, both in and out of Congress, than ever before. And just now it is perplexing the mighty ones as no subject ever did before. Nor is it confined to politics alone. Presbyterian assemblies, Methodist conferences, Unitarian gatherings, and single churches to an indefinite extent, are wrangling, and cracking, and going to pieces on the same question. Why, Kansas is neither the whole nor a tithe of the real question.

A house divided against itself cannot stand.[4]

I believe the government cannot endure permanently half slave and half free. I expressed this belief a year ago; and subsequent developments

---

2. Lewis Cass.
3. Benjamin Silliman (1779–1864), Yale professor, wrote President James Buchanan a letter, signed by forty-two other Connecticut citizens, protesting against Kansas governor Robert J. Walker's invasion of the town of Lawrence, a center of antislavery activity. In his reply to Silliman, published in the *Washington Union*, Buchanan cited the *Dred Scott* decision in arguing that slavery had always been legal in the territory.
4. Cf. Matthew 12:25 and Mark 3:25.

have but confirmed me. I do not expect the Union to be dissolved. I do not expect the house to fall; but I do expect it will cease to be divided. It will become all one thing or all the other. Either the opponents of slavery will arrest the further spread of it, and put it in course of ultimate extinction; or its advocates will push it forward till it shall become alike lawful in all the States, old as well as new. Do you doubt it? Study the Dred Scott decision, and then see how little even now remains to be done. That decision may be reduced to three points.

The first is that a negro cannot be a citizen. That point is made in order to deprive the negro, in every possible event, of the benefit of that provision of the United States Constitution which declares that "the citizens of each State shall be entitled to all privileges and immunities of citizens in the several States."

The second point is that the United States Constitution protects slavery, as property, in all the United States territories, and that neither Congress, nor the people of the Territories, nor any other power, can prohibit it at any time prior to the formation of State constitutions.

This point is made in order that the Territories may safely be filled up with slaves, before the formation of State constitutions, thereby to embarrass the free-State sentiment, and enhance the chances of slave constitutions being adopted.

The third point decided is that the voluntary bringing of Dred Scott into Illinois by his master, and holding him here a long time as a slave, did not operate his emancipation—did not make him free.

This point is made, not to be pressed immediately; but if acquiesced in for a while, then to sustain the logical conclusion that what Dred Scott's master might lawfully do with Dred in the free State of Illinois, every other master may lawfully do with any other one or one hundred slaves in Illinois, or in any other free State. Auxiliary to all this, and working hand in hand with it, the Nebraska doctrine is to educate and mold public opinion to "not care whether slavery is voted up or voted down." At least Northern public opinion must cease to care anything about it. Southern public opinion may, without offense, continue to care as much as it pleases.

Welcome, or unwelcome, agreeable, or disagreeable, whether this shall be an entire slave nation, is the issue before us. Every incident—every little shifting of scenes or of actors—only clears away the intervening trash, compacts and consolidates the opposing hosts, and brings them more and more distinctly face to face.

The conflict will be a severe one; and it will be fought through by those who do care for the result, and not by those who do not care—by those who are for, and those who are against a legalized national slavery. The combined charge of Nebraskaism, and Dred Scottism must be repulsed, and rolled back. The deceitful cloak of "self-government" wherewith "the sum of all villanies" seeks to protect and adorn itself, must be torn from it's hateful carcass. That burlesque upon judicial decisions, and slander and profanation upon the honored names, and sacred history of republican America, must be overruled, and expunged from the books of authority.

To give the victory to the right, not bloody bullets, but peaceful ballots only, are necessary. Thanks to our good old constitution, and organization under it, these alone are necessary. It only needs that every right thinking man, shall go to the polls, and without fear or prejudice, vote as he thinks.

ca. December 28, 1857

First Lecture on Discoveries and Inventions, Bloomington, Indiana[1]

All creation is a mine, and every man, a miner.

The whole earth, and all *within* it, *upon* it, and *round about* it, including *himself*, in his physical, moral, and intellectual nature, and his susceptabilities, are the infinitely various "leads" from which, man, from the first, was to dig out his destiny.

In the beginning, the mine was unopened, and the miner stood *naked*, and *knowledgeless*, upon it.

Fishes, birds, beasts, and creeping things, are not miners, but *feeders* and *lodgers*, merely. Beavers build houses; but they build them in nowise differently, or better now, than they did, five thousand years ago. Ants, and honey-bees, provide food for winter; but just in the *same way* they did, when Solomon refered the sluggard to them as patterns of prudence.[2]

Man is not the only animal who labors; but he is the only one who *improves* his workmanship. This improvement, he effects by *Discoveries*, and *Inventions*. His first important discovery was the fact that he was naked; and his first invention was the fig-leaf-apron. This simple article—the apron—made of leaves, seems to have been the origin of *clothing*—the one thing for which nearly half of the toil and care of the human race has ever since been expended. The most important improvement ever made in connection with clothing, was the invention of *spinning* and *weaving*. The spinning jenny, and power-loom, invented in modern times, though great *improvements*, do not, *as inventions*, rank with the ancient arts of spinning and weaving. Spinning and weaving brought into the department of clothing such abundance and variety of material. Wool, the hair of several species of animals, hemp, flax, cotten, silk, and perhaps other articles, were all suited to it, affording garments not only adapted to wet and dry, heat and cold, but also susceptable of high degrees of ornamental finish. Exactly *when*, or *where*, spinning and weaving originated is not known. At the first interview of the Almighty with Adam and Eve, after the fall, He made "coats of skins, and clothed them" Gen: 3-21.[3]

The Bible makes no other alusion to clothing, *before* the flood. Soon *after* the deluge Noah's two sons covered him with a *garment*; but of what *material* the garment was made is not mentioned. Gen. 9-23.

Abraham mentions "*thread*" in such connection as to indicate that spinning and weaving were in use in his day—Gen. 14.23—and soon after,

---

1. Lincoln delivered this lecture at Bloomington before the Young Men's Association on April 6, 1858.
2. "Go to the ant, O sluggard; and see, and emulate his ways, and become wiser than he. For whereas he has no husbandry, nor any one to compel him, and is under no master, he prepares food for himself in the summer, and lays by abundant store in harvest. Or go to the bee, and learn how diligent she is, and how earnestly she is engaged in her work" (Proverbs 6:6–7).
3. The biblical citations in the text are Lincoln's.

reference to the art is frequently made. "*Linen breeches*," are mentioned,—Exod. 28.42—and it is said "all the women that were wise hearted, did *spin* with their hands" (35-25) and, "all the women whose hearts stirred them up in wisdom, *spun* goat's hair" (35-26). The work of the "*weaver*" is mentioned—(35-35). In the book of Job, a very old book, date not exactly known, the "*weavers shuttle*" is mentioned.

The above mention of "*thread*" by Abraham is the oldest recorded alusion to spinning and weaving; and *it* was made about two thousand years after the creation of man, and now, near four thousand years ago. Profane authors think these arts originated in Egypt; and this is not contradicted, or made improbable, by any thing in the Bible; for the alusion of Abraham, mentioned, was not made until after he had sojourned in Egypt.

The discovery of the properties of *iron*, and the making of *iron tools*, must have been among the earliest of important discoveries and inventions. We can scarcely conceive the possibility of making much of anything else, without the use of iron tools. Indeed, an iron *hammer* must have been very much needed to make the *first* iron hammer with. A *stone* probably served as a substitute. How could the "*gopher wood*"[4] for the Ark, have been gotten out without an axe? It seems to me an axe, or a miracle, was indispensable. Corresponding with the prime necessity for iron, we find at least one very early notice of it. Tubal-cain[5] was "an instructer of every artificer in *brass* and *iron*"—Gen: 4-22. Tubal-cain was the seventh in decent from Adam; and his birth was about one thousand years before the flood. *After* the flood, frequent mention is made of *iron*, and *instruments* made of iron. Thus "instrument of iron" at Num: 35-16; "bed-stead of iron" at Deut. 3-11—"the iron furnace" at 4-20—and "iron tool" at 27-5. At 19-5—very distinct mention of "the ax to cut down the tree" is made; and also at 8-9, the promised land is described as "a land whose stones are iron, and out of whose hills thou mayest dig brass." From the somewhat frequent mention of brass in connection with iron, it is not improbable that brass—perhaps what we now call copper—was used by the ancients for some of the same purposes as iron.

Transportation—the removal of person, and goods—from place to place—would be an early *object*, if not a *necessity*, with man. By his natural powers of locomotion, and without much assistance from Discovery and invention, he could move himself about with considerable facility; and even, could carry small burthens with him. But very soon he would wish to lessen the labor, while he might, at the same time, extend, and expedite the business. For this object, wheel-carriages, and water-crafts—wagons and boats—are the most important inventions. The use of the wheel & axle, has been so long known, that it is difficult, without reflection, to estimate it at it's true value.

The oldest recorded allusion to the wheel and axle is the mention of a "chariot" Gen: 41-43. This was in Egypt, upon the occasion of Joseph being made Governor by Pharaoh. It was about twentyfive hundred years after the creation of Adam. That the chariot then mentioned was a wheel-carriage drawn by animals, is sufficiently evidenced by the mention of

---

4. The wood (probably cedar) mentioned in the Bible as the material used by Noah to build his ark (Genesis 6:14).
5. A descendant of Cain, Tubal-Cain is commonly considered to have been the first metalsmith.

chariot-*wheels*, at Exod. 14-25, and the mention of chariots in connection with *horses*, in the same chapter, verses 9 & 23. So much, at present, for land-transportation.

Now, as to transportation by *water*, I have concluded, without sufficient authority perhaps, to use the term "boat" as a general name for all water-craft. The boat is indispensable to navigation. It is not probable that the philosophical principle upon which the use of the boat primarily depends—towit, the *principle*, that any thing will float, which can not sink without displacing more than it's own *weight* of water—was known, or even thought of, before the first boats were made. The sight of a crow standing on a piece of drift-wood floating down the swolen current of a creek or river, might well enough suggest the specific idea to a savage, that he could himself get upon a log, or on two logs tied together, and somehow work his way to the opposite shore of the same stream. Such a suggestion, so taken, would be the birth of navigation; and such, not improbably, it really was. The leading idea was thus caught; and whatever came afterwards, were but improvements upon, and auxiliaries to, it.

As man is a land animal, it might be expected he would learn to travel by land somewhat earlier than he would by water. Still the crossing of streams, somewhat too deep for wading, would be an early necessity with him. If we pass by the Ark, which may be regarded as belonging rather to the *miracalous*, than to *human* invention the first notice we have of water-craft, is the mention of "ships" by Jacob–Gen: 49-13. It is not till we reach the book of Isaiah that we meet with the mention of "oars" and "sails."

As mans *food*—his first necessity—was to be derived from the vegitation of the earth, it was natural that his first care should be directed to the assistance of that vegitation. And accordingly we find that, even before the fall, the man was put into the garden of Eden "to dress it, and to keep it." And when afterwards, in consequence of the first transgression, *labor* was imposed on the race, as a *penalty*—a *curse*—we find the first born man—the first heir of the curse—was "a tiller of the ground." This was the beginning of agriculture; and although, both in point of time, and of importance, it stands at the head of all branches of human industry, it has derived less direct advantage from Discovery and Invention, than almost any other. The plow, of very early origin; and reaping, and threshing, machines, of modern invention are, at this day, the principle improvements in agriculture. And even the oldest of these, the plow, could not have been conceived of, until a precedent conception had been caught, and put into practice—I mean the conception, or idea, of substituting other forces in nature, for man's own muscular power. These other forces, as now used, are principally, the *strength* of animals, and the *power* of the wind, of running streams, and of steam.

Climbing upon the back of an animal, and making it carry us, might not, occur very readily. I think the back of the camel would never have suggested it. It was, however, a matter of vast importance.

The earliest instance of it mentioned, is when "Abraham rose up early in the morning, and saddled his ass," Gen. 22-3 preparatory to sacraficing Isaac as a burnt-offering; but the allusion to the *saddle* indicates that riding had been in use some time; for it is quite probable they rode bare-backed awhile, at least, before they invented saddles.

The *idea*, being once conceived, of riding *one* species of animals, would soon be extended to others. Accordingly we find that when the servant of Abraham went in search of a wife for Isaac, he took ten *camels* with him; and, on his return trip, "Rebekah arose, and her damsels, and they rode upon the camels, and followed the man" Gen 24-61.

The *horse*, too, as a riding animal, is mentioned early. The Redsea being safely passed, Moses and the children of Israel sang to the Lord "the *horse*, and his *rider* hath he thrown into the sea." Exo. 15-1.

Seeing that animals could bear *man* upon their backs, it would soon occur that they could also bear other burthens. Accordingly we find that Joseph's bretheren, on their first visit to Egypt, "laded their asses with the corn, and departed thence" Gen. 42-26.

Also it would occur that animals could be made to *draw* burthens *after* them, as well as to bear them upon their backs; and hence plows and chariots came into use early enough to be often mentioned in the books of Moses—Deut. 22-10. Gen. 41-43. Gen. 46-29. Exo. 14-25.

Of all the forces of nature, I should think the *wind* contains the largest amount of *motive power*—that is, power to move things. Take any given space of the earth's surface—for instance, Illinois—and all the power exerted by all the men, and beasts, and running-water, and steam, over and upon it, shall not equal the one hundredth part of what is exerted by the blowing of the wind over and upon the same space. And yet it has not, so far in the world's history, become proportionably *valuable* as a motive power. It is applied extensively, and advantageously, to sail-vessels in navigation. Add to this a few wind-mills, and pumps, and you have about all. That, as yet, no very successful mode of *controlling*, and *directing* the wind, has been discovered; and that, naturally, it moves by fits and starts—now so gently as to scarcely stir a leaf, and now so roughly as to level a forest—doubtless have been the insurmountable difficulties. As yet, the wind is an *untamed*, and *unharnessed* force; and quite possibly one of the greatest discoveries hereafter to be made, will be the taming, and harnessing of the wind. That the difficulties of controlling this power are very great is quite evident by the fact that they have already been perceived, and struggled with more than three thousand years; for that power was applied to sail-vessels, at least as early as the time of the prophet Isaiah.

In speaking of *running streams*, as a motive power, I mean it's application to mills and other machinery by means of the *"water wheel"*—a thing now well known, and extensively used; but, of which, no mention is made in the bible, though it is thought to have been in use among the romans—(Am. Ency.[6] tit—Mill). The language of the Saviour "Two women shall be grinding at the mill &c"[7] indicates that, even in the populous city of Jerusalem, at that day, mills were operated by hand—having, as yet had no other than human power applied to them.

The advantageous use of *Steam-power* is, unquestionably, a modern discovery.

And yet, as much as two thousand years ago the power of steam was not only observed, but an ingenius toy was actually made and put in motion by it, at Alexandria in Egypt.

6. Probably *Encyclopaedia Americana: A Popular Dictionary of Arts, Sciences, Literature, History, Politics and Biography*, edited by Francis Lieber et al. (Philadelphia: Lea & Blanchard, 1849).
7. "Two women will be grinding at the mill; one will be taken and one left" (Matthew 24:41).

What appears strange is, that neither the inventor of the toy, nor any one else, for so long a time afterwards, should perceive that steam would move *useful* machinery as well as a toy.

April 6, 1858

"House Divided" Speech at Springfield, Illinois

The Speech, immediately succeeding, was delivered, June 16, 1858 at Springfield Illinois, at the close of the Republican State convention held at that time and place; and by which convention Mr. Lincoln had been named as their candidate for U. S. Senator.

Senator Douglas was not present.[1]

Mr. President and Gentlemen of the Convention.

If we could first know *where* we are, and *whither* we are tending, we could then better judge *what* to do, and *how* to do it.

We are now far into the *fifth* year, since a policy was initiated, with the *avowed* object, and *confident* promise, of putting an end to slavery agitation.

Under the operation of that policy, that agitation has not only, *not ceased*, but has *constantly augmented*.

In *my* opinion, it *will* not cease, until a *crisis* shall have been reached, and passed.

"A house divided against itself cannot stand."

I believe this government cannot endure, permanently half *slave* and half *free*.

I do not expect the Union to be *dissolved*—I do not expect the house to *fall*—but I *do* expect it will cease to be divided.

It will become *all* one thing, or *all* the other.

Either the *opponents* of slavery, will arrest the further spread of it, and place it where the public mind shall rest in the belief that it is in course of ultimate extinction; or its *advocates* will push it forward, till it shall become alike lawful in *all* the States, *old* as well as *new*—*North* as well as *South*.

Have we no *tendency* to the latter condition?

Let any one who doubts, carefully contemplate that now almost complete legal combination—piece of *machinery* so to speak—compounded of the Nebraska doctrine, and the Dred Scott decision. Let him consider not only *what work* the machinery is adapted to do, and *how well* adapted; but also, let him study the *history* of its construction, and trace, if he can, or rather *fail*, if he can, to trace the evidences of design, and concert of action, among its chief bosses, from the beginning.

The new year of 1854 found slavery excluded from more than half the States by State Constitutions, and from most of the national territory by Congressional prohibition.

Four days later, commenced the struggle, which ended in repealing that Congressional prohibition.

---

1. This preface and the ones that appear in the Lincoln-Douglas debates were written by Lincoln in a scrapbook he kept of newspaper clippings of the debates.

This opened all the national territory to slavery; and was the first point gained.

But, so far, *Congress* only, had acted; and an *indorsement* by the people, *real* or apparent, was indispensable, to *save* the point already gained, and give chance for more.

This necessity had not been overlooked; but had been provided for, as well as might be, in the notable argument of "*squatter sovereignty*," otherwise called "*sacred right of self government*," which latter phrase, though expressive of the only rightful basis of any government, was so perverted in this attempted use of it as to amount to just this: That if any *one* man, choose to enslave *another*, no *third* man shall be allowed to object.

That argument was incorporated into the Nebraska bill itself, in the language which follows: "*It being the true intent and meaning of this act not to legislate slavery into any Territory or state, nor to exclude it therefrom; but to leave the people thereof perfectly free to form and regulate their domestic institutions in their own way, subject only to the Constitution of the United States.*"

Then opened the roar of loose declamation in favor of "Squatter Sovereignty," and "Sacred right of self government."

"But," said opposition members, "let us be more *specific*—let us *amend* the bill so as to expressly declare that the people of the territory *may* exclude slavery." "Not we," said the friends of the measure; and down they voted the amendment.

While the Nebraska bill was passing through congress, a *law case*, involving the question of a negroe's freedom, by reason of his owner having voluntarily taken him first into a free state and then a territory covered by the congressional prohibition, and held him as a slave, for a long time in each, was passing through the U.S. Circuit Court for the District of Missouri; and both Nebraska bill and law suit were brought to a decision in the same month of May, 1854. The negroe's name was "Dred Scott," which name now designates the decision finally made in the case.

Before the *then* next Presidential election, the law case came *to*, and was argued *in* the Supreme Court of the United States; but the *decision* of it was deferred until *after* the election. Still, *before* the election, Senator Trumbull, on the floor of the Senate, requests the leading advocate of the Nebraska bill to state *his opinion* whether the people of a territory can constitutionally exclude slavery from their limits; and the latter answers, "That is a question for the Supreme Court."

The election came. Mr. Buchanan was elected, and the *indorsement*, such as it was, secured. That was the *second* point gained. The indorsement, however, fell short of a clear popular majority by nearly four hundred thousand votes, and so, perhaps, was not overwhelmingly reliable and satisfactory.

The *outgoing* President,[2] in his last annual message, as impressively as possible *echoed back* upon the people the *weight* and *authority* of the indorsement.

2. Franklin Pierce.

The Supreme Court met again; *did not* announce their decision, but ordered a re-argument.

The Presidential inauguration came, and still no decision of the court; but the *incoming* President, in his inaugural address, fervently exhorted the people to abide by the forthcoming decision, *whatever it might be.*

Then, in a few days, came the decision.

The reputed author of the Nebraska bill finds an early occasion to make a speech at this capitol indorsing the Dred Scott Decision, and vehemently denouncing all opposition to it.

The new President, too, seizes the early occasion of the Silliman letter to *indorse* and strongly *construe* that decision, and to express his *astonishment* that any different view had ever been entertained.

At length a squabble springs up between the President and the author of the Nebraska bill, on the *mere* question of *fact*, whether the Lecompton constitution was or was not, in any just sense, made by the people of Kansas; and in that squabble the latter declares that all he wants is a fair vote for the people, and that he *cares* not whether slavery be voted *down* or voted *up.* I do not understand his declaration that he cares not whether slavery be voted down or voted up, to be intended by him other than as an *apt definition* of the *policy* he would impress upon the public mind—the *principle* for which he declares he has suffered much, and is ready to suffer to the end.

And well may he cling to that principle. If he has any parental feeling, well may he cling to it. That principle, is the only *shred* left of his original Nebraska doctrine. Under the Dred Scott decision, "squatter sovereignty" squatted out of existence, tumbled down like temporary scaffolding—like the mould at the foundry served through one blast and fell back into loose sand—helped to carry an election, and then was kicked to the winds. His late *joint* struggle with the Republicans, against the Lecompton Constitution, involves nothing of the original Nebraska doctrine. That struggle was made on a point, the right of a people to make their own constitution, upon which he and the Republicans have never differed.

The several points of the Dred Scott decision, in connection with Senator Douglas' "care not" policy, constitute the piece of machinery, in its *present* state of advancement. This was the third point gained.

The *working* points of that machinery are:

First, that no negro slave, imported as such from Africa, and no descendant of such slave can ever be a *citizen* of any State, in the sense of that term as used in the Constitution of the United States.

This point is made in order to deprive the negro, in every possible event, of the benefit of this provision of the United States Constitution, which declares that—

"The citizens of each State shall be entitled to all privileges and immunities of citizens in the several States."

Secondly, that "subject to the Constitution of the United States," neither *Congress* nor a *Territorial Legislature* can exclude slavery from any United States territory.

This point is made in order that individual men may *fill up* the territories with slaves, without danger of losing them as property, and thus to enhance the chances of *permanency* to the institution through all the future.

Thirdly, that whether the holding a negro in actual slavery in a free State, makes him free, as against the holder, the United States courts will not decide, but will leave to be decided by the courts of any slave State the negro may be forced into by the master.

This point is made, not to be pressed *immediately*; but, if acquiesced in for a while, and apparently *indorsed* by the people at an election, *then* to sustain the logical conclusion that what Dred Scott's master might lawfully do with Dred Scott, in the free State of Illinois, every other master may lawfully do with any other *one*, or one *thousand* slaves, in Illinois, or in any other free State.

Auxiliary to all this, and working hand in hand with it, the Nebraska doctrine, or what is left of it, is to *educate* and *mould* public opinion, at least *Northern* public opinion, to not *care* whether slavery is voted *down* or voted *up*.

This shows exactly where we now *are*; and *partially* also, whither we are tending.

It will throw additional light on the latter, to go back, and run the mind over the string of historical facts already stated. Several things will *now* appear less *dark* and *mysterious* than they did *when* they were transpiring. The people were to be left "perfectly free" "subject only to the Constitution." What the *Constitution* had to do with it, outsiders could not *then* see. Plainly enough *now*, it was an exactly fitted *niche*, for the Dred Scott decision to afterwards come in, and declare the *perfect freedom* of the people, to be just no freedom at all.

Why was the amendment, expressly declaring the right of the people to exclude slavery, voted down? Plainly enough *now*, the adoption of it, would have spoiled the niche for the Dred Scott decision.

Why was the court decision held up? Why, even a Senator's individual opinion withheld, till *after* the Presidential election? Plainly enough *now*, the speaking out *then* would have damaged the *"perfectly free"* argument upon which the election was to be carried.

Why the *outgoing* President's felicitation on the indorsement? Why the delay of a reargument? Why the incoming President's *advance* exhortation in favor of the decision?

These things *look* like the cautious *patting* and *petting* a spirited horse, preparatory to mounting him, when it is dreaded that he may give the rider a fall.

And why the hasty after indorsements of the decision by the President and others?

We can not absolutely *know* that all these exact adaptations are the result of preconcert. But when we see a lot of framed timbers, different portions of which we know have been gotten out at different times and places and by different workmen—Stephen, Franklin, Roger and James,[3] for instance—and when we see these timbers joined together, and see they exactly make the frame of a house or a mill, all the tenons and mortices exactly fitting, and all the lengths and proportions of the different pieces exactly adapted to their respective places, and not a piece too many or too few—not omitting even scaffolding—or, if a single piece be

---

3. Senator Stephen A. Douglas, President Franklin Pierce, Chief Justice Roger B. Taney, and President James Buchanan.

lacking, we can see the place in the frame exactly fitted and prepared to yet bring such piece in—in *such* a case, we find it impossible to not *believe* that Stephen and Franklin and Roger and James all understood one another from the beginning, and all worked upon a common *plan* or *draft* drawn up before the first lick was struck.

It should not be overlooked that, by the Nebraska bill, the people of a *State* as well as *Territory*, were to be left *"perfectly free"* *"subject only to the Constitution."*

Why mention a *State?* They were legislating for *territories*, and not *for* or *about* States. Certainly the people of a State *are* and *ought to be* subject to the Constitution of the United States; but why is mention of this *lugged* into this merely *territorial* law? Why are the people of a *territory* and the people of a *state* therein *lumped* together, and their relation to the Constitution therein treated as being *precisely* the same?

While the opinion of *the Court*, by Chief Justice Taney, in the Dred Scott case, and the separate opinions of all the concurring Judges, expressly declare that the Constitution of the United States neither permits Congress nor a Territorial legislature to exclude slavery from any United States territory, they all *omit* to declare whether or not the same Constitution permits a *state*, or the people of a State, to exclude it.

Possibly, this was a mere *omission*; but who can be *quite* sure, if McLean or Curtis had sought to get into the opinion a declaration of unlimited power in the people of a *state* to exclude slavery from their limits, just as Chase and Macy[4] sought to get such declaration, in behalf of the people of a territory, into the Nebraska bill—I ask, who can be quite *sure* that it would not have been voted down, in the one case, as it had been in the other.

The nearest approach to the point of declaring the power of a State over slavery, is made by Judge Nelson.[5] He approaches it more than once, using the precise idea, and *almost* the language too, of the Nebraska act. On one occasion his exact language is, "except in cases where the power is restrained by the Constitution of the United States, the law of the State is supreme over the subject of slavery within its jurisdiction."

In what *cases* the power of the *states is* so restrained by the U.S. Constitution, is left an *open* question, precisely as the same question, as to the restraint on the power of the *territories* was left open in the Nebraska act. Put *that* and *that* together, and we have another nice little niche, which we may, ere long, see filled with another Supreme Court decision, declaring that the Constitution of the United States does not permit a *state* to exclude slavery from its limits.

And this may especially be expected if the doctrine of "care not whether slavery be voted *down* or voted *up*," shall gain upon the public mind sufficiently to give promise that such a decision can be maintained when made.

Such a decision is all that slavery now lacks of being alike lawful in all the States.

---

4. Daniel Macy (1840–1864), representative from Indiana. Salmon P. Chase (1808–1873), senator from Ohio.
5. Samuel Nelson (1792–1873), Supreme Court justice and New York Democrat, wrote a concurring opinion in the *Dred Scott* decision in which he focused on the point that Missouri could make up its own mind about the status of blacks in its jurisdiction. Other justices on the court wanted a more strongly proslavery statement, which they got from Taney.

Welcome or unwelcome, such decision *is* probably coming, and will soon be upon us, unless the power of the present political dynasty shall be met and overthrown.

We shall *lie down* pleasantly dreaming that the people of *Missouri* are on the verge of making their State *free*; and we shall *awake* to the *reality*, instead, that the *Supreme* Court has made *Illinois* a *slave* State.

To meet and overthrow the power of that dynasty, is the work now before all those who would prevent that consummation.

That is *what* we have to do.

But *how* can we best do it?

There are those who denounce us *openly* to their *own* friends, and yet whisper *us softly*, that *Senator Douglas* is the *aptest* instrument there is, with which to effect that object. *They* do *not* tell us, nor has *he* told us, that he *wishes* any such object to be effected. They wish us to *infer* all, from the facts, that he now has a little quarrel with the present head of the dynasty; and that he has regularly voted with us, on a single point, upon which, he and we, have never differed.

They remind us that *he* is a very *great man*, and that the largest of *us* are very small ones. Let this be granted. But "a *living dog* is better than a *dead lion*."[6] Judge Douglas, if not a *dead* lion *for this work*, is at least a *caged* and *toothless* one. How can he oppose the advances of slavery? He don't *care* anything about it. His avowed *mission is impressing* the "public heart" to *care* nothing about it.

A leading Douglas Democratic newspaper thinks Douglas' superior talent will be needed to resist the revival of the African slave trade.

Does Douglas believe an effort to revive that trade is approaching? He has not said so. Does he *really* think so? But if it is, how can he resist it? For years he has labored to prove it a *sacred right* of white men to take negro slaves into the new territories. Can he possibly show that it is *less* a sacred right to *buy* them where they can be bought cheapest? And, unquestionably they can be bought *cheaper in Africa* than in *Virginia*.

He has done all in his power to reduce the whole question of slavery to one of a mere *right of property*; and as such, how can *he* oppose the foreign slave trade—how can he refuse that trade in that "property" shall be "perfectly free"—unless he does it as a *protection* to the home production? And as the home *producers* will probably not *ask* the protection, he will be wholly without a ground of opposition.

Senator Douglas holds, we know, that a man may rightfully be *wiser today* than he was *yesterday*—that he may rightfully *change* when he finds himself wrong.

But, can we for that reason, run ahead, and *infer* that he *will* make any particular change, of which he, himself, has given no intimation? Can we *safely* base *our* action upon any such *vague* inference?

Now, as ever, I wish to not *misrepresent* Judge Douglas' *position*, question his *motives*, or do ought that can be personally offensive to him.

Whenever, *if ever*, he and we can come together on *principle* so that *our great cause* may have assistance from *his great ability*, I hope to have interposed no adventitious obstacle.

---

6. Ecclesiastes 9:4: "For to him that is joined to all the living there is hope: for a living dog is better than a dead lion."

But clearly, he is not *now* with us—he does not *pretend* to be—he does not *promise* to *ever* be.

Our cause, then, must be intrusted to, and conducted by its own undoubted friends—those whose hands are free, whose hearts are in the work—who *do care* for the result.

Two years ago the Republicans of the nation mustered over thirteen hundred thousand strong.

We did this under the single impulse of resistance to a common danger, with every external circumstance against us.

Of *strange, discordant,* and even, *hostile* elements, we gathered from the four winds, and *formed* and fought the battle through, under the constant hot fire of a disciplined, proud, and pampered enemy.

Did we brave all *then,* to *falter* now?—*now*—when that same enemy is *wavering,* dissevered and belligerent?

The result is not doubtful. We shall not fail—if we stand firm, we shall not fail.

Wise councils may *accelerate* or *mistakes delay* it, but, sooner or later the victory is *sure* to come.

June 16, 1858

Fragment on the Struggle against Slavery

I have never professed an indifference to the honors of official station; and were I to do so now, I should only make myself ridiculous. Yet I have never failed—do not now fail—to remember that in the republican cause there is a higher aim than that of mere office. I have not allowed myself to forget that the abolition of the Slave-trade by Great Brittain, was agitated a hundred years before it was a final success; that the measure had it's open fire-eating opponents; it's stealthy "dont care" opponents; it's dollar and cent opponents; it's inferior race opponents; its negro equality opponents; and its religion and good order opponents; that all these opponents got offices, and their adversaries got none. But I have also remembered that though they blazed, like tallow-candles for a century, at last they flickered in the socket, died out, stank in the dark for a brief season, and were remembered no more, even by the smell. School-boys know that Wilberforce, and Granville Sharpe,[1] helped that cause forward; but who can now name a single man who labored to retard it? Remembering these things I can not but regard it as possible that the higher object of this contest may not be completely attained within the term of my natural life. But I can not doubt either that it will come in due time. Even in this view, I am proud, in my passing speck of time, to contribute an humble mite to that glorious consummation, which my own poor eyes may not last to see.

ca. July 1858

---

1. William Wilberforce (1759–1833) and Granville Sharp (1735–1813), English reformers who led the campaign to abolish the British slave trade.

From Speech at Chicago, Illinois

The succeeding speech was delivered by Mr. Lincoln, on Saturday Evening, July 10, 1858, at Chicago, Illinois.

Senator Douglas was not present.[1]

* * *

What Is Popular Sovereignty?

Popular sovereignty! everlasting popular sovereignty! [Laughter and continued cheers.] Let us for a moment inquire into this vast matter of popular sovereignty. What is popular sovereignty? We recollect that at an early period in the history of this struggle, there was another name for this same thing—*Squatter Sovereignty.* It was not exactly Popular Sovereignty but Squatter Sovereignty. What do those terms mean? What do those terms mean when used now? And vast credit is taken by our friend, the Judge[2], in regard to his support of it, when he declares the last years of his life have been, and all the future years of his life shall be, devoted to this matter of popular sovereignty. What is it? Why, it is the sovereignty of the people! What was Squatter Sovereignty? I suppose if it had any significance at all it was the right of the people to govern themselves, to be sovereign of their own affairs while they were squatted down in a country not their own, while they had squatted on a territory that did not belong to them, in the sense that a State belongs to the people who inhabit it—when it belonged to the nation—such right to govern themselves was called "Squatter Sovereignty."

Now I wish you to mark. What has become of that Squatter Sovereignty? What has become of it? Can you get anybody to tell you now that the people of a territory have any authority to govern themselves, in regard to this mooted question of Slavery, before they form a State Constitution? No such thing at all, although there is a general running fire, and although there has been a hurrah made in every speech on that side, assuming that policy had given the people of a territory the right to govern themselves upon this question; yet the point is dodged. To-day it has been decided—no more than a year ago it was decided by the Supreme Court of the United States, and is insisted upon to-day, that the people of a territory have no right to exclude Slavery from a territory, that if any one man chooses to take slaves into a territory, all the rest of the people have no right to keep them out. This being so, and this decision being made one of the points that the Judge approved, and one in the approval of which he says he means to keep me down—put me down I should not say, for I have never been up. He says he is in favor of it, and sticks to it, and expects to win his battle on that decision, which says that there is no such thing as Squatter Sovereignty; but that any one man may take slaves into a territory, and all the other men in the territory may be opposed to it, and yet by reason of the constitution they cannot prohibit it. When

---

1. Lincoln's note in the debate's scrap book.
2. Stephen A. Douglas, Lincoln's opponent in the race in Illinois for the U.S. Senate.

that is so, how much is left of this vast matter of Squatter Sovereignty I should like to know?—(a voice)—"it has all gone."

When we get back, we get to the point of the right of the people to make a constitution. Kansas was settled, for example, in 1854. It was a territory yet, without having formed a Constitution, in a very regular way, for three years. All this time negro slavery could be taken in by any few individuals, and by that decision of the Supreme Court, which the Judge approves, all the rest of the people cannot keep it out; but when they come to make a Constitution they may say they will not have Slavery. But it is there; they are obliged to tolerate it in some way, and all experience shows that it will be so—for they will not take the negro slaves and absolutely deprive the owners of them. All experience shows this to be so. All that space of time that runs from the beginning of the settlement of the Territory until there is sufficiency of people to make a State Constitution—all that portion of time popular sovereignty is given up. The seal is absolutely put down upon it by the Court decision, and Judge Douglas puts his own upon the top of that, yet he is appealing to the people to give him vast credit for his devotion to popular sovereignty. (Applause.)

Again, when we get to the question of the right of the people to form a State Constitution as they please, to form it with Slavery or without Slavery—if that is anything new, I confess I don't know it. Has there ever been a time when anybody said that any other than the people of a Territory itself should form a Constitution? What is now in it, that Judge Douglas should have fought several years of his life, and pledged himself to fight all the remaining years of his life for? Can Judge Douglas find anybody on earth that said that anybody else should form a constitution for a people? (A voice, "Yes.") Well, I should like you to name him; I should like to know who he was. (Same voice—"John Calhoun.")[3]

Mr. Lincoln—No, sir, I never heard of even John Calhoun saying such a thing. He insisted on the same principle as Judge Douglas; but his mode of applying it in fact, was wrong. It is enough for my purpose to ask this crowd, when ever a Republican said anything against it? They never said anything against it, but they have constantly spoken for it; and whosoever will undertake to examine the platform, and the speeches of responsible men of the party, and of irresponsible men, too, if you please, will be unable to find one word from anybody in the Republican ranks, opposed to that Popular Sovereignty which Judge Douglas thinks that he has invented. [Applause.] I suppose that Judge Douglas will claim in a little while, that he is the inventor of the idea that the people should govern themselves: [cheers and laughter]; that nobody ever thought of such a thing until he brought it forward. We do remember, that in that old Declaration of Independence, it is said that "We hold these truths to be self-evident that all men are created equal; that they are endowed by their Creator with certain inalienable rights; that among these are life, liberty, and the pursuit of happiness; that to secure these rights, governments are instituted among men, deriving their just powers from the consent of the governed." There is the origin of Popular Sovereignty. [Loud applause].

3. Illinois Democrat (1806–1859), who in 1857 presided over the convention in Kansas that produced the proslavery Lecompton Constitution. (Not to be confused with Senator John C. Calhoun of South Carolina.)

Who, then, shall come in at this day and claim that he invented it. [Laughter and applause.]

* * *

Lincoln and Douglas

Gentlemen: I fear that I shall become tedious, (Go on, go on.) I leave this branch of the subject to take hold of another. I take up that part of Judge Douglas' speech in which he respectfully attended to me. [Laughter.]

Judge Douglas made two points upon my recent speech at Springfield. He says they are to be the issues of this campaign. The first one of these points he bases upon the language in a speech which I delivered at Springfield, which I believe I can quote correctly from memory. I said there that "we are now far into the fifth year since a policy was instituted for the avowed object and with the confident promise of putting an end to slavery agitation; under the operation of that policy, that agitation had only not ceased, but has constantly augmented."[4]—(A voice)—"That's the very language." "I believe it will not cease until a crisis shall have been reached and passed. A house divided against itself cannot stand. I believe this government cannot endure permanently half slave and half free." [Applause.] "I do not expect the Union to be dissolved,"—I am quoting from my speech—"I do not expect the house to fall, but I do expect it will cease to be divided. It will become all one thing or the other. Either the opponents of slavery will arrest the spread of it, and place it where the public mind shall rest in the belief that it is in the course of ultimate extinction, or its advocates will push it forward until it shall become alike lawful in all the States, North as well as South." [Good, good.]

What is the paragraph. In this paragraph which I have quoted in your hearing, and to which I ask the attention of all, Judge Douglas thinks he discovers great political heresy. I want your attention particularly to what he has inferred from it. He says I am in favor of making all the States of this Union uniform in all their internal regulations; that in all their domestic concerns I am in favor of making them entirely uniform. He draws this inference from the language I have quoted to you. He says that I am in favor of making war by the North upon the South for the extinction of slavery; that I am also in favor of inviting (as he expresses it) the South to a war upon the North, for the purpose of nationalizing slavery. Now, it is singular enough, if you will carefully read that passage over, that I did not say that I was in favor of anything in it. I only said what I expected would take place. I made a prediction only—it may have been a foolish one perhaps. I did not even say that I desired that slavery should be put in course of ultimate extinction. I do say so now, however, [great applause] so there need be no longer any difficulty about that. It may be written down in the great speech. [Applause and laughter.]

Gentlemen, Judge Douglas informed you that this speech of mine was probably carefully prepared. I admit that it was. I am not master of language; I have not a fine education; I am not capable of entering into a disquisition upon dialectics, as I believe you call it; but I do not believe

---

4. Reference to the battles between proslavery and free-state forces in Kansas, which had come to be known as Bleeding Kansas.

the language I employed bears any such construction as Judge Douglas put upon it. But I don't care about a quibble in regard to words. I know what I meant, and I will not leave this crowd in doubt, if I can explain it to them, what I really meant in the use of that paragraph.

I am not, in the first place, unaware that this Government has endured eighty-two years, half slave and half free. I know that. I am tolerably well acquainted with the history of the country, and I know that it has endured eighty-two years, half slave and half free. I *believe*—and that is what I meant to allude to there—I *believe* it has endured because, during all that time, until the introduction of the Nebraska Bill, the public mind did rest, all the time, in the belief that slavery was in course of ultimate extinction. ["Good!" "Good!" and applause.] That was what gave us the rest that we had through that period of eighty-two years; at least, so I believe. I have always hated slavery, I think as much as any Abolitionist. [Applause.] I have been an Old Line Whig. I have always hated it, but I have always been quiet about it until this new era of the introduction of the Nebraska Bill began. I always believed that everybody was against it, and that it was in course of ultimate extinction. (Pointing to Mr. Browning,[5] who stood near by.) Browning thought so; the great mass of the nation have rested in the belief that slavery was in course of ultimate extinction. They had reason so to believe.

The adoption of the Constitution and its attendant history led the people to believe so; and that such was the belief of the framers of the Constitution itself. Why did those old men, about the time of the adoption of the Constitution, decree that Slavery should not go into the new Territory, where it had not already gone? Why declare that within twenty years the African Slave Trade, by which slaves are supplied, might be cut off by Congress? Why were all these acts? I might enumerate more of these acts— but enough. What were they but a clear indication that the framers of the Constitution intended and expected the ultimate extinction of that institution. [Cheers.] And now, when I say, as I said in my speech that Judge Douglas has quoted from, when I say that I think the opponents of slavery will resist the farther spread of it, and place it where the public mind shall rest with the belief that it is in course of ultimate extinction, I only mean to say, that they will place it where the founders of this Government originally placed it.

I have said a hundred times, and I have now no inclination to take it back, that I believe there is no right, and ought to be no inclination in the people of the free States to enter into the slave States, and interfere with the question of slavery at all. I have said that always. Judge Douglas has heard me say it—if not quite a hundred times, at least as good as a hundred times; and when it is said that I am in favor of interfering with slavery where it exists, I know it is unwarranted by anything I have ever *intended*, and, as I believe, by anything I have ever *said*. If, by any means, I have ever used language which could fairly be so construed, (as, however, I believe I never have,) I now correct it.

[Here the shouts of the Seventh Ward Delegation[6] announced that they were coming in procession. They were received with enthusiastic cheers.]

---

5. Orville Browning, Illinois politician and Lincoln's close friend.
6. A group of some four hundred Lincoln supporters from Chicago's seventh ward.

So much, then, for the inference that Judge Douglas draws, that I am in favor of setting the sections at war with one another. I know that I never meant any such thing, and I believe that no fair mind can infer any such thing from anything I have ever said. ["Good," "good."]

Now in relation to his inference that I am in favor of a general consolidation of all the local institutions of the various States. I will attend to that for a little while, and try to inquire, if I can, how on earth it could be that any man could draw such an inference from anything I said. I have said, very many times, in Judge Douglas' hearing, that no man believed more than I in the principle of self-government; that it lies at the bottom of all my ideas of just government, from beginning to end.

* * *

* * * I think that the Republican party is made up of those who, as far as they can peaceably, will oppose the extension of slavery, and who will hope for its ultimate extinction. If they believe it is wrong in grasping up the new lands of the continent, and keeping them from the settlement of free white laborers, who want the land to bring up their families upon; if they are in earnest, although they may make a mistake, they will grow restless, and the time will come when they will come back again and re-organize, if not by the same name, at least upon the same principles as their party now has. It is better, then, to save the work while it is begun. You have done the labor; maintain it—keep it. If men choose to serve you, go with them; but as you have made up your organization upon principle, stand by it; for, as surely as God reigns over you, and has inspired your mind, and given you a sense of propriety, and continues to give you hope, so surely you will still cling to these ideas, and you will at last come back again after your wanderings, merely to do your work over again. [Loud applause.]

We were often—more than once at least—in the course of Judge Douglas' speech last night, reminded that this government was made for white men—that he believed it was made for white men. Well, that is putting it into a shape in which no one wants to deny it, but the Judge then goes into his passion for drawing inferences that are not warranted. I protest, now and forever, against that counterfeit logic which presumes that because I do not want a negro woman for a slave, I do necessarily want her for a wife. [Laughter and cheers.] My understanding is that I need not have her for either, but as God made us separate, we can leave one another alone and do one another much good thereby. There are white men enough to marry all the white women, and enough black men to marry all the black women, and in God's name let them be so married. The Judge regales us with the terrible enormities that take place by the mixture of races; that the inferior race bears the superior down. Why, Judge, if we do not let them get together in the Territories they won't mix there. [Immense applause.]

A voice—"Three cheers for Lincoln." [The cheers were given with a hearty good will.]

Mr. Lincoln—I should say at least that that is a self evident truth.

Now, it happens that we meet together once every year, sometime about the 4th of July, for some reason or other. These 4th of July gatherings I suppose have their uses. If you will indulge me, I will state what I suppose to be some of them.

We are now a mighty nation, we are thirty—or about thirty millions of people, and we own and inhabit about one-fifteenth part of the dry land of the whole earth. We run our memory back over the pages of history for about eighty-two years and we discover that we were then a very small people in point of numbers, vastly inferior to what we are now, with a vastly less extent of country,—with vastly less of everything we deem desirable among men,—we look upon the change as exceedingly advantageous to us and to our posterity, and we fix upon something that happened away back, as in some way or other being connected with this rise of prosperity. We find a race of men living in that day whom we claim as our fathers and grandfathers; they were iron men, they fought for the principle that they were contending for; and we understood that by what they then did it has followed that the degree of prosperity that we now enjoy has come to us. We hold this annual celebration to remind ourselves of all the good done in this process of time of how it was done and who did it, and how we are historically connected with it; and we go from these meetings in better humor with ourselves—we feel more attached the one to the other, and more firmly bound to the country we inhabit. In every way we are better men in the age, and race, and country in which we live for these celebrations. But after we have done all this we have not yet reached the whole. There is something else connected with it. We have besides these men—descended by blood from our ancestors—among us perhaps half our people who are not descendants at all of these men, they are men who have come from Europe—German, Irish, French and Scandinavian—men that have come from Europe themselves, or whose ancestors have come hither and settled here, finding themselves our equals in all things. If they look back through this history to trace their connection with those days by blood, they find they have none, they cannot carry themselves back into that glorious epoch and make themselves feel that they are part of us, but when they look through that old Declaration of Independence they find that those old men say that "We hold these truths to be self-evident, that all men are created equal," and then they feel that that moral sentiment taught in that day evidences their relation to those men, that it is the father of all moral principle in them, and that they have a right to claim it as though they were blood of the blood, and flesh of the flesh of the men who wrote that Declaration, (loud and long continued applause) and so they are. That is the electric cord in that Declaration that links the hearts of patriotic and liberty-loving men together, that will link those patriotic hearts as long as the love of freedom exists in the minds of men throughout the world. [Applause.]

Now, sirs, for the purpose of squaring things with this idea of "don't care if slavery is voted up or voted down," for sustaining the Dred Scott decision [A voice—"Hit him again"], for holding that the Declaration of Independence did not mean anything at all, we have Judge Douglas giving his exposition of what the Declaration of Independence means, and we have him saying that the people of America are equal to the people of England. According to his construction, you Germans are not connected with it. Now I ask you in all soberness, if all these things, if indulged in, if ratified, if confirmed and endorsed, if taught to our children, and repeated to them, do not tend to rub out the sentiment of liberty in the country, and to transform this Government into a government of some other form.

Those arguments that are made, that the inferior race are to be treated with as much allowance as they are capable of enjoying; that as much is to be done for them as their condition will allow. What are these arguments? They are the arguments that kings have made for enslaving the people in all ages of the world. You will find that all the arguments in favor of king-craft were of this class; they always bestrode the necks of the people, not that they wanted to do it, but because the people were better off for being ridden. That is their argument, and this argument of the Judge is the same old serpent that says you work and I eat, you toil and I will enjoy the fruits of it. Turn in whatever way you will—whether it come from the mouth of a King, an excuse for enslaving the people of his country, or from the mouth of men of one race as a reason for enslaving the men of another race, it is all the same old serpent, and I hold if that course of argumentation that is made for the purpose of convincing the public mind that we should not care about this, should be granted, it does not stop with the negro. I should like to know if taking this old Declaration of Independence, which declares that all men are equal upon principle and making exceptions to it where will it stop. If one man says it does not mean a negro, why not another say it does not mean some other man? If that declaration is not the truth, let us get the Statute book, in which we find it and tear it out! Who is so bold as to do it! [Voices—"me" "no one," &c.] If it is not true let us tear it out! [cries of "no, no,"] let us stick to it then, [cheers] let us stand firmly by it then. [Applause.]

It may be argued that there are certain conditions that make necessities and impose them upon us, and to the extent that a necessity is imposed upon a man he must submit to it. I think that was the condition in which we found ourselves when we established this government. We had slavery among us, we could not get our constitution unless we permitted them to remain in slavery, we could not secure the good we did secure if we grasped for more, and having by necessity submitted to that much, it does not destroy the principle that is the charter of our liberties. Let that charter stand as our standard.

My friend has said to me that I am a poor hand to quote Scripture. I will try it again, however. It is said in one of the admonitions of the Lord, "As your Father in Heaven is perfect, be ye also perfect." The Savior, I suppose, did not expect that any human creature could be perfect as the Father in Heaven; but He said, "As your Father in Heaven is perfect, be ye also perfect."[7] He set that up as a standard, and he who did most towards reaching that standard, attained the highest degree of moral perfection. So I say in relation to the principle that all men are created equal, let it be as nearly reached as we can. If we cannot give freedom to every creature, let us do nothing that will impose slavery upon any other creature. [Applause.] Let us then turn this government back into the channel in which the framers of the Constitution originally placed it. Let us stand firmly by each other. If we do not do so we are turning in the contrary direction, that our friend Judge Douglas proposes—not intentionally—as working in the traces tend to make this one universal slave nation. [A voice—"that is so."] He is one that runs in that direction, and as such I resist him.

---

7. Cf. Matthew 5:48.

My friends, I have detained you about as long as I desired to do, and I have only to say, let us discard all this quibbling about this man and the other man—this race and that race and the other race being inferior, and therefore they must be placed in an inferior position—discarding our standard that we have left us. Let us discard all these things, and unite as one people throughout this land, until we shall once more stand up declaring that all men are created equal.

My friends, I could not, without launching off upon some new topic, which would detain you too long, continue tonight. [Cries of "go on."] I thank you for this most extensive audience that you have furnished me to-night. I leave you, hoping that the lamp of liberty will burn in your bosoms until there shall no longer be a doubt that all men are created free and equal.

July 10, 1858

On Slavery and Democracy

As I would not be a *slave*, so I would not be a *master*. This expresses my idea of democracy. Whatever differs from this, to the extent of the difference, is no democracy.

ca. August 1, 1858

From Portion of Speech at Edwardsville, Illinois

✲   ✲   ✲

The difference between the Republican and the Democratic parties on the leading issue of this contest, as I understand it, is, that the former consider slavery a moral, social and political wrong, while the latter *do not* consider it either a moral, social or political wrong; and the action of each, as respects the growth of the country and the expansion of our population, is squared to meet these views. I will not allege that the Democratic party consider slavery morally, socially and politically *right*; though their tendency to that view has, in my opinion, been constant and unmistakable for the past five years. I prefer to take, as the accepted maxim of the party, the idea put forth by Judge Douglas, that he "don't care whether slavery is voted down or voted up." I am quite willing to believe that many Democrats would prefer that slavery be always voted down, and I am sure that some prefer that it be always "voted up"; but I have a right to insist that their action, especially if it be their *constant and unvarying* action, shall determine their ideas and preferences on the subject. Every measure of the Democratic party of late years, bearing directly or indirectly on the slavery question, has corresponded with this notion of utter indifference whether slavery or freedom shall outrun in the race of empire across the Pacific—every measure, I say, up to the Dred Scott decision, where, it seems to me, the idea is boldly suggested that slavery is *better* than freedom. The Republican party, on the contrary, hold that this government was

instituted to secure the blessings of freedom, and that slavery is an unqualified evil to the negro, to the white man, to the soil, and to the State.
Regarding it an evil, they will not molest it in the States where it exists;
they will not overlook the constitutional guards which our forefathers have
placed around it; they will do nothing which can give proper offence to
those who hold slaves by legal sanction; but they will use every constitutional method to prevent the evil from becoming larger and involving more
negroes, more white men, more soil, and more States in its deplorable consequences. They will, if possible, place it where the public mind shall rest
in the belief that it is in course of ultimate peaceable extinction, in God's
own good time. And to this end they will, if possible, restore the government to the policy of the fathers—the policy of preserving the new territories from the baneful influence of human bondage, as the Northwestern
territories were sought to be preserved by the ordinance of 1787 and the
compromise act of 1820. They will oppose, in all its length and breadth,
the modern Democratic idea that slavery is as good as freedom, and ought
to have room for expansion all over the continent, if people can be found to
carry it. All, or very nearly all, of Judge Douglas' arguments about "Popular
Sovereignty," as he calls it, are logical if you admit that slavery is as good
and as right as freedom; and not one of them is worth a rush if you deny it.
This is the difference, as I understand it, between the Republican and the
Democratic parties; and I ask the gentleman, and all of you, whether his
question is not satisfactorily answered.—[Cries of "Yes, yes."]

*   *   *

September 11, 1858

On Pro-Slavery Theology

Suppose it is true, that the negro is inferior to the white, in the gifts of
nature; is it not the exact reverse justice that the white should, for that
reason, take from the negro, any part of the little which has been given
him? "*Give* to him that is needy" is the christian rule of charity; but "Take
from him that is needy" is the rule of slavery.

Pro-Slavery Theology

The sum of pro-slavery theology seems to be this: "Slavery is not universally *right*, nor yet universally *wrong*; it is better for *some* people to be
slaves; and, in such cases, it is the Will of God that they be such."

Certainly there is no contending against the Will of God; but still there
is some difficulty in ascertaining, and applying it, to particular cases. For
instance we will suppose the Rev. Dr. Ross[1] has a slave named Sambo, and
the question is "Is it the Will of God that Sambo shall remain a slave, or
be set free?" The Almighty gives no audable answer to the question, and
his revelation—the Bible—gives none—or, at most, none but such as
admits of a squabble, as to it's meaning. No one thinks of asking Sambo's

---

1. Apparent reference to Frederick A. Ross (1796–1883), Alabama Presbyterian clergyman and
   author of *Slavery Ordained by God* (1857).

opinion on it. So, at last, it comes to this, that *Dr. Ross* is to decide the question. And while he considers it, he sits in the shade, with gloves on his hands, and subsists on the bread that Sambo is earning in the burning sun. If he decides that God Wills Sambo to continue a slave, he thereby retains his own comfortable position; but if he decides that God will's Sambo to be free, he thereby has to walk out of the shade, throw off his gloves, and delve for his own bread. Will Dr. Ross be actuated by that perfect impartiality, which has ever been considered most favorable to correct decisions?

But, slavery is good for some people!!! As a *good* thing, slavery is strikingly peculiar, in this, that it is the only good thing which no man ever seeks the good of, *for himself.*

Nonsense! Wolves devouring lambs, not because it is good for their own greedy maws, but because it is good for the lambs!!!

October 1, 1858?

From The Lincoln-Douglas Debates

From *First Lincoln-Douglas Debate, Ottawa, Illinois*

FIRST JOINT DEBATE:—AUGUST 21– 1858, AT OTTAWA, ILLINOIS.
SENATOR DOUGLAS' TWO SPEECHES TAKEN FROM THE CHICAGO TIMES;
MR. LINCOLN'S, FROM THE PRESS & TRIBUNE.

FROM MR. DOUGLAS'S SPEECH

[Douglas portrays Lincoln as the leader of an antislavery cabal that in 1854 transformed the Whig Party into what Douglas calls "Black Republican" Party. Douglas reads an excerpt from Lincoln's "House Divided" speech and says:]

* * *

Mr. Lincoln, in the extract from which I have read, says that this Government cannot endure permanently in the same condition in which it was made by its framers—divided into free and slave States. He says that it has existed for about seventy years thus divided, and yet he tells you that it cannot endure permanently on the same principles and in the same relative condition in which our fathers made it. ("Neither can it.") Why can it not exist divided into free and slave States? Washington, Jefferson, Franklin,[1] Madison, Hamilton, Jay, and the great men of that day, made this Government divided into free States and slave States, and left each State perfectly free to do as it pleased on the subject of slavery. ("Right, right.") Why can it not exist on the same principles on which our fathers made it? ("It can.") They knew when they framed the Constitution that in a country as wide and broad as this, with such a variety of climate, production and interest, the people necessarily required different laws and institutions in different localities. They knew that the laws and regulations

---

1. Benjamin Franklin (1706–1790), political leader, scientist, and signer of the Declaration of Independence. Jay: John Jay (1745–1829), a delegate to the First Continental Congress and the first chief justice of the United States.

which would suit the granite hills of New Hampshire would be unsuited to the rice plantations of South Carolina, ("right, right,") and they, therefore, provided that each State should retain its own Legislature, and its own sovereignty with the full and complete power to do as it pleased within its own limits, in all that was local and not national. (Applause.) One of the reserved rights of the States, was the right to regulate the relations between Master and Servant, on the slavery question. At the time the Constitution was formed, there were thirteen States in the Union, twelve of which were slaveholding States and one a free State. Suppose this doctrine of uniformity preached by Mr. Lincoln, that the States should all be free or all be slave had prevailed and what would have been the result? Of course, the twelve slaveholding States would have overruled the one free State, and slavery would have been fastened by a Constitutional provision on every inch of the American Republic, instead of being left as our fathers wisely left it, to each State to decide for itself. ("Good, good," and three cheers for Douglas.) Here I assert that uniformity in the local laws and institutions of the different States is neither possible or desirable. If uniformity had been adopted when the government was established, it must inevitably have been the uniformity of slavery everywhere, or else the uniformity of negro citizenship and negro equality everywhere.

We are told by Lincoln that he is utterly opposed to the Dred Scott decision, and will not submit to it, for the reason that he says it deprives the negro of the rights and privileges of citizenship. (Laughter and applause.) That is the first and main reason which he assigns for his warfare on the Supreme Court of the United States and its decision. I ask you, are you in favor of conferring upon the negro the rights and privileges of citizenship? ("No, no.") Do you desire to strike out of our State Constitution that clause which keeps slaves and free negroes out of the State, and allow the free negroes to flow in, ("never,") and cover your prairies with black settlements? Do you desire to turn this beautiful State into a free negro colony, ("no, no,") in order that when Missouri abolishes slavery she can send one hundred thousand emancipated slaves into Illinois, to become citizens and voters, on an equality with yourselves? ("Never," "no.") If you desire negro citizenship, if you desire to allow them to come into the State and settle with the white man, if you desire them to vote on an equality with yourselves, and to make them eligible to office, to serve on juries, and to adjudge your rights, then support Mr. Lincoln and the Black Republican party, who are in favor of the citizenship of the negro. ("Never, never.") For one, I am opposed to negro citizenship in any and every form. (Cheers.) I believe this government was made on the white basis. ("Good.") I believe it was made by white men, for the benefit of white men and their posterity for ever, and I am in favor of confining citizenship to white men, men of European birth and descent, instead of conferring it upon negroes, Indians and other inferior races. ("Good for you." "Douglas forever.")

Mr. Lincoln, following the example and lead of all the little Abolition orators, who go around and lecture in the basements of schools and churches, reads from the Declaration of Independence, that all men were created equal, and then asks how can you deprive a negro of that equality which God and the Declaration of Independence awards to him. He and they maintain that negro equality is guarantied by the laws of God, and that it is asserted in the Declaration of Independence. If they think so, of course they have a right to say so, and so vote. I do not question Mr. Lincoln's conscientious belief that the negro was made his equal, and hence is his brother, (laughter,) but for my own part, I do not regard the negro as my equal, and positively deny that he is my brother or any kin to me whatever. ("Never." "Hit him again," and cheers.) Lincoln has evidently learned by heart Parson Lovejoy's[2] catechism. (Laughter and applause.) He can repeat it as well as Farnsworth, and he is worthy of a medal from father Giddings and Fred Douglass[3] for his Abolitionism. (Laughter.) He holds that the negro was born his equal and yours, and that he was endowed with equality by the Almighty, and that no human law can deprive him of these rights which were guarantied to him by the Supreme ruler of the Universe. Now, I do not believe that the Almighty ever intended the negro to be the equal of the white man. ("Never, never.") If he did, he has been a long time demonstrating the fact. (Cheers.) For thousands of years the negro has been a race upon the earth, and during all that time, in all latitudes and climates, wherever he has wandered or been taken, he has been inferior to the race which he has there met. He belongs to an inferior race, and must always occupy an inferior position. ("Good," "that's so," &c.) I do not hold that because the negro is our inferior that therefore he ought to be a slave. By no means can such a conclusion be drawn from what I have said. On the contrary, I hold that humanity and Christianity both require that the negro shall have and enjoy every right, every privilege, and every immunity consistent with the safety of the society in which he lives. (That's so.) On that point, I presume, there can be no diversity of opinion. You and I are bound to extend to our inferior and dependent being every right, every privilege, every facility and immunity consistent with the public good. The question then arises what rights and privileges are consistent with the public good. This is a question which each State and each Territory must decide for itself—Illinois has decided it for herself. We have provided that the negro shall not be a slave, and we have also provided that he shall not be a citizen, but protect him in his civil rights, in his life, his person and his property, only depriving him of all political rights whatsoever, and refusing to put him on an equality with the white man. ("Good.") That policy of Illinois is satisfactory to the Democratic party and to me, and if it were to the Republicans, there would then be no question upon the subject; but the Republicans say that he ought to be made a citizen, and when he becomes a citizen he becomes your equal, with all your rights and privileges. ("He never shall.") They assert the Dred Scott decision to be monstrous because it denies that the negro is or can be a citizen under the Constitution. Now, I hold that Illinois had a right to abolish and prohibit slavery as she did, and I hold that Kentucky has the same right to continue and protect slavery that Illinois

2. Owen Lovejoy (1811–1864), brother of the antislavery martyr Elijah Lovejoy and conductor on the Underground Railroad. A longtime Congregational minister, he turned to antislavery politics and served as a Republican congressman from Illinois from 1857 until his death.
3. Frederick Douglass (1818–1895) escaped from slavery in 1838 and became established in the North as the era's leading African American abolitionist. John Franklin Farnsworth (1820–1897), a seven-term Republican U.S. Representative from Illinois. Joshua Giddings (1795–1864), a prominent antislavery politician who was a U.S. Representative from Ohio from 1838 to 1859.

had to abolish it. I hold that New York had as much right to abolish slavery as Virginia has to continue it, and that each and every State of this Union is a sovereign power, with the right to do as it pleases upon this question of slavery, and upon all its domestic institutions. * * * Why should Illinois be at war with Missouri, or Kentucky with Ohio, or Virginia with New York, merely because their institutions differ? Our fathers intended that our institutions should differ. They knew that the North and the South having different climates, productions and interests, required different institutions. This doctrine of Mr. Lincoln's of uniformity among the institutions of the different States is a new doctrine, never dreamed of by Washington, Madison, or the framers of this Government. Mr. Lincoln and the Republican party set themselves up as wiser than these men who made this government, which has flourished for seventy years under the principle of popular sovereignty, recognizing the right of each State to do as it pleased. Under that principle, we have grown from a nation of three or four millions to a nation of about thirty millions of people; we have crossed the Allegheny mountains and filled up the whole North West, turning the prairie into a garden, and building up churches and schools, thus spreading civilization and christianity where before there was nothing but savage-barbarism. Under that principle we have become from a feeble nation, the most powerful on the face of the earth, and if we only adhere to that principle, we can go forward increasing in territory, in power, in strength and in glory until the Republic of America shall be the North Star that shall guide the friends of freedom throughout the civilized world. ("Long may you live," and great applause.) And why can we not adhere to the great principle of self-government government, upon which our institutions were originally based. ("We can.") I believe that this new doctrine preached by Mr. Lincoln and his party will dissolve the Union if it succeeds. They are trying to array all the Northern States in one body against the South, to excite a sectional war between the free States and the slave States, in order that the one or the other may be driven to the wall.

*   *   *

FROM MR. LINCOLN'S REPLY

Mr. Lincoln then came forward and was greeted with loud and protracted cheers from fully two-thirds of the audience. This was admitted by the Douglas men on the platform. It was some minutes before he could make himself heard, even by those on the stand. At last he said:

MY FELLOW-CITIZENS: When a man hears himself somewhat misrepresented, it provokes him—at least, I find it so with myself; but when the misrepresentation becomes very gross and palpable, it is more apt to amuse him. [Laughter.] * * *

*   *   *

[Lincoln denies Douglas's charge that he and others conspired to "Abolitionize" the Whig Party. Then Lincoln reads a long passage from his 1854 speech in the Kansas Nebraska Act (pp. 81–98 above) in which he declared that, while he opposed slavery on moral grounds, he did not envisage the possibility of social or political equality for blacks. Lincoln resumes:]

Now gentlemen, I don't want to read at any greater length, but this is the true complexion of all I have ever said in regard to the institution of slavery and the black race. This is the whole of it, and anything that argues me into his idea of perfect social and political equality with the negro, is but a specious and fantastic arrangement of words, by which a man can prove a horse chestnut to be a chestnut horse. [Laughter.] I will say here, while upon this subject, that I have no purpose directly or indirectly to interfere with the institution of slavery in the States where it exists. I believe I have no lawful right to do so, and I have no inclination to do so. I have no purpose to introduce political and social equality between the white and the black races. There is a physical difference between the two, which in my judgment will probably forever forbid their living together upon the footing of perfect equality, and inasmuch as it becomes a necessity that there must be a difference, I, as well as Judge Douglas, am in favor of the race to which I belong, having the superior position. I have never said anything to the contrary, but I hold that notwithstanding all this, there is no reason in the world why the negro is not entitled to all the natural rights enumerated in the Declaration of Independence, the right to life, liberty and the pursuit of happiness. [Loud cheers.] I hold that he is as much entitled to these as the white man. I agree with Judge Douglas he is not my equal in many respects—certainly not in color, perhaps not in moral or intellectual endowment. But in the right to eat the bread, without leave of anybody else, which his own hand earns, *he is my equal and the equal of Judge Douglas, and the equal of every living man.* [Great applause.]

Now I pass on to consider one or two more of these little follies. The Judge is wofully at fault about his early friend Lincoln being a "grocery keeper." [Laughter.] I don't know as it would be a great sin, if I had been, but he is mistaken. Lincoln never kept a grocery anywhere in the world. [Laughter.] It is true that Lincoln did work the latter part of one winter in a small still house, up at the head of a hollow. [Roars of laughter.] And so I think my friend, the Judge, is equally at fault when he charges me at the time when I was in Congress of having opposed our soldiers who were fighting in the Mexican war. The Judge did not make his charge very distinctly but I can tell you what he can prove by referring to the record. You remember I was an old Whig, and whenever the Democratic party tried to get me to vote that the war had been righteously begun by the President, I would not do it. But whenever they asked for any money, or land warrants, or anything to pay the soldiers there, during all that time, I gave the same votes that Judge Douglas did. [Loud applause.] You can think as you please as to whether that was consistent. Such is the truth; and the Judge has the right to make all he can out of it. But when he, by a general charge, conveys the idea that I withheld supplies from the soldiers who were fighting in the Mexican war, or did anything else to hinder the soldiers, he is, to say the least, grossly and altogether mistaken, as a consultation of the records will prove to him.

As I have not used up so much of my time as I had supposed, I will dwell a little longer upon one or two of these minor topics upon which the Judge has spoken. He has read from my speech in Springfield, in which I say that "a house divided against itself cannot stand." Does the Judge say it *can* stand? [Laughter.] I don't know whether he does or not. The Judge does not seem to be attending to me just now, but I would like to know if it is his opinion that a house divided against itself *can stand*. If he does, then there is a question of veracity, not between him and me, but between the Judge and an authority of a somewhat higher character. [Laughter and applause.]

Now, my friends, I ask your attention to this matter for the purpose of saying something seriously. I know that the Judge may readily enough agree with me that the maxim which was put forth by the Saviour is true, but he may allege that I misapply it; and the Judge has a right to urge that, in my application, I do misapply it, and then I have a right to show that I do *not* misapply it. When he undertakes to say that because I think this nation, so far as the question of Slavery is concerned, will all become one thing or all the other, I am in favor of bringing about a dead uniformity in the various States, in all their institutions, he argues erroneously. The great variety of the local institutions in the States, springing from differences in the soil, differences in the face of the country, and in the climate, are bonds of Union. They do not make "a house divided against itself," but they make a house united. If they produce in one section of the country what is called for by the wants of another section, and this other section can supply the wants of the first, they are not matters of discord but bonds of union, true bonds of union. But can this question of slavery be considered as among *these* varieties in the institutions of the country? I leave it to you to say whether, in the history of our government, this institution of slavery has not always failed to be a bond of union, and, on the contrary, been an apple of discord and an element of division in the house. [Cries of "Yes, yes," and applause.] I ask you to consider whether, so long as the moral constitution of men's minds shall continue to be the same, after this generation and assemblage shall sink into the grave, and another race shall arise, with the same moral and intellectual development we have—whether, if that institution is standing in the same irritating position in which it now is, it will not continue an element of division? [Cries of "Yes, yes."] If so, then I have a right to say that in regard to this question, the Union is a house divided against itself, and when the Judge reminds me that I have often said to him that the institution of slavery has existed for eighty years in some States, and yet it does not exist in some others, I agree to the fact, and I account for it by looking at the position in which our fathers originally placed it—restricting it from the new Territories where it had not gone, and legislating to cut off its source by the abrogation of the slave trade,[4] thus putting the seal of legislation *against its spread*. The public mind *did* rest in the belief that it was in the course of ultimate extinction. [Cries of "Yes, yes."] But lately, I think—and in this I charge nothing on the Judge's motives—lately, I think, that he, and those acting with him, have placed that institution on a new basis, which looks to the *perpetuity and nationalization of slavery*. [Loud cheers.] And while it is placed upon this new basis, I say, and I have said, that I believe we shall not have peace upon the question until the opponents of slavery arrest the further spread of it, and place it where the public mind shall rest in the belief that it is in the course of ultimate extinction; or, on the other hand, that its advocates will push it forward until it shall become alike

---

4. The Constitution prohibited the importation of slaves as of 1808.

lawful in all the States, old as well as new, North as well as South. Now, I believe if we could arrest the spread, and place it where Washington, and Jefferson, and Madison placed it, it *would be* in the course of ultimate extinction, and the public mind *would*, as for eighty years past, believe that it was in the course of ultimate extinction. The crisis would be past and the institution might be let alone for a hundred years, if it should live so long, in the States where it exists, yet it would be going out of existence in the way best for both the black and the white races. [Great cheering.]

A VOICE—Then do you repudiate Popular Sovereignty?

MR. LINCOLN—Well, then, let us talk about Popular Sovereignty! [Laughter.] What is Popular Sovereignty? [Cries of "A humbug," "a humbug."] Is it the right of the people to have Slavery or not have it, as they see fit, in the territories? I will state—and I have an able man to watch me—my understanding is that Popular Sovereignty, as now applied to the question of Slavery, does allow the people of a Territory to have Slavery if they want to, but does not allow them *not* to have it if they *do not* want it. [Applause and laughter.] I do not mean that if this vast concourse of people were in a Territory of the United States, any one of them would be obliged to have a slave if he did not want one; but I do say that, as I understand the Dred Scott decision, if any one man wants slaves, all the rest have no way of keeping that one man from holding them.

When I made my speech at Springfield, of which the Judge complains, and from which he quotes, I really was not thinking of the things which he ascribes to me at all. I had no thought in the world that I was doing anything to bring about a war between the free and slave States. I had no thought in the world that I was doing anything to bring about a political and social equality of the black and white races. It never occurred to me that I was doing anything or favoring anything to reduce to a dead uniformity all the local institutions of the various States. But I must say, in all fairness to him, if he thinks I am doing something which leads to these bad results, it is none the better that I did not mean it. It is just as fatal to the country, if I have any influence in producing it, whether I intend it or not. But can it be true, that placing this institution upon the original basis—the basis upon which our fathers placed it—can have any tendency to set the Northern and the Southern States at war with one another, or that it can have any tendency to make the people of Vermont raise sugar cane, because they raise it in Louisiana, or that it can compel the people of Illinois to cut pine logs on the Grand Prairie, where they will not grow, because they cut pine logs in Maine, where they do grow? [Laughter.] The Judge says this is a new principle started in regard to this question. Does the Judge claim that he is working on the plan of the founders of government? I think he says in some of his speeches—indeed I have one here now—that he saw evidence of a policy to allow slavery to be south of a certain line, while north of it should be excluded, and he saw an indisposition on the part of the country to stand upon that policy, and therefore he set about studying the subject upon *original principles*, and upon *original principles* he got up the Nebraska bill! I am fighting it upon these "original principles"—fighting it in the Jeffersonian, Washingtonian, and Madisonian fashion. [Laughter and applause.]

* * *

* * * I ask the attention of the people here assembled and elsewhere, to the course that Judge Douglas is pursuing every day as bearing upon this question of making slavery national. Not going back to the records but taking the speeches he makes, the speeches he made yesterday and day before and makes constantly all over the country—I ask your attention to them. In the first place what is necessary to make the institution national? Not war. There is no danger that the people of Kentucky will shoulder their muskets and with a young nigger stuck on every bayonet march into Illinois and force them upon us. There is no danger of our going over there and making war upon them. Then what is necessary for the nationalization of slavery? It is simply the next Dred Scott decision. It is merely for the Supreme Court to decide that no *State* under the Constitution can exclude it, just as they have already decided that under the Constitution neither Congress nor the Territorial Legislature can do it. When that is decided and acquiesced in, the whole thing is done. This being true, and this being the way as I think that slavery is to be made national, let us consider what Judge Douglas is doing every day to that end. In the first place, let us see what influence he is exerting on public sentiment. In this and like communities, public sentiment is everything. With public sentiment, nothing can fail; without it nothing can succeed. Consequently he who moulds public sentiment, goes deeper than he who enacts statutes or pronounces decisions. He makes statutes and decisions possible or impossible to be executed. This must be borne in mind, as also the additional fact that Judge Douglas is a man of vast influence, so great that it is enough for many men to profess to believe anything, when they once find out that Judge Douglas professes to believe it. Consider also the attitude he occupies at the head of a large party—a party which he claims has a majority of all the voters in the country. This man sticks to a decision which forbids the people of a Territory from excluding slavery, and he does so not because he says it is right in itself—he does not give any opinion on that—but because it has been *decided by the court*, and being decided by the court, he is, and you are bound to take it in your political action as *law*—not that he judges at all of its merits, but because a decision of the court is to him a *"Thus saith the Lord."* [Applause.] He places it on that ground alone, and you will bear in mind that thus committing himself unreservedly to this decision, *commits him to the next one* just as firmly as to this. He did not commit himself on account of the merit or demerit of the decision, but it is a *Thus saith the Lord.* The next decision, as much as this, will be a *thus saith the Lord.* There is nothing that can divert or turn him away from this decision. It is nothing that I point out to him that his great prototype, Gen. Jackson, did not believe in the binding force of decisions. It is nothing to him that Jefferson did not so believe. I have said that I have often heard him approve of Jackson's course in disregarding the decision of the Supreme Court pronouncing a National Bank constitutional.[5] He says, I did not hear him say so. He denies the accuracy of my recollection. I say he ought to know better than I, but I will make no question about this thing, though it still seems to me that I heard him say it twenty times. [Applause and laughter.] I will tell him though, that he

---

5. At its 1856 convention in Cincinnati, the Democratic Party adopted a platform that decried a national bank as oppressive and unconstitutional.

now claims to stand on the Cincinnati platform, which affirms that Congress *cannot* charter a National Bank, in the teeth of that old standing decision that Congress *can* charter a bank. [Loud applause.] And I remind him of another piece of history on the question of respect for judicial decisions, and it is a piece of Illinois history, belonging to a time when the large party to which Judge Douglas belonged, were displeased with a decision of the Supreme Court of Illinois, because they had decided that a Governor could not remove a Secretary of State. You will find the whole story in Ford's History of Illinois, and I know that Judge Douglas will not deny that he was then in favor of over-slaughing[6] that decision by the mode of adding five new Judges, so as to vote down the four old ones. Not only so, but it ended in *the Judge's sitting down on that very bench as one of the five new Judges to break down the four old ones.* [Cheers and laughter.] It was in this way precisely that he got his title of Judge. Now, when the Judge tells me that men appointed conditionally to sit as members of a court, will have to be catechised beforehand upon some subject, I say "You know Judge; you have tried it." [Laughter.] When he says a court of this kind will lose the confidence of all men, will be prostituted and disgraced by such a proceeding, I say, "You know best, Judge; you have been through the mill." [Great laughter.] But I cannot shake Judge Douglas' teeth loose from the Dred Scott decision. Like some obstinate animal (I mean no disrespect,) that will hang on when he has once got his teeth fixed, you may cut off a leg, or you may tear away an arm, still he will not relax his hold. And so I may point out to the Judge, and say that he is bespattered all over, from the beginning of his political life to the present time, with attacks upon judicial decisions—I may cut off limb after limb of his public record, and strive to wrench him from a single dictum of the Court—yet I cannot divert him from it. He hangs to the last, to the Dred Scott decision. [Loud cheers.] These things show there is a purpose *strong as death and eternity* for which he adheres to this decision, and for which he will adhere to *all other decisions* of the same Court. [Vociferous applause.]

A HIBERNIAN.—Give us something besides Dred Scott.

MR. LINCOLN.—Yes; no doubt you want to hear something that don't hurt. [Laughter and applause.] Now, having spoken of the Dred Scott decision, one more word and I am done. Henry Clay, my beau ideal of a statesman, the man for whom I fought all my humble life—Henry Clay once said of a class of men who would repress all tendencies to liberty and ultimate emancipation, that they must, if they would do this, go back to the era of our Independence, and muzzle the cannon which thunders its annual joyous return; they must blow out the moral lights around us; they must penetrate the human soul, and eradicate there the love of liberty; and then and not till then, could they perpetuate slavery in this country! [Loud cheers.] To my thinking, Judge Douglas is, by his example and vast influence, doing that very thing in this community, [cheers,] when he says that the negro has nothing in the Declaration of Independence. Henry Clay plainly understood the contrary. Judge Douglas is going back to the era of our Revolution, and to the extent of his ability, muzzling the cannon which thunders its annual joyous return. When he

6. Ignoring. "Ford's History": Thomas Ford, *A History of Illinois, from Its Commencement as a State in 1818 to 1847* (1854).

invites any people willing to have slavery, to establish it, he is blowing out the moral lights around us. [Cheers.] When he says he "cares not whether slavery is voted down or voted up,"—that it is a sacred right of self government—he is in my judgment penetrating the human soul and eradicating the light of reason and the love of liberty in this American people. [Enthusiastic and continued applause.] * * *

August 21, 1858

From *Second Lincoln-Douglas Debate, Freeport, Illinois*

SECOND JOINT DEBATE, AUGUST 27, 1858 AT FREEPORT,
ILLINOIS. LINCOLN, AS REPORTED IN THE PRESS & TRIBUNE. DOUGLAS,
AS REPORTED IN THE CHICAGO TIMES.

FROM MR. LINCOLN'S SPEECH

☼   ☼   ☼

* * * I will take up the Judge's interrogatories as I find them printed in the Chicago *Times*, and answer them *seriatim*.[7] In order that there may be no mistake about it, I have copied the interrogatories in writing, and also my answers to them. The first one of these interrogatories is in these words:

Question 1. "I desire to know whether Lincoln to-day stands, as he did in 1854, in favor of the unconditional repeal of the fugitive slave law?"

Answer. I do not now, nor ever did, stand in favor of the unconditional repeal of the fugitive slave law. [Cries of "Good," "Good."]

Q. 2. "I desire him to answer whether he stands pledged to-day, as he did in 1854, against the admission of any more slave States into the Union, even if the people want them?"

A. I do not now, nor ever did, stand pledged against the admission of any more slave States into the Union.

Q. 3. "I want to know whether he stands pledged against the admission of a new State into the Union with such a Constitution as the people of that State may see fit to make."

A. I do not stand pledged against the admission of a new State into the Union, with such a Constitution as the people of that State may see fit to make. [Cries of "good," "good."]

Q. 4. "I want to know whether he stands to-day pledged to the abolition of slavery in the District of Columbia?"

A. I do not stand to-day pledged to the abolition of slavery in the District of Columbia.

Q. 5. "I desire him to answer whether he stands pledged to the prohibition of the slave trade between the different States?"

A. I do not stand pledged to the prohibition of the slave trade between the different States.

Q. 6. "I desire to know whether he stands pledged to prohibit slavery in all the Territories of the United States, North as well as South of the Missouri Compromise line."

---

7. In a series.

A.   I am impliedly, if not expressly, pledged to a belief in the *right* and *duty* of Congress to prohibit slavery in all the United States Territories. [Great applause.]

Q. 7.   "I desire him to answer whether he is opposed to the acquisition of any new territory unless slavery is first prohibited therein."

A.   I am not generally opposed to honest acquisition of territory; and, in any given case, I would or would not oppose such acquisition, accordingly as I might think such acquisition would or would not agravate the slavery question among ourselves. [Cries of good, good.]

Now, my friends, it will be perceived upon an examination of these questions and answers, that so far I have only answered that I was not *pledged* to this, that or the other. The Judge has not framed his interrogatories to ask me anything more than this, and I have answered in strict accordance with the interrogatories, and have answered truly that I am not *pledged* at all upon any of the points to which I have answered. But I am not disposed to hang upon the exact form of his interrogatory. I am rather disposed to take up at least some of these questions, and state what I really think upon them.

As to the first one, in regard to the Fugitive Slave Law, I have never hesitated to say, and I do not now hesitate to say, that I think, under the Constitution of the United States, the people of the Southern States are entitled to a Congressional Fugitive Slave Law. Having said that, I have had nothing to say in regard to the existing Fugitive Slave Law further than that I think it should have been framed so as to be free from some of the objections that pertain to it, without lessening its efficiency. And inasmuch as we are not now in an agitation in regard to an alteration or modification of that law, I would not be the man to introduce it as a new subject of agitation upon the general question of slavery.

* * *

FROM MR. DOUGLAS'S SPEECH

* * *

I trust now that Mr. Lincoln will deem himself answered on his four points. He racked his brain so much in devising these four questions that he exhausted himself, and had not strength enough to invent the others. (Laughter.) As soon as he is able to hold a council with his advisers, Lovejoy, Farnsworth, and Fred. Douglass, he will frame and propound others. (Good, good, &c. Renewed laughter, in which Mr. Lincoln feebly joined, saying that he hoped with their aid to get seven questions, the number asked him by Judge Douglas, and so make *conclusions* even.) You Black Republicans who say good, I have no doubt think that they are all good men. (White, white.) I have reason to recollect that some people in this country think that Fred. Douglass is a very good man. The last time I came here to make a speech, while talking from the stand to you, people of Freeport, as I am doing to-day, I saw a carriage and a magnificent one it was, drive up and take a position on the outside of the crowd; a beautiful young lady was sitting on the box seat, whilst Fred. Douglass and her mother reclined inside, and the owner of the carriage acted as driver. (Laughter, cheers, cries of right, what have you to say against it, &c.) I saw this in your own town. ("What of it.") All I have to say of it is this, that if you, Black Republicans, think that the negro ought to be on a social equality with your wives and daughters, and ride in a carriage with your wife, whilst you drive the team, you have a perfect right to do so. (Good, good, and cheers, mingled with hooting and cries of white, white.) I am told that one of Fred. Douglass' kinsmen, another rich black negro, is now traveling in this part of the State making speeches for his friend Lincoln as the champion of black men. ("White men, white men," and "what have you got to say against it." That's right, &c.) All I have to say on that subject is that those of you who believe that the negro is your equal and ought to be on an equality with you socially, politically, and legally; have a right to entertain those opinions, and of course will vote for Mr. Lincoln. ("Down with the negro," no, no, &c.)

* * *

August 27, 1858

From *Third Lincoln-Douglas Debate, Jonesboro, Illinois*

FROM MR. DOUGLAS'S SPEECH

* * *

* * * I hold that a negro is not and never ought to be a citizen of the United States. (Good, good, and tremendous cheers.) I hold that this government was made on the white basis, by white men, for the benefit of white men and their posterity forever, and should be administered by white men and none others. I do not believe that the Almighty made the negro capable of self-government. I am aware that all the abolition lecturers that you find traveling about through the country are in the habit of reading the Declaration of Independence to prove that all men were created equal and endowed by their Creator with certain inalienable rights, among which are life, liberty, and the pursuit of happiness. Mr. Lincoln is very much in the habit of following in the track of Lovejoy in this particular, by reading that part of the Declaration of Independence to prove that the negro was endowed by the Almighty with the inalienable right of equality with white men. Now, I say to you, my fellow-citizens, that in my opinion the signers of the Declaration had no reference to the negro whatever when they declared all men to be created equal. They desired to express by that phrase, white men, men of European birth and European descent, and had no reference either to the negro, the savage Indians, the Fejee, the Malay, or any other inferior and degraded race, when they spoke of the equality of men. One great evidence that such was their understanding, is to be found in the fact that at that time every one of the thirteen colonies was a slaveholding colony, every signer of the Declaration represented a slaveholding constituency, and we know that no one of them emancipated his slaves, much less offered citizenship to them when they signed the Declaration, and yet, if they had intended to declare that the negro was the equal of the white man, and entitled by divine right to an equality with him, they were bound, as honest men, that day and hour to have put their negroes on an equality with themselves. (Cheers.) Instead of doing so, with uplifted eyes to Heaven they implored the Divine blessing upon them, during the seven years' bloody war they had to fight to maintain that Declaration, never dreaming that they were violating divine law by still holding the negroes in bondage and depriving them of equality.

My friends, I am in favor of preserving this government as our fathers made it. It does not follow by any means that because a negro is not your equal or mine that hence he must necessarily be a slave. On the contrary, it does follow that we ought to extend to the negro every right, every privilege, every immunity which he is capable of enjoying consistent with the good of society. When you ask me what these rights are, what their nature and extent is, I tell you that that is a question which each State of this Union must decide for itself. Illinois has already decided the question. We have decided that the negro must not be a slave within our limits, but we have also decided that the negro shall not be a citizen within our limits; that he shall not vote, hold office, or exercise any political rights. I maintain that Illinois, as a sovereign State, has a right thus to fix her policy with reference to the relation between the white man and the negro; but while we had the right to decide the question for ourselves we must recognize the same right in Kentucky and in every other State to make the same decision, or a different one. Having decided our own policy with reference to the black race, we must leave Kentucky and Missouri and every other State perfectly free to make just such a decision as they see proper on that question.

Kentucky has decided that question for herself. She has said that within her limits a negro shall not exercise any political rights, and she has also said that a portion of the negroes under the laws of that State shall be slaves. She had as much right to adopt that as her policy as we had to adopt the contrary for our policy. New York has decided that in that State a negro may vote if he has $250 worth of property, and if he owns that much he may vote upon an equality with the white man. I, for one, am utterly opposed to negro suffrage anywhere and under any circumstances; yet, inasmuch as the Supreme Court have decided in the celebrated Dred Scott case that a State has a right to confer the privilege of voting upon free negroes, I am not going to make war upon New York because she has adopted a policy repugnant to my feelings. (That's good.) But New York must mind her own business, and keep her negro suffrage to herself and not attempt to force it upon us. (Great applause.)

In the State of Maine they have decided that a negro may vote and hold office on an equality with a white man. I had occasion to say to the Senators from Maine in a discussion last session, that if they thought that the white people within the limits of their State were no better than negroes, I would not quarrel with them for it, but they must not say that my white constituents of Illinois were no better than negroes, or we would be sure to quarrel. (Cheers.)

The Dred Scott decision covers the whole question, and declares that each State has the right to settle this question of suffrage for itself, and all questions as to the relations between the white man and the negro. Judge Taney expressly lays down the doctrine. I receive it as law, and I say that while those States are adopting regulations on that subject disgusting and abhorrent, according to my views, I will not make war on them if they will mind their own business and let us alone. (Bravo, and cheers.)

I now come back to the question, why cannot this Union exist forever divided into free and slave States as our fathers made it? It can thus exist if each State will carry out the principles upon which our institutions were founded, to wit: the right of each State to do as it pleases, without meddling with its neighbors. Just act upon that great principle, and this Union will not only live forever, but it will extend and expand until it covers the whole continent, and make this confederacy one grand ocean-bound republic. We must bear in mind that we are yet a young nation growing with a rapidity unequalled in the history of the world, that our national increase is great, and that the emigration from the old world is increasing, requiring us to expand and acquire new territory from time to time in order to give our people land to live upon. If we live upon the principle of State rights and State sovereignty, each State regulating its own affairs and minding its own business, we can go on and extend indefinitely, just as fast and as far as we need the territory. The time may come, indeed has now come, when our interests would be advanced by the acquisition of the island of Cuba. (Terrific applause.) When we get Cuba we must take it as we find it, leaving the people to decide the question of slavery for themselves, without interference on the part of the federal government, or of any State of this Union. So, when it becomes necessary to acquire any portion of Mexico or Canada, or of this continent or the adjoining islands, we must take them as we find them, leaving the people free to do as they please, to have slavery or not, as they choose. * * *

*   *   *

September 15, 1858

From *Fourth Lincoln-Douglas Debate,* Charleston, Illinois

FOURTH JOINT DEBATE SEPTEMBER 18. 1858. LINCOLN, AS REPORTED IN THE PRESS & TRIBUNE. DOUGLAS, AS REPORTED IN THE CHICAGO TIMES.

FROM MR. LINCOLN'S SPEECH

*   *   *

While I was at the hotel to-day an elderly gentleman called upon me to know whether I was really in favor of producing a perfect equality between the negroes and white people. [Great laughter.] While I had not proposed to myself on this occasion to say much on that subject, yet as the question was asked me I thought I would occupy perhaps five minutes in saying something in regard to it. I will say then that I am not, nor ever have been in favor of bringing about in any way the social and political equality of the white and black races, [applause]—that I am not nor ever have been in favor of making voters or jurors of negroes, nor of qualifying them to hold office, nor to intermarry with white people; and I will say in addition to this that there is a physical difference between the white and black races which I believe will for ever forbid the two races living together on terms of social and political equality. And inasmuch as they cannot so live, while they do remain together there must be the position of superior and inferior, and I as much as any other man am in favor of having the superior position assigned to the white race. I say upon this occasion I do not perceive that because the white man is to have the superior position the negro should be denied everything. I do not understand that because I do not want a negro woman for a slave I must necessarily want her for a wife. [Cheers and laughter.] My understanding is that I can just let her alone. I am now in my fiftieth year, and I certainly never have had a black woman for either a slave or a wife. So it seems to me quite possible for us to get along without making either slaves or wives of negroes. I will add to this that I have never seen to my knowledge a man, woman or child who was in favor of producing a perfect equality, social and political, between negroes and white men. I recollect of but one distinguished instance that I ever heard of so frequently as to be entirely satisfied of its correctness—and that is the case of Judge Douglas' old friend Col. Richard M. Johnson.[8] [Laughter.] I will also add to the remarks I have made, (for I am not going to enter at large upon this subject,) that I have never had the least apprehension that I or my friends would marry negroes if there was no law to keep them from it, [laughter] but as Judge Douglas and his friends seem to be in great apprehension that they might, if there were no law to keep them from it, [roars of laughter] I give him the most solemn pledge that I will to the very last stand by the law of this State, which forbids the marrying of white people with negroes. [Continued laughter and applause.] I will add one further word, which is this, that I do not understand there is any place where an alteration of the social and political relations of the negro and the white man can be made except in the State Legislature—not in the Congress of the United States—and as I do not really apprehend the approach of any such thing myself, and as Judge Douglas seems to be in constant horror that some such danger is rapidly approaching, I propose as the best means to prevent it that the Judge be kept at home and placed in the State Legislature to fight the measure. [Uproarious laughter and applause.] I do not propose dwelling longer at this time on this subject.

*   *   *

FROM MR. DOUGLAS'S REPLY

*   *   *

Lincoln maintains there that the Declaration of Independence asserts that the negro is equal to the white man, and that under Divine law, and if he believes so it was rational for him to advocate negro citizenship, which, when allowed, puts the negro on an equality under the law. (No negro equality for us; down with Lincoln.) I say to you in all frankness, gentlemen, that in my opinion a negro is not a citizen, cannot be, and ought not to be, under the constitution of the United States. (That's the doctrine.) I will not even qualify my opinion to meet the declaration of one of the Judges of the Supreme Court in the Dred Scott case, "that a negro descended from African parents, who was imported into this country as a slave, is not a citizen,

8. Kentucky Democrat and Martin Van Buren's vice president (1780–1850), who had sired two children out of wedlock with an octoroon slave and, after she died, had taken another black mistress.

and cannot be." I say that this government was established on the white basis. It was made by white men, for the benefit of white men and their posterity forever, and never should be administered by any except white men. (Cheers.) I declare that a negro ought not to be a citizen, whether his parents were imported into this country as slaves or not, or whether or not he was born here. It does not depend upon the place a negro's parents were born, or whether they were slaves or not, but upon the fact that he is a negro, belonging to a race incapable of self government, and for that reason ought not to be on an equality with white men. (Immense applause.)

*　*　*

FROM MR. LINCOLN'S REJOINDER

*　*　*

Judge Douglas has said to you that he has not been able to get from me an answer to the question whether I am in favor of negro-citizenship. So far as I know, the Judge never asked me the question before. [Applause.] He shall have no occasion to ever ask it again, for I tell him very frankly that I am not in favor of negro citizenship. [Renewed applause.] This furnishes me an occasion for saying a few words upon the subject. I mentioned in a certain speech of mine which has been printed, that the Supreme Court had decided that a negro could not possibly be made a citizen, and without saying what was my ground of complaint in regard to that, or whether I had any ground of complaint, Judge Douglas has from that thing manufactured nearly every thing that he ever says about my disposition to produce an equality between the negroes and the white people. [Laughter and applause.] If any one will read my speech, he will find I mentioned that as one of the points decided in the course of the Supreme Court opinions, but I did not state what objection I had to it. But Judge Douglas tells the people what my objection was when I did not tell them myself. [Loud applause and laughter.] Now my opinion is that the different States have the power to make a negro a citizen under the Constitution of the United States if they choose. The Dred Scott decision decides that they have not that power. If the State of Illinois had that power I should be opposed to the exercise of it. [Cries of "good," "good," and applause.] That is all I have to say about it.

Judge Douglas has told me that he heard my speeches north and my speeches south—that he had heard me at Ottawa and at Freeport in the north, and recently at Jonesboro in the south, and there was a very different cast of sentiment in the speeches made at the different points. I will not charge upon Judge Douglas that he wilfully misrepresents me, but I call upon every fair-minded man to take these speeches and read them, *and I dare him to point out any difference between my printed speeches north and south.* [Great cheering.] While I am here perhaps I ought to say a word, if I have the time, in regard to the latter portion of the Judge's speech, which was a sort of declamation in reference to my having said I entertained the belief that this government would not endure, half slave and half free. I have said so and I did not say it without what seemed to me to be good reasons. It perhaps would require more time than I have now to set forth these reasons in detail; but let me ask you a few questions. Have we ever had any peace on this slavery question? [No, no.] When are we to

have peace upon it if it is kept in the position it now occupies? [Never.]
How are we ever to have peace upon it? That is an important question. To
be sure if we will all stop and allow Judge Douglas and his friends to
march on in their present career until they plant the institution all over
the nation, here and wherever else our flag waves, and we acquiesce in
it, there will be peace. But let me ask Judge Douglas how he is going to
get the people to do that? [Applause.] They have been wrangling over this
question for at least forty years. This was the cause of the agitation resulting in the Missouri Compromise—this produced the troubles at the
annexation of Texas, in the acquisition of the territory acquired in the
Mexican war. Again, this was the trouble which was quieted by the Compromise of 1850, when it was settled "*forever*," as both the great political
parties declared in their National Conventions. That "forever" turned out
to be just four years, [laughter] *when Judge Douglas himself re-opened it.*
[Immense applause, cries of "hit him again," &c.] When is it likely to come
to an end? He introduced the Nebraska bill in 1854 to put *another end* to
the slavery agitation. He promised that it would finish it all up immediately, and he has never made a speech since until he got into a quarrel
with the President about the Lecompton Constitution, in which he has
not declared that we are *just at the end* of the slavery agitation. But in one
speech, I think last winter, he did say that he didn't quite see when the
end of the slavery agitation would come. [Laughter and cheers.] Now he
tells us again that it is all over, and the people of Kansas have voted down
the Lecompton Constitution. How is it over? That was only one of the
attempts at putting an end to the slavery agitation—one of these "final
settlements." [Renewed laughter.] Is Kansas in the Union? Has she formed
a Constitution that she is likely to come in under? Is not the slavery agitation still an open question in that Territory? Has the voting down of that
Constitution put an end to all the trouble? Is that more likely to settle it
than every one of these previous attempts to settle the slavery agitation.
[Cries of "No," "No."] Now, at this day in the history of the world we can
no more foretell where the end of this slavery agitation will be than we
can see the end of the world itself. The Nebraska-Kansas bill was introduced four years and a half ago, and if the agitation is ever to come to an
end, we may say we are four years and a half nearer the end. So, too, we
can say we are four years and a half nearer the end of the world; and we
can just as clearly see the end of the world as we can see the end of this
agitation. [Applause.] The Kansas settlement did not conclude it. If Kansas should sink to-day, and leave a great vacant space in the earth's surface, this vexed question would still be among us. I say, then, there is no
way of putting an end to the slavery agitation amongst us but to put it back
upon the basis where our fathers placed it, [applause] no way but to keep
it out of our new Territories [renewed applause]—to restrict it forever to
the old States where it now exists. [Tremendous and prolonged cheering;
cries of "That's the doctrine," "Good," "Good," &c.] Then the public mind
will rest in the belief that it is in the course of ultimate extinction. That is
one way of putting an end to the slavery agitation. [Applause.]

The other way is for us to surrender and let Judge Douglas and his
friends have their way and plant slavery over all the States—cease speaking of it as in any way a wrong—regard slavery as one of the common matters of property, and speak of negroes as we do of our horses and cattle.

But while it drives on in its state of progress as it is now driving, and as it has driven for the last five years, I have ventured the opinion, and I say to-day, that we will have no end to the slavery agitation until it takes one turn or the other. [Applause.] I do not mean that when it takes a turn towards ultimate extinction it will be in a day, nor in a year, nor in two years. I do not suppose that in the most peaceful way ultimate extinction would occur in less than a hundred years at the least; but that it will occur in the best way for both races in God's own good time, I have no doubt. [Applause.] * * *

* * *

September 18, 1858

From *Fifth Lincoln-Douglas Debate, Galesburg, Illinois*

FIFTH JOINT DEBATE OCTOBER 7. 1858, AT GALESBURG, ILLINOIS
DOUGLAS, AS REPORTED IN THE CHICAGO TIMES. LINCOLN, AS REPORTED
IN THE PRESS & TRIBUNE.

FROM MR. LINCOLN'S REPLY

* * *

The Judge has alluded to the Declaration of Independence, and insisted that negroes are not included in that Declaration; and that it is a slander upon the framers of that instrument, to suppose that negroes were meant therein; and he asks you: Is it possible to believe that Mr. Jefferson, who penned the immortal paper, could have supposed himself applying the language of that instrument to the negro race, and yet held a portion of that race in slavery? Would he not at once have freed them? I only have to remark upon this part of the Judge's speech, (and that, too, very briefly, for I shall not detain myself, or you, upon that point for any great length of time,) that I believe the entire records of the world, from the date of the Declaration of Independence up to within three years ago, may be searched in vain for one single affirmation, from one single man, that the negro was not included in the Declaration of Independence. I think I may defy Judge Douglas to show that he ever said so, that Washington ever said so, that any President ever said so, that any member of Congress ever said so, or that any living man upon the whole earth ever said so, until the necessities of the present policy of the Democratic party, in regard to slavery, had to invent that affirmation. [Tremendous applause.] And I will remind Judge Douglas and this audience, that while Mr. Jefferson was the owner of slaves, as undoubtedly he was, in speaking upon this very subject, he used the strong language that "he trembled for his country when he remembered that God was just;"[9] and I will offer the highest premium in my power to Judge Douglas if he will show that he, in all his life, ever uttered a sentiment at all akin to that of Jefferson. [Great applause and cries of "Hit him again," "good," "good."]

The next thing to which I will ask your attention is the Judge's comments upon the fact, as he assumes it to be, that we cannot call our public meetings as Republican meetings; and he instances Tazewell county

9. Jefferson, *Notes on the State of Virginia* (1785), Query XVIII.

as one of the places where the friends of Lincoln have called a public
meeting and have not dared to name it a Republican meeting. He instances
Monroe county as another where Judge Trumbull[1] and Jehu Baker
addressed the persons whom the Judge assumes to be the friends of Lincoln, calling them the "Free Democracy." I have the honor to inform Judge
Douglas that he spoke in that very county of Tazewell last Saturday, and I
was there on Tuesday last, and when he spoke there he spoke under a call
not venturing to use the word "Democrat." [Cheers and laughter.] (Turning to Judge Douglas.) What do you think of this? [Immense applause and
roars of laughter.]

So again, there is another thing to which I would ask the Judge's attention upon this subject. In the contest of 1856 his party delighted to call
themselves together as the "National Democracy,"[2] but now, if there
should be a notice put up anywhere for a meeting of the "National Democracy," Judge Douglas and his friends would not come. [Laughter.] They
would not suppose themselves invited. [Renewed laughter and cheers.]
They would understand that it was a call for those hateful Postmasters
whom he talks about. [Uproarious laughter.]

Now a few words in regard to these extracts from speeches of mine,
which Judge Douglas has read to you, and which he supposes are in very
great contrast to each other. Those speeches have been before the public
for a considerable time, and if they have any inconsistency in them, if
there is any conflict in them the public have been able to detect it. When
the Judge says, in speaking on this subject, that I make speeches of one
sort for the people of the Northern end of the State, and of a different
sort for the Southern people, he assumes that I do not understand that
my speeches will be put in print and read North and South. I knew all the
while that the speech that I made at Chicago and the one I made at
Jonesboro and the one at Charleston, would all be put in print and all the
reading and intelligent men in the community would see them and know
all about my opinions. And I have not supposed, and do not now suppose,
that there is any conflict whatever between them. ["They are all good
speeches!" "Hurrah for Lincoln!"] But the Judge will have it that if we do
not confess that there is a sort of inequality between the white and black
races, which justifies us in making them slaves, we must, then, insist that
there is a degree of equality that requires us to make them our wives.
[Loud applause, and cries, "Give it to him;" "Hit him again."] Now, I have
all the while taken a broad distinction in regard to that matter; and that
is all there is in these different speeches which he arrays here, and the
entire reading of either of the speeches will show that that distinction
was made. Perhaps by taking two parts of the same speech, he could have
got up as much of a conflict as the one he has found. I have all the while
maintained, that in so far as it should be insisted that there was an equality between the white and black races that should produce a perfect social

1. A U.S. Senator (1813–1896) from Illinois who served in the Senate from 1855 through 1873.
Baker: an Illinois Republican (1822–1903) who served in the U.S. House of Representatives
(1865–69 and 1887–89).
2. In the 1856 election, Democrats had unified around a national ticket headed by James
Buchanan, but Douglas distanced himself from the national party when he disagreed with its
leaders over the proslavery Lecompton Constitution. Thereafter, government officials, including postmasters, known to be associated with Douglas were in jeopardy of losing their jobs at
the hands of the Buchanan administration.

and political equality, it was an impossibility. This you have seen in my printed speeches, and with it I have said, that in their right to "life, liberty and the pursuit of happiness," as proclaimed in that old Declaration, the inferior races are our equals. [Long-continued cheering.] And these declarations I have constantly made in reference to the abstract moral question, to contemplate and consider when we are legislating about any new country which is not already cursed with the actual presence of the evil—slavery. I have never manifested any impatience with the necessities that spring from the actual presence of black people amongst us, and the actual existence of slavery amongst us where it does already exist; but I have insisted that, in legislating for new countries, where it does not exist, there is no just rule other than that of moral and abstract right! With reference to those new countries, those maxims as to the right of a people to "life, liberty and the pursuit of happiness," were the just rules to be constantly referred to. There is no misunderstanding this, except by men interested to misunderstand it. [Applause.] I take it that I have to address an intelligent and reading community, who will peruse what I say, weigh it, and then judge whether I advance improper or unsound views, or whether I advance hypocritical, and deceptive, and contrary views in different portions of the country. I believe myself to be guilty of no such thing as the latter, though, of course, I cannot claim that I am entirely free from all error in the opinions I advance.

The Judge has also detained us a while in regard to the distinction between his party and our party. His he assumes to be a national party—ours, a sectional one. He does this in asking the question whether this country has any interest in the maintenance of the Republican party? He assumes that our party is altogether sectional—that the party to which he adheres is national; and the argument is, that no party can be a rightful party—can be based upon rightful principles—unless it can announce its principles everywhere. I presume that Judge Douglas could not go into Russia and announce the doctrine of our national democracy; he could not denounce the doctrine of kings, and emperors, and monarchies, in Russia; and it may be true of this country, that in some places we may not be able to proclaim a doctrine as clearly true as the truth of democracy, because there is a section so directly opposed to it that they will not tolerate us in doing so. Is it the true test of the soundness of a doctrine, that in some places people won't let you proclaim it? [No, no, no.] Is that the way to test the truth of any doctrine? [No, no, no.] Why, I understood that at one time the people of Chicago would not let Judge Douglas preach a certain favorite doctrine of his. [Laughter and cheers.] I commend to his consideration the question, whether he takes that as a test of the unsoundness of what he wanted to preach. [Loud cheers.]

*   *   *

FROM MR. DOUGLAS'S REPLY

*   *   *

Mr. Lincoln asserts to-day as he did at Chicago, that the negro was included in that clause of the Declaration of Independence which says that all men were created equal and endowed by the Creator with certain inalienable rights, among which are life, liberty and the pursuit of happiness. (Ain't that so?) If the negro was made his equal and mine, if that equality was established by Divine law, and was the negro's inalienable right, how came he to say at Charleston to the Kentuckians residing in that section of our State, that the negro was physically inferior to the white man, belonged to an inferior race, and he was for keeping him always in that inferior condition? (Good.) I wish you to bear these things in mind. At Charleston he said that the negro belonged to an inferior race, and that he was for keeping him in that inferior condition. There he gave the people to understand that there was no moral question involved, because the inferiority being established, it was only a question of degree and not a question of right; here, to-day, instead of making it a question of degree, he makes it a moral question, says that it is a great crime to hold the negro in that inferior condition. (He's right.) Is he right now or was he right in Charleston? (Both.) He is right then, sir, in your estimation, not because he is consistent, but because he can trim his principles any way in any section, so as to secure votes. All I desire of him is that he will declare the same principles in the South that he does in the North.

But did you notice how he answered my position that a man should hold the same doctrines throughout the length and breadth of this republic? He said, "Would Judge Douglas go to Russia and proclaim the same principles he does here?" I would remind him that Russia is not under the American constitution. ("Good," and laughter.) If Russia was a part of the American republic, under our federal constitution, and I was sworn to support that constitution, I would maintain the same doctrine in Russia that I do in Illinois. (Cheers.) The slaveholding States are governed by the same federal constitution as ourselves, and hence a man's principles, in order to be in harmony with the constitution, must be the same in the South as they are in the North, the same in the free States as they are in the slave States. Whenever a man advocates one set of principles in one section, and another set in another section, his opinions are in violation of the spirit of the constitution which he has sworn to support. ("That's so.") When Mr. Lincoln went to Congress in 1847, and laying his hand upon the holy evangelists, made a solemn vow in the presence of high Heaven that he would be faithful to the constitution,—what did he mean? the constitution as he expounds it in Galesburg, or the constitution as he expounds it in Charleston? (Cheers.)

*　*　*

October 7, 1858

From *Sixth Lincoln-Douglas Debate, Quincy, Illinois*

SIXTH JOINT DEBATE. OCTOBER 13. 1858 AT QUINCY, ILLINOIS.
LINCOLN AS REPORTED IN THE PRESS & TRIBUNE. DOUGLAS
AS REPORTED IN THE CHICAGO TIMES.

FROM MR. LINCOLN'S SPEECH

*　*　*

* * * [Douglas] brought forward a quotation or two from a speech of mine delivered at Chicago, and then to contrast with it he brought for-

ward an extract from a speech of mine at Charleston, in which he insisted that I was greatly inconsistent, and insisted that his conclusion followed that I was playing a double part, and speaking in one region one way and in another region another way. I have not time now to dwell on this as long as I would like, and I wish only now to re-quote that portion of my speech at Charleston which the Judge quoted, and then make some comments upon it. This he quotes from me as being delivered at Charleston, and I believe correctly: "I will say, then, that I am not, nor ever have been, in favor of bringing about in any way the social and political equality of the white and black races—that I am not nor ever have been in favor of making voters or jurors of negroes, nor of qualifying them to hold office, nor to intermarry with white people; and I will say in addition to this that there is a physical difference between the white and black races which will ever forbid the two races living together on terms of social and political equality. And inasmuch as they cannot so live, while they do remain together, there must be the position of superior & inferior. I am as much as any other man in favor of having the superior position assigned to the white race." ["Good," "Good," and loud cheers.] This, I believe, is the entire quotation from the Charleston speech as the Judge made it. His comments are as follows:

> Yes, here you find men who hurrah for Lincoln, and say he is right when he discards all distinction between races, or when he declares that he discards the doctrine that there is such a thing as a superior and inferior race; and Abolitionists are required and expected to vote for Mr. Lincoln because he goes for the equality of the races, holding that in the Declaration of Independence the white man and the negro were declared equal, and endowed by Divine law with equality. And down South with the Old Line Whigs, with the Kentuckians, the Virginians, and the Tennesseeans, he tells you that there is a physical difference between the races, making the one superior, the other inferior, and he is in favor of maintaining the superiority of the white race over the negro.

Those are the Judge's comments. Now I wish to show you, that a month, or only lacking three days of a month, before I made the speech at Charleston, which the Judge quotes from, he had himself heard me say substantially the same thing. It was in our first meeting, at Ottawa—and I will say a word about where it was and the atmosphere it was in, after a while—but, at our first meeting, at Ottawa, I read an extract from an old speech of mine, made nearly four years ago, not merely to show my sentiments, but to show that my sentiments were long entertained and openly expressed; in which extract I expressly declared that my own feelings would not admit a social and political equality between the white and black races, and that even if my own feelings would admit of it, I still knew that the public sentiment of the country would not, and that such a thing was an utter impossibility, or substantially that. That extract from my old speech the reporters, by some sort of accident, passed over, and it was not reported. I lay no blame upon anybody. I suppose they thought that I would hand it over to them, and dropped reporting while I was reading it, but afterwards went away without getting it from me. At the end of that quotation from my old speech, which I read at Ottawa, I made the comments which were reported at that time, and which I will now read, and ask you to notice how very nearly they are the same as Judge Douglas says were delivered by me down in Egypt. After reading I added these words: "Now, gentlemen, I don't want to read at any great length, but this is the true complexion of all I have ever said in regard to the institution of slavery or the black race, and this is the whole of it; and anything that argues me into his idea of perfect social and political equality with the negro is but a specious and fantastical arrangement of words by which a man can prove a horse-chestnut to be a chestnut horse. I will say here, while upon this subject, that I have no purpose directly or indirectly to interfere with the institution in the States where it exists. I believe I have no right to do so. I have no inclination to do so. I have no purpose to introduce political and social equality between the white and black races. There is a physical difference between the two, which, in my judgment, will probably forever forbid their living together on the footing of perfect equality, and inasmuch as it becomes a necessity that there must be a difference, I as well as Judge Douglas am in favor of the race to which I belong having the superior position." [Cheers, "That's the doctrine."] "I have never said anything to the contrary, but I hold that, notwithstanding all this, there is no reason in the world why the negro is not entitled to all the rights enumerated in the Declaration of Independence—the right of life, liberty and the pursuit of happiness. I hold that he is as much entitled to these as the white man. I agree with Judge Douglas that he is not my equal in many respects, certainly not in color—perhaps not in intellectual and moral endowments; but in the right to eat the bread without leave of anybody else which his own hand earns, he is my equal and the equal of Judge Douglas, and the equal of every other man." [Loud cheers.]

*   *   *

We have in this nation this element of domestic slavery. It is a matter of absolute certainty that it is a disturbing element. It is the opinion of all the great men who have expressed an opinion upon it, that it is a dangerous element. We keep up a controversy in regard to it. That controversy necessarily springs from difference of opinion, and if we can learn exactly— can reduce to the lowest elements—what that difference of opinion is, we perhaps shall be better prepared for discussing the different systems of policy that we would propose in regard to that disturbing element. I suggest that the difference of opinion, reduced to its lowest terms, is no other than the difference between the men who think slavery a wrong and those who do not think it wrong. The Republican party think it wrong—we think it is a moral, a social and a political wrong. We think it is a wrong not confining itself merely to the persons or the States where it exists, but that it is a wrong in its tendency, to say the least, that extends itself to the existence of the whole nation. Because we think it wrong, we propose a course of policy that shall deal with it as a wrong. We deal with it as with any other wrong, in so far as we can prevent its growing any larger, and so deal with it that in the run of time there may be some promise of an end to it. We have a due regard to the actual presence of it amongst us and the difficulties of getting rid of it in any satisfactory way, and all the constitutional obligations thrown about it. I suppose that in reference both to its actual existence in the nation, and to our constitutional obligations, we have no right at all to disturb it in the States where it exists, and we profess that we have no more inclination to disturb it than we have the right to do it. We go further than that; we don't propose to disturb it where, in one instance, we think the Constitution would permit us. We think the Constitution would permit us to disturb it in the District of Columbia. Still we do not propose to do that, unless it should be in terms which I don't suppose the nation is very likely soon to agree to—the terms of making the emancipation gradual and compensating the unwilling owners. Where we suppose we have the constitutional right, we restrain ourselves in reference to the actual existence of the institution and the difficulties thrown about it. We also oppose it as an evil so far as it seeks to spread itself. We insist on the policy that shall restrict it to its present limits. We don't suppose that in doing this we violate anything due to the actual presence of the institution, or anything due to the constitutional guarantees thrown around it.

*　*　*

October 13, 1858

From *Seventh Lincoln-Douglas Debate, Alton, Illinois*

SEVENTH, AND LAST JOINT DEBATE. OCTOBER 15. 1858. DOUGLAS
AS REPORTED IN THE CHICAGO TIMES. LINCOLN
AS REPORTED IN THE PRESS & TRIBUNE.

FROM MR. LINCOLN'S REPLY

*　*　*

At Galesburg the other day, I said in answer to Judge Douglas, that three years ago there never had been a man, so far as I knew or believed, in the whole world, who had said that the Declaration of Independence did not include negroes in the term "all men." I re-assert it to-day. I assert that Judge Douglas and all his friends may search the whole records of the country, and it will be a matter of great astonishment to me if they shall be able to find that one human being three years ago had ever uttered the astounding sentiment that the term "all men" in the Declaration did not include the negro. Do not let me be misunderstood. I know that more than three years ago there were men who, finding this assertion constantly in the way of their schemes to bring about the ascendancy and perpetuation of slavery, *denied the truth of it.* I know that Mr. Calhoun and all the politicians of his school denied the truth of the Declaration. I know that it ran along in the mouths of some Southern men for a period of years, ending at last in that shameful though rather forcible declaration of Pettit[3] of Indiana, upon the floor of the United States Senate, that the Declaration of Independence was in that respect "a self-evident lie," rather than a self-evident truth. But I say, with a perfect knowledge of all this hawking at the Declaration without directly attacking it, that three years ago there never had lived a man who had ventured to assail it in the sneaking way of pretending to believe it and then asserting it did not include the negro. [Cheers.] I believe the first man who ever said it was

---

3. John Pettit, Democratic Senator, made this statement about the Declaration of Independence in an 1854 speech.

Chief Justice Taney in the Dred Scott case, and the next to him was our friend Stephen A. Douglas. [Cheers and laughter.] And now it has become the catch-word of the entire party. * * *

* * *

Again; the institution of slavery is only mentioned in the Constitution of the United States two or three times, and in neither of these cases does the word "slavery" or "negro race" occur; but covert language is used each time, and for a purpose full of significance. What is the language in regard to the prohibition of the African slave trade? It runs in about this way: "The migration or importation of such persons as any of the States now existing shall think proper to admit, shall not be prohibited by the Congress prior to the year one thousand eight hundred and eight."

The next allusion in the Constitution to the question of slavery and the black race, is on the subject of the basis of representation, and there the language used is, "Representatives and direct taxes shall be apportioned among the several States which may be included within this Union, according to their respective numbers, which shall be determined by adding to the whole number of free persons, including those bound to service for a term of years, and excluding Indians not taxed—three-fifths of all other persons."

It says "persons," not slaves, not negroes; but this "three-fifths" can be applied to no other class among us than the negroes.

Lastly, in the provision for the reclamation of fugitive slaves it is said: "No person held to service or labor in one State under the laws thereof escaping into another, shall in consequence of any law or regulation therein, be discharged from such service or labor, but shall be delivered up, on claim of the party to whom such service or labor may be due." There again there is no mention of the word "negro" or of slavery. In all three of these places, being the only allusions to slavery in the instrument, covert language is used. Language is used not suggesting that slavery existed or that the black race were among us. And I understand the contemporaneous history of those times to be that covert language was used with a purpose, and that purpose was that in our Constitution, which it was hoped and is still hoped will endure forever—when it should be read by intelligent and patriotic men, after the institution of slavery had passed from among us—there should be nothing on the face of the great charter of liberty suggesting that such a thing as negro slavery had ever existed among us. [Enthusiastic applause.] This is part of the evidence that the fathers of the Government expected and intended the institution of slavery to come to an end. They expected and intended that it should be in the course of ultimate extinction. And when I say that I desire to see the further spread of it arrested I only say I desire to see that done which the fathers have first done. When I say I desire to see it placed where the public mind will rest in the belief that it is in the course of ultimate extinction, I only say I desire to see it placed where they placed it. It is not true that our fathers, as Judge Douglas assumes, made this government part slave and part free. Understand the sense in which he puts it. He assumes that slavery is a rightful thing within itself,—was introduced by the framers of the Constitution. The exact truth is, that they found the institution existing among us, and they left it as they found it. But in making the government they left this institution with many clear marks of disapprobation upon it. They found slavery among them and they left it among them because of the difficulty—the absolute impossibility of its immediate removal. And when Judge Douglas asks me why we cannot let it remain part slave and part free as the fathers of the government made, he asks a question based upon an assumption which is itself a falsehood; and I turn upon him and ask him the question, when the policy that the fathers of the government had adopted in relation to this element among us was the best policy in the world—the only wise policy—the only policy that we can ever safely continue upon—that will ever give us peace unless this dangerous element masters us all and becomes a national institution—*I turn upon him and ask him why he could not let it alone?* [Great and prolonged cheering.] I turn and ask him why he was driven to the necessity of introducing a *new policy*[4] in regard to it? He has himself said he introduced a new policy. He said so in his speech on the 22d of March of the present year, 1858. I ask him why he could not let it remain where our fathers placed it? I ask too of Judge Douglas and his friends why we shall not again place this institution upon the basis on which the fathers left it? I ask you when he infers that I am in favor of setting the free and slave States at war, when the institution was placed in that attitude by those who made the constitution, *did they make any war?* ["No;" "no;" and cheers.] If we had no war out of it when thus placed, wherein is the ground of belief that we shall have war out of it if we return to that policy? Have we had any peace upon this matter springing from any other basis? ["No, no."] I maintain that we have not. I have proposed nothing more than a return to the policy of the fathers.

I confess, when I propose a certain measure of policy, it is not enough for me that I do not intend anything evil in the result, but it is incumbent on me to show that it has not a *tendency* to that result. I have met Judge Douglas in that point of view. I have not only made the declaration that I do not *mean* to produce a conflict between the States, but I have tried to show by fair reasoning, and I think I have shown to the minds of fair men, that I propose nothing but what has a most peaceful tendency. The quotation that I happened to make in that Springfield speech, that "a house divided against itself cannot stand," and which has proved so offensive to the Judge, was part and parcel of the same thing. He tries to show that variety in the domestic institutions of the different States is necessary and indispensable. I do not dispute it. I have no controversy with Judge Douglas about that. I shall very readily agree with him that it would be foolish for us to insist upon having a cranberry law here, in Illinois, where we have no cranberries, because they have a cranberry law in Indiana, where they have cranberries. [Laughter, "good, good."] I should insist that it would be exceedingly wrong in us to deny to Virginia the right to enact oyster laws where they have oyster, because we want no such laws here. [Renewed laughter.] I understand, I hope, quite as well as Judge Douglas or anybody else, that the variety in the soil and climate and face of the country, and consequent variety in the industrial pursuits and productions of a country, require systems of law conforming to this variety in the natural features of the country. I understand quite as well as Judge

4. The Kansas Nebraska Act of 1854, which Douglas authored.

Douglas, that if we here raise a barrel of flour more than we want, and the Louisianians raise a barrel of sugar more than they want, it is of mutual advantage to exchange. That produces commerce, brings us together, and makes us better friends. We like one another the more for it. And I understand as well as Judge Douglas, or anybody else, that these mutual accommodations are the cements which bind together the different parts of this Union—that instead of being a thing to "divide the house"—figuratively expressing the Union,—they tend to sustain it; they are the props of the house tending always to hold it up.

But when I have admitted all this, I ask if there is any parallel between these things and this institution of slavery? I do not see that there is any parallel at all between them. Consider it. When have we had any difficulty or quarrel amongst ourselves about the cranberry laws of Indiana, or the oyster laws of Virginia, or the pine lumber laws of Maine, or the fact that Louisiana produces sugar, and Illinois flour? When have we had any quarrels over these things? When have we had perfect peace in regard to this thing which I say is an element of discord in this Union? We have sometimes had peace, but when was it? It was when the institution of slavery remained quiet where it was. We have had difficulty and turmoil whenever it has made a struggle to spread itself where it was not. I ask then, if experience does not speak in thunder tones, telling us that the policy which has given peace to the country heretofore, being returned to, gives the greatest promise of peace again. ["Yes;" "yes;" "yes."] You may say and Judge Douglas has intimated the same thing, that all this difficulty in regard to the institution of slavery is the mere agitation of office seekers and ambitious Northern politicians. He thinks we want to get "his place," I suppose. [Cheers and laughter.] I agree that there are office seekers amongst us. The Bible says somewhere that we are desperately selfish. I think we would have discovered that fact without the Bible. I do not claim that I am any less so than the average of men, but I do claim that I am not more selfish than Judge Douglas. [Roars of laughter and applause.]

But is it true that all the difficulty and agitation we have in regard to this institution of slavery springs from office seeking—from the mere ambition of politicians? Is that the truth? How many times have we had danger from this question? Go back to the day of the Missouri Compromise. Go back to the Nullification question, at the bottom of which lay this same slavery question. Go back to the time of the Annexation of Texas. Go back to the troubles that led to the Compromise of 1850. You will find that every time, with the single exception of the Nullification question, they sprung from an endeavor to spread this institution. There never was a party in the history of this country, and there probably never will be of sufficient strength to disturb the general peace of the country. Parties themselves may be divided and quarrel on minor questions, yet it extends not beyond the parties themselves. But does not this question make a disturbance outside of political circles? Does it not enter into the churches and rend them asunder?[5] What divided the great Methodist Church into two parts, North and South? What has raised this constant disturbance

5. Christian religious bodies that split into Northern and Southern branches over slavery included the Methodist (1844), Baptist (1845), New School Presbyterian (1857), and Old School Presbyterian (1861) churches.

in every Presbyterian General Assembly that meets? What disturbed the
Unitarian Church in this very city two years ago?[6] What has jarred and
shaken the great American Tract Society[7] recently, not yet splitting it, but
sure to divide it in the end. Is it not this same mighty, deep seated power
that somehow operates on the minds of men, exciting and stirring them
up in every avenue of society—in politics, in religion, in literature, in morals, in all the manifold relations of life? [Applause.] Is this the work of politicians? Is that irresistible power which for fifty years has shaken the
government and agitated the people to be stilled and subdued by pretending that it is an exceedingly simple thing, and we ought not to talk about
it? [Great cheers and laughter.] If you will get everybody else to stop talking about it, I assure I will quit before they have half done so. [Renewed
laughter.] But where is the philosophy or statesmanship which assumes
that you can quiet that disturbing element in our society which has disturbed us for more than half a century, which has been the only serious
danger that has threatened our institutions—I say, where is the philosophy or the statesmanship based on the assumption that we are to quit
talking about it [applause], and that the public mind is all at once to cease
being agitated by it? Yet this is the policy here in the North that Douglas
is advocating—that we are to care nothing about it! I ask you if it is not a
false philosophy? Is it not a false statesmanship that undertakes to build
up a system of policy upon the basis of caring nothing about *the very thing
that every body does care the most about?* ["Yes, yes," and applause]—a thing
which all experience has shown we care a very great deal about? [Laughter
and applause.]

The Judge alludes very often in the course of his remarks to the exclusive right which the States have to decide the whole thing for themselves.
I agree with him very readily that the different States have that right. He
is but fighting a man of straw when he assumes that I am contending
against the right of the States to do as they please about it. Our controversy with him is in regard to the new Territories. We agree that when the
States come in as States they have the right and the power to do as they
please. We have no power as citizens of the free States or in our federal
capacity as members of the Federal Union through the general government, to disturb slavery in the States where it exists. We profess constantly
that we have no more inclination than belief in the power of the Government to disturb it; yet we are driven constantly to defend ourselves from
the assumption that we are warring upon the rights of the *States.* What I
insist upon is, that the new Territories shall be kept free from it while in
the Territorial condition. Judge Douglas assumes that we have no interest
in them—that we have no right whatever to interfere. I think we have
some interest. I think that as white men we have. Do we not wish for an
outlet for our surplus population, if I may so express myself? Do we not
feel an interest in getting to that outlet with such institutions as we would
like to have prevail there? If you go to the Territory opposed to slavery
and another man comes upon the same ground with his slave, upon the

6. In summer 1856, William D'Arcy Haley, a Unitarian minister in Alton, was forced to resign
after his church was ransacked as result of an antislavery sermon he had preached.
7. The society released a statement in March 1856 saying that on the subject of slavery the
group's charter "allows it to go so far as evangelical Christians in the Northern and in the
Southern states can approve the publications it may issue, and no farther."

assumption that the things are equal, it turns out that he has the equal right all his way and you have no part of it your way. If he goes in and makes it a slave Territory, and by consequence a slave State, is it not time that those who desire to have it a free State were on equal ground. Let me suggest it in a different way. How many Democrats are there about here ["a thousand"] who have left slave States and come into the free State of Illinois to get rid of the institution of slavery. [Another voice—"a thousand and one."] I reckon there are a thousand and one. [Laughter.] I will ask you, if the policy you are now advocating had prevailed when this country was in a Territorial condition, where would you have gone to get rid of it? [Applause.] Where would you have found your free State or Territory to go to? And when hereafter, for any cause, the people in this place shall desire to find new homes, if they wish to be rid of the institution, where will they find the place to go to? [Loud cheers.]

Now irrespective of the moral aspect of this question as to whether there is a right or wrong in enslaving a negro, I am still in favor of our new Territories being in such a condition that white men may find a home—may find some spot where they can better their condition—where they can settle upon new soil and better their condition in life. [Great and continued cheering.] I am in favor of this not merely, (I must say it here as I have elsewhere,) for our own people who are born amongst us, but as an outlet for *free white people everywhere*, the world over—in which Hans and Baptiste and Patrick, and all other men from all the world, may find new homes and better their conditions in life. [Loud and long continued applause.]

I have stated upon former occasions, and I may as well state again, what I understand to be the real issue in this controversy between Judge Douglas and myself. On the point of my wanting to make war between the free and the slave States, there has been no issue between us. So, too, when he assumes that I am in favor of introducing a perfect social and political equality between the white and black races. These are false issues, upon which Judge Douglas has tried to force the controversy. There is no foundation in truth for the charge that I maintain either of these propositions. The real issue in this controversy—the one pressing upon every mind—is the sentiment on the part of one class that looks upon the institution of slavery *as a wrong*, and of another class that *does not* look upon it as a wrong. The sentiment that contemplates the institution of slavery in this country as a wrong is the sentiment of the Republican party. It is the sentiment around which all their actions—all their arguments circle—from which all their propositions radiate. They look upon it as being a moral, social and political wrong; and while they contemplate it as such, they nevertheless have due regard for its actual existence among us, and the difficulties of getting rid of it in any satisfactory way and to all the constitutional obligations thrown about it. Yet having a due regard for these, they desire a policy in regard to it that looks to its not creating any more danger. They insist that it should as far as may be, *be treated* as a wrong, and one of the methods of treating it as a wrong is to *make provision that it shall grow no larger*. [Loud applause.] They also desire a policy that looks to a peaceful end of slavery at sometime, as being wrong. These are the views they entertain in regard to it as I understand them; and all their sentiments—all their arguments and propositions are brought within this range. I have said and I repeat it here, that if there be a man amongst us who does not think that the institution of slavery is wrong in any one of the aspects of which I have spoken, he is misplaced and ought not to be with us. And if there be a man amongst us who is so impatient of it as a wrong as to disregard its actual presence among us and the difficulty of getting rid of it suddenly in a satisfactory way, and to disregard the constitutional obligations thrown about it, that man is misplaced if he is on our platform. We disclaim sympathy with him in practical action. He is not placed properly with us.

On this subject of treating it as a wrong, and limiting its spread, let me say a word. Has any thing ever threatened the existence of this Union save and except this very institution of Slavery? What is it that we hold most dear amongst us? Our own liberty and prosperity. What has ever threatened our liberty and prosperity save and except this institution of Slavery? If this is true, how do you propose to improve the condition of things by enlarging Slavery—by spreading it out and making it bigger? You may have a wen or a cancer upon your person and not be able to cut it out lest you bleed to death; but surely it is no way to cure it, to engraft it and spread it over your whole body. That is no proper way of treating what you regard a wrong. You see this peaceful way of dealing with it as a wrong—restricting the spread of it, and not allowing it to go into new countries where it has not already existed. That is the peaceful way, the old-fashioned way, the way in which the fathers themselves set us the example.

On the other hand, I have said there is a sentiment which treats it as *not* being wrong. That is the Democratic sentiment of this day. I do not mean to say that every man who stands within that range positively asserts that it is right. That class will include all who positively assert that it is right, and all who like Judge Douglas treat it as indifferent and do not say it is either right or wrong. These two classes of men fall within the general class of those who do not look upon it as a wrong. And if there be among you anybody who supposes that he as a Democrat, can consider himself "as much opposed to slavery as anybody," I would like to reason with him. You never treat it as a wrong. What other thing that you consider as a wrong, do you deal with as you deal with that? Perhaps you *say* it is wrong, *but your leader never does, and you quarrel with anybody who says it is wrong.* Although you pretend to say so yourself you can find no fit place to deal with it as a wrong. You must not say anything about it in the free States, *because it is not here.* You must not say anything about it in the slave States, *because it is there.* You must not say anything about it in the pulpit, because that is religion and has nothing to do with it. You must not say anything about it in politics, *because that will disturb the security of "my place."* [Shouts of laughter and cheers.] There is no place to talk about it as being a wrong, although you say yourself it is a wrong. But finally you will screw yourself up to the belief that if the people of the slave States should adopt a system of gradual emancipation on the slavery question, you would be in favor of it. You would be in favor of it. You say that is getting it in the right place, and you would be glad to see it succeed. But you are deceiv-

8. Francis Preston Blair, Jr. (1821–1875), a U.S. congressman from Missouri who served as a Union general in the Civil War, and Benjamin Gratz Brown (1826–1885), a Missouri congressman.

ing yourself. You all know that Frank Blair and Gratz Brown,[8] down there in St. Louis, undertook to introduce that system in Missouri. They fought as valiantly as they could for the system of gradual emancipation which you pretend you would be glad to see succeed. Now I will bring you to the test. After a hard fight they were beaten, and when the news came over here you threw up your hats and *hurrahed for Democracy.* [Great applause and laughter.] More than that, take all the argument made in favor of the system you have proposed, and it carefully excludes the idea that there is anything wrong in the institution of slavery. The arguments to sustain that policy carefully excluded it. Even here to-day you heard Judge Douglas quarrel with me because I uttered a wish that it might sometime come to an end. Although Henry Clay could say he wished every slave in the United States was in the country of his ancestors, I am denounced by those pretending to respect Henry Clay for uttering a wish that it might sometime, in some peaceful way, come to an end. The Democratic policy in regard to that institution will not tolerate the merest breath, the slightest hint, of the least degree of wrong about it. Try it by some of Judge Douglas' arguments. He says he "don't care whether it is voted up or voted down" in the Territories. I do not care myself in dealing with that expression, whether it is intended to be expressive of his individual sentiments on the subject, or only of the national policy he desires to have established. It is alike valuable for my purpose. Any man can say that who does not see anything wrong in slavery, but no man can logically say it who does see a wrong in it; because no man can logically say he don't care whether a wrong is voted up or voted down. He may say he don't care whether an indifferent thing is voted up or down, but he must logically have a choice between a right thing and a wrong thing. He contends that whatever community wants slaves has a right to have them. So they have if it is not a wrong. But if it is a wrong, he cannot say people have a right to do wrong. He says that upon the score of equality, slaves should be allowed to go in a new Territory, like other property. This is strictly logical if there is no difference between it and other property. If it and other property are equal, his argument is entirely logical. But if you insist that one is wrong and the other right, there is no use to institute a comparison between right and wrong. You may turn over everything in the Democratic policy from beginning to end, whether in the shape it takes on the statute book, in the shape it takes in the Dred Scott decision, in the shape it takes in conversation or the shape it takes in short maxim-like arguments—it everywhere carefully excludes the idea that there is anything wrong in it.

That is the real issue. That is the issue that will continue in this country when these poor tongues of Judge Douglas and myself shall be silent. It is the eternal struggle between these two principles—right and wrong—throughout the world. They are the two principles that have stood face to face from the beginning of time; and will ever continue to struggle. The one is the common right of humanity and the other the divine right of kings. It is the same principle in whatever shape it develops itself. It is the same spirit that says, "You work and toil and earn bread, and I'll eat it." [Loud applause.] No matter in what shape it comes, whether from the mouth of a king who seeks to bestride the people of his own nation and live by the fruit of their labor, or from one race of men as an apology for enslaving another race, it is the same tyrannical principle. I was glad to express my gratitude at Quincy, and I reexpress it here to Judge Douglas— *that he looks to no end of the institution of slavery.* That will help the people to see where the struggle really is. It will hereafter place with us all men who really do wish the wrong may have an end. And whenever we can get rid of the fog which obscures the real question—when we can get Judge Douglas and his friends to avow a policy looking to its perpetuation—we can get out from among them that class of men and bring them to the side of those who treat it as a wrong. Then there will soon be an end of it, and that end will be its "ultimate extinction." Whenever the issue can be distinctly made, and all extraneous matter thrown out so that men can fairly see the real difference between the parties, this controversy will soon be settled, and it will be done peaceably too. There will be no war, no violence. It will be placed again where the wisest and best men of the world, placed it. Brooks[9] of South Carolina once declared that when this Constitution was framed, its framers did not look to the institution existing until this day. When he said this, I think he stated a fact that is fully borne out by the history of the times. But he also said they were better and wiser men than the men of these days; yet the men of these days had experience which they had not, and by the invention of the cotton gin it became a necessity in this country that slavery should be perpetual.[1] I now say that willingly or unwillingly, purposely or without purpose, Judge Douglas has been the most prominent instrument in changing the position of the institution of slavery which the fathers of the government expected to come to an end ere this—*and putting it upon Brooks' cotton gin basis,* [Great applause,]—placing it where he openly confesses he has no desire there shall ever be an end of it. [Renewed applause.]

I understand I have ten minutes yet. I will employ it in saying something about this argument Judge Douglas uses, while he sustains the Dred Scot decision, that the people of the Territories can still somehow exclude slavery. The first thing I ask attention to is the fact that Judge Douglas constantly said, before the decision, that whether they could or not, *was a question for the Supreme Court.* [Cheers.] But after the Court has made the decision he virtually says it is not a question for the Supreme Court, but for the people. [Renewed applause] And how is it he tells us they can exclude it? He says it needs "police regulations," and that admits of "unfriendly legislation." Although it is a right established by the constitution of the United States to take a slave into a Territory of the United States and hold him as property, yet unless the Territorial Legislature will give friendly legislation, and, more especially, if they adopt unfriendly legislation, they can practically exclude him. Now, without meeting this proposition as a matter of fact, I pass to consider the real constitutional obligation. Let me take the gentleman who looks me in the face before me, and let us suppose that he is a member of the Territorial Legislature. The first thing he will do will be to swear that he will support the Consti-

---

9. Preston S. Brooks (1819–1857), Democratic congressman and ardent defender of slavery who in 1856 pummeled Massachusetts Senator Charles Sumner (1811–1874) after the latter made an antislavery speech.
1. Brooks made his "cotton gin" argument for slavery in an 1854 speech.

tution of the United States. His neighbor by his side in the Territory has
slaves and needs Territorial legislation to enable him to enjoy that constitutional right. Can he withhold the legislation which his neighbor needs
for the enjoyment of a right which is fixed in his favor in the Constitution
of the United States which he has sworn to support? Can he withhold it
without violating his oath? And more especially, can he pass unfriendly
legislation to violate his oath? Why this is a *monstrous* sort of talk about
the Constitution of the United States! [Great applause.] *There has never
been as outlandish or lawless a doctrine from the mouth of any respectable
man on earth.* [Tremendous cheers.] I do not believe it is a constitutional
right to hold slaves in a Territory of the United States. I believe the decision
was improperly made and I go for reversing it. Judge Douglas is furious
against those who go for reversing a decision. But he is for legislating it
out of all force while the law itself stands. I repeat that there has never
been so monstrous a doctrine uttered from the mouth of a respectable
man. [Loud cheers.]

I suppose most of us, (I know it of myself,) believe that the people of the
Southern States are entitled to a Congressional fugitive slave law—that it
is a right fixed in the Constitution. But it cannot be made available to them
without Congressional legislation. In the Judge's language, it is a "barren
right" which needs legislation before it can become efficient and valuable
to the persons to whom it is guaranteed. And as the right is constitutional
I agree that the legislation shall be granted to it—and that not that we like
the institution of slavery. We profess to have no taste for running and
catching niggers—at least I profess no taste for that job at all. Why then do
I yield support to a fugitive slave law? Because I do not understand that the
Constitution, which guarantees that right, can be supported without it.
And if I believed that the right to hold a slave in a Territory was equally
fixed in the Constitution with the right to reclaim fugitives, I should be
bound to give it the legislation necessary to support it. I say that no man
can deny his obligation to give the necessary legislation to support slavery
in a Territory, who believes it is a constitutional right to have it there. No
man can, who does not give the Abolitionist an argument to deny the obligation enjoined by the constitution to enact a fugitive slave law. Try it now.
It is the strongest abolition argument ever made. I say if that Dred Scott
decision is correct then the right to hold slaves in a Territory is equally a
constitutional right with the right of a slaveholder to have his runaway
returned. No one can show the distinction between them. The one is
express, so that we cannot deny it. The other is construed to be in the constitution, so that he who believes the decision to be correct believes in the
right. And the man who argues that by unfriendly legislation, in spite of
that constitutional right, slavery may be driven from the Territories, cannot
avoid furnishing an argument by which Abolitionists may deny the obligation to return fugitives, and claim the power to pass laws unfriendly to the
right of the slaveholder to reclaim his fugitive. I do not know how such an
argument may strike a popular assembly like this, but I defy anybody to
go before a body of men whose minds are educated to estimating evidence
and reasoning, and show that there is an iota of difference between the
constitutional right to reclaim a fugitive, and the constitutional right to
hold a slave, in a Territory, provided this Dred Scott decision is correct.
[Cheers.] I defy any man to make an argument that will justify unfriendly

legislation to deprive a slaveholder of his right to hold his slave in a Territory, that will not equally, in all its length, breadth and thickness furnish an argument for nullifying the fugitive slave law. Why there is not such an Abolitionist in the nation as Douglas, after all. [Loud and enthusiastic applause.]

October 15, 1858

Speech at Meredosia, Illinois[1]

On Monday night last [Lincoln] addressed a small meeting at Meredosia. His object was to convert two or three Germans at that place to the republican faith. To effect this object, we are informed he took for his text the Declaration of Independence and labored for an hour to prove by that instrument that the negro was born with rights equal with the whites; thus by implication assailing the Constitution of the United States, which protects the institution of negro servitude in the slave states.

In the course of his speech he remarked that, while at Naples on the preceding day he had noticed about a dozen Irishmen on the levee, and it had occurred to him that those Irishmen had been imported expressly to vote him down.

Doubtless Mr. Lincoln entertains a holy horror of all Irishmen and other adopted citizens who have sufficient self-respect to believe themselves superior to the negro. What right have adopted citizens to vote Mr. Lincoln and his negro equality doctrines down? He would doubtless disfranchise every one of them if he had the power. His reference to the danger of his being voted down by foreigners, was a cue to his followers, similar in character to the intimation of the Chicago Press a few days since, that the republicans of the interior counties should protect their rights; in other words, that under the pretext of protecting their rights, they should keep adopted citizens from the polls. We hope no adopted citizen will attempt to put in an illegal vote; yet every adopted citizen, be a democrat or republican, should have his vote. And every foreigner in old Morgan who is a legal voter, *will have his vote* in spite of Mr. Lincoln.

The effect produced by Mr. Lincoln's significant reference to the danger he apprehended from the foreign vote, was manifested before the close of the meeting. Dr. Wackly,[2] a highly respectable merchant of Meredosia, who is an influential German, and also a German speaker of considerable talent, a few evenings before, in a speech had expressed the opinion that Mr. Lincoln was a knownothing. Mr. Lincoln referred to this charge, and retorted on to the Dr. in severe, personal manner.

October 18, 1858

1. This summary of Lincoln's speech at Meredosia appeared in the Jacksonville, Illinois, *Sentinel*, October 22, 1858.
2. Probably a reference to Dr. W. J. Wackerle of Meredosia.

To James N. Brown[1]

Hon. J. N. Brown   Springfield,
My dear Sir   Oct. 18. 1858
I do not perceive how I can express myself, more plainly, than I have done in the foregoing extracts. In four of them I have expressly disclaimed all intention to bring about social and political equality between the white and black races, and, in all the rest, I have done the same thing by clear implication.

I have made it equally plain that I think the negro is included in the word "men" used in the Declaration of Independence.

I believe the declaration that "all men are created equal" is the great fundamental principle upon which our free institutions rest; that negro slavery is violative of that principle; but that, by our frame of government, that principle has not been made one of legal obligation; that by our frame of government, the States which have slavery are to retain it, or surrender it at their own pleasure; and that all others—individuals, free-states and national government—are constitutionally bound to leave them alone about it.

I believe our government was thus framed because of the *necessity* springing from the actual presence of slavery, when it was framed.

That such necessity does not exist in the teritories, where slavery is not present.[2]

In his Mendenhall speech Mr. Clay says

"Now, as an abstract principle, there is no doubt of the truth of that declaration (all men created equal) and it is desireable, in the original construction of society, and in organized societies, to keep it in view, as a great fundamental principle"

Again, in the same speech Mr. Clay says

"If a state of nature existed, and we were about to lay the foundations of society, no man would be more strongly opposed than I should to incorporate the institution of slavery among it's elements;"

Exactly so. In our new free teritories, a state of nature *does* exist. In them Congress lays the foundations of society; and, in laying those foundations, I say, with Mr. Clay, it is desireable that the declaration of the equality of all men shall be kept in view, as a great fundamental principle; and that Congress, which lays the foundations of society, should, like Mr. Clay, be strongly opposed to the incorporation of slavery among it's elements.

But it does not follow that social and political equality between whites and blacks, *must* be incorporated, because slavery must *not*. The declaration does not so require. Yours as ever

---

1. Illinois Republican (1806–1868) who, at Lincoln's urging, ran for the state legislature in 1858. During the campaign, Brown, a former Kentuckian, was unsure how to confront the charge that Republicans advocated "negro equality."
2. An address about slavery that Henry Clay gave in Richmond, Indiana, in October 1842 at the behest of Quaker abolitionist Hiram Menendhall (1801–1852) and others.

To Edward Lusk[1]

Edward Lusk, Esq   Springfield,
Dear Sir   Oct. 30, 1858
I understand the story is still being told, and insisted upon, that I have
been a Know-Nothing. I repeat, what I stated in a public speech at Meredosia,[2] that I am not, nor ever have been, connected with the party called
the Know-Nothing party, or party calling themselves the American party.
Certainly no man of truth, and I believe, no man of good character for
truth can be found to say on his own knowledge that I ever was connected
with that party. Yours very truly

Portion of Last Speech in Campaign of 1858, Springfield, Illinois

My friends, to-day closes the discussions of this canvass. The planting
and the culture are over; and there remains but the preparation, and the
harvest.

I stand here surrounded by friends—some *political, all personal* friends,
I trust. May I be indulged, in this closing scene, to say a few words of
myself. I have borne a laborious, and, in some respects to myself, a painful part in the contest. Through all, I have neither assailed, nor wrestled
with any part of the constitution. The legal right of the Southern people
to reclaim their fugitives I have constantly admitted. The legal right of
Congress to interfere with their institution in the states, I have constantly
denied. In resisting the spread of slavery to new teritory, and with that,
what appears to me to be a tendency to subvert the first principle of free
government itself my whole effort has consisted. To the best of my judgment I have labored *for*, and not *against* the Union. As I have not felt, so I
have not expressed any harsh sentiment towards our Southern bretheren.
I have constantly declared, as I really believed, the only difference between
them and us, is the difference of circumstances.

I have meant to assail the motives of no party, or individual; and if I have,
in any instance (of which I am not conscious) departed from my purpose,
I regret it.

I have said that in some respects the contest has been painful to me.
Myself, and those with whom I act have been constantly accused of a
purpose to destroy the union; and bespattered with every imaginable
odious epithet; and some who were friends, as it were but yesterday have
made themselves most active in this. I have cultivated patience, and
made no attempt at a retort.

Ambition has been ascribed to me. God knows how sincerely I prayed
from the first that this field of ambition might not be opened. I claim no
insensibility to political honors; but today could the Missouri restriction
be restored, and the whole slavery question replaced on the old ground of
"toleration by *necessity*" where it exists, with unyielding hostility to the

---

1. A farmer in Meredosia, Illinois.
2. See p. 178.

spread of it, on principle, I would, in consideration, gladly agree, that Judge Douglas should never be *out*, and I never *in*, an office, so long as we both or either, live.

October 30, 1858

To W. H. Wells[1]

W. H. Wells, Esq.   Springfield, Ills.
My dear Sir: Jany. 8, 1859.
Yours of the 3rd. Inst. is just received. I regret to say that the joint discussions between Judge Douglas and myself have been published in no shape except in the first newspaper reports; and that I have no copy of them, or even of the single one at Freeport, which I could send you. By dint of great labor since the election, I have got together a nearly, (not quite) complete single set to preserve myself. I shall preserve your address, and if I can, in a reasonable time, lay my hand on an old paper containing the Freeport discussion, I will send it to you.

All dallying with Douglas by Republicans, who are such at heart, is, at the very least, time, and labor lost; and all such, who so dally with him, will yet bite their lips in vexation for their own folly. His policy, which rigourously excludes all idea of there being any *wrong* in slavery, does lead inevitably to the nationalization of the Institution; and all who deprecate that consummation, and yet are seduced into his support, do but cut their own throats. True, Douglas *has* opposed the administration on one measure, and yet *may* on some other; but while he upholds the Dred Scott decision, declares that he cares not whether slavery be voted down or voted up; that it is simply a question of dollars and cents, and that the Almighty has drawn a line on one side of which labor *must* be performed by slaves; to support him or Buchanan, is simply to reach the same goal by only slightly different roads. Very Respectfully

Second Lecture on Discoveries and Inventions, Jacksonville, Illinois[1]

We have all heard of Young America.[2] He is the most *current* youth of the age. Some think him conceited, and arrogant; but has he not reason to entertain a rather extensive opinion of himself? Is he not the inventor and owner of the *present*, and sole hope of the *future*? Men, and things, everywhere, are ministering unto him. Look at his apparel, and you shall see cotten fabrics from Manchester and Lowell; flax-linen from Ireland; wool-cloth from Spain; silk from France; furs from the Arctic regions, with a

---

1. A young printer in Waynesburg, Pennsylvania, who had asked for a copy of the Lincoln-Douglas debates; he had a special interest in the debate at Freeport.
1. Lincoln gave this speech in three Illinois locations—Jacksonville, Decatur, and Springfield—in February 1859.
2. A social movement of the 1840s and 1850s that championed American expansion, free trade, and a rejection of the past.

buffalo-robe from the Rocky Mountains, as a general out-sider. At his table, besides plain bread and meat made at home, are sugar from Louisiana; coffee and fruits from the tropics; salt from Turk's Island; fish from New-foundland; tea from China, and spices from the Indies. The whale of the Pacific furnishes his candle-light; he has a diamond-ring from Brazil; a gold-watch from California, and a Spanish cigar from Havanna. He not only has a present supply of all these, and much more; but thousands of hands are engaged in producing fresh supplies, and other thousands, in bringing them to him. The iron horse is panting, and impatient, to carry him everywhere, in no time; and the lightening stands ready harnessed to take and bring his tidings in a trifle less than no time. He owns a large part of the world, by right of possessing it; and all the rest by right of *wanting* it, and *intending* to have it. As Plato[3] had for the immortality of the soul, so Young America has "a pleasing hope—a fond desire—a longing after"[4] teritory. He has a great passion—a perfect rage—for the *"new"*; particularly new men for office, and the new earth mentioned in the revelations, in which, being no more sea, there must be about three times as much land as in the present. He is a great friend of humanity; and his desire for land is not selfish, but merely an impulse to extend the area of freedom. He is very anxious to fight for the liberation of enslaved nations and colonies, provided, always, they *have* land, and have *not* any liking for his interference. As to those who have no land, and would be glad of help from any quarter, he considers *they* can afford to wait a few hundred years longer. In knowledge he is particularly rich. He knows all that can possibly be known; inclines to believe in spiritual rappings, and is the unquestioned inventor of *"Manifest Destiny."*[5] His horror is for all that is old, particularly "Old Fogy"; and if there be any thing old which he can endure, it is only old whiskey and old tobacco.

If the said Young America really is, as he claims to be, the owner of all present, it must be admitted that he has considerable advantage of Old Fogy. Take, for instance, the first of all fogies, father Adam. There he stood, a very perfect physical man, as poets and painters inform us; but he must have been very ignorant, and simple in his habits. He had had no sufficient time to learn much by observation; and he had no near neighbors to teach him anything. No part of his breakfast had been brought from the other side of the world; and it is quite probable, he had no conception of the world having any other side. In all of these things, it is very plain, he was no equal of Young America; the most that can be said is, that *according to his chance* he may have been quite as much of a man as his very self-complaisant descendant. Little as was what he knew, let the Youngster discard all he has learned from others, and then show, if he can, any advantage on his side. In the way of *land*, and *live stock*, Adam was quite in the ascendant. He had dominion over all the earth, and all the living things upon, and round about it. The land has been sadly divided out since; but never fret, Young America will *re-annex* it.

3. Ancient Greek philosopher (429–347 B.C.E.).
4. Joseph Addison (1672–1719), *Cato*, 5.1.
5. Coined in 1845 by Democratic journalist John L. O'Sullivan, the phrase signified the desire to spread American institutions and values westward to the Pacific and elsewhere. "Spiritual rappings": or spiritualism, a popular movement that believed that spirits of the dead communicate with the living through such signs as rapping sounds.

The great difference between Young America and Old Fogy, is the result of *Discoveries, Inventions*, and *Improvements*. These, in turn, are the result of *observation, reflection* and *experiment*. For instance, it is quite certain that ever since water has been boiled in covered vessels, men have seen the lids of the vessels rise and fall a little, with a sort of fluttering motion, by force of the steam; but so long as this was not specially observed, and reflected and experimented upon, it came to nothing. At length however, after many thousand years, some man observes this long-known effect of hot water lifting a pot-lid, and begins a train of reflection upon it. He says "Why, to be sure, the force that lifts the pot-lid, will lift any thing else, which is no heavier than the pot-lid." "And, as man has much hard lifting to do, can not this hot-water power be made to help him?" He has become a little excited on the subject, and he fancies he hears a voice answering "Try me" He does try it; and the *observation, reflection*, and *trial* gives to the world the control of that tremendous, and now well known agent, called steam-power. This is not the actual history in detail, but the general principle.

But was this first inventor of the application of steam, wiser or more ingenious than those who had gone before him? Not at all. Had he not learned much of them, he never would have succeeded—probably, never would have thought of making the attempt. To be fruitful in invention, it is indispensable to have a *habit* of observation and reflection; and this *habit*, our steam friend acquired, no doubt, from those who, to him, were old fogies. But for the difference in *habit* of observation, why did yankees, almost instantly, discover gold in California, which had been trodden upon, and overlooked by indians and Mexican greasers, for centuries? Goldmines are not the only mines overlooked in the same way. There are more mines above the Earth's surface than below it. All nature—the whole world, material, moral, and intellectual,—is a mine; and, in Adam's day, it was a wholly unexplored mine. Now, it was the destined work of Adam's race to develope, by discoveries, inventions, and improvements, the hidden treasures of this mine. But Adam had nothing to turn his attention to the work. If he should do anything in the way of invention, he had first to invent the art of invention—the *instance* at least, if not the *habit* of observation and reflection. As might be expected he seems not to have been a very observing man at first; for it appears he went about naked a considerable length of time, before he even noticed that obvious fact. But when he did observe it, the observation was not lost upon him; for it immediately led to the first of all inventions, of which we have any direct account—*the fig-leaf apron*.

The inclination to exchange thoughts with one another is probably an original impulse of our nature. If I be in pain I wish to let you know it, and to ask your sympathy and assistance; and my pleasurable emotions also, I wish to communicate to, and share with you. But to carry on such communication, some *instrumentality* is indispensable. Accordingly speech—articulate sounds rattled off from the tongue—was used by our first parents, and even by Adam, before the creation of Eve. He gave names to the animals while she was still a bone in his side; and he broke out quite volubly when she first stood before him, the best present of his maker. From this it would appear that speech was not an invention of man, but rather the direct gift of his Creator. But whether Divine gift, or invention, it is still plain that if a mode of communication had been left to invention, *speech* must have been the first, from the superior adaptation to the end, of the organs of speech, over every other means within the whole range of nature. Of the organs of speech the tongue is the principal; and if we shall test it, we shall find the capacities of the tongue, in the utterance of articulate sounds, absolutely wonderful. You can count from one to one hundred, quite distinctly in about forty seconds. In doing this two hundred and eighty three distinct sounds or syllables are uttered, being seven to each second; and yet there shall be enough difference between every two, to be easily recognized by the ear of the hearer. What other *signs* to represent *things* could possibly be produced so rapidly? or, even, if ready made, could be *arranged* so rapidly to express the sense? *Motions* with the hands, are no adequate substitute. *Marks* for the recognition of the eye—*writing*—although a wonderful auxiliary for speech, is no worthy substitute for it. In addition to the more slow and laborious process of getting up a communication in writing, the materials—pen, ink, and paper—are not always at hand. But one always has his tongue with him, and the breath of his life is the ever-ready material with which it works. Speech, then, by enabling different individuals to interchange thoughts, and thereby to combine their powers of observation and reflection, greatly facilitates useful discoveries and inventions. What one observes, and would himself infer nothing from, he tells to another, and that other at once sees a valuable hint in it. A result is thus reached which neither *alone* would have arrived at.

And this reminds me of what I passed unnoticed before, that the very first invention was a joint operation, Eve having shared with Adam in the getting up of the apron. And, indeed, judging from the fact that sewing has come down to our times as "woman's work" it is very probable she took the leading part; he, perhaps, doing no more than to stand by and thread the needle. That proceeding may be reckoned as the mother of all "Sewing societies"; and the first and most perfect "world's fair" all inventions and all inventors then in the world, being on the spot.

But speech alone, valuable as it ever has been, and is, has not advanced the condition of the world much. This is abundantly evident when we look at the degraded condition of all those tribes of human creatures who have no considerable additional means of communicating thoughts. *Writing*—the art of communicating thoughts to the mind, through the eye—is the great invention of the world. Great in the astonishing range of analysis and combination which necessarily underlies the most crude and general conception of it—great, very great in enabling us to converse with the dead, the absent, and the unborn, at all distances of time and of space; and great, not only in its direct benefits, but greatest help, to all other inventions. Suppose the art, with all conception of it, were this day lost to the world, how long, think you, would it be, before even Young America could get up the letter A. with any adequate notion of using it to advantage? The precise period at which writing was invented, is not known; but it certainly was as early as the time of Moses; from which we may safely infer that it's inventors were very old fogies.

Webster,[6] at the time of writing his Dictionary, speaks of the English Language as then consisting of seventy or eighty thousand words. If so,

6. Noah Webster (1758–1843), author of *An American Dictionary of the English Language* (1828).

the language in which the five books of Moses were written must, at that time, now thirtythree or four hundred years ago, have consisted of at least one quarter as many, or, twenty thousand. When we remember that words are *sounds* merely, we shall conclude that the idea of representing those sounds by *marks*, so that whoever should at any time after see the marks, would understand what sounds they meant, was a bold and ingenius conception, not likely to occur to one man of a million, in the run of a thousand years. And, when it did occur, a distinct mark for each word, giving twenty thousand different marks first to be learned, and afterwards remembered, would follow as the second thought, and would present such a difficulty as would lead to the conclusion that the whole thing was impracticable. But the *necessity* still would exist; and we may readily suppose that the idea was conceived, and lost, and reproduced, and dropped, and taken up again and again, until at last, the thought of dividing sounds into parts, and making a mark, not to represent a whole sound, but only a part of one, and then of combining these marks, not very many in number, upon the principles of permutation, so as to represent any and all of the whole twenty thousand words, and even any additional number was somehow conceived and pushed into practice. This was the invention of *phoenetic* writing, as distinguished from the clumsy picture writing of some of the nations. That it was difficult of conception and execution, is apparant, as well by the foregoing reflections, as by the fact that so many tribes of men have come down from Adam's time to ours without ever having possessed it. It's utility may be conceived, by the reflection that, to *it* we owe everything which distinguishes us from savages. Take it from us, and the Bible, all history, all science, all government, all commerce, and nearly all social intercourse go with it.

The great activity of the tongue, in articulating sounds, has already been mentioned; and it may be of some passing interest to notice the wonderful powers of the *eye*, in conveying ideas to the mind from writing. Take the same example of the numbers from *one* to *one hundred*, written down, and you can run your eye over the list, and be assured that every number is in it, in about one half the time it would require to pronounce the words with the voice; and not only so, but you can, in the same short time, determine whether every word is spelled correctly, by which it is evident that every separate letter, amounting to eight hundred and sixty four, has been recognized, and reported to the mind, within the incredibly short space of twenty seconds, or one third of a minute.

I have already intimated my opinion that in the world's history, certain inventions and discoveries occurred, of peculiar value, on account of their great efficiency in facilitating all other inventions and discoveries. Of these were the arts of writing and of printing—the discovery of America, and the introduction of Patent-laws. The date of the first, as already stated, is unknown; but it certainly was as much as fifteen hundred years before the Christian era; the second—printing—came in 1436, or nearly three thousand years after the first. The others followed more rapidly— the discovery of America in 1492, and the first patent laws in 1624. Though not apposite to my present purpose, it is but justice to the fruitfulness of that period, to mention two other important events—the Lutheran Reformation in 1517, and, still earlier, the invention of negroes, or, of the present mode of using them, in 1434. But, to return to the consideration of printing, it is plain that it is but the *other* half—and in real utility, the *better* half—of writing; and that both together are but the assistants of speech in the communication of thoughts between man and man. When man was possessed of speech alone, the chances of invention, discovery, and improvement, were very limited; but by the introduction of each of these, they were greatly multiplied. When writing was invented, any important observation, likely to lead to a discovery, had at least a chance of being written down, and consequently, a better chance of never being forgotten; and of being seen, and reflected upon, by a much greater number of persons; and thereby the chances of a valuable hint being caught, proportionably augmented. By this means the observation of a single individual might lead to an important invention, years, and even centuries after he was dead. In one word, by means of writing, the seeds of invention were more permanently preserved, and more widely sown. And yet, for the three thousand years during which printing remained undiscovered after writing was in use, it was only a small portion of the people who could write, or read writing; and consequently the field of invention, though much extended, still continued very limited. At length printing came. It gave ten thousand copies of any written matter, quite as cheaply as ten were given before; and consequently a thousand minds were brought into the field where there was but one before. This was a great *gain*; and history shows a great *change* corresponding to it, in point of time. I will venture to consider *it*, the true termination of that period called "the dark ages." Discoveries, inventions, and improvements followed rapidly, and have been increasing their rapidity ever since. The effects could not come, all at once. It required time to bring them out; and they are still coming. The *capacity* to read, could not be multiplied as fast as the *means* of reading. Spelling-books just began to go into the hands of the children; but the teachers were not very numerous, or very competent; so that it is safe to infer they did not advance so speedily as they do now-a-days. It is very probable—almost certain—that the great mass of men, at that time, were utterly unconscious, that their *conditions*, or their *minds* were capable of improvement. They not only looked upon the educated few as superior beings; but they supposed themselves to be naturally incapable of rising to equality. To immancipate the mind from this false and under estimate of itself, is the great task which printing came into the world to perform. It is difficult for us, *now* and *here*, to conceive how strong this slavery of the mind was; and how long it did, of necessity, take, to break it's shackles, and to get a habit of freedom of thought, established. It is, in this connection, a curious fact that a new country is most favorable—almost necessary—to the immancipation of thought, and the consequent advancement of civilization and the arts. The human family originated as is thought, somewhere in Asia, and have worked their way principally Westward. Just now, in civilization, and the arts, the people of Asia are entirely behind those of Europe; those of the East of Europe behind those of the West of it; while we, here in America, *think* we discover, and invent, and improve, faster than any of them. *They* may think this is arrogance; but they can not deny that Russia has called on us to show her how to build steam-boats and railroads—while in the older parts of Asia, they scarcely know that such things as S.Bs &

RR.s.[7] exist. In anciently inhabited countries, the dust of ages—a real downright old-fogyism—seems to settle upon, and smother the intellects and energies of man. It is in this view that I have mentioned the discovery of America as an event greatly favoring and facilitating useful discoveries and inventions.

Next came the Patent laws. These began in England in 1624; and, in this country, with the adoption of our constitution. Before then, any man might instantly use what another had invented; so that the inventor had no special advantage from his own invention. The patent system changed this; secured to the inventor, for a limited time, the exclusive use of his invention; and thereby added the fuel of *interest* to the *fire* of genius, in the discovery and production of new and useful things.

February 11, 1859

From Speech at Chicago, Illinois[1]

* * *

* * * Never forget that we have before us this whole matter of the right or wrong of slavery in this Union, though the immediate question is as to its spreading out into new Territories and States.

I do not wish to be misunderstood upon this subject of slavery in this country. I suppose it may long exist, and perhaps the best way for it to come to an end peaceably is for it to exist for a length of time. But I say that the spread and strengthening and perpetuation of it is an entirely different proposition. There we should in every way resist it as a wrong, treating it as a wrong, with the fixed idea that it must and will come to an end. If we do not allow ourselves to be allured from the strict path of our duty by such a device as shifting our ground and throwing ourselves into the rear of a leader who denies our first principle, denies that there is an absolute wrong in the institution of slavery, then the future of the Republican cause is safe and victory is assured. You Republicans of Illinois have deliberately taken your ground; you have heard the whole subject discussed again and again; you have stated your faith, in platforms laid down in a State Convention, and in a National Convention; you have heard and talked over and considered it until you are now all of opinion that you are on a ground of unquestionable right. All you have to do is to keep the faith, to remain steadfast to the right, to stand by your banner. Nothing should lead you to leave your guns. Stand together, ready, with match in hand. Allow nothing to turn you to the right or to the left. Remember how long you have been in setting out on the true course; how long you have been in getting your neighbors to understand and believe as you now do. Stand by your principles; stand by your guns; and victory complete and permanent is sure at the last.

March 1, 1859

---

7. Steamboats and railroads.
1. This speech was written down by a reporter but was not published until 1893, when it appeared in the *North American Review*.

To Henry L. Pierce[1] and Others

Messrs. Henry L. Pierce, & others.   Springfield, Ills.
Gentlemen   April 6. 1859
Your kind note inviting me to attend a Festival in Boston, on the 13th. Inst. in honor of the birth-day of Thomas Jefferson, was duly received. My engagements are such that I can not attend.

Bearing in mind that about seventy years ago, two great political parties were first formed in this country, that Thomas Jefferson was the head of one of them, and Boston the headquarters of the other, it is both curious and interesting that those supposed to descend politically from the party opposed to Jefferson, should now be celebrating his birth-day in their own original seat of empire, while those claiming political descent from him have nearly ceased to breathe his name everywhere.

Remembering too, that the Jefferson party were formed upon their supposed superior devotion to the *personal* rights of men, holding the rights of *property* to be secondary only, and greatly inferior, and then assuming that the so-called democracy of to-day, are the Jefferson, and their opponents, the anti-Jefferson parties, it will be equally interesting to note how completely the two have changed hands as to the principle upon which they were originally supposed to be divided.

The democracy of to-day hold the *liberty* of one man to be absolutely nothing, when in conflict with another man's right of *property*. Republicans, on the contrary, are for both the *man* and the *dollar*; but in cases of conflict, the man *before* the dollar.

I remember once being much amused at seeing two partially intoxicated men engage in a fight with their great-coats on, which fight, after a long, and rather harmless contest, ended in each having fought himself *out* of his own coat, and *into* that of the other. If the two leading parties of this day are really identical with the two in the days of Jefferson and Adams, they have performed about the same feat as the two drunken men.

But soberly, it is now no child's play to save the principles of Jefferson from total overthrow in this nation.

One would start with great confidence that he could convince any sane child that the simpler propositions of Euclid are true; but, nevertheless, he would fail, utterly, with one who should deny the definitions and axioms. The principles of Jefferson are the definitions and axioms of free society. And yet they are denied, and evaded, with no small show of success. One dashingly calls them "glittering generalities"; another bluntly calls them "self evident lies"; and still others insidiously argue that they apply only to "superior races."

These expressions, differing in form, are identical in object and effect—the supplanting the principles of free government, and restoring those of classification, caste, and legitimacy. They would delight a convocation of crowned heads, plotting against the people. They are the van-guard—the miners, and sappers—of returning despotism. We must repulse them, or they will subjugate us.

---

1. A Republican representative (1825–1896) from Massachusetts.

This is a world of compensations; and he who would *be* no slave, must consent to *have* no slave. Those who deny freedom to others, deserve it not for themselves; and, under a just God, can not long retain it.

All honor to Jefferson—to the man who, in the concrete pressure of a struggle for national independence by a single people, had the coolness, forecast, and capacity to introduce into a merely revolutionary document, an abstract truth, applicable to all men and all times, and so to embalm it there, that to-day, and in all coming days, it shall be a rebuke and a stumbling-block to the very harbingers of re-appearing tyrany and oppression. Your obedient Servant

To Thomas J. Pickett[1]

T.J. Pickett, Esq   Springfield,
My dear Sir.   April 16. 1859.
Yours of the 13th. is just received. My engagements are such that I can not, at any very early day, visit Rock-Island, to deliver a lecture, or for any other object.

As to the other matter you kindly mention, I must, in candor, say I do not think myself fit for the Presidency. I certainly am flattered, and gratified, that some partial friends think of me in that connection; but I really think it best for our cause that no concerted effort, such as you suggest, should be made.

Let this be considered confidential. Yours very truly

To Salmon P. Chase[1]

Hon. S. P. Chase   Springfield, Ills.
My dear Sir   June 20. 1859
Yours of the 13th. Inst. is received. You say you would be glad to have my views. Although I think congress has constitutional authority to enact a Fugitive Slave law, I have never elaborated an opinion upon the subject. My view has been, and is, simply this: The U.S. constitution says the fugitive slave *"shall be delivered up"* but it does not expressly say *who* shall deliver him up. Whatever the constitution says *"shall be done"* and has omitted saying who shall do it, the government established by that constitution, *ex vi termini*,[2] is vested with the power of doing; and congress is, by the constitution, expressly empowered to make all laws which shall be necessary and proper for carrying into execution all powers vested by the constitution in the government of the United States. This would be my view, on a simple reading of the constitution; and it is greatly strengthened by the historical fact that the constitution was adopted, in great part, in order to get a government which could execute it's own behests, in con-

1. Editor of the *Rock Island Register* who had written Lincoln asking if he could promote him in Illinois newspapers as a possible presidential candidate.
1. An Ohio Republican (1808–1873) who had a long history of speaking out against slavery and served as a U.S. Senator (1849–55) and the governor of Ohio (1856–60). He became Lincoln's secretary of the treasury (1861–64) and was later Chief Justice of the Supreme Court.
2. From the force of the term (Latin).

tradistinction to that under the Articles of confederation, which depended, in many respects, upon the States, for its' execution; and the other fact that one of the earliest congresses, under the constitution, did enact a Fugitive Slave law.

But I did not write you on this subject, with any view of discussing the constitutional question. My only object was to impress you with what I believe is true, that the introduction of a proposition for repeal of the Fugitive Slave law, into the next Republican National convention, will explode the convention and the party. Having turned your attention to the point, I wish to do no more. Yours very truly

To Schuyler Colfax[1]

Hon: Schuyler Colfax: Springfield, Ills, July 6, 1859.
My dear Sir: I much regret not seeing you while you were here among us. Before learning that you were to be at Jacksonville on the 4th. I had given my word to be at another place. Besides a strong desire to make your personal acquaintance, I was anxious to speak with you on politics, a little more fully than I can well do in a letter. My main object in such conversation would be to hedge against divisions in the Republican ranks generally, and particularly for the contest of 1860. The point of danger is the temptation in different localities to *"platform"* for something which will be popular just there, but which, nevertheless, will be a firebrand elsewhere, and especially in a National convention. As instances, the movement against foreigners in Massachusetts; in New-Hampshire, to make obedience to the Fugitive Slave law, punishable as a crime; in Ohio, to repeal the Fugitive Slave law; and squatter sovereignty in Kansas. In these things there is explosive matter enough to blow up half a dozen national conventions, if it gets into them; and what gets very rife outside of conventions is very likely to find it's way into them. What is desirable, if possible, is that in every local convocation of Republicans, a point should be made to avoid everything which will distract republicans elsewhere. Massachusetts republicans should have looked beyond their noses; and then they could not have failed to see that tilting against foreigners would ruin us in the whole North-West. New-Hampshire and Ohio should forbear tilting against the Fugitive Slave law in such way as to utterly overwhelm us in Illinois with the charge of enmity to the constitution itself. Kansas, in her confidence that she can be saved to freedom on "squatter sovereignty"—ought not to forget that to prevent the spread and nationalization of slavery is a national concern, and must be attended to by the nation. In a word, in every locality we should look beyond our noses; and at least say nothing on points where it is probable we shall disagree.

I write this for your eye only; hoping however that if you see danger as I think I do, you will do what you can to avert it. Could not suggestions be made to the leading men in the State and congressional conventions; and so avoid, to some extent at least, these apples of discord? Yours very truly

---

1. An Indiana congressman (1823–1885) who had written Lincoln about the great difficulty of coordinating disparate antislavery factions.

From Notes for Speeches

* * *

Negro equality! Fudge!! How long, in the government of a God, great enough to make and maintain this Universe, shall there continue knaves to vend, and fools to gulp, so low a piece of demagougeism as this.

ca. September 1859

From Address before the Wisconsin State Agricultural Society, Milwaukee, Wisconsin

* * *

The world is agreed that *labor* is the source from which human wants are mainly supplied. There is no dispute upon this point. From this point, however, men immediately diverge. Much disputation is maintained as to the best way of applying and controlling the labor element. By some it is assumed that labor is available only in connection with capital—that nobody labors, unless somebody else, owning capital, somehow, by the use of that capital, induces him to do it. Having assumed this, they proceed to consider whether it is best that capital shall *hire* laborers, and thus induce them to work by their own consent; or *buy* them, and drive them to it without their consent. Having proceeded so far they naturally conclude that all laborers are necessarily either *hired* laborers, or *slaves*. They further assume that whoever is once a *hired* laborer, is fatally fixed in that condition for life; and thence again that his condition is as bad as, or worse than that of a slave. This is the *"mud-sill"* theory.[1]

But another class of reasoners hold the opinion that there is no *such* relation between capital and labor, as assumed; and that there is no such thing as a freeman being fatally fixed for life, in the condition of a hired laborer, that both these assumptions are false, and all inferences from them groundless.[2] They hold that labor is prior to, and independent of, capital; that, in fact, capital is the fruit of labor, and could never have existed if labor had not *first* existed—that labor can exist without capital, but that capital could never have existed without labor. Hence they hold that labor is the superior—greatly the superior—of capital.

They do not deny that there is, and probably always will be, *a* relation between labor and capital. The error, as they hold, is in assuming that the *whole* labor of the world exists within that relation. A few men own capital; and that few avoid labor themselves, and with their capital, hire, or buy, another few to labor for them. A large majority belong to neither class— neither work for others, nor have others working for them. Even in all our

---

1. Held that a class of menial workers—enslaved and free—was necessary for enabling the higher classes to advance civilization. It was introduced by South Carolina Senator James Henry Hammond (1807–1864) in an 1858 speech.
2. In the so-called labor theory of value, a commodity is valued according to the labor required to make that commodity. This principle had been articulated by classical economists Adam Smith (1723–1790) and David Ricardo (1772–1823).

slave States, except South Carolina, a majority of the whole people of all colors, are neither slaves nor masters. In these Free States, a large majority are neither *hirers* nor *hired*. Men, with their families—wives, sons and daughters—work for themselves, on their farms, in their houses and in their shops, taking the whole product to themselves, and asking no favors of capital on the one hand, nor of hirelings or slaves on the other. It is not forgotten that a considerable number of persons mingle their own labor with capital; that is, labor with their own hands, and also buy slaves or hire freemen to labor for them; but this is only a *mixed*, and not a *distinct* class. No principle stated is disturbed by the existence of this mixed class. Again, as has already been said, the opponents of the *"mud-sill"* theory insist that there is not, of necessity, any such thing as the free hired laborer being fixed to that condition for life. There is demonstration for saying this. Many independent men, in this assembly, doubtless a few years ago were hired laborers. And their case is almost if not quite the general rule.

The prudent, penniless beginner in the world, labors for wages awhile, saves a surplus with which to buy tools or land, for himself; then labors on his own account another while, and at length hires another new beginner to help him. This, say its advocates, is *free* labor—the just and generous, and prosperous system, which opens the way for all—gives hope to all, and energy, and progress, and improvement of condition to all. If any continue through life in the condition of the hired laborer, it is not the fault of the system, but because of either a dependent nature which prefers it, or improvidence, folly, or singular misfortune. I have said this much about the elements of labor generally, as introductory to the consideration of a new phase which that element is in process of assuming. The old general rule was that *educated* people did not perform manual labor. They managed to eat their bread, leaving the toil of producing it to the uneducated. This was not an insupportable evil to the working bees, so long as the class of drones remained very small. But *now*, especially in these free States, nearly all are educated—quite too nearly all, to leave the labor of the uneducated, in any wise adequate to the support of the whole. It follows from this that henceforth educated people must labor. Otherwise, education itself would become a positive and intolerable evil. No country can sustain, in idleness, more than a small per centage of its numbers. The great majority must labor at something productive. From these premises the problem springs, "How can *labor* and *education* be the most satisfactorily combined?"

By the *"mud-sill"* theory it is assumed that labor and education are incompatible; and any practical combination of them impossible. According to that theory, a blind horse upon a tread-mill, is a perfect illustration of what a laborer should be—all the better for being blind, that he could not tread out of place, or kick understandingly. According to that theory, the education of laborers, is not only useless, but pernicious, and dangerous. In fact, it is, in some sort, deemed a misfortune that laborers should have heads at all. Those same heads are regarded as explosive materials, only to be safely kept in damp places, as far as possible from that peculiar sort of fire which ignites them. A Yankee who could invent a strong *handed* man without a head would receive the everlasting gratitude of the "mud-sill" advocates.

But Free Labor says "no!" Free Labor argues that, as the Author of man makes every individual with one head and one pair of hands, it was probably intended that heads and hands should cooperate as friends; and that that particular head, should direct and control that particular pair of hands. As each man has one mouth to be fed, and one pair of hands to furnish food, it was probably intended that that particular pair of hands should feed that particular mouth—that each head is the natural guardian, director, and protector of the hands and mouth inseparably connected with it; and that being so, every head should be cultivated, and improved, by whatever will add to its capacity for performing its charge. In one word Free Labor insists on universal education.

I have so far stated the opposite theories of *"Mud-Sill"* and "Free Labor" without declaring any preference of my own between them. On an occasion like this I ought not to declare any. I suppose, however, I shall not be mistaken, in assuming as a fact, that the people of Wisconsin prefer free labor, with its natural companion, education.

This leads to the further reflection, that no other human occupation opens so wide a field for the profitable and agreeable combination of labor with cultivated thought, as agriculture. I know of nothing so pleasant to the mind, as the discovery of anything which is at once *new* and *valuable*—nothing which so lightens and sweetens toil, as the hopeful pursuit of such discovery. And how vast, and how varied a field is agriculture, for such discovery. The mind, already trained to thought, in the country school, or higher school, cannot fail to find there an exhaustless source of profitable enjoyment. Every blade of grass is a study; and to produce two, where there was but one, is both a profit and a pleasure. And not grass alone; but soils, seeds, and seasons—hedges, ditches, and fences, draining, droughts, and irrigation—plowing, hoeing, and harrowing—reaping, mowing, and threshing—saving crops, pests of crops, diseases of crops, and what will prevent or cure them—implements, utensils, and machines, their relative merits, and how to improve them—hogs, horses, and cattle—sheep, goats, and poultry—trees, shrubs, fruits, plants, and flowers—the thousand things of which these are specimens—each a world of study within itself.

*   *   *

September 30, 1859

Speech at Elwood, Kansas[1]

Mr. Lincoln was received with great enthusiasm. He stated the reasons why he was unable to make a speech this evening. He could only say a few words to us who had come out to meet him the first time he had placed his foot upon the soil of Kansas. Mr. Lincoln said that it was possible that we had local questions in regard to Railroads, Land Grants and internal improvements which were matters of deeper interest to us than the questions arising out of national politics, but of these local interests he knew nothing and should say nothing. We had, however, just adopted a State Constitution, and it was probable, that, under that Constitution, we should

1. This summary of Lincoln's speech appeared in the Elwood, Kansas, *Free Press* on December 3, 1859.

soon cease our Territorial existence, and come forward to take our place in the brotherhood of States, and act our parts as a member of the confederation. Kansas would be Free, but the same questions we had had here in regard to Freedom or Slavery would arise in regard to other Territories and we should have to take our part in deciding them. People often ask, "why make such a fuss about a few niggers?" I answer the question by asking what will you do to dispose of this question? The Slaves constitute one seventh of our entire population. Wherever there is an element of this magnitude in a government it will be talked about. The general feeling in regard to Slavery had changed entirely since the early days of the Republic. You may examine the debates under the Confederation, in the Convention that framed the Constitution and in the first session of Congress and you will not find a single man saying that Slavery is a good thing. They all believed it was an evil. They made the Northwest Territory—the only Territory then belonging to the government—forever free. They prohibited the African Slave trade. Having thus prevented its extension and cut off the supply, the Fathers of the Republic believed Slavery must soon disappear. There are only three clauses in the Constitution which refer to Slavery, and in neither of them is the word Slave or Slavery mentioned. The word is not used in the clause prohibiting the African Slave trade; it is not used in the clause which makes Slaves a basis of representation; it is not used in the clause requiring the return of fugitive Slaves. And yet in all the debates in the Convention the question was discussed and Slaves and Slavery talked about. Now why was this word kept out of that instrument and so carefully kept out that a European, be he ever so intelligent, if not familiar with our institutions, might read the Constitution over and over again and never learn that Slavery existed in the United States. The reason is this. The Framers of the Organic Law believed that the Constitution would outlast Slavery and they did not want a word there to tell future generations that Slavery had ever been legalized in America.

Your Territory has had a marked history—no other Territory has ever had such a history. There had been strife and bloodshed here, both parties had been guilty of outrages; he had his opinions as to the relative guilt of the parties, but he would not say who had been most to blame. One fact was certain—there had been loss of life, destruction of property; our material interests had been retarded. Was this desirable? There is a peaceful way of settling these questions—the way adopted by government until a recent period. The bloody code has grown out of the new policy in regard to the government of Territories.

Mr. Lincoln in conclusion adverted briefly to the Harper's Ferry Affair.[2] He believed the attack of Brown wrong for two reasons. It was a violation of law and it was, as all such attacks must be, futile as far as any effect it might have on the extinction of a great evil.

We have a means provided for the expression of our belief in regard to Slavery—it is through the ballot box—the peaceful method provided by the

---

2. In October 1859, militant abolitionist John Brown (1800–1859) raided Harpers Ferry, Virginia, with the aim of freeing slaves in the region, escaping with them to the mountains, and sparking a series of events that, he hoped, would lead to the fall of slavery. Brown stalled too long and, after a bloody battle with federal troops, was captured, brought to trial, and executed. Though unsuccessful, Brown created panic in the South, where his scheme was wrongly attributed to the Republican Party.

Constitution. John Brown has shown great courage, rare unselfishness, as even Gov. Wise[3] testifies. But no man, North or South, can approve of violence or crime. Mr. Lincoln closed his brief speech by wishing all to go out to the election on Tuesday and to vote as became the Freemen of Kansas.

ca. December 1, 1859

To Jesse W. Fell,[1] Enclosing Autobiography

J. W. Fell, Esq   Springfield,
My dear Sir: Dec. 20. 1859
Herewith is a little sketch, as you requested. There is not much of it, for the reason, I suppose, that there is not much of me.

If any thing be made out of it, I wish it to be modest, and not to go beyond the materials. If it were thought necessary to incorporate any thing from any of my speeches, I suppose there would be no objection. Of course it must not appear to have been written by myself. Yours very truly

I was born Feb. 12, 1809, in Hardin County, Kentucky. My parents were both born in Virginia, of undistinguished families—second families, perhaps I should say. My mother, who died in my tenth year, was of a family of the name of Hanks, some of whom now reside in Adams, and others in Macon counties, Illinois. My paternal grandfather, Abraham Lincoln, emigrated from Rockingham County, Virginia, to Kentucky, about 1781 or 2, where, a year or two later, he was killed by indians, not in battle, but by stealth, when he was laboring to open a farm in the forest. His ancestors, who were quakers, went to Virginia from Berks County, Pennsylvania. An effort to identify them with the New-England family of the same name ended in nothing more definite, than a similarity of Christian names in both families, such as Enoch, Levi, Mordecai, Solomon, Abraham, and the like.

My father, at the death of his father, was but six years of age; and he grew up, litterally without education. He removed from Kentucky to what is now Spencer county, Indiana, in my eighth year. We reached our new home about the time the State came into the Union. It was a wild region, with many bears and other wild animals still in the woods. There I grew up. There were some schools, so called; but no qualification was ever required of a teacher, beyond "*readin, writin, and cipherin*," to the Rule of Three. If a straggler supposed to understand latin, happened to so-journ in the neighborhood, he was looked upon as a wizzard. There was absolutely nothing to excite ambition for education. Of course when I came of age I did not know much. Still somehow, I could read, write, and cipher to the Rule of Three; but that was all. I have not been to school since. The little advance I now have upon this store of education, I have picked up from time to time under the pressure of necessity.

I was raised to farm work, which I continued till I was twenty two. At twenty one I came to Illinois, and passed the first year in Macon county.

3. John A. Wise (1806–1876), governor of Virginia when John Brown invaded Harpers Ferry. Despite his proslavery stance, Wise strongly disagreed with those who called Brown insane, describing him as "a man of clear head, of courage, fortitude, . . . firm, truthful, and intelligent."
1. A Bloomington, Illinois, businessman and a longtime friend of Lincoln (1808–1887).

Then I got to New-Salem (at that time in Sangamon, now in Menard county, where I remained a year as a sort of Clerk in a store. Then came the Black-Hawk war; and I was elected a Captain of Volunteers—a success which gave me more pleasure than any I have had since. I went the campaign, was elated, ran for the Legislature the same year (1832) and was beaten—the only time I ever have been beaten by the people. The next, and three succeeding biennial elections, I was elected to the Legislature. I was not a candidate afterwards. During this Legislative period I had studied law, and removed to Springfield to practice it. In 1846 I was once elected to the lower House of Congress. Was not a candidate for re-election. From 1849 to 1854, both inclusive, practiced law more assiduously than ever before. Always a whig in politics, and generally on the whig electoral tickets, making active canvasses. I was losing interest in politics, when the repeal of the Missouri Compromise aroused me again. What I have done since then is pretty well known.

If any personal description of me is thought desirable, it may be said, I am, in height, six feet, four inches, nearly; lean in flesh, weighing, on an average, one hundred and eighty pounds; dark complexion, with coarse black hair, and grey eyes—no other marks or brands recollected. Yours very truly

Address at Cooper Institute, New York City

Mr. President and Fellow-citizens of New-York:—The facts with which I shall deal this evening are mainly old and familiar; nor is there anything new in the general use I shall make of them. If there shall be any novelty, it will be in the mode of presenting the facts, and the inferences and observations following that presentation.

In his speech last autumn, at Columbus, Ohio, as reported in "The New-York Times," Senator Douglas said:

"Our fathers, when they framed the Government under which we live, understood this question just as well, and even better, than we do now."

I fully indorse this, and I adopt it as a text for this discourse. I so adopt it because it furnishes a precise and an agreed starting point for a discussion between Republicans and that wing of the Democracy headed by Senator Douglas. It simply leaves the inquiry: *"What was the understanding those fathers had of the question mentioned?"*

What is the frame of Government under which we live?

The answer must be: "The Constitution of the United States." That Constitution consists of the original, framed in 1787, (and under which the present government first went into operation,) and twelve subsequently framed amendments, the first ten of which were framed in 1789.

Who were our fathers that framed the Constitution? I suppose the "thirty-nine" who signed the original instrument may be fairly called our fathers who framed that part of the present Government. It is almost exactly true to say they framed it, and it is altogether true to say they fairly represented the opinion and sentiment of the whole nation at that time. Their names, being familiar to nearly all, and accessible to quite all, need not now be repeated.

I take these "thirty-nine" for the present, as being "our fathers who framed the Government under which we live."

What is the question which, according to the text, those fathers understood "just as well, and even better than we do now?"

It is this: Does the proper division of local from federal authority, or anything in the Constitution, forbid *our Federal Government* to control as to slavery in *our Federal Territories?*

Upon this, Senator Douglas holds the affirmative, and Republicans the negative. This affirmation and denial form an issue; and this issue—this question—is precisely what the text declares our fathers understood "better than we."

Let us now inquire whether the "thirty-nine," or any of them, ever acted upon this question; and if they did, how they acted upon it—how they expressed that better understanding?

In 1784, three years before the Constitution—the United States then owning the Northwestern Territory, and no other, the Congress of the Confederation had before them the question of prohibiting slavery in that Territory; and four of the "thirty-nine," who afterward framed the Constitution, were in that Congress, and voted on that question. Of these, Roger Sherman, Thomas Mifflin, and Hugh Williamson[1] voted for the prohibition, thus showing that, in their understanding, no line dividing local from federal authority, nor anything else, properly forbade the Federal Government to control as to slavery in federal territory. The other of the four—James M'Henry[2]—voted against the prohibition, showing that, for some cause, he thought it improper to vote for it.

In 1787, still before the Constitution, but while the Convention was in session framing it, and while the Northwestern Territory still was the only territory owned by the United States, the same question of prohibiting slavery in the territory again came before the Congress of the Confederation; and two more of the "thirty-nine" who afterward signed the Constitution, were in that Congress, and voted on the question. They were William Blount and William Few,[3] and they both voted for the prohibition—thus showing that, in their understanding, no line dividing local from federal authority, nor anything else, properly forbade the Federal Government to control as to slavery in federal territory. This time the prohibition became a law, being part of what is now well known as the Ordinance of '87.

The question of federal control of slavery in the territories, seems not to have been directly before the Convention which framed the original Constitution; and hence it is not recorded that the "thirty-nine," or any of them, while engaged on that instrument, expressed any opinion of that precise question.

In 1789, by the first Congress which sat under the Constitution, an act was passed to enforce the Ordinance of '87, including the prohibition of slavery in the Northwestern Territory. The bill for this act was reported by one of the "thirty-nine," Thomas Fitzsimmons, then a member of the House of Representatives from Pennsylvania. It went through all its stages

---

1. Representative of North Carolina at the Continental Congress and the Constitutional Convention (1735–1819). Sherman (1721–93), Connecticut politician and signer of the Declaration of Independence, the Articles of Confederation, and the Constitution. Mifflin (1744–1800), Continental Congressman from Pennsylvania.
2. James McHenry (1753–1816), Maryland delegate to the Continental Congress, signer of the Constitution, and secretary of war under George Washington and John Adams.
3. Georgia delegate at the convention (1748–1828). Blount (1749–1800), member of the North Carolina delegation at the Constitutional Convention of 1787.

without a word of opposition, and finally passed both branches without yeas and nays, which is equivalent to an unanimous passage. In this Congress there were sixteen of the thirty-nine fathers who framed the original Constitution. They were John Langdon, Nicholas Gilman, Wm. S. Johnson, Roger Sherman, Robert Morris, Thos. Fitzsimmons, William Few, Abraham Baldwin, Rufus King, William Paterson, George Clymer, Richard Bassett, George Read, Pierce Butler, Daniel Carroll, James Madison.

This shows that, in their understanding, no line dividing local from federal authority, nor anything in the Constitution, properly forbade Congress to prohibit slavery in the federal territory; else both their fidelity to correct principle, and their oath to support the Constitution, would have constrained them to oppose the prohibition.

Again, George Washington, another of the "thirty-nine," was then President of the United States, and, as such, approved and signed the bill; thus completing its validity as a law, and thus showing that, in his understanding, no line dividing local from federal authority, nor anything in the Constitution, forbade the Federal Government, to control as to slavery in federal territory.

No great while after the adoption of the original Constitution, North Carolina ceded to the Federal Government the country now constituting the State of Tennessee; and a few years later Georgia ceded that which now constitutes the States of Mississippi and Alabama. In both deeds of cession it was made a condition by the ceding States that the Federal Government should not prohibit slavery in the ceded country. Besides this, slavery was then actually in the ceded country. Under these circumstances, Congress, on taking charge of these countries, did not absolutely prohibit slavery within them. But they did interfere with it—take control of it—even there, to a certain extent. In 1798, Congress organized the Territory of Mississippi. In the act of organization, they prohibited the bringing of slaves into the Territory, from any place without the United States, by fine, and giving freedom to slaves so brought. This act passed both branches of Congress without yeas and nays. In that Congress were three of the "thirty-nine" who framed the original Constitution. They were John Langdon, George Read and Abraham Baldwin.[4] They all, probably, voted for it. Certainly they would have placed their opposition to it upon record, if, in their understanding, any line dividing local from federal authority, or anything in the Constitution, properly forbade the Federal Government to control as to slavery in federal territory.

In 1803, the Federal Government purchased the Louisiana country. Our former territorial acquisitions came from certain of our own States; but this Louisiana country was acquired from a foreign nation. In 1804, Congress gave a territorial organization to that part of it which now constitutes the State of Louisiana. New Orleans, lying within that part, was an old and comparatively large city. There were other considerable towns and settlements, and slavery was extensively and thoroughly intermingled with the people. Congress did not, in the Territorial Act, prohibit slavery;

---

4. Langdon (1741–1819), congressman from New Hampshire; Read (1733–1798), lawyer from Delaware, member of the Federalist party, and signer of the Declaration of Independence; Baldwin (1754–1807), minister and statesman who represented Georgia in the Continental Congress and founded the University of Georgia.

but they did interfere with it—take control of it—in a more marked and extensive way than they did in the case of Mississippi. The substance of the provision therein made, in relation to slaves, was:

First. That no slave should be imported into the territory from foreign parts.

Second. That no slave should be carried into it who had been imported into the United States since the first day of May, 1798.

Third. That no slave should be carried into it, except by the owner, and for his own use as a settler; the penalty in all the cases being a fine upon the violator of the law, and freedom to the slave.

This act also was passed without yeas and nays. In the Congress which passed it, there were two of the "thirty-nine." They were Abraham Baldwin and Jonathan Dayton.[5] As stated in the case of Mississippi, it is probable they both voted for it. They would not have allowed it to pass without recording their opposition to it, if, in their understanding, it violated either the line properly dividing local from federal authority, or any provision of the Constitution.

In 1819–20, came and passed the Missouri question. Many votes were taken, by yeas and nays, in both branches of Congress, upon the various phases of the general question. Two of the "thirty-nine"—Rufus King and Charles Pinckney[6]—were members of that Congress. Mr. King steadily voted for slavery prohibition and against all compromises, while Mr. Pinckney as steadily voted against slavery prohibition and against all compromises. By this, Mr. King showed that, in his understanding, no line dividing local from federal authority, nor anything in the Constitution, was violated by Congress prohibiting slavery in federal territory; while Mr. Pinckney, by his votes, showed that, in his understanding, there was some sufficient reason for opposing such prohibition in that case.

The cases I have mentioned are the only acts of the "thirty-nine," or of any of them, upon the direct issue, which I have been able to discover.

To enumerate the persons who thus acted, as being four in 1784, two in 1787, seventeen in 1789, three in 1798, two in 1804, and two in 1819–20—there would be thirty of them. But this would be counting John Langdon, Roger Sherman, William Few, Rufus King, and George Read, each twice, and Abraham Baldwin, three times. The true number of those of the "thirty-nine" whom I have shown to have acted upon the question, which, by the text, they understood better than we, is twenty-three, leaving sixteen not shown to have acted upon it in any way.

Here, then, we have twenty-three out of our thirty-nine fathers "who framed the Government under which we live," who have, upon their official responsibility and their corporal oaths, acted upon the very question which the text affirms they "understood just as well, and even better than we do now;" and twenty-one of them—a clear majority of the whole "thirty-nine"—so acting upon it as to make them guilty of gross political impropriety and wilful perjury, if, in their understanding, any proper

---

5. A Federalist from New Jersey, Dayton (1760–1824), served in the American Revolutionary War and was the youngest signer of the U.S. Constitution.
6. King (1755–1827), congressman from Massachusetts known for his opposition to the expansion of slavery; Pinckney (1757–1824), Federalist congressman from South Carolina who, along with fellow South Carolinian Pierce Butler (1744–1822), introduced the fugitive slave clause (Article IV, Section 2, Clause 3) to the Constitutional Convention.

division between local and federal authority, or anything in the Constitution they had made themselves, and sworn to support, forbade the Federal Government to control as to slavery in the federal territories. Thus the twenty-one acted; and, as actions speak louder than words, so actions, under such responsibility, speak still louder.

Two of the twenty-three voted against Congressional prohibition of slavery in the federal territories, in the instances in which they acted upon the question. But for what reasons they so voted is not known. They may have done so because they thought a proper division of local from federal authority, or some provision or principle of the Constitution, stood in the way; or they may, without any such question, have voted against the prohibition, on what appeared to them to be sufficient grounds of expediency. No one who has sworn to support the Constitution, can conscientiously vote for what he understands to be an unconstitutional measure, however expedient he may think it; but one may and ought to vote against a measure which he deems constitutional, if, at the same time, he deems it inexpedient. It, therefore, would be unsafe to set down even the two who voted against the prohibition, as having done so because, in their understanding, any proper division of local from federal authority, or anything in the Constitution, forbade the Federal Government to control as to slavery in federal territory.

The remaining sixteen of the "thirty-nine," so far as I have discovered, have left no record of their understanding upon the direct question of federal control of slavery in the federal territories. But there is much reason to believe that their understanding upon that question would not have appeared different from that of their twenty-three compeers, had it been manifested at all.

For the purpose of adhering rigidly to the text, I have purposely omitted whatever understanding may have been manifested by any person, however distinguished, other than the thirty-nine fathers who framed the original Constitution; and, for the same reason, I have also omitted whatever understanding may have been manifested by any of the "thirty-nine" even, on any other phase of the general question of slavery. If we should look into their acts and declarations on those other phases, as the foreign slave trade, and the morality and policy of slavery generally, it would appear to us that on the direct question of federal control of slavery in federal territories, the sixteen, if they had acted at all, would probably have acted just as the twenty-three did. Among that sixteen were several of the most noted anti-slavery men of those times—as Dr. Franklin, Alexander Hamilton and Gouverneur Morris[7]—while there was not one now known to have been otherwise, unless it may be John Rutledge, of South Carolina.[8]

The sum of the whole is, that of our thirty-nine fathers who framed the original Constitution, twenty-one—a clear majority of the whole—certainly understood that no proper division of local from federal authority, nor any part of the Constitution, forbade the Federal Government to control slavery

---

7. A representative of Pennsylvania at the Constitutional Convention in 1787, Morris (1752–1816) has been called the "Penman of the Constitution" because he wrote large sections of that founding document, including its preamble.
8. A congressman, slave owner, and judge from South Carolina (1739–1800), known for his support of slave ownership at the Constitutional Convention and his opposition to the Jay Treaty with Great Britain.

in the federal territories; while all the rest probably had the same understanding. Such, unquestionably, was the understanding of our fathers who framed the original Constitution; and the text affirms that they understood the question "better than we."

But, so far, I have been considering the understanding of the question manifested by the framers of the original Constitution. In and by the original instrument, a mode was provided for amending it; and, as I have already stated, the present frame of "the Government under which we live" consists of that original, and twelve amendatory articles framed and adopted since. Those who now insist that federal control of slavery in federal territories violates the Constitution, point us to the provisions which they suppose it thus violates; and, as I understand, they all fix upon provisions in these amendatory articles, and not in the original instrument. The Supreme Court, in the Dred Scott case, plant themselves upon the fifth amendment, which provides that no person shall be deprived of "life, liberty or property without due process of law;" while Senator Douglas and his peculiar adherents plant themselves upon the tenth amendment, providing that "the powers not delegated to the United States by the Constitution," "are reserved to the States respectively, or to the people."

Now, it so happens that these amendments were framed by the first Congress which sat under the Constitution—the identical Congress which passed the act already mentioned, enforcing the prohibition of slavery in the Northwestern Territory. Not only was it the same Congress, but they were the identical, same individual men who, at the same session, and at the same time within the session, had under consideration, and in progress toward maturity, these Constitutional amendments, and this act prohibiting slavery in all the territory the nation then owned. The Constitutional amendments were introduced before, and passed after the act enforcing the Ordinance of '87; so that, during the whole pendency of the act to enforce the Ordinance, the Constitutional amendments were also pending.

The seventy-six members of that Congress, including sixteen of the framers of the original Constitution, as before stated, were preeminently our fathers who framed that part of "the Government under which we live," which is now claimed as forbidding the Federal Government to control slavery in the federal territories.

Is it not a little presumptuous in any one at this day to affirm that the two things which that Congress deliberately framed, and carried to maturity at the same time, are absolutely inconsistent with each other? And does not such affirmation become impudently absurd when coupled with the other affirmation from the same mouth, that those who did the two things, alleged to be inconsistent, understood whether they really were inconsistent better than we—better than he who affirms that they are inconsistent?

It is surely safe to assume that the thirty-nine framers of the original Constitution, and the seventy-six members of the Congress which framed the amendments thereto, taken together, do certainly include those who may be fairly called "our fathers who framed the Government under which we live." And so assuming, I defy any man to show that any one of them ever, in his whole life, declared that, in his understanding, any proper division of local from federal authority, or any part of the Constitution, forbade the Federal Government to control as to slavery in the federal territories. I go a step further. I defy any one to show that any living man in the whole world ever did, prior to the beginning of the present century, (and I might almost say prior to the beginning of the last half of the present century,) declare that, in his understanding, any proper division of local from federal authority, or any part of the Constitution, forbade the Federal Government to control as to slavery in the federal territories. To those who now so declare, I give, not only "our fathers who framed the Government under which we live," but with them all other living men within the century in which it was framed, among whom to search, and they shall not be able to find the evidence of a single man agreeing with them.

Now, and here, let me guard a little against being misunderstood. I do not mean to say we are bound to follow implicitly in whatever our fathers did. To do so, would be to discard all the lights of current experience—to reject all progress—all improvement. What I do say is, that if we would supplant the opinions and policy of our fathers in any case, we should do so upon evidence so conclusive, and argument so clear, that even their great authority, fairly considered and weighed, cannot stand; and most surely not in a case whereof we ourselves declare they understood the question better than we.

If any man at this day sincerely believes that a proper division of local from federal authority, or any part of the Constitution, forbids the Federal Government to control as to slavery in the federal territories, he is right to say so, and to enforce his position by all truthful evidence and fair argument which he can. But he has no right to mislead others, who have less access to history, and less leisure to study it, into the false belief that "our fathers, who framed the Government under which we live," were of the same opinion—thus substituting falsehood and deception for truthful evidence and fair argument. If any man at this day sincerely believes "our fathers who framed the Government under which we live," used and applied principles, in other cases, which ought to have led them to understand that a proper division of local from federal authority or some part of the Constitution, forbids the Federal Government to control as to slavery in the federal territories, he is right to say so. But he should, at the same time, brave the responsibility of declaring that, in his opinion, he understands their principles better than they did themselves; and especially should he not shirk that responsibility by asserting that they "understood the question just as well, and even better, than we do now."

But enough! Let all who believe that "our fathers, who framed the Government under which we live, understood this question just as well, and even better, than we do now," speak as they spoke, and act as they acted upon it. This is all Republicans ask—all Republicans desire—in relation to slavery. As those fathers marked it, so let it be again marked, as an evil not to be extended, but to be tolerated and protected only because of and so far as its actual presence among us makes that toleration and protection a necessity. Let all the guaranties those fathers gave it, be, not grudgingly, but fully and fairly maintained. For this Republicans contend, and with this, so far as I know or believe, they will be content.

And now, if they would listen—as I suppose they will not—I would address a few words to the Southern people.

I would say to them:—You consider yourselves a reasonable and a just people; and I consider that in the general qualities of reason and justice you are not inferior to any other people. Still, when you speak of us Republicans, you do so only to denounce us as reptiles, or, at the best, as no better than outlaws. You will grant a hearing to pirates or murderers, but nothing like it to "Black Republicans." In all your contentions with one another, each of you deems an unconditional condemnation of "Black Republicanism" as the first thing to be attended to. Indeed, such condemnation of us seems to be an indispensable prerequisite—license, so to speak—among you to be admitted or permitted to speak at all. Now, can you, or not, be prevailed upon to pause and to consider whether this is quite just to us, or even to yourselves? Bring forward your charges and specifications, and then be patient long enough to hear us deny or justify.

You say we are sectional. We deny it. That makes an issue; and the burden of proof is upon you. You produce your proof; and what is it? Why, that our party has no existence in your section—gets no votes in your section. The fact is substantially true; but does it prove the issue? If it does, then in case we should, without change of principle, begin to get votes in your section, we should thereby cease to be sectional. You cannot escape this conclusion; and yet, are you willing to abide by it? If you are, you will probably soon find that we have ceased to be sectional, for we shall get votes in your section this very year. You will then begin to discover, as the truth plainly is, that your proof does not touch the issue. The fact that we get no votes in your section, is a fact of your making, and not of ours. And if there be fault in that fact, that fault is primarily yours, and remains so until you show that we repel you by some wrong principle or practice. If we do repel you by any wrong principle or practice, the fault is ours; but this brings you to where you ought to have started—to a discussion of the right or wrong of our principle. If our principle, put in practice, would wrong your section for the benefit of ours, or for any other object, then our principle, and we with it, are sectional, and are justly opposed and denounced as such. Meet us, then, on the question of whether our principle, put in practice, would wrong your section; and so meet us as if it were possible that something may be said on our side. Do you accept the challenge? No! Then you really believe that the principle which "our fathers who framed the Government under which we live" thought so clearly right as to adopt it, and indorse it again and again, upon their official oaths, is in fact so clearly wrong as to demand your condemnation without a moment's consideration.

Some of you delight to flaunt in our faces the warning against sectional parties given by Washington in his Farewell Address. Less than eight years before Washington gave that warning, he had, as President of the United States, approved and signed an act of Congress, enforcing the prohibition of slavery in the Northwestern Territory, which act embodied the policy of the Government upon that subject up to and at the very moment he penned that warning; and about one year after he penned it, he wrote La Fayette that he considered that prohibition a wise measure, expressing in the same connection his hope that we should at some time have a confederacy of free States.

Bearing this in mind, and seeing that sectionalism has since arisen upon this same subject, is that warning a weapon in your hands against us, or in our hands against you? Could Washington himself speak, would he cast the blame of that sectionalism upon us, who sustain his policy, or upon you who repudiate it? We respect that warning of Washington, and we commend it to you, together with his example pointing to the right application of it.

But you say you are conservative—eminently conservative—while we are revolutionary, destructive, or something of the sort. What is conservatism? Is it not adherence to the old and tried, against the new and untried? We stick to, contend for, the identical old policy on the point in controversy which was adopted by "our fathers who framed the Government under which we live;" while you with one accord reject, and scout, and spit upon that old policy, and insist upon substituting something new. True, you disagree among yourselves as to what that substitute shall be. You are divided on new propositions and plans, but you are unanimous in rejecting and denouncing the old policy of the fathers. Some of you are for reviving the foreign slave trade; some for a Congressional Slave-Code for the Territories; some for Congress forbidding the Territories to prohibit Slavery within their limits; some for maintaining Slavery in the Territories through the judiciary; some for the "gur-reat pur-rinciple" that "if one man would enslave another, no third man should object," fantastically called "Popular Sovereignty;" but never a man among you in favor of federal prohibition of slavery in federal territories, according to the practice of "our fathers who framed the Government under which we live." Not one of all your various plans can show a precedent or an advocate in the century within which our Government originated. Consider, then, whether your claim of conservatism for yourselves, and your charge of destructiveness against us, are based on the most clear and stable foundations.

Again, you say we have made the slavery question more prominent than it formerly was. We deny it. We admit that it is more prominent, but we deny that we made it so. It was not we, but you, who discarded the old policy of the fathers. We resisted, and still resist, your innovation; and thence comes the greater prominence of the question. Would you have that question reduced to its former proportions? Go back to that old policy. What has been will be again, under the same conditions. If you would have the peace of the old times, readopt the precepts and policy of the old times.

You charge that we stir up insurrections among your slaves. We deny it; and what is your proof? Harper's Ferry! John Brown!! John Brown was no Republican; and you have failed to implicate a single Republican in his Harper's Ferry enterprise. If any member of our party is guilty in that matter, you know it or you do not know it. If you do know it, you are inexcusable for not designating the man and proving the fact. If you do not know it, you are inexcusable for asserting it, and especially for persisting in the assertion after you have tried and failed to make the proof. You need not be told that persisting in a charge which one does not know to be true, is simply malicious slander.

Some of you admit that no Republican designedly aided or encouraged the Harper's Ferry affair; but still insist that our doctrines and declarations necessarily lead to such results. We do not believe it. We know we hold to no doctrine, and make no declaration, which were not held to and made by "our fathers who framed the Government under which we live." You never dealt fairly by us in relation to this affair. When it occurred, some important State elections were near at hand, and you were in evident glee with the belief that, by charging the blame upon us, you could get an advantage of us in those elections. The elections came, and your expectations were not quite fulfilled. Every Republican man knew that, as to himself at least, your charge was a slander, and he was not much inclined by it to cast his vote in your favor. Republican doctrines and declarations are accompanied with a continual protest against any interference whatever with your slaves, or with you about your slaves. Surely, this does not encourage them to revolt. True, we do, in common with "our fathers, who framed the Government under which we live," declare our belief that slavery is wrong; but the slaves do not hear us declare even this. For anything we say or do, the slaves would scarcely know there is a Republican party. I believe they would not, in fact, generally know it but for your misrepresentations of us, in their hearing. In your political contests among yourselves, each faction charges the other with sympathy with Black Republicanism; and then, to give point to the charge, defines Black Republicanism to simply be insurrection, blood and thunder among the slaves.

Slave insurrections are no more common now than they were before the Republican party was organized. What induced the Southampton insurrection,[9] twenty-eight years ago, in which, at least, three times as many lives were lost as at Harper's Ferry? You can scarcely stretch your very elastic fancy to the conclusion that Southampton was "got up by Black Republicanism." In the present state of things in the United States, I do not think a general, or even a very extensive slave insurrection, is possible. The indispensable concert of action cannot be attained. The slaves have no means of rapid communication; nor can incendiary freemen, black or white, supply it. The explosive materials are everywhere in parcels; but there neither are, nor can be supplied, the indispensable connecting trains.

Much is said by Southern people about the affection of slaves for their masters and mistresses; and a part of it, at least, is true. A plot for an uprising could scarcely be devised and communicated to twenty individuals before some one of them, to save the life of a favorite master or mistress, would divulge it. This is the rule; and the slave revolution in Hayti[1] was not an exception to it, but a case occurring under peculiar circumstances. The gunpowder plot[2] of British history, though not connected with slaves, was more in point. In that case, only about twenty were admitted to the secret; and yet one of them, in his anxiety to save a friend, betrayed the plot to that friend, and, by consequence, averted the calamity. Occasional poisonings from the kitchen, and open or stealthy assassinations in the field, and local revolts extending to a score or so, will continue to occur as the natural results of slavery; but no general insurrection of slaves, as I think, can happen in this country for a long time. Whoever much fears, or much hopes for such an event, will be alike disappointed.

9. In 1831, Nat Turner (1800–1831), an enslaved black in Southampton, Virginia, led a slave rebellion in which fifty-five whites and numerous blacks were killed.
1. In the French island of Saint-Domingue, enslaved blacks rose up in a prolonged rebellion (1791–1804) against European colonizers, who were driven from the island. This insurrection led to the establishment of the Haitian republic.
2. A failed assassination attempt of 1605 in which a group of British Catholics tried to kill King James I of England. The scheme was foiled when the authorities received a tip from an anonymous source.

In the language of Mr. Jefferson, uttered many years ago, "It is still in our power to direct the process of emancipation, and deportation, peaceably, and in such slow degrees, as that the evil will wear off insensibly; and their places be, *pari passu*, filled up by free white laborers. If, on the contrary, it is left to force itself on, human nature must shudder at the prospect held up."[3]

Mr. Jefferson did not mean to say, nor do I, that the power of emancipation is in the Federal Government. He spoke of Virginia; and, as to the power of emancipation, I speak of the slaveholding States only. The Federal Government, however, as we insist, has the power of restraining the extension of the institution—the power to insure that a slave insurrection shall never occur on any American soil which is now free from slavery.

John Brown's effort was peculiar. It was not a slave insurrection. It was an attempt by white men to get up a revolt among slaves, in which the slaves refused to participate. In fact, it was so absurd that the slaves, with all their ignorance, saw plainly enough it could not succeed. That affair, in its philosophy, corresponds with the many attempts, related in history, at the assassination of kings and emperors. An enthusiast broods over the oppression of a people till he fancies himself commissioned by Heaven to liberate them. He ventures the attempt, which ends in little else than his own execution. Orsini's[4] attempt on Louis Napoleon, and John Brown's attempt at Harper's Ferry were, in their philosophy, precisely the same. The eagerness to cast blame on old England in the one case, and on New England in the other, does not disprove the sameness of the two things.

And how much would it avail you, if you could, by the use of John Brown, Helper's Book,[5] and the like, break up the Republican organization? Human action can be modified to some extent, but human nature cannot be changed. There is a judgment and a feeling against slavery in this nation, which cast at least a million and a half of votes. You cannot destroy that judgment and feeling—that sentiment—by breaking up the political organization which rallies around it. You can scarcely scatter and disperse an army which has been formed into order in the face of your heaviest fire; but if you could, how much would you gain by forcing the sentiment which created it out of the peaceful channel of the ballot-box, into some other channel? What would that other channel probably be? Would the number of John Browns be lessened or enlarged by the operation?

But you will break up the Union rather than submit to a denial of your Constitutional rights.

That has a somewhat reckless sound; but it would be palliated, if not fully justified, were we proposing, by the mere force of numbers, to deprive you of some right, plainly written down in the Constitution. But we are proposing no such thing.

When you make these declarations, you have a specific and well-understood allusion to an assumed Constitutional right of yours, to take slaves into the federal territories, and to hold them there as property. But

---

3. From Jefferson's *Autobiography*.
4. Felice Orsini (1819–1858), Italian revolutionary who tried to assassinate Napoleon III.
5. *The Impending Crisis of the South* (1857), a widely read antislavery book by Southerner Hinton Rowan Helper (1829–1909), who argued that chattel slavery would ruin the South economically.

no such right is specifically written in the Constitution. That instrument is literally silent about any such right. We, on the contrary, deny that such a right has any existence in the Constitution, even by implication.

Your purpose, then, plainly stated, is, that you will destroy the Government, unless you be allowed to construe and enforce the Constitution as you please, on all points in dispute between you and us. You will rule or ruin in all events.

This, plainly stated, is your language. Perhaps you will say the Supreme Court has decided the disputed Constitutional question in your favor.[6] Not quite so. But waiving the lawyer's distinction between dictum and decision, the Court have decided the question for you in a sort of way. The Court have substantially said, it is your Constitutional right to take slaves into the federal territories, and to hold them there as property. When I say the decision was made in a sort of way, I mean it was made in a divided Court, by a bare majority of the Judges, and they not quite agreeing with one another in the reasons for making it; that it is so made as that its avowed supporters disagree with one another about its meaning, and that it was mainly based upon a mistaken statement of fact—the statement in the opinion that "the right of property in a slave is distinctly and expressly affirmed in the Constitution."

An inspection of the Constitution will show that the right of property in a slave is not "*distinctly* and *expressly* affirmed" in it. Bear in mind, the Judges do not pledge their judicial opinion that such right is *impliedly* affirmed in the Constitution; but they pledge their veracity that it is "*distinctly* and *expressly*" affirmed there—"distinctly," that is, not mingled with anything else—"expressly," that is, in words meaning just that, without the aid of any inference, and susceptible of no other meaning.

If they had only pledged their judicial opinion that such right is affirmed in the instrument by implication, it would be open to others to show that neither the word "slave" nor "slavery" is to be found in the Constitution, nor the word "property" even, in any connection with language alluding to the things slave, or slavery, and that wherever in that instrument the slave is alluded to, he is called a "person;"—and wherever his master's legal right in relation to him is alluded to, it is spoken of as "service or labor which may be due,"—as a debt payable in service or labor. Also, it would be open to show, by contemporaneous history, that this mode of alluding to slaves and slavery, instead of speaking of them, was employed on purpose to exclude from the Constitution the idea that there could be property in man.

To show all this, is easy and certain.

When this obvious mistake of the Judges shall be brought to their notice, is it not reasonable to expect that they will withdraw the mistaken statement, and reconsider the conclusion based upon it?

And then it is to be remembered that "our fathers, who framed the Government under which we live"—the men who made the Constitution—decided this same Constitutional question in our favor, long ago—decided it without division among themselves, when making the decision; without division among themselves about the meaning of it after it was made, and, so far as any evidence is left, without basing it upon any mistaken statement of facts.

6. A reference to the *Dred Scott* decision.

Under all these circumstances, do you really feel yourselves justified to break up this Government, unless such a court decision as yours is, shall be at once submitted to as a conclusive and final rule of political action? But you will not abide the election of a Republican President! In that supposed event, you say, you will destroy the Union; and then, you say, the great crime of having destroyed it will be upon us! That is cool. A highwayman holds a pistol to my ear, and mutters through his teeth, "Stand and deliver, or I shall kill you, and then you will be a murderer!"

To be sure, what the robber demanded of me—my money—was my own; and I had a clear right to keep it; but it was no more my own than my vote is my own; and the threat of death to me, to extort my money, and the threat of destruction to the Union, to extort my vote, can scarcely be distinguished in principle.

A few words now to Republicans. *It is exceedingly desirable that all parts of this great Confederacy shall be at peace, and in harmony, one with another. Let us Republicans do our part to have it so. Even though much provoked, let us do nothing through passion and ill temper. Even though the southern people will not so much as listen to us, let us calmly consider their demands, and yield to them if, in our deliberate view of our duty, we possibly can.* Judging by all they say and do, and by the subject and nature of their controversy with us, let us determine, if we can, what will satisfy them.

Will they be satisfied if the Territories be unconditionally surrendered to them? We know they will not. In all their present complaints against us, the Territories are scarcely mentioned. Invasions and insurrections are the rage now. Will it satisfy them, if, in the future, we have nothing to do with invasions and insurrections? We know it will not. We so know, because we know we never had anything to do with invasions and insurrections; and yet this total abstaining does not exempt us from the charge and the denunciation.

The question recurs, what will satisfy them? Simply this: We must not only let them alone, but we must, somehow, convince them that we do let them alone. This, we know by experience, is no easy task. We have been so trying to convince them from the very beginning of our organization, but with no success. In all our platforms and speeches we have constantly protested our purpose to let them alone; but this has had no tendency to convince them. Alike unavailing to convince them, is the fact that they have never detected a man of us in any attempt to disturb them.

These natural, and apparently adequate means all failing, what will convince them? This, and this only: cease to call slavery *wrong*, and join them in calling it *right*. And this must be done thoroughly—done in *acts* as well as in *words*. Silence will not be tolerated—we must place ourselves avowedly with them. Senator Douglas's new sedition law[7] must be enacted and enforced, suppressing all declarations that slavery is wrong, whether made in politics, in presses, in pulpits, or in private. We must arrest and return their fugitive slaves with greedy pleasure. We must pull down our Free State constitutions. The whole atmosphere must be disinfected from all taint of opposition to slavery, before they will cease to believe that all their troubles proceed from us.

---

7. In March 1860, Stephen A. Douglas endorsed a bill to criminalize public criticism of slavery.

I am quite aware they do not state their case precisely in this way. Most of them would probably say to us, "Let us alone, *do* nothing to us, and *say* what you please about slavery." But we do let them alone—have never disturbed them—so that, after all, it is what we say, which dissatisfies them. They will continue to accuse us of doing, until we cease saying.

I am also aware they have not, as yet, in terms, demanded the overthrow of our Free-State Constitutions. Yet those Constitutions declare the wrong of slavery, with more solemn emphasis, than do all other sayings against it; and when all these other sayings shall have been silenced, the overthrow of these Constitutions will be demanded, and nothing be left to resist the demand. It is nothing to the contrary, that they do not demand the whole of this just now. Demanding what they do, and for the reason they do, they can voluntarily stop nowhere short of this consummation. Holding, as they do, that slavery is morally right, and socially elevating, they cannot cease to demand a full national recognition of it, as a legal right, and a social blessing.

Nor can we justifiably withhold this, on any ground save our conviction that slavery is wrong. If slavery is right, all words, acts, laws, and constitutions against it, are themselves wrong, and should be silenced, and swept away. If it is right, we cannot justly object to its nationality—its universality; if it is wrong, they cannot justly insist upon its extension—its enlargement. All they ask, we could readily grant, if we thought slavery right; all we ask, they could as readily grant, if they thought it wrong. Their thinking it right, and our thinking it wrong, is the precise fact upon which depends the whole controversy. Thinking it right, as they do, they are not to blame for desiring its full recognition, as being right; but, thinking it wrong, as we do, can we yield to them? Can we cast our votes with their view, and against our own? In view of our moral, social, and political responsibilities, can we do this?

Wrong as we think slavery is, we can yet afford to let it alone where it is, because that much is due to the necessity arising from its actual presence in the nation; but can we, while our votes will prevent it, allow it to spread into the National Territories, and to overrun us here in these Free States? If our sense of duty forbids this, then let us stand by our duty, fearlessly and effectively. Let us be diverted by none of those sophistical contrivances wherewith we are so industriously plied and belabored—contrivances such as groping for some middle ground between the right and the wrong, vain as the search for a man who should be neither a living man nor a dead man— such as a policy of "don't care" on a question about which all true men do care—such as Union appeals beseeching true Union men to yield to Disunionists, reversing the divine rule, and calling, not the sinners, but the righteous to repentance—such as invocations to Washington, imploring men to unsay what Washington said, and undo what Washington did.

Neither let us be slandered from our duty by false accusations against us, nor frightened from it by menaces of destruction to the Government nor of dungeons to ourselves. LET US HAVE FAITH THAT RIGHT MAKES MIGHT, AND IN THAT FAITH, LET US, TO THE END, DARE TO DO OUR DUTY AS WE UNDERSTAND IT.

February 27, 1860

From Speech at New Haven, Connecticut

*   *   *

Look at the magnitude of this subject! One sixth of our population, in round numbers—not quite one sixth, and yet more than a seventh,—about one sixth of the whole population of the United States are slaves! The owners of these slaves consider them property. The effect upon the minds of the owners is that of property, and nothing else—it induces them to insist upon all that will favorably affect its value as property, to demand laws and institutions and a public policy that shall increase and secure its value, and make it durable, lasting and universal. The effect on the minds of the owners is to persuade them that there is no wrong in it. The slaveholder does not like to be considered a mean fellow, for holding that species of property, and hence he has to struggle within himself and sets about arguing himself into the belief that Slavery is right. The property influences his mind. The dissenting minister, who argued some theological point with one of the established church, was always met by the reply, "I can't see it so." He opened the Bible, and pointed him to a passage, but the orthodox minister replied, "I can't see it so." Then he showed him a single word—"Can you see that?" "Yes, I see it," was the reply. The dissenter laid a guinea over the word and asked, "Do you see it now?" [Great laughter.] So here. Whether the owners of this species of property do really see it as it is, it is not for me to say, but if they do, they see it as it is through 2,000,000,000 of dollars, and that is a pretty thick coating. [Laughter.] Certain it is, that they do not see it as we see it. Certain it is, that this two thousand million of dollars, invested in this species of property, all so concentrated that the mind can grasp it at once—this immense pecuniary interest, has its influence upon their minds.

But here in Connecticut and at the North Slavery does not exist, and we see it through no such medium. To us it appears natural to think that slaves are human beings; *men*, not property; that some of the things, at least, stated about men in the Declaration of Independence apply to them as well as to us. [Applause.] I say, we think, most of us, that this Charter of Freedom applies to the slave as well as to ourselves, that the class of arguments put forward to batter down that idea, are also calculated to break down the very idea of a free government, even for white men, and to undermine the very foundations of free society. [Continued applause.] We think Slavery a great moral wrong, and while we do not claim the right to touch it where it exists, we wish to treat it as a wrong in the Territories, where our votes will reach it. We think that a respect for ourselves, a regard for future generations and for the God that made us, require that we put down this wrong where our votes will properly reach it. We think that species of labor an injury to free white men—in short, we think Slavery a great moral, social and political evil, tolerable only because, and so far as its actual existence makes it necessary to tolerate it, and that beyond that, it ought to be treated as a wrong.

Now these two ideas, the property idea that Slavery is right, and the idea that it is wrong, come into collision, and do actually produce that irrepressible conflict which Mr. Seward[1] has been so roundly abused for mentioning. The two ideas conflict, and must conflict.

Again, in its political aspect, does anything in any way endanger the perpetuity of this Union but that single thing, Slavery? Many of our adversaries are anxious to claim that they are specially devoted to the Union, and take pains to charge upon us hostility to the Union. Now we claim that we are the only true Union men, and we put to them this one proposition: What ever endangered this Union, save and except Slavery? Did any other thing ever cause a moment's fear? All men must agree that this thing alone has ever endangered the perpetuity of the Union. But if it was threatened by any other influence, would not all men say that the best thing that could be done, if we could not or ought not to destroy it, would be at least to keep it from growing any larger? Can any man believe that the way to save the Union is to extend and increase the only thing that threatens the Union, and to suffer it to grow bigger and bigger? [Great applause.]

Whenever this question shall be settled, it must be settled on some philosophical basis. No policy that does not rest upon some philosophical public opinion can be permanently maintained. And hence, there are but two policies in regard to Slavery that can be at all maintained. The first, based on the property view that Slavery is right, conforms to that idea throughout, and demands that we shall do everything for it that we ought to do if it were right. We must sweep away all opposition, for opposition to the right is wrong; we must agree that Slavery is right, and we must adopt the idea that property has persuaded the owner to believe— that Slavery is morally right and socially elevating. This gives a philosophical basis for a permanent policy of encouragement.

The other policy is one that squares with the idea that Slavery is wrong, and it consists in doing everything that we ought to do if it is wrong. Now, I don't wish to be misunderstood, nor to leave a gap down to be misrepresented, even. I don't mean that we ought to attack it where it exists. To me it seems that if we were to form a government anew, in view of the actual presence of Slavery we should find it necessary to frame just such a government as our fathers did; giving to the slaveholder the entire control where the system was established, while we possessed the power to restrain it from going outside those limits. [Applause.] From the necessities of the case we should be compelled to form just such a government as our blessed fathers gave us; and, surely, if they have so made it, that adds another reason why we should let Slavery alone where it exists.

If I saw a venomous snake crawling in the road, any man would say I might seize the nearest stick and kill it; but if I found that snake in bed with my children, that would be another question. [Laughter.] I might hurt the children more than the snake, and it might bite them. [Applause.] Much more, if I found it in bed with my neighbor's children, and I had bound myself by a solemn compact not to meddle with his children under any circumstances, it would become me to let that particular mode of getting rid of the gentleman alone. [Great laughter.] But if there was a bed newly made up, to which the children were to be taken, and it was proposed to take a batch of young snakes and put them there with them, I

---

1. William H. Seward (1801–1872), antislavery New York politician and later Lincoln's secretary of state, who predicted in an 1858 speech "an irrepressible conflict" between freedom and slavery.

take it no man would say there was any question how I ought to decide! [Prolonged applause and cheers.]

That is just the case! The new Territories are the newly made bed to which our children are to go, and it lies with the nation to say whether they shall have snakes mixed up with them or not. It does not seem as if there could be much hesitation what our policy should be! [Applause.]

Now I have spoken of a policy based on the idea that Slavery is wrong, and a policy based upon the idea that it is right. But an effort has been made for a policy that shall treat it as neither right or wrong. It is based upon utter indifference. Its leading advocate has said "I don't care whether it be voted up or down." [Laughter.] "It is merely a matter of dollars and cents." "The Almighty has drawn a line across this continent, on one side of which all soil must forever be cultivated by slave labor, and on the other by free;" "when the struggle is between the white man and the negro, I am for the white man; when it is between the negro and the crocodile, I am for the negro." Its central idea is indifference. It holds that it makes no more difference to us whether the Territories become free or slave States, than whether my neighbor stocks his farm with horned cattle or puts it into tobacco. All recognize this policy, the plausible sugar-coated name of which is *popular sovereignty.*" [Laughter.]

March 6, 1860

To George Ashmun[1]

Springfield, Ills.
May 23. 1860

Hon: George Ashmun:
President of the Republican National Convention.
Sir: I accept the nomination tendered me by the Convention over which you presided, and of which I am formally apprized in the letter of yourself and others, acting as a committee of the convention, for the purpose.

The declaration of principles and sentiments, which accompanies your letter, meets my approval; and it shall be my care not to violate, or disregard it, in any part.

Imploring the assistance of Divine Providence, and with due regard to the views and feelings of all who were represented in the convention; to the rights of all the states, and territories, and people of the nation; to the inviolability of the constitution, and the perpetual union, harmony, and prosperity of all, I am most happy to co-operate for the practical success of the principles declared by the convention. Your obliged friend, and fellow citizen

Autobiography Written for Campaign[1]

Abraham Lincoln was born Feb. 12, 1809, then in Hardin, now in the more recently formed county of Larue, Kentucky. His father, Thomas, &

1. A former Whig congressman from Massachusetts (1804–1870) who had served in the House of Representatives from 1845 to 1851.
1. At the request of the Chicago journalist John L. Scripps, Lincoln wrote this sketch, which was the basis of Scripps's campaign biography *Life of Abraham Lincoln* (July 1860).

grand-father, Abraham, were born in Rockingham county Virginia, whither their ancestors had come from Berks county Pennsylvania. His lineage has been traced no farther back than this. The family were originally quakers, though in later times they have fallen away from the peculiar habits of that people. The grand-father Abraham, had four brothers—Isaac, Jacob, John & Thomas. So far as known, the descendants of Jacob and John are still in Virginia. Isaac went to a place near where Virginia, North Carolina, and Tennessee, join; and his decendants are in that region. Thomas came to Kentucky, and after many years, died there, whence his decendants went to Missouri. Abraham, grandfather of the subject of this sketch, came to Kentucky, and was killed by indians about the year 1784. He left a widow, three sons and two daughters. The eldest son, Mordecai, remained in Kentucky till late in life, when he removed to Hancock county, Illinois, where soon after he died, and where several of his descendants still reside. The second son, Josiah, removed at an early day to a place on Blue River, now within Harrison county, Indiana; but no recent information of him, or his family, has been obtained. The eldest sister, Mary, married Ralph Crume and some of her descendants are how known to be in Breckenridge county Kentucky. The second sister, Nancy, married William Brumfield, and her family are not known to have left Kentucky, but there is no recent information from them. Thomas, the youngest son, and father of the present subject, by the early death of his father, and very narrow circumstances of his mother, even in childhood was a wandering laboring boy, and grew up litterally without education. He never did more in the way of writing than to bunglingly sign his own name. Before he was grown, he passed one year as a hired hand with his uncle Isaac on Wataga, a branch of the Holsteen River. Getting back into Kentucky, and having reached his 28th. year, he married Nancy Hanks—mother of the present subject—in the year 1806. She also was born in Virginia; and relatives of hers of the name of Hanks, and of other names, now reside in Coles, in Macon, and in Adams counties, Illinois, and also in Iowa. The present subject has no brother or sister of the whole or half blood. He had a sister, older than himself, who was grown and married, but died many years ago, leaving no child. Also a brother, younger than himself, who died in infancy. Before leaving Kentucky he and his sister were sent for short periods, to A.B.C. schools, the first kept by Zachariah Riney, and the second by Caleb Hazel.

At this time his father resided on Knob-creek, on the road from Bardstown Ky. to Nashville Tenn. at a point three, or three and a half miles South or South-West of Atherton's ferry on the Rolling Fork. From this place he removed to what is now Spencer county Indiana, in the autumn of 1816, A. then being in his eigth year. This removal was partly on account of slavery; but chiefly on account of the difficulty in land titles in Ky. He settled in an unbroken forest; and the clearing away of surplus wood was the great task a head. A. though very young, was large of his age, and had an axe put into his hands at once; and from that till within his twentythird year, he was almost constantly handling that most useful instrument— less, of course, in plowing and harvesting seasons. At this place A. took an early start as a hunter, which was never much improved afterwards. (A few days before the completion of his eigth year, in the absence of his father, a flock of wild turkeys approached the new log-cabin, and A. with a rifle gun, standing inside, shot through a crack, and killed one of them.

He has never since pulled a trigger on any larger game.) In the autumn of 1818 his mother died; and a year afterwards his father married Mrs. Sally Johnston, at Elizabeth-Town, Ky—a widow, with three children of her first marriage. She proved a good and kind mother to A. and is still living in Coles Co. Illinois. There were no children of this second marriage. His father's residence continued at the same place in Indiana, till 1830. While here A. went to A.B.C. schools by littles, kept successively by Andrew Crawford, —— Sweeney, and Azel W. Dorsey. He does not remember any other. The family of Mr. Dorsey now reside in Schuyler Co. Illinois. A. now thinks that the agregate of all his schooling did not amount to one year. He was never in a college or Academy as a student; and never inside of a college or accademy building till since he had a law-license. What he has in the way of education, he has picked up. After he was twentythree, and had separated from his father, he studied English grammar, imperfectly of course, but so as to speak and write as well as he now does. He studied and nearly mastered the Six-books of Euclid, since he was a member of Congress. He regrets his want of education, and does what he can to supply the want. In his tenth year he was kicked by a horse, and apparently killed for a time. When he was nineteen, still residing in Indiana, he made his first trip upon a flat-boat to New-Orleans. He was a hired hand merely; and he and a son of the owner, without other assistance, made the trip. The nature of part of the cargo-load, as it was called—made it necessary for them to linger and trade along the Sugar coast—and one night they were attacked by seven negroes with intent to kill and rob them. They were hurt some in the melee, but succeeded in driving the negroes from the boat, and then "cut cable" "weighed anchor" and left.

March 1st. 1830—A. having just completed his 21st. year, his father and family, with the families of the two daughters and sons-in-law, of his stepmother, left the old homestead in Indiana, and came to Illinois. Their mode of conveyance was waggons drawn by ox-teams, or A. drove one of the teams. They reached the county of Macon, and stopped there some time within the same month of March. His father and family settled a new place on the North side of the Sangamon river, at the junction of the timber-land and prairie, about ten miles Westerly from Decatur. Here they built a log-cabin, into which they removed, and made sufficient of rails to fence ten acres of ground, fenced and broke the ground, and raised a crop of sown corn upon it the same year. These are, or are supposed to be, the rails about which so much is being said just now, though they are far from being the first, or only rails ever made by A.

The sons-in-law, were temporarily settled at other places in the county. In the autumn all hands were greatly afflicted with augue and fever, to which they had not been used, and by which they were greatly discouraged—so much so that they determined on leaving the county. They remained however, through the succeeding winter, which was the winter of the very celebrated "deep snow" of Illinois. During that winter, A. together with his step-mother's son, John D. Johnston, and John Hanks, yet residing in Macon county, hired themselves to one Denton Offutt, to take a flat boat from Beards-town Illinois to New-Orleans; and for that purpose, were to join him—Offut—at Springfield, Ills so soon as the snow should go off. When it did go off which was about the 1st. of March 1831— the county was so flooded, as to make traveling by land impracticable; to obviate which difficulty they purchased a large canoe and came down the Sangamon river in it. This is the time and the manner of A's first entrance into Sangamon County. They found Offutt at Springfield, but learned from him that he had failed in getting a boat at Beardstown. This lead to their hiring themselves to him at $12 per month, each; and getting the timber out of the trees and building a boat at old Sangamon Town on the Sangamon river, seven miles N.W. of Springfield, which boat they took to New-Orleans, substantially upon the old contract. It was in connection with this boat that occurred the ludicrous incident of sewing up the hogs eyes. Offutt bought thirty odd large fat live hogs, but found difficulty in driving them from where he purchased them to the boat, and thereupon conceived the whim that he could sew up their eyes and drive them where he pleased. No sooner thought of than decided, he put his hands, including A. at the job, which they completed—all but the driving. In their blind condition they could not be driven out of the lot or field they were in. This expedient failing, they were tied and hauled on carts to the boat. It was near the Sangamon River, within what is now Menard county.

During this boat enterprize acquaintance with Offutt, who was previously an entire stranger, he conceved a liking for A. and believing he could turn him to account, he contracted with him to act as clerk for him, on his return from New-Orleans, in charge of a store and Mill at New-Salem, then in Sangamon, now in Menard county. Hanks had not gone to New-Orleans, but having a family, and being likely to be detained from home longer than at first expected, had turned back from St. Louis. He is the same John Hanks[2] who now engineers the "rail enterprize" at Decatur; and is a first cousin to A's mother. A's father, with his own family & others mentioned, had, in pursuance of their intention, removed from Macon to Coles county. John D. Johnston, the step-mother's son, went to them; and A. stopped indefinitely, and, for the first time, as it were, by himself at New-Salem, before mentioned. This was in July 1831. Here he rapidly made acquaintances and friends. In less than a year Offutt's business was failing—had almost failed,—when the Black-Hawk war of 1832—broke out. A joined a volunteer company, and to his own surprize, was elected captain of it. He says he has not since had any success in life which gave him so much satisfaction. He went the campaign, served near three months, met the ordinary hardships of such an expedition, but was in no battle. He now owns in Iowa, the land upon which his own warrants for this service, were located. Returning from the campaign, and encouraged by his great popularity among his immediate neighbors, he, the same year, ran for the Legislature and was beaten—his own precinct, however, casting it's votes 277 for and 7, against him. And this too while he was an avowed Clay man, and the precinct the autumn afterwards, giving a majority of 115 to Genl. Jackson over Mr. Clay. This was the only time A was ever beaten on a direct vote of the people. He was now without means and out of business, but was anxious to remain with his friends who had treated him with so much generosity, especially as he had nothing elsewhere to go to.

2. Lincoln's second cousin who on May 9, 1860, caused a sensation at the Decatur, Illinois, Republican convention when he carried onstage two fence rails draped with a banner that read "Abraham Lincoln, the Rail Candidate for President in 1860. Two rails from a lot of three thousand made in 1830 by John Hanks and Abe Lincoln." The incident bolstered Lincoln's populist image as the "Rail Splitter."

He studied what he should do—thought of learning the black-smith trade—thought of trying to study law—rather thought he could not succeed at that without a better education. Before long, strangely enough, a man offered to sell and did sell, to A. and another as poor as himself, an old stock of goods, upon credit. They opened as merchants; and he says that was *the* store. Of course they did nothing but get deeper and deeper in debt. He was appointed Postmaster at New-Salem—the office being too insignificant, to make his politics an objection. The store winked out. The Surveyor of Sangamon, offered to depute to A that portion of his work which was within his part of the county. He accepted, procured a compass and chain, studied Flint, and Gibson a little, and went at it. This procured bread, and kept soul and body together. The election of 1834 came, and he was then elected to the Legislature by the highest vote cast for any candidate. Major John T. Stuart, then in full practice of the law, was also elected. During the canvass, in a private conversation he encouraged A. to study law. After the election he borrowed books of Stuart, took them home with him, and went at it in good earnest. He studied with nobody. He still mixed in the surveying to pay board and clothing bills. When the Legislature met, the law books were dropped, but were taken up again at the end of the session. He was re-elected in 1836, 1838, and 1840. In the autumn of 1836 he obtained a law licence, and on April 15, 1837 removed to Springfield, and commenced the practice, his old friend, Stuart taking him into partnership. March 3rd. 1837, by a protest[3] entered upon the Ills. House Journal of that date, at pages 817, 818, A. with Dan Stone, another representative of Sangamon, briefly defined his position on the slavery question; and so far as it goes, it was then the same that it is now. The protest is as follows—(Here insert it) In 1838, & 1840 Mr. L's party in the Legislature voted for him as Speaker; but being in the minority, he was not elected. After 1840 he declined a re-election to the Legislature. He was on the Harrison electoral ticket in 1840, and on that of Clay in 1844, and spent much time and labor in both those canvasses. In Nov. 1842 he was married to Mary, daughter of Robert S. Todd, of Lexington, Kentucky. They have three living children, all sons—one born in 1843, one in 1850, and one in 1853. They lost one, who was born in 1846. In 1846, he was elected to the lower House of Congress, and served one term only, commencing in Dec. 1847 and ending with the inauguration of Gen. Taylor, in March 1849. All the battles of the Mexican war had been fought before Mr. L. took his seat in congress, but the American army was still in Mexico, and the treaty of peace was not fully and formally ratified till the June afterwards. Much has been said of his course in Congress in regard to this war. A careful examination of the Journals and Congressional Globe shows, that he voted for all the supply measures which came up, and for all the measures in any way favorable to the officers, soldiers, and their families, who conducted the war through; with this exception that some of these measures passed without yeas and nays, leaving no record as to how particular men voted. The Journals and Globe also show him voting that the war was unnecessarily and unconstitutionally begun by the President of the United States. This is the language of Mr. Ashmun's

3. See p. 6.

amendment, for which Mr. L. and nearly or quite all, other whigs of the H. R. voted.

Mr. L's reasons for the opinion expressed by this vote were briefly that the President had sent Genl. Taylor into an inhabited part of the country belonging to Mexico, and not to the U.S. and thereby had provoked the first act of hostility—in fact the commencement of the war; that the place, being the country bordering on the East bank of the Rio Grande, was inhabited by native Mexicans, born there under the Mexican government; and had never submitted to, nor been conquered by Texas, or the U.S. nor transferred to either by treaty—that although Texas claimed the Rio Grande as her boundary, Mexico had never recognized it, the people on the ground had never recognized it, and neither Texas nor the U.S. had ever enforced it—that there was a broad desert between that, and the country over which Texas had actual control—that the country where hostilities commenced, having once belonged to Mexico, must remain so, until it was somehow legally transferred, which had never been done.

Mr. L. thought the act of sending an armed force among the Mexicans, was *unnecessary*, inasmuch as Mexico was in no way molesting, or menacing the U.S. or the people thereof; and that it was *unconstitutional*, because the power of levying war is vested in Congress, and not in the President. He thought the principal motive for the act, was to divert public attention from the surrender of "Fifty-four, forty, or fight" to Great Brittain, on the Oregon boundary question.

Mr. L. was not a candidate for re-election. This was determined upon, and declared before he went to Washington, in accordance with an understanding among whig friends, by which Col. Hardin, and Col. Baker had each previously served a single term in the same District.

In 1848, during his term in congress, he advocated Gen. Taylor's nomination for the Presidency, in opposition to all others, and also took an active part for his election, after his nomination—speaking a few times in Maryland, near Washington, several times in Massachusetts, and canvassing quite fully his own district in Illinois, which was followed by a majority in the district of over 1500 for Gen. Taylor.

Upon his return from Congress he went to the practice of the law with greater earnestness than ever before. In 1852 he was upon the Scott electoral ticket, and did something in the way of canvassing, but owing to the hopelessness of the cause in Illinois, he did less than in previous presidential canvasses.

In 1854, his profession had almost superseded the thought of politics in his mind, when the repeal of the Missouri compromise aroused him as he had never been before.

In the autumn of that year he took the stump with no broader practical aim or object than to secure, if possible, the re-election of Hon Richard Yates to congress. His speeches at once attracted a more marked attention than they had ever before done. As the canvass proceeded, he was drawn to different parts of the state, outside of Mr. Yates' district. He did not abandon the law, but gave his attention, by turns, to that and politics. The State agricultural fair was at Springfield that year, and Douglas was announced to speak there.

In the canvass of 1856, Mr. L. made over fifty speeches, no one of which, so far as he remembers, was put in print. One of them was made at Galena,[4] but Mr. L. has no recollection of any part of it being printed; nor does he remember whether in that speech he said anything about a Supreme court decision. He may have spoken upon that subject; and some of the newspapers may have reported him as saying what is now ascribed to him; but he thinks he could not have expressed himself as represented.

ca. June 1860

To Abraham Jonas[1]

Confidential

Hon. A. Jonas: Springfield, Ills.
My dear Sir   July 21,1860
Yours of the 20th. is received. I suppose as good, or even better, men than I may have been in American, or Know-Nothing lodges; but in point of fact, I never was in one, at Quincy, or elsewhere. I was never in Quincy but one day and two nights, while Know-Nothing lodges were in existence, and you were with me that day and both those nights. I had never been there before in my life; and never afterwards, till the joint debate with Douglas in 1858. It was in 1854, when I spoke in some Hall there,[2] and after the speaking, you, with others, took me to, an oyster saloon, passed an hour there, and you walked with me to, and parted with me at, the Quincy-House, quite late at night. I left by stage for Naples before day-light in the morning, having come in by the same route, after dark, the evening previous to the speaking, when I found you waiting at the Quincy House to meet me. A few days after I was there, Richardson,[3] as I understood, started this same story about my having been in a Know-Nothing lodge. When I heard of the charge, as I did soon after, I taxed my recollection for some incident which could have suggested it; and I remembered that on parting with you the last night, I went to the Office of the Hotel to take my stage passage for the morning, was told that no stage office for that line was kept there, and that I must see the driver, before retiring, to insure his calling for me in the morning; and a servant was sent with me to find the driver, who after taking me a square or two, stopped me, and stepped perhaps a dozen steps farther, and in my hearing called to some one, who answered him apparently from the upper part of a building, and promised to call with the stage for me at the Quincy House. I returned and went to bed; and before day the stage called and took me. This is all.

4. On July 26, 1856, the Galena Daily Advertiser reported a speech Lincoln had given three days earlier in which he allegedly said that only a Supreme Court decision could open up the western territories for slavery.
1. A Quincy, Illinois, lawyer and a close friend of Lincoln's (1801–1864) who reported that a mutual acquaintance, Isaac N. Morris, was collecting affidavits from Irishmen that Lincoln had been spotted in a Know Nothing lodge in Quincy.
2. Lincoln spoke in Kendall's Hall in Quincy on November 1, 1854.
3. William A. Richardson (1811–1875), a prominent Illinois Democrat who served in the U.S. House of Representatives (1847–56; 1861–63) and the Senate (1863–65).

That I never was in a Know-Nothing lodge in Quincy, I should expect, could be easily proved, by respectable men, who were always in the lodges and never saw me there. An affidavit of one or two such would put the matter at rest.

And now, a word of caution. Our adversaries think they can gain a point, if they could force me to openly deny this charge, by which some degree of offence would be given to the Americans. For this reason, it must not publicly appear that I am paying any attention to the charge. Yours truly

To George T. M. Davis[1]

Private & confidential.

Geo. T. M. Davis, Esq   Springfield, Ills.
My dear Sir: Oct. 27. 1860

Mr. Dubois has shown me your letter of the 20th.; and I promised him to write you. What is it I could say which would quiet alarm? Is it that no interference by the government, with slaves or slavery within the states, is intended? I have said this so often already, that a repetition of it is but mockery, bearing an appearance of weakness, and cowardice, which perhaps should be avoided. Why do not uneasy men *read* what I have already said? and what our *platform* says? If they will not read, or heed, then, would they read, or heed, a repetition of them? Of course the declaration that there is no intention to interfere with slaves or slavery, in the states, with all that is fairly implied in such declaration, is true; and I should have no objection to make, and repeat the declaration a thousand times, if there were no danger of encouraging bold bad men to believe they are dealing with one who can be scared into anything.

I have some reason to believe the Sub-National committee, at the Astor House, may be considering this question; and if their judgment should be different from mine, mine might be modified by theirs. Yours very truly

Passage Written for Lyman Trumbull's[1] Speech at Springfield, Illinois

I have labored in, and for, the Republican organization with entire confidence that whenever it shall be in power, each and all of the States will be left in as complete control of their own affairs respectively, and at as perfect liberty to choose, and employ, their own means of protecting property, and preserving peace and order within their respective limits, as they have ever been under any administration. Those who have voted for Mr. Lincoln, have expected, and still expect this; and they would not have voted for him had they expected otherwise. I regard it as extremely

---

1. George Turnbull Moore Davis (1810–1888), an Illinois lawyer, and later a New York business-man who notified Illinois politician Jesse K. Dubois (1811–1876) of an alleged plan in New York and several Southern cities to create a financial panic in the event of Lincoln's election.
1. Illinois lawyer and politician (1813–1896) who incorporated parts of this passage in a speech made November 20, 1860. He served in the U.S. Senate from 1855 to 1873 and in 1865 co-wrote the Thirteenth Amendment to the Constitution, which abolished slavery.

fortunate for the peace of the whole country, that this point, upon which the Republicans have been so long, and so persistently misrepresented, is now to be brought to a practical test, and placed beyond the possibility of doubt. Disunionists *per se*, are now in hot haste to get out of the Union, precisely because they perceive they can not, much longer, maintain apprehension among the Southern people that their homes, and firesides, and lives, are to be endangered by the action of the Federal Government. With such *"Now, or never"* is the maxim.

I am rather glad of this military preparation in the South. It will enable the people the more easily to suppress any uprisings there, which their misrepresentations of purposes may have encouraged.

November 20, 1860

To John A. Gilmer[1]

Strictly confidential.

Hon. John A. Gilmer: Springfield, Ill. Dec 15, 1860.
My dear Sir—Yours of the 10th is received. I am greatly disinclined to write a letter on the subject embraced in yours; and I would not do so, even privately as I do, were it not that I fear you might misconstrue my silence. Is it desired that I shall shift the ground upon which I have been elected? I can not do it. You need only to acquaint yourself with that ground, and press it on the attention of the South. It is all in print and easy of access. May I be pardoned if I ask whether even you have ever attempted to procure the reading of the Republican platform, or my speeches, by the Southern people? If not, what reason have I to expect that any additional production of mine would meet a better fate? It would make me appear as if I repented for the crime of having been elected, and was anxious to apologize and beg forgiveness. To so represent me, would be the principal use made of any letter I might now thrust upon the public. My old record cannot be so used; and that is precisely the reason that some new declaration is so much sought.

Now, my dear sir, be assured, that I am not questioning *your* candor; I am only pointing out, that, while a new letter would hurt the cause which I think a just one, you can quite as well effect every patriotic object with the old record. Carefully read pages 18, 19, 74, 75, 88, 89, & 267 of the volume of Joint Debates between Senator Douglas and myself, with the Republican Platform adopted at Chicago, and all your questions will be substantially answered. I have no thought of recommending the abolition of slavery in the District of Columbia, nor the slave trade among the slave states, even on the conditions indicated; and if I were to make such recommendation, it is quite clear Congress would not follow it.

As to employing slaves in Arsenals and Dockyards, it is a thing I never thought of in my life, to my recollection, till I saw your letter; and I may say of it, precisely as I have said of the two points above.

---

1. A U.S. Representative from South Carolina (1805–1868) who in 1860–61 opposed secession; he later served in the Confederate Congress.

As to the use of patronage in the slave states, where there are few or no Republicans, I do not expect to inquire for the politics of the appointee, or whether he does or not own slaves. I intend in that matter to accommodate the people in the several localities, if they themselves will allow me to accommodate them. In one word, I never have been, am not now, and probably never shall be, in a mood of harassing the people, either North or South.

On the territorial question, I am inflexible, as you see my position in the book. On that, there is a difference between you and us; and it is the only substantial difference. You think slavery is right and ought to be extended; we think it is wrong and ought to be restricted. For this, neither has any just occasion to be angry with the other.

As to the state laws, mentioned in your sixth question, I really know very little of them. I never have read one. If any of them are in conflict with the fugitive slave clause, or any other part of the constitution, I certainly should be glad of their repeal; but I could hardly be justified, as a citizen of Illinois, or as President of the United States, to recommend the repeal of a statute of Vermont, or South Carolina.

With the assurance of my highest regards I subscribe myself Your obt. Servt.,

P.S. The documents referred to, I suppose you will readily find in Washington.

To Thurlow Weed[1]

Private & Confidential.

Hon. Thurlow Weed   Springfield, Ills- Dec. 17-1860

My dear Sir Yours of the 11th. was received two days ago. Should the convocation of Governors, of which you speak, seem desirous to know my views on the present aspect of things, tell them you judge from my speeches that I will be inflexible on the territorial question; that I probably think either the Missouri line extended, or Douglas' and Eli Thayer's[2] Pop. Sov. would lose us every thing we gained by the election; that filibustering for all South of us, and making slave states of it, would follow in spite of us, under either plan.

Also, that I probably think all opposition, real and apparant, to the fugitive slave clause of the constitution ought to be withdrawn.

I believe you can pretend to find but little, if any thing, in my speeches, about secession; but my opinion is that no state can, in any way lawfully, get out of the Union, without the consent of the others; and that it is the duty of the President, and other government functionaries to run the machine as it is. Yours very truly

---

1. An influential New York Republican (1797–1882), who had written Lincoln suggesting a meeting of governors in New York City to form a plan of action in light of the intensifying national crisis.
2. U.S. representative from Massachusetts (1819–1899). "Pop. Sov.": popular sovereignty, the idea that settlers of western territories should be left to decide for themselves about slavery.

To Henry J. Raymond[1]

Confidential

Hon. H. J. Raymond   Springfields, Ills.
My dear Sir   Dec. 18, 1860

Yours of the 14th. is received. What a very mad-man your correspondent, Smedes is. Mr. Lincoln is not pledged to the ultimate extinction of slavery; does not hold the black man to be the equal of the white, unqualifiedly as Mr. S. states it; and never did stigmatize their white people as immoral & unchristian; and Mr. S. can not prove one of his assertions true.

Mr. S. seems sensitive on the questions of morals and christianity. What does he think of a man who makes charges against another which he does not know to be true, and could easily learn to be false?

As to the pitcher story, it is a forgery out and out. I never made but one speech in Cincinnati—the last speech in the volume containing the Joint Debates between Senator Douglas and myself. I have never yet seen Gov. Chase. I was never in a meeting of negroes in my life; and never saw a pitcher presented by anybody to anybody.

I am much obliged by your letter, and shall be glad to hear from you again when you have anything of interest. Yours truly

To Alexander H. Stephens[1]

For your own eye only.

Hon. A. H. Stephens—   Springfield, Ills.
My dear Sir   Dec. 22, 1860

Your obliging answer to my short note is just received, and for which please accept my thanks. I fully appreciate the present peril the country is in, and the weight of responsibility on me.

Do the people of the South really entertain fears that a Republican administration would, *directly*, or *indirectly*, interfere with their slaves, or with them, about their slaves? If they do, I wish to assure you, as once a friend, and still, I hope, not an enemy, that there is no cause for such fears.

The South would be in no more danger in this respect, than it was in the days of Washington. I suppose, however, this does not meet the case. You think slavery is *right* and ought to be extended; while we think it is *wrong* and ought to be restricted. That I suppose is the rub. It certainly is the only substantial difference between us. Yours very truly

1. A prominent journalist and founder of the *New York Times* (1820–1869) who had received a virulent letter from William C. Smedes, a Mississippi legislator, reporting a speech Lincoln had allegedly once given in Cincinnati, Ohio, where free blacks presented a pitcher to Salmon P. Chase. The evidence indicates that Lincoln was not present at the speech, which was actually given on May 6, 1842, by Chase himself.
1. A Georgia politician (1812–1883) who had formerly served as a Whig representative in Congress, became the vice president of the Confederate States of America. In 1861, he delivered his so-called Cornerstone Speech, in which he praised the South as a society founded on "the great truth that the negro is not equal to the white man; that slavery, subordination to the superior race, is his natural and normal condition."

Farewell Address at Springfield, Illinois

My friends—No one, not in my situation, can appreciate my feeling of sadness at this parting. To this place, and the kindness of these people, I owe every thing. Here I have lived a quarter of a century, and have passed from a young to an old man. Here my children have been born, and one is buried. I now leave, not knowing when, or whether ever, I may return, with a task before me greater than that which rested upon Washington. Without the assistance of that Divine Being, who ever attended him, I cannot succeed. With that assistance I cannot fail. Trusting in Him, who can go with me, and remain with you and be every where for good, let us confidently hope that all will yet be well. To His care commending you, as I hope in your prayers you will commend me, I bid you an affectionate farewell

February 11, 1861

From Speech at Indianapolis, Indiana

※　※　※

The words "coercion" and "invasion" are in great use about these days. Suppose we were simply to try if we can, and ascertain what, is the meaning of these words. Let us get, if we can, the exact definitions of these words—not from dictionaries, but from the men who constantly repeat them—what things they mean to express by the words. What, then, is "coercion"? What is "invasion"? Would the marching of an army into South Carolina, for instance, without the consent of her people, and in hostility against them, be coercion or invasion? I very frankly say, I think it would be invasion, and it would be coercion too, if the people of that country were forced to submit. But if the Government, for instance, but simply insists upon holding its own forts, or retaking those forts which belong to it,—[cheers,]—or the enforcement of the laws of the United States in the collection of duties upon foreign importations,—[renewed cheers,]—or even the withdrawal of the mails from those portions of the country where the mails themselves are habitually violated; would any or all of these things be coercion? Do the lovers of the Union contend that they will resist coercion or invasion of any State, understanding that any or all of these would be coercing or invading a State? If they do, then it occurs to me that the means for the preservation of the Union they so greatly love, in their own estimation, is of a very thin and airy character. [Applause.] If sick, they would consider the little pills of the homœopathist as already too large for them to swallow. In their view, the Union, as a family relation, would not be anything like a regular marriage at all, but only as a sort of free-love arrangement,[1]—[laughter,]—to be maintained

1. The antebellum period witnessed several communitarian experiments in free love, based on French utopian socialist Charles Fourier's notion that conventional marriage should be abolished and replaced by relationships based on what was called "passional [or passionate] attraction." "Homœopathist": practitioner of a form of alternative medicine, homeopathy, by which illness is treated with small doses of substances that create symptoms of the very illness being treated, on the theory that "like cures like."

on what that sect calls passionate attraction. [Continued laughter.] But, my friends, enough of this.

What is the particular sacredness of a State? I speak not of that position which is given to a State in and by the Constitution of the United States, for that all of us agree to—we abide by; but that position assumed, that a State can carry with it out of the Union that which it holds in sacredness by virtue of its connection with the Union. I am speaking of that assumed right of a State, as a primary principle, that the Constitution should rule all that is less than itself, and ruin all that is bigger than itself. [Laughter.] But, I ask, wherein does consist that right? If a State, in one instance, and a county in another, should be equal in extent of territory, and equal in the number of people, wherein is that State any better than the county? Can a change of name change the right? By what principle of original right is it that one-fiftieth or one-ninetieth of a great nation, by calling themselves a State, have the right to break up and ruin that nation as a matter of original principle? Now, I ask the question—I am not deciding anything—[laughter,]—and with the request that you will think somewhat upon that subject and decide for yourselves, if you choose, when you get ready,—where is the mysterious, original right, from principle, for a certain district of country with inhabitants, by merely being called a State, to play tyrant over all its own citizens, and deny the authority of everything greater than itself. [Laughter.] I say I am deciding nothing, but simply giving something for you to reflect upon; and, with having said this much, and having declared, in the start, that I will make no long speeches, I thank you again for this magnificent welcome, and bid you an affectionate farewell. [Cheers.]

February 11, 1861

From Speech at Cleveland, Ohio

* * *

I think that there is no occasion for any excitement. The crisis, as it is called, is altogether an artificial crisis. In all parts of the nation there are differences of opinion and politics. There are differences of opinion even here. You did not all vote for the person who now addresses you. What is happening now will not hurt those who are farther away from here. Have they not all their rights now as they ever have had? Do they not have their fugitive slaves returned now as ever? Have they not the same constitution that they have lived under for seventy odd years? Have they not a position as citizens of this common country, and have we any power to change that position? (Cries of "No.") What then is the matter with them? Why all this excitement? Why all these complaints? As I said before, this crisis is all artificial. It has no foundation in facts. It was not argued up, as the saying is, and cannot, therefore, be argued down. Let it alone and it will go down of itself (Laughter). Mr. Lincoln said they must be content with but a few words from him. He was very much fatigued, and had spoken so frequently that he was already hoarse. He thanked them for the cordial and magnificent reception they had given him. Not less did he thank them for the votes they gave him last fall, and quite as much he thanked them for the efficient aid they had given the cause which he represented—a cause which he would say was a good one. He had one more word to say. He was given to understand that this reception was not tendered by his own party supporters, but by men of all parties. This is as it should be. If Judge Douglas had been elected and had been here on his way to Washington, as I am to-night, the republicans should have joined his supporters in welcoming him, just as his friends have joined with mine tonight. If all do not join now to save the good old ship of the Union this voyage nobody will have a chance to pilot her on another voyage. He concluded by thanking all present for the devotion they have shown to the cause of the Union.

February 15, 1861

Address to the New Jersey Senate at Trenton, New Jersey

Mr. President and Gentlemen of the Senate of the State of New-Jersey: I am very grateful to you for the honorable reception of which I have been the object. I cannot but remember the place that New-Jersey holds in our early history. In the early Revolutionary struggle, few of the States among the old Thirteen had more of the battle-fields of the country within their limits than old New-Jersey. May I be pardoned if, upon this occasion, I mention that away back in my childhood, the earliest days of my being able to read, I got hold of a small book, such a one as few of the younger members have ever seen, "Weem's Life of Washington."[1] I remember all the accounts there given of the battle fields and struggles for the liberties of the country, and none fixed themselves upon my imagination so deeply as the struggle here at Trenton, New-Jersey. The crossing of the river; the contest with the Hessians; the great hardships endured at that time, all fixed themselves on my memory more than any single revolutionary event; and you all know, for you have all been boys, how these early impressions last longer than any others. I recollect thinking then, boy even though I was, that there must have been something more than common that those men struggled for. I am exceedingly anxious that that thing which they struggled for; that something even more than National Independence; that something that held out a great promise to all the people of the world to all time to come; I am exceedingly anxious that this Union, the Constitution, and the liberties of the people shall be perpetuated in accordance with the original idea for which that struggle was made, and I shall be most happy indeed if I shall be an humble instrument in the hands of the Almighty, and of this, his almost chosen people, for perpetuating the object of that great struggle. You give me this reception, as I understand, without distinction of party. I learn that this body is composed of a majority of gentlemen who, in the exercise of their best judgment in the choice of a Chief Magistrate, did not think I was the man. I understand, never-

1. *The Life of Washington*, by Mason Locke Weems (1759–1825), first published in 1800.

theless, that they came forward here to greet me as the constitutional President of the United States—as citizens of the United States, to meet the man who, for the time being, is the representative man of the nation, united by a purpose to perpetuate the Union and liberties of the people. As such, I accept this reception more gratefully than I could do did I believe it was tendered to me as an individual.

February 21, 1861

Address to the New Jersey General Assembly at Trenton, New Jersey

Mr. Speaker and Gentlemen: I have just enjoyed the honor of a reception by the other branch of this Legislature, and I return to you and them my thanks for the reception which the people of New-Jersey have given, through their chosen representatives, to me, as the representative, for the time being, of the majesty of the people of the United States. I appropriate to myself very little of the demonstrations of respect with which I have been greeted. I think little should be given to any man, but that it should be a manifestation of adherence to the Union and the Constitution. I understand myself to be received here by the representatives of the people of New-Jersey, a majority of whom differ in opinion from those with whom I have acted. This manifestation is therefore to be regarded by me as expressing their devotion to the Union, the Constitution and the liberties of the people. You, Mr. Speaker,[1] have well said that this is a time when the bravest and wisest look with doubt and awe upon the aspect presented by our national affairs. Under these circumstances, you will readily see why I should not speak in detail of the course I shall deem it best to pursue. It is proper that I should avail myself of all the information and all the time at my command, in order that when the time arrives in which I must speak officially, I shall be able to take the ground which I deem the best and safest, and from which I may have no occasion to swerve. I shall endeavor to take the ground I deem most just to the North, the East, the West, the South, and the whole country. I take it, I hope, in good temper— certainly no malice toward any section. I shall do all that may be in my power to promote a peaceful settlement of all our difficulties. The man does not live who is more devoted to peace than I am. [Cheers.] None who would do more to preserve it. But it may be necessary to put the foot down firmly. [Here the audience broke out into cheers so loud and long that for some moments it was impossible to hear Mr. L.'s voice.] He continued: And if I do my duty, and do right, you will sustain me, will you not? [Loud cheers, and cries of "Yes," "Yes," "We will."] Received, as I am, by the members of a Legislature the majority of whom do not agree with me in political sentiments, I trust that I may have their assistance in piloting the ship of State through this voyage, surrounded by perils as it is; for, if it should suffer attack now, there will be no pilot ever needed for another voyage.

1. Charles Haight (1838–1891), a Democrat who served as speaker of the state's General Assembly from 1860 through 1861.

Gentlemen, I have already spoken longer than I intended, and must beg leave to stop here.

February 21, 1861

Speech at Independence Hall, Philadelphia, Pennsylvania

Mr. Cuyler[1]:—I am filled with deep emotion at finding myself standing here in the place where were collected together the wisdom, the patriotism, the devotion to principle, from which sprang the institutions under which we live. You have kindly suggested to me that in my hands is the task of restoring peace to our distracted country. I can say in return, sir, that all the political sentiments I entertain have been drawn, so far as I have been able to draw them, from the sentiments which originated, and were given to the world from this hall in which we stand. I have never had a feeling politically that did not spring from the sentiments embodied in the Declaration of Independence. (Great cheering.) I have often pondered over the dangers which were incurred by the men who assembled here and adopted that Declaration of Independence—I have pondered over the toils that were endured by the officers and soldiers of the army, who achieved that Independence. (Applause.) I have often inquired of myself, what great principle or idea it was that kept this Confederacy so long together. It was not the mere matter of the separation of the colonies from the mother land; but something in that Declaration giving liberty, not alone to the people of this country, but hope to the world for all future time. (Great applause.) It was that which gave promise that in due time the weights should be lifted from the shoulders of all men, and that *all* should have an equal chance. (Cheers.) This is the sentiment embodied in that Declaration of Independence.

Now, my friends, can this country be saved upon that basis? If it can, I will consider myself one of the happiest men in the world if I can help to save it. If it can't be saved upon that principle, it will be truly awful. But, if this country cannot be saved without giving up that principle—I was about to say I would rather be assassinated on this spot than to surrender it:[2] (Applause.)

Now, in my view of the present aspect of affairs, there is no need of bloodshed and war. There is no necessity for it. I am not in favor of such a course, and I may say in advance, there will be no blood shed unless it be forced upon the Government. The Government will not use force unless force is used against it. (Prolonged applause and cries of "That's the proper sentiment.")

My friends, this is a wholly unprepared speech. I did not expect to be called upon to say a word when I came here—I supposed I was merely to do something towards raising a flag. I may, therefore, have said something indiscreet, (cries of "no, no"), but I have said nothing but what I am willing to live by, and, in the pleasure of Almighty God, die by.

February 22, 1861

1. The president (1819–1876) of the Select Council of Philadelphia.
2. The night before this speech, Lincoln had been informed of a plot to assassinate him on his way through Baltimore.

First Inaugural Address

Fellow citizens of the United States:

In compliance with a custom as old as the government itself, I appear before you to address you briefly, and to take, in your presence, the oath prescribed by the Constitution of the United States, to be taken by the President "before he enters on the execution of his office."

I do not consider it necessary, at present, for me to discuss those matters of administration about which there is no special anxiety, or excitement.

Apprehension seems to exist among the people of the Southern States, that by the accession of a Republican Administration, their property, and their peace, and personal security, are to be endangered. There has never been any reasonable cause for such apprehension. Indeed, the most ample evidence to the contrary has all the while existed, and been open to their inspection. It is found in nearly all the published speeches of him who now addresses you. I do but quote from one of those speeches when I declare that "I have no purpose, directly or indirectly, to interfere with the institution of slavery in the States where it exists. I believe I have no lawful right to do so, and I have no inclination to do so." Those who nominated and elected me did so with full knowledge that I had made this, and many similar declarations, and had never recanted them. And more than this, they placed in the platform, for my acceptance, and as a law to themselves, and to me, the clear and emphatic resolution which I now read:

"*Resolved*, That the maintenance inviolate of the rights of the States, and especially the right of each State to order and control its own domestic institutions according to its own judgment exclusively, is essential to that balance of power on which the perfection and endurance of our political fabric depend; and we denounce the lawless invasion by armed force of the soil of any State or Territory, no matter under what pretext, as among the gravest of crimes."

I now reiterate these sentiments: and in doing so, I only press upon the public attention the most conclusive evidence of which the case is susceptible, that the property, peace and security of no section are to be in anywise endangered by the now incoming Administration. I add too, that all the protection which, consistently with the Constitution and the laws, can be given, will be cheerfully given to all the States when lawfully demanded, for whatever cause—as cheerfully to one section, as to another.

There is much controversy about the delivering up of fugitives from service or labor. The clause I now read is as plainly written in the Constitution as any other of its provisions:

"No person held to service or labor in one State, under the laws thereof, escaping into another, shall, in consequence of any law or regulation therein, be discharged from such service or labor, but shall be delivered up on claim of the party to whom such service or labor may be due."

It is scarcely questioned that this provision was intended by those who made it, for the reclaiming of what we call fugitive slaves; and the intention of the law-giver is the law. All members of Congress swear their support to the whole Constitution—to this provision as much as to any other. To the proposition, then, that slaves whose cases come within the terms of this clause, "shall be delivered up," their oaths are unanimous.

Now, if they would make the effort in good temper, could they not, with nearly equal unanimity, frame and pass a law, by means of which to keep good that unanimous oath?

There is some difference of opinion whether this clause should be enforced by national or by state authority; but surely that difference is not a very material one. If the slave is to be surrendered, it can be of but little consequence to him, or to others, by which authority it is done. And should any one, in any case, be content that his oath shall go un-kept, on a merely unsubstantial controversy as to *how* it shall be kept?

Again, in any law upon this subject, ought not all the safeguards of liberty known in civilized and humane jurisprudence to be introduced, so that a free man be not, in any case, surrendered as a slave? And might it not be well, at the same time, to provide by law for the enforcement of that clause in the Constitution which guaranties that "The citizens of each State shall be entitled to all previleges and immunities of citizens in the several States?"

I take the official oath to-day, with no mental reservations, and with no purpose to construe the Constitution or laws, by any hypercritical rules. And while I do not choose now to specify particular acts of Congress as proper to be enforced, I do suggest, that it will be much safer for all, both in official and private stations, to conform to, and abide by, all those acts which stand unrepealed, than to violate any of them, trusting to find impunity in having them held to be unconstitutional.

It is seventy-two years since the first inauguration of a President under our national Constitution. During that period fifteen different and greatly distinguished citizens, have, in succession, administered the executive branch of the government. They have conducted it through many perils; and, generally, with great success. Yet, with all this scope for precedent, I now enter upon the same task for the brief constitutional term of four years, under great and peculiar difficulty. A disruption of the Federal Union heretofore only menaced, is now formidably attempted.

I hold, that in contemplation of universal law, and of the Constitution, the Union of these States is perpetual. Perpetuity is implied, if not expressed, in the fundamental law of all national governments. It is safe to assert that no government proper, ever had a provision in its organic law for its own termination. Continue to execute all the express provisions of our national Constitution, and the Union will endure forever—it being impossible to destroy it, except by some action not provided for in the instrument itself.

Again, if the United States be not a government proper, but an association of States in the nature of contract merely, can it, as a contract, be peaceably unmade, by less than all the parties who made it? One party to a contract may violate it—break it, so to speak; but does it not require all to lawfully rescind it?

Descending from these general principles, we find the proposition that, in legal contemplation, the Union is perpetual, confirmed by the history of the Union itself. The Union is much older than the Constitution. It was formed in fact, by the Articles of Association in 1774. It was matured and continued by the Declaration of Independence in 1776. It was further matured and the faith of all the then thirteen States expressly plighted and engaged that it should be perpetual, by the Articles of Confederation in 1778. And finally, in 1787, one of the declared objects for ordaining and establishing the Constitution, was *"to form a more perfect union."*

But if destruction of the Union, by one, or by a part only, of the States, be lawfully possible, the Union is *less* perfect than before the Constitution, having lost the vital element of perpetuity.

It follows from these views that no State, upon its own mere motion, can lawfully get out of the Union,—that *resolves* and *ordinances* to that effect are legally void; and that acts of violence, within any State or States, against the authority of the United States, are insurrectionary or revolutionary, according to circumstances.

I therefore consider that, in view of the Constitution and the laws, the Union is unbroken; and, to the extent of my ability, I shall take care, as the Constitution itself expressly enjoins upon me, that the laws of the Union be faithfully executed in all the States. Doing this I deem to be only a simple duty on my part; and I shall perform it, so far as practicable, unless my rightful masters, the American people, shall withhold the requisite means, or, in some authoritative manner, direct the contrary. I trust this will not be regarded as a menace, but only as the declared purpose of the Union that it *will* constitutionally defend, and maintain itself.

In doing this there needs to be no bloodshed or violence; and there shall be none, unless it be forced upon the national authority. The power confided to me, will be used to hold, occupy, and possess the property, and places belonging to the government, and to collect the duties and imposts; but beyond what may be necessary for these objects, there will be no invasion—no using of force against, or among the people anywhere. Where hostility to the United States, in any interior locality, shall be so great and so universal, as to prevent competent resident citizens from holding the Federal offices, there will be no attempt to force obnoxious strangers among the people for that object. While the strict legal right may exist in the government to enforce the exercise of these offices, the attempt to do so would be so irritating, and so nearly impracticable with all, that I deem it better to forego, for the time, the uses of such offices.

The mails, unless repelled, will continue to be furnished in all parts of the Union. So far as possible, the people everywhere shall have that sense of perfect security which is most favorable to calm thought and reflection. The course here indicated will be followed, unless current events, and experience, shall show a modification, or change, to be proper; and in every case and exigency, my best discretion will be exercised, according to circumstances actually existing, and with a view and a hope of a peaceful solution of the national troubles, and the restoration of fraternal sympathies and affections.

That there are persons in one section, or another who seek to destroy the Union at all events, and are glad of any pretext to do it, I will neither affirm or deny; but if there be such, I need address no word to them. To those, however, who really love the Union, may I not speak?

Before entering upon so grave a matter as the destruction of our national fabric, with all its benefits, its memories, and its hopes, would it not be wise to ascertain precisely why we do it? Will you hazard so desperate a step, while there is any possibility that any portion of the ills you fly from, have no real existence? Will you, while the certain ills you fly to, are greater than all the real ones you fly from? Will you risk the commission of so fearful a mistake?

All profess to be content in the Union, if all constitutional rights can be maintained. Is it true, then, that any right, plainly written in the Constitution, has been denied? I think not. Happily the human mind is so constituted, that no party can reach to the audacity of doing this. Think, if you can, of a single instance in which a plainly written provision of the Constitution has ever been denied. If, by the mere force of numbers, a majority should deprive a minority of any clearly written constitutional right, it might, in a moral point of view, justify revolution—certainly would, if such right were a vital one. But such is not our case. All the vital rights of minorities, and of individuals, are so plainly assured to them, by affirmations and negations, guarranties and prohibitions, in the Constitution, that controversies never arise concerning them. But no organic law can ever be framed with a provision specifically applicable to every question which may occur in practical administration. No foresight can anticipate, nor any document of reasonable length contain express provisions for all possible questions. Shall fugitives from labor be surrendered by national or by State authority? The Constitution does not expressly say. *May* Congress prohibit slavery in the territories? The Constitution does not expressly say. *Must* Congress protect slavery in the territories? The Constitution does not expressly say.

From questions of this class spring all our constitutional controversies, and we divide upon them into majorities and minorities. If the minority will not acquiesce, the majority must, or the government must cease. There is no other alternative; for continuing the government, is acquiescence on one side or the other. If a minority, in such case, will secede[1] rather than acquiesce, they make a precedent which, in turn, will divide and ruin them; for a minority of their own will secede from them, whenever a majority refuses to be controlled by such minority. For instance, why may not any portion of a new confederacy, a year or two hence, arbitrarily secede again, precisely as portions of the present Union now claim to secede from it. All who cherish disunion sentiments, are now being educated to the exact temper of doing this. Is there such perfect identity of interests among the States to compose a new Union, as to produce harmony only, and prevent renewed secession?

Plainly, the central idea of secession, is the essence of anarchy. A majority, held in restraint by constitutional checks, and limitations, and always changing easily, with deliberate changes of popular opinions and sentiments, is the only true sovereign of a free people. Whoever rejects it, does, of necessity, fly to anarchy or to despotism. Unanimity is impossible; the rule of a minority, as a permanent arrangement, is wholly inadmissable; so that, rejecting the majority principle, anarchy, or despotism in some form, is all that is left.

I do not forget the position assumed by some, that constitutional questions are to be decided by the Supreme Court; nor do I deny that such decisions must be binding in any case, upon the parties to a suit, as to the

---

1. Seven Southern states—South Carolina, Mississippi, Florida, Alabama, Georgia, Louisiana, and Texas—had already seceded from the Union; they were later followed by Virginia, Arkansas, Tennessee, and North Carolina.

object of that suit, while they are also entitled to very high respect and consideration, in all paralel cases, by all other departments of the government. And while it is obviously possible that such decision may be erroneous in any given case, still the evil effect following it, being limited to that particular case, with the chance that it may be over-ruled, and never become a precedent for other cases, can better be borne than could the evils of a different practice. At the same time the candid citizen must confess that if the policy of the government, upon vital questions, affecting the whole people, is to be irrevocably fixed by decisions of the Supreme Court, the instant they are made, in ordinary litigation between parties, in personal actions, the people will have ceased, to be their own rulers, having, to that extent, practically resigned their government, into the hands of that eminent tribunal. Nor is there, in this view, any assault upon the court, or the judges. It is a duty, from which they may not shrink, to decide cases properly brought before them; and it is no fault of theirs, if others seek to turn their decisions to political purposes.

One section of our country believes slavery is *right*, and ought to be extended, while the other believes it is *wrong*, and ought not to be extended. This is the only substantial dispute. The fugitive slave clause of the Constitution, and the law for the suppression of the foreign slave trade, are each as well enforced, perhaps, as any law can ever be in a community where the moral sense of the people imperfectly supports the law itself. The great body of the people abide by the dry legal obligation in both cases, and a few break over in each. This, I think, cannot be perfectly cured; and it would be worse in both cases *after* the separation of the sections, than before. The foreign slave trade, now imperfectly suppressed, would be ultimately revived without restriction, in one section; while fugitive slaves, now only partially surrendered, would not be surrendered at all, by the other.

Physically speaking, we cannot separate. We cannot remove our respective sections from each other, nor build an impassable wall between them. A husband and wife may be divorced, and go out of the presence, and beyond the reach of each other; but the different parts of our country cannot do this. They cannot but remain face to face; and intercourse, either amicable or hostile, must continue between them. Is it possible then to make that intercourse more advantageous, or more satisfactory, *after* separation than *before*? Can aliens make treaties easier than friends can make laws? Can treaties be more faithfully enforced between aliens, than laws can among friends? Suppose you go to war, you cannot fight always; and when, after much loss on both sides, and no gain on either, you cease fighting, the identical old questions, as to terms of intercourse, are again upon you.

This country, with its institutions, belongs to the people who inhabit it. Whenever they shall grow weary of the existing government, they can exercise their *constitutional* right of amending it, or their *revolutionary* right to dismember, or overthrow it. I can not be ignorant of the fact that many worthy, and patriotic citizens are desirous of having the national constitution amended. While I make no recommendation of amendments, I fully recognize the rightful authority of the people over the whole subject, to be exercised in either of the modes prescribed in the instrument itself; and I should, under existing circumstances, favor, rather than oppose, a fair oppertunity being afforded the people to act upon it.

I will venture to add that, to me, the convention mode seems preferable, in that it allows amendments to originate with the people themselves, instead of only permitting them to take, or reject, propositions, originated by others, not especially chosen for the purpose, and which might not be precisely such, as they would wish to either accept or refuse. I understand a proposed amendment to the Constitution—which amendment, however, I have not seen, has passed Congress, to the effect that the federal government, shall never interfere with the domestic institutions of the States, including that of persons held to service. To avoid misconstruction of what I have said, I depart from my purpose not to speak of particular amendments, so far as to say that, holding such a provision to now be implied constitutional law, I have no objection to its being made express, and irrevocable.

The Chief Magistrate derives all his authority from the people, and they have conferred none upon him to fix terms for the separation of the States. The people themselves can do this also if they choose; but the executive, as such, has nothing to do with it. His duty is to administer the present government, as it came to his hands, and to transmit it, unimpaired by him, to his successor.

Why should there not be a patient confidence in the ultimate justice of the people? Is there any better, or equal hope, in the world? In our present differences, is either party without faith of being in the right? If the Almighty Ruler of nations, with his eternal truth and justice, be on your side of the North, or on yours of the South, that truth, and that justice, will surely prevail, by the judgment of this great tribunal, the American people.

By the frame of the government under which we live, this same people have wisely given their public servants but little power for mischief; and have, with equal wisdom, provided for the return of that little to their own hands at very short intervals.

While the people retain their virtue, and vigilence, no administration, by any extreme of wickedness or folly, can very seriously injure the government, in the short space of four years.

My countrymen, one and all, think calmly and *well*, upon this whole subject. Nothing valuable can be lost by taking time. If there be an object to *hurry* any of you, in hot haste, to a step which you would never take *deliberately*, that object will be frustrated by taking time; but no good object can be frustrated by it. Such of you as are now dissatisfied, still have the old Constitution unimpaired, and, on the sensitive point, the laws of your own framing under it; while the new administration will have no immediate power, if it would, to change either. If it were admitted that you who are dissatisfied, hold the right side in the dispute, there still is no single good reason for precipitate action. Intelligence, patriotism, Christianity, and a firm reliance on Him, who has never yet forsaken this favored land, are still competent to adjust, in the best way, all our present difficulty.

In *your* hands, my dissatisfied fellow countrymen, and not in *mine*, is the momentous issue of civil war. The government will not assail *you*. You can have no conflict, without being yourselves the aggressors. *You* have no oath registered in Heaven to destroy the government, while *I* shall have the most solemn one to "preserve, protect and defend" it.

I am loth to close. We are not enemies, but friends. We must not be enemies. Though passion may have strained, it must not break our bonds of affection. The mystic chords of memory, streching from every battle-field, and patriot grave, to every living heart and hearthstone, all over this broad land, will yet swell the chorus of the Union, when again touched, as surely they will be, by the better angels of our nature.

March 4, 1861

Reply to the Virginia Convention

Hon: William Ballard Preston, Alexander H. H. Stuart, & George W. Randolph, Esq[1]—

Gentlemen: As a committee of the Virginia convention, now in session, you present me a preamble and resolution, in these words:

Whereas, in the opinion of this Convention the uncertainty which pre-vails in the public mind as to the policy which the Federal Executive intends to pursue toward the seceded States is extremely injurious to the industrial and commercial interests of the country; tends to keep up an excitement which is unfavorable to the adjustment of pending difficulties, and threatens a disturbance of the public peace; therefore

Resolved, that a committee of three delegates be appointed by this Con-vention to wait upon the President of the United States, present to him this preamble and resolution, and respectfully ask of him to communicate to this Convention the policy which the Federal Executive intends to pur-sue in regard to the Confederate States.

Adopted by the Convention of the State of Virginia, Richmond, April 8th 1861

In pursuance of the foregoing resolution, the following delegates were appointed to constitute said committee.

Hon. William Ballard Preston.

Hon. Alexander H. H. Stuart.

George W. Randolph Esq.

JOHN JANNEY[2]   PRESIDENT

JNO. L. EUBANK[3]   SECRETARY.

In answer I have to say, that having, at the beginning of my official term, expressed my intended policy, as plainly as I was able, it is with deep regret, and some mortification, I now learn, that there is great, and injurious uncertainty, in the public mind, as to what that policy is, and what course I intend to pursue. Not having, as yet, seen occasion to change, it is now my purpose to pursue the course marked out in the inaugeral address. I com-mend a careful consideration of the whole document, as the best expression I can give of my purposes. As I then, and therein, said, I now repeat:

---

1. Lawyer, planter, and later, general and statesman for the Confederacy (1818–1867). Preston (1805–1862), secretary of the navy under Zachary Taylor and later served as a Confederate States senator. Stuart (1807–1891), Millard Fillmore's secretary of the interior.
2. Janney (1798–1872) was the president of the Virginia Secession Convention in 1861.
3. John A. Eubank of Richmond, Virginia was a supporter of secession.

"The power confided to me will be used to hold, occupy, and possess, the property, and places belonging to the Government, and to collect the duties, and imposts; but, beyond what is necessary for these objects, there will be no invasion—no using of force against, or among the people anywhere"

By the words "property, and places, belonging to the Government" I chiefly allude to the military posts, and property, which were in the possession of the Government when it came to my hands. But if, as now appears to be true, in pursuit of a purpose to drive the United States authority from these places, an unprovoked assault, has been made upon Fort-Sumpter, I shall hold myself at liberty to re-possess, if I can, like places which had been seized before the Government was devolved upon me.

And, in every event, I shall, to the extent of my ability, repel force by force.

In case it proves true, that Fort-Sumpter has been assaulted, as is reported, I shall perhaps, cause the United States mails to be withdrawn from all the States which claim to have seceded—believing that the commencement of actual war against the Government, justifies and possibly demands this.

I scarcely need to say that I consider the Military posts and property situated within the states, which claim to have seceded, as yet belonging to the Government of the United States, as much as they did before the supposed secession.

Whatever else I may do for the purpose, I shall not attempt to collect the duties, and imposts, by any armed invasion of any part of the country—not meaning by this, however, that I may not land a force, deemed necessary, to relieve a fort upon a border of the country. From the fact, that I have quoted a part of the inaugeral address, it must not be infered that I repudiate any other part, the whole of which I reaffirm, except so far as what I now say of the mails, may be regarded as a modification.

April 13, 1861

Proclamation Calling Militia and Convening Congress

April 15, 1861
By the President of the United States

A Proclamation.

Whereas the laws of the United States have been for some time past, and now are opposed, and the execution thereof obstructed in the States of South Carolina, Georgia, Alabama, Florida, Mississippi, Louisiana and Texas, by combinations too powerful to be suppressed by the ordinary course of judicial proceedings, or by the powers vested in the Marshals by law,

Now therefore, I, Abraham Lincoln, President of the United States, in virtue of the power in me vested by the Constitution, and the laws, have thought fit to call forth, and hereby do call forth, the militia of the several States of the Union, to the aggregate number of seventy-five thousand, in order to suppress said combinations, and to cause the laws to be duly executed. The details, for this object, will be immediately communicated to the State authorities through the War Department.

I appeal to all loyal citizens to favor, facilitate and aid this effort to maintain the honor, the integrity, and the existence of our National Union, and the perpetuity of popular government; and to redress wrongs already long enough endured.

I deem it proper to say that the first service assigned to the forces hereby called forth will probably be to re-possess the forts, places, and property which have been seized from the Union; and in every event, the utmost care will be observed, consistently with the objects aforesaid, to avoid any devastation, any destruction of, or interference with, property, or any disturbance of peaceful citizens in any part of the country.

And I hereby command the persons composing the combinations aforesaid to disperse, and retire peaceably to their respective abodes within twenty days from this date.

Deeming that the present condition of public affairs presents an extraordinary occasion, I do hereby, in virtue of the power in me vested by the constitution, convene both Houses of Congress. Senators and Representatives are therefore summoned to assemble at their respective chambers, at 12 o'clock, noon, on Thursday, the fourth day of July, next, then and there to consider and determine, such measures, as, in their wisdom, the public safety, and interest may seem to demand.

In Witness Whereof I have hereunto set my hand, and caused the Seal of the United States to be affixed.

Done at the city of Washington this fifteenth day of April in the year of our Lord One thousand, Eight hundred and Sixty-one, and of the Independence of the United States the Eighty-fifth.

ABRAHAM LINCOLN

By the President
WILLIAM H. SEWARD, Secretary of State.

April 15, 1861

Proclamation of Blockade

By the President of the United States of America: A Proclamation

Whereas an insurrection against the Government of the United States has broken out in the States of South Carolina, Georgia, Alabama, Florida, Mississippi, Louisiana, and Texas, and the laws of the United States for the collection of the revenue cannot be effectually executed therein comformably to that provision of the Constitution which requires duties to be uniform throughout the United States:

And whereas a combination of persons engaged in such insurrection, have threatened to grant pretended letters of marque to authorize the bearers thereof to commit assaults on the lives, vessels, and property of good citizens of the country lawfully engaged in commerce on the high seas, and in waters of the United States: And whereas an Executive Proclamation has been already issued, requiring the persons engaged in these disorderly proceedings to desist therefrom, calling out a militia force for the purpose of repressing the same, and convening Congress in extraordinary session, to deliberate and determine thereon:

Now, therefore, I, Abraham Lincoln, President of the United States, with a view to the same purposes before mentioned, and to the protection of the public peace, and the lives and property of quiet and orderly citizens pursuing their lawful occupations, until Congress shall have assembled and deliberated on the said unlawful proceedings, or until the same shall have ceased, have further deemed it advisable to set on foot a blockade of the ports within the States aforesaid, in pursuance of the laws of the United States, and of the law of Nations, in such case provided. For this purpose a competent force will be posted so as to prevent entrance and exit of vessels from the ports aforesaid. If, therefore, with a view to violate such blockade, a vessel shall approach, or shall attempt to leave either of the said ports, she will be duly warned by the Commander of one of the blockading vessels, who will endorse on her register the fact and date of such warning, and if the same vessel shall again attempt to enter or leave the blockaded port, she will be captured and sent to the nearest convenient port, for such proceedings against her and her cargo as prize, as may be deemed advisable.

And I hereby proclaim and declare that if any person, under the pretended authority of the said States, or under any other pretense, shall molest a vessel of the United States, or the persons or cargo on board of her, such person will be held amenable to the laws of the United States for the prevention and punishment of piracy.

In witness whereof, I have hereunto set my hand, and caused the seal of the United States to be affixed.

Done at the City of Washington, this nineteenth day of April, in the year of our Lord one thousand eight hundred and sixty-one, and of the Independence of the United States the eighty-fifth.

ABRAHAM LINCOLN

By the President:
WILLIAM H. SEWARD, Secretary of State

April 19, 1861

To Reverdy Johnson[1]

Confidential.

Executive Mansion, April 24th 1861.

Hon. Reverdy Johnson
My dear Sir: Your note of this morning is just received. I forebore to answer yours of the 22d because of my aversion (which I thought you understood,) to getting on paper, and furnishing new grounds for misunderstanding.

1. A Maryland attorney and statesman (1796–1876) who had represented the slave-holding defendant in the *Dred Scott* case and yet who opposed slavery and helped prevent Maryland from seceding from the Union during the Civil War.

I *do* say the sole purpose of bringing troops *here* is to defend this capital.

I *do* say I have no purpose to *invade* Virginia, with them or any other troops, as I understand the word *invasion*. But suppose Virginia sends her troops, or admits others through her borders, to assail this capital, am I not to repel them, even to the crossing of the Potomac if I can?

Suppose Virginia erects, or permits to be erected, batteries on the opposite shore, to bombard the city, are we to stand still and see it done? In a word, if Virginia strikes us, are we not to strike back, and as effectively as we can?

Again, are we not to hold Fort Monroe (for instance) if we can? I have no objection to declare a thousand times that I have no purpose to *invade* Virginia or any other State, but I do not mean to let them invade us without striking back. Yours truly

April 24, 1861

To Winfield Scott[1]

To the Commanding General of the Army
  of the United States:
You are engaged in repressing an insurrection against the laws of the United States. If at any point on or in the vicinity of the military line, which is now used between the City of Philadelphia and the City of Washington, via Perryville, Annapolis City, and Annapolis Junction, you find resistance which renders it necessary to suspend the writ of Habeas Corpus[2] for the public safety, you, personally or through the officer in command at the point where the resistance occurs, are authorized to suspend that writ.

April 27, 1861

Message to Congress in Special Session

Fellow-citizens of the Senate and House of Representatives:
Having been convened on an extraordinary occasion, as authorized by the Constitution, your attention is not called to any ordinary subject of legislation.

At the beginning of the present Presidential term, four months ago, the functions of the Federal Government were found to be generally suspended within the several States of South Carolina, Georgia, Alabama, Mississippi, Louisiana, and Florida, excepting only those of the Post Office Department.

1. Time-tested military commander (1796–1876) and the Whig candidate for president in 1852 who, early in the Civil War, conceived the so-called Anaconda Plan, which involved a naval blockade of Southern ports combined with a campaign down the Mississippi River aimed at dividing the South.
2. May you have the body (Latin); the law stipulates that an arrested person has the right to know why he or she is being arrested.

Within these States, all the Forts, Arsenals, Dock-yards, Custom-houses, and the like, including the movable and stationary property in, and about them, had been seized, and were held in open hostility to this Government, excepting only Forts Pickens, Taylor, and Jefferson, on, and near the Florida coast, and Fort Sumter, in Charleston harbor, South Carolina. The Forts thus seized had been put in improved condition; new ones had been built; and armed forces had been organized, and were organizing, all avowedly with the same hostile purpose.

The Forts remaining in the possession of the Federal government, in, and near, these States, were either besieged or menaced by warlike preparations; and especially Fort Sumter was nearly surrounded by well-protected hostile batteries, with guns equal in quality to the best of its own, and outnumbering the latter as perhaps ten to one. A disproportionate share, of the Federal muskets and rifles, had somehow found their way into these States, and had been seized, to be used against the government. Accumulations of the public revenue, lying within them, had been seized for the same object. The Navy was scattered in distant seas; leaving but a very small part of it within the immediate reach of the government. Officers of the Federal Army and Navy, had resigned in great numbers; and, of those resigning, a large proportion had taken up arms against the government. Simultaneously, and in connection, with all this, the purpose to sever the Federal Union, was openly avowed. In accordance with this purpose, an ordinance had been adopted in each of these States, declaring the States, respectively, to be separated from the National Union. A formula for instituting a combined government of these states had been promulgated; and this illegal organization, in the character of confederate States was already invoking recognition, aid, and intervention, from Foreign Powers.

Finding this condition of things, and believing it to be an imperative duty upon the incoming Executive, to prevent, if possible, the consummation of such attempt to destroy the Federal Union, a choice of means to that end became indispensable. This choice was made; and was declared in the Inaugural address. The policy chosen looked to the exhaustion of all peaceful measures, before a resort to any stronger ones. It sought only to hold the public places and property, not already wrested from the Government, and to collect the revenue; relying for the rest, on time, discussion, and the ballot-box. It promised a continuance of the mails, at government expense, to the very people who were resisting the government; and it gave repeated pledges against any disturbance to any of the people, or any of their rights. Of all that which a president might constitutionally, and justifiably, do in such a case, everything was foreborne, without which, it was believed possible to keep the government on foot.

On the 5th of March, (the present incumbent's first full day in office) a letter of Major Anderson,[1] commanding at Fort Sumter, written on the

---

1. Robert Anderson (1805–1871) remained loyal to the Union even though he was a former slave holder from Kentucky. After South Carolina seceded from the Union, he secretly moved from Fort Moultrie, an indefensible garrison in Charleston Harbor, to the nearby Fort Sumter. In reaction to this pro-Union move, Southern forces opened fire on Fort Sumter on April 14, 1861, and two days later Anderson surrendered. The incident triggered the Civil War.

28th of February, and received at the War Department on the 4th of March, was, by that Department, placed in his hands. This letter expressed the professional opinion of the writer, that re-inforcements could not be thrown into that Fort within the time for his relief, rendered necessary by the limited supply of provisions, and with a view of holding possession of the same, with a force of less than twenty thousand good, and well-disciplined men. This opinion was concurred in by all the officers of his command; and their *memoranda* on the subject, were made enclosures of Major Anderson's letter. The whole was immediately laid before Lieutenant General Scott, who at once concurred with Major Anderson in opinion. On reflection, however, he took full time, consulting with other officers, both of the Army and the Navy; and, at the end of four days, came reluctantly, but decidedly, to the same conclusion as before. He also stated at the same time that no such sufficient force was then at the control of the Government, or could be raised, and brought to the ground, within the time when the provisions in the Fort would be exhausted. In a purely military point of view, this reduced the duty of the administration, in the case, to the mere matter of getting the garrison safely out of the Fort.

It was believed, however, that to so abandon that position, under the circumstances, would be utterly ruinous; that the *necessity* under which it was to be done, would not be fully understood—that, by many, it would be construed as a part of a *voluntary* policy—that, at home, it would discourage the friends of the Union, embolden its adversaries, and go far to insure to the latter, a recognition abroad—that, in fact, it would be our national destruction consummated. This could not be allowed. Starvation was not yet upon the garrison; and ere it would be reached, *Fort Pickens* might be reinforced. This last, would be a clear indication of *policy*, and would better enable the country to accept the evacuation of Fort Sumter, as a military *necessity*. An order was at once directed to be sent for the landing of the troops from the Steamship Brooklyn, into Fort Pickens. This order could not go by land, but must take the longer, and slower route by sea. The first return news from the order was received just one week before the fall of Fort Sumter. The news itself was, that the officer commanding the Sabine, to which vessel the troops had been transferred from the Brooklyn, acting upon some *quasi* armistice of the late administration, (and of the existence of which, the present administration, up to the time the order was despatched, had only too vague and uncertain rumors, to fix attention) had refused to land the troops. To now re-inforce Fort Pickens, before a crisis would be reached at Fort Sumter was impossible—rendered so by the near exhaustion of provisions in the latter-named Fort. In precaution against such a conjuncture, the government had, a few days before, commenced preparing an expedition, as well adapted as might be, to relieve Fort Sumter, which expedition was intended to be ultimately used, or not, according to circumstances. The strongest anticipated case, for using it, was now presented; and it was resolved to send it forward. As had been intended, in this contingency, it was also resolved to notify the Governor of South Carolina,[2] that he might expect an attempt would be made to provision the Fort; and that, if the attempt should not be resisted, there would be no effort to throw in men, arms, or ammunition, without

2. Francis W. Pickens (1805–1869), who was governor from 1860 to 1862.

further notice, or in case of an attack upon the Fort. This notice was accordingly given; whereupon the Fort was attacked, and bombarded to its fall, without even awaiting the arrival of the provisioning expedition.

It is thus seen that the assault upon, and reduction of, Fort Sumter, was, in no sense, a matter of self defence on the part of the assailants. They well knew that the garrison in the Fort could, by no possibility, commit aggression upon them. They knew—they were expressly notified— that the giving of bread to the few brave and hungry men of the garrison, was all which would on that occasion be attempted, unless themselves, by resisting so much, should provoke more. They knew that this Government desired to keep the garrison in the Fort, not to assail them, but merely to maintain visible possession, and thus to preserve the Union from actual, and immediate dissolution—trusting, as herein-before stated, to time, discussion, and the ballot-box, for final adjustment; and they assailed, and reduced the Fort, for precisely the reverse object—to drive out the visible authority of the Federal Union, and thus force it to immediate dissolution.

That this was their object, the Executive well understood; and having said to them in the inaugural address, "You can have no conflict without being yourselves the aggressors," he took pains, not only to keep this declaration good, but also to keep the case so free from the power of ingenious sophistry, as that the world should not be able to misunderstand it. By the affair at Fort Sumter, with its surrounding circumstances, that point was reached. Then, and thereby, the assailants of the Government, began the conflict of arms, without a gun in sight, or in expectancy, to return their fire, save only the few in the Fort, sent to that harbor, years before, for their own protection, and still ready to give that protection, in whatever was lawful. In this act, discarding all else, they have forced upon the country, the distinct issue: "Immediate dissolution, or blood."

And this issue embraces more than the fate of these United States. It presents to the whole family of man, the question, whether a constitutional republic, or a democracy—a government of the people, by the same people—can, or cannot, maintain its territorial integrity, against its own domestic foes. It presents the question, whether discontented individuals, too few in numbers to control administration, according to organic law, in any case, can always, upon the pretences made in this case, or on any other pretences, or arbitrarily, without any pretence, break up their Government, and thus practically put an end to free government upon the earth. It forces us to ask: "Is there, in all republics, this inherent, and fatal weakness?" "Must a government, of necessity, be too *strong* for the liberties of its own people, or too *weak* to maintain its own existence?"

So viewing the issue, no choice was left but to call out the war power of the Government; and so to resist force, employed for its destruction, by force, for its preservation.

The call was made; and the response of the country was most gratifying; surpassing, in unanimity and spirit, the most sanguine expectation. Yet none of the States commonly called Slave-states, except Delaware, gave a Regiment through regular State organization. A few regiments have been organized within some others of those states, by individual enterprise, and received into the government service. Of course the seceded

States, so called, (and to which Texas had been joined about the time of the inauguration,) gave no troops to the cause of the Union. The border States, so called, were not uniform in their actions; some of them being almost *for* the Union, while in others—as Virginia, North Carolina, Tennessee, and Arkansas—the Union sentiment was nearly repressed, and silenced. The course taken in Virginia was the most remarkable—perhaps the most important. A convention, elected by the people of that State, to consider this very question of disrupting the Federal Union, was in session at the capital of Virginia when Fort Sumter fell. To this body the people had chosen a large majority of *professed* Union men. Almost immediately after the fall of Sumter, many members of that majority went over to the original disunion minority, and, with them, adopted an ordinance for withdrawing the State from the Union. Whether this change was wrought by their great approval of the assault upon Sumter, or their great resentment at the government's resistance to that assault, is not definitely known. Although they submitted the ordinance, for ratification, to a vote of the people, to be taken on a day then somewhat more than a month distant, the convention, and the Legislature, (which was also in session at the same time and place) with leading men of the State, not members of either, immediately commenced acting, as if the State were already out of the Union. They pushed military preparations vigorously forward all over the state. They seized the United States Armory at Harper's Ferry, and the Navy-yard at Gosport, near Norfolk. They received—perhaps invited— into their state, large bodies of troops, with their warlike appointments, from the so-called seceded States. They formally entered into a treaty of temporary alliance, and co-operation with the so-called "Confederate States," and sent members to their Congress at Montgomery. And, finally, they permitted the insurrectionary government to be transferred to their capital at Richmond.

The people of Virginia have thus allowed this giant insurrection to make its nest within her borders; and this government has no choice left but to deal with it, *where* it finds it. And it has the less regret, as the loyal citizens have, in due form, claimed its protection. Those loyal citizens, this government is bound to recognize, and protect, as being Virginia.

In the border States, so called—in fact, the middle states—there are those who favor a policy which they call "armed neutrality"—that is, an arming of those states to prevent the Union forces passing one way, or the disunion, the other, over their soil. This would be disunion completed. Figuratively speaking, it would be the building of an impassable wall along the line of separation. And yet, not quite an impassable one; for, under the guise of neutrality, it would tie the hands of the Union men, and freely pass supplies from among them, to the insurrectionists, which it could not do as an open enemy. At a stroke, it would take all the trouble off the hands of secession, except only what proceeds from the external blockade. It would do for the disunionists that which, of all things, they most desire—feed them well, and give them disunion without a struggle of their own. It recognizes no fidelity to the Constitution, no obligation to maintain the Union; and while very many who have favored it are, doubtless, loyal citizens, it is, nevertheless, treason in effect.

Recurring to the action of the government, it may be stated that, at first, a call was made for seventy-five thousand militia; and rapidly following this, a proclamation was issued for closing the ports of the insurrectionary districts by proceedings in the nature of Blockade.[3] So far all was believed to be strictly legal. At this point the insurrectionists announced their purpose to enter upon the practice of privateering.

Other calls were made for volunteers, to serve three years, unless sooner discharged; and also for large additions to the regular Army and Navy. These measures, whether strictly legal or not, were ventured upon, under what appeared to be a popular demand, and a public necessity; trusting, then as now, that Congress would readily ratify them. It is believed that nothing has been done beyond the constitutional competency of Congress.

Soon after the first call for militia, it was considered a duty to authorize the Commanding General,[4] in proper cases, according to his discretion, to suspend the privilege of the writ of habeas corpus; or, in other words, to arrest, and detain, without resort to the ordinary processes and forms of law, such individuals as he might deem dangerous to the public safety. This authority has purposely been exercised but very sparingly. Nevertheless, the legality and propriety of what has been done under it, are questioned; and the attention of the country has been called to the proposition that one who is sworn to "take care that the laws be faithfully executed," should not himself violate them. Of course some consideration was given to the questions of power, and propriety, before this matter was acted upon. The whole of the laws which were required to be faithfully executed, were being resisted, and failing of execution, in nearly one-third of the States. Must they be allowed to finally fail of execution, even had it been perfectly clear, that by the use of the means necessary to their execution, some single law, made in such extreme tenderness of the citizen's liberty, that practically, it relieves more of the guilty, than of the innocent, should, to a very limited extent, be violated? To state the question more directly, are all the laws, *but one*, to go unexecuted, and the government itself go to pieces, lest that one be violated? Even in such a case, would not the official oath be broken, if the government should be overthrown, when it was believed that disregarding the single law, would tend to preserve it? But it was not believed that this question was presented. It was not believed that any law was violated. The provision of the Constitution that "The privilege of the writ of habeas corpus, shall not be suspended unless when, in cases of rebellion or invasion, the public safety may require it," is equivalent to a provision—is a provision—that such privilege may be suspended when, in cases of rebellion, or invasion, the public safety *does* require it. It was decided that we have a case of rebellion, and that the public safety does require the qualified suspension of the privilege of the writ which was authorized to be made. Now it is insisted that Congress, and not the Executive, is vested with this power. But the Constitution itself, is silent as to which, or who, is to exercise the power; and as the provision was

3. On April 15, 1861, in response to the Confederate attack on Fort Sumter, Lincoln called up 75,000 militia. On May 3 he issued another proclamation that increased the regular army by 22,714 and enlisted 42,034 additional army volunteers as well as 18,000 men in the naval service.
4. George B. McClellan (1826–1885), the General-in-Chief of the Union Army in 1861–62.

plainly made for a dangerous emergency, it cannot be believed the framers of the instrument intended, that in every case, the danger should run its course, until Congress could be called together; the very assembling of which might be prevented, as was intended in this case, by the rebellion.

No more extended argument is now offered; as an opinion, at some length, will probably be presented by the Attorney General.[5] Whether there shall be any legislation upon the subject, and if any, what, is submitted entirely to the better judgment of Congress.

The forbearance of this government had been so extraordinary, and so long continued, as to lead some foreign nations to shape their action as if they supposed the early destruction of our national Union was probable. While this, on discovery, gave the Executive some concern, he is now happy to say that the sovereignty, and rights of the United States, are now everywhere practically respected by foreign powers; and a general sympathy with the country is manifested throughout the world.

The reports of the Secretaries of the Treasury, War, and the Navy,[6] will give the information in detail deemed necessary, and convenient for your deliberation, and action; while the Executive, and all the Departments, will stand ready to supply omissions, or to communicate new facts, considered important for you to know.

It is now recommended that you give the legal means for making this contest a short, and a decisive one; that you place at the control of the government, for the work, at least four hundred thousand men, and four hundred millions of dollars. That number of men is about one tenth of those of proper ages within the regions where, apparently, *all* are willing to engage; and the sum is less than a twentythird part of the money value owned by the men who seem ready to devote the whole. A debt of six hundred millions of dollars *now*, is a less sum per head, than was the debt of our revolution, when we came out of that struggle; and the money value in the country now, bears even a greater proportion to what it was *then*, than does the population. Surely each man has as strong a motive *now*, to *preserve* our liberties, as each had *then*, to *establish* them.

A right result, at this time, will be worth more to the world, than ten times the men, and ten times the money. The evidence reaching us from the country, leaves no doubt, that the material for the work is abundant; and that it needs only the hand of legislation to give it legal sanction, and the hand of the Executive to give it practical shape and efficiency. One of the greatest perplexities of the government, is to avoid receiving troops faster than it can provide for them. In a word, the people will save their government, if the government itself, will do its part, only indifferently well.

It might seem, at first thought, to be of little difference whether the present movement at the South be called "secession" or "rebellion." The movers, however, well understand the difference. At the beginning, they knew they could never raise their treason to any respectable magnitude, by any name which implies *violation* of law. They knew their people possessed as much of moral sense, as much of devotion to law and order, and as much pride in, and reverence for, the history, and government, of their

5. Edward Bates (1793–1869), attorney general from 1861 to 1864.
6. Secretary of the Treasury Salmon P. Chase (1808–1873), Secretary of War Edwin M. Stanton (1814–1869), and Secretary of the Navy Gideon Welles (1802–1878).

common country, as any other civilized, and patriotic people. They knew they could make no advancement directly in the teeth of these strong and noble sentiments. Accordingly they commenced by an insidious debauching of the public mind. They invented an ingenious sophism, which, if conceded, was followed by perfectly logical steps, through all the incidents, to the complete destruction of the Union. The sophism itself is, that any state of the Union may, *consistently* with the national Constitution, and therefore *lawfully*, and *peacefully*, withdraw from the Union, without the consent of the Union, or of any other state. The little disguise that the supposed right is to be exercised only for just cause, themselves to be the sole judge of its justice, is too thin to merit any notice.

With rebellion thus sugar-coated, they have been drugging the public mind of their section for more than thirty years; and, until at length, they have brought many good men to a willingness to take up arms against the government the day *after* some assemblage of men have enacted the farcical pretence of taking their State out of the Union, who could have been brought to no such thing the day *before*.

This sophism derives much—perhaps the whole—of its currency, from the assumption, that there is some omnipotent, and sacred supremacy, pertaining to a *State*—to each State of our Federal Union. Our States have neither more, nor less power, than that reserved to them, in the Union, by the Constitution—no one of them ever having been a State *out* of the Union. The original ones passed into the Union even *before* they cast off their British colonial dependence; and the new ones each came into the Union directly from a condition of dependence, excepting Texas. And even Texas, in its temporary independence, was never designated a State. The new ones only took the designation of States, on coming into the Union, while that name was first adopted for the old ones, in, and by, the Declaration of Independence. Therein the "United Colonies" were declared to be "Free and Independent States"; but, even then, the object plainly was not to declare their independence of *one another*, or of the *Union*; but directly the contrary, as their mutual pledge, and their mutual action, before, at the time, and afterwards, abundantly show. The express plighting of faith, by each and all of the original thirteen, in the Articles of Confederation, two years later, that the Union shall be perpetual, is most conclusive. Having never been States, either in substance, or in name, *outside* of the Union, whence this magical omnipotence of "State rights," asserting a claim of power to lawfully destroy the Union itself? Much is said about the "sovereignty" of the States; but the word, even, is not in the national Constitution; nor, as is believed, in any of the State constitutions. What is a "sovereignty," in the political sense of the term? Would it be far wrong to define it "A political community, without a political superior"? Tested by this, no one of our States, except Texas, ever was a sovereignty. And even Texas gave up the character on coming into the Union; by which act, she acknowledged the Constitution of the United States, and the laws and treaties of the United States made in pursuance of the Constitution, to be, for her, the supreme law of the land. The States have their *status* in the Union, and they have no other *legal status*. If they break from this, they can only do so against law, and by revolution. The Union, and not themselves separately, procured their independence, and their liberty. By conquest, or purchase, the Union gave each of them, whatever of independence, and liberty, it has. The Union is older than any of the States; and, in fact, it created them as States. Originally, some dependent colonies made the Union; and, in turn, the Union threw off their old dependence, for them, and made them States, such as they are. Not one of them ever had a State constitution, independent of the Union. Of course, it is not forgotten that all the new States framed their constitutions, before they entered the Union; nevertheless, dependent upon, and preparatory to, coming into the Union.

Unquestionably the States have the powers, and rights, reserved to them in, and by the National Constitution; but among these, surely, are not included all conceivable powers, however mischievous, or destructive; but, at most, such only, as were known in the world, at the time, as governmental powers; and certainly, a power to destroy the government itself, had never been known as a governmental—as a merely administrative power. This relative matter of National power, and State rights, as a principle, is no other than the principle of *generality*, and *locality*. Whatever concerns the whole, should be confided to the whole—to the general government; while, whatever concerns *only* the State, should be left exclusively, to the State. This is all there is of original principle about it. Whether the National Constitution, in defining boundaries between the two, has applied the principle with exact accuracy, is not to be questioned. We are all bound by that defining, without question.

What is now combatted, is the position that secession is *consistent* with the Constitution—is *lawful*, and *peaceful*. It is not contended that there is any express law for it; and nothing should ever be implied as law, which leads to unjust, or absurd consequences. The nation purchased, with money, the countries out of which several of these States were formed. Is it just that they shall go off without leave, and without refunding? The nation paid very large sums, (in the aggregate, I believe, nearly a hundred millions) to relieve Florida of the aboriginal tribes. Is it just that she shall now be off without consent, or without making any return? The nation is now in debt for money applied to the benefit of these so-called seceding States, in common with the rest. Is it just, either that creditors shall go unpaid, or the remaining States pay the whole? A part of the present national debt was contracted to pay the old debts of Texas. Is it just that she shall leave, and pay no part of this herself?

Again, if one State may secede, so may another; and when all shall have seceded, none is left to pay the debts. Is this quite just to creditors? Did we notify them of this sage view of ours, when we borrowed their money? If we now recognize this doctrine, by allowing the seceders to go in peace, it is difficult to see what we can do, if others choose to go, or to extort terms upon which they will promise to remain.

The seceders insist that our Constitution admits of secession. They have assumed to make a National Constitution of their own, in which, of necessity, they have either *discarded*, or *retained*, the right of secession, as they insist, it exists in ours. If they have discarded it, they thereby admit that, on principle, it ought not to be in ours. If they have retained it, by their own construction of ours they show that to be consistent they must secede from one another, whenever they shall find it the easiest way of settling their debts, or effecting any other selfish, or unjust object. The principle itself is one of disintegration, and upon which no government can possibly endure.

If all the States, save one, should assert the power to *drive* that one out of the Union, it is presumed the whole class of seceder politicians would at once deny the power, and denounce the act as the greatest outrage upon State rights. But suppose that precisely the same act, instead of being called "driving the one out," should be called "the seceding of the others from that one," it would be exactly what the seceders claim to do; unless, indeed, they make the point, that the one, because it is a minority, may rightfully do, what the others, because they are a majority, may not rightfully do. These politicians are subtle, and profound, on the rights of minorities. They are not partial to that power which made the Constitution, and speaks from the preamble, calling itself "We, the People."

It may well be questioned whether there is, to-day, a majority of the legally qualified voters of any State, except perhaps South Carolina, in favor of disunion. There is much reason to believe that the Union men are the majority in many, if not in every other one, of the so-called seceded States. The contrary has not been demonstrated in any one of them. It is ventured to affirm this, even of Virginia and Tennessee; for the result of an election, held in military camps, where the bayonets are all on one side of the question voted upon, can scarcely be considered as demonstrating popular sentiment. At such an election, all that large class who are, at once, *for* the Union, and *against* coercion, would be coerced to vote against the Union.

It may be affirmed, without extravagance, that the free institutions we enjoy, have developed the powers, and improved the condition, of our whole people, beyond any example in the world. Of this we now have a striking, and an impressive illustration. So large an army as the government has now on foot, was never before known, without a soldier in it, but who had taken his place there, of his own free choice. But more than this: there are many single Regiments whose members, one and another, possess full practical knowledge of all the arts, sciences, professions, and whatever else, whether useful or elegant, is known in the world; and there is scarcely one, from which there could not be selected, a President, a Cabinet, a Congress, and perhaps a Court, abundantly competent to administer the government itself. Nor do I say this is not true, also, in the army of our late friends, now adversaries, in this contest; but if it is, so much better the reason why the government, which has conferred such benefits on both them and us, should not be broken up. Whoever, in any section, proposes to abandon such a government, would do well to consider, in deference to what principle it is, that he does it—what better he is likely to get in its stead—whether the substitute will give, or be intended to give, so much of good to the people. There are some fore-shadowings on this subject. Our adversaries have adopted some Declarations of Independence; in which, unlike the good old one, penned by Jefferson, they omit the words "all men are created equal." Why? They have adopted a temporary national constitution, in the preamble of which, unlike our good old one, signed by Washington, they omit "We, the People," and substitute "We, the deputies of the sovereign and independent States." Why? Why this deliberate pressing out of view, the rights of men, and the authority of the people?

This is essentially a People's contest. On the side of the Union, it is a struggle for maintaining in the world, that form, and substance of government, whose leading object is, to elevate the condition of men—to lift artificial weights from all shoulders—to clear the paths of laudable pursuit for all—to afford all, an unfettered start, and a fair chance, in the race of life. Yielding to partial, and temporary departures, from necessity, this is the leading object of the government for whose existence we contend.

I am most happy to believe that the plain people understand, and appreciate this. It is worthy of note, that while in this, the government's hour of trial, large numbers of those in the Army and Navy, who have been favored with the offices, have resigned, and proved false to the hand which had pampered them, not one common soldier, or common sailor is known to have deserted his flag.

Great honor is due to those officers who remain true, despite the example of their treacherous associates; but the greatest honor, and most important fact of all, is the unanimous firmness of the common soldiers, and common sailors. To the last man, so far as known, they have successfully resisted the traitorous efforts of those, whose commands, but an hour before, they obeyed as absolute law. This is the patriotic instinct of the plain people. They understand, without an argument, that destroying the government, which was made by Washington, means no good to them.

Our popular government has often been called an experiment. Two points in it, our people have already settled—the successful *establishing*, and the successful *administering* of it. One still remains—its successful *maintenance* against a formidable internal attempt to overthrow it. It is now for them to demonstrate to the world, that those who can fairly carry an election, can also suppress a rebellion—that ballots are the rightful, and peaceful, successors of bullets; and that when ballots have fairly, and constitutionally, decided, there can be no successful appeal, back to bullets; that there can be no successful appeal, except to ballots themselves, at succeeding elections. Such will be a great lesson of peace; teaching men that what they cannot take by an election, neither can they take it by a war—teaching all, the folly of being the beginners of a war.

Lest there be some uneasiness in the minds of candid men, as to what is to be the course of the government, towards the Southern States, *after* the rebellion shall have been suppressed, the Executive deems it proper to say, it will be his purpose then, as ever, to be guided by the Constitution, and the laws; and that he probably will have no different understanding of the powers, and duties of the Federal government, relatively to the rights of the States, and the people, under the Constitution, than that expressed in the inaugural address.

He desires to preserve the government, that it may be administered for all, as it was administered by the men who made it. Loyal citizens everywhere, have the right to claim this of their government; and the government has no right to withhold, or neglect it. It is not perceived that, in giving it, there is any coercion, any conquest, or any subjugation, in any just sense of those terms.

The Constitution provides, and all the States have accepted the provision, that "The United States shall guarantee to every State in this Union a republican form of government." But, if a State may lawfully go out of the Union, having done so, it may also discard the republican form of government; so that to prevent its going out, is an indispensable *means*, to the *end*, of maintaining the guaranty mentioned; and when an end is lawful and obligatory, the indispensable means to it, are also lawful, and obligatory.

It was with the deepest regret that the Executive found the duty of employing the war-power, in defence of the government, forced upon him. He could but perform this duty, or surrender the existence of the government. No compromise, by public servants, could, in this case, be a cure; not that compromises are not often proper, but that no popular government can long survive a marked precedent, that those who carry an election, can only save the government from immediate destruction, by giving up the main point, upon which the people gave the election. The people themselves, and not their servants, can safely reverse their own deliberate decisions. As a private citizen, the Executive could not have consented that these institutions shall perish; much less could he, in betrayal of so vast, and so sacred a trust, as these free people had confided to him. He felt that he had no moral right to shrink; nor even to count the chances of his own life, in what might follow. In full view of his great responsibility, he has, so far, done what he has deemed his duty. You will now, according to your own judgment, perform yours. He sincerely hopes that your views, and your action, may so accord with his, as to assure all faithful citizens, who have been disturbed in their rights, of a certain, and speedy restoration to them, under the Constitution, and the laws.

And having thus chosen our course, without guile, and with pure purpose, let us renew our trust in God, and go forward without fear, and with manly hearts.

July 4, 1861.

Proclamation of a National Fast Day

By the President of the United States of America:
A Proclamation

Whereas a joint Committee of both Houses of Congress has waited on the President of the United States, and requested him to "recommend a day of public humiliation, prayer and fasting, to be observed by the people of the United States with religious solemnities, and the offering of fervent supplications to Almighty God for the safety and welfare of these States, His blessings on their arms, and a speedy restoration of peace:"—

And whereas it is fit and becoming in all people, at all times, to acknowledge and revere the Supreme Government of God; to bow in humble submission to his chastisements; to confess and deplore their sins and transgressions in the full conviction that the fear of the Lord is the beginning of wisdom; and to pray, with all fervency and contrition, for the pardon of their past offences, and for a blessing upon their present and prospective action:

And whereas, when our own beloved Country, once, by the blessing of God, united, prosperous and happy, is now afflicted with faction and civil war, it is peculiarly fit for us to recognize the hand of God in this terrible visitation, and in sorrowful remembrance of our own faults and crimes as a nation and as individuals, to humble ourselves before Him, and to pray for His mercy,—to pray that we may be spared further punishment, though most justly deserved; that our arms may be blessed and made effectual for the re-establishment of law, order and peace, throughout the wide extent of our country; and that the inestimable boon of civil and religious liberty, earned under His guidance and blessing, by the labors and sufferings of our fathers, may be restored in all its original excellence:—

Therefore, I, Abraham Lincoln, President of the United States, do appoint the last Thursday in September next, as a day of humiliation, prayer and fasting for all the people of the nation. And I do earnestly recommend to all the People, and especially to all ministers and teachers of religion of all denominations, and to all heads of families, to observe and keep that day according to their several creeds and modes of worship, in all humility and with all religious solemnity, to the end that the united prayer of the nation may ascend to the Throne of Grace and bring down plentiful blessings upon our Country.

In testimony whereof, I have hereunto set my hand, and caused the Seal of the United States to be affixed, this 12th, day of August A.D. 1861, and of the Independence of the United States of America the 86th.

By the President: ABRAHAM LINCOLN.
    WILLIAM H. SEWARD, Secretary of State.

August 12, 1861

To John C. Frémont[1]

Private and confidential

Major General Fremont: Washington D.C. Sept. 2, 1861.
My dear Sir: Two points in your proclamation of August 30th give me some anxiety. First, should you shoot a man, according to the proclamation, the Confederates would very certainly shoot our best man in their hands in retaliation; and so, man for man, indefinitely. It is therefore my order that you allow no man to be shot, under the proclamation, without first having my approbation or consent.

Secondly, I think there is great danger that the closing paragraph, in relation to the confiscation of property, and the liberating slaves of traiterous owners, will alarm our Southern Union friends, and turn them against us—perhaps ruin our rather fair prospect for Kentucky. Allow me therefore to ask, that you will as of your own motion, modify that paragraph so as to conform to the *first* and *fourth* sections of the act of Congress, entitled, "An act to confiscate property used for insurrectionary purposes," approved August, 6th, 1861, and a copy of which act I herewith send you. This letter is written in a spirit of caution and not of censure.

I send it by a special messenger, in order that it may certainly and speedily reach you. Yours very truly

Copy of letter sent to Gen. Fremont, by special messenger leaving Washington Sep. 3. 1861.

September 2, 1861

1. As commander of the Union campaign in Missouri, he issued a proclamation stating that Missourians found carrying arms were subject to imprisonment and, if found guilty, execution. Frémont also ordered that enemies of the Union be punished by the confiscation of their property and the emancipation of their slaves.

To John C. Frémont

Washington, D.C.
Sep. 11. 1861.

Major General John C. Fremont.

Sir: Yours of the 8th. in answer to mine of 2nd. Inst. is just received. Assuming that you, upon the ground, could better judge of the necessities of your position than I could at this distance, on seeing your proclamation of August 30th. I perceived no general objection to it. The particular clause, however, in relation to the confiscation of property and the liberation of slaves, appeared to me to be objectionable, in it's non-conformity to the Act of Congress passed the 6th. of last August upon the same subjects; and hence I wrote you expressing my wish that that clause should be modified accordingly. Your answer, just received, expresses the preference on your part, that I should make an open order for the modification, which I very cheerfully do. It is therefore ordered that the said clause of said proclamation be so modified, held, and construed, as to conform to, and not to transcend, the provisions on the same subject contained in the act of Congress entitled "An Act to confiscate property used for insurrectionary purposes" Approved, August 6. 1861; and that said act be published at length with this order. Your Obt. Servt

To Orville H. Browning[1]

Private & confidential.

Hon. O. H. Browning

My Dear Sir:

Executive Mansion
Washington Sept 22d 1861.

Yours of the 17th is just received; and coming from you, I confess it astonishes me. That you should object to my adhering to a law, which you had assisted in making, and presenting to me, less than a month before, is odd enough. But this is a very small part. Genl. Fremont's proclamation, as to confiscation of property, and the liberation of slaves, is *purely political*, and not within the range of *military law*, or necessity. If a commanding General finds a necessity to seize the farm of a private owner, for a pasture, an encampment, or a fortification, he has the right to do so, and to so hold it, as long as the necessity lasts; and this is within military law, because within military necessity. But to say the farm shall no longer belong to the owner, or his heirs forever; and this as well when the farm is not needed for military purposes as when it is, is purely political, without the savor of military law about it. And the same is true of slaves. If the General needs them, he can seize them, and use them; but when the need is past, it is not for him to fix their permanent future condition. That must be settled according to laws made by law-makers, and not by military proclamations. The proclamation in the point in question, is simply "dictatorship." It assumes that the general may do *anything* he pleases— confiscate the lands and free the slaves of *loyal* people, as well as of disloyal

---

1. After the death of Stephen A. Douglas on June 3, 1861, Browning took Douglas's place in the Senate, serving until 1863.

ones. And going the whole figure I have no doubt would be more popular with some thoughtless people, than that which has been done! But I cannot assume this reckless position; nor allow others to assume it on my responsibility. You speak of it as being the only means of *saving* the government. On the contrary it is itself the surrender of the government. Can it be pretended that it is any longer the government of the U.S.—any government of Constitution and laws,—wherein a General, or a President, may make permanent rules of property by proclamation?

I do not say Congress might not with propriety pass a law, on the point, just such as General Fremont proclaimed. I do not say I might not, as a member of Congress, vote for it. What I object to, is, that I as President, shall expressly or impliedly seize and exercise the permanent legislative functions of the government.

So much as to principle. Now as to policy. No doubt the thing was popular in some quarters, and would have been more so if it had been a general declaration of emancipation. The Kentucky Legislature would not budge till that proclamation was modified; and Gen. Anderson telegraphed me that on the news of Gen. Fremont having actually issued deeds of manumission, a whole company of our Volunteers threw down their arms and disbanded. I was so assured, as to think it probable, that the very arms we had furnished Kentucky would be turned against us. I think to lose Kentucky is nearly the same as to lose the whole game. Kentucky gone, we can not hold Missouri, nor, as I think, Maryland. These all against us, and the job on our hands is too large for us. We would as well consent to separation at once, including the surrender of this capitol. On the contrary, if you will give up your restlessness for new positions, and back me manfully on the grounds upon which you and other kind friends gave me the election, and have approved in my public documents, we shall go through triumphantly.

You must not understand I took my course on the proclamation *because* of Kentucky. I took the same ground in a private letter to General Fremont before I heard from Kentucky.

You think I am inconsistent because I did not also forbid Gen. Fremont to shoot men under the proclamation. I understand that part to be within military law; but I also think, and so privately wrote Gen. Fremont, that it is impolitic in this, that our adversaries have the power, and will certainly exercise it, to shoot as many of our men as we shoot of theirs. I did not say this in the public letter, because it is a subject I prefer not to discuss in the hearing of our enemies.

There has been no thought of removing Gen. Fremont on any ground connected with his proclamation; and if there has been any wish for his removal on any ground, our mutual friend Sam. Glover can probably tell you what it was. I hope no real necessity for it exists on any ground.

Suppose you write to Hurlbut[2] and get him to resign. Your friend as ever

---

2. General Stephen A. Hurlbut (1815–1882), an Illinoisan who served under Frémont in Missouri, was charged with habitual intoxication. He did not resign and served through the remainder of the war.

Drafts of a Bill for Compensated Emancipation in Delaware[1]

Be it enacted by the State of Delaware, that on condition the United States of America will, at the present session of Congress, engage by law to pay, and thereafter faithfully pay to the said State of Delaware, in the six per cent bonds of said United States, the sum of seven hundred and nineteen thousand and two hundred dollars, in five equal annual instalments, there shall be neither slavery nor involuntary servitude, at any time after the first day of January in the year of our Lord one thousand, eight hundred and sixtyseven, within the said State of Delaware, except in the punishment of crime, whereof the party shall have been duly convicted: Provided, that said State shall, in good faith prevent, so far as possible, the carrying of any person out of said State, into involuntary servitude, beyond the limits of said State, at any time after the passage of this act; and shall also provide for one fifth of the adult slavery becoming free at the middle of the year one thousand eight hundred and sixtytwo; one fourth of the remainder of said adults, at the middle of the year one thousand eight hundred and sixtythree; one third of the remainder of said adults, at the middle of the year one thousand eight hundred and sixty four; one half the remainder of said adults at the middle of the year one thousand eight hundred and sixtyfive; and the entire remainder of adults, together with all minors, at the beginning of the year one thousand eight hundred and sixtyseven, as hereinbefore indicated. And provided also that said State may make provision of apprenticeship, not to extend beyond the age of twentyone years for males, nor eighteen for females, for all minors whose mothers were not free, at the respective births of such minors.

Be it enacted by the State of Delaware that on condition the United States of America will, at the present session of Congress, engage by law to pay, and thereafter faithfully pay to the said State of Delaware, in the six per cent bonds of said United States, the sum of seven hundred and nineteen thousand, and two hundred dollars, in thirty one equal annual instalments, there shall be neither slavery nor involuntary servitude, at any time after the first day of January in the year of our Lord one thousand eight hundred and ninety three, within the said State of Delaware, except in the punishment of crime, whereof the party shall have been duly convicted; nor, except in the punishment of crime as aforesaid, shall any person who shall be born after the passage of this act, nor any person above the age of thirty five years, be held in slavery, or to involuntary servitude, within said State of Delaware, at any time after the passage of this act.

And be it further enacted that said State shall, in good faith prevent, so far as possible, the carrying of any person out of said state, into involuntary servitude, beyond the limits of said State, at any time after the passage of this act.

And be it further enacted that said State may make provision of apprenticeship, not to extend beyond the age of twentyone years for males, nor

---

1. Such a bill was never introduced into the Delaware legislature.

eighteen for females, for all minors whose mothers were not free at the respective births of such minors.

On reflection, I like No. 2 the better. By it the Nation would pay the State $23,200 per annum for thirtyone years—and

All born after the passage of the act would be born free—and

All slaves above the age of 35 years would become free on the passage of the act—and

All others would become free on arriving at the age of 35 years, until January 1893—when

All remaining of all ages would become free, subject to apprenticeship for minors born of slave mothers, up to the respective ages of 21 and 18.

If the State would desire to have the money sooner, let the bill be altered only in fixing the time of final emancipation earlier, and making the annual instalments correspondingly fewer in number, by which they would also be correspondingly larger in amount. For instance, strike out "1893," and insert "1872"; and strike out "thirtyone" annual instalments, and insert "ten" annual instalments. The instalments would then be $71,920 instead of $23,200 as now. In all other particulars let the bill stand precisely as it is.

ca. November 26, 1861

From Annual Message to Congress

Fellow Citizens of the Senate and House of Representatives:

In the midst of unprecedented political troubles, we have cause of great gratitude to God for unusual good health, and most abundant harvests.

You will not be surprised to learn that, in the peculiar exigencies of the times, our intercourse with foreign nations has been attended with profound solicitude, chiefly turning upon our own domestic affairs.

A disloyal portion of the American people have, during the whole year, been engaged in an attempt to divide and destroy the Union. * * *

* * *

Under and by virtue of the act of Congress entitled "An act to confiscate property used for insurrectionary purposes," approved August, 6, 1861, the legal claims of certain persons to the labor and service of certain other persons have become forfeited; and numbers of the latter, thus liberated, are already dependent on the United States, and must be provided for in some way. Besides this, it is not impossible that some of the States will pass similar enactments for their own benefit respectively, and by operation of which persons of the same class will be thrown upon them for disposal. In such case I recommend that Congress provide for accepting such persons from such States, according to some mode of valuation, in lieu, *pro tanto*,[1] of direct taxes, or upon some other plan to be agreed on with such States respectively; that such persons, on such acceptance by the general government, be at once deemed free; and that, in any event,

---

1. To that extent (Latin).

steps be taken for colonizing both classes, (or the one first mentioned, if the other shall not be brought into existence,) at some place, or places, in a climate congenial to them. It might be well to consider, too,—whether the free colored people already in the United States could not, so far as individuals may desire, be included in such colonization.

To carry out the plan of colonization may involve the acquiring of territory, and also the appropriation of money beyond that to be expended in the territorial acquisition. Having practiced the acquisition of territory for nearly sixty years, the question of constitutional power to do so is no longer an open one with us. The power was questioned at first by Mr. Jefferson, who, however, in the purchase of Louisiana, yielded his scruples on the plea of great expediency. If it be said that the only legitimate object of acquiring territory is to furnish homes for white men, this measure effects that object; for the emigration of colored men leaves additional room for white men remaining or coming here. Mr. Jefferson, however, placed the importance of procuring Louisiana more on political and commercial grounds than on providing room for population.

On this whole proposition,—including the appropriation of money with the acquisition of territory, does not the expediency amount to absolute necessity—that, without which the government itself cannot be perpetuated? The war continues. In considering the policy to be adopted for suppressing the insurrection, I have been anxious and careful that the inevitable conflict for this purpose shall not degenerate into a violent and remorseless revolutionary struggle. I have, therefore, in every case, thought it proper to keep the integrity of the Union prominent as the primary object of the contest on our part, leaving all questions which are not of vital military importance to the more deliberate action of the legislature.

In the exercise of my best discretion I have adhered to the blockade of the ports held by the insurgents, instead of putting in force, by proclamation, the law of Congress enacted at the late session, for closing those ports.

So, also, obeying the dictates of prudence, as well as the obligations of law, instead of transcending, I have adhered to the act of Congress to confiscate property used for insurrectionary purposes. If a new law upon the same subject shall be proposed, its propriety will be duly considered.

The Union must be preserved, and hence, all indispensable means must be employed. We should not be in haste to determine that radical and extreme measures, which may reach the loyal as well as the disloyal, are indispensable.

The inaugural address at the beginning of the Administration, and the message to Congress at the late special session, were both mainly devoted to the domestic controversy out of which the insurrection and consequent war have sprung. Nothing now occurs to add or subtract, to or from, the principles or general purposes stated and expressed in those documents.

The last ray of hope for preserving the Union peaceably, expired at the assault upon Fort Sumter; and a general review of what has occurred since may not be unprofitable. What was painfully uncertain then, is much better defined and more distinct now; and the progress of events is plainly in the right direction. The insurgents confidently claimed a strong support from north of Mason and Dixon's line; and the friends of the

Union were not free from apprehension on the point. This, however, was soon settled definitely and on the right side. South of the line, noble little Delaware led off right from the first. Maryland was made to *seem* against the Union. Our soldiers were assaulted, bridges were burned, and railroads torn up, within her limits; and we were many days, at one time, without the ability to bring a single regiment over her soil to the capital. Now, her bridges and railroads are repaired and open to the government; she already gives seven regiments to the cause of the Union and none to the enemy; and her people, at a regular election, have sustained the Union, by a larger majority, and a larger aggregate vote than they ever before gave to any candidate, or any question. Kentucky, too, for some time in doubt, is now decidedly, and, I think, unchangeably, ranged on the side of the Union. Missouri is comparatively quiet; and I believe cannot again be overrun by the insurrectionists. These three States of Maryland, Kentucky, and Missouri, neither of which would promise a single soldier at first, have now an aggregate of not less than forty thousand in the field, for the Union; while, of their citizens, certainly not more than a third of that number, and they of doubtful whereabouts, and doubtful existence, are in arms against it. After a somewhat bloody struggle of months, winter closes on the Union people of western Virginia, leaving them masters of their own country.

An insurgent force of about fifteen hundred, for months dominating the narrow peninsular region, constituting the counties of Accomac and Northampton, and known as eastern shore of Virginia, together with some contiguous parts of Maryland, have laid down their arms; and the people there have renewed their allegiance to, and accepted the protection of, the old flag. This leaves no armed insurrectionist north of the Potomac, or east of the Chesapeake.

Also we have obtained a footing at each of the isolated points, on the southern coast, of Hatteras, Port Royal, Tybee Island, near Savannah, and Ship Island; and we likewise have some general accounts of popular movements, in behalf of the Union, in North Carolina and Tennessee.

These things demonstrate that the cause of the Union is advancing steadily and certainly southward.

Since your last adjournment, Lieutenant General Scott has retired from the head of the army. During his long life, the nation has not been unmindful of his merit; yet, on calling to mind how faithfully, ably and brilliantly he has served the country, from a time far back in our history, when few of the now living had been born, and thenceforward continually, I cannot but think we are still his debtors. I submit, therefore, for your consideration, what further mark of recognition is due to him, and to ourselves, as a grateful people.

With the retirement of General Scott came the executive duty of appointing, in his stead, a general-in-chief of the army. It is a fortunate circumstance that neither in council nor country was there, so far as I know, any difference of opinion as to the proper person to be selected. The retiring chief repeatedly expressed his judgment in favor of General McClellan[2] for

2. George B. McClellan (1826–1885) formed the Army of the Potomac and was its general-in-chief from November 1861 to March 1862. Lincoln removed him from command after the Peninsula Campaign, when he failed to take the Confederate capital of Richmond and to defeat the smaller Army of Virginia, led by General Robert E. Lee (1807–1870).

the position; and in this the nation seemed to give a unanimous concurrence. The designation of General McClellan is therefore in considerable degree, the selection of the Country as well as of the Executive; and hence there is better reason to hope there will be given him, the confidence, and cordial support thus, by fair implication, promised, and without which, he cannot, with so full efficiency, serve the country.

It has been said that one bad general is better than two good ones; and the saying is true, if taken to mean no more than that an army is better directed by a single mind, though inferior, than by two superior ones, at variance, and cross-purposes with each other.

And the same is true, in all joint operations wherein those engaged, *can* have none but a common end in view, and *can* differ only as to the choice of means. In a storm at sea, no one on board *can* wish the ship to sink; and yet, not unfrequently, all go down together, because too many will direct, and no single mind can be allowed to control.

It continues to develop that the insurrection is largely, if not exclusively, a war upon the first principle of popular government—the rights of the people. Conclusive evidence of this is found in the most grave and maturely considered public documents, as well as in the general tone of the insurgents. In those documents we find the abridgement of the existing right of suffrage and the denial to the people of all right to participate in the selection of public officers, except the legislative boldly advocated, with labored arguments to prove that large control of the people in government, is the source of all political evil. Monarchy itself is sometimes hinted at as a possible refuge from the power of the people.

In my present position, I could scarcely be justified were I to omit raising a warning voice against this approach of returning despotism.

It is not needed, nor fitting here, that a general argument should be made in favor of popular institutions; but there is one point, with its connexions, not so hackneyed as most others, to which I ask a brief attention. It is the effort to place *capital* on an equal footing with, if not above *labor*, in the structure of government. It is assumed that labor is available only in connexion with capital; that nobody labors unless somebody else, owning capital, somehow by the use of it, induces him to labor. This assumed, it is next considered whether it is best that capital shall *hire* laborers, and thus induce them to work by their own consent, or *buy* them, and drive them to it without their consent. Having proceeded so far, it is naturally concluded that all laborers are either *hired* laborers, or what we call slaves. And further it is assumed that whoever is once a hired laborer, is fixed in that condition for life.

Now, there is no such relation between capital and labor as assumed; nor is there any such thing as a free man being fixed for life in the condition of a hired laborer. Both these assumptions are false, and all inferences from them are groundless.

Labor is prior to, and independent of, capital. Capital is only the fruit of labor, and could never have existed if labor had not first existed. Labor is the superior of capital, and deserves much the higher consideration. Capital has its rights, which are as worthy of protection as any other rights. Nor is it denied that there is, and probably always will be, a relation between labor and capital, producing mutual benefits. The error is in assuming that the whole labor of community exists within that relation. A few men own capital, and that few avoid labor themselves, and, with their capital, hire or buy another few to labor for them. A large majority belong to neither class—neither work for others, nor have others working for them. In most of the southern States, a majority of the whole people of all colors are neither slaves nor masters; while in the northern a large majority are neither hirers nor hired. Men with their families—wives, sons, and daughters—work for themselves, on their farms, in their houses, and in their shops, taking the whole product to themselves, and asking no favors of capital on the one hand, nor of hired laborers or slaves on the other. It is not forgotten that a considerable number of persons mingle their own labor with capital—that is, they labor with their own hands, and also buy or hire others to labor for them; but this is only a mixed, and not a distinct class. No principle stated is disturbed by the existence of this mixed class.

Again: as has already been said, there is not, of necessity, any such thing as the free hired laborer being fixed to that condition for life. Many independent men everywhere in these States, a few years back in their lives, were hired laborers. The prudent, penniless beginner in the world, labors for wages awhile, saves a surplus with which to buy tools or land for himself; then labors on his own account another while, and at length hires another new beginner to help him. This is the just, and generous, and prosperous system, which opens the way to all—gives hope to all, and consequent energy, and progress, and improvement of condition to all. No men living are more worthy to be trusted than those who toil up from poverty—none less inclined to take, or touch, aught which they have not honestly earned. Let them beware of surrendering a political power which they already possess, and which, if surrendered, will surely be used to close the door of advancement against such as they, and to fix new disabilities and burdens upon them, till all of liberty shall be lost.

From the first taking of our national census to the last are seventy years; and we find our population at the end of the period eight times as great as it was at the beginning. The increase of those other things which men deem desirable has been even greater. We thus have at one view, what the popular principle applied to government, through the machinery of the States and the Union, has produced in a given time; and also what, if firmly maintained, it promises for the future. There are already among us those, who, if the Union be preserved, will live to see it contain two hundred and fifty millions. The struggle of today, is not altogether for today—it is for a vast future also. With a reliance on Providence, all the more firm and earnest, let us proceed in the great task which events have devolved upon us.

December 3, 1861

President's General War Order No. 1

President's general ⎱   Executive Mansion,
War Order No. 1 ⎰   Washington, January 27, 1862.
Ordered that the 22nd. day of February 1862, be the day for a general movement of the Land and Naval forces of the United States against the insurgent forces.

That especially—

The Army at & about, Fortress Monroe.
The Army of the Potomac.
The Army of Western Virginia
The Army near Munfordsville, Ky.
The Army and Flotilla at Cairo.
And a Naval force in the Gulf of Mexico,
      be ready for a movement on that day.

That all other forces, both Land and Naval, with their respective commanders, obey existing orders, for the time, and be ready to obey additional orders when duly given.

That the Heads of Departments, and especially the Secretaries of War and of the Navy, with all their subordinates; and the General-in-Chief, with all other commanders and subordinates, of Land and Naval forces, will severally be held to their strict and full responsibilities, for the prompt execution of this order.

January 27, 1862

To George B. McClellan

Executive Mansion,
Major General McClellan   Washington, Feb. 3, 1862.
My dear Sir: You and I have distinct, and different plans for a movement of the Army of the Potomac—yours to be down the Chesapeake, up the Rappahannock to Urbana, and across land to the terminus of the Railroad on the York River—, mine to move directly to a point on the Railroad South West of Manassas.

If you will give me satisfactory answers to the following questions, I shall gladly yield my plan to yours.

1st. Does not your plan involve a greatly larger expenditure of *time*, and *money* than mine?

2nd. Wherein is a victory *more certain* by your plan than mine?

3rd. Wherein is a victory *more valuable* by your plan than mine?

4th. In fact, would it not be *less* valuable, in this, that it would break no great line of the enemie's communications, while mine would?

5th. In case of disaster, would not a safe retreat be more difficult by your plan than by mine? Yours truly

———

1. Suppose the enemy should attack us in force *before* we reach the Ocoquan, what? In view of the possibility of this, might it not be safest to have our entire force to move together from above the Ocoquan.

2. Suppose the enemy, in force, shall dispute the crossing of the Ocoquan, what? In view of this, might it not be safest for us to cross the Ocoquan at Colchester rather than at the village of Ocoquan? This would cost the enemy two miles more of travel to meet us, but would, on the contrary, leave us two miles further from our ultimate destination.

3. Suppose we reach Maple valley without an attack, will we not be attacked there, in force, by the enemy marching by the several roads from Manassas? and if so, what?

February 3, 1862

Message to Congress

Fellow-citizens of the Senate, and House of Representatives,

I recommend the adoption of a Joint Resolution[1] by your honorable bodies which shall be substantially as follows:

"Resolved that the United States ought to co-operate with any state which may adopt gradual abolishment of slavery, giving to such state pecuniary aid, to be used by such state in it's discretion, to compensate for the inconveniences public and private, produced by such change of system"

If the proposition contained in the resolution does not meet the approval of Congress and the country, there is the end; but if it does command such approval, I deem it of importance that the states and people immediately interested, should be at once distinctly notified of the fact, so that they may begin to consider whether to accept or reject it. The federal government would find it's highest interest in such a measure, as one of the most efficient means of self-preservation. The leaders of the existing insurrection entertain the hope that this government will ultimately be forced to acknowledge the independence of some part of the disaffected region, and that all the slave states North of such part will then say "the Union, for which we have struggled, being already gone, we now choose to go with the Southern section." To deprive them of this hope, substantially ends the rebellion; and the initiation of emancipation completely deprives them of it, as to all the states initiating it. The point is not that *all* the states tolerating slavery would very soon, if at all, initiate emancipation; but that, while the offer is equally made to all, the more Northern shall, by such initiation, make it certain to the more Southern, that in no event, will the former ever join the latter, in their proposed confederacy. I say "initiation" because, in my judgment, gradual, and not sudden emancipation, is better for all. In the mere financial, or pecuniary view, any member of Congress, with the census-tables and Treasury-reports before him, can readily see for himself how very soon the current expenditures of this war would purchase, at fair valuation, all the slaves in any named State. Such a proposition, on the part of the general government, sets up no claim of a right, by federal authority, to interfere with slavery within state limits, referring, as it does, the absolute control of the subject, in each case, to the state and it's people, immediately interested. It is proposed as a matter of perfectly free choice with them.

In the annual message last December, I thought fit to say "The Union must be preserved; and hence all indispensable means must be employed." I said this, not hastily, but deliberately. War has been made, and continues to be, an indispensable means to this end. A practical re-acknowledgement of the national authority would render the war unnecessary, and it would at once cease. If, however, resistance continues, the war must also continue; and it is impossible to foresee all the incidents, which may attend and all the ruin which may follow it. Such as may seem indispensable, or may obviously promise great efficiency towards ending the struggle, must and will come.

1. The resolution was passed by Congress on April 10.

The proposition now made, though an offer only, I hope it may be esteemed no offence to ask whether the pecuniary consideration tendered would not be of more value to the States and private persons concerned, than are the institution, and property in it, in the present aspect of affairs.

While it is true that the adoption of the proposed resolution would be merely initiatory, and not within itself a practical measure, it is recommended in the hope that it would soon lead to important practical results. In full view of my great responsibility to my God, and to my country, I earnestly beg the attention of Congress and the people to the subject.

March 6. 1862.

To James A. McDougall[1]

Hon. James A. McDougal   Executive Mansion
U.S. Senate   Washington, March 14, 1862
My dear Sir: As to the expensiveness of the plan of gradual emancipation with compensation, proposed in the late Message, please allow me one or two brief suggestions.

Less than one half-day's cost of this war would pay for all the slaves in Delaware at four hundred dollars per head:

Thus, all the slaves in Delaware,
    by the Census of 1860, are.   1798
                                                                                400

Cost of the slaves, ... \$ 719,200.
One day's cost of the war . . . . "2,000,000.

Again, less than eighty seven days cost of this war would, at the same price, pay for all in Delaware, Maryland, District of Columbia, Kentucky, and Missouri.

Thus, slaves in Delaware   1798
    "   " Maryland   87,188
    "   " Dis. of Col.   3,181
    "   " Kentucky   225,490
    "   " Missouri   114,965

                                                                        432,622
                                                                     400

Cost of the slaves \$173,048,800
Eightyseven days' cost of the war . . . . "174,000,000.

Do you doubt that taking the initiatory steps on the part of those states and this District, would shorten the war more than eightyseven days, and thus be an actual saving of expense?

A word as to the *time* and *manner* of incurring the expence. Suppose, for instance, a State devises and adopts a system by which the institution

---

1. Senator from California from 1861 to 1867 and war Democrat (1817–1867), who supported the Union cause but opposed the plan for compensated emancipation that Lincoln had proposed in his message to Congress on March 6, 1862 (p. 260).

absolutely ceases therein by a named day—say January 1st. 1882. Then, let the sum to be paid to such state by the United States, be ascertained by taking from the Census of 1860, the number of slaves within the state, and multiplying that number by four hundred—the United States to pay such sum to the state in twenty equal annual instalments, in six per cent. bonds of the United States.

The sum thus given, as to *time* and *manner*, I think would not be half as onerous, as would be an equal sum, raised *now*, for the indefinite prosse-cution of the war; but of this you can judge as well as I.

I inclose a Census-table for your convenience. Yours very truly

To Horace Greeley[1]

Private

Hon. Horace Greeley—   Executive Mansion,
My dear Sir: Washington, March 24, 1862.
Your very kind letter of the 16th. to Mr. Colfax, has been shown me by him. I am grateful for the generous sentiments and purposes expressed towards the administration. Of course I am anxious to see the policy proposed in the late special message, go forward; but you have advo-cated it from the first, so that I need to say little to you on the subject. If I were to suggest anything it would be that as the North are already for the measure, we should urge it *persuasively*, and not *menacingly*, upon the South. I am a little uneasy about the abolishment of slavery in this District, not but I would be glad to see it abolished, but as to the time and manner of doing it. If some one or more of the border-states would move fast, I should greatly prefer it; but if this can not be in a reasonable time, I would like the bill to have the three main features—gradual—compensation—and vote of the people—I do not talk to mem-bers of congress on the subject, except when they ask me. I am not prepared to make any suggestion about confiscation. I may drop you a line hereafter. Yours truly

To George B. McClellan

Major General McClellan.   Washington,
My dear Sir.   April 9. 1862
Your despatches complaining that you are not properly sustained, while they do not offend me, do pain me very much.

Blencker's Division[1] was withdrawn from you before you left here; and you knew the pressure under which I did it, and, as I thought, acquiesced in it—certainly not without reluctance.

After you left, I ascertained that less than twenty thousand unorga-nized men, without a single field battery, were all you designed to be left for the defence of Washington, and Manassas Junction; and part of this

---

1. Editor (1811–1872) of the *New York Tribune*, a leading antislavery newspaper, had written Congressman Colfax in support of Lincoln's emancipation goals.
1. Louis Blencker (1812–1863), colonel in the 8th New York Volunteer Infantry Regiment.

even, was to go to Gen. Hooker's[2] old position. Gen. Banks' corps, once designed for Manassas Junction, was diverted, and tied up on the line of Winchester and Strausburg, and could not leave it without again exposing the upper Potomac, and the Baltimore and Ohio Railroad. This presented, (or would present, when McDowell and Sumner[3] should be gone) a great temptation to the enemy to turn back from the Rappahanock, and sack Washington. My explicit order that Washington should, by the judgment of *all* the commanders of Army corps, be left entirely secure, had been neglected. It was precisely this that drove me to detain McDowell.

I do not forget that I was satisfied with your arrangement to leave Banks at Mannassas Junction; but when that arrangement was broken up, and *nothing* was substituted for it, of course I was not satisfied. I was constrained to substitute something for it myself. And now allow me to ask "Do you really think I should permit the line from Richmond, *via* Mannassas Junction, to this city to be entirely open, except what resistance could be presented by less than twenty thousand unorganized troops?" This is a question which the country will not allow me to evade.

There is a curious mystery about the *number* of the troops now with you. When I telegraphed you on the 6th. saying you had over a hundred thousand with you, I had just obtained from the Secretary of War, a statement, taken as he said, from your own returns, making 108,000 then with you, and *en route* to you. You now say you will have but 85,000, when all *en route* to you shall have reached you. How can the discrepancy of 23,000 be accounted for?

As to Gen. Wool's[4] command, I understand it is doing for you precisely what a like number of your own would have to do, if that command was away.

I suppose the whole force which has gone forward for you, is with you by this time; and if so, I think it is the precise time for you to strike a blow. By delay the enemy will relatively gain upon you—that is, he will gain faster, by *fortifications* and *re-inforcements*, than you can by re-inforcements alone.

And, once more let me tell you, it is indispensable to *you* that you strike a blow. *I* am powerless to help this. You will do me the justice to remember I always insisted, that going down the Bay in search of a field, instead of fighting at or near Mannassas, was only shifting, and not surmounting, a difficulty—that we would find the same enemy, and the same, or equal, intrenchments, at either place. The country will not fail to note—is now noting—that the present hesitation to move upon an intrenched enemy, is but the story of Manassas repeated.

I beg to assure you that I have never written you, or spoken to you, in greater kindness of feeling than now, nor with a fuller purpose to sustain you, so far as in my most anxious judgment, I consistently can. *But you must act.* Yours very truly

2. Joseph Hooker (1814–1879), a Union Army general. Nathaniel P. Banks (1816–1894), a major general of volunteers in the Union Army.
3. Irvin McDowell (1818–1885), a brigadier general who was initially charged with supporting McClellan's Peninsula Campaign but who later stayed behind to defend Washington. Edwin V. Sumner (1797–1863), a Union brigadier general who commanded one of Maj. Gen. McClellan's corps in the Peninsula Campaign.
4. John E. Wool (1784–1869), a Union Army general who secured Fort Monroe, Virginia, a principal storehouse for supplies in McClellan's Peninsula Campaign.

Message to Congress

Fellow citizens of the Senate, and House of Representatives.

The Act entitled "An Act for the release of certain persons held to service, or labor in the District of Columbia" has this day been approved, and signed.

I have never doubted the constitutional authority of congress to abolish slavery in this District; and I have ever desired to see the national capital freed from the institution in some satisfactory way. Hence there has never been, in my mind, any question upon the subject, except the one of expediency, arising in view of all the circumstances. If there be matters within and about this act, which might have taken a course or shape, more satisfactory to my judgment, I do not attempt to specify them. I am gratified that the two principles of compensation, and colonization, are both recognized, and practically applied in the act.

In the matter of compensation, it is provided that claims may be presented within ninety days from the passage of the act "but not thereafter"; and there is no saving for minors, femes-covert,[1] insane, or absent persons. I presume this is an omission by mere over-sight, and I recommend that it be supplied by an amendatory or supplemental act.[2]

April 16. 1862.

Response to Evangelical Lutherans[1]

Gentlemen: I welcome here the representatives of the Evangelical Lutherans of the United States. I accept with gratitude their assurances of the sympathy and support of that enlightened, influential, and loyal class of my fellow-citizens in an important crisis which involves, in my judgment, not only the civil and religious liberties of our own dear land, but in a large degree the civil and religious liberties of mankind in many countries and through many ages. You well know, gentlemen, and the world knows, how reluctantly I accepted this issue of battle forced upon me, on my advent to this place, by the internal enemies of our country. You all know, the world knows the forces and resources the public agents have brought into employment to sustain a Government against which there has been brought not one complaint of real injury committed against society, at home or abroad. You all may recollect that in taking up the sword thus forced into our hands this Government appealed to the prayers of the pious and the good, and declared that it placed its whole dependence upon the favor of God. I now humbly and reverently, in your presence, reiterate the acknowledgment of that dependence, not doubting that, if it shall please the Divine Being who determines the destinies of nations that this shall remain a united people, they will, humbly seeking

---

1. Married women.
2. Congress did pass such legislation.
1. A committee of the General Synod of the Evangelical Lutheran Church presented Lincoln with resolutions supporting his war efforts and his maintenance of the Constitution and Union.

the Divine guidance, make their prolonged national existence a source of new benefits to themselves and their successors, and to all classes and conditions of mankind.

May 13, 1862

Proclamation Revoking General Hunter's Emancipation Order

By the President of the United States of America.
A Proclamation

Whereas there appears in the public prints, what purports to be a proclamation, of Major General Hunter,[1] in the words and figures following, towit:

> *Headquarters Department of the South,* ⎫
> Hilton Head, S.C., May 9, 1862.⎰
> General Orders No. 11.—The three States of Georgia, Florida and South Carolina, comprising the military department of the south, having deliberately declared themselves no longer under the protection of the United States of America, and having taken up arms against the said United States, it becomes a military necessity to declare them under martial law. This was accordingly done on the 25th day of April, 1862. Slavery and martial law in a free country are altogether incompatible; the persons in these three States—Georgia, Florida and South Carolina—heretofore held as slaves, are therefore declared forever free.
>
> DAVID HUNTER,
> (Official)   Major General Commanding.
> ED. W. SMITH, Acting Assistant Adjutant General.

And whereas the same is producing some excitement, and misunderstanding: therefore

I, Abraham Lincoln, president of the United States, proclaim and declare, that the government of the United States, had no knowledge, information, or belief, of an intention on the part of General Hunter to issue such a proclamation; nor has it yet, any authentic information that the document is genuine. And further, that neither General Hunter, nor any other commander, or person, has been authorized by the Government of the United States, to make proclamations declaring the slaves of any State free; and that the supposed proclamation, now in question, whether genuine or false, is altogether void, so far as respects such declaration.

I further make known that whether it be competent for me, as Commander-in-Chief of the Army and Navy, to declare the Slaves of any state or states, free, and whether at any time, in any case, it shall have become a necessity indispensable to the maintenance of the government, to exercise such supposed power, are questions which, under my respon-

---

1. David Hunter (1802–1886), Union general in the Department of the South, was a strong advocate of emancipation and of enlisting blacks into the Union Army.

sibility, I reserve to myself, and which I can not feel justified in leaving to the decision of commanders in the field. These are totally different questions from those of police regulations in armies and camps.

On the sixth day of March last, by a special message, I recommended to Congress the adoption of a joint resolution to be substantially as follows:

> *Resolved*, That the United States ought to co-operate with any State which may adopt a gradual abolishment of slavery, giving to such State pecuniary aid, to be used by such State in its discretion to compensate for the inconveniences, public and private, produced by such change of system.

The resolution, in the language above quoted, was adopted by large majorities in both branches of Congress, and now stands an authentic, definite, and solemn proposal of the nation to the States and people most immediately interested in the subject matter. To the people of those states I now earnestly appeal. I do not argue. I beseech you to make the arguments for yourselves. You can not if you would, be blind to the signs of the times. I beg of you a calm and enlarged consideration of them, ranging, if it may be, far above personal and partizan politics. This proposal makes common cause for a common object, casting no reproaches upon any. It acts not the pharisee. The change it contemplates would come gently as the dews of heaven, not rending or wrecking anything. Will you not embrace it? So much good has not been done, by one effort, in all past time, as, in the providence of God, it is now your high previlege to do. May the vast future not have to lament that you have neglected it.

In witness whereof, I have hereunto set my hand, and caused the seal of the United States to be affixed.

Done at the City of Washington this nineteenth day of May, in the year of our Lord one thousand eight hundred and sixty-two, and of the Independence of the United States the eighty-sixth.   ABRAHAM LINCOLN.

By the President:

WILLIAM H. SEWARD, Secretary of State.

May 19, 1862

To George B. McClellan

Washington City, D.C.

Major Gen. McClellan   June 28– 1862

Save your Army at all events.[1] Will send re-inforcements as fast as we can. Of course they can not reach you to-day, tomorrow, or next day. I have not said you were ungenerous for saying you needed re-inforcement. I thought you were ungenerous in assuming that I did not send them as fast as I could. I feel any misfortune to you and your Army quite as keenly as you feel it yourself. If you have had a drawn battle, or a repulse, it is the price we pay for the enemy not being in Washington. We protected

---

1. McClellan was in the midst of a protracted engagement against Lee, known as the Seven Days Battle, that resulted in a Union retreat and the temporary saving of Richmond for the Confederacy.

Washington, and the enemy concentrated on you; had we stripped Washington, he would have been upon us before the troops sent could have got to you. Less than a week ago you notified us that re-inforcements were leaving Richmond to come in front of us. It is the nature of the case, and neither you or the government that is to blame. Please tell at once the present condition and aspect of things.

P.S. Gen. Pope[2] thinks if you fall back, it would be much better towards York River, than towards the James. As Pope now has charge of the Capital, please confer with him through the telegraph.

Appeal to Border-State Representatives for Compensated Emancipation, Washington, D.C.

Gentlemen. After the adjournment of Congress, now very near, I shall have no opportunity of seeing you for several months. Believing that you of the border-states hold more power for good than any other equal number of members, I feel it a duty which I can not justifiably waive, to make this appeal to you. I intend no reproach or complaint when I assure you that in my opinion, if you all had voted for the resolution in the gradual emancipation message of last March, the war would now be substantially ended. And the plan therein proposed is yet one of the most potent, and swift means of ending it. Let the states which are in rebellion see, definitely and certainly, that, in no event, will the states you represent ever join their proposed Confederacy, and they can not, much longer maintain the contest. But you can not divest them of their hope to ultimately have you with them so long as you show a determination to perpetuate the institution within your own states. Beat them at elections, as you have overwhelmingly done, and, nothing daunted, they still claim you as their own. You and I know what the lever of their power is. Break that lever before their faces, and they can shake you no more forever.

Most of you have treated me with kindness and consideration; and I trust you will not now think I improperly touch what is exclusively your own, when, for the sake of the whole country I ask "Can you, for your states, do better than to take the course I urge?" Discarding *punctillio*,[1] and maxims adapted to more manageable times, and looking only to the unprecedentedly stern facts of our case, can you do better in any possible event? You prefer that the constitutional relation of the states to the nation shall be practically restored, without disturbance of the institution; and if this were done, my whole duty, in this respect, under the constitution, and my oath of office, would be performed. But it is not done, and we are trying to accomplish it by war. The incidents of the war can not be avoided. If the war continue long, as it must, if the object be not sooner attained, the institution in your states will be extinguished by mere friction and abrasion—by the mere incidents of the war. It will be gone, and you will have

2. John Pope (1822–1892), commander of the Army of the Mississippi and later the Army of Virginia.
1. Petty points of conduct.

nothing valuable in lieu of it. Much of it's value is gone already. How much better for you, and for your people, to take the step which, at once, shortens the war, and secures substantial compensation for that which is sure to be wholly lost in any other event. How much better to thus save the money which else we sink forever in the war. How much better to do it while we can, lest the war ere long render us pecuniarily unable to do it. How much better for you, as seller, and the nation as buyer, to sell out, and buy out, that without which the war could never have been, than to sink both the thing to be sold, and the price of it, in cutting one another's throats.

I do not speak of emancipation *at once*, but of a *decision* at once to emancipate *gradually*. Room in South America for colonization, can be obtained cheaply, and in abundance; and when numbers shall be large enough to be company and encouragement for one another, the freed people will not be so reluctant to go.

I am pressed with a difficulty not yet mentioned—one which threatens division among those who, united are none too strong. An instance of it is known to you. Gen. Hunter is an honest man. He was, and I hope, still is, my friend. I valued him none the less for his agreeing with me in the general wish that all men everywhere, could be free. He proclaimed all men free within certain states, and I repudiated the proclamation. He expected more good, and less harm from the measure, than I could believe would follow. Yet in repudiating it, I gave dissatisfaction, if not offence, to many whose support the country can not afford to lose. And this is not the end of it. The pressure, in this direction, is still upon me, and is increasing. By conceding what I now ask, you can relieve me, and much more, can relieve the country, in this important point. Upon these considerations I have again begged your attention to the message of March last. Before leaving the Capital, consider and discuss it among yourselves. You are patriots and statesmen; and, as such, I pray you, consider this proposition; and, at the least, commend it to the consideration of your states and people. As you would perpetuate popular government for the best people in the world, I beseech you that you do in no wise omit this. Our common country is in great peril, demanding the loftiest views, and boldest action to bring it speedy relief. Once relieved, it's form of government is saved to the world; it's beloved history, and cherished memories, are vindicated; and it's happy future fully assured, and rendered inconceivably grand. To you, more than to any others, the previlege is given, to assure that happiness, and swell that grandeur, and to link your own names therewith forever.

July 12, 1862

Draft of the Emancipation Proclamation[1]

In pursuance of the sixth section of the act of Congress entitled "An Act to suppress the insurrection and to punish treason and rebellion, to seize and confiscate property of rebels, and for other purposes" Approved July

---

1. Lincoln presented this draft of the Emancipation Proclamation to his cabinet on July 22 but postponed issuing it; apparently he agreed with William H. Seward that it should be made public only after a Union victory so that it didn't seem like a desperate war strategy.

17. 1862, and which act, and the Joint Resolution explanatory thereof, are herewith published, I, ABRAHAM LINCOLN, President of the United States, do hereby proclaim to, and warn all persons within the contemplation of said sixth section to cease participating in, aiding, countenancing, or abetting the existing rebellion, or any rebellion against the government of the United States, and to return to their proper allegiance to the United States, on pain of the forfeiture and seizure, as within and by said sixth section provided.

And I hereby make known that it is my purpose, upon the next meeting of congress, to again recommend the adoption of a practical measure for tendering pecuniary aid to the free choice or rejection, of any and all States which may then be recognizing and practically sustaining the authority of the United States, and which may then have voluntarily adopted, or therefore may voluntarily adopt, gradual adoption abolishment of slavery within such State or States—that the object is to practically restore, thenceforward to be maintained, the constitutional relation between the general government, and each, and all the states, wherein that relation is now suspended, or disturbed; and that, for this object, the war, as it has been, will be, prossecuted. And, as a fit and necessary military measure for effecting this object, I, as Commander-in-Chief of the Army and Navy of the United States, do order and declare that on the first day of January in the year of Our Lord one thousand, eight hundred and sixtythree, all persons held as slaves within any state or states, wherein the constitutional authority of the United States shall not then be practically recognized, submitted to, and maintained, shall then, thenceforward, and forever, be free.

July 22, 1862

To William H. Seward

Hon. W. H. Seward Executive Mansion
My dear Sir June 28. 1862.
My view of the present condition of the War is about as follows:

The evacuation of Corinth, and our delay by the flood in the Chicahominy, has enabled the enemy to concentrate too much force in Richmond for McClellan to successfully attack. In fact there soon will be no substantial rebel force any where else. But if we send all the force from here to McClellan, the enemy will, before we can know of it, send a force from Richmond and take Washington. Or, if a large part of the Western Army be brought here to McClellan, they will let us have Richmond, and retake Tennessee, Kentucky, Missouri &c. What should be done is to hold what we have in the West, open the Mississippi, and, take Chatanooga & East Tennessee, without more—a reasonable force should, in every event, be kept about Washington for it's protection. Then let the country give us a hundred thousand new troops in the shortest possible time, which added to McClellan, directly or indirectly, will take Richmond, without endangering any other place which we now hold—and will substantially end the war. I expect to maintain this contest until successful, or till I die, or am conquered, or my term expires, or Congress or the country forsakes me; and I would publicly appeal to the country for this new force, were it not that I fear a general panic and stampede would follow—so hard is it to have a thing understood as it really is. I think the new force should be all, or nearly all infantry, principally because such can be raised most cheaply and quickly. Yours very truly

To Reverdy Johnson[1]

private

Hon Reverdy Johnson   Executive Mansion,
                                       Washington, July 26, 1862.
My Dear Sir. Yours of the 16th. by the hand of Governor Shepley[2] is received. It seems the Union feeling in Louisiana is being crushed out by the course of General Phelps.[3] Please pardon me for believing that is a false pretense. The people of Louisiana—all intelligent people every where—know full well, that I never had a wish to touch the foundations of their society, or any right of theirs. With perfect knowledge of this, they forced a necessity upon me to send armies among them, and it is their own fault, not mine, that they are annoyed by the presence of General Phelps. They also know the remedy—know how to be cured of General Phelps. Remove the necessity of his presence. And might it not be well for them to consider whether they have not already had *time* enough to do this? If they can conceive of anything worse than General Phelps, within my power, would they not better be looking out for it? They very well know the way to avert all this is simply to take their place in the Union upon the old terms. If they will not do this, should they not receive harder blows rather than lighter ones?

You are ready to say I apply to *friends* what is due only to *enemies*. I distrust the *wisdom* if not the *sincerity* of friends, who would hold my hands while my enemies stab me. This appeal of professed friends has paralyzed me more in this struggle than any other one thing. You remember telling me the day after the Baltimore mob in April 1861,[4] that it would crush all Union feeling in Maryland for me to attempt bringing troops over Maryland soil to Washington. I brought the troops notwithstanding, and yet there was Union feeling enough left to elect a Legislature the next autumn which in turn elected a very excellent Union U.S. Senator![5]

I am a patient man—always willing to forgive on the Christian terms of repentance; and also to give ample *time* for repentance. Still I must save this government if possible. What I *cannot* do, of course I *will* not

---

1. As result of complaints by foreign consuls about the Union's military occupation of New Orleans, the State Department had sent Johnson to investigate conditions there.
2. George Foster Shepley (1819–1878), a colonel in the Union Army, was military governor of Louisiana from May 20 to July 11, 1862.
3. John W. Phelps (1813–1885), a brigadier general, participated in the seizure of Forts Jackson and St. Philip on the Mississippi River Delta, leading to the takeover of New Orleans by Union forces.
4. On April 19, 1861, Confederate sympathizers attacked Union troops that were on their way to Washington, D.C. The mob action resulted in more than fifty casualties.
5. I.e., Reverdy Johnson.

do; but it may as well be understood, once for all, that I shall not surrender this game leaving any available card unplayed. Yours truly

Address on Colonization to a Committee of Colored Men, Washington, D.C.

This afternoon the President of the United States gave audience to a Committee of colored men at the White House. They were introduced by the Rev. J. Mitchell,[1] Commissioner of Emigration. E. M. Thomas,[2] the Chairman, remarked that they were there by invitation to hear what the Executive had to say to them. Having all been seated, the President, after a few preliminary observations, informed them that a sum of money had been appropriated by Congress, and placed at his disposition for the purpose of aiding the colonization in some country of the people, or a portion of them, of African descent, thereby making it his duty, as it had for a long time been his inclination, to favor that cause; and why, he asked, should the people of your race be colonized, and where? Why should they leave this country? This is, perhaps, the first question for proper consideration. You and we are different races. We have between us a broader difference than exists between almost any other two races. Whether it is right or wrong I need not discuss, but this physical difference is a great disadvantage to us both, as I think your race suffer very greatly, many of them by living among us, while ours suffer from your presence. In a word we suffer on each side. If this is admitted, it affords a reason at least why we should be separated. You here are freemen I suppose.

A Voice: Yes, sir.

The President—Perhaps you have long been free, or all your lives. Your race are suffering, in my judgment, the greatest wrong inflicted on any people. But even when you cease to be slaves, you are yet far removed from being placed on an equality with the white race. You are cut off from many of the advantages which the other race enjoy. The aspiration of men is to enjoy equality with the best when free, but on this broad continent, not a single man of your race is made the equal of a single man of ours. Go where you are treated the best, and the ban is still upon you.

I do not propose to discuss this, but to present it as a fact with which we have to deal. I cannot alter it if I would. It is a fact, about which we all think and feel alike, I and you. We look to our condition, owing to the existence of the two races on this continent. I need not recount to you the effects upon white men, growing out of the institution of Slavery. I believe in its general evil effects on the white race. See our present condition—the country engaged in war!—our white men cutting one another's throats, none knowing how far it will extend; and then consider what we know to be the truth. But for your race among us there could not be war, although many men engaged on either side do not care for you one way or the other.

---

1. James Mitchell (1818–1903), a Methodist minister active in the American Colonization Society; on August 4, 1862, Lincoln appointed him U. S. Commissioner of Emigration.
2. Edward M. Thomas (d. 1863?), a well-known African American intellectual, was the chairman of the five-member delegation of free blacks that met with Lincoln in the White House to discuss colonization.

Nevertheless, I repeat, without the institution of Slavery and the colored race as a basis, the war could not have an existence.

It is better for us both, therefore, to be separated. I know that there are free men among you, who even if they could better their condition are not as much inclined to go out of the country as those, who being slaves could obtain their freedom on this condition. I suppose one of the principal difficulties in the way of colonization is that the free colored man cannot see that his comfort would be advanced by it. You may believe you can live in Washington or elsewhere in the United States the remainder of your life, perhaps more so than you can in any foreign country, and hence you may come to the conclusion that you have nothing to do with the idea of going to a foreign country. This is (I speak in no unkind sense) an extremely selfish view of the case.

But you ought to do something to help those who are not so fortunate as yourselves. There is an unwillingness on the part of our people, harsh as it may be, for you free colored people to remain with us. Now, if you could give a start to white people, you would open a wide door for many to be made free. If we deal with those who are not free at the beginning, and whose intellects are clouded by Slavery, we have very poor materials to start with. If intelligent colored men, such as are before me, would move in this matter, much might be accomplished. It is exceedingly important that we have men at the beginning capable of thinking as white men, and not those who have been systematically oppressed.

There is much to encourage you. For the sake of your race you should sacrifice something of your present comfort for the purpose of being as grand in that respect as the white people. It is a cheering thought throughout life that something can be done to ameliorate the condition of those who have been subject to the hard usage of the world. It is difficult to make a man miserable while he feels he is worthy of himself, and claims kindred to the great God who made him. In the American Revolutionary war sacrifices were made by men engaged in it; but they were cheered by the future. Gen. Washington himself endured greater physical hardships than if he had remained a British subject. Yet he was a happy man, because he was engaged in benefiting his race—something for the children of his neighbors, having none of his own.

The colony of Liberia has been in existence a long time. In a certain sense it is a success. The old President of Liberia, Roberts,[3] has just been with me—the first time I ever saw him. He says they have within the bounds of that colony between 300,000 and 400,000 people, or more than in some of our old States, such as Rhode Island or Delaware, or in some of our newer States, and less than in some of our larger ones. They are not all American colonists, or their descendants. Something less than 12,000 have been sent thither from this country. Many of the original settlers have died, yet, like people elsewhere, their offspring outnumber those deceased.

The question is if the colored people are persuaded to go anywhere, why not there? One reason for an unwillingness to do so is that some of you would rather remain within reach of the country of your nativity. I do not know how much attachment you may have toward our race. It does

3. Joseph Jenkins Roberts (1809–1876), a Virginia-born free black, emigrated to Liberia in 1829 and served as its president from 1847 to 1856.

not strike me that you have the greatest reason to love them. But still you are attached to them at all events.

The place I am thinking about having for a colony is in Central America.[4] It is nearer to us than Liberia—not much more than one-fourth as far as Liberia, and within seven days' run by steamers. Unlike Liberia it is on a great line of travel—it is a highway. The country is a very excellent one for any people, and with great natural resources and advantages, and especially because of the similarity of climate with your native land—thus being suited to your physical condition.

The particular place I have in view is to be a great highway from the Atlantic or Caribbean Sea to the Pacific Ocean, and this particular place has all the advantages for a colony. On both sides there are harbors among the finest in the world. Again, there is evidence of very rich coal mines. A certain amount of coal is valuable in any country, and there may be more than enough for the wants of the country. Why I attach so much importance to coal is, it will afford an opportunity to the inhabitants for immediate employment till they get ready to settle permanently in their homes.

If you take colonists where there is no good landing, there is a bad show; and so where there is nothing to cultivate, and of which to make a farm. But if something is started so that you can get your daily bread as soon as you reach there, it is a great advantage. Coal land is the best thing I know of with which to commence an enterprise.

To return, you have been talked to upon this subject, and told that a speculation is intended by gentlemen, who have an interest in the country, including the coal mines. We have been mistaken all our lives if we do not know whites as well as blacks look to their self-interest. Unless among those deficient of intellect everybody you trade with makes something. You meet with these things here as elsewhere.

If such persons have what will be an advantage to them, the question is whether it cannot be made of advantage to you. You are intelligent, and know that success does not as much depend on external help as on self-reliance. Much, therefore, depends upon yourselves. As to the coal mines, I think I see the means available for your self-reliance.

I shall, if I get a sufficient number of you engaged, have provisions made that you shall not be wronged. If you will engage in the enterprise I will spend some of the money intrusted to me. I am not sure you will succeed. The Government may lose the money, but we cannot succeed unless we try; but we think, with care, we can succeed.

The political affairs in Central America are not in quite as satisfactory condition as I wish. There are contending factions in that quarter; but it is true all the factions are agreed alike on the subject of colonization, and want it, and are more generous than we are here. To your colored race they have no objection. Besides, I would endeavor to have you made equals, and have the best assurance that you should be the equals of the best.

The practical thing I want to ascertain is whether I can get a number of able-bodied men, with their wives and children, who are willing to go,

---

4. The establishment of a colony for American blacks in Central or South America had been discussed since 1858, when Representative Francis P. Blair Jr. (1791–1876) of Missouri and Senator James R. Dolittle (1815–1897) of Wisconsin introduced the idea to Congress.

when I present evidence of encouragement and protection. Could I get a hundred tolerably intelligent men, with their wives and children, to "cut their own fodder," so to speak? Can I have fifty? If I could find twenty-five able-bodied men, with a mixture of women and children, good things in the family relation, I think I could make a successful commencement.

I want you to let me know whether this can be done or not. This is the practical part of my wish to see you. These are subjects of very great importance, worthy of a month's study, instead of a speech delivered in an hour. I ask you then to consider seriously not pertaining to yourselves merely, nor for your race, and ours, for the present time, but as one of the things, if successfully managed, for the good of mankind—not confined to the present generation, but as

> "From age to age descends the lay,
>   To millions yet to be,
> Till far its echoes roll away,
>   Into eternity."[5]

The above is merely given as the substance of the President's remarks.

The Chairman of the delegation briefly replied that "they would hold a consultation and in a short time give an answer." The President said: "Take your full time—no hurry at all."

The delegation then withdrew.

                                                    August 14, 1862

To Horace Greeley[1]

Hon. Horace Greely: Executive Mansion,
Dear Sir   Washington, August 22, 1862.

I have just read yours of the 19th. addressed to myself through the New-York Tribune. If there be in it any statements, or assumptions of fact, which I may know to be erroneous, I do not, now and here, controvert them. If there be in it any inferences which I may believe to be falsely drawn, I do not now and here, argue against them. If there be perceptable in it an impatient and dictatorial tone, I waive it in deference to an old friend, whose heart I have always supposed to be right.

As to the policy I "seem to be pursuing" as you say, I have not meant to leave any one in doubt.

I would save the Union. I would save it the shortest way under the Constitution. The sooner the national authority can be restored; the nearer the Union will be "the Union as it was." If there be those who would not save the Union, unless they could at the same time *save* slavery, I do not agree with them. If there be those who would not save the Union unless they could at the same time *destroy* slavery, I do not agree with them. My paramount object in this struggle *is* to save the Union, and is *not* either to

---

5. Robert Grant's "Hosanna in the Highest" (1839).
1. This is a reply to Greeley's open letter to Lincoln, published as "The Prayer of Twenty Millions" in the *New York Tribune* on August 19, 1862 (pp. 391–95). In the letter, Greeley urged the president to free the slaves in order to weaken the Confederacy.

save or to destroy slavery. If I could save the Union without freeing *any* slave I would do it, and if I could save it by freeing *all* the slaves I would do it; and if I could save it by freeing some and leaving others alone I would also do that. What I do about slavery, and the colored race, I do because I believe it helps to save the Union; and what I forbear, I forbear because I do *not* believe it would help to save the Union. I shall do *less* whenever I shall believe what I am doing hurts the cause, and I shall do *more* whenever I shall believe doing more will help the cause. I shall try to correct errors when shown to be errors; and I shall adopt new views so fast as they shall appear to be true views.

I have here stated my purpose according to my view of *official* duty; and I intend no modification of my oft-expressed *personal* wish that all men every where could be free. Yours,

Meditation on the Divine Will

The will of God prevails. In great contests each party claims to act in accordance with the will of God. Both *may* be, and one *must* be wrong. God can not be *for*, and *against* the same thing at the same time. In the present civil war it is quite possible that God's purpose is something different from the purpose of either party—and yet the human instrumentalities, working just as they do, are of the best adaptation to effect His purpose. I am almost ready to say this is probably true—that God wills this contest, and wills that it shall not end yet. By his mere quiet power, on the minds of the now contestants, He could have either *saved* or *destroyed* the Union without a human contest. Yet the contest began. And having begun He could give the final victory to either side any day. Yet the contest proceeds.

September 2, 1862?

Reply to Chicago Emancipation Memorial, Washington, D.C.[1]

"The subject presented in the memorial is one upon which I have thought much for weeks past, and I may even say for months. I am approached with the most opposite opinions and advice, and that by religious men, who are equally certain that they represent the Divine will. I am sure that either the one or the other class is mistaken in that belief, and perhaps in some respects both. I hope it will not be irreverent for me to say that if it is probable that God would reveal his will to others, on a point so connected with my duty, it might be supposed he would reveal it directly to me; for, unless I am more deceived in myself than I often am, it is my earnest desire to know the will of Providence in this matter. *And if I can learn what it is I will do it!* These are not, however, the days of miracles,

---

1. This report, published in the Chicago *Tribune* on September 23, 1862, reproduces an exchange between Lincoln and a delegation representing a group of Chicago Christians who had issued a memorial in favor of national emancipation.

and I suppose it will be granted that I am not to expect a direct revelation. I must study the plain physical facts of the case, ascertain what is
possible and learn what appears to be wise and right. The subject is difficult, and good men do not agree. For instance, the other day four gentlemen of standing and intelligence (naming one or two of the number)
from New York called, as a delegation, on business connected with the
war; but, before leaving, two of them earnestly beset me to proclaim general emancipation, upon which the other two at once attacked them! You
know, also, that the last session of Congress had a decided majority of
anti-slavery men, yet they could not unite on this policy. And the same is
true of the religious people. Why, the rebel soldiers are praying with a
great deal more earnestness, I fear, than our own troops, and expecting
God to favor their side; for one of our soldiers, who had been taken prisoner, told Senator Wilson, a few days since, that he met with nothing so
discouraging as the evident sincerity of those he was among in their
prayers. But we will talk over the merits of the case.

"What *good* would a proclamation of emancipation from me do, especially as we are now situated? I do not want to issue a document that the
whole world will see must necessarily be inoperative, like the Pope's bull
against the comet![2] Would *my word* free the slaves, when I cannot even
enforce the Constitution in the rebel States? Is there a single court, or
magistrate, or individual that would be influenced by it there? And what
reason is there to think it would have any greater effect upon the slaves
than the late law of Congress, which I approved, and which offers protection and freedom to the slaves of rebel masters who come within our
lines? Yet I cannot learn that that law has caused a single slave to come
over to us. And suppose they could be induced by a proclamation of freedom from me to throw themselves upon us, *what should we do with them?*
How can we feed and care for such a multitude? Gen. Butler[3] wrote me a
few days since that he was issuing more rations to the slaves who have
rushed to him than to all the white troops under his command. They *eat*,
and that is all, though it is true Gen. Butler is feeding the whites also by
the thousand; for it nearly amounts to a famine there. If, now, the pressure of the war should call off our forces from New Orleans to defend
some other point, what is to prevent the masters from reducing the blacks
to slavery again; for I am told that whenever the rebels take any black prisoners, free or slave, they immediately auction them off! They did so with
those they took from a boat that was aground in the Tennessee river a few
days ago. And then *I am very ungenerously attacked for it!* For instance,
when, after the late battles at and near Bull Run, an expedition went out
from Washington under a flag of truce to bury the dead and bring in the
wounded, and the rebels seized the blacks who went along to help and
sent them into slavery, Horace Greeley said in his paper that the Government would probably do nothing about it. What *could* I do? [Here your
delegation suggested that this was a gross outrage on a flag of truce,
which covers and protects all over which it waves, and that whatever he

2. According to popular legend, a medieval pope, Callixtus III (1378–1458), had excommunicated
   the "apparition" of Halley's comet in 1456.
3. General Benjamin F. Butler (1818–1893) had seized New Orleans in May 1862 and served as
   its military commander until November of that year.

could do if *white* men had been similarly detained he *could* do in this case.]

"Now, then, tell me, if you please, what possible result of good would follow the issuing of such a proclamation as you desire? Understand, I raise no objections against it on legal or constitutional grounds; for, as commander-in-chief of the army and navy, in time of war, I suppose I have a right to take any measure which may best subdue the enemy. Nor do I urge objections of a moral nature, in view of possible consequences of insurrection and massacre at the South. I view the matter as a practical war measure, to be decided upon according to the advantages or disadvantages it may offer to the suppression of the rebellion."

Thus invited, your delegation very willingly made reply to the following effect; it being understood that a portion of the remarks were intermingled by the way of conversation with those of the President just given.

We observed (taking up the President's ideas in order) that good men indeed differed in their opinions on this subject; nevertheless *the truth was somewhere*, and it was a matter of solemn moment for him to ascertain it; that we had not been so wanting in respect, alike to ourselves and to him, as to come a thousand miles to bring merely *our opinion* to be set over against the *opinion* of other parties; that the memorial contained facts, principles, and arguments which appealed to the intelligence of the President and to his faith in Divine Providence; that he could not deny that the Bible denounced oppression as one of the highest of crimes, and threatened Divine judgments against nations that practice it; that our country had been exceedingly guilty in this respect, both at the North and South; that our just punishment has come by a slaveholder's rebellion; that the virus of secession is found wherever the virus of slavery extends, and no farther; so that there is the amplest reason for expecting to avert Divine judgments by putting away the sin, and for hoping to remedy the national troubles by striking at their cause.

We observed, further, that we freely admitted the probability, and even the certainty, that God would reveal the path of duty to the President as well as to others, provided he sought to learn it in the appointed way; but, as according to his own remark, Providence wrought by means and not miraculously, it might be, God would use the suggestions and arguments of other minds to secure that result. We felt the deepest personal interest in the matter as of national concern, and would fain aid the thoughts of our President by communicating the convictions of the Christian community from which we came, with the ground upon which they were based.

That it was true he could not now enforce the Constitution at the South; but we could see in that fact no reason whatever for not proclaiming emancipation, but rather the contrary. The two appealed to different classes; the latter would aid, and in truth was necessary to re-establish the former; and the two could be made operative together as fast as our armies fought their way southward; while we had yet to hear that he proposed to abandon the Constitution because of the present difficulty of enforcing it.

As to the inability of Congress to agree on this policy at the late session, it was quite possible, in view of subsequent events, there might be more unanimity at another meeting. The members have met their constituents and learned of marvellous conversions to the wisdom of emancipation, especially since late reverses have awakened thought as to the extreme peril of the nation, and made bad men as well as good men realize that we have to deal with God in this matter. Men of the most opposite previous views were now uniting in calling for this measure.

That to proclaim emancipation would secure the sympathy of Europe and the whole civilized world, which now saw no other reason for the strife than national pride and ambition, an unwillingness to abridge our domain and power. No other step would be so potent to prevent foreign intervention.

Furthermore, it would send a thrill through the entire North, firing every patriotic heart, giving the people a glorious principle for which to suffer and to fight, and assuring them that the work was to be so thoroughly done as to leave our country free forever from danger and disgrace in this quarter.

We added, that when the proclamation should become widely known (as the law of Congress has *not* been) it would withdraw the slaves from the rebels, leaving them without laborers, and giving us *both laborers and soldiers*. That the difficulty experienced by Gen. Butler and other Generals arose from the fact that *half-way measures could never avail*. It is the inherent vice of half-way measures that they create as many difficulties as they remove. It is folly merely to receive and feed the slaves. They should be welcomed and fed, and then, according to Paul's doctrine,[4] that they who eat must work, be made to labor and to fight for their liberty and ours. With such a policy the blacks would be no incumbrance and their rations no waste. In this respect we should follow the ancient maxim, and learn of the enemy. What the rebels most fear is what we should be most prompt to do; and what they most fear is evident from the hot haste with which, on the first day of the present session of the Rebel Congress, bills were introduced threatening terrible vengeance if we used the blacks in the war.

The President rejoined from time to time in about these terms:

"I admit that slavery is the root of the rebellion, or at least its *sine qua non*. The ambition of politicians may have instigated them to act, but they would have been impotent without slavery as their instrument. I will also concede that emancipation would help us in Europe, and convince them that we are incited by something more than ambition. I grant further that it would help *somewhat* at the North, though not so much, I fear, as you and those you represent imagine. Still, some additional strength would be added in that way to the war. And then unquestionably it would weaken the rebels by drawing off their laborers, which is of great importance. But I am not so sure we could do much with the blacks. If we were to arm them, I fear that in a few weeks the arms would be in the hands of the rebels; and indeed thus far we have not had arms enough to equip our white troops. I will mention another thing, though it meet only your scorn and contempt: There are fifty thousand bayonets in the Union armies from the Border Slave States. It would be a serious matter if, in consequence of a proclamation such as you desire, they should go over to the rebels. I do not think they all would—not so many indeed as a year ago, or as six months ago—not so many to-day as yesterday. Every day increases

---

4. "For even when we were with you, this we commanded you, that if any would not work, neither should he eat" (2 Thessalonians 3:10).

their Union feeling. They are also getting their pride enlisted, and want to beat the rebels. Let me say one thing more: I think you should admit that we already have an important principle to rally and unite the people in the fact that constitutional government is at stake. This is a fundamental idea, going down about as deep as any thing."

We answered that, being fresh from the people, we were naturally more hopeful than himself as to the necessity and probable effect of such a proclamation. The value of constitutional government is indeed a grand idea for which to contend; but the people know that *nothing else has put constitutional government in danger but slavery*; that the toleration of that aristocratic and despotic element among our free institutions was the inconsistency that had nearly wrought our ruin and caused free government to appear a failure before the world, and therefore the people demand emancipation to preserve and perpetuate constitutional government. Our idea would thus be found to go deeper than this, and to be armed with corresponding power. ("Yes," interrupted Mr. Lincoln, "that is the true ground of our difficulties.") That a proclamation of general emancipation, "giving Liberty and Union" as the national watch-word, would rouse the people and rally them to his support beyond any thing yet witnessed—appealing alike to conscience, sentiment, and hope. He must remember, too, that present manifestations are no index of what would then take place. If the leader will but utter a trumpet call the nation will respond with patriotic ardor. No one can tell the power of the right word from the right man to develop the latent fire and enthusiasm of the masses. ("I know it," exclaimed Mr. Lincoln.) That good sense must of course be exercised in drilling, arming, and using black as well as white troops to make them efficient; and that in a scarcity of arms it was at least worthy of inquiry whether it were not wise to place a portion of them in the hands of those nearest to the seat of the rebellion and able to strike the deadliest blow.

That in case of a proclamation of emancipation we had no fear of serious injury from the desertion of Border State troops. The danger was greatly diminished, as the President had admitted. But let the desertions be what they might, the increased spirit of the North would replace them two to one. One State alone, if necessary, would compensate the loss, were the whole 50,000 to join the enemy. The struggle has gone too far, and cost too much treasure and blood, to allow of a partial settlement. Let the line be drawn at the same time between freedom and slavery, and between loyalty and treason. The sooner we know who are our enemies the better.

In bringing our interview to a close, after an hour of earnest and frank discussion, of which the foregoing is a specimen, Mr. Lincoln remarked: "Do not misunderstand me, because I have mentioned these objections. They indicate the difficulties that have thus far prevented my action in some such way as you desire. I have not decided against a proclamation of liberty to the slaves, but hold the matter under advisement. And I can assure you that the subject is on my mind, by day and night, more than any other. Whatever shall appear to be God's will I will do. I trust that, in the freedom with which I have canvassed your views, I have not in any respect injured your feelings."

September 13, 1862

Preliminary Emancipation Proclamation

By the President of the United States of America
A Proclamation

I, Abraham Lincoln, President of the United States of America, and Commander-in-chief of the Army and Navy thereof, do hereby proclaim and declare that hereafter, as heretofore, the war will be prossecuted for the object of practically restoring the constitutional relation between the United States, and each of the states, and the people thereof, in which states that relation is, or may be suspended, or disturbed.

That it is my purpose, upon the next meeting of Congress to again recommend the adoption of a practical measure tendering pecuniary aid to the free acceptance or rejection of all slave-states, so called, the people whereof may not then be in rebellion against the United States, and which states, may then have voluntarily adopted, or thereafter may voluntarily adopt, immediate, or gradual abolishment of slavery within their respective limits; and that the effort to colonize persons of African descent, with their consent, upon this continent, or elsewhere, with the previously obtained consent of the Governments existing there, will be continued.

That on the first day of January in the year of our Lord, one thousand eight hundred and sixty-three, all persons held as slaves within any state, or designated part of a state, the people whereof shall then be in rebellion against the United States shall be then, thenceforward, and forever free; and the executive government of the United States, including the military and naval authority thereof, will recognize and maintain the freedom of such persons, and will do no act or acts to repress such persons, or any of them, in any efforts they may make for their actual freedom.

That the executive will, on the first day of January aforesaid, by proclamation, designate the States, and parts of states, if any, in which the people thereof respectively, shall then be in rebellion against the United States; and the fact that any state, or the people thereof shall, on that day be, in good faith represented in the Congress of the United States, by members chosen thereto, at elections wherein a majority of the qualified voters of such state shall have participated, shall, in the absence of strong countervailing testimony, be deemed conclusive evidence that such state and the people thereof, are not then in rebellion against the United States.

That attention is hereby called to an act of Congress entitled "An act to make an additional Article of War" approved March 13, 1862, and which act is in the words and figure following:

> Be it enacted by the Senate and House of Representatives of the United States of America in Congress assembled, That hereafter the following shall be promulgated as an additional article of war for the government of the army of the United States, and shall be obeyed and observed as such:
>
> Article—. All officers or persons in the military or naval service of the United States are prohibited from employing any of the forces under their respective commands for the purpose of returning fugitives from service or labor, who may have escaped from any persons to whom such service or labor is claimed to be due, and any officer

who shall be found guilty by a court-martial of violating this article shall be dismissed from the service.

SEC. 2. *And be it further enacted,* That this act shall take effect from and after its passage.

Also to the ninth and tenth sections of an act entitled "An Act to suppress Insurrection, to punish Treason and Rebellion, to seize and confiscate property of rebels, and for other purposes," approved July 17, 1862, and which sections are in the words and figures following:

SEC. 9. *And be it further enacted,* That all slaves of persons who shall hereafter be engaged in rebellion against the government of the United States, or who shall in any way give aid or comfort thereto, escaping from such persons and taking refuge within the lines of the army; and all slaves captured from such persons or deserted by them and coming under the control of the government of the United States; and all slaves of such persons found *on* (or) being within any place occupied by rebel forces and afterwards occupied by the forces of the United States, shall be deemed captives of war, and shall be forever free of their servitude and not again held as slaves.

SEC. 10. *And be it further enacted,* That no slave escaping into any State, Territory, or the District of Columbia, from any other State, shall be delivered up, or in any way impeded or hindered of his liberty, except for crime, or some offence against the laws, unless the person claiming said fugitive shall first make oath that the person to whom the labor or service of such fugitive is alleged to be due is his lawful owner, and has not borne arms against the United States in the present rebellion, nor in any way given aid and comfort thereto; and no person engaged in the military or naval service of the United States shall, under any pretence whatever, assume to decide on the validity of the claim of any person to the service or labor of any other person, or surrender up any such person to the claimant, on pain of being dismissed from the service.

And I do hereby enjoin upon and order all persons engaged in the military and naval service of the United States to observe, obey, and enforce, within their respective spheres of service, the act, and sections above recited.

And the executive will in due time recommend that all citizens of the United States who shall have remained loyal thereto throughout the rebellion, shall (upon the restoration of the constitutional relation between the United States, and their respective states, and people, if that relation shall have been suspended or disturbed) be compensated for all losses by acts of the United States, including the loss of slaves.

In witness whereof, I have hereunto set my hand, and caused the seal of the United States to be affixed.

Done at the City of Washington, this twenty second day of September, in the year of our Lord, one thousand eight hundred and sixty two, and of the Independence of the United States, the eighty seventh.

ABRAHAM LINCOLN

By the President:

WILLIAM H. SEWARD, Secretary of State.

September 22, 1862

Proclamation Suspending the Writ of Habeas Corpus

By the President of the United States of America:
A Proclamation

Whereas, it has become necessary to call into service not only volunteers but also portions of the militia of the States by draft in order to suppress the insurrection existing in the United States, and disloyal persons are not adequately restrained by the ordinary processes of law from hindering this measure and from giving aid and comfort in various ways to the insurrection;

Now, therefore, be it ordered, first, that during the existing insurrection and as a necessary measure for suppressing the same, all Rebels and Insurgents, their aiders and abettors within the United States, and all persons discouraging volunteer enlistments, resisting militia drafts, or guilty of any disloyal practice, affording aid and comfort to Rebels against the authority of the United States, shall be subject to martial law and liable to trial and punishment by Courts Martial or Military Commission:

Second. That the Writ of Habeas Corpus is suspended in respect to all persons arrested, or who are now, or hereafter during the rebellion shall be, imprisoned in any fort, camp, arsenal, military prison, or other place of confinement by any military authority or by the sentence of any Court Martial or Military Commission.

In witness whereof, I have hereunto set my hand, and caused the seal of the United States to be affixed.

Done at the City of Washington this twenty fourth day of September, in the year of our Lord one thousand eight hundred and sixty-two, and of the Independence of the United States the 87th.   ABRAHAM LINCOLN.

By the President:

WILLIAM H. SEWARD, Secretary of State.

September 24, 1862

To George B. McClellan

Major General McClellan   Executive Mansion,
My dear Sir   Washington, Oct. 13, 1862.
You remember my speaking to you of what I called your over-cautiousness. Are you not over-cautious when you assume that you can not do what the enemy is constantly doing? Should you not claim to be at least his equal in prowess, and act upon the claim?

As I understand, you telegraph Gen. Halleck[1] that you can not subsist your army at Winchester unless the Railroad from Harper's Ferry to that point be put in working order. But the enemy does now subsist his army at

---

1. Henry W. Halleck (1815–1872), appointed General-in-Chief of all Union forces by Lincoln in July 1862.

Winchester at a distance nearly twice as great from railroad transportation as you would have to do without the railroad last named. He now wagons from Culpepper C.H.[2] which is just about twice as far as you would have to do from Harper's Ferry. He is certainly not more than half as well provided with wagons as you are. I certainly should be pleased for you to have the advantage of the Railroad from Harper's Ferry to Winchester, but it wastes all the remainder of autumn to give it to you; and, in fact ignores the question of *time*, which can not, and must not be ignored.

Again, one of the standard maxims of war, as you know, is "to operate upon the enemy's communications as much as possible without exposing your own." You seem to act as if this applies *against* you, but can not apply in your *favor*. Change positions with the enemy, and think you not he would break your communication with Richmond within the next twenty-four hours? You dread his going into Pennsylvania. But if he does so in full force, he gives up his communications to you absolutely, and you have nothing to do but to follow, and ruin him; if he does so with less than full force, fall upon, and beat what is left behind all the easier.

Exclusive of the water line, you are now nearer Richmond than the enemy is by the route that you *can*, and he *must* take. Why can you not reach there before him, unless you admit that he is more than your equal on a march. His route is the arc of a circle, while yours is the chord. The roads are as good on yours as on his.

You know I desired, but did not order, you to cross the Potomac below, instead of above the Shenandoah and Blue Ridge. My idea was that this would at once menace the enemies' communications, which I would seize if he would permit. If he should move Northward I would follow him closely, holding his communications. If he should prevent our seizing his communications, and move towards Richmond, I would press closely to him, fight him if a favorable opportunity should present, and, at least, try to beat him to Richmond on the inside track. I say "try"; if we never try, we shall never succeed. If he make a stand at Winchester, moving neither North or South, I would fight him there, on the idea that if we can not beat him when he bears the wastage of coming to us, we never can when we bear the wastage of going to him. This proposition is a simple truth, and is too important to be lost sight of for a moment. In coming to us, he tenders us an advantage which we should not waive. We should not so operate as to merely drive him away. As we must beat him somewhere, or fail finally, we can do it, if at all, easier near to us, than far away. If we can not beat the enemy where he now is, we never can, he again being within the entrenchments of Richmond.

Recurring to the idea of going to Richmond on the inside track, the facility of supplying from the side away from the enemy is remarkable—as it were, by the different spokes of a wheel extending from the hub towards the rim—and this whether you move directly by the chord, or on the inside arc, hugging the Blue Ridge more closely. The chord-line, as you see, carries you by Aldie, Hay-Market, and Fredericksburg; and you see how turn-pikes, railroads, and finally, the Potomac by Acquia Creek, meet you at all points from Washington. The same, only the lines lengthened a

2. Culpeper Court House, Virginia.

little, if you press closer to the Blue Ridge part of the way. The gaps through the Blue Ridge I understand to be about the following distances from Harper's Ferry, towit: Vestal's five miles; Gregorie's, thirteen, Snicker's eighteen, Ashby's, twenty-eight, Mannassas, thirty-eight, Chester forty-five, and Thornton's fifty-three.[3] I should think it preferable to take the route nearest the enemy, disabling him to make an important move without your knowledge, and compelling him to keep his forces together, for dread of you. The gaps would enable you to attack if you should wish. For a great part of the way, you would be practically between the enemy and both Washington and Richmond, enabling us to spare you the greatest number of troops from here. When at length, running for Richmond ahead of him enables him to move this way; if he does so, turn and attack him in rear. But I think he should be engaged long before such point is reached. It is all easy if our troops march as well as the enemy; and it is unmanly to say they can not do it.

This letter is in no sense an order. Yours truly

Order for Sabbath Observance[1]

Executive Mansion, Washington, November 15, 1862

The President, Commander-in-Chief of the Army and Navy, desires and enjoins the orderly observance of the Sabbath by the officers and men in the military and naval service. The importance for man and beast of the prescribed weekly rest, the sacred rights of Christian soldiers and sailors, a becoming deference to the best sentiment of a Christian people, and a due regard for the Divine will, demand that Sunday labor in the Army and Navy be reduced to the measure of strict necessity.

The discipline and character of the national forces should not suffer, nor the cause they defend be imperiled, by the profanation of the day or name of the Most High. "At this time of public distress"—adopting the words of Washington in 1776[2]—"men may find enough to do in the service of God and their country without abandoning themselves to vice and immorality." The first General Order issued by the Father of his Country after the Declaration of Independence, indicates the spirit in which our institutions were founded and should ever be defended: "*The General hopes and trusts that every officer and man will endeavor to live and act as becomes a Christian soldier defending the dearest rights and liberties of his country.*"

November 15, 1862

---

3. Various mountain gaps or valleys in Northern Virginia.
1. Lincoln evidently issued this order at the request of Christian ministers who visited him. The *New York Tribune* on November 14, 1862, reported that "Messrs. Fred. Winston, David Hoodley, Foster, Booth, and another gentleman, representing religious bodies in New-York City, called upon the President and heads of departments today to urge upon him the propriety of enforcing a better observance of the Sabbath in the army. The interviews are represented as agreeable and satisfactory."
2. July 9, 1776.

To Carl Schurz[1]

Gen. Carl Schurz   Executive Mansion,
My dear Sir   Washington, Nov. 24. 1862.
I have just received, and read, your letter of the 20th. The purport of it is
that we lost the late elections,[2] and the administration is failing, because
the war is unsuccessful; and that I must not flatter myself that I am not
justly to blame for it. I certainly know that if the war fails, the administration fails, and that I *will* be blamed for it, whether I deserve it or not.
And I ought to be blamed, if I could do better. You think I could do better;
therefore you blame me already. I think I could not do better; therefore I
blame you for blaming me. I understand you *now* to be willing to accept
the help of men, who are not republicans, provided they have "heart in it."
Agreed. I want no others. But who is to be the judge of hearts, or of "heart
in it"? If I must discard my own judgment, and take yours, I must also take
that of others; and by the time I should reject all I should be advised to
reject, I should have none left, republicans, or others—not even yourself.
For, be assured, my dear sir, there are men who have "heart in it" that
think you are performing your part as poorly as you think I am performing mine. I certainly have been dissatisfied with the slowness of Buell[3]
and McClellan; but before I relieved them I had great fears I should not
find successors to them, who would do better; and I am sorry to add,
that I have seen little since to relieve those fears. I do not clearly see the
prospect of any more rapid movements. I fear we shall at last find out
that the difficulty is in our case, rather than in particular generals. I
wish to disparage no one—certainly not those who sympathize with me;
but I must say I need success more than I need sympathy, and that I have
not seen the so much greater evidence of getting success from my sympathizers, than from those who are denounced as the contrary. It does seem
to me that in the field the two classes have been very much alike, in what
they have done, and what they have failed to do. In sealing their faith
with their blood, Baker, and Lyon, and Bohlen, and Richardson, republicans, did all that men could do; but did they any more than Kearney, and
Stevens, and Reno, and Mansfield,[4] none of whom were republicans, and
some, at least of whom, have been bitterly, and repeatedly, denounced to
me as secession sympathizers? I will not perform the ungrateful task of
comparing cases of failure.

In answer to your question "Has it not been publicly stated in the newspapers, and apparently proved as a fact, that from the commencement of
the war, the enemy was continually supplied with information by some of
the confidential subordinates of as important an officer as Adjutant

---

1. Former German revolutionary (1829–1906) who emigrated to the United States and became a
   Republican supporter of Lincoln. During the Civil War, he was a commissioned officer who
   served in the Second Battle of Bull Run, Chancellorsville, Gettysburg, and other battles.
2. The Republicans had fared poorly in the congressional elections that fall, losing 22 seats (out
   of total House membership of 185), while the Democrats gained 28.
3. Don Carlos Buell (1818–1898), a Union general who participated in two of the war's major
   battles, Shiloh and Perryville. In the latter battle, his cautiousness in the face of outnumbered
   Confederate forces angered many Americans.
4. Lincoln here mentions seven generals and one colonel who were killed or mortally wounded in
   battle.

General Thomas?" I must say "no" so far as my knowledge extends. And I add that if you can give any tangible evidence upon that subject, I will thank you to come to the City and do so. Very truly Your friend

From Annual Message to Congress

Fellow-citizens of the Senate and House of Representatives:
Since your last annual assembling another year of health and bountiful harvests has passed. And while it has not pleased the Almighty to bless us with a return of peace, we can but press on, guided by the best light He gives us, trusting that in His own good time, and wise way, all will yet be well.

The correspondence touching foreign affairs which has taken place during the last year is herewith submitted, in virtual compliance with a request to that effect, made by the House of Representatives near the close of the last session of Congress.

If the condition of our relations with other nations is less gratifying than it has usually been at former periods, it is certainly more satisfactory than a nation so unhappily distracted as we are, might reasonably have apprehended. In the month of June last there were some grounds to expect that the maritime powers which, at the beginning of our domestic difficulties, so unwisely and unnecessarily, as we think, recognized the insurgents as a belligerent, would soon recede from that position, which has proved only less injurious to themselves, than to our own country. But the temporary reverses which afterwards befell the national arms, and which were exaggerated by our own disloyal citizens abroad have hitherto delayed that act of simple justice.

The civil war, which has so radically changed for the moment, the occupations and habits of the American people, has necessarily disturbed the social condition, and affected very deeply the prosperity of the nations with which we have carried on a commerce that has been steadily increasing throughout a period of half a century. It has, at the same time, excited political ambitions and apprehensions which have produced a profound agitation throughout the civilized world. In this unusual agitation we have forborne from taking part in any controversy between foreign states, and between parties or factions in such states. We have attempted no propagandism, and acknowledged no revolution. But we have left to every nation the exclusive conduct and management of its own affairs. Our struggle has been, of course, contemplated by foreign nations with reference less to its own merits, than to its supposed, and often exaggerated effects and consequences resulting to those nations themselves. Nevertheless, complaint on the part of this government, even if it were just, would certainly be unwise.

The treaty with Great Britain for the suppression of the slave trade has been put into operation with a good prospect of complete success. It is an occasion of special pleasure to acknowledge that the execution of it, on the part of Her Majesty's government, has been marked with a jealous respect for the authority of the United States, and the rights of their moral and loyal citizens.

The convention with Hanover for the abolition of the stade dues[1] has been carried into full effect, under the act of Congress for that purpose.

A blockade of three thousand miles of sea-coast could not be established, and vigorously enforced, in a season of great commercial activity like the present, without committing occasional mistakes, and inflicting unintentional injuries upon foreign nations and their subjects.

A civil war occurring in a country where foreigners reside and carry on trade under treaty stipulations, is necessarily fruitful of complaints of the violation of neutral rights. All such collisions tend to excite misapprehensions, and possibly to produce mutual reclamations between nations which have a common interest in preserving peace and friendship. In clear cases of these kinds I have, so far as possible, heard and redressed complaints which have been presented by friendly powers. There is still, however, a large and an augmenting number of doubtful cases upon which the government is unable to agree with the governments whose protection is demanded by the claimants. There are, moreover, many cases in which the United States, or their citizens, suffer wrongs from the naval or military authorities of foreign nations, which the governments of those states are not at once prepared to redress. I have proposed to some of the foreign states, thus interested, mutual conventions to examine and adjust such complaints. This proposition has been made especially to Great Britain, to France, to Spain, and to Prussia. In each case it has been kindly received, but has not yet been formally adopted.

I deem it my duty to recommend an appropriation in behalf of the owners of the Norwegian bark Admiral P. Tordenskiold, which vessel was, in May, 1861, prevented by the commander of the blockading force off Charleston from leaving that port with cargo, notwithstanding a similar privilege had, shortly before, been granted to an English vessel. I have directed the Secretary of State to cause the papers in the case to be communicated to the proper committees.

Applications have been made to me by many free Americans of African descent to favor their emigration, with a view to such colonization as was contemplated in recent acts of Congress. Other parties, at home and abroad—some from interested motives, others upon patriotic considerations, and still others influenced by philanthropic sentiments—have suggested similar measures; while, on the other hand, several of the Spanish-American republics have protested against the sending of such colonies to their respective territories. Under these circumstances, I have declined to move any such colony to any state, without first obtaining the consent of its government, with an agreement on its part to receive and protect such emigrants in all the rights of freemen; and I have, at the same time, offered to the several states situated within the tropics, or having colonies there, to negotiate with them, subject to the advice and consent of the Senate, to favor the voluntary emigration of persons of that class to their respective territories, upon conditions which shall be equal, just, and humane. Liberia and Hayti are, as yet, the only countries to

---

1. Tolls levied on ships going up the Elbe and passing the mouth of the Schwinge River. A bill passed by Congress in March 1862 provided funds supporting a treaty by which the tolls were abolished by the king of Hanover in exchange for a lump payment by the United States.

which colonists of African descent from here, could go with certainty of being received and adopted as citizens; and I regret to say such persons, contemplating colonization, do not seem so willing to migrate to those countries, as to some others, nor so willing as I think their interest demands. I believe, however, opinion among them, in this respect, is improving; and that, ere long, there will be an augmented, and considerable migration to both these countries, from the United States.

The new commercial treaty between the United States and the Sultan of Turkey has been carried into execution.

A commercial and consular treaty has been negotiated, subject to the Senate's consent, with Liberia; and a similar negotiation is now pending with the republic of Hayti. A considerable improvement of the national commerce is expected to result from these measures.

Our relations with Great Britain, France, Spain, Portugal, Russia, Prussia, Denmark, Sweden, Austria, the Netherlands, Italy, Rome, and the other European states, remain undisturbed. Very favorable relations also continue to be maintained with Turkey, Morocco, China and Japan.

During the last year there has not only been no change of our previous relations with the independent states of our own continent, but, more friendly sentiments than have heretofore existed, are believed to be entertained by these neighbors, whose safety and progress, are so intimately connected with our own. This statement especially applies to Mexico, Nicaragua, Costa Rica, Honduras, Peru, and Chile.

The commission under the convention with the republic of New Granada closed its session, without having audited and passed upon, all the claims which were submitted to it. A proposition is pending to revive the convention, that it may be able to do more complete justice. The joint commission between the United States and the republic of Costa Rica has completed its labors and submitted its report.

I have favored the project for connecting the United States with Europe by an Atlantic telegraph, and a similar project to extend the telegraph from San Francisco, to connect by a Pacific telegraph with the line which is being extended across the Russian empire.

The Territories of the United States, with unimportant exceptions, have remained undisturbed by the civil war, and they are exhibiting such evidence of prosperity as justifies an expectation that some of them will soon be in a condition to be organized as States, and be constitutionally admitted into the federal Union.

*   *   *

The Indian tribes upon our frontiers have, during the past year, manifested a spirit of insubordination, and, at several points, have engaged in open hostilities against the white settlements in their vicinity. The tribes occupying the Indian country south of Kansas, renounced their allegiance to the United States, and entered into treaties with the insurgents. Those who remained loyal to the United States were driven from the country. The chief of the Cherokees has visited this city for the purpose of restoring the former relations of the tribe with the United States. He alleges that they were constrained, by superior force, to enter into treaties with the insurgents, and that the United States neglected to furnish the protection which their treaty stipulations required.

In the month of August last the Sioux Indians, in Minnesota, attacked the settlements in their vicinity with extreme ferocity, killing, indiscriminately, men, women, and children.[2] This attack was wholly unexpected, and, therefore, no means of defence had been provided. It is estimated that not less than eight hundred persons were killed by the Indians, and a large amount of property was destroyed. How this outbreak was induced is not definitely known, and suspicions, which may be unjust, need not to be stated. Information was received by the Indian bureau, from different sources, about the time hostilities were commenced, that a simultaneous attack was to be made upon the white settlements by all the tribes between the Mississippi river and the Rocky mountains. The State of Minnesota has suffered great injury from this Indian war. A large portion of her territory has been depopulated, and a severe loss has been sustained by the destruction of property. The people of that State manifest much anxiety for the removal of the tribes beyond the limits of the State as a guarantee against future hostilities. The Commissioner of Indian Affairs will furnish full details. I submit for your especial consideration whether our Indian system shall not be remodelled. Many wise and good men have impressed me with the belief that this can be profitably done.

I submit a statement of the proceedings of commissioners, which shows the progress that has been made in the enterprise of constructing the Pacific railroad. And this suggests the earliest completion of this road, and also the favorable action of Congress upon the projects now pending before them for enlarging the capacities of the great canals in New York and Illinois, as being of vital, and rapidly increasing importance to the whole nation, and especially to the vast interior region hereinafter to be noticed at some greater length. I purpose having prepared and laid before you at an early day some interesting and valuable statistical information upon this subject. The military and commercial importance of enlarging the Illinois and Michigan canal, and improving the Illinois river, is presented in the report of Colonel Webster to the Secretary of War, and now transmitted to Congress. I respectfully ask attention to it.

* * *

On the twenty-second day of September last a proclamation was issued by the Executive, a copy of which is herewith submitted.

In accordance with the purpose expressed in the second paragraph of that paper, I now respectfully recall your attention to what may be called "compensated emancipation."

A nation may be said to consist of its territory, its people, and its laws. The territory is the only part which is of certain durability. "One generation passeth away, and another generation cometh, but the earth abideth forever."[3] It is of the first importance to duly consider, and estimate, this ever-enduring part. That portion of the earth's surface which is owned and inhabited by the people of the United States, is well adapted to be the

---

2. Known as the Dakota War of 1862, this string of Indian attacks caused the deaths of over eight hundred whites and the displacement of some forty thousand settlers, who fled from their homes.
3. Ecclesiastes 1:4.

home of one national family; and it is not well adapted for two, or more. Its vast extent, and its variety of climate and productions, are of advantage, in this age, for one people, whatever they might have been in former ages. Steam, telegraphs, and intelligence, have brought these, to be an advantageous combination, for one united people.

In the inaugural address I briefly pointed out the total inadequacy of disunion, as a remedy for the differences between the people of the two sections. I did so in language which I cannot improve, and which, therefore, I beg to repeat:

"One section of our country believes slavery is *right*, and ought to be extended, while the other believes it is *wrong*, and ought not to be extended. This is the only substantial dispute. The fugitive slave clause of the Constitution, and the law for the suppression of the foreign slave trade, are each as well enforced, perhaps, as any law can ever be in a community where the moral sense of the people imperfectly supports the law itself. The great body of the people abide by the dry legal obligation in both cases, and a few break over in each. This, I think, cannot be perfectly cured; and it would be worse in both cases *after* the separation of the sections, than before. The foreign slave trade, now imperfectly suppressed, would be ultimately revived without restriction in one section; while fugitive slaves, now only partially surrendered, would not be surrendered at all by the other.

"Physically speaking, we cannot separate. We cannot remove our respective sections from each other, nor build an impassable wall between them. A husband and wife may be divorced, and go out of the presence, and beyond the reach of each other; but the different parts of our country cannot do this. They cannot but remain face to face; and intercourse, either amicable or hostile, must continue between them. Is it possible, then, to make that intercourse more advantageous, or more satisfactory, *after* separation than *before*? Can aliens make treaties, easier than friends can make laws? Can treaties be more faithfully enforced between aliens, than laws can among friends? Suppose you go to war, you cannot fight always; and when, after much loss on both sides, and no gain on either, you cease fighting, the identical old questions, as to terms of intercourse, are again upon you."

There is no line, straight or crooked, suitable for a national boundary, upon which to divide. Trace through, from east to west, upon the line between the free and slave country, and we shall find a little more than one-third of its length are rivers, easy to be crossed, and populated, or soon to be populated, thickly upon both sides; while nearly all its remaining length, are merely surveyor's lines, over which people may walk back and forth without any consciousness of their presence. No part of this line can be made any more difficult to pass, by writing it down on paper, or parchment, as a national boundary. The fact of separation, if it comes, gives up, on the part of the seceding section, the fugitive slave clause, along with all other constitutional obligations upon the section seceded from, while I should expect no treaty stipulation would ever be made to take its place.

But there is another difficulty. The great interior region, bounded east by the Alleghanies, north by the British dominions, west by the Rocky mountains, and south by the line along which the culture of corn and cotton meets, and which includes part of Virginia, part of Tennessee, all of Kentucky, Ohio, Indiana, Michigan, Wisconsin, Illinois, Missouri, Kansas,

Iowa, Minnesota and the Territories of Dakota, Nebraska, and part of Colorado, already has above ten millions of people, and will have fifty millions within fifty years, if not prevented by any political folly or mistake. It contains more than one-third of the country owned by the United States—certainly more than one million of square miles. Once half as populous as Massachusetts already is, it would have more than seventy-five millions of people. A glance at the map shows that, territorially speaking, it is the great body of the republic. The other parts are but marginal borders to it, the magnificent region sloping west from the rocky mountains to the Pacific, being the deepest, and also the richest, in undeveloped resources. In the production of provisions, grains, grasses, and all which proceed from them, this great interior region is naturally one of the most important in the world. Ascertain from the statistics the small proportion of the region which has, as yet, been brought into cultivation, and also the large and rapidly increasing amount of its products, and we shall be overwhelmed with the magnitude of the prospect presented. And yet this region has no sea-coast, touches no ocean anywhere. As part of one nation, its people now find, and may forever find, their way to Europe by New York, to South America and Africa by New Orleans, and to Asia by San Francisco. But separate our common country into two nations, as designed by the present rebellion, and every man of this great interior region is thereby cut off from some one or more of these outlets, not, perhaps, by a physical barrier, but by embarrassing and onerous trade regulations.

And this is true, *wherever* a dividing, or boundary line, may be fixed. Place it between the now free and slave country, or place it south of Kentucky, or north of Ohio, and still the truth remains, that none south of it, can trade to any port or place north of it, and none north of it, can trade to any port or place south of it, except upon terms dictated by a government foreign to them. These outlets, cast, west, and south, are indispensable to the well-being of the people inhabiting, and to inhabit, this vast interior region. *Which* of the three may be the best, is no proper question. All, are better than either, and all, of right, belong to that people, and to their successors forever. True to themselves, they will not ask *where* a line of separation shall be, but will vow, rather, that there shall be no such line. Nor are the marginal regions less interested in these communications to, and through them, to the great outside world. They too, and each of them, must have access to this Egypt of the West, without paying toll at the crossing of any national boundary.

Our national strife springs not from our permanent part; not from the land we inhabit; not from our national homestead. There is no possible severing of this, but would multiply, and not mitigate, evils among us. In all its adaptations and aptitudes, it demands union, and abhors separation. In fact, it would, ere long, force reunion, however much of blood and treasure the separation might have cost.

Our strife pertains to ourselves—to the passing generations of men; and it can, without convulsion, be hushed forever with the passing of one generation.

In this view, I recommend the adoption of the following resolution and articles amendatory to the Constitution of the United States:

"*Resolved by the Senate and House of Representatives of the United States of America in Congress assembled,* (two thirds of both houses concurring,)

That the following articles be proposed to the legislatures (or conventions) of the several States as amendments to the Constitution of the United States, all or any of which articles when ratified by three-fourths of the said legislatures (or conventions) to be valid as part or parts of the said Constitution, viz:

"Article———.

"Every State, wherein slavery now exists, which shall abolish the same therein, at any time, or times, before the first day of January, in the year of our Lord one thousand and nine hundred, shall receive compensation from the United States as follows, to wit:

"The President of the United States shall deliver to every such State, bonds of the United States, bearing interest at the rate of —— per cent, per annum, to an amount equal to the aggregate sum of   for each slave shown to have been therein, by the eighth census of the United States, said bonds to be delivered to such State by instalments, or in one parcel, at the completion of the abolishment, accordingly as the same shall have been gradual, or at one time, within such State; and interest shall begin to run upon any such bond, only from the proper time of its delivery as aforesaid. Any State having received bonds as aforesaid, and afterwards reintroducing or tolerating slavery therein, shall refund to the United States the bonds so received, or the value thereof, and all interest paid thereon.

"Article———.

"All slaves who shall have enjoyed actual freedom by the chances of the war, at any time before the end of the rebellion, shall be forever free; but all owners of such, who shall not have been disloyal, shall be compensated for them, at the same rates as is provided for States adopting abolishment of slavery, but in such way, that no slave shall be twice accounted for.

"Article———.

"Congress may appropriate money, and otherwise provide, for coloniz-ing free colored persons, with their own consent, at any place or places without the United States."

I beg indulgence to discuss these proposed articles at some length. Without slavery the rebellion could never have existed; without slavery it could not continue.

Among the friends of the Union there is great diversity, of sentiment, and of policy, in regard to slavery, and the African race amongst us. Some would perpetuate slavery; some would abolish it suddenly, and without compensation; some would abolish it gradually, and with com-pensation; some would remove the freed people from us, and some would retain them with us; and there are yet other minor diversities. Because of these diversities, we waste much strength in struggles among ourselves. By mutual concession we should harmonize, and act together. This would be compromise; but it would be compromise among the friends, and not with the enemies of the Union. These articles are intended to embody a plan of such mutual concessions. If the plan shall be adopted, it is assumed that emancipation will follow, at least, in several of the States.

As to the first article, the main points are: first, the emancipation; secondly, the length of time for consummating it—thirty-seven years; and thirdly, the compensation.

The emancipation will be unsatisfactory to the advocates of perpetual slavery; but the length of time should greatly mitigate their dissatisfaction. The time spares both races from the evils of sudden derangement—in fact, from the necessity of any derangement—while most of those whose habitual course of thought will be disturbed by the measure will have passed away before its consummation. They will never see it. Another class will hail the prospect of emancipation, but will deprecate the length of time. They will feel that it gives too little to the now living slaves. But it really gives them much. It saves them from the vagrant destitution which must largely attend immediate emancipation in localities where their numbers are very great; and it gives the inspiring assurance that their posterity shall be free forever. The plan leaves to each State, choosing to act under it, to abolish slavery now, or at the end of the century, or at any intermediate time, or by degrees, extending over the whole or any part of the period; and it obliges no two states to proceed alike. It also provides for compensation, and generally the mode of making it. This, it would seem, must further mitigate the dissatisfaction of those who favor perpetual slavery, and especially of those who are to receive the compensation. Doubtless some of those who are to pay, and not to receive will object. Yet the measure is both just and economical. In a certain sense the liberation of slaves is the destruction of property—property acquired by descent, or by purchase, the same as any other property. It is no less true for having been often said, that the people of the south are not more responsible for the original introduction of this property, than are the people of the north; and when it is remembered how unhesitatingly we all use cotton and sugar, and share the profits of dealing in them, it may not be quite safe to say, that the south has been more responsible than the north for its continuance. If then, for a common object, this property is to be sacrificed is it not just that it be done at a common charge?

And if, with less money, or money more easily paid, we can preserve the benefits of the Union by this means, than we can by the war alone, is it not also economical to do it? Let us consider it then. Let us ascertain the sum we have expended in the war since compensated emancipation was proposed last March, and consider whether, if that measure had been promptly accepted, by even some of the slave States, the same sum would not have done more to close the war, than has been otherwise done. If so the measure would save money, and, in that view, would be a prudent and economical measure. Certainly it is not so easy to pay *something* as it is to pay *nothing*; but it is easier to pay a *large* sum than it is to pay a larger one. And it is easier to pay any sum *when* we are able, than it is to pay it *before* we are able. The war requires large sums, and requires them at once. The aggregate sum necessary for compensated emancipation, of course, would be large. But it would require no ready cash; nor the bonds even, any faster than the emancipation progresses. This might not, and probably would not, close before the end of the thirty-seven years. At that time we shall probably have a hundred millions of people to share the burden, instead of thirty one millions, as now. And not only so, but the increase of our population may be expected to continue for a long time after that period, as rapidly as before; because our territory will not have become full. I do not state this inconsiderately. At the same ratio of increase which we have maintained, on an average, from our first national census, in 1790, until that of 1860, we should, in 1900, have a population of 103,208,415. And why may we not continue that ratio far beyond that period? Our abundant room—our broad national homestead—is our ample resource.* * *

* * *

The proposed emancipation would shorten the war, perpetuate peace, insure this increase of population, and proportionately the wealth of the country. With these, we should pay all the emancipation would cost, together with our other debt, easier than we should pay our other debt, without it. If we had allowed our old national debt to run at six per cent, per annum, simple interest, from the end of our revolutionary struggle until to day, without paying anything on either principal or interest, each man of us would owe less upon that debt now, than each man owed upon it then; and this because our increase of men, through the whole period, has been greater than six per cent.; has run faster than the interest upon the debt. Thus, time alone relieves a debtor nation, so long as its population increases faster than unpaid interest accumulates on its debt.

This fact would be no excuse for delaying payment of what is justly due; but it shows the great importance of time in this connexion—the great advantage of a policy by which we shall not have to pay until we number a hundred millions, what, by a different policy, we would have to pay now, when we number but thirty one millions. In a word, it shows that a dollar will be much harder to pay for the war, than will be a dollar for emancipation on the proposed plan. And then the latter will cost no blood, no precious life. It will be a saving of both.

As to the second article, I think it would be impracticable to return to bondage the class of persons therein contemplated. Some of them, doubtless, in the property sense, belong to loyal owners; and hence, provision is made in this article for compensating such.

The third article relates to the future of the freed people. It does not oblige, but merely authorizes, Congress to aid in colonizing such as may consent. This ought not to be regarded as objectionable, on the one hand, or on the other, in so much as it comes to nothing, unless by the mutual consent of the people to be deported, and the American voters, through their representatives in Congress.

I cannot make it better known than it already is, that I strongly favor colonization. And yet I wish to say there is an objection urged against free colored persons remaining in the country, which is largely imaginary, if not sometimes malicious.

It is insisted that their presence would injure, and displace white labor and white laborers. If there ever could be a proper time for mere catch arguments, that time surely is not now. In times like the present, men should utter nothing for which they would not willingly be responsible through time and in eternity. Is it true, then, that colored people can displace any more white labor, by being free, than by remaining slaves? If they stay in their old places, they jostle no white laborers; if they leave their old places, they leave them open to white laborers. Logically, there is neither more nor less of it. Emancipation, even without deportation, would probably enhance the wages of white labor, and, very surely, would not reduce them. Thus, the customary amount of labor would still have to be performed; the freed people would surely not do more than their old proportion of it, and very probably, for a time, would do less, leaving an increased part to white laborers, bringing their labor into greater demand, and, consequently, enhancing the wages of it. With deportation, even to a limited extent, enhanced wages to white labor is mathematically certain. Labor is like any other commodity in the market—increase the demand for it, and you increase the price of it. Reduce the supply of black labor, by colonizing the black laborer out of the country, and, by precisely so much, you increase the demand for, and wages of, white labor.

But it is dreaded that the freed people will swarm forth, and cover the whole land? Are they not already in the land? Will liberation make them any more numerous? Equally distributed among the whites of the whole country, and there would be but one colored to seven whites. Could the one, in any way, greatly disturb the seven? There are many communities now, having more than one free colored person, to seven whites; and this, without any apparent consciousness of evil from it. The District of Columbia, and the States of Maryland and Delaware, are all in this condition. The District has more than one free colored to six whites; and yet, in its frequent petitions to Congress, I believe it has never presented the presence of free colored persons as one of its grievances. But why should emancipation south, send the free people north? People, of any color, seldom run, unless there be something to run from. *Heretofore* colored people, to some extent, have fled north from bondage; and *now*, perhaps, from both bondage and destitution. But if gradual emancipation and deportation be adopted, they will have neither to flee from. Their old masters will give them wages at least until new laborers can be procured; and the freed men, in turn, will gladly give their labor for the wages, till new homes can be found for them, in congenial climes, and with people of their own blood and race. This proposition can be trusted on the mutual interests involved. And, in any event, cannot the north decide for itself, whether to receive them?

Again, as practice proves more than theory, in any case, has there been any irruption of colored people northward, because of the abolishment of slavery in this District last spring?

What I have said of the proportion of free colored persons to the whites, in the District, is from the census of 1860, having no reference to persons called contrabands, nor to those made free by the act of Congress abolishing slavery here.

The plan consisting of these articles is recommended, not but that a restoration of the national authority would be accepted without its adoption.

Nor will the war, nor proceedings under the proclamation of September 22, 1862, be stayed because of the *recommendation* of this plan. Its timely *adoption*, I doubt not, would bring restoration and thereby stay both.

And, notwithstanding this plan, the recommendation that Congress provide by law for compensating any State which may adopt emancipation, before this plan shall have been acted upon, is hereby earnestly renewed. Such would be only an advance part of the plan, and the same arguments apply to both.

This plan is recommended as a means, not in exclusion of, but additional to, all others for restoring and preserving the national authority throughout the Union. The subject is presented exclusively in its economical aspect. The plan would, I am confident, secure peace more speedily, and maintain it more permanently, than can be done by force alone; while all it would cost, considering amounts, and manner of payment, and times of payment, would be easier paid than will be the additional cost of the war, if we rely solely upon force. It is much—very much—that it would cost no blood at all.

The plan is proposed as permanent constitutional law. It cannot become such without the concurrence of, first, two-thirds of Congress, and, afterwards, three-fourths of the States. The requisite three-fourths of the States will necessarily include seven of the Slave states. Their concurrence, if obtained, will give assurance of their severally adopting emancipation, at no very distant day, upon the new constitutional terms. This assurance would end the struggle now, and save the Union forever.

I do not forget the gravity which should characterize a paper addressed to the Congress of the nation by the Chief Magistrate of the nation. Nor do I forget that some of you are my seniors, nor that many of you have more experience than I, in the conduct of public affairs. Yet I trust that in view of the great responsibility resting upon me, you will perceive no want of respect to yourselves, in any undue earnestness I may seem to display.

Is it doubted, then, that the plan I propose, if adopted, would shorten the war, and thus lessen its expenditure of money and of blood? Is it doubted that it would restore the national authority and national prosperity, and perpetuate both indefinitely? Is it doubted that we here—Congress and Executive—can secure its adoption? Will not the good people respond to a united, and earnest appeal from us? Can we, can they, by any other means, so certainly, or so speedily, assure these vital objects? We can succeed only by concert. It is not "can *any* of us *imagine* better?" but "can we *all* do better?" Object whatsoever is possible, still the question recurs "can we do better?" The dogmas of the quiet past, are inadequate to the stormy present. The occasion is piled high with difficulty, and we must rise with the occasion. As our case is new, so we must think anew, and act anew. We must disenthrall ourselves, and then we shall save our country.

Fellow-citizens, *we* cannot escape history. We of this Congress and this administration, will be remembered in spite of ourselves. No personal significance, or insignificance, can spare one or another of us. The fiery trial through which we pass, will light us down, in honor or dishonor, to the latest generation. We *say* we are for the Union. The world will not forget that we say this. We know how to save the Union. The world knows we do know how to save it. We—even *we here*—hold the power, and bear the responsibility. In *giving* freedom to the *slave*, we *assure* freedom to the *free*—honorable alike in what we give, and what we preserve. We shall nobly save, or meanly lose, the last best, hope of earth. Other means may succeed; this could not fail. The way is plain, peaceful, generous, just—a way which, if followed, the world will forever applaud, and God must forever bless.

December 1, 1862.

Congratulations to the Army of the Potomac

Executive Mansion, Washington, December 22, 1862

To the Army of the Potomac: I have just read your Commanding General's preliminary report of the battle of Fredericksburg.[1] Although you were not successful, the attempt was not an error, nor the failure other than an accident. The courage with which you, in an open field, maintained the contest against an entrenched foe, and the consummate skill and success with which you crossed and re-crossed the river, in face of the enemy, show that you possess all the qualities of a great army, which will yet give victory to the cause of the country and of popular government. Condoling with the mourners for the dead, and sympathizing with the severely wounded, I congratulate you that the number of both is comparatively so small.

I tender to you, officers and soldiers, the thanks of the nation.

December 22, 1862

Final Emancipation Proclamation

By the President of the United States of America:
A Proclamation

Whereas, on the twentysecond day of September, in the year of our Lord one thousand eight hundred and sixty two, a proclamation was issued by the President of the United States, containing, among other things, the following, towit:

> "That on the first day of January, in the year of our Lord one thousand eight hundred and sixty-three, all persons held as slaves within any State or designated part of a State, the people whereof shall then be in rebellion against the United States, shall be then, thenceforward, and forever free; and the Executive Government of the United States, including the military and naval authority thereof, will recognize and maintain the freedom of such persons, and will do no act or acts to repress such persons, or any of them, in any efforts they may make for their actual freedom.
>
> "That the Executive will, on the first day of January aforesaid, by proclamation, designate the States and parts of States, if any, in which the people thereof, respectively, shall then be in rebellion against the United States; and the fact that any State, or the people thereof, shall on that day be, in good faith, represented in the Congress of the United States by members chosen thereto at elections wherein a majority of the qualified voters of such State shall have participated, shall, in the absence of strong countervailing testimony, be deemed conclusive evidence that such State, and the people thereof, are not then in rebellion against the United States."

---

1. The Battle of Fredericksburg, Virginia (December 11–15, 1862) was a lopsided victory for the South. Confederate forces under Robert E. Lee, protected by a stone wall atop a ridge known as Marye's Heights, resisted a frontal assault by the Union Army under Ambrose Burnside (1824–1881), which stormed the hill bravely but futilely. The Union suffered 12,653 casualties, the Confederacy 5,377.

Now, therefore I, Abraham Lincoln, President of the United States, by virtue of the power in me vested as Commander-in-Chief, of the Army and Navy of the United States in time of actual armed rebellion against authority and government of the United States, and as a fit and necessary war measure for suppressing said rebellion, do, on this first day of January, in the year of our Lord one thousand eight hundred and sixty three, and in accordance with my purpose so to do publicly proclaimed for the full period of one hundred days, from the day first above mentioned, order and designate as the States and parts of States wherein the people thereof respectively, are this day in rebellion against the United States, the following, towit:

Arkansas, Texas, Louisiana, (except the Parishes of St. Bernard, Plaquemines, Jefferson, St. Johns, St. Charles, St. James, Ascension, Assumption, Terrebonne, Lafourche, St. Mary, St. Martin, and Orleans, including the City of New-Orleans) Mississippi, Alabama, Florida, Georgia, South-Carolina, North-Carolina, and Virginia, (except the fortyeight counties designated as West Virginia, and also the counties of Berkley, Accomac, Northampton, Elizabeth-City, York, Princess Ann, and Norfolk, including the cities of Norfolk & Portsmouth); and which excepted parts are, for the present, left precisely as if this proclamation were not issued.

And by virtue of the power, and for the purpose aforesaid, I do order and declare that all persons held as slaves within said designated States, and parts of States, are, and hence-forward shall be free; and that the Executive government of the United States, including the military and naval authorities thereof, will recognize and maintain the freedom of said persons.

And I hereby enjoin upon the people so declared to be free to abstain from all violence, unless in necessary self-defence; and I recommend to them that, in all cases when allowed, they labor faithfully for reasonable wages.

And I further declare and make known, that such persons of suitable condition, will be received into the armed service of the United States to garrison forts, positions, stations, and other places, and to man vessels of all sorts in said service.

And upon this act, sincerely believed to be an act of justice, warranted by the Constitution, upon military necessity, I invoke the considerate judgment of mankind, and the gracious favor of Almighty God.

In witness whereof, I have hereunto set my hand and caused the seal of the United States to be affixed.

Done at the City of Washington, this first day of January, in the year of our Lord one thousand eight hundred and sixty three, and of the Independence of the United States of America the eighty-seventh.

By the President: ABRAHAM LINCOLN

WILLIAM H. SEWARD, Secretary of State.

January 1, 1863

To Caleb Russell and Sallie A. Fenton[1]

Executive Mansion,
My Good Friends   Washington, January 5, 1863
The Honorable Senator Harlan has just placed in my hands your letter of
the 27th of December which I have read with pleasure and gratitude.

It is most cheering and encouraging for me to know that in the efforts
which I have made and am making for the restoration of a righteous peace
to our country, I am upheld and sustained by the good wishes and prayers
of God's people. No one is more deeply than myself aware that without
His favor our highest wisdom is but as foolishness and that our most
strenuous efforts would avail nothing in the shadow of His displeasure. I
am conscious of no desire for my country's welfare, that is not in consonance with His will, and of no plan upon which we may not ask His blessing. It seems to me that if there be one subject upon which all good men
may unitedly agree, it is imploring the gracious favor of the God of Nations
upon the struggles our people are making for the preservation of their precious birthright of civil and religious liberty. Very truly Your friend

To John A. McClernand[1]

                                            Executive Mansion,
Major General McClernand   Washington, January 8. 1863.
My dear Sir Your interesting communication by the hand of Major
Scates[2] is received. I never did ask more, nor ever was willing to accept
less, than for all the States, and the people thereof, to take and hold their
places, and their rights, in the Union, under the Constitution of the
United States. For this alone have I felt authorized to struggle; and I seek
neither more nor less now. Still, to use a coarse, but an expressive figure,
broken eggs can not be mended. I have issued the emancipation proclamation, and I can not retract it.

After the commencement of hostilities I struggled nearly a year and a
half to get along without touching the "institution"; and when finally I
conditionally determined to touch it, I gave a hundred days fair notice of
my purpose, to all the States and people, within which time they could
have turned it wholly aside, by simply again becoming good citizens of the
United States. They chose to disregard it, and I made the peremptory proclamation on what appeared to me to be a military necessity. And being
made, it must stand. As to the States not included in it, of course they can
have their rights in the Union as of old. Even the people of the states
included, if they choose, need not to be hurt by it. Let them adopt systems
of apprenticeship for the colored people, conforming substantially to the
most approved plans of gradual emancipation; and, with the aid they can
have from the general government, they may be nearly as well off, in this

---

1. Iowa Quakers wrote a letter on December 27, 1862, to Senator James Harlan of Iowa (1820–
1899), expressing approval of the then-forthcoming Emancipation Proclamation.
1. Union general (1812–1900) who had strongly criticized the Emancipation Proclamation.
2. Walter B. Scates (1808–1886), a major who served under General McClernand.

respect, as if the present trouble had not occurred, and much better off than they can possibly be if the contest continues persistently.

As to any dread of my having a "purpose to enslave, or exterminate, the whites of the South," I can scarcely believe that such dread exists. It is too absurd. I believe you can be my personal witness that no man is less to be dreaded for undue severity, in any case.

If the friends you mention really wish to have peace upon the old terms, they should act at once. Every day makes the case more difficult. They can so act, with entire safety, so far as I am concerned.

I think you would better not make this letter public; but you may rely confidently on my standing by whatever I have said in it. Please write me if any thing more comes to light. Yours very truly

To Joseph Hooker[1]

Major General Hooker: Executive Mansion,
General.   Washington, January 26, 1863.
I have placed you at the head of the Army of the Potomac. Of course I have done this upon what appear to me to be sufficient reasons. And yet I think it best for you to know that there are some things in regard to which, I am not quite satisfied with you. I believe you to be a brave and a skilful soldier, which, of course, I like. I also believe you do not mix politics with your profession, in which you are right. You have confidence in yourself, which is a valuable, if not an indispensable quality. You are ambitious, which, within reasonable bounds, does good father than harm. But I think that during Gen. Burnside's[2] command of the Army, you have taken counsel of your ambition, and thwarted him as much as you could, in which you did a great wrong to the country, and to a most meritorious and honorable brother officer. I have heard, in such way as to believe it, of your recently saying that both the Army and the Government needed a Dictator. Of course it was not *for* this, but in spite of it, that I have given you the command. Only those generals who gain successes, can set up dictators. What I now ask of you is military success, and I will risk the dictatorship. The government will support you to the utmost of it's ability, which is neither more nor less than it has done and will do for all commanders. I much fear that the spirit which you have aided to infuse into the Army, of criticising their Commander, and withholding confidence from him, will now turn upon you. I shall assist you as far as I can, to put it down. Neither you, nor Napoleon, if he were alive again, could get any good out of an army, while such a spirit prevails in it.

And now, beware of rashness. Beware of rashness, but with energy, and sleepless vigilance, go forward, and give us victories. Yours very truly

---

1. Union general (1814–1879) who had several successes in the war but who in May 1863 would suffer a major defeat at the hands of Robert E. Lee at Chancellorsville.
2. Ambrose E. Burnside (1824–1881) commanded an expeditionary force that secured part of North Carolina, leading to his promotion to Major General on March 19, 1862.

To William S. Rosecrans[1]

Executive Mansion, Washington,
Major General Rosecrans.   February 17, 1863.
My dear Sir: In no other way does the enemy give us so much trouble, at so little expence to himself, as by the *raids* of rapidly moving small bodies of troops (largely, if not wholly, mounted) harrassing, and discouraging loyal residents, supplying themselves with provisions, clothing, horses, and the like, surprising and capturing small detachments of our forces, and breaking our communications. And this will increase just in proportion as his larger armies shall weaken, and wane. Nor can these raids be successfully met by even larger forces of our own, of the same kind, acting merely on the *defensive*. I think we should organize proper forces, and make *counter-raids*. We should not capture so much of supplies from them, as they have done from us; but it would trouble them more to repair railroads and bridges than it does us. What think you of trying to get up such a corps in your army? Could you do it without any, or many additional troops (which we have not to give you) provided we furnish horses, suitable arms, and other appointments? Please consider this, not as an order, but as a suggestion. Yours truly

> While I wish the required arms to be furnished to Gen. Rosecrans, I have made no promise on the subject, except what you can find in the within copy of letter

March 27, 1863.

To Andrew Johnson[1]

Private
Hon. Andrew Johnson   Executive Mansion,
My dear Sir: Washington, March 26. 1863.
I am told you have at least *thought* of raising a negro military force. In my opinion the country now needs no specific thing so much as some man of your ability, and position, to go to this work. When I speak of your position, I mean that of an eminent citizen of a slave-state, and himself a slaveholder. The colored population is the great *available* and yet *unavailed* of, force for restoring the Union. The bare sight of fifty thousand armed, and drilled black soldiers on the banks of the Mississippi, would end the rebellion at once. And who doubts that we can present that sight, if we but take hold in earnest? If you *have* been thinking of it please do not dismiss the thought. Yours truly

---

1. Union general (1819–1898) who, like Hooker, was generally successful in the western theater but had one notorious defeat; in Rosencrans's case, at Chickamauga in September 1863.
1. A Tennessee Democrat (1808–1875) who was Lincoln's running mate in 1864 and served as his vice president, succeeding him as president after the assassination of Lincoln in April 1865.

Speech to Indian Chiefs, Washington, D.C.[1]

"You have all spoken of the strange sights you see here, among your pale-faced brethren; the very great number of people that you see; the big wigwams; the difference between our people and your own. But you have seen but a very small part of the pale-faced people. You may wonder when I tell you that there are people here in this wigwam, now looking at you, who have come from other countries a great deal farther off than you have come.

"We pale-faced people think that this world is a great, round ball, and we have people here of the pale-faced family who have come almost from the other side of it to represent their nations here and conduct their friendly intercourse with us, as you now come from your part of the round ball."

Here a globe was introduced, and the President, laying his hand upon it, said:

"One of our learned men will now explain to you our notions about this great ball, and show you where you live."

Professor Henry[2] then gave the delegation a detailed and interesting explanation of the formation of the earth, showing how much of it was water and how much was land; and pointing out the countries with which we had intercourse. He also showed them the position of Washington and that of their own country, from which they had come.

The President then said:

"We have people now present from all parts of the globe—here, and here, and here. There is a great difference between this pale-faced people and their red brethren, both as to numbers and the way in which they live. We know not whether your own situation is best for your race, but this is what has made the difference in our way of living.

"The pale-faced people are numerous and prosperous because they cultivate the earth, produce bread, and depend upon the products of the earth rather than wild game for a subsistence.

"This is the chief reason of the difference; but there is another. Although we are now engaged in a great war between one another, we are not, as a race, so much disposed to fight and kill one another as our red brethren.

"You have asked for my advice. I really am not capable of advising you whether, in the providence of the Great Spirit, who is the great Father of us all, it is best for you to maintain the habits and customs of your race, or adopt a new mode of life.

"I can only say that I can see no way in which your race is to become as numerous and prosperous as the white race except by living as they do, by the cultivation of the earth.

"It is the object of this Government to be on terms of peace with you, and with all our red brethren. We constantly endeavor to be so. We make treaties with you, and will try to observe them; and if our children should sometimes behave badly, and violate these treaties, it is against our wish.

---

1. Among the delegation addressed here are chiefs from the Apache, Arapaho, Caddo, Cheyenne, Comanche, and Kiowa tribes.
2. Joseph Henry (1797–1878), physicist, secretary of the Smithsonian Institution, and Professor of Natural Philosophy at Princeton.

"You know it is not always possible for any father to have his children do precisely as he wishes them to do.

"In regard to being sent back to your own country, we have an officer, the Commissioner of Indian Affairs, who will take charge of that matter, and make the necessary arrangements."

The President's remarks were received with frequent marks of applause and approbation. "Ugh," "Aha" sounded along the line as the interpreter proceeded, and their countenances gave evident tokens of satisfaction.

March 27, 1863

Proclamation Appointing a National Fast Day[1]

By the President of the United States of America.

A Proclamation.

Whereas, the Senate of the United States, devoutly recognizing the Supreme Authority and just Government of Almighty God, in all the affairs of men and of nations, has, by a resolution, requested the President to designate and set apart a day for National prayer and humiliation:

And whereas it is the duty of nations as well as of men, to own their dependence upon the overruling power of God, to confess their sins and transgressions, in humble sorrow, yet with assured hope that genuine repentance will lead to mercy and pardon; and to recognize the sublime truth, announced in the Holy Scriptures and proven by all history, that those nations only are blessed whose God is the Lord:

And, insomuch as we know that, by His divine law, nations like individuals are subjected to punishments and chastisements in this world, may we not justly fear that the awful calamity of civil war, which now desolates the land, may be but a punishment, inflicted upon us, for our presumptuous sins, to the needful end of our national reformation as a whole People? We have been the recipients of the choicest bounties of Heaven. We have been preserved, these many years, in peace and prosperity. We have grown in numbers, wealth and power, as no other nation has ever grown. But we have forgotten God. We have forgotten the gracious hand which preserved us in peace, and multiplied and enriched and strengthened us; and we have vainly imagined, in the deceitfulness of our hearts, that all these blessings were produced by some superior wisdom and virtue of our own. Intoxicated with unbroken success, we have become too self-sufficient to feel the necessity of redeeming and preserving grace, too proud to pray to the God that made us!

It behooves us then, to humble ourselves before the offended Power, to confess our national sins, and to pray for clemency and forgiveness.

Now, therefore, in compliance with the request, and fully concurring in the views of the Senate, I do, by this my proclamation, designate and set apart Thursday, the 30th. day of April, 1863, as a day of national humiliation, fasting, and prayer. And I do hereby request all the People to abstain, on that day, from their ordinary secular pursuits, and to unite, at

1. This proclamation resulted from a Senate resolution, passed on March 3, asking the president to proclaim a day of "national prayer and humiliation." The resolution was introduced by Senator James Harlan, a devout Methodist.

their several places of public worship and their respective homes, in keeping the day holy to the Lord, and devoted to the humble discharge of the religious duties proper to that solemn occasion.

All this being done, in sincerity and truth, let us then rest humbly in the hope authorized by the Divine teachings, that the united cry of the Nation will be heard on high, and answered with blessings, no less than the pardon of our national sins, and the restoration of our now divided and suffering Country, to its former happy condition of unity and peace.

In witness whereof, I have hereunto set my hand and caused the seal of the United States to be affixed.

Done at the City of Washington, this thirtieth day of March, in the year of our Lord one thousand eight hundred and sixty-three, and of the Independence of the United States the eighty seventh.

By the President: ABRAHAM LINCOLN

WILLIAM H. SEWARD, Secretary of State.

March 30, 1863

Resolution on Slavery

Whereas, while *heretofore*, States, and Nations, have tolerated slavery, *recently*, for the first in the world, an attempt has been made to construct a new Nation, upon the basis of, and with the primary, and fundamental object to maintain, enlarge, and perpetuate human slavery, therefore,

Resolved, That no such embryo State should ever be recognized by, or admitted into, the family of christian and civilized nations; and that all christian and civilized men everywhere should, by all lawful means, resist to the utmost, such recognition or admission.

April 15, 1863

To Joseph Hooker

Head-Quarters,
Major General Hooker.   Army of the Potomac,
My dear Sir   May. 7 1863.

The recent movement of your army is ended without effecting it's object, except perhaps some important breakings of the enemies communications. What next? If possible I would be very glad of another movement early enough to give us some benefit from the fact of the enemies communications being broken, but neither for this reason or any other, do I wish anything done in desperation or rashness. An early movement would also help to supersede the bad moral effect of the recent one, which is sure to be considerably injurious. Have you already in your mind a plan wholly, or partially formed? If you have, prossecute it without interference from me. If you have not, please inform me, so that I, incompetent as I may be, can try assist in the formation of some plan for the Army. Yours as ever

Reply to Members of the Presbyterian General Assembly[1]

It has been my happiness to receive testimonies of a similar nature, from I believe, all denominations of Christians. They are all loyal, but perhaps not in the same degree, or in the same numbers; but I think they all claim to be loyal. This to me is most gratifying, because from the beginning I saw that the issues of our great struggle depended on the Divine interposition and favor. If we had that, all would be well. The proportions of this rebellion were not for a long time understood. I saw that it involved the greatest difficulties, and would call forth all the powers of the whole country. The end is not yet.

The point made in your paper is well taken as to "the Government" and the "administration" in whose hands are those interests. I fully appreciate its correctness and justice. In my administration I might have committed some errors. It would be, indeed, remarkable if I had not. I have acted according to my best judgment in every case. The views expressed by the Committee accord with my own; and on this principle "the Government" is to be supported though the administration may not in every case wisely act. As a pilot, I have used my best exertions to keep afloat our ship of State, and shall be glad to resign my trust at the appointed time to another pilot more skillful and successful than I may prove. In every case, and at all hazards, the Government must be perpetuated. Relying, as I do, upon the Almighty Power, and encouraged as I am by these resolutions which you have just read, with the support which I receive from Christian men, I shall not hesitate to use all the means at my control to secure the termination of this rebellion, and will hope for success.

I sincerely thank you for this interview, this pleasant mode of presentation, and the General Assembly for their patriotic support in these resolutions.

June 2, 1863

To Erastus Corning[1] and Others

Executive Mansion
Washington
Hon. Erastus Corning & others   June 12, 1863.
Gentlemen Your letter of May 19th. inclosing the resolutions of a public meeting held at Albany, N.Y. on the 16th. of the same month, was received several days ago.

The resolutions, as I understand them, are resolvable into two propositions—first, the expression of a purpose to sustain the cause of the

1. A response to resolutions in support of the administration presented to Lincoln on June 2 by a committee of sixty-five members of the General Assembly of the Presbyterian Church.
1. An Albany, New York, businessman and Democratic politician (1794–1872) who had organized a protest meeting against Lincoln's military arrests and his suspension of habeas corpus, which Corning's group considered despotic and unconstitutional. Lincoln, in this long letter of reply, defended his actions on constitutional grounds, but Corning was not convinced. He and his committee wrote Lincoln on June 30: "Your claim to have found not outside, but within the

Union, to secure peace through victory, and to support the administration in every constitutional, and lawful measure to suppress the rebellion; and secondly, a declaration of censure upon the administration for supposed unconstitutional action such as the making of military arrests. And, from the two propositions a third is deduced, which is, that the gentlemen composing the meeting are resolved on doing their part to maintain our common government and country, despite the folly or wickedness, as they may conceive, of any administration. This position is eminently patriotic, and as such, I thank the meeting, and congratulate the nation for it. My own purpose is the same; so that the meeting and myself have a common object, and can have no difference, except in the choice of means or measures, for effecting that object.

And here I ought to close this paper, and would close it, if there were no apprehension that more injurious consequences, than any merely personal to myself, might follow the censures systematically cast upon me for doing what, in my view of duty, I could not forbear. The resolutions promise to support me in every constitutional and lawful measure to suppress the rebellion; and I have not knowingly employed, nor shall knowingly employ, any other. But the meeting, by their resolutions, assert and argue, that certain military arrests and proceedings following them for which I am ultimately responsible, are unconstitutional. I think they are not. The resolutions quote from the constitution, the definition of treason; and also the limiting safe-guards and guarantees therein provided for the citizen, on trials for treason, and on his being held to answer for capital or otherwise infamous crimes, and, in criminal prosecutions, his right to a speedy and public trial by an impartial jury. They proceed to resolve "That these safe-guards of the rights of the citizen against the pretentions of arbitrary power, were intended more *especially* for his protection in times of civil commotion." And, apparently, to demonstrate the proposition, the resolutions proceed "They were secured substantially to the English people, *after* years of protracted civil war, and were adopted into our constitution at the *close* of the revolution." Would not the demonstration have been better, if it could have been truly said that these safe-guards had been adopted, and applied *during* the civil wars and *during* our Revolution, instead of *after* the one, and at the *close* of the other. I too am devotedly for them after civil war, and before civil war, and at all times "except when, in cases of Rebellion or Invasion, the public Safety may require" their suspension. The resolutions proceed to tell us that these safe-guards "have stood the test of seventysix years of trial, under our republican system, under circumstances which show that while they constitute the foundation of all free government, they are the elements of the enduring stability of the Republic." No one denies that they have so stood the test up to the beginning of the present rebellion if we except a certain matter at New-Orleans hereafter to be mentioned; nor does any

---

Constitution, a principle or germ of arbitrary power, which in time of war expands at once into an absolute sovereignty, wielded by one man; so that liberty perishes, or is dependent on his will, his discretion or his caprice. This extraordinary doctrine, you claim to derive wholly from that clause of the Constitution, which, in case of invasion or rebellion, permits the writ of habeas corpus to be suspended. Upon this ground your whole argument is based. You must permit us, to say to you with all due respect, but with the earnestness demanded by the occasion, that the American people will never acquiesce in this doctrine."

one question that they will stand the same test much longer after the rebellion closes. But these provisions of the constitution have no application to the case we have in hand, because the arrests complained of were not made for treason—that is, not for *the* treason defined in the constitution, and upon the conviction of which, the punishment is death—nor yet were they made to hold persons to answer for any capital, or otherwise infamous crimes; nor were the proceedings following, in any constitutional or legal sense, "criminal prossecutions." The arrests were made on totally different grounds, and the proceedings following, accorded with the grounds of the arrests. Let us consider the real case with which we are dealing, and apply to it the parts of the constitution plainly made for such cases.

Prior to my instalation here it had been inculcated that any State had a lawful right to secede from the national Union, and that it would be expedient to exercise the right, whenever the devotees of the doctrine should fail to elect a President to their own liking. I was elected contrary to their liking; and accordingly, so far as it was legally possible, they had taken seven states out of the Union, had seized many of the United States Forts, and had fired upon the United States' Flag, all before I was inaugerated, and, of course, before I had done any official act whatever. The rebellion, thus began, soon ran into the present civil war; and, in certain respects, it began on very unequal terms between the parties. The insurgents had been preparing for it more than thirty years, while the government had taken no steps to resist them. The former had carefully considered all the means which could be turned to their account. It undoubtedly was a well pondered reliance with them that in their own unrestricted effort to destroy Union, constitution, and law, all together, the government would, in great degree, be restrained by the same constitution and law, from arresting their progress. Their sympathizers pervaded all departments of the government and nearly all communities of the people. From this material, under cover of "Liberty of speech," "Liberty of the press," and "Habeas corpus," they hoped to keep on foot amongst us a most efficient corps of spies, informers, suppliers, and aiders and abettors of their cause in a thousand ways. They knew that in times such as they were inaugerating, by the constitution itself, the "Habeas corpus" might be suspended; but they also knew they had friends who would make a question as to *who* was to suspend it; meanwhile their spies and others might remain at large to help on their cause. Or if, as has happened, the executive should suspend the writ, without ruinous waste of time, instances of arresting innocent persons might occur, as are always likely to occur in such cases; and then a clamor could be raised in regard to this, which might be, at least, of some service to the insurgent cause. It needed no very keen perception to discover this part of the enemies' programme, so soon as by open hostilities their machinery was fairly put in motion. Yet, thoroughly imbued with a reverence for the guaranteed rights of individuals, I was slow to adopt the strong measures, which by degrees I have been forced to regard as being within the exceptions of the constitution, and as indispensable to the public Safety. Nothing is better known to history than that courts of justice are utterly incompetent to such cases. Civil courts are organized chiefly for trials of individuals, or, at most, a few individuals acting in concert; and this in quiet times, and on charges of crimes well defined in the law. Even in times of peace, bands of horse-thieves and robbers frequently grow too numerous and powerful for the ordinary courts of justice. But what comparison, in numbers, have such bands ever borne to the insurgent sympathizers even in many of the loyal States? Again, a jury too frequently have at least one member, more ready to hang the panel than to hang the traitor. And yet, again, he who dissuades one man from volunteering, or induces one soldier to desert, weakens the Union cause as much as he who kills a union soldier in battle. Yet this dissuasion, or inducement, may be so conducted as to be no defined crime of which any civil court would take cognizance.

Ours is a case of Rebellion—so called by the resolutions before me—in fact, a clear, flagrant, and gigantic case of Rebellion; and the provision of the constitution that "The privilege of the writ of Habeas corpus shall not be suspended, unless when in cases of Rebellion or Invasion, the public Safety may require it" is *the* provision which specially applies to our present case. This provision plainly attests the understanding of those who made the constitution that ordinary courts of justice are inadequate to "cases of Rebellion"—attests their purpose that in such cases, men may be held in custody whom the courts acting on ordinary rules, would discharge. Habeas corpus, does not discharge men who are proved to be guilty of defined crime; and its suspension is allowed by the constitution on purpose that men may be arrested and held, who cannot be proved to be guilty of defined crime, "when, in cases of Rebellion or Invasion the public Safety may require it." This is precisely our present case—a case of Rebellion, wherein the public Safety *does* require the suspension. Indeed, arrests by process of courts, and arrests in cases of rebellion, do not proceed altogether upon the same basis. The former is directed at the small per centage of ordinary and continuous perpetration of crime; while the latter is directed at sudden and extensive uprisings against the government, which, at most, will succeed or fail, in no great length of time. In the latter case, arrests are made, not so much for what has been done, as for what probably would be done. The latter is more for the preventive and less for the vindictive than the former. In such cases the purposes of men are much more easily understood, than in cases of ordinary crime. The man who stands by and says nothing when the peril of his government is discussed, can not be misunderstood. If not hindered, he is sure to help the enemy. Much more, if he talks ambiguously—talks for his country with "buts" and "ifs" and "ands." Of how little value the constitutional provision I have quoted will be rendered, if arrests shall never be made until defined crimes shall have been committed, may be illustrated by a few notable examples. Gen. John C. Breckinridge, Gen. Robert E. Lee, Gen. Joseph E. Johnston, Gen. John B. Magruder, Gen. William B. Preston, Gen. Simon B. Buckner, and Commodore Franklin Buchanan,[2] now occupying the very highest places in the rebel war service, were all within the power of the government since the rebellion began, and were

2. Joseph E. Johnston (1807–1891), Confederate general; John B. Magruder (1807–1871), Confederate general; William B. Preston (1805–1862), Virginia lawyer who submitted the state's ordinance for secession on April 16, 1861, and later served in the Confederate States Congress; Simon B.. Buckner (1823–1914), Kentuckian who declined service in the Union Army and later served as a Confederate brigadier general; Franklin Buchanan (1800–1874), Confederate Navy captain.

nearly as well known to be traitors then as now. Unquestionably if we had seized and held them, the insurgent cause would be much weaker. But no one of them had then committed any crime defined in the law. Every one of them if arrested would have been discharged on Habeas Corpus, were the writ allowed to operate. In view of these and similar cases, I think the time not unlikely to come when I shall be blamed for having made too few arrests rather than too many.

By the third resolution, the meeting indicate their opinion that military arrests may be constitutional in localities where rebellion actually exists; but that such arrests are unconstitutional in localities where rebellion or insurrection does not actually exist. They insist that such arrests shall not be made "outside of the lines of necessary military occupation, and the scenes of insurrection." In asmuch, however, as the constitution itself makes no such distinction, I am unable to believe that there is any such constitutional distinction. I concede that the class of arrests complained of, can be constitutional only when, in cases of Rebellion or Invasion, the public Safety may require them; and I insist that in such cases they are constitutional *wherever* the public safety does require them—as well in places to which they may prevent the rebellion extending, as in those where it may be already prevailing—as well where they may restrain mischievous interference with the raising and supplying of armies, to suppress the rebellion, as where the rebellion may actually be—as well where they may restrain the enticing men out of the army, as where they would prevent mutiny in the army—equally constitutional at all places where they will conduce to the public Safety, as against the dangers of Rebellion or Invasion.

Take the particular case mentioned by the meeting. They assert in substance that Mr. Vallandigham[3] was by a military commander, seized and tried "for no other reason than words addressed to a public meeting, in criticism of the course of the administration, and in condemnation of the military orders of that general." Now, if there be no mistake about this—if this assertion is the truth and the whole truth—if there was no other reason for the arrest, then I concede that the arrest was wrong. But the arrest, as I understand, was made for a very different reason. Mr. Vallandigham avows his hostility to the war on the part of the Union; and his arrest was made because he was laboring, with some effect, to prevent the raising of troops; to encourage desertions from the army; and to leave the rebellion without an adequate military force to suppress it. He was not arrested because he was damaging the political prospects of the administration, or the personal interests of the commanding general, but because he was damaging the army, upon the existence and vigor of which the life of the nation depends. He was warring upon the military, and this gave the military constitutional jurisdiction to lay hands upon him. If Mr. Vallandigham was not damaging the military power of the country, then his arrest was made on mistake of fact, which I would be glad to correct on reasonably satisfactory evidence.

3. Clement L. Vallandigham (1820–1871), antiwar Ohio Democrat and the leader of the so-called Copperheads, had given a speech at Mount Vernon, Ohio, on May 1, 1863, describing Lincoln's war policies as dictatorial and illegal. General Ambrose Burnside considered the speech in violation of his General Order Number 38, which mandated that expressions of sympathy for the enemy were punishable by death or banishment. Vallandigham was arrested, court-martialed, jailed, and later banished to the Confederacy by Lincoln.

I understand the meeting, whose resolutions I am considering, to be in favor of suppressing the rebellion by military force—by armies. Long experience has shown that armies can not be maintained unless desertion shall be punished by the severe penalty of death. The case requires, and the law and the constitution, sanction this punishment. Must I shoot a simple-minded soldier boy who deserts, while I must not touch a hair of a wily agitator who induces him to desert? This is none the less injurious when effected by getting a father, or brother, or friend, into a public meeting, and there working upon his feeling, till he is persuaded to write the soldier boy, that he is fighting in a bad cause, for a wicked administration of a contemptible government, too weak to arrest and punish him if he shall desert. I think that in such a case, to silence the agitator, and save the boy, is not only constitutional, but, withal, a great mercy.

If I be wrong on this question of constitutional power, my error lies in believing that certain proceedings are constitutional when, in cases of rebellion or Invasion, the public Safety requires them, which would not be constitutional when, in absence of rebellion or invasion, the public Safety does not require them—in other words, that the constitution is not in its application in all respects the same, in cases of Rebellion or invasion involving the public Safety, as it is in times of profound peace and public security. The constitution itself makes the distinction; and I can no more be persuaded that the government can constitutionally take no strong measure in time of rebellion, because it can be shown that the same could not be lawfully taken in time of peace, than I can be persuaded that a particular drug is not good medicine for a sick man, because it can be shown to not be good food for a well one. Nor am I able to appreciate the danger, apprehended by the meeting, that the American people will, by means of military arrests during the rebellion, lose the right of public discussion, the liberty of speech and the press, the law of evidence, trial by jury, and Habeas corpus, throughout the indefinite peaceful future which I trust lies before them, any more than I am able to believe that a man could contract so strong an appetite for emetics during temporary illness, as to persist in feeding upon them through the remainder of his healthful life.

In giving the resolutions that earnest consideration which you request of me, I can not overlook the fact that the meeting speak as "Democrats." Nor can I, with full respect for their known intelligence, and the fairly presumed deliberation with which they prepared their resolutions, be permitted to suppose that this occurred by accident, or in any way other than that they preferred to designate themselves "democrats" rather than "American citizens." In this time of national peril I would have preferred to meet you upon a level one step higher than any party platform; because I am sure that from such more elevated position, we could do better battle for the country we all love than we possibly can from those lower ones, where from the force of habit, the prejudices of the past, and selfish hopes of the future, we are sure to expend much of our ingenuity and strength in finding fault with, and aiming blows at each other. But since you have denied me this, I will yet be thankful, for the country's sake, that not all democrats have done so. He on whose discretionary judgment Mr. Vallandigham was arrested and tried, is a democrat, having no old party affinity with me; and the judge who rejected the constitutional view expressed in these resolutions, by refusing to discharge Mr. V. on Habeas

Corpus, is a democrat of better days than these, having received his judicial mantle at the hands of President Jackson. And still more, of all those democrats who are nobly exposing their lives and shedding their blood on the battle-field, I have learned that many approve the course taken with Mr. V., while I have not heard of a single one condemning it. I can not assert that there are none such.

And the name of President Jackson recalls an instance of pertinent history. After the battle of New-Orleans, and while the fact that the treaty of peace had been concluded, was well known in the city, but before official knowledge of it had arrived, Gen. Jackson still maintained martial or military law. Now, that it could be said the war was over, the clamor against martial law, which had existed from the first, grew more furious. Among other things, a Mr. Louiaillier[4] published a denunciatory newspaper article. Gen. Jackson arrested him. A lawyer by the name of Morel procured the U.S. Judge Hall to order a writ of Habeas Corpus to release Mr. Louiaillier. Gen. Jackson arrested both the lawyer and the judge. A Mr. Hollander ventured to say of some part of the matter that "it was a dirty trick." Gen. Jackson arrested him. When the officer undertook to serve the writ of Habeas Corpus, Gen. Jackson took it from him, and sent him away with a copy. Holding the judge in custody a few days, the General sent him beyond the limits of his encampment, and set him at liberty, with an order to remain till the ratification of peace should be regularly announced, or until the British should have left the Southern coast. A day or two more elapsed, the ratification of the treaty of peace was regularly announced, and the judge and others were fully liberated. A few days more, and the judge called Gen. Jackson into court and fined him $1,000 for having arrested him and the others named. The General paid the fine, and there the matter rested for nearly thirty years, when congress refunded principal and interest. The late Senator Douglas, then in the House of Representatives, took a leading part in the debate, in which the constitutional question was much discussed. I am not prepared to say whom the journals would show to have voted for the measure.

It may be remarked: First, that we had the same constitution then, as now. Secondly, that we then had a case of Invasion, and now we have a case of Rebellion, and: Thirdly, that the permanent right of the people to public discussion, the liberty of speech and the press, the trial by jury, the law of evidence, and the Habeas Corpus, suffered no detriment whatever by that conduct of Gen. Jackson, or its subsequent approval by the American Congress.

And yet, let me say that in my own discretion, I do not know whether I would have ordered the arrest of Mr. V. While I cannot shift the responsibility from myself, I hold that, as a general rule, the commander in the field is the better judge of the necessity in any particular case. Of course, I must practice a general directory and revisory power in the matter.

---

4. Louis Louaillier, a Louisiana legislator who in January 1815 had published an article criticizing General Andrew Jackson for not suspending martial law after America's victory over the British in the Battle of New Orleans. Jackson ordered the arrest of Louaillier, whose lawyer who appealed to U.S. District Judge Dominick A. Hall. When Judge Hall obtained a writ of habeas corpus for Louaillier, Jackson had the judge imprisoned and then removed four miles outside of New Orleans and freed.

One of the resolutions expresses the opinion of the meeting that arbitrary arrests will have the effect to divide and distract those who should be united in suppressing the rebellion, and I am specifically called on to discharge Mr. Vallandigham. I regard this as, at least, a fair appeal to me on the expediency of exercising a constitutional power which I think exists. In response to such appeal I have to say it gave me pain when I learned that Mr. V. had been arrested—that is, I was pained that there should have seemed to be a necessity for arresting him—and that it will afford me great pleasure to discharge him so soon as I can, by any means, believe the public safety will not suffer by it. I further say, that as the war progress, it appears to me, opinion, and action, which were in great confusion at first, take shape, and fall into more regular channels, so that the necessity for strong dealing with them gradually decreases. I have every reason to desire that it would cease altogether, and far from the least is my regard for the opinions and wishes of those who, like the meeting at Albany, declare their purpose to sustain the government in every constitutional and lawful measure to suppress the rebellion. Still, I must continue to do so much as may seem to be required by the public safety.

Response to Serenade, Washington, D.C.[1]

Fellow-citizens: I am very glad indeed to see you to-night, and yet I will not say I thank you for this call, but I do most sincerely thank Almighty God for the occasion on which you have called. [Cheers.] How long ago is it?—eighty odd years—since on the Fourth of July for the first time in the history of the world a nation by its representatives, assembled and declared as a self-evident truth that "all men are created equal." [Cheers.] That was the birthday of the United States of America. Since then the Fourth of July has had several peculiar recognitions. The two most distinguished men in the framing and support of the Declaration were Thomas Jefferson and John Adams[2]—the one having penned it and the other sustained it the most forcibly in debate—the only two of the fifty-five who sustained it being elected President of the United States. Precisely fifty years after they put their hands to the paper it pleased Almighty God to take both from the stage of action. This was indeed an extraordinary and remarkable event in our history. Another President,[3] five years after, was called from this stage of existence on the same day and month of the year; and now, on this last Fourth of July just passed, when we have a gigantic Rebellion, at the bottom of which is an effort to overthrow the principle that all men were created equal, we have the surrender of a most powerful position and army on that very day, [cheers] and not only so, but in a succession of battles in Pennsylvania,[4] near to us, through three days, so rapidly fought

---

1. In response to the Union victory at Vicksburg, cheering crowds and bands gathered outside the White House, prompting these remarks by Lincoln from an upper widow.
2. The second president of the United States, known for assisting Thomas Jefferson in drafting the Declaration of Independence and promoting it in Congress.
3. I.e., James Monroe.
4. In early July, the Army of the Potomac under George Gordon Meade (1815–1872) stopped Robert E. Lee's attempted invasion of the North in a series of battles near Gettysburg, Pennsylvania.

that they might be called one great battle on the 1st, 2d and 3d of the month of July; and on the 4th the cohorts of those who opposed the declaration that all men are created equal, "turned tail" and run. [Long and continued cheers.] Gentlemen, this is a glorious theme, and the occasion for a speech, but I am not prepared to make one worthy of the occasion. I would like to speak in terms of praise due to the many brave officers and soldiers who have fought in the cause of the Union and liberties of the country from the beginning of the war. There are trying occasions, not only in success, but for the want of success. I dislike to mention the name of one single officer lest I might do wrong to those I might forget. Recent events bring up glorious names, and particularly prominent ones, but these I will not mention. Having said this much, I will now take the music.

July 7, 1863

To Ulysses S. Grant[1]

Major General Grant   Executive Mansion,
My dear General   Washington, July 13, 1863.
I do not remember that you and I ever met personally. I write this now as a grateful acknowledgment for the almost inestimable service you have done the country. I wish to say a word further. When you first reached the vicinity of Vicksburg, I thought you should do, what you finally did— march the troops across the neck, run the batteries with the transports, and thus go below; and I never had any faith, except a general hope that you knew better than I, that the Yazoo Pass expedition, and the like, could succeed. When you got below, and took Port-Gibson, Grand Gulf, and vicinity, I thought you should go down the river and join Gen. Banks;[2] and when you turned Northward East of the Big Black, I feared it was a mistake. I now wish to make the personal acknowledgment that you were right, and I was wrong. Yours very truly

To George G. Meade

Executive Mansion,
Major General Meade   Washington, July 14, 1863.
I have just seen your despatch to Gen. Halleck,[1] asking to be relieved of your command, because of a supposed censure of mine. I am very— very—grateful to you for the magnificent success you gave the cause of the country at Gettysburg; and I am sorry now to be the author of the slightest pain to you.[2] But I was in such deep distress myself that I could

1. Plain-spoken, cigar-smoking general (1822–1885) whose victories at Vicksburg and Chattanooga later led Lincoln to appoint him as the commander of all the Union armies. His aggressive tactics against the Confederacy would help win the war.
2. General Nathaniel P. Banks (1816–1894) lay siege to Port Hudson, Louisiana, between May 22 and July 9, 1863.
1. Henry Halleck (1815–1872), a Union commander in the western theater of the war.
2. Lincoln had expressed displeasure that Meade did not follow up his success at Gettysburg by pursuing and defeating Lee's retreating forces.

not restrain some expression of it. I had been oppressed nearly ever since the battles at Gettysburg, by what appeared to be evidences that yourself, and Gen. Couch, and Gen. Smith,[3] were not seeking a collision with the enemy, but were trying to get him across the river without another battle. What these evidences were, if you please, I hope to tell you at some time, when we shall both feel better. The case, summarily stated is this. You fought and beat the enemy at Gettysburg; and, of course, to say the least, his loss was as great as yours. He retreated; and you did not, as it seemed to me, pressingly pursue him; but a flood in the river detained him, till, by slow degrees, you were again upon him. You had at least twenty thousand veteran troops directly with you, and as many more raw ones within supporting distance, all in addition to those who fought with you at Gettysburg; while it was not possible that he had received a single recruit; and yet you stood and let the flood run down, bridges be built, and the enemy move away at his leisure, without attacking him. And Couch and Smith! The latter left Carlisle in time, upon all ordinary calculation, to have aided you in the last battle at Gettysburg; but he did not arrive. At the end of more than ten days, I believe twelve, under constant urging, he reached Hagerstown from Carlisle, which is not an inch over fiftyfive miles, if so much. And Couch's movement was very little different.

Again, my dear general, I do not believe you appreciate the magnitude of the misfortune involved in Lee's escape. He was within your easy grasp, and to have closed upon him would, in connection with our other late successes, have ended the war. As it is, the war will be prolonged indefinitely. If you could not safely attack Lee last monday, how can you possibly do so South of the river, when you can take with you very few more than two thirds of the force you then had in hand? It would be unreasonable to expect, and I do not expect you can now effect much. Your golden opportunity is gone, and I am distressed immeasureably because of it.

I beg you will not consider this a prossecution, or persecution of yourself. As you had learned that I was dissatisfied, I have thought it best to kindly tell you why.

Proclamation of Thanksgiving

By the President of the United States of America.

A Proclamation.

It has pleased Almighty God to hearken to the supplications and prayers of an afflicted people, and to vouchsafe to the army and the navy of the United States victories on land and on the sea so signal and so effective as to furnish reasonable grounds for augmented confidence that the Union of these States will be maintained, their constitution preserved, and their peace and prosperity permanently restored. But these victories have been accorded not without sacrifices of life, limb, health and liberty

---

3. Darius N. Couch (1822–1897) and William Farrar Smith (1824–1903).

incurred by brave, loyal and patriotic citizens. Domestic affliction in every part of the country follows in the train of these fearful bereavements. It is meet and right to recognize and confess the presence of the Almighty Father and the power of His Hand equally in these triumphs and in these sorrows:

Now, therefore, be it known that I do set apart Thursday the 6th. day of August next, to be observed as a day for National Thanksgiving, Praise and Prayer, and I invite the People of the United States to assemble on that occasion in their customary places of worship, and in the forms approved by their own consciences, render the homage due to the Divine Majesty, for the wonderful things he has done in the Nation's behalf, and invoke the influence of His Holy Spirit to subdue the anger, which has produced, and so long sustained a needless and cruel rebellion, to change the hearts of the insurgents, to guide the counsels of the Government with wisdom adequate to so great a national emergency, and to visit with tender care and consolation throughout the length and breadth of our land all those who, through the vicissitudes of marches, voyages, battles and sieges, have been brought to suffer in mind, body or estate, and finally to lead the whole nation, through the paths of repentance and submission to the Divine Will, back to the perfect enjoyment of Union and fraternal peace.

In witness whereof, I have hereunto set my hand and caused the seal of the United States to be affixed.

Done at the city of Washington, this fifteenth day of July, in the year of our Lord one thousand eight hundred and sixty-three, and of the Independence of the United States of America the eighty-eighth.

By the President: ABRAHAM LINCOLN

WILLIAM H. SEWARD, Secretary of State.

July 15, 1863

Verse on Lee's Invasion of the North

Gen. Lees invasion of the North written by himself—

> In eighteen sixty three, with pomp,
>   and mighty swell,
> Me and Jeff's[1] Confederacy, went
>   forth to sack Phil-del,
> 5 The Yankees they got arter us, and
>   giv us particular hell,
> And we skedaddled back again,
>   and didn't sack Phil-del.

July 19, 1863

---

1. Jefferson Davis (1808–1889) of Mississippi, president of the Confederate States of America.

Order of Retaliation

Executive Mansion, Washington D.C July 30. 1863

It is the duty of every government to give protection to its citizens, of whatever class, color, or condition, and especially to those who are duly organized as soldiers in the public service. The law of nations and the usages and customs of war as carried on by civilized powers, permit no distinction as to color in the treatment of prisoners of war as public enemies. To sell or enslave any captured person, on account of his color, and for no offence against the laws of war, is a relapse into barbarism and a crime against the civilization of the age.

The government of the United States will give the same protection to all its soldiers, and if the enemy shall sell or enslave anyone because of his color, the offense shall be punished by retaliation upon the enemy's prisoners in our possession.

It is therefore ordered that for every soldier of the United States killed in violation of the laws of war, a rebel soldier shall be executed; and for every one enslaved by the enemy or sold into slavery, a rebel soldier shall be placed at hard labor on the public works and continued at such labor until the other shall be released and receive the treatment due to a prisoner of war

July 30, 1863

To Nathaniel P. Banks[1]

Executive Mansion, Washington,
My dear General Banks   August 5, 1863.
Being a poor correspondent is the only apology I offer for not having sooner tendered my thanks for your very successful, and very valuable military operations this year. The final stroke in opening the Mississippi never should, and I think never will, be forgotten.

Recent events in Mexico,[2] I think, render early action in Texas more important than ever. I expect, however, the General-in-Chief, will address you more fully upon this subject.

Governor Boutwell[3] read me to-day that part of your letter to him, which relates to Louisiana affairs. While I very well know what I would be glad for Louisiana to do, it is quite a different thing for me to assume direction of the matter. I would be glad for her to make a new Constitution recognizing the emancipation proclamation, and adopting emancipation in those parts of the state to which the proclamation does not apply. And while she is at it, I think it would not be objectionable for her to adopt some practical system by which the two races could gradually

---

1. Banks's successful siege of Port Hudson on the Mississippi, in combination with Grant's victory at Vicksburg, won the Mississippi River Valley for the Union, thus cutting the Confederacy in two.
2. France, reacting to Mexico's suspension of interest payments to foreign nations, invaded Mexico and occupied its capital, Mexico City, in the summer of 1863.
3. George S. Boutwell (1818–1905), Republican congressman and former governor of Massachusetts.

live themselves out of their old relation to each other, and both come out better prepared for the new. Education for young blacks should be included in the plan. After all, the power, or element, of "contract" may be sufficient for this probationary period; and, by it's simplicity, and flexibility, may be the better.

As an anti-slavery man I have a motive to desire emancipation, which pro-slavery men do not have; but even they have strong enough reason to thus place themselves again under the shield of the Union; and to thus perpetually hedge against the recurrence of the scenes through which we are now passing.

Gov. Shepley[4] has informed me that Mr. Durant is now taking a registry, with a view to the election of a Constitutional convention in Louisiana. This, to me, appears proper. If such convention were to ask my views, I could present little else than what I now say to you. I think the thing should be pushed forward, so that if possible, it's mature work may reach here by the meeting of Congress.

For my own part I think I shall not, in any event, retract the emancipation proclamation; nor, as executive, ever return to slavery any person who is free by the terms of that proclamation, or by any of the acts of Congress.

If Louisiana shall send members to Congress, their admission to seats will depend, as you know, upon the respective Houses, and not upon the President.

If these views can be of any advantage in giving shape, and impetus, to action there, I shall be glad for you to use them prudently for that object. Of course you will confer with intelligent and trusty citizens of the State, among whom I would suggest Messrs. Flanders, Hahn,[5] and Durant; and to each of whom I now think I may send copies of this letter. Still it is perhaps better to not make the letter generally public. Yours very truly

Copies sent to Messrs. Flanders, Hahn & Durant, each indorsed as follows.

The within is a copy of a letter to Gen. Banks. Please observe my directions to him. Do not mention the paragraph about Mexico.

Aug. 6. 1863.

To Ulysses S. Grant

Executive Mansion,
My dear General Grant: Washington, August 9, 1863.
I see by a despatch of yours that you incline quite strongly towards an expedition against Mobile. This would appear tempting to me also, were it not that in view of recent events in Mexico, I am greatly impressed with the importance of re-establishing the national authority in Western Texas as soon as possible. I am not making an order, however. That I leave, for the present at least, to the General-in-Chief.

4. George F. Shepley (1819–1878), a Union colonel who served as military governor of New Orleans from 1862 to 1864. Durant: Thomas Jefferson Durant (1817–1882), a leading Mississippi Unionist.
5. Benjamin Franklin Flanders (1816–1896) and Michael Hahn (1830–1886), leading Mississippi Unionists.

A word upon another subject. Gen. Thomas[1] has gone again to the Mississippi Valley, with the view of raising colored troops. I have no reason to doubt that you are doing what you reasonably can upon the same subject. I believe it is a resource which, if vigorously applied now, will soon close the contest. It works doubly, weakening the enemy and strengthening us. We were not fully ripe for it until the river was opened. Now, I think at least a hundred thousand can, and ought to be rapidly organized along it's shores, relieving all the white troops to serve elsewhere.

Mr. Dana[2] understands you as believing that the emancipation proclamation has helped some in your military operations. I am very glad if this is so. Did you receive a short letter from me, dated the 13th. of July? Yours very truly

To James H. Hackett[1]

Executive Mansion,
My dear Sir: Washington, August 17, 1863.
Months ago I should have acknowledged the receipt of your book,[2] and accompanying kind note; and I now have to beg your pardon for not having done so.

For one of my age, I have seen very little of the drama. The first presentation of Falstaff I ever saw was yours here, last winter or spring. Perhaps the best compliment I can pay is to say, as I truly can, I am very anxious to see it again. Some of Shakspeare's plays I have never read; while others I have gone over perhaps as frequently as any unprofessional reader. Among the latter are Lear, Richard Third, Henry Eighth, Hamlet, and especially Macbeth. I think nothing equals Macbeth. It is wonderful. Unlike you gentlemen of the profession, I think the soliloquy in Hamlet commencing "O, my offence is rank" surpasses that commencing "To be, or not to be." But pardon this small attempt at criticism. I should like to hear you pronounce the opening speech of Richard the Third. Will you not soon visit Washington again? If you do, please call and let me make your personal acquaintance. Yours truly

To James C. Conkling[1]

Hon. James C. Conkling   Executive Mansion,
My Dear Sir.   Washington, August 26, 1863.
Your letter inviting me to attend a mass-meeting of unconditional Union-men, to be held at the Capital of Illinois, on the 3d day of September, has been received.

1. Lorenzo Thomas (1804–1875), an adjutant general in the Union Army.
2. Charles A. Dana (1819–1897), who represented Secretary of War Edwin Stanton (1814–1869) at Grant's headquarters.
1. An actor (1800–1871) known especially for his role as Falstaff in Shakespeare's Henry IV plays.
2. *Notes and Comments upon Certain Plays and Actors of Shakespeare: With Criticisms and Correspondence* (1863).
1. An Illinois lawyer and Republican politician (1816–1899) whom Lincoln had known since the early 1840s.

It would be very agreeable to me, to thus meet my old friends, at my own home; but I can not, just now, be absent from here, so long as a visit there, would require.

The meeting is to be of all those who maintain unconditional devotion to the Union; and I am sure my old political friends will thank me for tendering, as I do, the nation's gratitude to those other noble men, whom no partizan malice, or partizan hope, can make false to the nation's life.

There are those who are dissatisfied with me. To such I would say: You desire peace; and you blame me that we do not have it. But how can we attain it? There are but three conceivable ways. First, to suppress the rebellion by force of arms. This, I am trying to do. Are you for it? If you are, so far we are agreed. If you are not for it, a second way is, to give up the Union. I am against this. Are you for it? If you are, you should say so plainly. If you are not for *force*, nor yet for *dissolution*, there only remains some imaginable *compromise*. I do not believe any compromise, embracing the maintenance of the Union, is now possible. All I learn, leads to a directly opposite belief. The strength of the rebellion, is its military—its army. That army dominates all the country, and all the people, within its range. Any offer of terms made by any man or men within that range, in opposition to that army, is simply nothing for the present; because such man or men, have no power whatever to enforce their side of a compromise, if one were made with them. To illustrate—Suppose refugees from the South, and peace men of the North, get together in convention, and frame and proclaim a compromise embracing a restoration of the Union; in what way can that compromise be used to keep Lee's army out of Pennsylvania? Meade's army can keep Lee's army out of Pennsylvania;[2] and, I think, can ultimately drive it out of existence. But no paper compromise, to which the controllers of Lee's army are not agreed, can, at all, affect that army. In an effort at such compromise we should waste time, which the enemy would improve to our disadvantage; and that would be all. A compromise, to be effective, must be made either with those who control the rebel army, or with the people first liberated from the domination of that army, by the success of our own army. Now allow me to assure you, that no word or intimation, from that rebel army, or from any of the men controlling it, in relation to any peace compromise, has ever come to my knowledge or belief. All charges and insinuations to the contrary, are deceptive and groundless. And I promise you, that if any such proposition shall hereafter come, it shall not be rejected, and kept a secret from you. I freely acknowledge myself the servant of the people, according to the bond of service—the United States constitution; and that, as such, I am responsible to them.

But, to be plain, you are dissatisfied with me about the negro. Quite likely there is a difference of opinion between you and myself upon that subject. I certainly wish that all men could be free, while I suppose you do not. Yet I have neither adopted, nor proposed any measure, which is not consistent with even your view, provided you are for the Union. I suggested compensated emancipation; to which you replied you wished not

2. General George Meade (1815–1872) was famous for his victory over Lee at Gettysburg.

to be taxed to buy negroes. But I had not asked you to be taxed to buy negroes, except in such way, as to save you from greater taxation to save the Union exclusively by other means.

You dislike the emancipation proclamation; and, perhaps, would have it retracted. You say it is unconstitutional—I think differently. I think the constitution invests its commander-in-chief, with the law of war, in time of war. The most that can be said, if so much, is, that slaves are property. Is there—has there ever been—any question that by the law of war, property, both of enemies and friends, may be taken when needed? And is it not needed whenever taking it, helps us, or hurts the enemy? Armies, the world over, destroy enemies' property when they can not use it; and even destroy their own to keep it from the enemy. Civilized belligerents do all in their power to help themselves, or hurt the enemy, except a few things regarded as barbarous or cruel. Among the exceptions are the massacre of vanquished foes, and noncombatants, male and female.

But the proclamation, as law, either is valid, or is not valid. If it is not valid, it needs no retraction. If it is valid, it can not be retracted, any more than the dead can be brought to life. Some of you profess to think its retraction would operate favorably for the Union. Why better *after* the retraction, than *before* the issue? There was more than a year and a half of trial to suppress the rebellion before the proclamation issued, the last one hundred days of which passed under an explicit notice that it was coming, unless averted by those in revolt, returning to their allegiance. The war has certainly progressed as favorably for us, since the issue of the proclamation as before. I know as fully as one can know the opinions of others, that some of the commanders of our armies in the field who have given us our most important successes, believe the emancipation policy, and the use of colored troops, constitute the heaviest blow yet dealt to the rebellion; and that, at least one of those important successes, could not have been achieved when it was, but for the aid of black soldiers. Among the commanders holding these views are some who have never had any affinity with what is called abolitionism, or with republican party politics; but who hold them purely as military opinions. I submit these opinions as being entitled to some weight against the objections, often urged, that emancipation, and arming the blacks, are unwise as military measures, and were not adopted, as such, in good faith.

You say you will not fight to free negroes. Some of them seem willing to fight for you; but, no matter. Fight you, then, exclusively to save the Union. I issued the proclamation on purpose to aid you in saving the Union. Whenever you shall have conquered all resistance to the Union, if I shall urge you to continue fighting, it will be an apt time, then, for you to declare you will not fight to free negroes.

I thought that in your struggle for the Union, to whatever extent the negroes should cease helping the enemy, to that extent it weakened the enemy in his resistance to you. Do you think differently? I thought that whatever negroes can be got to do as soldiers, leaves just so much less for white soldiers to do, in saving the Union. Does it appear otherwise to you? But negroes, like other people, act upon motives. Why should they do any thing for us, if we will do nothing for them? If they stake their lives for us, they must be prompted by the strongest motive—even the promise of freedom. And the promise being made, must be kept.

The signs look better. The Father of Waters[3] again goes unvexed to the sea. Thanks to the great North-West for it. Nor yet wholly to them. Three hundred miles up, they met New-England, Empire, Key-Stone,[4] and Jersey, hewing their way right and left. The Sunny South too, in more colors than one, also lent a hand. On the spot, their part of the history was jotted down in black and white. The job was a great national one; and let none be banned who bore an honorable part in it. And while those who have cleared the great river may well be proud, even that is not all. It is hard to say that anything has been more bravely, and well done, than at Antietam, Murfreesboro, Gettysburg, and on many fields of lesser note. Nor must Uncle Sam's Web-feet[5] be forgotten. At all the watery margins they have been present. Not only on the deep sea, the broad bay, and the rapid river, but also up the narrow muddy bayou, and wherever the ground was a little damp, they have been, and made their tracks. Thanks to all. For the great republic—for the principle it lives by, and keeps alive—for man's vast future,—thanks to all.

Peace does not appear so distant as it did. I hope it will come soon, and come to stay; and so come as to be worth the keeping in all future time. It will then have been proved that, among free men, there can be no successful appeal from the ballot to the bullet; and that they who take such appeal are sure to lose their case, and pay the cost. And then, there will be some black men who can remember that, with silent tongue, and clenched teeth, and steady eye, and well-poised bayonet, they have helped mankind on to this great consummation; while, I fear, there will be some white ones, unable to forget that, with malignant heart, and deceitful speech, they have strove to hinder it.

Still let us not be over-sanguine of a speedy final triumph. Let us be quite sober. Let us diligently apply the means, never doubting that a just God, in his own good time, will give us the rightful result. Yours very truly

To Salmon P. Chase

Hon. S. P. Chase.   Executive Mansion,
My dear Sir: Washington, September 2. 1863.
Knowing your great anxiety that the emancipation proclamation shall now be applied to certain parts of Virginia and Louisiana which were exempted from it last January, I state briefly what appear to me to be difficulties in the way of such a step. The original proclamation has no constitutional or legal justification, except as a military measure. The exemptions were made because the military necessity did not apply to the exempted localities. Nor does that necessity apply to them now any more than it did then. If I take the step must I not do so, without the argument of military necessity, and so, without any argument, except the one that I think the measure politically expedient, and morally right? Would I not thus give up all footing upon constitution or law? Would I not thus be in the boundless field of absolutism? Could this pass unno-

3. I.e., the Mississippi River.
4. New York, nicknamed the Empire State, and Pennsylvania, the Keystone State.
5. The U.S. Navy.

ticed, or unresisted? Could it fail to be perceived that without any further stretch, I might do the same in Delaware, Maryland, Kentucky, Tennessee, and Missouri; and even change any law in any state? Would not many of our own friends shrink away appalled? Would it not lose us the elections, and with them, the very cause we seek to advance?

From Opinion on the Draft[1]

* * *

It is clear that a constitutional law may not be expedient or proper. Such would be a law to raise armies when no armies were needed. But this is not such. The republican institutions, and territorial integrity of our country can not be maintained without the further raising and supporting of armies. There can be no army without men. Men can be had only voluntarily, or involuntarily. We have ceased to obtain them voluntarily; and to obtain them involuntarily, is the draft—the conscription. If you dispute the feets, and declare that men can still be had voluntarily in sufficient numbers prove the assertion by yourselves volunteering in such numbers, and I shall gladly give up the draft. Or if not a sufficient number, but any one of you will volunteer, he for his single self, will escape all the horrors of the draft; and will thereby do only what each one of at least a million of his manly brethren have already done. Their toil and blood have been given as much for you as for themselves. Shall it all be lost rather than you too, will bear your part?

I do not say that all who would avoid serving in the war, are unpatriotic; but I do think every patriot should willingly take his chance under a law made with great care in order to secure entire fairness. This law was considered, discussed, modified, and amended, by congress, at great length, and with much labor; and was finally passed, by both branches, with a near approach to unanimity. At last, it may not be exactly such as any one man out of congress, or even in congress, would have made it. It has been said, and I believe truly, that the constitution itself is not altogether such as any one of it's framers would have preferred. It was the joint work of all; and certainly the better that it was so.

Much complaint is made of that provision of the conscription law which allows a drafted man to substitute three hundred dollars for himself; while, as I believe, none is made of that provision which allows him to substitute another man for himself. Nor is the three hundred dollar provision objected to for unconstitutionality; but for inequality—for favoring the rich against the poor. The substitution of men is the provision if any, which favors the rich to the exclusion of the poor. But this being a provision in accordance with an old and well known practice, in the raising of armies, is not objected to. There would have been great objection if that provision had been omitted. And yet being in, the money provision really modifies the inequality which the other introduces. It allows men to escape the service, who are too poor to escape but for it. Without the money provision, competition among the more wealthy might,

1. Lincoln evidently wrote this piece as a public letter, but he never issued it.

and probably would, raise the price of substitutes above three hundred dollars, thus leaving the man who could raise only three hundred dollars, no escape from personal service. True, by the law as it is, the man who can not raise so much as three hundred dollars, nor obtain a personal substitute for less, can not escape; but he can come quite as near escaping as he could if the money provision were not in the law. To put it another way, is an unobjectionable law which allows only the man to escape who can pay a thousand dollars, made objectionable by adding a provision that any one may escape who can pay the smaller sum of three hundred dollars? This is the exact difference at this point between the present law and all former draft laws. It is true that by this law a some what larger number will escape than could under a law allowing personal substitutes only; but each additional man thus escaping will be a poorer man than could have escaped by the law in the other form. The money provision enlarges the class of exempts from actual service simply by admitting poorer men into it. How, then can this money provision be a wrong to the poor man? The inequality complained of pertains in greater degree to the substitution of men, and is really modified and lessened by the money provision. The inequality could only be perfectly cured by sweeping both provisions away. This being a great innovation, would probably leave the law more distasteful than it now is.

The principle of the draft, which simply is involuntary, or enforced service, is not new. It has been practiced in all ages of the world. It was well known to the framers of our constitution as one of the modes of raising armies, at the time they placed in that instrument the provision that "the congress shall have power to raise and support armies." It has been used, just before, in establishing our independence; and it was also used under the constitution in 1812. Wherein is the peculiar hardship now? Shall we shrink from the necessary means to maintain our free government, which our grand-fathers employed to establish it, and our own fathers have already employed once to maintain it? Are we degenerate? Has the manhood of our race run out?

✻   ✻   ✻

ca. mid-September 1863

Proclamation Suspending Writ of Habeas Corpus

By the President of the United States of America.
A Proclamation

Whereas the Constitution of the United States has ordained that the privilege of the Writ of Habeas Corpus shall not be suspended unless when in cases or rebellion or invasion the public safety may require it, And whereas a rebellion was existing on the third day of March, 1863, which rebellion is still existing; and whereas by a statute which was approved on that day, it was enacted by the Senate and House of Representatives of the United States in Congress assembled, that, during the present insurrection, the President of the United States, whenever, in his judgment, the Public safety may require, is authorized to suspend the privilege of the Writ of Habeas Corpus in any case throughout the United States or any part thereof; and whereas in the judgment of the President the public safety does require that the privilege of the said writ shall now be suspended throughout the United States in the cases where, by the authority of the President of the United States, military, naval and civil officers of the United States or any of them hold persons under their command or in their custody either as prisoners of war, spies, or aiders or abettors of the enemy; or officers, soldiers or seamen enrolled or drafted or mustered or enlisted in or belonging to the land or naval forces of the United States or as deserters therefrom or otherwise amenable to military law, or the Rules and Articles of War or the rules or regulations prescribed for the military or naval services by authority of the President of the United States or for resisting a draft or for any other offence against the military or naval service. Now, therefore, I, Abraham Lincoln, President of the United States, do hereby proclaim and make known to all whom it may concern, that the privilege of the Writ of Habeas Corpus is suspended throughout the United States in the several cases before mentioned, and that this suspension will continue throughout the duration of the said rebellion, or until this proclamation shall, by a subsequent one to be issued by the President of the United States, be modified or revoked. And I do hereby require all magistrates, attorneys and other civil officers within the United States, and all officers and others in the military and naval services of the United States, to take distinct notice of this suspension, and to give it full effect, and all citizens of the United States to conduct and govern themselves accordingly and in conformity with the Constitution of the United States and the laws of Congress in such case made and provided.

In testimony whereof, I have hereunto set my hand, and caused the Seal of the United States to be affixed, this Fifteenth day of September, in the year of our Lord one thousand eight hundred and sixty three and of the Independence of the United States of America the Eighty-eighth. By the President: ABRAHAM LINCOLN

WILLIAM H. SEWARD, Secretary of State.

September 15, 1863

Reply to Sons of Temperance, Washington, D.C.

As a matter of course, it will not be possible for me to make a response coextensive with the address which you have presented to me. If I were better known than I am, you would not need to be told that in the advocacy of the cause of temperance you have a friend and sympathizer in me. [Applause.]

When I was a young man, long ago, before the Sons of Temperance as an organization, had an existence, I in an humble way, made temperance speeches, [applause] and I think I may say that to this day I have never, by my example, belied what I then said. [Loud applause.]

In regard to the suggestions which you make for the purpose of the advancement of the cause of temperance in the army, I cannot make particular responses to them at this time. To prevent intemperance in the army is even a part of the articles of war. It is part of the law of the land—and was so, I presume, long ago—to dismiss officers for drunkenness. I am not sure that consistently with the public service, more can be done than has been done. All, therefore, that I can promise you is, (if you will be pleased to furnish me with a copy of your address) to have it submitted to the proper Department and have it considered, whether it contains any suggestions which will improve the cause of temperance and repress the cause of drunkenness in the army any better than it is already done. I can promise no more than that.

I think that the reasonable men of the world have long since agreed that intemperance is one of the greatest, if not the very greatest of all evils amongst mankind. That is not a matter of dispute, I believe. That the disease exists, and that it is a very great one is agreed upon by all.

The mode of cure is one about which there may be differences of opinion. You have suggested that in an army—our army—drunkenness is a great evil, and one which, while it exists to a very great extent, we cannot expect to overcome so entirely as to have such successes in our arms as we might have without it. This undoubtedly is true, and while it is, perhaps, rather a bad source to derive comfort from, nevertheless, in a hard struggle, I do not know but what it is some consolation to be aware that there is some intemperance on the other side, too, and that they have no right to beat us in physical combat on that ground. [Laughter and applause.]

But I have already said more than I expected to be able to say when I began, and if you please to hand me a copy of your address it shall be considered. I thank you very heartily, gentlemen, for this call, and for bringing with you these very many pretty ladies.

September 29, 1863

Proclamation of Thanksgiving

By the President of the United States of America.
A Proclamation

The year that is drawing towards its close, has been filled with the blessings of fruitful fields and healthful skies. To these bounties, which are so constantly enjoyed that we are prone to forget the source from which they come, others have been added, which are of so extraordinary a nature, that they cannot fail to penetrate and soften even the heart which is habitually insensible to the ever watchful providence of Almighty God. In the midst of a civil war of unequalled magnitude and severity, which has sometimes seemed to foreign States to invite and to provoke their aggression, peace has been preserved with all nations, order has been maintained, the laws have been respected and obeyed, and harmony has prevailed everywhere except in the theatre of military conflict; while that theatre has been greatly contracted by the advancing armies and navies of the Union. Needful diversions of wealth and of strength from the fields of peaceful industry to the national defence, have not arrested the plough, the shuttle or the ship; the axe has enlarged the borders of our settlements, and the mines, as well of iron and coal as of the precious metals, have yielded even more abundantly than heretofore. Population has steadily increased, notwithstanding the waste that has been made in the camp, the siege and the battle-field; and the country, rejoicing in the consciousness of augmented strength and vigor, is permitted to expect continuance of years with large increase of freedom. No human counsel hath devised nor hath any mortal hand worked out these great things. They are the gracious gifts of the Most High God, who, while dealing with us in anger for our sins, hath nevertheless remembered mercy. It has seemed to me fit and proper that they should be solemnly, reverently and gratefully acknowledged as with one heart and one voice by the whole American People. I do therefore invite my fellow citizens in every part of the United States, and also those who are at sea and those who are sojourning in foreign lands, to set apart and observe the last Thursday of November next, as a day of Thanksgiving and Praise to our beneficent Father who dwelleth in the Heavens. And I recommend to them that while offering up the ascriptions justly due to Him for such singular deliverances and blessings, they do also, with humble penitence for our national perverseness and disobedience, commend to His tender care all those who have become widows, orphans, mourners or sufferers in the lamentable civil strife in which we are unavoidably engaged, and fervently implore the interposition of the Almighty Hand to heal the wounds of the nation and to restore it as soon as may be consistent with the Divine purposes to the full enjoyment of peace, harmony, tranquillity and Union.

In testimony whereof, I have hereunto set my hand and caused the Seal of the United States to be affixed.

Done at the city of Washington, this Third day of October, in the year of our Lord one thousand eight hundred and sixty-three, and of the Independence of the United States the Eighty-eighth.

By the President: ABRAHAM LINCOLN
WILLIAM H. SEWARD, Secretary of State.

October 3, 1863

From To Charles D. Drake[1] and Others

Hon. Charles D. Drake &   Executive Mansion
others, Committee   Washington D.C. Oct. 5. 1863

*   *   *

* * * We are in civil war. In such cases there always is a main question; but in this case that question is a perplexing compound—Union and Slavery. It thus becomes a question not of two sides merely, but of at least four sides, even among those who are for the Union, saying nothing of those who are against it. Thus, those who are for the Union *with*, but not *without* slavery—those for it *without*, but not *with*—those for it *with* or *without*, but prefer it *with*—and those for it *with* or *without*, but prefer it *without*. Among these again, is a subdivision of those who are for *gradual*

---

1. A lawyer (1811–1892) and U.S. senator from Missouri.

but not for *immediate*, and those who are for *immediate*, but not for *gradual* extinction of slavery. It is easy to conceive that all these shades of opinion, and even more, may be sincerely entertained by honest and truthful men. Yet, all being for the Union, by reason of these differences, each will prefer a different way of sustaining the Union. At once sincerity is questioned, and motives are assailed. Actual war coming, blood grows hot, and blood is spilled. Thought is forced from old channels into confusion. Deception breeds and thrives. Confidence dies, and universal suspicion reigns. Each man feels an impulse to kill his neighbor, lest he be first killed by him. Revenge and retaliation follow. And all this, as before said, may be among honest men only. But this is not all. Every foul bird comes abroad, and every dirty reptile rises up. These add crime to confusion. Strong measures, deemed indispensable but harsh at best, such men make worse by mal-administration. Murders for old grudges, and murders for pelf, proceed under any cloak that will best cover for the ocasion. These causes amply account for what has occurred in Missouri,[1] without ascribing it to the weakness, or wickedness of any general. * * *

* * *

Remarks to Baltimore Presbyterian Synod: Two Versions[1]

I can only say in this case, as in so many others, that I am profoundly grateful for the respect given in every variety of form in which it can be given from the religious bodies of the country. I saw, upon taking my position here, that I was going to have an administration, if an administration at all, of extraordinary difficulty. It was, without exception, a time of the greatest difficulty that this country ever saw. I was early brought to a living reflection that nothing in my power whatever, in others to rely upon, would succeed without the direct assistance of the Almighty, but all must fail.

I have often wished that I was a more devout man than I am.

Nevertheless, amid the greatest difficulties of my Administration, when I could not see any other resort, I would place my whole reliance in God, knowing that all would go well, and that He would decide for the right.

I thank you, gentlemen, in the name of the religious bodies which you represent, and in the name of the Common Father, for this expression of your respect. I cannot say more.

Gentlemen of the Baltimore Synod: I can only say that in this case, as in many others, I am profoundly grateful for the support given me in every field of labor in which it can be given, and which has ever been extended to me by the religious community of the country. I saw before taking my posi-

---

1. Apparently a reference to the brutal cavalry raid (Sept. 22–Oct. 26) made in Missouri by the confederate officer Joseph Shelby (1830–1897).
1. Representatives of the Baltimore synod were presented in the White House on October 1863 by the Reverend Phineas D. Gurley, pastor of Washington's New York Avenue Presbyterian Church, which Lincoln occasionally attended. The two slightly varying reports of this meeting appeared in the Washington *National Republican*, October 24, 1863, and *National Intelligencer*, October 26, 1863, respectively.

tion here that I was to have an administration, if it could be called such, of extraordinary difficulty, and it seems to me that it was ever present with me as an extraordinary matter that in the time of the greatest difficulty that this country had ever experienced, or was likely to experience, the man who, at the least of it, gave poor promise of ability, was brought out for duty at that time. I was early brought to the living reflection that there was nothing in the arms of this man, however there might be in others, to rely upon for such difficulties, and that without the direct assistance of the Almighty I was certain of failing. I sincerely wish that I was a more devoted man than I am. Sometimes in my difficulties I have been driven to the last resort to say God is still my only hope. It is still all the world to me.

I again say that I thank you in the name of the religious people of the country generally, and in the name of our common Father of returning you my thanks for the encouraging and most unanimous support that has been constantly given me. I know not that I can say more.

October 24, 1863

To Benjamin F. Flanders

Hon. B. F. Flanders   Executive Mansion
My dear Sir: Washington, D.C. Nov. 9. 1863
In a conversation with Gen. Butler he made a suggestion which impressed me a good deal at the time. It was that, as a preliminary step, a vote be taken, yea or nay, whether there shall be a State convention to repeal the Ordinance of secession, and remodel the State constitution. I send it merely as a suggestion for your consideration, not having considered it maturely myself. The point which impressed me was, not so much the questions to be voted on, as the effect of chrystallizing, so to speak, in taking such popular vote on any proper question. In fact, I have always thought the act of secession is legally nothing, and needs no repealing. Turn the thought over in your mind, and see if in your own judgment, you can make any thing of it. Yours very truly

Address at Gettysburg, Pennsylvania[1]

Address delivered at the dedication of the Cemetery at Gettysburg.

Four score and seven years ago our fathers brought forth on this continent, a new nation, conceived in Liberty, and dedicated to the proposition that all men are created equal.

Now we are engaged in a great civil war, testing whether that nation, or any nation so conceived and so dedicated, can long endure. We are met on a great battle-field of that war. We have come to dedicate a portion of that field, as a final resting place for those who here gave their lives that that nation might live. It is altogether fitting and proper that we should do this.

---

1. This is Lincoln's final text of the Gettysburg Address, published in the 1864 volume *Autograph Leaves of Our Country's Authors.*

But, in a larger sense, we can not dedicate—we can not consecrate—we can not hallow—this ground. The brave men, living and dead, who struggled here, have consecrated it, far above our poor power to add or detract. The world will little note, nor long remember what we say here, but it can never forget what they did here. It is for us the living, rather, to be dedicated here to the unfinished work which they who fought here have thus far so nobly advanced. It is rather for us to be here dedicated to the great task remaining before us—that from these honored dead we take increased devotion to that cause for which they gave the last full measure of devotion—that we here highly resolve that these dead shall not have died in vain—that this nation, under God,[2] shall have a new birth of freedom—and that government of the people, by the people, for the people, shall not perish from the earth.

Abraham Lincoln.[3]

November 19. 1863.

From Annual Message to Congress

*   *   *

The report of the Secretary of War is a document of great interest. It consists of—

1. The military operations of the year, detailed in the report of the general-in-chief.

2. The organization of colored persons into the war service.

3. The exchange of prisoners, fully set forth in the letter of General Hitchcock.

4. The operations under the act for enrolling and calling out the national forces, detailed in the report of the provost marshal general.

5. The organization of the invalid corps; and

6. The operation of the several departments of the quartermaster general, commissary general, paymaster general, chief of engineers, chief of ordnance, and surgeon general.

It has appeared impossible to make a valuable summary of this report except such as would be too extended for this place, and hence I content myself by asking your careful attention to the report itself.

*   *   *

2. The phrase "under God" seems to have been added spontaneously by Lincoln as he spoke, for it is absent from two drafts of the speech he wrote before November 19. Three newspaper transcriptions of the address, written on the scene, include the phrase; see, for example, the *New York Times* report ("Lincoln in His Era," pp. 405–7). Lincoln, evidently caught up in the reverent spirit of the occasion, paused after "shall" and added "under God" before continuing with "have a new birth of freedom . . ." He corrected this rather awkward placement of the phrase in three later handwritten copies of the speech, moving it to its current position, after the word "nation." For further discussion of the different drafts and the day's ceremonies, see the excerpt from Gabor S. Boritt's *The Gettysburg Gospel* ("Modern Views," pp. 514–22).

3. Of the five extant drafts in Lincoln's hand, this, the final one—known as the Bliss copy because Lincoln penned it in 1864 for the publisher Alexander Bliss for inclusion in *Autograph Leaves*—is the only one signed by the president. This copy now hangs in the Lincoln Room of the White House.

The measures provided at your last session for the removal of certain Indian tribes have been carried into effect. Sundry treaties have been negotiated which will, in due time, be submitted for the constitutional action of the Senate. They contain stipulations for extinguishing the possessory rights of the Indians to large and valuable tracts of land. It is hoped that the effect of these treaties will result in the establishment of permanent friendly relations with such of these tribes as have been brought into frequent and bloody collision with our outlying settlements and emigrants.[1]

Sound policy and our imperative duty to these wards of the government demand our anxious and constant attention to their material well-being, to their progress in the arts of civilization, and, above all, to that moral training which, under the blessing of Divine Providence, will confer upon them the elevated and sanctifying influences, the hopes and consolation of the Christian faith.

*   *   *

Of those who were slaves at the beginning of the rebellion, full one hundred thousand are now in the United States military service, about one-half of which number actually bear arms in the ranks; thus giving the double advantage of taking so much labor from the insurgent cause, and supplying the places which otherwise must be filled with so many white men. So far as tested, it is difficult to say they are not as good soldiers as any. No servile insurrection, or tendency to violence or cruelty, has marked the measures of emancipation and arming the blacks. These measures have been much discussed in foreign countries, and contemporary with such discussion the tone of public sentiment there is much improved. At home the same measures have been fully discussed, supported, criticised, and denounced, and the annual elections following are highly encouraging to those whose official duty it is to bear the country through this great trial. Thus we have the new reckoning. The crisis which threatened to divide the friends of the Union is past.

Looking now to the present and future, and with reference to a resumption of the national authority within the States wherein that authority has been suspended, I have thought fit to issue a proclamation,[2] a copy of which is herewith transmitted. On examination of this proclamation it will appear, as is believed, that nothing is attempted beyond what is amply justified by the Constitution. True, the form of an oath is given, but no man is coerced to take it. The man is only promised a pardon in case he voluntarily takes the oath. The Constitution authorizes the Executive to grant or withhold the pardon at his own absolute discretion; and this includes the power to grant on terms, as is fully established by judicial and other authorities.

*   *   *

An attempt to guaranty and protect a revived State government, constructed in whole, or in preponderating part, from the very element against

---

1. In the aftermath of the Sioux Uprising of 1862, in which insurgent Indians killed some 350 whites, Lincoln ordered the removal of a number of tribes to South Dakota. Also, at his order, thirty-eight Sioux males were hanged on December 26, 1862, in Mankato, Minnesota, in the largest mass execution in U.S. history.
2. See "Proclamation of Amnesty and Reconstruction" on pp. 332–34.

whose hostility and violence it is to be protected, is simply absurd. There must be a test by which to separate the opposing elements, so as to build only from the sound; and that test is a sufficiently liberal one, which accepts as sound whoever will make a sworn recantation of his former unsoundness.

But if it be proper to require, as a test of admission to the political body, an oath of allegiance to the Constitution of the United States, and to the Union under it, why also to the laws and proclamations in regard to slavery? Those laws and proclamations were enacted and put forth for the purpose of aiding in the suppression of the rebellion. To give them their fullest effect, there had to be a pledge for their maintenance. In my judgment they have aided, and will further aid, the cause for which they were intended. To now abandon them would be not only to relinquish a lever of power, but would also be a cruel and an astounding breach of faith. I may add at this point, that while I remain in my present position I shall not attempt to retract or modify the emancipation proclamation; nor shall I return to slavery any person who is free by the terms of that proclamation, or by any of the acts of Congress.

*   *   *

The suggestion in the proclamation as to maintaining the political framework of the States on what is called reconstruction, is made in the hope that it may do good without danger of harm. It will save labor and avoid great confusion.

But why any proclamation now upon this subject? This question is beset with the conflicting views that the step might be delayed too long or be taken too soon. In some States the elements for resumption seem ready for action, but remain inactive, apparently for want of a rallying point—a plan of action. Why shall A adopt the plan of B, rather than B that of A? And if A and B should agree, how can they know but that the general government here will reject their plan? By the proclamation a plan is presented which may be accepted by them as a rallying point, and which they are assured in advance will not be rejected here. This may bring them to act sooner than they otherwise would.

The objections to a premature presentation of a plan by the national Executive consists in the danger of committals on points which could be more safely left to further developments. Care has been taken to so shape the document as to avoid embarrassments from this source. Saying that, on certain terms, certain classes will be pardoned, with rights restored, it is not said that other classes, or other terms, will never be included. Saying that reconstruction will be accepted if presented in a specified way, it is not said it will never be accepted in any other way.

The movements, by State action, for emancipation in several of the States, not included in the emancipation proclamation, are matters of profound gratulation. And while I do not repeat in detail what I have heretofore so earnestly urged upon this subject, my general views and feelings remain unchanged; and I trust that Congress will omit no fair opportunity of aiding these important steps to a great consummation.

In the midst of other cares, however important, we must not lose sight of the fact that the war power is still our main reliance. To that power alone can we look, yet for a time, to give confidence to the people in the contested regions, that the insurgent power will not again overrun them. Until that confidence shall be established, little can be done anywhere for what is called reconstruction. Hence our chiefest care must still be directed to the army and navy, who have thus far borne their harder part so nobly and well. And it may be esteemed fortunate that in giving the greatest efficiency to these indispensable arms, we do also honorably recognize the gallant men, from commander to sentinel, who compose them, and to whom, more than to others, the world must stand indebted for the home of freedom disenthralled, regenerated, enlarged, and perpetuated.

Washington, December 8, 1863.

Proclamation of Amnesty and Reconstruction

By the President of the United States of America:
A Proclamation

Whereas, in and by the Constitution of the United States, it is provided that the President "shall have power to grant reprieves and pardons for offences against the United States, except in cases of impeachment;" and

Whereas a rebellion now exists whereby the loyal State governments of several States have for a long time been subverted, and many persons have committed and are now guilty of treason against the United States; and

Whereas, with reference to said rebellion and treason, laws have been enacted by Congress declaring forfeitures and confiscation of property and liberation of slaves, all upon terms and conditions therein stated, and also declaring that the President was thereby authorized at any time thereafter, by proclamation, to extend to persons who may have participated in the existing rebellion, in any State or part thereof, pardon and amnesty, with such exceptions and at such times and on such conditions as he may deem expedient for the public welfare; and

Whereas the congressional declaration for limited and conditional pardon accords with well-established judicial exposition of the pardoning power; and

Whereas, with reference to said rebellion, the President of the United States has issued several proclamations, with provisions in regard to the liberation of slaves; and

Whereas it is now desired by some persons heretofore engaged in said rebellion to resume their allegiance to the United States, and to reinaugurate loyal State governments within and for their respective States; therefore,

I, Abraham Lincoln, President of the United States, do proclaim, declare, and make known to all persons who have, directly or by implication, participated in the existing rebellion, except as hereinafter excepted, that a full pardon is hereby granted to them and each of them, with restoration of all rights of property, except as to slaves, and in property cases where rights of third parties shall have intervened, and upon the condition that every such person shall take and subscribe an oath, and thenceforward keep and maintain said oath inviolate; and which oath shall be registered for permanent preservation, and shall be of the tenor and effect following, to wit:

"I, ———, do solemnly swear, in presence of Almighty God, that I will henceforth faithfully support, protect and defend the Constitution of the United States, and the union of the States thereunder; and that I will, in like manner, abide by and faithfully support all acts of Congress passed during the existing rebellion with reference to slaves, so long and so far as not repealed, modified or held void by Congress, or by decision of the Supreme Court; and that I will, in like manner, abide by and faithfully support all proclamations of the President made during the existing rebellion having reference to slaves, so long and so far as not modified or declared void by decision of the Supreme Court. So help me God."

The persons excepted from the benefits of the foregoing provisions are all who are, or shall have been, civil or diplomatic officers or agents of the so-called confederate government; all who have left judicial stations under the United States to aid the rebellion; all who are, or shall have been, military or naval officers of said so-called confederate government above the rank of colonel in the army, or of lieutenant in the navy; all who left seats in the United States Congress to aid the rebellion; all who resigned commissions in the army or navy of the United States, and afterwards aided the rebellion; and all who have engaged in any way in treating colored persons or white persons, in charge of such, otherwise than lawfully as prisoners of war, and which persons may have been found in the United States service, as soldiers, seamen, or in any other capacity.

And I do further proclaim, declare, and make known, that whenever, in any of the States of Arkansas, Texas, Louisiana, Mississippi, Tennessee, Alabama, Georgia, Florida, South Carolina, and North Carolina, a number of persons, not less than one-tenth in number of the votes cast in such State at the Presidential election of the year of our Lord one thousand eight hundred and sixty, each having taken the oath aforesaid and not having since violated it, and being a qualified voter by the election law of the State existing immediately before the so-called act of secession, and excluding all others, shall re-establish a State government which shall be republican, and in no wise contravening said oath, such shall be recognized as the true government of the State, and the State shall receive thereunder the benefits of the constitutional provision which declares that "The United States shall guaranty to every State in this union a republican form of government, and shall protect each of them against invasion; and, on application of the legislature, or the executive, (when the legislature cannot be convened,) against domestic violence."

And I do further proclaim, declare, and make known that any provision which may be adopted by such State government in relation to the freed people of such State, which shall recognize and declare their permanent freedom, provide for their education, and which may yet be consistent, as a temporary arrangement, with their present condition as a laboring, landless, and homeless class, will not be objected to by the national Executive. And it is suggested as not improper, that, in constructing a loyal State government in any State, the name of the State, the boundary, the subdivisions, the constitution, and the general code of laws, as before the rebellion, be maintained, subject only to the modifications made necessary by the conditions hereinbefore stated, and such others, if any, not contravening said conditions, and which may be deemed expedient by those framing the new State government.

To avoid misunderstanding, it may be proper to say that this proclamation, so far as it relates to State governments, has no reference to States wherein loyal State governments have all the while been maintained. And for the same reason, it may be proper to further say that whether members sent to Congress from any State shall be admitted to seats, constitutionally rests exclusively with the respective Houses, and not to any extent with the Executive. And still further, that this proclamation is intended to present the people of the States wherein the national authority has been suspended, and loyal State governments have been subverted, a mode in and by which the national authority and loyal State governments may be re-established within said States, or in any of them; and, while the mode presented is the best the Executive can suggest, with his present impressions, it must not be understood that no other possible mode would be acceptable.

Given under my hand at the city, of Washington, the 8th. day of December, A.D. one thousand eight hundred and sixty-three, and of the independence of the United States of America the eighty-eighth.

By the President: ABRAHAM LINCOLN
WILLIAM H. SEWARD, Secretary of State.

December 8, 1863

To Oliver D. Filley[1]

O. D. Filley   Executive Mansion,
St. Louis, Mo.   Washington, Dec. 22. 1863.
I have just looked over a petition signed by some three dozen citizens of St. Louis, and three accompanying letters, one by yourself, one by a Mr. Nathan Ranney, and one by a Mr. John D. Coalter, the whole relating to the Rev. Dr. McPheeters.[2] The petition prays, in the name of justice and mercy that I will restore Dr. McPheeters to all his ecclesiastical rights.

This gives no intimation as to what ecclesiastical rights are withheld. Your letter states that Provost Marshal Dick, about a year ago, ordered the arrest of Dr. McPheters, Pastor of the Vine Street Church, prohibited him from officiating, and placed the management of the affairs of the church out of the control of it's chosen Trustees; and near the close you state that a certain course "would insure his release." Mr. Ranney's letter says "Dr. Saml. S. McPheeters is enjoying all the rights of a civilian, but can not preach the gospel!!!" Mr. Coalter, in his letter, asks "Is it not a strange illustration of the condition of things that the question of who shall be allowed to preach in a church in St. Louis, shall be decided by the President of the United States?"

---

1. Mayor of St. Louis, Missouri (1806–1881).
2. Samuel B. McPheeters (1828–1901) had been removed from his pulpit at the Pine (not Vine) Street Presbyterian Church in St. Louis by provost marshal Franklin A. Dick for sermonizing on behalf of the Confederacy. Through Lincoln's intervention, McPheeters was restored to his pastorate, although his own congregation eventually expelled him.

Now, all this sounds very strangely; and withal, a little as if you gentlemen making the application, do not understand the case alike, one affirming that the Dr. is enjoying all the rights of a civilian, and another pointing out to me what will secure his release! On the 2nd. day of January last I wrote Gen. Curtis in relation to Mr. Dick's order upon Dr. McPheeters, and, as I suppose the Dr. is enjoying all the rights of a civilian, I only quote that part of my letter which relates to the church. It is as follows: "But I must add that the U.S. government must not, as by this order, undertake to run the churches. When an individual, in a church or out of it, becomes dangerous to the public interest, he must be checked; but the churches, as such must take care of themselves. It will not do for the U.S. to appoint Trustees, Supervisors, or other agents for the churches." This letter going to Gen. Curtis, then in command there I supposed of course it was obeyed, especially as I heard no further complaint from Dr. M. or his friends for nearly an entire year.

I have never interfered, nor thought of interfering as to who shall or shall not preach in any church; nor have I knowingly, or believingly, tolerated any one else to so interfere by my authority. If any one is so interfering, by color of my authority, I would like to have it specifically made known to me.

If, after all, what is now sought, is to have me put Dr. M. back, over the heads of a majority of his own congregation, that too, will be declined. I will not have control of any church on any side. Yours Respectfully

Endorsement on Petition Concerning Samuel B. McPheeters

The assumptions of this paper, so far as I know, or believe are entirely false. I have never deprived Dr. McPheters of any ecclesiastical right, or authorized, or excused its' being done by any one deriving authority from me. On the contrary, in regard to this very case, I directed, a long time ago, that Dr. McPheters was to be arrested, or remain at large, upon the same rule as any one else; and that, in no event, was any one to interfere by my authority, as to who should, or should not preach in any church. This was done, I think, in a letter, in the nature of an order, to Mr. Dick. The assumption that I am keeping Dr. M. from preaching in his church is monstrous. If any one is doing this, by pretense of my authority, I will thank any one who can, to make out and present me, a specific case against him. If, after all, the Dr. is kept out by the majority of his own parishioners, and my official power is sought to force him in over their heads, I decline that also.

December 22. 1863

To Edwin M. Stanton[1]

Executive Mansion,   February 1, 1864.
Sir: You are directed to have a transport (either a steam or sailing vessel
as may be deemed proper by the Quartermaster-General) sent to the
colored colony established by the United States at the island of Vache,
on the coast of San Domingo, to bring back to this country such of the
colonists there as desire to return. You will have the transport furnished
with suitable supplies for that purpose, and detail an officer of the Quartermaster's Department who, under special instructions to be given,
shall have charge of the business. The colonists will be brought to
Washington, unless otherwise hereafter directed, and be employed and
provided for at the camps for colored persons around that city. Those only
will be brought from the island who desire to return, and their effects will
be brought with them.

To John A. Andrew[1]

His Excellency. John A. Andrew   Executive Mansion,
Governor of Massachusetts   Washington, February 18. 1864.
Yours of the 12th. was received yesterday. If I were to judge from the letter, without any external knowledge, I should suppose that all the colored
people South of Washington were struggling to get to Massachusetts;
that Massachusetts was anxious to receive and retain the whole of them
as permanent citizens; and that the United States Government here was
interposing and preventing this. But I suppose these are neither really the
facts, nor meant to be asserted as true by you. Coming down to what I
suppose to be the real facts, you are engaged in trying to raise colored
troops for the U.S. and wish to take recruits from Virginia, through Washington, to Massachusetts for that object; and the loyal Governor of Virginia, also trying to raise troops for us, objects to your taking his material
away; while we, having to care for all, and being responsible alike to all,
have to do as much for him, as we would have to do for you, if he was, by our
authority, taking men from Massachusetts to fill up Virginia regiments. No
more than this has been intended by me; nor, as I think, by the Secretary of
War. There may have been some abuses of this, as a rule, which, if known,
should be prevented in future.

If, however, it be really true that Massachusetts wishes to afford a permanent home within her borders, for all, or even a large number of colored
persons who will come to her, I shall be only too glad to know it. It would
give relief in a very difficult point; and I would not for a moment hinder
from going, any person who is free by the terms of the proclamation or any
of the acts of Congress.

1. Lincoln's secretary of war during most of the Civil War (1814–1869).
1. Governor of Massachusetts (1818–1867) between 1861 and 1866 who was instrumental in
   creating African American units for the Union Army, including the Fifty-Fourth Massachusetts Infantry under Robert Gould Shaw.

To John A. J. Creswell[1]

Hon. John A. J. Creswell   Executive Mansion,
My dear Sir: Washington, March 7, 1864.
I am very anxious for emancipation to be effected in Maryland in some substantial form. I think it probable that my expressions of a preference for *gradual* over *immediate* emancipation, are misunderstood. I had thought the *gradual* would produce less confusion, and destitution, and therefore would be more satisfactory; but if those who are better acquainted with the subject, and are more deeply interested in it, prefer the *immediate*, most certainly I have no objection to their judgment prevailing. My wish is that all who are for emancipation *in any form*, shall co-operate, all treating all respectfully, and all adopting and acting upon the major opinion, when fairly ascertained. What I have dreaded is the danger that by jealousies, rivalries, and consequent ill-blood—driving one another out of meetings and conventions—perchance from the polls—the friends of emancipation themselves may divide, and lose the measure altogether. I wish this letter to not be made public; but no man representing me as I herein represent myself, will be in any danger of contradiction by me. Yours truly

Presentation of Commission to Ulysses S. Grant, Washington. D.C.

General Grant
The nation's appreciation of what you have done, and it's reliance upon you for what remains to do, in the existing great struggle, are now presented with this commission, constituting you Lieutenant General in the Army of the United States. With this high honor devolves upon you also, a corresponding responsibility. As the country herein trusts you, so, under God, it will sustain you. I scarcely need to add that with what I here speak for the nation goes my own hearty personal concurrence.

March 9, 1864

To Michael Hahn

Private

            Executive Mansion,
Hon. Michael Hahn   Washington,
My dear Sir: March 13. 1864.
I congratulate you on having fixed your name in history as the first-free-state Governor of Louisiana. Now you are about to have a Convention which, among other things, will probably define the elective franchise.[1] I

---

1. Republican congressman (1828–1891) from Maryland.
1. Louisiana adopted a state constitution restricting the franchise to whites but leaving open the possibility of awarding it to blacks in the future.

barely suggest for your private consideration, whether some of the colored people may not be let in—as, for instance, the very intelligent, and especially those who have fought gallantly in our ranks. They would probably help, in some trying time to come, to keep the jewel of liberty within the family of freedom. But this is only a suggestion, not to the public, but to you alone. Yours truly

To Albert G. Hodges[1]

A. G. Hodges, Esq   Executive Mansion,
Frankfort, Ky.   Washington, April 4, 1864.
My dear Sir: You ask me to put in writing the substance of what I verbally said the other day, in your presence, to Governor Bramlette and Senator Dixon.[2] It was about as follows:

"I am naturally anti-slavery. If slavery is not wrong, nothing is wrong. I can not remember when I did not so think, and feel. And yet I have never understood that the Presidency conferred upon me an unrestricted right to act officially upon this judgment and feeling. It was in the oath I took that I would, to the best of my ability, preserve, protect, and defend the Constitution of the United States. I could not take the office without taking the oath. Nor was it my view that I might take an oath to get power, and break the oath in using the power. I understood, too, that in ordinary civil administration this oath even forbade me to practically indulge my primary abstract judgment on the moral question of slavery. I had publicly declared this many times, and in many ways. And I aver that, to this day, I have done no official act in mere deference to my abstract judgment and feeling on slavery. I did understand however, that my oath to preserve the constitution to the best of my ability, imposed upon me the duty of preserving, by every indispensable means, that government—that nation—of which that constitution was the organic law. Was it possible to lose the nation, and yet preserve the constitution? By general law life *and* limb must be protected; yet often a limb must be amputated to save a life; but a life is never wisely given to save a limb. I felt that measures, otherwise unconstitutional, might become lawful, by becoming indispensable to the preservation of the constitution, through the preservation of the nation. Right or wrong, I assumed this ground, and now avow it. I could not feel that, to the best of my ability, I had even tried to preserve the constitution, if, to save slavery, or any minor matter, I should permit the wreck of government, country, and Constitution all together. When, early in the war, Gen. Fremont attempted military emancipation, I forbade it, because I did not then think it an indispensable necessity. When a little later, Gen. Cameron,[3] then Secretary of War, suggested the arming of the blacks, I objected, because I did not yet think it an indispensable necessity. When, still later, Gen. Hunter attempted military emancipation, I again forbade

---

1. Editor of the Frankfort, Kentucky, *Commonwealth* (1802–1881).
2. Archibald Dixon (1802–1876), a U.S. senator from Kentucky from 1852 to 1855. Thomas E. Bramlette (1817–75), governor of Kentucky, who had opposed the recruiting of black troops in his state.
3. Simon Cameron (1799–1889), Pennsylvania Republican who had been Lincoln's secretary of war until 1862.

it, because I did not yet think the indispensable necessity had come. When, in March, and May, and July 1862 I made earnest, and successive appeals to the border states to favor compensated emancipation, I believed the indispensable necessity for military emancipation, and arming the blacks would come, unless averted by that measure. They declined the proposition; and I was, in my best judgment, driven to the alternative of either surrendering the Union, and with it, the Constitution, or of laying strong hand upon the colored element. I chose the latter. In choosing it, I hoped for greater gain than loss; but of this, I was not entirely confident. More than a year of trial now shows no loss by it in our foreign relations, none in our home popular sentiment, none in our white military force,—no loss by it any how or any where. On the contrary, it shows a gain of quite a hundred and thirty thousand soldiers, seamen, and laborers. These are palpable facts, about which, as facts, there can be no cavilling. We have the men; and we could not have had them without the measure.

"And now let any Union man who complains of the measure, test himself by writing down in one line that he is for subduing the rebellion by force of arms; and in the next, that he is for taking these hundred and thirty thousand men from the Union side, and placing them where they would be but for the measure he condemns. If he can not face his case so stated, it is only because he can not face the truth."

I add a word which was not in the verbal conversation. In telling this tale I attempt no compliment to my own sagacity. I claim not to have controlled events, but confess plainly that events have controlled me. Now, at the end of three years struggle the nation's condition is not what either party, or any man devised, or expected. God alone can claim it. Whither it is tending seems plain. If God now wills the removal of a great wrong, and wills also that we of the North as well as you of the South, shall pay fairly for our complicity in that wrong, impartial history will find therein new cause to attest and revere the justice and goodness of God. Yours truly

Address at Sanitary Fair,
Baltimore, Maryland

Ladies and Gentlemen—Calling to mind that we are in Baltimore, we can not fail to note that the world moves. Looking upon these many people, assembled here, to serve, as they best may, the soldiers of the Union, it occurs at once that three years ago, the same soldiers could not so much as pass through Baltimore. The change from then till now, is both great, and gratifying. Blessings on the brave men who have wrought the change, and the fair women who strive to reward them for it.

But Baltimore suggests more than could happen within Baltimore. The change within Baltimore is part only of a far wider change. When the war began, three years ago, neither party, nor any man, expected it would last till now. Each looked for the end, in some way, long ere to-day. Neither did any anticipate that domestic slavery would be much affected by the war. But here we are; the war has not ended, and slavery has been much affected— how much needs not now to be recounted. So true is it that man proposes, and God disposes.

But we can see the past, though we may not claim to have directed it; and seeing it, in this case, we feel more hopeful and confident for the future.

The world has never had a good definition of the word liberty, and the American people, just now, are much in want of one. We all declare for liberty; but in using the same *word* we do not all mean the same *thing*. With some the word liberty may mean for each man to do as he pleases with himself, and the product of his labor; while with others the same word may mean for some men to do as they please with other men, and the product of other men's labor. Here are two, not only different, but incompatable things, called by the same name—liberty. And it follows that each of the things is, by the respective parties, called by two different and incompatable names—liberty and tyranny.

The shepherd drives the wolf from the sheep's throat, for which the sheep thanks the shepherd as a *liberator*, while the wolf denounces him for the same act as the destroyer of liberty, especially as the sheep was a black one. Plainly the sheep and the wolf are not agreed upon a definition of the word liberty; and precisely the same difference prevails to-day among us human creatures, even in the North, and all professing to love liberty. Hence we behold the processes by which thousands are daily passing from under the yoke of bondage, hailed by some as the advance of liberty, and bewailed by others as the destruction of all liberty. Recently, as it seems, the people of Maryland have been doing something to define liberty; and thanks to them that, in what they have done, the wolf's dictionary, has been repudiated.

It is not very becoming for one in my position to make speeches at great length; but there is another subject upon which I feel that I ought to say a word. A painful rumor, true I fear, has reached us of the massacre, by the rebel forces, at Fort Pillow,[1] in the West end of Tennessee, on the Mississippi river, of some three hundred colored soldiers and white officers, who had just been overpowered by their assailants. There seems to be some anxiety in the public mind whether the government is doing it's duty to the colored soldier, and to the service, at this point. At the beginning of the war, and for some time, the use of colored troops was not contemplated; and how the change of purpose was wrought, I will not now take time to explain. Upon a clear conviction of duty I resolved to turn that element of strength to account; and I am responsible for it to the American people, to the christian world, to history, and on my final account to God. Having determined to use the negro as a soldier, there is no way but to give him all the protection given to any other soldier. The difficulty is not in stating the principle, but in practically applying it. It is a mistake to suppose the government is indifferent to this matter, or is not doing the best it can in regard to it. We do not to-day *know* that a colored soldier, or white officer commanding colored soldiers, has been massacred by the rebels when made a prisoner. We fear it, believe it, I may say, but we do not *know* it. To take the life of one of their prisoners, on the assumption that they murder ours, when it is short of certainty that they do murder ours, might be too serious, too cruel a mistake. We are having the Fort-Pillow affair thoroughly investigated; and such investigation will probably show conclusively how

---

1. Many black Union soldiers who surrendered to Southern troops after the battle at Fort Pillow in Tennessee were executed, apparently at the order of General Nathan B. Forrest.

the truth is. If, after all that has been said, it shall turn out that there has been no massacre at Fort-Pillow, it will be almost safe to say there has been none, and will be none elsewhere. If there has been the massacre of three hundred there, or even the tenth part of three hundred, it will be conclusively proved; and being so proved, the retribution shall as surely come. It will be matter of grave consideration in what exact course to apply the retribution; but in the supposed case, it must come.

April 18, 1864

To Ulysses S. Grant

Executive Mansion Washington,
Lieutenant General Grant.   April 30, 1864
Not expecting to see you again before the Spring campaign opens, I wish to express, in this way, my entire satisfaction with what you have done up to this time, so far as I understand it. The particulars of your plans I neither know, or seek to know. You are vigilant and self-reliant; and, pleased with this, I wish not to obtrude any constraints or restraints upon you. While I am very anxious that any great disaster, or the capture of our men in great numbers, shall be avoided, I know these points are less likely to escape your attention than they would be mine. If there is anything wanting which is within my power to give, do not fail to let me know it.

And now with a brave Army, and a just cause, may God sustain you. Yours very truly

To Cabinet Members

Executive Mansion,
Sir: Washington, May 3, 1864.
It is now quite certain that a large number of our colored soldiers, with their white officers, were, by the rebel force, massacred after they had surrendered, at the recent capture of Fort-Pillow. So much is known, though the evidence is not yet quite ready to be laid before me. Meanwhile I will thank you to prepare, and give me in writing your opinion as to what course, the government should take in the case. Yours truly

Response to Serenade

Fellow-citizens: I am very much obliged to you for the compliment of this call, though I apprehend it is owing more to the good news[1] received to-day from the army than to a desire to see me. I am, indeed, very grateful to the brave men who have been struggling with the enemy in the field, to their noble commanders who have directed them, and especially to our Maker. Our commanders are following up their victories resolutely and

---

1. Reports that Grant had defeated Lee in the Battle of the Wilderness and was now moving on Spotsylvania courthouse caused premature rejoicing in Washington, including this serenade at the White House. It was soon learned that the battles were tactically inconclusive.

successfully. I think, without knowing the particulars of the plans of Gen. Grant, that what has been accomplished is of more importance than at first appears. I believe I know, (and am especially grateful to know) that Gen. Grant has not been jostled in his purposes; that he has made all his points, and to-day he is on his line as he purposed before he moved his armies. I will volunteer to say that I am very glad at what has happened; but there is a great deal still to be done. While we are grateful to all the brave men and officers for the events of the past few days, we should, above all, be very grateful to Almighty God, who gives us victory.

There is enough yet before us requiring all loyal men and patriots to perform their share of the labor and follow the example of the modest General at the head of our armies, and sink all personal considerations for the sake of the country. I commend you to keep yourselves in the same tranquil mood that is characteristic of that brave and loyal man. I have said more than I expected when I came before you; repeating my thanks for this call, I bid you good-bye. [Cheers.]

May 9, 1864

To the Friends of Union and Liberty

Executive Mansion, Washington,
To the friends of Union & Liberty.   May 9, 1864.
Enough is known of Army operations within the last five days to claim our especial gratitude to God; while what remains undone demands our most sincere prayers to, and reliance upon, Him, without whom, all human effort is vain. I recommend that all patriots, at their homes, in their places of public worship, and wherever they may be, unite in common thanksgiving and prayer to Almighty God.

Response to Methodists[1]

Gentlemen.   May 18, 1864.
In response to your address, allow me to attest the accuracy of it's historical statements; indorse the sentiments it expresses; and thank you, in the nation's name, for the sure promise it gives.

Nobly sustained as the government has been by all the churches, I would utter nothing which might, in the least, appear invidious against any. Yet, without this, it may fairly be said that the Methodist Episcopal Church, not less devoted than the best, is, by it's greater numbers, the most important of all. It is no fault in others that the Methodist Church sends more soldiers to the field, more nurse to the hospital, and more prayers to

1. A response to an address from the General Conference of the Methodist Episcopal Church, presented by a committee composed of Bishop Edward R. Ames and the Reverends Joseph Cummings, Granville Moody, Charles Elliott, and George Peck, who pointed to the Methodist record of loyalty to the Union and support of the administration and pledged continued prayers for the "preservation of our country undivided, for the triumph of our cause, and for a permanent peace, gained by the sacrifice of no moral principles, but founded on the Word of God, and securing, in righteousness, liberty and equal rights to all."

Heaven than any. God bless the Methodist Church—bless all the churches—and blessed be God, Who, in this our great trial, giveth us the churches.

To George B. Ide, James R. Doolittle, and A. Hubbell[1]

Rev. Dr. Ide ⎫   Executive Mansion,
Hon. J. R. Doolittle ⎬ Committee   Washington,
& Hon. A. Hubbell ⎭   May 30, 1864.

In response to the preamble and resolutions of the American Baptist Home Mission Society, which you did me the honor to present, I can only thank you for thus adding to the effective and almost unanamous support which the Christian communities are so zealously giving to the country, and to liberty. Indeed it is difficult to conceive how it could be otherwise with any one professing Christianity, or even having ordinary perceptions of right and wrong. To read in the Bible, as the word of God himself, that "In the sweat of *thy* face shalt thou eat bread,"[2] and to preach there-from that, "In the sweat of *other mans* faces shalt thou eat bread," to my mind can scarcely be reconciled with honest sincerity. When brought to my final reckoning, may I have to answer for robbing no man of his goods; yet more tolerable even this, than for robbing one of himself, and all that was his. When, a year or two ago, those professedly holy men of the South, met in the semblance of prayer and devotion, and, in the name of Him who said "As ye would all men should do unto you, do ye even so unto them"[3] appealed to the christian world to aid them in doing to a whole race of men, as they would have no man do unto themselves, to my thinking, they contemned and insulted God and His church, far more than did Satan when he tempted the Saviour with the Kingdoms of the earth. The devils attempt was no more false, and far less hypocritical. But let me forbear, remembering it is also written "Judge not, lest ye be judged."[4]

Reply to Committee of the National Union Convention, Washington, D.C.

Gentlemen of the Committee: I will neither conceal my gratification, nor restrain the expression of my gratitude, that the Union people, through their convention, in their continued effort to save, and advance the nation, have deemed me not unworthy to remain in my present position.

I know no reason to doubt that I shall accept the nomination tendered; and yet perhaps I should not declare definitely before reading and considering what is called the Platform.

---

1. Maybe Alrich [Aldrich?] Hubbell, a businessman from Utica, New York. George B. Ide (1804–1872), pastor of the First Baptist Church in Springfield, Massachusetts. James R. Doolittle (1815–1897), U.S. Senator from Wisconsin, a devout Baptist and a fervent supporter of Lincoln.
2. Genesis 3:19.
3. Matthew 7:12; Luke 6:31.
4. Matthew 7:1; Luke 6:37.

I will say now, however, I approve the declaration in favor of so amend-ing the Constitution as to prohibit slavery throughout the nation. When the people in revolt, with a hundred days of explicit notice, that they could, within those days, resume their allegiance, without the overthrow of their institution, and that they could not so resume it afterwards, elected to stand out, such amendment of the Constitution as now proposed, became a fitting, and necessary conclusion to the final success of the Union cause. Such alone can meet and cover all cavils. Now, the unconditional Union men, North and South, perceive its importance, and embrace it. In the joint names of Liberty and Union, let us labor to give it legal form, and practical effect.

June 9, 1864

Speech at Great Central Sanitary Fair, Philadelphia, Pennsylvania[1]

I suppose that this toast was intended to open the way for me to say something. [Laughter.] War, at the best, is terrible, and this war of ours, in its magnitude and in its duration, is one of the most terrible. It has deranged business, totally in many localities, and partially in all locali-ties. It has destroyed property, and ruined homes; it has produced a national debt and taxation unprecedented, at least in this country. It has carried mourning to almost every home, until it can almost be said that the "heavens are hung in black."[2] Yet it continues, and several relieving coincidents have accompanied it from the very beginning, which have not been known, as I understood, or have any knowledge of, in any for-mer wars in the history of the world. The Sanitary Commission, with all its benevolent labors, the Christian Commission, with all its Christian and benevolent labors, and the various places, arrangements, so to speak, and institutions, have contributed to the comfort and relief of the soldiers. You have two of these places in this city—the Cooper-Shop and Union Volunteer Refreshment Saloons. [Great applause and cheers.] And lastly, these fairs, which, I believe, began only in last August, if I mistake not, in Chicago; then at Boston, at Cincinnati, Brooklyn, New York, at Baltimore, and those at present held at St. Louis, Pittsburg, and Philadelphia. The motive and object that lie at the bottom of all these are most worthy; for, say what you will, after all the most is due to the soldier, who takes his life in his hands and goes to fight the battles of his country. [Cheers.] In what is contributed to his comfort when he passes to and fro, and in what is contributed to him when he is sick and wounded, in whatever shape it comes, whether from the fair and tender hand of woman, or from any other source, is much, very much; but, I think there is still that which has as much value to him—he is not forgotten. [Cheers.] Another view of these various institutions is worthy of consideration, I think; they are voluntary contributions, given freely, zealously, and earnestly, on top of all the dis-turbances of business, the taxation and burdens that the war has imposed

1. This is a version of Lincoln's speech as reported in the Philadelphia *Press* on June 14, 1864.
2. *Henry IV*, 1.1.

upon us, giving proof that the national resources are not at all exhausted, [cheers;] that the national spirit of patriotism is even stronger than at the commencement of the rebellion.

It is a pertinent question often asked in the mind privately, and from one to the other, when is the war to end? Surely I feel as deep an interest in this question as any other can, but I do not wish to name a day, or month, or a year when it is to end. I do not wish to run any risk of seeing the time come, without our being ready for the end, and for fear of disappointment, because the time had come and not the end. We accepted this war for an object, a worthy object, and the war will end when that object is attained. Under God, I hope it never will until that time. [Great cheering.] Speaking of the present campaign, General Grant is reported to have said, I am going through on this line if it takes all summer. [Cheers.] This war has taken three years; it was begun or accepted upon the line of restoring the national authority over the whole national domain, and for the American people, as far as my knowledge enables me to speak, I say we are going through on this line if it takes three years more. [Cheers.] My friends, I did not know but that I might be called upon to say a few words before I got away from here, but I did not know it was coming just here. [Laughter.] I have never been in the habit of making predictions in regard to the war, but I am almost tempted to make one.—If I were to hazard it, it is this: That Grant is this evening, with General Meade and General Hancock, of Pennsylvania, and the brave officers and soldiers with him, in a position from whence he will never be dislodged until Richmond is taken [loud cheering], and I have but one single proposition to put now, and, perhaps, I can best put it in form of an interrogative. If I shall discover that General Grant and the noble officers and men under him can be greatly facilitated in their work by a sudden pouring forward of men and assistance, will you give them to me? [Cries of "yes."] Then, I say, stand ready, for I am watching for the chance. [Laughter and cheers.] I thank you, gentlemen.

June 16, 1864

Proclamation of a Day of Prayer

*By the President of the United States of America:
A Proclamation.*

Whereas, the Senate and House of Representatives at their last Session adopted a Concurrent Resolution, which was approved on the second day of July instant, and which was in the words following, namely:

"That, the President of the United States be requested to appoint a day for humiliation and prayer by the people of the United States; that he request his constitutional advisers at the head of the executive departments to unite with him as Chief Magistrate of the Nation, at the City of Washington, and the members of Congress, and all magistrates, all civil, military and naval officers,—all soldiers, sailors, and marines, with all loyal and law-abiding people, to convene at their usual places of worship, or wherever they may be, to confess and to repent of their manifold sins;

to implore the compassion and forgiveness of the Almighty, that, if consistent with His will, the existing rebellion may be speedily suppressed, and the supremacy of the Constitution and laws of the United States may be established throughout all the States; to implore Him as the Supreme Ruler of the World, not to destroy us as a people, nor suffer us to be destroyed by the hostility or connivance of other Nations, or by obstinate adhesion to our own counsels, which may be in conflict with His eternal purposes, and to implore Him to enlighten the mind of the Nation to know and do His will; humbly believing that it is in accordance with His will that our place should be maintained as a united people among the family of nations; to implore Him to grant to our armed defenders and the masses of the people that courage, power of resistance and endurance necessary to secure that result; to implore Him in His infinite goodness to soften the hearts, enlighten the minds, and quicken the consciences of those in rebellion, that they may lay down their arms and speedily return to their allegiance to the United States, that they may not be utterly destroyed, that the effusion of blood may be stayed, and that unity and fraternity may be restored, and peace established throughout all our borders."

Now, therefore, I, Abraham Lincoln, President of the United States, cordially concurring with the Congress of the United States in the penitential and pious sentiments expressed in the aforesaid Resolution, and heartily approving of the devotional design and purpose thereof, do, hereby, appoint the first Thursday of August next, to be observed by the People of the United States as a day of national humiliation and prayer.

I do, hereby, further invite and request the Heads of the Executive Departments of this Government, together with all Legislators,—all Judges and Magistrates, and all other persons exercising authority in the land, whether civil, military or naval,—and all soldiers, seamen and marines in the national service,—and all the other loyal and law-abiding People of the United States, to assemble in their preferred places of public worship on that day, and there and then to render to the Almighty and Merciful Ruler of the Universe, such homages and such confessions, and to offer to Him such supplications, as the Congress of the United States have, in their aforesaid Resolution, so solemnly, so earnestly, and so earnestly, and so reverently recommended.

In testimony whereof, I have hereunto set my hand and caused the seal of the United States to be affixed.

Done at the City of Washington, this seventh day of July, in the year of our Lord, one thousand eight hundred and sixtyfour, and of the Independence of the United States the eighty-ninth.   ABRAHAM LINCOLN
By the President:
WILLIAM H. SEWARD, Secretary of State.

July 7, 1864

Proclamation Concerning Reconstruction

By the President of the United States.
A Proclamation

Whereas, at the late Session, Congress passed a Bill,[1] "To guarantee to certain States, whose governments have been usurped or overthrown, a republican form of Government," a copy of which is hereunto annexed:

And whereas, the said Bill was presented to the President of the United States, for his approval, less than one hour before the *sine die*[2] adjournment of said Session, and was not signed by him:

And whereas, the said Bill contains, among other things, a plan for restoring the States in rebellion to their proper practical relation in the Union, which plan expresses the sense of Congress upon that subject, and which plan it is now thought fit to lay before the people for their consideration:

Now, therefore, I, Abraham Lincoln, President of the United States, do proclaim, declare, and make known, that, while I am, (as I was in December last, when by proclamation I propounded a plan for restoration) unprepared, by a formal approval of this Bill, to be inflexibly committed to any single plan of restoration; and, while I am also unprepared to declare, that the free-state constitutions and governments, already adopted and installed in Arkansas and Louisiana, shall be set aside and held for nought, thereby repelling and discouraging the loyal citizens who have set up the same, as to further effort; or to declare a constitutional competency in Congress to abolish slavery in States, but am at the same time sincerely hoping and expecting that a constitutional amendment, abolishing slavery throughout the nation, may be adopted, nevertheless, I am fully satisfied with the system for restoration contained in the Bill, as one very proper plan for the loyal people of any State choosing to adopt it; and that I am, and at all times shall be, prepared to give the Executive aid and assistance to any such people, so soon as the military resistance to the United States shall have been suppressed in any such State, and the people thereof shall have sufficiently returned to their obedience to the Constitution and the laws of the United States,—in which cases, military Governors will be appointed, with directions to proceed according to the Bill.

In testimony whereof, I have hereunto set my hand and caused the Seal of the United States to be affixed.

Done at the City of Washington this eighth day of July, in the year of Our Lord, one thousand eight hundred and sixty-four, and of the Independence of the United States the eighty-ninth.

By the President: ABRAHAM LINCOLN.

WILLIAM H. SEWARD, Secretary of State.

July 8, 1864

---

1. On July 2, Congress had passed the Wade-Davis Bill, which stipulated that a state that had seceded could rejoin the Union only after it had formed a constitutional convention and freed all its slaves, and 50 percent of its citizens had sworn allegiance to the United States. Lincoln pocket-vetoed the bill.
2. Indefinitely postponed (Latin).

Proclamation Calling for 500,000 Volunteers

By the President of the United States of America:
A Proclamation

Whereas, by the act approved July 4, 1864, entitled "an act further to regulate and provide for the enrolling and calling out the National forces and for other purposes," it is provided that the President of the United States may, "at his discretion, at any time hereafter, call for any number of men as volunteers, for the respective terms of one, two and three years for military service," and "that in case the quota of or any part thereof, of any town, township, ward of a city, precinct, or election district, or of a county not so subdivided, shall not be filled within the space of fifty days after such call, then the President shall immediately order a draft for one year to fill such quota or any part thereof which may be unfilled."

And whereas, the new enrolment, heretofore ordered, is so far completed as that the aforementioned act of Congress may now be put in operation for recruiting and keeping up the strength of the armies in the field for garrisons, and such military operations as may be required for the purpose of suppressing the rebellion, and restoring the authority of the United States Government in the insurgent States:

Now, therefore, I, Abraham Lincoln, President of the United States, do issue this my call for five hundred thousand volunteers for the military service, Provided, nevertheless, that this call shall be reduced by all credits which may be established under section 8 of the aforesaid act on account of persons who have entered the naval service during the present rebellion, and by credits for men furnished to the military service in excess of calls heretofore made. Volunteers will be accepted under this call for one, two, or three years, as they may elect, and will be entitled to the bounty provided by the law, for the period of service for which they enlist.

And I hereby proclaim, order and direct, that immediately after the fifth day of September, 1864, being fifty days from the date of this call, a draft for troops to serve for one year shall be had in every town, township, ward of a city, precinct or election district or county not so subdivided to fill the quota which shall be assigned to it under this call, or any part thereof, which may be unfilled, by volunteers on the said fifth day of September 1864.

In testimony whereof, I have hereunto set my hand and caused the seal of the United States to be affixed.

Done at the city of Washington, this eighteenth day of July, in the year of our Lord one thousand eight hundred and sixty four, and of the Independence of the United States the eighty-ninth.

By the President: ABRAHAM LINCOLN
   WILLIAM H. SEWARD Secretary of State.

July 18, 1864

Memorandum on Clement C. Clay[1]

Executive Mansion,
Washington, 1864

Hon. Clement C. Clay, one of the Confederate gentlemen who recently, at Niagara Falls, in a letter to Mr. Greeley, declared that they were *not* empowered to negotiate for peace, but that they *were*, however, in the confidential employment of their government, has prepared a Platform and an Address to be adopted by the Democracy at the Chicago Convention, the preparing of these, and conferring with the democratic leaders in regard to the same, being the confidential employment of their government, in which he, and his confreres are engaged. The following planks are in the Platform—

5. The war to be further prossecuted only to restore the *Union as it was*, and only in such manner, that no further detriment to slave property shall be effected.

6. All negro soldiers and seamen to be at once disarmed and degraded to menial service in the Army and Navy; and no additional negroes to be, on any pretence whatever, taken from their masters.

7 All negroes not having enjoyed actual freedom during the war to be held permanently as slaves; and whether those who shall have enjoyed actual freedom during the war, shall be free to be a legal question.

The following paragraphs are in the Address—

"Let all who are in favor of peace; of arresting the slaughter of our countrymen, of saving the country from bankruptcy & ruin, of securing food & raiment & good wages for the laboring classes; of disappointing the enemies of Democratic & Republican Government who are rejoicing in the overthrow of their proudest monuments; of vindicating our capacity for self-government, arouse and maintain these principles, and elect these candidates."

+ + + + +

"The stupid tyrant who now disgraces the Chair of Washington and Jackson could, any day, have peace and restoration of the Union; and would have them, only that he persists in the war merely to free the slaves."

The convention may not litterally adopt Mr. Clay's Platform and Address, but we predict it will do so substantially. We shall see.

Mr. Clay confesses to his Democratic friends that he is for *peace* and *disunion*; but, he says "You can not elect without a cry of war for the union; but, once elected, we are friends, and can adjust matters somehow." He also says "You will find some difficulty in proving that Lincoln could, if he would, have peace and re-union, because Davis has not said so, and will not say so; but you must assert it, and re-assert it, and stick to it, and it will pass as at least half proved."

ca. July 25, 1864

1. An Alabama senator (1816–1882) in the First Confederate Congress, Clay, along with other Confederate representatives, visited Niagara Falls in July 1864 and engaged in brief, fruitless peace negotiations with the antislavery editor Horace Greeley, who served as a conduit to President Lincoln.

To Abram Wakeman[1]

Private

Abram Wakeman, Esq

My dear Sir:

Executive Mansion,
Washington,
July 25, 1864.

I feel that the subject which you pressed upon my attention in our recent conversation is an important one. The men of the South, recently (and perhaps still) at Niagara Falls, tell us distinctly that they *are* in the confidential employment of the rebellion; and they tell us as distinctly that they are *not* empowered to offer terms of peace. Does any one doubt that what they *are* empowered to do, is to assist in selecting and arranging a candidate and a platform for the Chicago convention? Who could have given them this confidential employment but he who only a week since declared to Jaquess[2] and Gilmore that he had no terms of peace but the independence of the South—the dissolution of the Union? Thus the present presidential contest will almost certainly be no other than a contest between a Union and a Disunion candidate, disunion certainly following the success of the latter. The issue is a mighty one for all people and all time; and whoever aids the right, will be appreciated and remembered. Yours truly

To Edwin M. Stanton[1]

I know not how much is within the legal power of the government in this case; but it is certainly true in equity, that the laboring women in our employment, should be paid at the least as much as they were at the beginning of the war. Will the Secretary of War please have the case fully examined, and so much relief given as can be consistently with the law and the public service.

July 27. 1864

To Ulysses S. Grant

"Cypher"

Lieut. Genl. Grant

City-Point, Va.

Office U.S. Military Telegraph,
War Department,
Washington, D.C., August 14 1864.

The Secretary of War and I concur that you better confer with Gen. Lee and stipulate for a mutual discontinuance of house-burning and other destruc-

---

1. New York City postmaster (1824–1889).
2. Union colonel and Methodist minister James F. Jaquess (1819–1898) and journalist James R. Gilmore (1822–1903) had recently been sent by Lincoln to the South to explore possible peace terms with Jefferson Davis and other Confederate leaders. Lincoln, who correctly assumed the negotiations would fail, had sent the two emissaries in order to quiet critics like Horace Greeley who believed a peaceful settlement could be achieved.
1. Lincoln here brings to the attention of his secretary of war that salaries for women working at the U.S. arsenal in Philadelphia had decreased since 1861, despite a steep rise in cost of living.

tion of private property. The time and manner of conference, and particulars of stipulation we leave, on our part, to your convenience and judgment.

To Charles D. Robinson[1]

Hon. Charles D. Robinson   Executive Mansion,
My dear Sir: Washington, August 17, 1864.
Your letter of the 7th. was placed in my hand yesterday by Gov. Randall.

To me it seems plain that saying re-union and abandonment of slavery would be considered, if offered, is not saying that nothing *else* or *less* would be considered, if offered. But I will not stand upon the mere construction of language. It is true, as you remind me, that in the Greeley letter of 1862, I said: "If I could save the Union without freeing any slave I would do it; and if I could save it by freeing all the slaves I would do it; and if I could save it by freeing some, and leaving others alone I would also do that." I continued in the same letter as follows: "What I do about slavery and the colored race, I do because I believe it helps to save the Union; and what I forbear I forbear because I do not believe it would help to save the Union. I shall do less whenever I shall believe what I am doing hurts the cause; and I shall do more whenever I shall believe doing more will help the cause." All this I said in the utmost sincerity; and I am as true to the whole of it now, as when I first said it. When I afterwards proclaimed emancipation, and employed colored soldiers, I only followed the declaration just quoted from the Greeley letter that "I shall do *more* whenever I shall believe *doing* more will help the cause." The way these measures were to help the cause, was not to be by magic, or miracles, but by inducing the colored people to come bodily over from the rebel side to ours. On this point, nearly a year ago, in a letter to Mr. Conkling, made public at once,[2] I wrote as follows: "But negroes, like other people, act upon motives. Why should they do anything for us if we will do nothing for them? If they stake their lives for us they must be prompted by the strongest motive—even the promise of freedom. And the promise, being made, must be kept." I am sure you will not, on due reflection, say that the promise being made, must be *broken* at the first opportunity. I am sure you would not desire me to say, or to leave an inference, that I am ready, whenever convenient, to join in re-enslaving those who shall have served us in consideration of our promise. As matter of morals, could such treachery by any possibility, escape the curses of Heaven, or of any good man? As matter of policy, to *announce* such a purpose, would ruin the Union cause itself. All recruiting of colored men would instantly cease, and all colored men now in our service, would instantly desert us. And rightfully too. Why should they give their lives for us, with full notice of our purpose to betray them? Drive back to the support of the rebellion the physical force which the colored people now give, and promise us, and neither the present, nor any coming administration, *can* save the Union. Take from

1. A Green Bay, Wisconsin, editor (1822–1886) who, as a war Democrat, supported Lincoln but was concerned about the president's current goal of abolishing slavery as a precondition for restoring the Union. Apparently this letter was never sent.
2. Lincoln's letter of August 26, 1863, to James C. Conkling (see pp. 318–21), intended to be read before a Union meeting in Springfield, Ill., was leaked to the press before the meeting.

us, and give to the enemy, the hundred and thirty, forty, or fifty thousand colored persons now serving us as soldiers, seamen, and laborers, and we can not longer maintain the contest. The party who could elect a President on a War & Slavery Restoration platform, would, of necessity, lose the colored force; and that force being lost, would be as powerless to save the Union as to do any other impossible thing. It is not a question of sentiment or taste, but one of physical force, which may be measured, and estimated as horse-power, and steam power, are measured and estimated. And by measurement, it is more than we can lose, and live. Nor can we, by discarding it, get a white force in place of it. There is a witness in every white mans bosom that he would rather go to the war having the negro to help him, than to help the enemy against him. It is not the giving of one class for another. It is simply giving a large force to the enemy, for *nothing* in return.

In addition to what I have said, allow me to remind you that no one, having control of the rebel armies, or, in fact, having any influence whatever in the rebellion, has offered, or intimated a willingness to, a restoration of the Union, in any event, or on any condition whatever. Let it be constantly borne in mind that no such offer has been made or intimated. Shall we be weak enough to allow the enemy to distract us with an abstract question which he himself refuses to present as a practical one? In the Conkling letter before mentioned, I said: "Whenever you shall have conquered all resistance to the Union, if I shall urge you to continue fighting, it will be an apt time *then* to declare that you will not fight to free negroes." I repeat this now. If Jefferson Davis wishes, for himself, or for the benefit of his friends at the North, to know what I would do if he were to offer peace and re-union, saying nothing about slavery, let him try me.

Speech to the 166th Ohio Regiment

I suppose you are going home to see your families and friends. For the service you have done in this great struggle in which we are engaged I present you sincere thanks for myself and the country. I almost always feel inclined, when I happen to say anything to soldiers, to impress upon them in a few brief remarks the importance of success in this contest. It is not merely for to-day, but for all time to come that we should perpetuate for our children's children this great and free government, which we have enjoyed all our lives. I beg you to remember this, not merely for my sake, but for yours. I happen temporarily to occupy this big White House. I am a living witness that any one of your children may look to come here as my father's child has. It is in order that each of you may have through this free government which we have enjoyed, an open field and a fair chance for your industry, enterprise and intelligence; that you may all have equal privileges in the race of life, with all its desirable human aspirations. It is for this the struggle should be maintained, that we may not lose our birthright—not only for one, but for two or three years. The nation is worth fighting for, to secure such an inestimable jewel.

August 22, 1864

Memorandum on Probable Failure of Re-election

Executive Mansion
Washington, Aug. 23, 1864.

This morning, as for some days past, it seems exceedingly probable that this Administration will not be re-elected. Then it will be my duty to so co-operate with the President elect, as to save the Union between the election and the inauguration; as he will have secured his election on such ground that he can not possibly save it afterwards.

Proclamation of Thanksgiving and Prayer

Executive Mansion,
Washington City September 3d. 1864

The signal success that Divine Providence has recently vouchsafed to the operations of the United States fleet and army in the harbor of Mobile and the reduction of Fort-Powell, Fort-Gaines, and Fort-Morgan, and the glorious achievements of the Army under Major General Sherman in the State of Georgia,[1] resulting in the capture of the City of Atlanta, call for devout acknowledgement to the Supreme Being in whose hands are the destinies of nations. It is therefore requested that on next Sunday, in all places of public worship in the United-States, thanksgiving be offered to Him for His mercy in preserving our national existence against the insurgent rebels who so long have been waging a cruel war against the Government of the United-States, for its overthrow; and also that prayer be made for the Divine protection to our brave soldiers and their leaders in the field, who have so often and so gallantly perilled their lives in battling with the enemy; and for blessing and comfort from the Father of Mercies to the sick, wounded, and prisoners, and to the orphans and widows of those who have fallen in the service of their country, and that he will continue to uphold the Government of the United-States against all the efforts of public enemies and secret foes.

September 3, 1864

To Eliza P. Gurney[1]

Eliza P. Gurney.   Executive Mansion,
My esteemed friend.   Washington, September 4. 1864.

I have not forgotten—probably never shall forget—the very impressive occasion when yourself and friends visited me on a Sabbath forenoon two years ago. Nor has your kind letter, written nearly a year later, ever been forgotten. In all, it has been your purpose to strengthen my reliance on God. I am much indebted to the good christian people of the country for

---

1. William Tecumseh Sherman (1820–1891) in the summer of 1864 had begun a vigorous, successful campaign in Georgia.
1. A pacifist Quaker (1801–1881) who expressed support of Lincoln's effort to end slavery but was ambivalent about his martial means of doing so.

their constant prayers and consolations; and to no one of them, more than to yourself. The purposes of the Almighty are perfect, and must prevail, though we erring mortals may fail to accurately perceive them in advance. We hoped for a happy termination of this terrible war long before this; but God knows best, and has ruled otherwise. We shall yet acknowledge His wisdom and our own error therein. Meanwhile we must work earnestly in the best light He gives us, trusting that so working still conduces to the great ends He ordains. Surely He intends some great good to follow this mighty convulsion, which no mortal could make, and no mortal could stay.

Your people—the Friends—have had, and are having, a very great trial. On principle, and faith, opposed to both war and oppression, they can only practically oppose oppression by war. In this hard dilemma, some have chosen one horn and some the other. For those appealing to me on conscientious grounds, I have done, and shall do, the best I could and can, in my own conscience, under my oath to the law. That you believe this I doubt not; and believing it, I shall still receive, for our country and myself, your earnest prayers to our Father in Heaven. Your sincere friend

Response to Presentation of a Bible by the Loyal Colored People of Baltimore, Washington, D.C.

This occasion would seem fitting for a lengthy response to the address which you have just made. I would make one, if prepared; but I am not. I would promise to respond in writing, had not experience taught me that business will not allow me to do so. I can only now say, as I have often before said, it has always been a sentiment with me that all mankind should be free. So far as able, within my sphere, I have always acted as I believed to be right and just; and I have done all I could for the good of mankind generally. In letters and documents sent from this office I have expressed myself better than I now can. In regard to this Great Book, I have but to say, it is the best gift God has given to man.

All the good the Saviour gave to the world was communicated through this book. But for it we could not know right from wrong. All things most desirable for man's welfare, here and hereafter, are to be found portrayed in it. To you I return my most sincere thanks for the very elegant copy of the great Book of God which you present.

September 7, 1864

Draft of Letter to Isaac M. Schermerhorn[1]

Isaac M. Schcmerhorn   Executive Mansion,
My dear Sir.   Washington, Sept. 12. 1864.
Yours inviting me to attend a Union Mass Meeting at Buffalo is received. Much is being said about peace; and no man desires peace more ardently than I. Still I am yet unprepared to give up the Union for a peace which,

---

1. A postmaster in Buffalo, New York, and a conservative Unionist.

so achieved, could not be of much duration. The preservation of our Union was *not* the sole avowed object for which the war was commenced. It was commenced for precisely the reverse object—*to destroy our Union.* The insurgents commenced it by firing upon the Star of the West, and on Fort Sumpter, and by other similar acts. It is true, however, that the administration accepted the war thus commenced, for the sole avowed object of preserving our Union; and it is not true that it has since been, or will be, prossecuted by this administration, for any other object. In declaring this, I only declare what I can know, and do know to be true, and what no other man can know to be false.

In taking the various steps which have led to my present position in relation to the war, the public interest and my private interest, have been perfectly paralel, because in no other way could I serve myself so well, as by truly serving the Union. The whole field has been open to me, where to choose. No place-hunting necessity has been upon me urging me to seek a position of antagonism to some other man, irrespective of whether such position might be favorable or unfavorable to the Union.

Of course I may err in judgment, but my present position in reference to the rebellion is the result of my best judgment, and according to that best judgment, it is the only position upon which any Executive can or could save the Union. Any substantial departure from it insures the success of the rebellion. An armistice—a cessation of hostilities—is the end of the struggle, and the insurgents would be in peaceable possession of all that has been struggled for. Any different policy in regard to the colored man, deprives us of his help, and this is more than we can bear. We can not spare the hundred and forty or fifty thousand now serving us as soldiers, seamen, and laborers. This is not a question of sentiment or taste, but one of physical force which may be measured and estimated as horse-power and Steam-power are measured and estimated. Keep it and you can save the Union. Throw it away, and the Union goes with it. Nor is it possible for any Administration to retain the service of these people with the express or implied understanding that upon the first convenient occasion, they are to be re-inslaved. It *can* not be; and it *ought* not to be.

To Henry W. Hoffman[1]

Executive Mansion,
Hon. Henry W Hoffman   Washington,
My dear Sir: October 10, 1864.

A convention of Maryland has framed a new constitution for the State; a public meeting is called for this evening, at Baltimore, to aid in securing its ratification by the people; and you ask a word from me, for the occasion. I presume the only feature of the instrument, about which there is serious controversy, is that which provides for the extinction of slavery. It needs not to be a secret, and I presume it is no secret, that I wish success to this provision. I desire it on every consideration. I wish all men to be free. I wish the

---

1. Maryland politician (1825–1895) whom Lincoln appointed as Baltimore's collector of customs, a position he held until 1866.

material prosperity of the already free which I feel sure the extinction of slavery would bring. I wish to see, in process of disappearing, that only thing which ever could bring this nation to civil war. I attempt no argument. Argument upon the question is already exhausted by the abler, better informed, and more immediately interested sons of Maryland herself. I only add that I shall be gratified exceedingly if the good people of the State shall, by their votes, ratify the new constitution. Yours truly

Proclamation of Thanksgiving

By the President of the United States of America:
A Proclamation

It has pleased Almighty God to prolong our national life another year, defending us with his guardian care against unfriendly designs from abroad, and vouchsafing to us in His mercy many and signal victories over the enemy, who is of our own household. It has also pleased our Heavenly Father to favor as well our citizens in their homes as our soldiers in their camps and our sailors on the rivers and seas with unusual health. He has largely augmented our free population by emancipation and by immigration, while he has opened to us new sources of wealth, and has crowned the labor of our working men in every department of industry with abundant rewards. Moreover, He has been pleased to animate and inspire our minds and hearts with fortitude, courage and resolution sufficient for the great trial of civil war into which we have been brought by our adherence as a nation to the cause of Freedom and Humanity, and to afford to us reasonable hopes of an ultimate and happy deliverance from all our dangers and afflictions.

Now, therefore, I, Abraham Lincoln, President of the United States, do, hereby, appoint and set apart the last Thursday in November next as a day, which I desire to be observed by all my fellow-citizens wherever they may then be as a day of Thanksgiving and Praise to Almighty God the beneficent Creator and Ruler of the Universe. And I do farther recommend to my fellow-citizens aforesaid that on that occasion they do reverently humble themselves in the dust and from thence offer up penitent and fervent prayers and supplications to the Great Disposer of events for a return of the inestimable blessings of Peace, Union and Harmony throughout the land, which it has pleased him to assign as a dwelling place for ourselves and for our posterity throughout all generations.

In testimony whereof, I have hereunto set my hand and caused the seal of the United States to be affixed.

Done at the city of Washington this twentieth day of October, in the year of our Lord one thousand eight hundred and sixty four, and, of the Independence of the United States the eighty-ninth.

By the President: Abraham Lincoln
William H Seward Secretary of State.

October 20, 1864

Response to Serenade, Washington, D.C.[1]

It has long been a grave question whether any government, not *too* strong for the liberties of its people, can be strong *enough* to maintain its own existence, in great emergencies.

On this point the present rebellion brought our republic to a severe test; and a presidential election occurring in regular course during the rebellion added not a little to the strain. If the loyal people, *united*, were put to the utmost of their strength by the rebellion, must they not fail when *divided*, and partially paralyzed, by a political war among themselves?

But the election was a necessity.

We can not have free government without elections; and if the rebellion could force us to forego, or postpone a national election, it might fairly claim to have already conquered and ruined us. The strife of the election is but human-nature practically applied to the facts of the case. What has occurred in this case, must ever recur in similar cases. Human-nature will not change. In any future great national trial, compared with the men of this, we shall have as weak, and as strong; as silly and as wise; as bad and good. Let us, therefore, study the incidents of this, as philosophy to learn wisdom from, and none of them as wrongs to be revenged.

But the election, along with its incidental, and undesirable strife, has done good too. It has demonstrated that a people's government can sustain a national election, in the midst of a great civil war. Until now it has not been known to the world that this was a possibility. It shows also how *sound*, and how *strong* we still are. It shows that, even among candidates of the same party, he who is most devoted to the Union, and most opposed to treason, can receive most of the people's votes. It shows also, to the extent yet known, that we have more men now, than we had when the war began. Gold is good in its place; but living, brave, patriotic men, are better than gold.

But the rebellion continues; and now that the election is over, may not all, having a common interest, re-unite in a common effort, to save our common country? For my own part I have striven, and shall strive to avoid placing any obstacle in the way. So long as I have been here I have not willingly planted a thorn in any man's bosom.

While I am deeply sensible to the high compliment of a re-election; and duly grateful, as I trust, to Almighty God for having directed my countrymen to a right conclusion, as I think, for their own good, it adds nothing to my satisfaction that any other man may be disappointed or pained by the result.

May I ask those who have not differed with me, to join with me, in this same spirit towards those who have?

And now, let me close by asking three hearty cheers for our brave soldiers and seamen and their gallant and skilful commanders.

November 10, 1864

1. Two days after Lincoln won the November 8 election, supporters gathered outside the White House to cheer and serenade him.

To Mrs. Lydia Bixby[1]

Executive Mansion,
Washington, Nov. 21, 1864.

Dear Madam,—I have been shown in the files of the War Department a statement of the Adjutant General of Massachusetts, that you are the mother of five sons who have died gloriously on the field of battle.

I feel how weak and fruitless must be any words of mine which should attempt to beguile you from the grief of a loss so overwhelming. But I cannot refrain from tendering to you the consolation that may be found in the thanks of the Republic they died to save.

I pray that our Heavenly Father may assuage the anguish of your bereavement, and leave you only the cherished memory of the loved and lost, and the solemn pride that must be yours, to have laid so costly a sacrifice upon the altar of Freedom. Yours, very sincerely and respectfully,

From Annual Message to Congress

*   *   *

Official correspondence has been freely opened with Liberia, and it gives us a pleasing view of social and political progress in that Republic. It may be expected to derive new vigor from American influence, improved by the rapid disappearance of slavery in the United States.

*   *   *

The act passed at the-last session for the encouragement of emigration has, so far as was possible, been put into operation. It seems to need amendment which will enable the officers of the government to prevent the practice of frauds against the immigrants while on their way and on their arrival in the ports, so as to secure them here a free choice of avocations and places of settlement. A liberal disposition towards this great national policy is manifested by most of the European States, and ought to be reciprocated on our part by giving the immigrants effective national protection. I regard our emigrants as one of the principal replenishing streams which are appointed by Providence to repair the ravages of internal war, and its wastes of national strength and health. All that is necessary is to secure the flow of that stream in its present fullness, and to that end the government must, in every way, make it manifest that it neither needs nor designs to impose involuntary military service upon those who come from other lands to cast their lot in our country.

1. This letter, no copy of which survives in Lincoln's hand, was printed in the *Boston Evening Transcript* on November 25, 1864, the day it was delivered to the widow Lydia Bixby. The letter was prompted by a note to Lincoln from Massachusetts governor John A. Andrew (1818–1867), who asked the president to write in condolence to Mrs. Bixby. Controversy surrounds the letter. Records reveal that three of Mrs. Bixby's sons were still living after the war. Reportedly, the Virginia-born Mrs. Bixby was a Confederate sympathizer who ran a Boston house of prostitution and destroyed Lincoln's letter after she received it. There is also debate over whether the letter was written by Lincoln or by his private assistant secretary John M. Hay (1838–1905).

The financial affairs of the government have been successfully administered during the last year. The legislation of the last session of Congress has beneficially affected the revenues, although sufficient time has not yet elapsed to experience the full effect of several of the provisions of the acts of Congress imposing increased taxation.

＊　＊　＊

The war continues. Since the last annual message all the important lines and positions then occupied by our forces have been maintained, and our arms have steadily advanced; thus liberating the regions left in rear, so that Missouri, Kentucky, Tennessee and parts of other States have again produced reasonably fair crops.

The most remarkable feature in the military operations of the year is General Sherman's attempted march of three hundred miles directly through the insurgent region.[1] It tends to show a great increase of our relative strength that our General-in-Chief should feel able to confront and hold in check every active force of the enemy, and yet to detach a well-appointed large army to move on such an expedition. The result not yet being known, conjecture in regard to it is not here indulged.

Important movements have also occurred during the year to the effect of moulding society for durability in the Union. Although short of complete success, it is much in the right direction, that twelve thousand citizens in each of the States of Arkansas and Louisiana have organized loyal State governments with free constitutions, and are earnestly struggling to maintain and administer them. The movements in the same direction, more extensive, though less definite in Missouri, Kentucky and Tennessee, should not be overlooked. But Maryland presents the example of complete success. Maryland is secure to Liberty and Union for all the future. The genius of rebellion will no more claim Maryland. Like another foul spirit, being driven out, it may seek to tear her, but it will woo her no more.

At the last session of Congress a proposed amendment of the Constitution abolishing slavery throughout the United States, passed the Senate, but failed for lack of the requisite two-thirds vote in the House of Representatives. Although the present is the same Congress, and nearly the same members, and without questioning the wisdom or patriotism of those who stood in opposition, I venture to recommend the reconsideration and passage of the measure at the present session. Of course the abstract question is not changed; but an intervening election shows, almost certainly, that the next Congress will pass the measure if this does not. Hence there is only a question of *time* as to when the proposed amendment will go to the States for their action. And as it is to so go, at all events, may we not agree that the sooner the better? It is not claimed that the election has imposed a duty on members to change their views or their votes, any further than, as an additional element to be considered, their judgment may be affected by it. It is the voice of the people now, for the first time, heard upon the question. In a great national crisis, like ours, unanimity of action among those seeking a common end is very desirable—almost

---

1. Sherman's famous March to the Sea (November 15 to December 21, 1864) from the captured Atlanta to the port of Savannah dealt a devastating blow to the Confederacy.

indispensable. And yet no approach to such unanimity is attainable, unless some deference shall be paid to the will of the majority, simply because it is the will of the majority. In this case the common end is the maintenance of the Union; and, among the means to secure that end, such will, through the election, is most clearly declared in favor of such constitutional amendment.

The most reliable indication of public purpose in this country is derived through our popular elections. Judging by the recent canvass and its result, the purpose of the people, within the loyal States, to maintain the integrity of the Union, was never more firm, nor more nearly unanimous, than now. The extraordinary calmness and good order with which the millions of voters met and mingled at the polls, give strong assurance of this. Not only all those who supported the Union ticket, so called, but a great majority of the opposing party also, may be fairly claimed to entertain, and to be actuated by, the same purpose. It is an unanswerable argument to this effect, that no candidate for any office whatever, high or low, has ventured to seek votes on the avowal that he was for giving up the Union. There have been much impugning of motives, and much heated controversy as to the proper means and best mode of advancing the Union cause; but on the distinct issue of Union or no Union, the politicians have shown their instinctive knowledge that there is no diversity among the people. In affording the people the fair opportunity of showing, one to another and to the world, this firmness and unanimity of purpose, the election has been of vast value to the national cause.

The election has exhibited another fact not less valuable to be known— the fact that we do not approach exhaustion in the most important branch of national resources—that of living men. While it is melancholy to reflect that the war has filled so many graves, and carried mourning to so many hearts, it is some relief to know that, compared with the surviving, the fallen have been so few. While corps, and divisions, and brigades, and regiments have formed, and fought, and dwindled, and gone out of existence, a great majority of the men who composed them are still living. The same is true of the naval service. The election returns prove this. So many voters could not else be found. The States regularly holding elections, both now and four years ago, to wit, California, Connecticut, Delaware, Illinois, Indiana, Iowa, Kentucky, Maine, Maryland, Massachusetts, Michigan, Minnesota, Missouri, New Hampshire, New Jersey, New York, Ohio, Oregon, Pennsylvania, Rhode Island, Vermont, West Virginia, and Wisconsin cast 3.982.011 votes now, against 3.870.222 cast then, showing an aggregate now of 3.982.011. To this is to be added 33.762 cast now in the new States of Kansas and Nevada, which States did not vote in 1860, thus swelling the aggregate to 4.015.773 and the net increase during the three years and a half of war to 145.551. A table is appended showing particulars. To this again should be added the number of all soldiers in the field from Massachusetts, Rhode Island, New Jersey, Delaware, Indiana, Illinois, and California, who, by the laws of those States, could not vote away from their homes, and which number cannot be less than 90.000. Nor yet is this all. The number in organized Territories is triple now what it was four years ago, while thousands, white and black, join us as the national arms press back the insurgent lines. So much is shown, affirmatively and negatively, by the election. It is not material to inquire *how* the increase has been produced, or to show that it would have been *greater* but for the war, which is probably true. The important fact remains demonstrated, that we have *more* men *now* than we had when the war *began*; that we are not exhausted, nor in process of exhaustion; that we are *gaining* strength, and may, if need be, maintain the contest indefinitely. This as to men. Material resources are now more complete and abundant than ever.

The national resources, then, are unexhausted, and, as we believe, inexhaustible. The public purpose to re-establish and maintain the national authority is unchanged, and, as we believe, unchangeable. The manner of continuing the effort remains to choose. On careful consideration of all the evidence accessible it seems to me that no attempt at negotiation with the insurgent leader[2] could result in any good. He would accept nothing short of severance of the Union—precisely what we will not and cannot give. His declarations to this effect are explicit and oft-repeated. He does not attempt to deceive us. He affords us no excuse to deceive ourselves. He cannot voluntarily reaccept the Union; we cannot voluntarily yield it. Between him and us the issue is distinct, simple, and inflexible. It is an issue which can only be tried by war, and decided by victory. If we yield, we are beaten; if the Southern people fail him, he is beaten. Either way, it would be the victory and defeat following war. What is true, however, of him who heads the insurgent cause, is not necessarily true of those who follow. Although he cannot reaccept the Union, they can. Some of them, we know, already desire peace and reunion. The number of such may increase. They can, at any moment, have peace simply by laying down their arms and submitting to the national authority under the Constitution. After so much, the government could not, if it would, maintain war against them. The loyal people would not sustain or allow it. If questions should remain, we would adjust them by the peaceful means of legislation, conference, courts, and votes, operating only in constitutional and lawful channels. Some certain, and other possible, questions are, and would be, beyond the Executive power to adjust; as, for instance, the admission of members into Congress, and whatever might require the appropriation of money. The Executive power itself would be greatly diminished by the cessation of actual war. Pardons and remissions of forfeitures, however, would still be within Executive control. In what spirit and temper this control would be exercised can be fairly judged of by the past.

A year ago general pardon and amnesty, upon specified terms, were offered to all, except certain designated classes;[3] and, it was, at the same time, made known that the excepted classes were still within contemplation of special clemency. During the year many availed themselves of the general provision, and many more would, only that the signs of bad faith in some led to such precautionary measures as rendered the practical process less easy and certain. During the same time also special pardons have been granted to individuals of the excepted classes, and no voluntary application has been denied. Thus, practically, the door has been, for a full year, open to all, except such as were not in condition to make free

2. Jefferson Davis, president of the Confederate States of America (1861–65).
3. See p. 332.

choice—that is, such as were in custody or under constraint. It is still so open to all. But the time may come—probably will come—when public duty shall demand that it be closed; and that, in lieu, more rigorous measures than heretofore shall be adopted.

In presenting the abandonment of armed resistance to the national authority on the part of the insurgents, as the only indispensable condition to ending the war on the part of the government, I retract nothing heretofore said as to slavery. I repeat the declaration made a year ago, that "while I remain in my present position I shall not attempt to retract or modify the emancipation proclamation, nor shall I return to slavery any person who is free by the terms of that proclamation, or by any of the Acts of Congress." If the people should, by whatever mode or means, make it an Executive duty to re-enslave such persons, another, and not I, must be their instrument to perform it.

In stating a single condition of peace, I mean simply to say that the war will cease on the part of the government, whenever it shall have ceased on the part of those who began it.

December 6. 1864.

Reply to a Southern Woman[1]

The President's last, shortest, and best speech.

On thursday of last week two ladies from Tennessee came before the President asking the release of their husbands held as prisoners of war at Johnson's Island. They were put off till friday, when they came again; and were again put off to Saturday. At each of the interviews one of the ladies urged that her husband was a religious man. On Saturday the President ordered the release of the prisoners, and then said to this lady "You say your husband is a religious man; tell him when you meet him, that I say I am not much of a judge of religion, but that, in my opinion, the religion that sets men to rebel and fight against their government, because, as they think, that government does not sufficiently help *some* men to eat their bread on the sweat of *other* men's faces, is not the sort of religion upon which people can get to heaven!"

December 6, 1864, or before

To William T. Sherman

Executive Mansion, Washington,
My dear General Sherman.   Dec. 26, 1864.
Many, many, thanks for your Christmas-gift[1]—the capture of Savannah.

When you were about leaving Atlanta for the Atlantic coast, I was *anxious*, if not fearful; but feeling that you were the better judge, and

1. This report of Lincoln's statement about religion appeared in the Washington *Chronicle* on December 7, 1864.
1. Sherman's army had captured Savannah, Georgia on December 21.

remembering that "nothing risked, nothing gained" I did not interfere. Now, the undertaking being a success, the honor is all yours; for I believe none of us went farther than to acquiesce. And, taking the work of Gen. Thomas[2] into the count, as it should be taken, it is indeed a great success. Not only does it afford the obvious and immediate military advantages; but, in showing to the world that your army could be divided, putting the stronger part to an important new service, and yet leaving enough to vanquish the old opposing force of the whole—Hood's army—it brings those who sat in darkness, to see a great light. But what next? I suppose it will be safer if I leave Gen. Grant and yourself to decide.

Please make my grateful acknowledgments to your whole army, officers and men. Yours very truly

Response to Serenade, Washington, D.C.[1]

The President said he supposed the passage through Congress of the Constitutional amendment for the abolishment of Slavery throughout the United States, was the occasion to which he was indebted for the honor of this call. [Applause.] The occasion was one of congratulation to the country and to the whole world. But there is a task yet before us—to go forward and consummate by the votes of the States that which Congress so nobly began yesterday. [Applause and cries—"They will do it," &c.] He had the honor to inform those present that Illinois had already to-day done the work. [Applause.] Maryland was about half through; but he felt proud that Illinois was a little ahead. He thought this measure was a very fitting if not an indispensable adjunct to the winding up of the great difficulty. He wished the reunion of all the States perfected and so effected as to remove all causes of disturbance in the future; and to attain this end it was necessary that the original disturbing cause should, if possible, be rooted out. He thought all would bear him witness that he had never shrunk from doing all that he could to eradicate Slavery by issuing an emancipation proclamation. [Applause.] But that proclamation falls far short of what the amendment will be when fully consummated. A question might be raised whether the proclamation was legally valid. It might be added that it only aided those who came into our lines and that it was inoperative as to those who did not give themselves up, or that it would have no effect upon the children of the slaves born hereafter. In fact it would be urged that it did not meet the evil. But this amendment is a King's cure for all the evils. [Applause.] It winds the whole thing up. He would repeat that it was the fitting if not indispensable adjunct to the consummation of the great game we are playing. He could not but congratulate all present, himself, the country and the whole world upon this great moral victory.

February 1, 1865

---

2. George H. Thomas (1816–1870) decisively defeated John Bell Hood (1831–1879) at Nashville in mid-December.
1. On the evening of February 1, 1865, a day after the passage of the Thirteenth Amendment, which abolished slavery, bands and a large crowd gathered outside the White House to salute the president.

To the Senate and House of Representatives

Fellow citizens of the Senate, and House of Representatives.

I respectfully recommend that a Joint Resolution, substantially as follows, be adopted so soon as practicable, by your honorable bodies.

"Resolved by the Senate and House of Representatives, of the United States of America in congress assembled: That the President of the United States is hereby empowered, in his discretion, to pay four hundred millions of dollars to the States of Alabama, Arkansas, Delaware, Florida, Georgia, Kentucky, Louisiana, Maryland Mississippi, Missouri, North Carolina, South Carolina, Tennessee, Texas, Virginia, and West-Virginia, in the manner, and on the conditions following, towit: The payment to be made in six per cent government bonds, and to be distributed among said States *pro rata* on their respective slave populations, as shown by the census of 1860; and no part of said sum to be paid unless all resistance to the national authority shall be abandoned and cease, on or before the first day of April next; and upon such abandonment and ceasing of resistance, one half of said sum to be paid in manner aforesaid, and the remaining half to be paid only upon the amendment of the national constitution recently proposed by congress, becoming valid law, on or before the first day of July next, by the action thereon of the requisite number of States"

The adoption of such resolution is sought with a view to embody it, with other propositions, in a proclamation looking to peace and re-union.

Whereas a Joint Resolution has been adopted by congress in the words following, towit

Now therefore I, Abraham Lincoln, President of the United States, do proclaim, declare, and make known, that on the conditions therein stated, the power conferred on the Executive in and by said Joint Resolution, will be fully exercised; that war will cease, and armies be reduced to a basis of peace; that all political offences will be pardoned; that all property, except slaves, liable to confiscation or forfeiture, will be released therefrom, except in cases of intervening interests of third parties; and that liberality will be recommended to congress upon all points not lying within executive control.

Feb. 5. 1865

To-day these papers, which explain themselves, were drawn up and submitted to the Cabinet & unanamously disapproved by them.

February 5, 1865

Second Inaugural Address

Fellow Countrymen:

At this second appearing to take the oath of the presidential office, there is less occasion for an extended address than there was at the first. Then a statement, somewhat in detail, of a course to be pursued, seemed fitting and proper. Now, at the expiration of four years, during which public declarations have been constantly called forth on every point and phase

Lincoln on February 5, 1865. Photo by Alexander Gardner. Known as the "last photograph of Lincoln from life," this was the last photo from the last session with Gardner at Gardner's Gallery in Washington, D.C., on that Sunday in February 1865. Library of Congress Prints and Photographs Division.

Lincoln on February 5, 1865. Photo by Alexander Gardner. Library of Congress Prints and Photographs Division.

of the great contest which still absorbs the attention, and engrosses the energies of the nation, little that is new could be presented. The progress of our arms, upon which all else chiefly depends, is as well known to the public as to myself; and it is, I trust, reasonably satisfactory and encouraging to all. With high hope for the future, no prediction in regard to it is ventured.

On the occasion corresponding to this four years ago, all thoughts were anxiously directed to an impending civil-war. All dreaded it—all sought to avert it. While the inaugeral address was being delivered from this place, devoted altogether to *saving* the Union without war, insurgent agents were in the city seeking to *destroy* it without war—seeking to dissolve the Union, and divide effects, by negotiation. Both parties deprecated war; but one of them would *make* war rather than let the nation survive; and the other would *accept* war rather than let it perish. And the war came.

One eighth of the whole population were colored slaves, not distributed generally over the Union, but localized in the Southern part of it. These slaves constituted a peculiar and powerful interest. All knew that this interest was, somehow, the cause of the war. To strengthen, perpetuate, and extend this interest was the object for which the insurgents would rend the Union, even by war; while the government claimed no right to do more than to restrict the territorial enlargement of it. Neither party expected for the war, the magnitude, or the duration, which it has already attained. Neither anticipated that the *cause* of the conflict might cease with, or even before, the conflict itself should cease. Each looked for an easier triumph, and a result less fundamental and astounding. Both read the same Bible, and pray to the same God; and each invokes His aid against the other. It may seem strange that any men should dare to ask a just God's assistance in wringing their bread from the sweat of other men's faces; but let us judge not that we be not judged. The prayers of both could not be answered; that of neither has been answered fully. The Almighty has His own purposes. "Woe unto the world because of offences! for it must needs be that offences come; but woe to that man by whom the offence cometh!"[1] If we shall suppose that American Slavery is one of those offences which, in the providence of God, must needs come, but which, having continued through His appointed time, He now wills to remove, and that He gives to both North and South, this terrible war, as the woe due to those by whom the offence came, shall we discern therein any departure from those divine attributes which the believers in a Living God always ascribe to Him? Fondly do we hope—fervently do we pray—that this mighty scourge of war may speedily pass away. Yet, if God wills that it continue, until all the wealth piled by the bond-man's two hundred and fifty years of unrequited toil shall be sunk, and until every drop of blood drawn with the lash, shall be paid by another drawn with the sword, as was said three thousand years ago, so still it must be said "the judgments of the Lord, are true and righteous altogether."[2]

With malice toward none; with charity for all; with firmness in the right, as God gives us to see the right, let us strive on to finish the work

1. Matthew 18:7.
2. Psalms 19:9.

we are in; to bind up the nation's wounds; to care for him who shall have borne the battle, and for his widow, and his orphan—to do all which may achieve and cherish a just, and a lasting peace, among ourselves, and with all nations.

March 4, 1865

Speech to the 140th Indiana Regiment, Washington, D.C.

FELLOW CITIZENS—It will be but a very few words that I shall undertake to say. I was born in Kentucky, raised in Indiana and lived in Illinois. (Laughter.) And now I am here, where it is my business to care equally for the good people of all the States. I am glad to see an Indiana regiment on this day able to present the captured flag to the Governor of Indiana. (Applause.) I am not disposed, in saying this, to make a distinction between the States, for all have done equally well. (Applause.) There are but few views or aspects of this great war upon which I have not said or written something whereby my own opinions might be known. But there is one— the recent attempt of our erring brethren, as they are sometimes called— (laughter)—to employ the negro to fight for them. I have neither written nor made a speech on that subject, because that was their business, not mine; and if I had a wish upon the subject I had not the power to intro- duce it, or make it effective. The great question with them was, whether the negro, being put into the army, would fight for them. I do not know, and therefore cannot decide. (Laughter.) They ought to know better than we. I have in my lifetime heard many arguments why the negroes ought to be slaves; but if they fight for those who would keep them in slavery it will be a better argument than any I have yet heard. (Laughter and applause.) He who will fight for that ought to be a slave. (Applause.) They have concluded at last to take one out of four of the slaves, and put them in the army; and that one out of the four who will fight to keep the others in slavery ought to be a slave himself unless he is killed in a fight. (Applause.) While I have often said that all men ought to be free, yet I would allow those colored persons to be slaves who want to be; and next to them those white persons who argue in favor of making other people slaves. (Applause.) I am in favor of giving an opportunity to such white men to try it on for themselves. (Applause.) I will say one thing in regard to the negro being employed to fight for them. I do know he cannot fight and stay at home and make bread too—(laughter and applause)—and as one is about as important as the other to them, I don't care which they do. (Renewed applause.) I am rather in favor of having them try them as soldiers. (Applause.) They lack one vote of doing that, and I wish I could send my vote over the river so that I might cast it in favor of allowing the negro to fight. (Applause.) But they cannot fight and work both. We must now see the bottom of the enemy's resources. They will stand out as long as they can, and if the negro will fight for them, they must allow him to fight. They have drawn upon their last branch of resources. (Applause.) And we can now see the bottom. (Applause.) I am glad to see the end so near at hand. (Applause.) I have said now more than I intended, and will therefore bid you goodby.

March 17, 1865

Response to Serenade, Washington, D.C.

"FELLOW CITIZENS: I am very greatly rejoiced to find that an occasion has occurred so pleasurable that the people cannot restrain themselves.[1] [Cheers.] I suppose that arrangements are being made for some sort of a formal demonstration, this, or perhaps, to-morrow night. [Cries of 'We can't wait,' 'We want it now,' &c.] If there should be such a demonstration, I, of course, will be called upon to respond, and I shall have nothing to say if you dribble it all out of me before. [Laughter and applause.] I see you have a band of music with you. [Voices, 'We have two or three.'] I propose closing up this interview by the band performing a particular tune which I will name. Before this is done, however, I wish to mention one or two little circumstances connected with it. I have always thought 'Dixie' one of the best tunes I have ever heard. Our adversaries over the way attempted to appropriate it, but I insisted yesterday that we fairly captured it. [Applause.] I presented the question to the Attorney General, and he gave it as his legal opinion that it is our lawful prize. [Laughter and applause.] I now request the band to favor me with its performance."

April 10, 1865

Speech on Reconstruction, Washington, D.C.

We meet this evening, not in sorrow, but in gladness of heart. The evacuation of Petersburg and Richmond, and the surrender of the principal insurgent army, give hope of a righteous and speedy peace whose joyous expression can not be restrained. In the midst of this, however, He, from Whom all blessings flow, must not be forgotten. A call for a national thanksgiving is being prepared, and will be duly promulgated. Nor must those whose harder part gives us the cause of rejoicing, be overlooked. Their honors must not be parcelled out with others. I myself, was near the front, and had the high pleasure of transmitting much of the good news to you; but no part of the honor, for plan or execution, is mine. To Gen. Grant, his skilful officers, and brave men, all belongs. The gallant Navy stood ready, but was not in reach to take active part.

By these recent successes the re-inauguration of the national authority—reconstruction—which has had a large share of thought from the first, is pressed much more closely upon our attention. It is fraught with great difficulty. Unlike the case of a war between independent nations, there is no authorized organ for us to treat with. No one man has authority to give up the rebellion for any other man. We simply must begin with, and mould

1. On April 9, Lee had surrendered to Grant at Appomattox.

from, disorganized and discordant elements. Nor is it a small additional embarrassment that we, the loyal people, differ among ourselves as to the mode, manner, and means of reconstruction.

As a general rule, I abstain from reading the reports of attacks upon myself, wishing not to be provoked by that to which I can not properly offer an answer. In spite of this precaution, however, it comes to my knowledge that I am much censured for some supposed agency in setting up, and seeking to sustain, the new State Government of Louisiana. In this I have done just so much as, and no more than, the public knows. In the Annual Message of Dec. 1863 and accompanying Proclamation, I presented *a* plan of reconstruction (as the phrase goes) which, I promised, if adopted by any State, should be acceptable to, and sustained by, the Executive government of the nation. I distinctly stated that this was not the only plan which might possibly be acceptable; and I also distinctly protested that the Executive claimed no right to say when, or whether members should be admitted to seats in Congress from such States. This plan was, in advance, submitted to the then Cabinet, and distinctly approved by every member of it. One of them[1] suggested that I should then, and in that connection, apply the Emancipation Proclamation to the theretofore excepted parts of Virginia and Louisiana; that I should drop the suggestion about apprenticeship for freed-people, and that I should omit the protest against my own power, in regard to the admission of members to Congress; but even he approved every part and parcel of the plan which has since been employed or touched by the action of Louisiana. The new constitution of Louisiana, declaring emancipation for the whole State, practically applies the Proclamation to the part previously excepted. It does not adopt apprenticeship for freed-people; and it is silent, as it could not well be otherwise, about the admission of members to Congress. So that, as it applies to Louisiana, every member of the Cabinet fully approved the plan. The Message went to Congress, and I received many commendations of the plan, written and verbal; and not a single objection to it, from any professed emancipationist, came to my knowledge, until after the news reached Washington that the people of Louisiana had begun to move in accordance with it. From about July 1862, I had corresponded with different persons, supposed to be interested, seeking a reconstruction of a State government for Louisiana. When the Message of 1863, with the plan before mentioned, reached New-Orleans, Gen. Banks wrote me that he was confident the people, with his military co-operation, would reconstruct, substantially on that plan. I wrote him, and some of them to try it; they tried it, and the result is known. Such only has been my agency in getting up the Louisiana government. As to sustaining it, my promise is out, as before stated. But, as bad promises are better broken than kept, I shall treat this as a bad promise, and break it, whenever I shall be convinced that keeping it is adverse to the public interest. But I have not yet been so convinced.

I have been shown a letter on this subject, supposed to be an able one, in which the writer expresses regret that my mind has not seemed to be definitely fixed on the question whether the seceded States, so called, are

---

1. Salmon P. Chase, who was secretary of the treasury from 1861 to 1864.

in the Union or out of it. It would perhaps, add astonishment to his regret, were he to learn that since I have found professed Union men endeavoring to make that question, I have *purposely* forborne any public expression upon it. As appears to me that question has not been, nor yet is, a practically material one, and that any discussion of it, while it thus remains practically immaterial, could have no effect other than the mischievous one of dividing our friends. As yet, whatever it may hereafter become, that question is bad, as the basis of a controversy, and good for nothing at all—a merely pernicious abstraction.

We all agree that the seceded States, so called, are out of their proper practical relation with the Union; and that the sole object of the government, civil and military, in regard to those States is to again get them into that proper practical relation. I believe it is not only possible, but in fact, easier, to do this, without deciding, or even considering, whether these states have even been out of the Union, than with it. Finding themselves safely at home, it would be utterly immaterial whether they had ever been abroad. Let us all join in doing the acts necessary to restoring the proper practical relations between these states and the Union; and each forever after, innocently indulge his own opinion whether, in doing the acts, he brought the States from without, into the Union, or only gave them proper assistance, they never having been out of it.

The amount of constituency, so to speak, on which the new Louisiana government rests, would be more satisfactory to all, if it contained fifty, thirty, or even twenty thousand, instead of only about twelve thousand, as it does. It is also unsatisfactory to some that the elective franchise is not given to the colored man. I would myself prefer that it were now conferred on the very intelligent, and on those who serve our cause as soldiers. Still the question is not whether the Louisiana government, as it stands, is quite all that is desirable. The question is "Will it be wiser to take it as it is, and help to improve it; or to reject, and disperse it?" "Can Louisiana be brought into proper practical relation with the Union *sooner* by *sustaining*, or by *discarding* her new State Government?"

Some twelve thousand voters in the heretofore slave-state of Louisiana have sworn allegiance to the Union, assumed to be the rightful political power of the State, held elections, organized a State government, adopted a free-state constitution, giving the benefit of public schools equally to black and white, and empowering the Legislature to confer the elective franchise upon the colored man. Their Legislature has already voted to ratify the constitutional amendment recently passed by Congress, abolishing slavery throughout the nation. These twelve thousand persons are thus fully committed to the Union, and to perpetual freedom in the state—committed to the very things, and nearly all the things the nation wants—and they ask the nations recognition, and it's assistance to make good their committal. Now, if we reject, and spurn them, we do our utmost to disorganize and disperse them. We in effect say to the white men "You are worthless, or worse—we will neither help you, nor be helped by you." To the blacks we say "This cup of liberty which these, your old masters, hold to your lips, we will dash from you, and leave you to the chances of gathering the spilled and scattered contents in some vague and undefined when, where, and how." If this course, discouraging and paralyzing both white and black, has any tendency to bring Louisiana into proper practical relations with the Union, I have, so far, been unable to perceive it. If, on the contrary, we recognize, and sustain the new government of Louisiana the converse of all this is made true. We encourage the hearts, and nerve the arms of the twelve thousand to adhere to their work, and argue for it, and proselyte for it, and fight for it, and feed it, and grow it, and ripen it to a complete success. The colored man too, in seeing all united for him, is inspired with vigilance, and energy, and daring, to the same end. Grant that he desires the elective franchise, will he not attain it sooner by saving the already advanced steps toward it, than by running backward over them? Concede that the new government of Louisiana is only to what it should be as the egg is to the fowl, we shall sooner have the fowl by hatching the egg than by smashing it? Again, if we reject Louisiana, we also reject one vote in favor of the proposed amendment to the national constitution. To meet this proposition, it has been argued that no more than three fourths of those States which have not attempted secession are necessary to validly ratify the amendment. I do not commit myself against this, further than to say that such a ratification would be questionable, and sure to be persistently questioned; while a ratification by three fourths of all the States would be unquestioned and unquestionable.

I repeat the question. "Can Louisiana be brought into proper practical relation with the Union *sooner* by *sustaining* or by *discording* her new State Government?

What has been said of Louisiana will apply generally to other States. And yet so great peculiarities pertain to each state; and such important and sudden changes occur in the same state; and, withal, so new and unprecedented is the whole case, that no exclusive, and inflexible plan can safely be prescribed as to details and colatterals. Such exclusive, and inflexible plan, would surely become a new entanglement. Important principles may, and must, be inflexible.

In the present *"situation"* as the phrase goes, it may be my duty to make some new announcement to the people of the South. I am considering, and shall not fail to act, when satisfied that action will be proper.

April 11, 1865

LINCOLN IN HIS ERA

Lincoln on February 9, 1864. Photo by Anthony Berger. This image was the basis of Lincoln's portrait on the five-dollar bill from 1914 to 2007. Library of Congress Prints and Photographs Division.

Commentary and Contexts

HORACE WHITE

[Lincoln Breaks Down in Debate with Douglas]†

THE CAMPAIGN

—

DOUGLAS AMONG THE PEOPLE

—

Joint Discussion at Ottawa![1]

—

LINCOLN BREAKS DOWN.

—

ENTHUSIASM OF THE PEOPLE!

—

The Battle Fought and Won.

—

Lincoln's Heart Fails Him!
Lincoln's Legs Fail Him!
Lincoln's Tongue Fails Him!
Lincoln's Arms Fail Him!
LINCOLN FAILS ALL OVER!!

—

The People Refuse to Support Him!
The People Laugh at Him!

—

DOUGLAS THE CHAMPION OF THE PEOPLE!

—

Douglas Skins the "Living Dog."

—

THE "DEAD LION" FRIGHTENS THE CANINE.
Douglas "Trotting" Lincoln Out.

—

DOUGLAS "CONCLUDES" ON ABE.

✳   ✳   ✳

---

† Headlines from article in the *Chicago Times*, August 22, 1858.
1. The debate at Ottawa, Illinois, on August 21, 1858, was the first of seven debates between Lincoln and Stephen A. Douglas in the race for the U.S. Senate. Douglas (1813–1861), a leading Democrat, had served continuously in the Senate since 1847.

HORACE GREELEY

[Two Master Debaters]†

Perhaps no local contest in this country ever excited so general or so profound an interest as that now waging in Illinois, with Senator Douglas, the Federal Administration, and the Republican party headed by Messrs. Lincoln and Trumbull[1] as the combatants. Apart from the eminent ability and ardent passions of Mr. Douglas, which must always excite attention to any struggle in which he may be engaged, his position as the object of Executive animosity and the uncertain character of his future relations to the Democratic party, draw toward him a degree of sympathy even from many who have been wont to regard him with very different feelings. It is true that this sympathy is diminished by the manner in which he has chosen to conduct the canvass, which reminds us more of the wild and unscrupulous athlete of his earlier days than of the noble displays of last Winter, when he stood forth in the Senate Chamber as the champion of popular rights against Executive usurpation, without the need of employing any other weapons than those of truth, and of a logic none the less conclusive because it was altogether honest.[2]

As our readers are already aware, one of the features of this remarkable contest is a series of public meetings in different parts of the State, where Mr. Douglas and Mr. Lincoln successively address the people—a mode of discussing political questions which might well be more generally adopted. The first of these meetings was held at Ottawa on Saturday, the 21st inst., and we publish on another page a full report of the speeches on both sides. Of the two, all partiality being left out of the question, we think Mr. Lincoln has decidedly the advantage. Not only are his doctrines better and truer than those of his antagonist, but he states them with more propriety and cogency, and with an infinitely better temper. More than this, in this discussion Mr. Douglas was betrayed into what was perhaps a fault as well as a blunder; at any rate, it was a blunder of a very gross character. He cited certain resolutions, which he alleged were adopted as the platform of the Illinois State Convention of 1854, and these alleged resolutions he made the text of a large portion of his speech. But it appears that no such resolutions were ever offered at any Republican State Convention in Illinois, or adopted by any such Convention. The Press and Tribune of Chicago charges that Mr. Douglas was aware of this, and that he committed an intentional fraud in producing the resolutions as he did. They were, it seems, really adopted at a small local meeting in Kane County; and yet the Senator brought them forward as the platform of a State Convention. Our Chicago cotemporary will have it that Mr. Douglas did this for effect at the moment, well knowing that the imposition must be exposed in due time. This is hardly credible; but there is no doubt that such a misrepre-

† New York Tribune, August 26, 1858.
1. A Republican senator from Illinois (1813–1896).
2. In 1857, Douglas led northern Democrats in protesting President James Buchanan's endorsement of Kansas's proslavery Lecompton Constitution, passed by a fraudulently elected territorial legislature.

sentation is, at least, a blunder, which must ultimately prove injurious to the party by which it is committed.

But it is not merely as a passage at arms between two eminent masters of the art of intellectual attack and defense that this discussion is worthy of study. It touches some of the most vital principles of our political system, and no man can carefully peruse it without some benefit, whatever his convictions as to the questions at issue between the disputants.

ANONYMOUS

[Lincoln Has Gained a National Reputation][†]

Mr. Lincoln is beaten.[1] Though Presidential management and the treachery of pretended friends may prevent Mr. Douglas' return, Mr. Lincoln cannot succeed. We know of no better time than the present to congratulate him on the memorable and brilliant canvass that he has made. He has fully vindicated the partialities of his friends, and has richly earned, though he has not achieved, success.

He has created for himself a national reputation that is both envied and deserved; and though he should hereafter fill no official station, he has done in the cause of Truth and Justice, what will aways entitle him to the gratitude of his party and to the admiration of all who respect the high moral qualities and the keen, comprehensive, and sound intellectual gifts that he has displayed. No man could have done more. His speeches will become landmarks in our political history; and we are sure that when the public mind is more fully aroused to the importance of the themes which he has so admirably discussed, the popular verdict will place him a long way in advance of the more fortunate champion by whom he has been overthrown.

The Republicans owe him much for his truthfulness, his courage, his self-command, and his consistency; but the weight of their debt is chiefly in this: that, under no temptation, no apprehension of defeat, in compliance with no solicitation, has he let down our standard in the least. That God-given and glorious principle which is the head and front of Republicanism, "All men are created equal, and are entitled to life, liberty and the pursuit of happiness," he has steadily upheld, defended, illustrated and applied in every speech which he has made. Men of his own faith may have differed with him when measures only were discussed; but the foundation of all—the principle which comprehends all—he has fought for with a zeal and courage that never flagged or quailed. In that was the pith and marrow of the contest.

Mr. Lincoln, at Springfield at peace with himself because he has been true to his convictions, enjoying the confidence and unfeigned respect of his peers, is more to be envied than Mr. Douglas in the Senate! Long live Honest Old Abe!

---

† From "Abraham Lincoln," *Chicago Press and Tribune*, November 10, 1858.
1. On November 2, 1858, Lincoln lost the race for the U.S. Senate in Illinois to Douglas.

ANONYMOUS

[A Great Statesman and a Popular Debater]†

The smoke of the battle has at length cleared away, and we are enabled to ascertain the exact condition of things in this State (Illinois). The Republicans have borne aloft their banner in triumph, and with all the free States (except California,) they are now enrolled on the side of the people, prepared to fight manfully in their behalf. When the first intelligence of the result came over the wires, it was loudly proclaimed that with the success of Douglas the popular vote was largely with his party, and subsequently that he had triumphed over both the Republican party and that of the General Administration. A slight alteration of the figures, however, puts this matter in a different light. It is now ascertained that on the Congressional ticket, the Republicans have a majority of the popular vote, over both branches of the Democratic party, (whilst Douglas is in a minority of 9,116 votes,) and that had it not been for the pelting storm with which the Northern part of the State was visited on the day of the election, that majority would have been increased by thousands. . . .

One word in regard to their standard-bearer in this exciting canvass. Though unsuccessful, Mr. Lincoln has made for himself a reputation as a great statesman and popular debater, as extensive as the country itself, whilst his earnest devotion to principle must have won the respect and admiration of the most determined opponents. His name, we perceive, has been mentioned in various parts of the country, in connection with the highest post in the gift of the people. A prominent candidate for the Vice Presidency before the Philadelphia Convention in 1856, it is only needed that, at the proper time, his friends should present an unbroken front for the ablest statesman of the West, and the East will delight to honor the man whose integrity and adherence to principle are as proverbial as his mental endowments have been rendered conspicuous in the brilliant canvass through which he has now just passed.

Three cheers for the Republicans of Illinois, and three times three for their gallant leader.

ANONYMOUS

[Nature's Orator: Lincoln at Cooper Union]†

The Speech of Abraham Lincoln at the Cooper Institute last evening was one of the happiest and most convincing political arguments ever made in this City, and was addressed to a crowded and most appreciating audience. Since the days of Clay and Webster,[1] no man has spoken to a larger assemblage of the intellect and mental culture of our City. Mr. Lincoln is

---

† From "The Republican of Illinois—Abraham Lincoln," *Reading* (Pennsylvania) *Journal*, reprinted in the *Chicago Press and Tribune*, December 16, 1858.
† *New York Tribune*, February 28, 1860.
1. Henry Clay (1777–1852) and Daniel Webster (1782–1852), eminent Whig politicians.

one of Nature's orators, using his rare powers solely and effectively to elucidate and to convince, though their inevitable effect is to delight and electrify as well. We present herewith a very full and accurate report of this Speech; yet the tones, the gestures, the kindling eye and the mirth-provoking look, defy the reporter's skill. The vast assemblage frequently rang with cheers and shouts of applause, which were prolonged and intensified at the close. No man ever before made such an impression on his first appeal to a New-York audience.

Mr. Lincoln speaks for the Republican cause tonight at Providence, R.I., and it is hoped that he will find time to speak once or more in Connecticut before he sets his face homeward.

We shall soon issue his Speech of last night in pamphlet form for cheap circulation.

ANONYMOUS

From The Winning Man—Abraham Lincoln[†]

In presenting Abraham Lincoln to the National Republican Convention, as a candidate for the Presidency, we are actuated not by our great love and esteem for the man, by any open or secret hostility to any other of the eminent gentlemen named for that high office, nor by a feeling of State pride or Western sectionalism, but by a profound and well-matured conviction that his unexceptionable record, his position between the extremes of opinion in the party, his spotless character as a citizen, and his acknowledged ability as a statesman, will, in the approaching canvass, give him an advantage before the people which no other candidate can claim. * * *

I. By his own motion, he is not a candidate. He has never sought, directly or indirectly, for the first or second place on the ticket. The movement in his favor is spontaneous. It has sprung up suddenly and with great strength, its roots being in the conviction that he is the man to reconcile all differences in our ranks, to conciliate all the now jarring elements, and to lead forward to certain victory. Having never entered into the field, he has put forth no personal effort for success, and he has never made, even by implication, a pledge of any sort by which his action, if he is President, will be influenced for any man, any measure, any policy. He will enter upon the contest with no clogs, no embarrassment; and this fact is a guaranty of a glorious triumph.

II. In all the fundamentals of Republicanism, he is radical up to the limit to which the party, with due respect for the rights of the South, proposes to go. But nature has given him that wise conservatism which has made his action and his expressed opinions so conform to the most mature sentiment of the country on this question of slavery, that no living man can put his finger on one of his speeches or any one of his public acts as a State legislator or as a member of Congress, to which valid objection can be raised. His avoidance of extremes has not been the result of ambition which measures words or regulates acts, but the natural consequence of an equable nature and in mental constitution that is never off its balance.

† *Chicago Press and Tribune,* May 15, 1860.

While no one doubts the strength of his attachments to the Republican cause, or doubts that he is a representative man, all who know him see that he occupies the happy mean between that alleged radicalism which binds the older Anti-Slavery men to Mr. Seward, and that conservatism which dictates the support of Judge Bates.[1] Seward men, Bates men, Cameron men and Chase[2] men can all accept him as their second choice, and be sure that in him they have the nearest approach to what they most admire in their respective favorites, which any possible compromise will enable them to obtain.

III. Mr. LINCOLN has no new record to make. Originally a Whig, though early a recruit of the great Republican party, he has nothing to explain for the satisfaction of New Jersey, Pennsylvania or the West. His opinions and votes on the Tariff will be acceptable to all sections except the extreme South, where Republicanism expects no support. Committed within proper limitations, set up by economy and constitutional obligation, to the improvement of rivers and harbors, to that most beneficent measure, the Homestead bill, and to the speedy construction of the Pacific Railroad,[3] he need write no letters to soften down old asperities, growing out of these questions, which must inevitably play their part in the canvass before us. He is all that Pennsylvania and the West have a right to demand.

IV. He is a Southern man by birth and education, who has never departed from the principles which he learned from the statesmen of the period in which he first saw the light. A Kentuckian, animated by the hopes that bring the Kentucky delegation here, a Western man, to whom sectionalism is unknown, he is that candidate around whom all opponents of the extension of Human Slavery, North and South, can rally.

*   *   *

JESSE HUTCHINSON[1]

Lincoln and Liberty [Campaign Song][†]

> Hurrah for the choice of the nation!
> Our chieftain so brave and so true;
> We'll go for the great Reformation—
> For Lincoln and Liberty too!
>
> 5   We'll go for the son of Kentucky—
> The hero of Hoosierdom[2] through—

1. Edward Bates (1793–1869), Missouri Republican and later Lincoln's attorney general. William H. Seward (1801–1872), later Lincoln's secretary of state.
2. Salmon Chase (1808–1873), later Lincoln's secretary of the treasury. Simon Cameron (1799–1889), later Lincoln's secretary of war.
3. Lincoln encouraged the building of the transcontinental railroad, completed in 1869. "Homestead bill": signed into law by Lincoln in 1862, it offered settlers free federal land west of the Mississippi River.
† From *Hutchinson's Republican Songster, for the Campaign of 1860* (New York: O. Hutchinson, 1860), pp. 71–72.
1. A singer, songwriter, and member of the Hutchinson Family singers, a popular vocal group of the era.
2. Indiana.

The pride of the Suckers[3] so lucky—
For Lincoln and Liberty too!

Our good David's sling is unerring,
10   The Slaveocrats' giant[4] he slew;
Then shout for the Freedom-preferring—
For Lincoln and Liberty too!

We'll go for the son of Kentucky,
The hero of Hoosierdom through;
15   The pride of the Suckers so lucky—
For Lincoln and Liberty too!

They'll find what, by felling and mauling,
Our rail-maker statesman can do;
For the People are everywhere calling
20   For Lincoln and Liberty too!

Then up with our banner so glorious,
The star-spangled red-white-and-blue,
We'll fight till out flag is victorious,
For Lincoln and Liberty too!

ANONYMOUS

The Lincoln Flag [Campaign Song][†]

1. Unroll the Lincoln flag, my boys,
Where freemen's sons are speeding,
And wave it, while a rag, my boys,
Remains where Freedom's bleeding.

5   Cho.—Our hearts are true as steel, my boys,
And every man's a brother;
While we have hearts to feel, my boys,
Our hands will help each other.

2. Up with the tapering mast, my boys,
10   As high as any steeple;
Then make our banner fast, my boys,
The standard of the people.—Chorus.

3. Free labor and free speech, my boys,
And LINCOLN for our leader,
15   And a free press to teach, my boys,
America, God speed her!—Chorus.

3. Illinoisans.
4. Stephen Douglas, known as the Little Giant.
† From *The Wide-Awake Vocalist; or, Rail Splitters' Songbook* (New York: E. A. Daggett, 1860), p. 7.

ANONYMOUS

[The Nation on the Verge of an Explosion]†

This day is the 4th of March—a day which has been looked forward to with intense anxiety by the country. It is the day of inauguration, when the President elect becomes President de facto. The ceremony will take place at twelve o'clock, and Mr. Lincoln, like Mr. Buchanan,[1] will deliver his inaugural before taking the oath of office. Never since the formation of the government was an inauguration day invested with so much of gloom. There is no longer any apprehension of disturbance at the capital; but the little cloud "the size of a man's hand" which appeared in the Southern horizon on the morning after the 6th of November has grown and spread and become darker and darker, till now the whole Southern heavens are overcast, and tempest seems almost inevitable.[2] The clouds at the North, too, have been ever since gathering and growing blacker, and moving forward in dense masses charged with electricity. It only needs a word and a blow from one man to produce a collision and make the theory of the irrepressible conflict a fearful practical reality. A word alone may be sufficient to precipitate the antagonistic elements upon each other, but, followed up by a blow, the result is certain.

No President of the United States has ever been inaugurated under such circumstances before. It is a new era in the history of the country—an unprecedented result of a Presidential election. It is the first time that a party organized on an issue involving a controverted question of morals and religion—a party organized moreover on a purely sectional issue, in opposition to the institutions of fifteen States, divided by a geographical line from the other States—was enabled to elect its candidate to rule over the whole Union, including those fifteen Southern States, not one of which gave him a vote. Upon this dangerous issue, therefore, Mr. Lincoln has been borne into power by a party whose principles are antagonistic to the principles of the people—whose combined opposition stands recorded in the ratio of three and a half to one. The popular vote for Mr. Lincoln was 1,865,840. The whole vote was 4,739,982. The official vote against him was thus 2,874,142.[3] If from those who voted for him we deduct the whigs and conservatives, who merely desired a change, and did not intend to endorse the Chicago platform,[4] and who if they had to vote now would throw their suffrages in a very different direction, the strictly republican vote was about one million, against upwards of 3,700,000 opposed to the Chicago platform. Yet it has been claimed, ever since the election, that the small republican minority have a right to enforce their policy over the large majority, to the overthrow of the constitution, to the disruption of the confederacy, and even to civil war. . . .

† From "The Inaugural of Mr. Lincoln," *New York Herald*, March 4, 1861.
1. James Buchanan (1791–1868), the fifteenth U.S. President (1857–61).
2. In the three months after November 6, the date of Lincoln's election, seven Southern states seceded from the Union.
3. Although Lincoln received only 39.7% of the popular vote in the four-party 1860 race, he won 180 electoral votes, for more than John C. Breckenridge's 72, John Bell's 39, and Stephen A. Douglas's 12.
4. The Republican Party platform of 1860 had expressed strong opposition to the western spread of slavery.

In consequence of the soothing tone of the speeches of Mr. Seward, who, it was known, was to be Premier in Mr. Lincoln's Cabinet, expectations of moderation were formed which are now dashed to earth by Mr. Seward's recent votes. And Mr. Lincoln himself, who had remained silent at Springfield when the people demanded his voice to still the rising storm, has lately spoken in words not calculated to reassure the country or disperse the clouds of war sweeping overhead. According to our best information, he persists in the revolutionary doctrines of the Chicago platform as the practical policy of his administration, and will neither make nor advise concessions. The radical wing of the republican party appears to have prevailed over the moderates, as the Jacobins[5] in the French Revolution prevailed over the Girondists of the party, and from the inaugural, therefore, to-day, nothing conciliatory is to be expected.

Now, if the tone of this official manifesto should turn out to be of the nature indicated by all our intelligence from Washington—holding out the sword and not the olive branch—and if that be the real expression of the new President's sentiments and the veritable programme of his policy, and not merely a bait to gain some point from the ultras of his own party, which would be playing an extremely foolish part, the ceremony to-day will be not only the inauguration of a President, but the inauguration of civil war, and it will give birth to a new conservative party at the North which will utterly rout and destroy the republican party, horse, foot and artillery. Mr. Lincoln had a glorious game in his hands, but we fear he has lost it forever. He might have saved the country and become second only to Washington in the hearts of the people; a few hours will tell whether he is the man for the occasion.

ANONYMOUS

[The Wisdom of the First Inaugural Address][†]

The almost universal satisfaction with which the Inaugural Address of President Lincoln is received is the strongest evidence of the anxiety with which it was waited for, as well as of the high character of the document itself. For nearly four months the people of this country, strong in the power of self-government to which our institutions have bred them, have sustained themselves, as no other nation could have done, virtually without a central government, and while all the evil elements in the discontented and vicious of the community were appealed to by an apparently successful rebellion. Undoubtedly we have been drifting fast into anarchy; the reign of scoundrelism was impending, and might have already overwhelmed us but for the patient forbearance of the people with an effete and expiring government, and the patient waiting for the government to come, on which all hopes and all fears were centered. But had it been evident that the incoming Administration was to be a mere continuation

---

5. A radical political group in France known for its Reign of Terror during the French Revolution, when many of the revolution's opponents were executed, including the Girondists, who favored ending the monarchy but resisted the revolution and the Jacobins.

† From the *New York Tribune*, March 6, 1861.

of the imbecile policy of the last three months, the country sustained no longer by the hope of something better to come, would have fallen presently into general wreck and ruin, at least for a season, incapable of holding together even by that powerful cohesion of popular government, which is at once the result and the test of the excellence of our Republican system. The feeling then would necessarily be one of great relief were the Address merely an assurance of some positive firmness on the part of the new Administration.

But how much more must it gratify the public expectation when the address is found to be marked by a sagacity as striking as its courage, and by an absence of all passion as remarkable as its keen division of the line of duty, its unequivocal statement of the issues at stake, and uncompromising admissions of their precise value. Upon the question of Slavery the President frankly acknowledges all that the Constitution requires, as the Republican party has done before him, and proclaims the duty of fulfiling those requirements. So there is no hypocritical profession of a hasty alacrity at performing what is the exceptional duty under a free government, and he is careful to characterize it as held by the majority of the people as strictly a "dry legal obligation." The question of Slavery in the Territories, inasmuch as the Constitution is silent in relation to it, he holds must be settled by the majority and their decision acquiesced in by the minority. Nor does he submit on this point to the dictum of the Supreme Court. In a few pregnant sentences, worthy the charge of a Chief Justice to a jury, and containing more sound law than is often found in charges twenty times its length, he clears away all the assumed settlement of the question by the Dred Scott decision. To the binding character of such decisions in private suits he assents, but he considers that the people would practically cease to be their own masters and resign the right of self-government into the hands of that tribunal, if they acknowledge that the policy of the Government is to be irrevocably fixed by the decisions of the Supreme Court, to which the Constitution gives no political power. And this is as sound common sense as it is good law, and sweeps away at a dash all the cobwebs of sophistry that have been woven over the public mind by the judgment in the case of Dred Scott.

But it is in the admirable treatment of the Secession question that Mr. Lincoln is most entitled to the gratitude of the country, and must certainly, it seems to us, command the support of all good citizens. The duty of the head of the Government to assert the rights of the Government itself is so self-evident a truth that the truth of the corollary is no less so—that those will be guilty of commencing civil war, if any shall arise, who shall attempt to hinder the Federal Government from occupying its own property. The avowal of his purpose, in this regard, is unequivocal, unhesitating, firm, and earnest. One thing only can be understood from it—he means to execute the laws. But as there is no hesitation, so there is no haste; and the firmness of his purpose is tempered by mercy. He means evidently to provoke no unnecessary hostilities, and only where his duty is perfectly clear to protect the rights of the whole will he assert the authority of the Federal Government. If in the interior of the Southern States foolish people will not permit the presence of Federal officers, they will be permitted to do without them, as they only are the losers; but where revenue is to be collected which belongs to the whole people, or where forts are to be reoccupied which no more belong to the section where they happen to be than they do to the people of the most distant corner of the Union, then the laws must be executed, and the power of the Federal Government asserted. But time, no doubt, will be given to the unhappy people, betrayed by an imbecile Government into excesses which four-months ago they never contemplated, to return to their allegiance, and restore the property of which they have possessed themselves under a lamentable delusion.

The clearness with which the President states his position on this point is as remarkable as its firmness, and so persuaded will the country be that it is a wise plan, and that it is a plan which must confine all further distur-bances to a few localities in settling the difference with the South, and that no disastrous consequences will follow it to any of the interests of the coun-try, that we predict that the people will now turn to their several affairs, the mechanic to his craft, the farmer to his plow, the merchant to his merchan-dise, all men to their usual callings, satisfied that they may safely leave the question in the hands of one perfectly able to manage it, who will bring order out of seeming chaos, reason out of folly, safety out of danger, and that in so doing he will not sacrifice the national honor or jeopard any of the national interests.

ANONYMOUS

Coercive Policy of the Inaugural[†]

We desire to repeat what we said on yesterday, that the coercive policy, foreshadowed in President Lincoln's Inaugural, towards the seceding States, will meet with the stern and unyielding resistance of a united South. The declaration confined in that document that the Federal Gov-ernment intends "to hold, occupy and possess the property and places belonging to the Government, and to collect the duties and imposts," nec-essarily involves war; and war, as remarked by Mr. Dorman[1] in his speech in Convention on yesterday, involves a total and permanent disruption of the Union.

It is too late now to discuss the rightfulness or the wrongfulness of the abstract doctrine of secession. Six or seven States have already proclaimed themselves independent of the Union, and have organized a Provisional Government, and are now in the act of discharging all the functions of a separate nationality. It is the part of wise and practical men, and it is especially the duty of the Federal Administration at Washington, to look facts in the face—to meet and accept facts as they find them, and dispose of them with a view to the interests of peace and harmony. Let Lincoln carry out the policy indicated in his Inaugural, and civil war will be inau-gurated forthwith throughout the length and breadth of the land. The Gulf States, in our judgment, have acted rashly, unneighborly, and improperly; but, considering them erring sisters, entitled to our sympathies and our aid

---

† From the *Richmond Whig*, reprinted in the *Charleston Mercury*, March 1, 1861.
1. James Baldwin Dorman (1823–1893), a Virginia politician who at first opposed secession but then supported it after the Fort Sumter incident in April 1861.

in an emergency, Virginia can never consent, and will never consent, for the Federal Government to employ coercive measures towards them. And the stupendous folly of such a policy is perfectly apparent. For, as we have said, it would lead to certain and inevitable war, and to the complete and eternal destruction of the Union. It would ultimately force all the Border States to make common cause with the Gulf States, and what would the Federal Government gain by such an operation? The thing is inadmissible—it is utterly absurd and ridiculous; and if Lincoln and his advisers wish to avoid serious trouble, and save the peace of the country, they will abandon their coercion policy, and take their stand on the broad platform of common-sense and common justice. "To hold, occupy, and possess the property and places belonging to the Government," within the limits of the seceded States, is a thing that can't be done—it is impracticable, and an attempt in that direction would be followed by an immediate collision between the State and Federal authorities, which would lead, in the end, to a general and disastrous civil war between the North and the South. Let President Lincoln reconsider his determination, and let him address himself to a peaceful solution of our national difficulties, and the Union may yet be restored in all its pristine dimensions, strength and glory.

In the Convention on yesterday the coercive doctrine of the Inaugural was the subject of extended debate. Many resolutions were offered in regard to it, all of which deprecated and denounced it in the strongest terms, and asserted the duty of Virginia to resist such policy by all the means at her command. It is manifest that the tone and language of the Inaugural on this point have created considerable excitement and indignation among the people of the State, and have aroused a spirit of resistance which will not tamely submit to see that policy carried into effect towards the seceding States. We are clearly of the opinion that the Convention should promptly and explicitly define the position of the State on this subject of coercion, and make it known to Lincoln and his Administration that any employment of force against the seceding States will be met by Virginians with instant and determined resistance. Let such formal and solemn declaration be unanimously made by the Convention, to-day, in the name of the people and the Commonwealth, and we feel sure it will exert the desired effect upon the Cabinet Councils at Washington. Let this declaration, too, be coupled with the earnest request, on the part of the State, that instead of "holding, occupying and possessing the property and places belonging to the Government," within the limits of the seceding States, the Federal Government should forthwith give them all up, as the only hope of preserving peace, preventing civil war and reconstructing the Union.

In conclusion, we express the earnest hope that President Lincoln and his advisers will perceive the impracticability and folly of attempting to carry out the coercive policy indicated in the Inaugural, and that they will forthwith abandon it, and forthwith announce to the country that it has been abandoned. For, let it be distinctly understood at Washington that, upon the abandonment of that unwise and insane policy depends the adherence of Virginia and the other Border States to the Union, and, consequently, the hope of a reconstruction of the Union and the prevention of civil war.

ANONYMOUS

[A Tyrant's Declaration of War][†]

President Abraham Lincoln reigns over all but six of the late United States. In the Inaugural Address which his Excellency (?) vouchsafed to deliver on yesterday, he manifested no disposition to relinquish the pleasure of reigning over all the States. He said plainly as a man could say anything, that the Union was intended to be, and should be, perpetual, and that his purpose was to "hold, occupy and possess," or in other words to hold, take and retain all the forts and arsenals that ever belonged to the late government, and to do this by force of arms, unless "the people, his masters," refuse to sustain him with men, money and munitions of war. When he uttered this fiat of war in an emphatic tone, a great and prolonged shout rose up from all the people, one half of whom could not hear him. Evidently he had a claque around him.

He will also "collect the duties and imposts." Beyond the power which may be necessary for these objects, there will be no invasion, no using of force. So there will be invasion, there will be force. But not in "interior localities." In plain terms, then, the navy will be used on the seacoasts and against the rebellious ports: but the army will be reserved as yet. People of Charleston prenez garde![1] Sumter will be reinforced, if possible. Men of Pensacola, keep a sleepless eye on Pickens.[2] I confess that this honest declaration of war is what I had not expected of Lincoln. Under Seward's adroit handling, I thought coercion would have been buttered over much more thickly. And it cannot be denied that sweet and suasive phrases are not wanting in the address; but the naked truth is none the less apparent and unmistakable for all that. King Lincoln—Rail Splitter Abraham—Imperator! We thank thee for this. It is the tocsin[3] of battle, but it is the signal of our freedom. Quickly, oh quickly begin the fray. Haste to levy tribute. "Enforce the laws" with all possible speed! We have no money to pay, but we have treasure enough—liquid wealth, redder than any gold and infinitely more precious. Be sure, be very sure, O! lowborn, despicable tyrant, that the price of liberty will be paid—good measure, heaped up, shaken down, running over, in hot streams fresh from hearts that will not, cannot beat in the breasts of slaves. Then shall we hear the thunder from Sumter, and the fierce reply from Moultrie and from Cumming's Point.[4]

Abraham still staggers to and fro like a drunken man under the intoxication of his new position, and the pressure of opposing forces. Such has been the strain upon the poor creature's nerves by the partizans of Chase and

† From "The Abolition Regime," *Charleston Mercury*, March 9, 1861.
1. Take guard! (French).
2. Fort Pickens in Pensacola, Florida, and Fort Sumter in Charleston, South Carolina, were two of four forts located on federal land in the South. The Civil War began at Fort Sumter when Southern forces began bombarding it on April 12, 1861.
3. Alarm bell.
4. Fort Moultrie and Cummings Point were locations in Charleston Harbor, South Carolina, from which Confederate shells were fired on the Union-held Fort Sumter.

Cameron, that a day or two ago he burst into tears and oaths, and cried, "My God! Gentlemen, what shall I do? How can I decide?" Unhappy being!

* * *

NATHANIEL HAWTHORNE[1]

[A Visit with Lincoln at the White House][†]

Of course, there was one other personage, in the class of statesmen, whom I should have been truly mortified to leave Washington without seeing; since (temporarily, at least, and by force of circumstances) he was the man of men. But a private grief had built up a barrier about him, impeding the customary free intercourse of Americans with their chief-magistrate; so that I might have come away without a glimpse of his very remarkable physiognomy,[2] save for a semi-official opportunity of which I was glad to take advantage. The fact is, we were invited to annex ourselves, as supernumeraries,[3] to a deputation that was about to wait upon the President, from a Massachusetts whip-factory, with a present of a splendid whip.

Our immediate party consisted only of four or five, (including Major Ben Perley Poore,[4] with his note-book and pencil,) but we were joined by several other persons, who seemed to have been lounging about the precincts of the White House, under the spacious porch, or within the hall, and who swarmed in with us to take the chances of a presentation. Nine o'clock[5] had been appointed as the time for receiving the deputation, and we were punctual to the moment, but not so the President, who sent us word that he was eating his breakfast, and would come as soon as he could. His appetite, we were glad to think, must have been a pretty fair one; for we waited about half-an-hour, in one of the ante-chambers, and then were ushered into a reception-room, in one corner of which sat the Secretaries of War and of the Treasury,[6] expecting, like ourselves, the termination of the presidential breakfast. During this interval, there were several new additions to our group, one or two of whom were in a working-garb; so that we formed a very miscellaneous collection of people, mostly unknown to each other, and without any common sponsor, but all with an equal right to look our head-servant in the face. By-and-by, there was a little stir on the staircase and in the passage-way; and in lounged a tall, loose-jointed figure, of an exaggerated Yankee port and demeanor, whom, (as being about the homeliest man I ever saw, yet by no means repulsive or disagreeable,) it was impossible not to recognize as Uncle Abe.

---

1. Novelist and story writer (1804–1864) whose works include *The Scarlet Letter* (1850) and *The House of the Seven Gables* (1852).
† From Nathaniel Hawthorne, "Chiefly About War-Matters. By a Peaceable Man," *The Atlantic Monthly* 10 (July 1862): 43–61.
2. Facial expression.
3. Superfluous visitors.
4. A popular journalist (1820–1887) who briefly led a battalion of Massachusetts volunteers during the Civil War.
5. On the morning of March 13, 1862.
6. Edwin M. Stanton (1814–1869) and Salmon P. Chase, respectively.

Unquestionably, Western man though he be, and Kentuckian by birth, President Lincoln is the essential representative of all Yankees, and the veritable specimen, physically, of what the world seems determined to regard as our characteristic qualities. It is the strangest, and yet the fittest thing in the jumble of human vicissitudes, that he, out of so many millions, unlooked-for, unselected by any intelligible process that could be based upon his genuine qualities, unknown to those who chose him, and unsuspected of what endowments may adapt him for his tremendous responsibility, should have found the way open for him to fling his lank personality into the chair of state—where, I presume, it was his first impulse to throw his legs on the council-table, and tell the cabinet-ministers a story. There is no describing his lengthy awkwardness, nor the uncouthness of his movement; and yet it seemed as if I had been in the habit of seeing him daily, and had shaken hands with him a thousand times in some village-street; so true was he to the aspect of the pattern American, though with a certain extravagance which, possibly, I exaggerated still further by the delighted eagerness with which I took it in. If put to guess his calling and livelihood, I should have taken him for a country-schoolmaster, as soon as anything else. He was dressed in a rusty black frock-coat and pantaloons, unbrushed, and worn so faithfully that the suit had adapted itself to the curves and angularities of his figure, and had grown to be an outer skin of the man. He had shabby slippers on his feet. His hair was black, still unmixed with gray, stiff, somewhat bushy, and had apparently been acquainted with neither brush nor comb, that morning, after the disarrangement of the pillow; and as to a night-cap, Uncle Abe probably knows nothing of such effeminacies. His complexion is dark and sallow, betokening, I fear, an insalubrious atmosphere around the White House; he has thick black eyebrows and an impending brow; his nose is large, and the lines about his mouth are very strongly defined.

The whole physiognomy is as coarse a one as you would meet anywhere in the length and breadth of the States; but, withal, it is redeemed, illuminated, softened, and brightened, by a kindly though serious look out of his eyes, and an expression of homely sagacity, that seems weighted with rich results of village-experience. A great deal of native sense; no bookish cultivation, no refinement; honest at heart, and thoroughly so, and yet, in some sort, sly—at least, endowed with a sort of tact and wisdom that are akin to craft, and would impel him, I think, to take an antagonist in flank, rather than to make a bull-run at him right in front. But, on the whole, I liked this sallow, queer, sagacious visage, with the homely human sympathies that warmed it; and, for my small share in the matter, would as lief have Uncle Abe for a ruler as any man whom it would have been practicable to put in his place.

* * *

JAMES SLOAN GIBBONS AND L. O. EMERSON

We Are Coming, Father Abraham
[Union Marching Song]†

We are coming, Father Abraham, 300,000 more,[1]
From Mississippi's winding stream and from New England's
    shore.
We leave our plows and workshops, our wives and children dear,
With hearts too full for utterance, with but a silent tear.
5 We dare not look behind us but steadfastly before.
We are coming, Father Abraham, 300,000 more!

CHORUS: We are coming, we are coming our Union to restore,
We are coming, Father Abraham, 300,000 more!

If you look across the hilltops that meet the northern sky,
10 Long moving lines of rising dust your vision may descry;
And now the wind, an instant, tears the cloudy veil aside,
And floats aloft our spangled flag in glory and in pride;
And bayonets in the sunlight gleam, and bands brave music
    pour,
We are coming, father Abr'am, three hundred thousand more!

Chorus

15 If you look up all our valleys where the growing harvests shine,
You may see our sturdy farmer boys fast forming into line;
And children from their mother's knees are pulling at the weeds,
And learning how to reap and sow against their country's needs;
And a farewell group stands weeping at every cottage door,
20 We are coming, Father Abr'am, three hundred thousand more!

Chorus

You have called us, and we're coming by Richmond's bloody tide,
To lay us down for freedom's sake, our brothers' bones beside;
Or from foul treason's savage group, to wrench the murderous
    blade;
And in the face of foreign foes its fragments to parade.
25 Six hundred thousand loyal men and true have gone before,
We are coming, Father Abraham, 300,000 more!

Chorus

† The lyrics are derived from a poem published anonymously in the *New York Evening Post* on July
16, 1862. The poem was by the Quaker abolitionist Gibbons but was commonly attributed to
the poet William Cullen Bryant, who was listed as the lyricist on some editions of the sheet
music. At least eight composers, including Stephen Foster, wrote music for the song. The most
popular version, with music by L. O. Emerson, sold an estimated two million copies in sheet
music form by the end of the Civil War.
1. In August 1862, Lincoln called up 300,000 militia from the Northern states.

HORACE GREELEY[1]

The Prayer of Twenty Millions[†]

To ABRAHAM LINCOLN, *President of the U. States:*
Dear Sir: I do not intrude to tell you—for you must know already—that a great proportion of those who triumphed in your election, and of all who desire the unqualified suppression of the Rebellion now desolating our country, are sorely disappointed and deeply pained by the policy you seem to be pursuing with regard to the slaves of Rebels. I write only to set succinctly and unmistakably before you what we require, what we think we have a right to expect, and of what we complain.

I. We require of you, as the first servant of the Republic, charged especially and preëminently with this duty, that you EXECUTE THE LAWS. Most emphatically do we demand that such laws as have been recently enacted, which therefore may fairly be presumed to embody the *present* will and to be dictated by the *present* needs of the Republic, and which, after due consideration have received your personal sanction, shall by you be carried into full effect, and that you publicly and decisively instruct your subordinates that such laws exist, that they are binding on all functionaries and citizens, and that they are to be obeyed to the letter.

II. We think you are strangely and disastrously remiss in the discharge of your official and imperative duty with regard to the emancipating provisions of the new Confiscation Act.[2] Those provisions were designed to fight Slavery with Liberty. They prescribe that men loyal to the Union, and willing to shed their blood in her behalf, shall no longer be held, with the Nation's consent, in bondage to persistent, malignant traitors, who for twenty years have been plotting and for sixteen months have been fighting to divide and destroy our country. Why these traitors should be treated with tenderness by you, to the prejudice of the dearest rights of loyal men, we cannot conceive.

III. We think you are unduly influenced by the counsels, the representations, the menaces, of certain fossil politicians hailing from the Border Slave States. Knowing well that the heartily, unconditionally loyal portion of the White citizens of those States do not expect nor desire that Slavery shall be upheld to the prejudice of the Union—(for the truth of which we appeal not only to every Republican residing in those States, but to such eminent loyalists as H. Winter Davis, Parson Brownlow, the Union Central Committee of Baltimore, and to *The Nashville Union*)[3]—we ask you to consider that Slavery is everywhere the inciting cause and sustaining base of treason: the most slaveholding sections of Maryland and

---

† *New York Tribune,* August 19, 1862.
1. A New York journalist, politician, and antislavery reformer (1811–1872).
2. The Second Confiscation Act, approved by Congress on June 16, 1862, freed slaves who sought refuge in Union camps. Emancipated blacks were given the option of being transported to countries where they would have the rights of free men. The bill applied only to states in open rebellion; slaves from border states were to be returned if their owners could prove loyalty to the Union.
3. I.e., *The Daily Nashville Union,* a pro-Union newspaper that started publication on April 10, 1862. Davis (1817–1865), a pro-Union congressman from Maryland. William G. "Parson" Brownlow (1805–1877), Tennessee newspaper editor, clergyman, and politician who was a strong opponent of secession and later became a Radical Republican.

Delaware being this day, though under the Union flag, in full sympathy with the Rebellion, while the Free-Labor portions of Tennessee and of Texas, though writhing under the bloody heel of Treason, are unconquerably loyal to the Union. So emphatically is this the case, that a most intelligent Union banker of Baltimore recently avowed his confident belief that a majority of the present Legislature of Maryland, though elected as and still professing to be Unionists, are at heart desirous of the triumph of the Jeff. Davis[4] conspiracy; and when asked how they could be won back to loyalty, replied—"Only by the complete Abolition of Slavery." It seems to us the most obvious truth, that whatever strengthens or fortifies Slavery in the Border States strengthens also Treason, and drives home the wedge intended to divide the Union. Had you from the first refused to recognize in those States, as here, any other than unconditional loyalty— that which stands for the Union, whatever may become of Slavery—those States would have been, and would be, far more helpful and less troublesome to the defenders of the Union than they have been, or now are.

IV. We think timid counsels in such a crisis calculated to prove perilous, and probably disastrous. It is the duty of a Government so wantonly, wickedly assailed by Rebellion as ours has been to oppose force to force in a defiant, dauntless spirit. It cannot afford to temporize with traitors nor with semi-traitors. It must not bribe them to behave themselves, nor make them fair promises in the hope of disarming their causeless hostility. Representing a brave and high-spirited people, it can afford to forfeit anything else better than its own self-respect, or their admiring confidence. For our Government even to see, after war has been made on it, to dispel the affected apprehensions of armed traitors that their cherished privileges may be assailed by it, is to invite insult and encourage hopes of its own downfall. The rush to arms of Ohio, Indiana, Illinois, is the true answer at once to the Rebel raids of John Morgan and the traitorous sophistries of Beriah Magoffin.[5]

V. We complain that the Union cause has suffered, and is now suffering immensely, from mistaken deference to Rebel Slavery. Had you, Sir, in your Inaugural Address, unmistakably given notice that, in case the Rebellion already commenced were persisted in, and your efforts to preserve the Union and enforce the laws should be resisted by armed force, *you would recognize no loyal person as rightfully held in Slavery by a traitor,* we believe the Rebellion would therein have received a staggering if not fatal blow. At that moment, according to the returns of the most recent elections, the Unionists were a large majority of the voters of the Slave States. But they were composed in good part of the aged, the feeble, the wealthy, the timid—the young, the reckless, the aspiring, the adventurous, had already been largely lured by the gamblers and negro-traders, the politicians by trade and the conspirators by instinct, into the toils of Treason. Had you then proclaimed that Rebellion would strike the shackles from the slaves of every traitor, the wealthy and the cautious would have been supplied with a powerful inducement to remain loyal. As it was, every

---

4. Jefferson Davis, president of the Confederacy.
5. Morgan (1825–1864), Confederate general who led cavalry raids in Tennessee Kentucky, Indiana, and Ohio, capturing over a thousand prisoners. Magoffin, governor of Kentucky (1815–1885) who briefly supported neutrality for his state during the Civil War.

coward in the South soon became a traitor from fear; for Loyalty was perilous, while Treason seemed comparatively safe. Hence the boasted unanimity of the South—a unanimity based on Rebel terrorism and the fact that immunity and safety were found on that side, danger and probable death on ours. The Rebels from the first have been eager to confiscate, imprison, scourge and kill: we have fought wolves with the devices of sheep. The result is just what might have been expected. Tens of thousands are fighting in the Rebel ranks to-day whose original bias and natural leanings would have led them into ours.

VI. We complain that the Confiscation Act which you approved is habitually disregarded by your Generals, and that no word of rebuke for them from you has yet reached the public ear. Fremont's Proclamation and Hunter's Order favoring Emancipation were promptly annulled by you; while Halleck's No. 3,[6] forbidding fugitives from Slavery to Rebels to come within his lines—an order as unmilitary as inhuman, and which received the hearty approbation of every traitor in America—with scores of like tendency, have never provoked even your remonstrance. We complain that the officers of your Armies have habitually repelled rather than invited the approach of slaves who would have gladly taken the risks of escaping from their Rebel masters to our camps, bringing intelligence often of inestimable value to the Union cause. We complain that those who *have* thus escaped to us, avowing a willingness to do for us whatever might be required, have been brutally and madly repulsed, and often surrendered to be scourged, maimed and tortured by the ruffian traitors, who pretend to own them. We complain that a large proportion of our regular Army Officers, with many of the Volunteers, evince far more solicitude to uphold Slavery than to put down the Rebellion. And finally, we complain that you, Mr. President, elected as a Republican, knowing well what an abomination Slavery is, and how emphatically it is the core and essence of this atrocious Rebellion, seem never to interfere with these atrocities, and never give a direction to your Military subordinates, which does not appear to have been conceived in the interest of Slavery rather than of Freedom.

VII. Let me call your attention to the recent tragedy in New-Orleans,[7] whereof the facts are obtained entirely through Pro-Slavery channels. A considerable body of resolute, able-bodied men, held in Slavery by two Rebel sugar-planters in defiance of the Confiscation Act which you have approved, left plantations thirty miles distant and made their way to the great mart of the South-West, which they knew to be in the undisputed possession of the Union forces. They made their way safely and quietly through thirty miles of Rebel territory, expecting to find freedom under the protection of our flag. Whether they had or had not heard of the passage of the Confiscation Act, they reasoned logically that we could not

<hr />

6. General Henry W. Halleck (1815–1872), fearing that some fugitive slaves might be spies for the Confederacy, in September 1861 issued an order preventing enslaved blacks from entering federal lines and expelling those who had already entered. Lincoln had revoked proclamations of emancipation of slaves issued by General John Frémont (1813–1890) in Missouri (August 1861) and by General David Hunter (1802–1886) in Georgia, Florida, and South Carolina (May 1862).

7. Greeley probably refers to an incident of August 4 involving a group of armed blacks, presumably runaway slaves, who were confronted by New Orleans police. The ensuing fray left three blacks killed and a number wounded.

kill them for deserting the service of their lifelong oppressors, who had through treason become our implacable enemies. They came to us for liberty and protection, for which they were willing to render their best service: they met with hostility, captivity, and murder. The barking of the base curs of Slavery in this quarter deceives no one—not even themselves. They say, indeed, that the negroes had no right to appear in New-Orleans armed (with their implements of daily labor in the cane-field); but no one doubts that they would gladly have laid these down if assured that they should be free. They were set upon and maimed, captured and killed, because they sought the benefit of that act of Congress which they may not specifically have heard of, but which was none the less the law of the land—which they had a clear *right* to the benefit of—which it was *somebody's* duty to publish far and wide, in order that so many as possible should be impelled to desist from serving Rebels and the Rebellion and come over to the side of the Union. They sought their liberty in strict accordance with the law of the land—they were butchered or reënslaved for so doing by the help of Union soldiers enlisted to fight against Slave-holding Treason. It was *somebody's* fault that they were so murdered—if others shall hereafter suffer in like manner, in default of explicit and public direction to your generals that they are to recognize and obey the Confiscation Act, the world will lay the blame on *you*. Whether you will choose to hear it through future History and at the bar of God, I will not judge. I can only hope.

VIII. On the face of this wide earth, Mr. President, there is not one disinterested, determined, intelligent champion of the Union cause who does not feel that all attempts to put down the Rebellion and at the same time uphold its inciting cause are preposterous and futile—that the Rebellion, if crushed out tomorrow, would be renewed within a year if Slavery were left in full vigor—that Army officers who remain to this day devoted to Slavery can at best be but half-way loyal to the Union—and that every hour of deference to Slavery is an hour of added and deepened peril to the Union. I appeal to the testimony of your Embassadors in Europe. It is freely at your service, not at mine. Ask them to tell you candidly whether the seeming subserviency of your policy to the slaveholding, slavery-upholding interest, is not the perplexity, the despair of statesmen of all parties, and be admonished by the general answer!

IX. I close as I began with the statement that what an immense majority of the Loyal Millions of your countrymen require of you is a frank, declared, unqualified, ungrudging execution of the laws of the land, more especially of the Confiscation Act. That Act gives freedom to the slaves of Rebels coming within our lines, or whom those lines may at any time inclose—we ask you to render it due obedience by publicly requiring all your subordinates to recognize and obey it. The Rebels are everywhere using the late anti-negro riots in the North, as they have long used your officers' treatment of negroes in the South, to convince the slaves that they have nothing to hope from a Union success—that we mean in that case to sell them into a bitterer bondage to defray the cost of the war. Let them impress this as a truth on the great mass of their ignorant and credulous bondmen, and the Union will never be restored—never. We cannot conquer Ten Millions of People united in solid phalanx against us, powerfully aided by Northern sympathizers and European allies. We must have scouts, guides, spies, cooks, teamsters, diggers and choppers from the Blacks of the South, whether we allow them to fight for us or not, or we shall be baffled and repelled. As one of the millions who would gladly have avoided this struggle at any sacrifice but that of Principle and Honor, but who now feel that the triumph of the Union is indispensable not only to the existence of our country but to the well-being of mankind, I entreat you to render a hearty and unequivocal obedience to the law of the land.

Yours,

New-York, August 19, 1862.   HORACE GREELEY.

KARL MARX

From Comments on North American Events[†]

The invasion of Maryland[1] was risked at a most favorable conjuncture. The North had suffered a disgraceful series of quite unprecedented defeats, the Federal army was demoralized, Stonewall Jackson the hero of the day, Lincoln and his government a universal laughing-stock, the Democratic Party, strong again in the North and people expecting Jefferson Davis to become president, France and England were openly preparing to proclaim the legitimacy—already recognized at home—of the slaveholders. "*Eppur si muove*."[2] Reason nevertheless prevails in world history.

Lincoln's proclamation[3] is even more important than the Maryland campaign. Lincoln is a *sui generis*[4] figure in the annals of history. He has no initiative, no idealistic impetus, cothurnus,[5] no historical trappings. He gives his most important actions always the most commonplace form. Other people claim to be "fighting for an idea," when it is for them a matter of square feet of land. Lincoln, even when he is motivated by an idea, talks about "square feet." He sings the bravura aria of his part hesitantly, reluctantly, and unwillingly, as though apologizing for being compelled by circumstances "to act the lion." The most formidable decrees—which will always remain remarkable historical documents—flung by him at the enemy all look like, and are intended to look like, routine summonses sent by a lawyer to the lawyer of the opposing party, legal chicaneries, involved, hidebound *actiones juris.*[6] His latest proclamation, which is drafted in the same style, the manifesto abolishing slavery, is the most important document in American history since the establishment of the Union, tantamount to the tearing up of the old American Constitution.

---

† In *Die Presse*, October 12, 1862. Translated by Peter Schneck for this edition.
1. Robert E. Lee's campaign in Maryland in September 1862 led to the bloody battle at Antietam. Though the battle was a draw, it stopped Lee's advance and was considered a tactical victory for the North.
2. This Italian phrase, which means "And yet it moves," was spoken before the Inquisition by the Italian scientist and philosopher Galileo when he was forced to recant his claim that the earth moves around the sun.
3. Lincoln took the opportunity of the North's success at Antietam to issue, on September 22, 1862, the preliminary Emancipation Proclamation (pp. 280–81), which declared freedom for enslaved blacks in states disloyal to the Union as of January 1, 1863.
4. Unique, unexampled.
5. Bombastic or overly dignified style, associated with inflated performances in classical tragedies.
6. Strictly legal actions, without regard to a cause.

Nothing is simpler than to show that Lincoln's principal political actions contain much that is aesthetically repulsive, logically inadequate, farcical in form and politically contradictory, as is done by the English Pindars[7] of slavery, *The Times, The Saturday Review* and *tutti quanti*. But Lincoln's place in the history of the United States and of mankind will nevertheless be next to that of Washington! Nowadays, when the insignificant struts about melodramatically on this side of the Atlantic, is it of no significance at all that the significant is clothed in everyday dress in the new world?

Lincoln is not the product of a popular revolution. This plebeian, who worked his way up from stone-breaker to senator in Illinois, without intellectual brilliance, without a particularly outstanding character, without exceptional importance—an average person of good will—was placed at the top by the interplay of the forces of general suffrage unaware of the great issues at stake. The new world has never achieved a greater triumph than by this demonstration that, given its political and social organization, ordinary people of good will can accomplish feats which only heroes could accomplish in the old world!

Hegel once observed that comedy is in fact superior to tragedy and humorous reasoning superior to grandiloquent reasoning. Although Lincoln does not possess the grandiloquence of historical action, as an average man of the people he has its humor. When did he issue the proclamation declaring that as of January 1, 1863, slavery in the Confederacy shall be abolished? At the very moment when the Confederacy as an independent state decided at its Richmond Congress on "peace negotiations." At the very moment when the slave-owners of the border states believed that the invasion of Kentucky by the armies of the South had made "the peculiar institution" just as safe as was their domination over their fellow countryman, President Abraham Lincoln in Washington.

RALPH WALDO EMERSON[1]

The President's Proclamation[†]

In so many arid forms which States incrust themselves with, once in a century, if so often, a poetic act and record occur. These are the jets of thought into affairs, when, roused by danger or inspired by genius, the political leaders of the day break the else insurmountable routine of class and local legislation, and take a step forward in the direction of catholic and universal interests. Every step in the history of political liberty is a sally of the human mind into the untried future, and has the interest of genius, and is fruitful in heroic anecdotes. Liberty is a slow fruit. It comes, like religion, for short periods, and in rare conditions, as if awaiting a culture of the race whch shall make it organic and permanent. Such moments of expansion in modern history were the Confession of Augsburg, the plantation of America, the English Commonwealth of 1648, the Declara-

---

7. Pindar (c. 522–443 B.C.E.), Greek poet known for his lush language. *Tutti quanti*: all of those.
1. Essayist, lecturer, and poet (1803–1882) who was the leading voice of Transcendentalist philosophy.
† *The Atlantic Monthly*, 10 (November 1862): 638–42.

tion of American Independence in 1776, the British emancipation of slaves in the West Indies, the passage of the Reform Bill, the repeal of the Corn-Laws, the Magnetic Ocean-Telegraph, though yet imperfect, the passage of the Homestead Bill in the last Congress, and now, eminently, President Lincoln's Proclamation on the twenty-second of September.[2] These are acts of great scope, working on a long future, and on permanent interests, and honoring alike those who initiate and those who receive them. These measures provoke no noisy joy, but are received into a sympathy so deep as to apprise us that mankind are greater and better than we know. At such times it appears as if a new public were created to greet the new event. It is as when an orator, having ended the compliments and pleasantries with which he conciliated attention, and having run over the superficial fitness and commodities of the measure he urges, suddenly, lending himself to some happy inspiration, announces with vibrating voice the grand human principles involved,—the bravoes and wits who greeted him loudly thus far are surprised and overawed; a new audience is found in the heart of the assembly,—an audience hitherto passive and unconcerned, now at last so searched and kindled that they come forward, every one a representative of mankind, standing for all nationalities.

The extreme moderation with which the President advanced to his design,—his long-avowed expectant policy, as if he chose to be strictly the executive of the best public sentiment of the country, waiting only till it should be unmistakably pronounced,—so fair a mind that none ever listened so patiently to such extreme variations of opinion,—so reticent that his decision has taken all parties by surprise, whilst yet it is the just sequel of his prior acts,—the firm tone in which he announces it, without inflation or surplusage,—all these have bespoken such favor to the act, that, great as the popularity of the President has been, we are beginning to think that we have underestimated the capacity and virtue which the Divine Providence has made an instrument of benefit so vast. He has been permitted to do more for America than any other American man. He is well entitled to the most indulgent construction. Forget all that we thought shortcomings, every mistake, every delay. In the extreme embarrassments of his part, call these endurance, wisdom, magnanimity, illuminated, as they now are, by this dazzling success.

When we consider the immense opposition that has been neutralized or converted by the progress of the war, (for it is not long since the President anticipated, the resignation of a large number of officers in the army, and the secession of three States, on the promulgation of this policy,)—when we see how the great stake which foreign nations hold in our affairs has recently brought every European power as a client into this court, and it became every day more apparent what gigantic and what remote

---

2. The preliminary Emancipation Proclamation. Emerson here mentions historical phenomena he considers liberating. "Confession of Augsburg": the Lutheran declaration of faith that helped spearhead the 16th-century Protestant Reformation. "English Commonwealth": a republic established after the civil wars had toppled the monarchy of Charles I. "British emancipation": Britain's abolition of slavery in its West Indies colonies in 1833. "Reform Bill": an 1832 act expanding suffrage in England. "Corn-Laws": laws that for three decades, beginning in 1815, protected English landowners by imposing heavy duties on imported grain. "Ocean-Telegraph": the transatlantic telegraph cable, which carried its first communication between North America and the British Isles in 1858.

interests were to be affected by the decision of the President,—one can hardly say the deliberation was too long. Against all timorous counsels he had the courage to seize the moment; and such was his position, and such the felicity attending the action, that he has replaced Government in the good graces of mankind. "Better is virtue in the sovereign than plenty in the season," say the Chinese. 'T is wonderful what power is, and how ill it is used, and how its ill use makes life mean, and the sunshine dark. Life in America had lost much of its attraction in the later years. The virtues of a good magistrate undo a world of mischief, and, because Nature works with rectitude, seem vastly more potent than the acts of bad governors, which are ever tempered by the good-nature in the people, and the incessant resistance which fraud and violence encounter. The acts of good governors work at a geometrical ratio, as one midsummer day seems to repair the damage of a year of war.

A day which most of us dared not hope to see, an event worth the dreadful war, worth its costs and uncertainties, seems now to be close before us. October, November, December will have passed over beating hearts and plotting brains: then the hour will strike, and all men of African descent who have faculty enough to find their way to our lines are assured of the protection of American law.

It is by no means necessary that this measure should be suddenly marked by any signal results on the negroes or on the Rebel masters. The force of the act is that it commits the country to this justice,—that it compels the innumerable officers, civil, military, naval, of the Republic to range themselves on the line of this equity. It draws the fashion to this side. It is not a measure that admits of being taken back. Done, it cannot be undone by a new Administration. For slavery overpowers the disgust of the moral sentiment only through immemorial usage. It cannot be introduced as an improvement of the nineteenth century. This act makes that the lives of our heroes have not been sacrificed in vain. It makes a victory of our defeats. Our hurts are healed; the health of the nation is repaired. With a victory like this, we can stand many disasters. It does not promise the redemption of the black race: that lies not with us: but it relieves it of our opposition. The President by this act has paroled all the slaves in America; they will no more fight against us; and it relieves our race once for all of its crime and false position. The first condition of success is secured in putting ourselves right. We have recovered ourselves from our false position, and planted ourselves on a law of Nature.

> "If that fail,
> The pillared firmament is rottenness,
> And earth's base built on stubble."[3]

The Government has assured itself of the best constituency in the world: every spark of intellect, every virtuous feeling, every religious heart, every man of honor, every poet, every philosopher, the generosity of the cities, the health of the country, the strong arms of the mechanics, the endur-

---

3. John Milton's *Comus* (1634), lines 597–98.

ance of farmers, the passionate conscience of women, the sympathy of distant nations,—all rally to its support.

Of course, we are assuming the firmness of the policy thus declared. It must not be a paper proclamation. We confide that Mr. Lincoln is in earnest, and, as he has been slow in making up his mind, has resisted the importunacy of parties and of events to the latest moment, he will be as absolute in his adhesion. Not only will he repeat and follow up his stroke, but the nation will add its irresistible strength. If the ruler has duties, so has the citizen. In times like these, when the nation is imperilled, what man can, without shame, receive good news from day to day, without giving good news of himself? What right has any one to read in the journals tidings of victories, if he has not bought them by his own valor, treasure, personal sacrifice, or by service as good in his own department? With this blot removed from our national honor, this heavy load lifted off the national heart, we shall not fear henceforward to show our faces among mankind. We shall cease to be hypocrites and pretenders, but what we have styled our free institutions will be such. . . .

Whilst we have pointed out the opportuneness of the Proclamation, it remains to be said that the President had no choice. He might look wistfully for what variety of courses lay open to him: every line but one was closed up with fire. This one, too, bristled with danger, but through it was the sole safety. The measure he has adopted was imperative. It is wonderful to see the unseasonable senility of what is called the Peace party, through all its masks, blinding their eyes to the main feature of the war, namely, its inevitableness. The war existed long before the cannonade of Sumter, and could not be postponed. It might have begun otherwise or elsewhere, but war was in the minds and bones of the combatants, it was written on the iron leaf, and you might as easily dodge gravitation. If we had consented to a peaceable secession of the Rebels, the divided sentiment of the Border States made peaceable secession impossible, the insatiable temper of the South made it impossible, and the slaves on the border, wherever the border might be, were an incessant fuel to rekindle the fire. Give the Confederacy New Orleans, Charleston, and Richmond, and they would have demanded St. Louis and Baltimore. Give them these, and they would have insisted on Washington. Give them Washington, and they would have assumed the army and navy, and, through these, Philadelphia, New York, and Boston. It looks as if the battle-field would have been at least as large in that event as it is now. The war was formidable, but could not be avoided. The war was and is an immense mischief, but brought with it the immense benefit of drawing a line, and rallying the Free States to fix it impassably,—preventing the whole force of Southern connection and influence throughout the North from distracting every city with endless confusion, detaching that force and reducing it to handfuls, and, in the progress of hostilities, disinfecting us of our habitual proclivity, throuh the affection of trade, and the traditions of the Democratic party, to follow Southern leading. . . .

. . . And the aim of the war on our part is indicated by the aim of the President's Proclamation, namely, to break up the false combination of Southern society, to destroy the piratic feature in it which makes it our enemy only as it is the enemy of the human race, and so allow its reconstruction on a just and healthful basis. Then new affinities will act, the old repulsions will cease, and, the cause of war being removed, Nature and trade may be trusted to establish a lasting peace.

We think we cannot overstate the wisdom and benefit of this act of the Government. The malignant cry of the Secession press within the Free States, and the recent action of the Confederate Congress, are decisive as to its efficiency and correctness of aim. Not less so is the silent joy which has greeted it in all generous hearts, and the new hope it has breathed into the world.

It was well to delay the steamers at the wharves, until this edict could be put on board. It will be an insurance to the ship as it goes plunging through the sea with glad tidings to all people. Happy are the young who find the pestilence cleansed out of the earth, leaving open to them an honest career. Happy the old, who see Nature purified before they depart. Do not let the dying die: hold them back to this world, until you have charged their ear and heart with this message to other spiritual societies, announcing the melioration of our planet.

> "Incertainties now crown themselves assured,
> And Peace proclaims olives of endless age."[4]

Meantime that ill-fated, much-injured race which the Proclamation respects will lose somewhat of the dejection sculptured for ages in their bronzed countenance, uttered in the wailing of their plaintive music,—a race naturally benevolent, joyous, docile, industrious, and whose very miseries sprang from their great talent for usefulness, which, in a more moral age, will not only defend their independence, but will give them a rank among nations.

ANONYMOUS

The Lincoln Catechism[†]

Question. What is the Constitution?
Answer. A league with hell—now obsolete.
Q. What is the Government?
A. Abraham Lincoln, Charles Sumner and Owen Lovejoy.[1]
Q. What is the President?
A. A general agent for negroes.
Q. What is Congress?
A. A body organized for the purpose of appropriating funds to buy Africans, and to make laws to protect the President from being punished for any violations of law he may be guilty of.
Q. What is an army?
A. A provost guard to arrest white men and set negroes free.

---

4. Shakespeare's Sonnet 107.
† *Southern Illustrated News* (Richmond), May 22, 1863.
1. Owen Lovejoy (1811–1864), a Republican congressman from Illinois, who consistently supported Lincoln during the war. Charles Sumner (1811–1874), a Radical Republican, senator from Massachusetts and a leader in political battles against slavery and the South.

Q. Whom are members of Congress supposed to represent?
A. The President and his Cabinet.
Q. What is understood by coining money?
A. Printing green paper.[2]
Q. What does the Constitution mean by "freedom of the press?"
A. The suppression of Conservative newspapers.
Q. What is the meaning of the word "liberty?"
A. Incarceration in a bastile.
Q. What is a Secretary of War?
A. A man who arrests people by telegraph.
Q. What are the duties of a Secretary of the Navy?
A. To build and sink gunboats.
Q. What is the business of a Secretary of the Treasury?
A. To destroy State Banks, and fill the pockets of the people with irredeemable U.S. shinplasters.[3]
Q. What is the meaning of the word "patriot?"
A. A man who loves his country less and the negro more.
Q. What is the meaning of the word "traitor?"
A. One who is a stickler for the Constitution and laws.
Q. What are the particular duties of a Commander-in-Chief?
A. To disgrace any General who does not believe that the negro is better than a white man.
Q. What is the meaning of the word "law?"
A. The will of the President.
Q. How were the States formed?
A. By the United States.
Q. Is the United States Government older than the States which made it?
A. It is.
Q. Have the States any rights?
A. None whatever, except what the General Government bestows.
Q. Have the people any rights?
A. None, except what the President gives.
Q. What is the *habeas corpus?*[4]
A. It is the power of the President to imprison whom he pleases.
Q. Who is the greatest martyr of history?
A. John Brown.[5]
Q. Who is the wisest man?
A. Abraham Lincoln.
Q. Who is Jeff Davis?
A. The Devil.

2. Beginning in 1862, paper bills known as greenbacks were issued in the North. Although the North saw inflation during the war, it was modest compared to the inflationary spiral in the South, where Confederate money steadily lost value due to ever-worsening economic conditions there.
3. Devalued paper money.
4. May you have the body (Latin); the law stipulates that an arrested person has the right to know why he or she is being arrested. Lincoln on September 24, 1862, had issued a sweeping proclamation imposing martial law and suspending habeas corpus.
5. Militant abolitionist (1800–1859) who in October 1859 raided Harpers Ferry, Virginia, with a small band in an effort to free slaves in the region and spark slave rebellions throughout the South. Brown was brought to trial, convicted of three crimes, and hanged on December 2, 1859. He was viewed in the South as a despicable madman and was widely revered in the North as an antislavery martyr.

BY A REBEL

Lines on the Proclamation[1] Issued
by the Tyrant Lincoln, April 1st, 1863[†]

"Are there no stones in heaven but what serve for the thunder, precious villain?"[2]

We have read the tyrant's order
  And the signet to the rule,
And thought the kingly jester meant
  To make an April fool,
5 For we knew that nothing better
  Than a joke in such a strain
Could e'er be made to emanate
  From his degraded brain;
For he orders every man and child,
10   In palace or in cot,
To *fast* and *pray* on such a day—
  To *fast* and *pray* for what?

• • •

To ask Almighty God to bless
  A despot's roll of crime;
15 To ask that he will bring distress
  On a more Christian clime;
To ask that murder, rapine, blood,
  May meet with more success;
That the noblest, fairest land on earth,
20   Be made a wilderness—
To ask the pure and holy God
  To bless his guilty plans,
And with approval sanctify
  The tyrant's blood-washed hands.

25 Pray that a mother's prayer be lost
  When dragged from home in chains;
The orphan's cry ascend unheard,
  When weeping it complains;
Pray that the tyrant's iron bands
30   May rust on maiden forms,
And that his galling manacles
  May bruise their fair white arms;
Pray that their tender voices die,
  Their tears in torrents pour,

---

1. The title slightly misdates Lincoln's "Proclamation Appointing a National Fast Day" (March 30, 1863; see p. 303), one of several such days of prayer, fasting, and humiliation proclaimed by Lincoln during the war.
† *Southern Illustrated News*, October 31, 1863.
2. Shakespeare, *Othello* 5.2.

35   And that their bleaching bones may strew
    The gloomy dungeon's floor.
Pray for a rack, a guillotine,
    On which to lash the free,
That the music of their torture
40   And their cries of agony,
May mingle with the stifled sob
    Of woman's broken heart,
To sate the maniac-tyrant's soul,
    And blunt remorse's dart;
45   Pray for more women searching,
    With their coward hireling band,
To degrade a helpless people,
    And insult a fallen land.

• • •

Oh, God! to thee thy people cry—
50   The God in whom they trust—
That thou wilt aid them in their need,
    And raise them from the dust;
And in thy vengeance, mighty God,
    Thy lightning dagger thrust
55   Into the shameless tyrant's heart,
    And drain its sordid lust;
Hurl down his broken sceptre,
    And break his blood-stained throne,
And applauding worlds shall clap their hands
60   To drown the tyrant's groan!

PETROLEUM V. NASBY [DAVID ROSS LOCKE][1]

Has an Interview with the President [†]

Church uv St._____ [2]
November the 1st, 1863.

I felt it my dooty to visit Washinton. The miserable condishon the Dimokrasy[3] find themselves into, since the elecshen, makes it necessary that suthin be

1. David Ross Locke (1830-1888), an Ohio newspaper editor and antislavery Republican who in his popular humor columns—reprinted nationwide and collected in volumes—assumed the persona of Nasby, an illiterate, drunken, racist Democrat who opposed Lincoln and the Emancipation Proclamation. By adopting this laughably abrasive persona, Locke satirically exposed Copperheads (Peace Democrats) as bigoted, pro-Southern white supremacists and thus contributed to Lincoln's reelection in 1864. Lincoln was so fond of the Nasby papers that he often read them aloud to others and once said that he would gladly give up his office if he could possess the latter's literary talent.
† From *The Nasby Papers: Letters and Sermons Containing the Views on the Topics of the Day.* Indianapolis: C. O. Perrine & Co., 1864. Pp. 45-7.
2. In the most of the early Petroleum Nasby letters, which had appeared in newspapers regularly since March 1861, Locke's speaker presented himself as the pastor of "The Church uv St. Vallandigum," a reference to Nasby's devotion to the Ohio anti-war Democrat Clement L. Vallandigham. In the current letter, the blank beside "Church uv St." points to Nasby's supposed repudiation of the disgraced Vallandigham, whom Lincoln had recently banished from the North because of his criticism of the Union cause.
3. The Democratic Party.

did, and therefore I determined to see wat cood be eifectid by a persnel interview with the President.

Interdoosin myself, I opened upon him delikitly, thus:—

"Linkin," sez I, "ez a Dimekrat, a free-born Dimekrat, who is prepared to die with neetnis and dispatch, and on short notis, for the inalienable rite uv free speech—knowin also that you er a goriller, a feendish ape, a thirster after blud, I speek."

"Speek on," says he.

"I am a Ohio Dimekrat' sez I, "who hez repoodiatid Vallandigum."

"Before or since the elecshin[4] did yoo repoodiate him ?" sez he.

"Since," retortid I.

"I thot so," sed he. "I would hev dun it, too, hed I bin you," continnered he, with a goriller-like grin.

"We air now in favor uv a viggerus prosecushen uv the war, and we want you to so alter yoor policy that we kin act with you corjelly," sez I.

"Say on," sez he.

"I will. We don't want yoo to change yoor policy materially. We are modrit. Anxshus to support yoo, we ask yoo to adopt the follerin trifling changis:—

"Restore to us our habis corpusses, as good ez new. Arrest no more men, wimmin, and children for opinyun's saik. Repele the ojus confisticashen bill, wich irritaits the Suthern mind and fires the Suthern hart. Do away with drafts and conskripshens. Revoke the Emansipashen Proclamashen, and give bonds that you'll never ishoo another. Do away with treasury noats and sich, and pay nuthin but gold. Protect our dawters from nigger equality. Disarm yoor nigger soljers, and send back the niggers to their owners, to conciliate them. Offer to assoom the war indetednis uv the South, and pledge the guvernment to remoonerate our Suthern brethren for the losses they hev sustaned in this onnatrel war. Call a convenshen uv Suthern men and sech gileless Northern men ez F. Peerce, J. Bookannun, Fernandywood,[5] and myself, to agree upon the terms uv reunion."

"Is that all?" sez the goriller.

"No," says I, promptly. "Ez a garantee uv good faith to us, we shel insist that the best haff uv the orifises[6] be given to Dimekrats who repoodiate Vallandigum. Do this, Linkin, and yoo throw lard ile on the troubled waters. Do this, and yoo rally to yoor support thowsends uv noble Dimokrats who went out uv offis with Bookannon, and hev bin gittin ther whisky on tick ever sinse. We hev made sakrifises. We hev repoodiatid Vallandigum,—we care not ef he rots in Canady ; we are willin to jine the war party, reservin to ourselvs the poor privilidge uv dictatin how and on wat principles it shel be carried on. Linkin ! Goriller ! Ape ! I hev dun."

The President replide that he would give the matter serious considerashen. He wood menshen the idee uv resinin to Seward, Chase, and Blair,[7] and wood address a circular to the postmasters, et settry, and see how

---

4. The October 13, 1863 gubernatorial election in Ohio in which the anstislavery candidate, John Brough, resoundingly defeated Clement Vallandigham, who ran for office in absentia from Canada.
5. Former Democratic presidents Franklin Pierce and James Buchanan and New York politician Fernando Wood (1812-1881), a leading Copperhead.
6. I.e., offices.
7. Secretary of State William H. Seward, Secretary of the Treasury Salmon P. Chase, and Union Army general Francis P. Blair, Jr.

menny uv urn wood be willin to resine to accommodait Dimekrats. He bed no dout several wood do it to-wunst.

"Is ther any littel thing I kin do for you ?"

"Nothin pertikler. I wood accept a small post-orifis, if sitooatid within easy range uv a distilry. My politikle days is well-nigh over. Let me but see the old party wunst moar in he assendency; let these old eyes wunst more behold the Constooshn ez it is, the Union ez it wuz, and the nigger ware he ought to be, and I will rap the mantel uv privit life around me, and go into delirum tremens happy. I hev no ambishen. I am in the seer and yellow leef. These whitnin lox, them sunken cheek, warn me that age and whisky hev done ther perfeck work, and that I shel soon go hents. Linkin, scorn not my words. I hev sed. Adoo."

So sayin, 1 wavd my hand impressively, and walkd away.

Petroleum V. Nasby,
Paster uv sed Church, in charge.

ANONYMOUS

[The Gettysburg Address as Reported by the *New York Times*][†]

THE HEROES OF JULY.

—

A Solemn and Imposing Event.

—

Dedication of the National Cemetery at Gettysburgh.

—

IMMENSE NUMBERS OF VISITORS.

—

Oration by Hon. Edward Everett[1]—Speeches of President Lincoln, Mr. Seward and Governor Seymour.[2]

—

THE PROGRAMME SUCCESSFULLY CARRIED OUT

—

The ceremonies attending the dedication of the National Cemetery commenced this morning by a grand military and civic display, under command of Maj.-Gen. Couch.[3] The line of march was taken up at 10 o'clock, and the procession marched through the principal streets to the cemetery, where the military formed in line and saluted the President. At 11½ the head of the procession arrived at the main stand. The President and members of the Cabinet, together with the chief military and civic dignitaries, took position on the stand. The President seated himself between

† *New York Times*, November 20, 1863.
1. Edward Everett (1794–1865), a prominent educator and politician from Massachusetts who was strongly devoted to preserving the Union.
2. A Democratic politician (1810–1886) who twice served as governor of New York.
3. Darius N. Couch (1822–1897) played a key role in defeating Lee during the Gettysburg campaign in the summer of 1863.

Mr. Seward and Mr. Everett after a reception marked with the respect and perfect silence due to the solemnity of the occasion, every man in the immense gathering uncovering on his appearance.

The military were formed in line extending around the stand, the area between the stand and military being occupied by civilians, comprising about 15,000 people and including men, women and children. The attendance of ladies was quite large. The military escort comprised one squadron of cavalry, two batteries of artillery and a regiment of infantry, which constitutes the regular funeral escort of honor for the highest officer in the service.

After the performance of a funeral dirge, by Birofield,[4] by the band, an eloquent prayer was delivered by Rev. Mr. Stockton.[5] . . .

Mr. Everett then commenced the delivery of his oration,[6] which was listened to with marked attention throughout. . . .

Although a heavy fog clouded the heavens in the morning during the procession, the sun broke out in all its brilliancy during the Rev. Mr. Stockton's prayer and shone upon the magnificent spectacle. The assemblage was of great magnitude, and was gathered within a circle of great extent around the stand, which was located on the highest point of ground on which the battle was fought. A long line of military surrounded the position taken by the immense multitude of people.

The Marshal took up a position on the left of the stand. Numerous flags and banners, suitably draped, were exhibited on the stand among the audience. The entire scene was one of grandeur due to the importance of the occasion. So quiet were the people that every word uttered by the orator of the day must have been heard by them all, notwithstanding the immensity of the concours. . . .

President Lincoln's Address

The President then delivered the following dedicatory speech:

> Fourscore and seven years ago our Fathers brought forth upon this Continent a new nation, conceived in liberty and dedicated to the proposition that all men are created equal. [Applause.] Now we are engaged in a great civil war, testing whether that nation, or any nation so conceived and so dedicated, can long endure. We are met on a great battle-field of that war. We are met to dedicate a portion of it as the final resting-place of those who here gave their lives that that nation might live. It is altogether fitting and proper that we should do this. But in a larger sense we cannot dedicate. We cannot consecrate, we cannot hallow this ground. The brave men, living and dead, who struggled here have consecrated it far above our power to add or detract. [Applause.] The world will little note nor long remember, what we say here, but it can never forget what they did here. [Applause.] It is for us, the living, rather to be dedicated here to the refinished work that they have thus so far nobly carried

---

4. Misspelling of Adolph Birgfeld (1828–1874), a prominent band-master and orchestra leader.
5. Thomas H. Stockton (1808–1868), Methodist minister who served as a congressional chaplain during the Civil War.
6. The two-hour oration was filled with references to ancient classics, European history, and details about the Civil War and contrasted sharply with Lincoln's pithy, eloquent speech.

on. [Applause.] It is rather for us to be here dedicated to the great task remaining before us, that from these honored dead we take increased devotion to that cause for which they here gave the last full measure of devotion; that we here highly resolve that the dead shall not have died in vain; [applause.] that the Nation shall under God have a new birth of freedom, and that Governments of the people, by the people and for the people, shall not perish from the earth. [Long continued applause.]

Three cheers were then given for the President and the Governors of the States.

After the delivery of the addresses, the dirge and the benediction closed the exercises, and the immense assemblage separated at about 4 o'clock. . . .

A subscription of $280 was made by the Marshals attending these ceremonies, to be devoted to the relief of the Richmond prisoners.

In the afternoon, the Lieutenant-Governor elect of Ohio, Col. Anderson,[7] delivered an oration at the Presbyterian Church.

The President and party returned to Washington at 6 o'clock this evening, followed by the Governors' trains. Thousands of persons were gathered at the depot, anxiously awaiting transportation to their homes, but they will probably be confined to the meagre accommodations of Gettysburgh till to-morrow.

ANONYMOUS

[The Gettysburg Address: An Insult to the Dead and a Libel on the Founding Fathers][†]

It is not supposed by any one, we believe, that Mr. Lincoln is possessed of much polish in manners or conversation. His adherents, however, claim for him an average amount of common sense, and more than an ordinarily kind and generous heart. We have failed to distinguish his pre-eminence in the latter, and apprehend the former to be somewhat mythical, but imagine that his deficiencies herein being less palpable than in other qualities constituting a statesman have led his admirers greatly to overestimate him in these regards. These qualities are unfailing guides to appropriateness of speech and action in mising with the world, however slight may have been the opportunities afforded their possessor for becoming acquainted with the usages of society.

The introduction of Dawdleism[1] in a funeral sermon is an innovation upon established conventionalities, which, a year or two ago, would have been regarded with scorn by all who thought custom should, to a greater or less extent, be consulted in determining social and public proprieties. And the custom which forbids its introduction is founded on the propriety which grows out of the fitness of things, and is not therefore merely arbitrary, or confined to special localities, but has suggested to all nations the

7. Charles Anderson (1814–1895), a Republican politician.
† From "The President at Gettysburg," *Chicago Times*, November 23, 1863.
1. Political partisanship.

exclusion of political partianship in funeral discourses. Common sense, then, should have taught Mr. Lincoln that its intrusion upon such an occasion was an offensive exhibition of boorishness and vulgarity. An Indian in eulogizing the memories of warriors who had fallen in battle would avoid allusion to differences in the tribe which had no connection with the prevailing circumstances, and which he knew would excite unnecessarily the bitter prejudices of his hearers. Is Mr. Lincoln less refined than a savage?

But aside from the ignorant rudeness manifest in the President's exhibition of Dawdleism at Gettysburg,—and which was an insult at least to the memories of a part of the dead, whom he was there professedly to honor,—in its misstatement of the cause for which they died, it was a perversion of history so flagrant that the most extended charity cannot regard it as otherwise than willful. That, if we do him injustice, our readers may make the needed correction, we append a portion of his eulogy on the dead at Gettysburg:

> "Four score and ten [sic] years ago our fathers brought forth upon this continent a nation consecrated [sic] to liberty and dedicated to the proposition that all men are created equal. [Cheers.] Now we are engaged in a great civil war, testing whether that nation or any other [sic] nation so consecrated [sic] and so dedicated can long endure."

As a refutation of this statement, we copy certain clauses in the Federal constitution:

> "Representatives and direct taxes shall be apportioned among the several States which may be included in this Union, according to their respective numbers, which shall be determined by adding to the whole number of free persons, including those bound to service for a term of years, and excluding Indians not taxed, three-fifths of all other persons."

> "The migration or importation of such persons as any of the States now existing shall think proper to admit shall not be prohibited by the Congress prior to the year 1808, but a tax or duty may be imposed on such importation, not exceeding ten dollars for each person."

> "No amendment to the constitution, made prior to 1808, shall affect the preceding clause."

> "No person held to service or labor in one State under the laws thereof, escaping into another, shall, in consequence of any law or regulation therein, be discharged from such service or labor, but shall be delivered up on claim of the party to whom such service or labor may be due."

Do these provisions in the constitution dedicate the nation to "the proposition that all men are created equal"? Mr. Lincoln occupies his present position by virtue of this constitution, and is sworn to the maintenance and enforcement of these provisions. It was to uphold this constitution, and the Union created by it, that our officers and soldiers gave their lives at Gettysburg. How dared he, then, standing on their graves, misstate the cause for which they died, and libel the statesmen who founded the government? They were men possessing too much self-respect to declare that negroes were their equals, or were entitled to equal privileges.

ANONYMOUS

[Lincoln as Absolute Dictator: A Copperhead's[1] Perspective][†]

By whom and when was Abraham Lincoln made dictator in this country? We are aware of no solemn vote of Congress declaring the Republic to be in danger, and the necessity for its salvation of suspending temporarily the normal function of the Constitution and the laws, that Abraham Lincoln may be invested with an absolute dictatorship. How, then, shall we qualify numerous acts of the President during the last three years, notoriously without the sphere of his executive duties, and some of them involving the highest legislative as well as executive powers, such as could be properly performed only by one invested with dictatorial authority. We must qualify such acts as sheer usurpation—audacious, criminal, perjured usurpation. President Lincoln has been guilty of usurpations, which if the dictatorial powers assumed were not used for his protection, would certainly subject him to impeachment and condign punishment.

Pretermitting all other arbitrary acts, we have now to do with one, than which none more high-handed, despotical and atrocious can be found in the history of usurpers; and we signalize it to the reprobation of his countrymen and the astonishment of the world. We allude to the recent annihilation by a stroke of his pen and the proclamation of a military lieutenant, of the sovereignty of Louisiana. No other authority than that possessed as President of the United States is alleged for this act. The proclamation begins: "I, Abraham Lincoln, President of the United States, do," &c., and the only "whereas" precedent to the enacting clause and justificatory of this annulment of the Constitution and laws of Louisiana, and the institution of a new government for that State is in these words: "And whereas, it is now desired by some persons heretofore engaged in said rebellion to resume their allegiance to the United States, and to reinaugurate loyal State governments within, and for their respective States; therefore," &c.

In this cavalier way is it that President Lincoln deals with State sovereignty! Louisiana and Arkansas[2] have thus fallen beneath his pen. Texas, Alabama, and Tennessee, Georgia, Florida, and the two Carolinas will soon follow. President Lincoln is in great haste now to make "loyal" States of these erring sisters, and to "restore the Union." Having been unable to effect it by force of arms and proclamations, during three years (those pestilent Southerners partaking in a provokingly slight degree of the nature of the spaniel that licks the hand which strikes him), the President is now getting up a trick of political hocus-pocus, by which, in the course of a few months, he hopes to make those now "rebellious" States seem to march in file harmoniously with these "loyal" States, exhibiting

---

1. An anti-war Democrat from the North.
† From "He Can't Do It," *New York Daily News*, February 15, 1864.
2. These states had recently formed Unionist governments and were permitted to hold elections under Lincoln's so-called Ten Per Cent Plan, whereby a Confederate state could reenter the Union if it adopted an antislavery constitution and at least a tenth of its population vowed loyalty to the Union.

to astonished and admiring Europe the charming spectacle of a "restored Union." He therefore "proclaims, declares, and makes known" that whenever in any of those now "rebellious" States a number of persons, not less than one-tenth in number of the votes cast in such States at the Presidential election of 1860, and having taken a certain "oath" prescribed, and not having violated it, &c., and "excluding all others," shall re-establish a State Government which shall be Republican—Black—(?)—and "in no wise contravening said oath," such "shall be recognized as the true Government of the State." The farce!

But why this crying anxiety, the curious may ask, to have those "rebellious" States made "loyal," and the "Union restored" in the course of a very few months from this current February? The Presidential election comes on next Autumn. President Lincoln means to be a candidate for re-election; and he hopes that the Electoral Colleges in those thus-to-be-recovered and thus-to-be-"loyal" States will, out of pure gratitude to him who has treated them so kindly these three years, aided by such military and functionary influence as perhaps he may be able to bring to bear upon them, cast their votes unanimously for him, and thus assure his re-election.

We say to President Lincoln that if he counts to foist himself in this manner upon the country for a second term he will be grievously disappointed. The people see through this game, and will not permit it to be successfully played. If he should venture, on the 4th of March, 1865, to reseat himself in the Presidential chair by virtue of an election secured by such shallow trick, we tell him plainly he cannot succeed. There will either be forcible resistance, or, as his first and legal election caused secession South, his second illegal election will cause secession North and West, and break up utterly this Union. The North and West have borne much; but they would not stand such impudent jugglery.

ANONYMOUS

[Lincoln and Satan]†

"Bully for you," cried Satan, enraptured, "you are the smartest pupil I ever had! I am afraid people will find you out after a while, though."

"Devil a fear, Old Boy. *As long a I'm called 'Honest Old Abe,' the people will swallow anything. There's nothing like having an honest name. It is a cloak for everything.*"

"True," said Beelzebub. He forbore to say any more. His mind was filled with uneasy suspicions. What if the cute[1] Bram should slip out of his bargain with *him*? "True," he continued, rolling this idea over in his mind; "if I hadn't tacked this name to you, you would have been nowhere to-day. It gave *confidence*, and you've profited well by it. But how about *our* arrangement. You don't expect to argue *me* out of *that*, do you?"

"Come, come, brother," said Bram with an affected air of honest indignation. "You don't suspect my *intentions* do you?"

---

† From *Abraham Africanus 1. His Secret Life, as Revealed under the Mesmeric Influence. Mysteries of the White House* (New York: J. F. Feeks, 1864).
1. Acute, clever.

ABRAHAM

AFRICANUS I.

His Secret Life,

AS REVEALED UNDER THE

MESMERIC INFLUENCE.

Mysteries of the White House.

J. F. FEEKS, PUBLISHER,

No. 26 ANN STREET, N. Y.

First title page from *Abraham Africanus I. His Secret Life, as Revealed under the Mesmeric Influence. Mysteries of the White House.* New York: J. F. Feeks, 1864. Reproduced by permission of HCL Widener Library US 6303.353.

"Hell is paved with them," said the Father of Lies, sententiously. "I want something more palpable than your assurances, Abe. Suppose we draw up a little memorandum of our agreement?"

So saying, he whipped out a little scroll of parchment, and tapping a hole in Bram's arm before he was sufficiently aware of his intention to prevent it, used his blood for ink. Then scribbling furiously for a few minutes, he covered the scroll with fine writing, and read the contract to his *confrere*:[2]

"'I hereby pledge to elevate Abraham Lincoln to a life Presidency of the United States of America—'"

"Stop, stop!" cried Bram, "you promised a Monarchy, or at least a First Consulship."

"Fool!" said the Devil. "Don't you perceive that if you call yourself a King or First Consul, the whole people will rise upon you?"

"Let them rise," said Bram, "I have my army. Every officer has been selected and appointed with that view. They are all men who believe the government needs to be *strengthened*."

"Your army wouldn't be worth a straw if you proceed so rudely. There are democrats enough in the country to eat up your army."

"But they're not organized," urged Bram, "and what's more, I don't intend to let them organize."

"Very strongly put, brother; but still there's nothing like doing things smoothly. My word for it, the easiest way is the best. You owe all your present success to four things. *First*, MY NOMINATION. *Second*, Your sobriquet of 'Honest.' *Third*, Those weak points of the Constitution which a little management converted into flaws, and a little stretching widened into fissures wide enough to drive a train of cars through. 'Military necessity' did the rest. *Fourth*, DOING THINGS QUIETLY. All these things combined have given you what I promised you in our first contract, POWER. In return you brought on a war which has made, taking both belligerents together, something like a million of victims."

"And out of that million," chuckled Abe, "of course, you reaped a plentiful harvest."

"Not so, Bram. I never was more deceived in my life. I GOT MY SHARE; but the majority of them were poor ignorant fools, infused with a false patriotism. I did well with the Abolitionists, and the men who accepted bounties; but the former were very scarce and the latter were hardly worth picking up. But to our contract. If you're elected for another term, you can easily get a law passed declaring the country in a state of permanent insurrection, and demanding more power to put it down. The first thing will be, a law to make the Presidency perpetual while the war lasts; the next, another making it perpetual during your life. Thus you will have got over the hardest part of it. The rest is easy enough. You can then have it entailed on your posterity, and change the title whenever you please. I should advise you to stick to that of President, though. There's nothing like a mild name. To continue:

"'I hereby pledge to elevate Abraham Lincoln to a life Presidency of the United States of America, and to stand by him and assist him to subvert the liberties of the American people and debauch their civic aspirations;

2. Colleague.

to impose upon them in every imaginable form of low cunning, and cheat them with words of double meaning and with false promises, until by these, and kindred means, that end is accomplished, and his dynasty firmly established.'"

While Satan was writing the contract, Bram held out his arm very patiently by way of inkstand; but now he withdrew it hastily, and looking at his watch, exclaimed:

"All right, my boy, I'll sign that, and then you'll please to consider this interview at an end, for some of my generals have been advancing too quickly, and if I don't relieve them of their commands the war will be over in a jiffy, and good-bye to my plans."

"You forget," said Beelzebub meaningly, and fixed his burning eyes upon Bram's till the latter winced and wiggled as though he was on a toasting fork, "you forget, my dear Bram."

"What?" stammered Bram, fearing he had been detected, yet hoping to escape, "What do I forget?"

"What!" roared the Evil One, "Do you pretend you don't know! you low, cunning, pettifogging, cringing, artful, Illinois stump lawyer! Would you cheat *me*? You know very well *there's no consideration expressed in that deed*, or you wouldn't have been in such a hurry to sign it, and run to look after your major-generals. But come, let us remain friends. I admire you the more for your dishonesty; only you musn't think to 'beat the Devil round a stump,' Honor amongst thieves, you know."

So saying, the worthy pair shook hands and *smiled*. The *elder one* then proceeded to finish the agreement:

"'In consideration whereof my friend promises, (no—pledges,) pledges to render unto me what he possesses (it ain't much, any how,) of a MORTAL SOUL, the same to be MINE forever!'

(Signed)   BAAL."

(Signed)   BRAM."

"Now," said Baal, as Old Abe with trembling fingers and face white as a sheet, signed the bond; "now, my dear Abe, if you want any advice, just let me know, for like yourself, I've other matters to attend to."

1864

HARRIET BEECHER STOWE[1]

[A Man of the Working Classes][†]

Abraham Lincoln is in the strictest sense *a man of the working classes*. All his advantages and abilities are those of a man of the working classes; all his disadvantages and disabilities are those of a man of the working classes; and his position now at the head of one of the most powerful nations of the earth, is a sign to all who live by labor that their day is

---

1. A prolific author (1811–1896) whose best-selling antislavery novel *Uncle Tom's Cabin* (1852) intensified the national debate over slavery that led to the Civil War.

† From "Abraham Lincoln," *Littell's Living Age*, February 6, 1864, p. 282.

coming. Lincoln was born to the inheritance of hard work as truly as the poorest laborer's son that digs in our fields. At seven years of age he was set to work, axe in hand, to clear up a farm in a Western forest. Until he was seventeen his life was that of a simple farm laborer, with only such intervals of schooling as farm laborers get. Probably the school instruction of his whole life would not amount to more than one year. At nineteen he made a trip to New Orleans as a hired hand on a flat boat, and on his return he split the rails for a log cabin and built it, and enclosed ten acres of land with a rail fence of his own handiwork. The next year he hired himself for twelve dollars a month to build a flat boat and take her to New Orleans; and any one who knows what the life of a Mississippi boatman was in those days, must know that it involved every land of labor. In 1832, in the Black Hawk Indian War, the hardy boatman volunteered to fight for his country, and was unanimously elected a captain, and served with honor for a season in frontier military life. After this, while serving as a postmaster, he began his law studies, borrowing the law books he was too poor to buy, and studying by the light of his evening fire. He acquired a name in the country about as a man of resources and shrewdness; he was one that people looked to for counsel in exigencies, and to whom they were ready to depute almost any enterprise which needed skill and energy. The surveyor of Sangamon County being driven with work, came to him to take the survey of a tract off from his hands.[2] True, he had never studied surveying—but what of that? He accepted the "job," procured a chain, a treatise on surveying, and *did the work.* Do we not see in this a parable of the wider wilderness which in later years he has undertaken to survey and fit for human habitation *without* chart or surveyor's chain?

In 1836 our backwoodsman, flat-boat hand, captain, surveyor, obtained a license to practise law, and, as might be expected, rose rapidly.

His honesty, shrewdness, energy, and keen practical insight into men and things soon made him the most influential man in his State. He became the reputed leader of the Whig party, and canvassed the State as stump speaker in time of Henry Clay, and in 1846 was elected representative to Congress. Here he met the grinding of the great question of the day—the upper and nether millstone of slavery and freedom revolving against each other. Lincoln's whole nature inclined him to be a harmonizer of conflicting parties rather than a committed combatant on either side. He was firmly and from principle an enemy to slavery—but the ground he occupied in Congress was in some respects a middle one between the advance guard of the anti-slavery and the spears of the fire-eaters. He voted with John Quincy Adams for the receipt of anti-slavery petitions;[3] he voted with Giddings[4] for a committee of inquiry into the constitutionality of slavery in the District of Columbia, and the expediency of abolishing slavery in that District; he voted for the various resolutions prohibiting slavery in the territories to be acquired from Mexico, and he voted forty-

2. In 1833, two years after moving to Sangamon County, Illinois, Lincoln was trained in surveying and put to work by the county surveyor John Calhoun (1808–1859).
3. Adams demanded that petitions against slavery be heard in the U.S. House of Representatives despite the gag rule that banned the discussion of slavery from the mid-1830s to the mid-1840s.
4. Joshua R. Giddings (1795–1864), an antislavery congressman from Ohio.

two times for the Wilmot Proviso.[5] In Jan. 16, 1849, he offered a plan for abolishing slavery in the District of Columbia, by compensation from the national treasury, with the consent of a majority of the citizens. He opposed the annexation of Texas, but voted for the bill to pay the expenses of the war.

But at the time of the repeal of the Missouri Compromise he took the field, heart and soul, against the plot to betray our territories to slavery. It was mainly owing to his exertions that at this critical period a Republican Senator was elected from Illinois, when a Republican Senator in the trembling national scales of the conflict was worth a thousand times his weight in gold.

Little did the Convention that nominated Abraham Lincoln for President know what they were doing. Little did the honest, fatherly, patriotic man, who stood in his simplicity on the platform at Springfield, asking the prayers of his townsmen and receiving their pledges to remember him, foresee how awfully he was to need those prayers, the prayers of all this nation, and the prayers of all the working, suffering common people throughout the world. * * *

Sooth to say, our own politicians were somewhat shocked with his state-papers at first. Why not let *us* make them a little more conventional, and file them to a classical pattern? "No," was his reply, "I shall write them myself. *The people will understand them.*" "But this or that form of expression is not elegant, not classical." "*The people will understand it,*" has been his invariable reply. And whatever may be said of his state-papers, as compared with the classic standards, it has been a fact that they have always been wonderfully well understood by the people, and that since the time of Washington, the state-papers of no President have more controlled the popular mind. And one reason for this is, that they have been informal and undiplomatic. They have more resembled a father's talks to his children than a state-paper. And they have had that relish and smack of the soil, that appeal to the simple human heart and head, which is a greater power in writing than the most artful devices of rhetoric. Lincoln might well say with the apostle, "But though I be rude in speech yet not in knowledge, but we have been thoroughly *made manifest among you* in all things."[6] His rejection of what is called fine writing was as deliberate as St. Paul's, and for the same reason—because he felt that he was speaking on a subject which must be made clear to the lowest intellect, though it should fail to captivate the highest. But we say of Lincoln's writing, that for all true, manly purposes of writing, there are passages in his state-papers that could not be better put; they are absolutely perfect. They are brief, condensed, intense, and with a power of insight and expression which make them worthy to be inscribed in letters of gold. Such are some passages of the celebrated Springfield letter, especially that masterly one where he compares the conduct of the patriotic and loyal blacks with that of the treacherous and disloyal whites. No one can read this letter without feeling the influence of a mind both strong and generous.

5. Introduced to the U.S. House of Representatives by David Wilmot (1814–1868) of Pennsylvania, the Wilmot Proviso would have banned slavery from the vast western territories acquired by the United States during the Mexican-American War (1846–48).
6. 2 Corinthians 11:6.

Lincoln is a strong man, but his strength is of a peculiar kind; it is not aggressive so much as passive, and among passive things, it is like the strength not so much of a stone buttress as of a wire cable. It is strength swaying to every influence, yielding on this side and on that to popular needs, yet tenaciously and inflexibly bound to carry its great end; and probably by no other kind of strength could our national ship have been drawn safely thus far during the tossings and tempests which beset her way.

Surrounded by all sorts of conflicting claims, by traitors, by half-hearted, timid men, by Border States men, and Free States men, by radical Abolitionists and Conservatives, he has listened to all, weighed the words of all, waited, observed, yielded now here and now there, but in the main kept one inflexible, honest purpose, and drawn the national ship through.

In times of our trouble Abraham Lincoln has had his turn of being the best abused man of our nation. Like Moses leading his Israel through the wilderness, he has seen the day when every man seemed ready to stone him, and yet, with simple, wiry, steady perseverance, he has held on, conscious of honest intentions, and looking to God for help. All the nation have felt, in the increasing solemnity of his proclamations and papers, how deep an education was being wrought in his mind by this simple faith in God, the ruler of nations, and this humble willingness to learn the awful lessons of his providence.

We do not mean to give the impression that Lincoln is a religious man in the sense in which that term is popularly applied. We believe he has never made any such profession, but we see evidence that in passing through this dreadful national crisis he has been forced by the very anguish of the struggle to look upward, where any rational creature must look for support. No man in this agony has suffered more and deeper, albeit with a dry, weary, patient pain, that seemed to some like insensibility. "Whichever way it ends," he said to the writer, "I have the impression that *I* sha'n't last long after it's over."[7] After the dreadful repulse of Fredericksburg, his heavy eyes and worn and weary air told how our reverses wore upon him, and yet there was a never-failing fund of patience at bottom that sometimes rose to the surface in some droll, quaint saying, or story, that forced a laugh even from himself.

There have been times with many, of impetuous impatience, when our national ship seemed to lie water-logged and we have called aloud for a deliverer of another fashion,—a brilliant general, a dashing, fearless statesman, a man who could dare and do, who would stake all on a die, and win or lose by a brilliant *coup de main*. It may comfort our minds that since He who ruleth in the armies of nations set no such man to this work, that perhaps He saw in the man whom He did send some peculiar fitness and aptitudes therefor.

Slow and careful in coming to resolutions, willing to talk with every person who has anything to show on any side of a disputed subject, long in weighing and pondering, attached to constitutional limits and time-honored landmarks, Lincoln certainly was the *safest* leader a nation could have at a time when the *habeas corpus* must be suspended, and all the constitutional and minor rights of citizens be thrown into the hands of their military

7. Presumably Lincoln said this to Stowe when she visited him in the White House in late 1862.

leader. A reckless, bold, theorizing dashing man of genius might have wrecked our Constitution and ended us in a splendid military despotism.

Among the many accusations which in hours of ill-luck have been thrown out upon Lincoln, it is remarkable that he has never been called self-seeking, or selfish. When we were troubled and sat in darkness, and looked doubtfully towards the presidential chair, it was never that we doubted the goodwill of our pilot—only the clearness of his eyesight. But Almighty God has granted to him that clearness of vision which he gives to the true-hearted, and enabled him to set his honest foot in that promised land of freedom which is to be the patrimony of all men, black and white—and from henceforth nations shall rise up to call him blessed.

ANONYMOUS

[The Second Inaugural: A Solemn, Charitable Speech][†]

Probably all men in all quarters of the world, who read President Lincoln's last Inaugural Address, were impressed by the evident tone of solemnity in it, and the want of any expression of personal exultation. There he stood, after four years of such trial, and exposed to such hate and obloquy as no other great leader in modern history has experienced, successful, reëlected, his policy approved by the people and by the greater test of events, the terrible rebellion evidently coming to its end, and he himself now certain of his grand position in the eyes of history—and yet not a word escaped him of triumph, or personal glory, or even of much hopefulness. We all expected more confidence—words promising the close of the war and speaking of the end of our difficulties. Many hoped for some definite line of policy to be laid out in this address. But instead, we heard a voice as if from some prophet, looking with solemn gaze down over the centuries, seeing that both sides in the great contest had their errors and sins, that no speedy victory could be looked for, and yet that the great Judge of the world would certainly give success to right and justice. The feeling for the bondmen and the sense of the great wrong done to them, with its inevitable punishment, seemed to rest with such solemn earnestness on his soul, that to the surprise of all and the derision of the flippant, an official speech became clothed in the language of the Bible. The English and French critics all observed this peculiar religious tone of the Inaugural, and nearly all sensible persons felt it not unsuited to the grandeur and momentous character of the events accompanying it. Many pronounced it a Cromwellian speech,[1] but it had one peculiarity, which Cromwell's speeches never possessed—a tone of perfect kindness and good-will to all, whether enemies or political opponents.

"With charity to all and malice for none," President Lincoln made his last speech to the world. Men will reperuse that solemn address with ever increasing interest and emotion, as if the shadow of his own tragic fate and the near and unseen dangers to the country, rested unconsciously on

† *New York Times*, April 17, 1865.
1. Sternly religious, referring to Oliver Cromwell (1599–1658), a devout Calvinistic Puritan who led the rebellion against the monarchy of Charles I during the English Civil War in the 1640s and then became Lord Protector of the Commonwealth of England.

its words. It will seem natural that no expression of exultation or personal triumph escaped the great leader of this revolution, but that his mind was filled with the impressive religious lessons of the times. It will be thought characteristic of his sense of justice and his sincere humanity, that his last public address to the country was most of all occupied by the wrongs done to the helpless race, whose friend and emancipator he had been. And it will seem but a part of his wonderful spirit of good-will to all, that not a syllable of bitterness toward the enemies of his country, to the traitors at home, or his personal revilers, passed his lips.

It is such a speech to the world as a Christian statesman would gladly have his last—earnest, humane, truly but not technically religious, filled with forgiveness and good will.

When generations have passed away, and the unhappy wounds of this war are healed, and the whole nation is united on a basis of universal liberty, our posterity will read the dying words of the great Emancipator and the leader of the people with new sympathy and reverence, thanking God that so honest and so pure a man, so true a friend of the oppressed, and so genuine a patriot, guided the nation in the time of its trial, and prepared the final triumph which he was never allowed to see.

ANONYMOUS

The Great National Calamity[†]

ABRAHAM LINCOLN IS DEAD! These portentious words, as they sped over the wires throughout the length and breadth of the land on Saturday morning last sent a thrill of agony through millions of loyal hearts and shrouded a nation, so lately rejoicing in the hour of victory, in the deepest sorrow. The blow came at a moment so unexpected and was so sudden and staggering— the crime by which he fell was so atrocious and the manner of it so revolting, that men were unable to realize the fact that one of the purest of citizens, the noblest of patriots, the most beloved and honored of Presidents, and the most forbearing and magnanimous of rulers had perished at the hands of an assassin. The horrifying details recalled only the scenes of blood which have disgraced barbaric ages. People were unwilling to believe that, in our own time, there could be found men capable of a crime so utterly fiendish and brutal. One of the assassins, in a crowded theater, stealthily approaches a man against whom he could have no just cause of enmity; a man so tender in his feelings and sympathies that all his errors were on the side of mercy; a man who had been twice elected to the highest office in the gift of a great people—and without giving any notice of his presence, while his victim, with his wife sitting by his side, is wholly unconscious of danger, deliberately discharges a pistol from behind, piercing the head of the President with the fatal ball, then availing himself of the bewilderment of the audience, leaps upon the stage, and makes his escape. The other assassin, at nearly the same moment, obtrudes himself into the sick chamber of a man who, but a few days before, had narrowly escaped death

† *Daily State Journal* (Sangomon County, Illinois), April 17, 1865.

by being thrown from his carriage, whose life is hardly yet free from danger, and commences a murderous assault upon his prostrate and helpless
victim, and the unarmed attendants.[1] It is impossible to conceive anything
more fiend-like and diabolical. And yet, this is called "chivalry!"—and the
perpetrators profess to be influenced by the love of liberty. It is the "chivalry" of the desperado, and the love of liberty which controls the highwayman and the enemy of humanity.

The nation is bereaved. Every loyal man and woman mourns the loss of
one whose unswerving justice, whose pure and unsullied honor and incor-
ruptible integrity, whose magnanimity of character and mercifulness
towards his enemies had won the respect even of those enemies themselves. All but traitors mourn him as a personal friend. At such an hour as
this and in sight of the fearful crime that has been committed, the spirit
of mere partisanship is disarmed and its voice silenced. Nothing but the
most uncontrollable and demoniac treason dares to assail a man so foully
dealt with, or gloat over the "deep damnation of his taking off."

President Lincoln died at the hand of Slavery. It was Slavery that conceived the fearful deed; it was Slavery that sought and found the willing
instrument and sped the fatal ball; it is Slavery alone that will justify the
act. Henceforth men will look upon slavery as indeed "the sum of all vil-
lainies," the fruitful parent of all crime. This murder was an assault upon
the principles of free Government, inasmuch as he was the choice of a
large majority of the nation for the office which he filled. He has fallen in
the very hour of victory, when constitutional free Government was being
vindicated, and when peace seemed just ready to return to a land torn and
distracted by civil war. Despite the calumnies of his enemies, his fame is
now secure. History and posterity will do him justice. His memory will be
a rich inheritance to our nation, attracting to his tomb the lovers of freedom from all lands, and dividing with that of Washington the admiration
of the world. With a slight change of phraseology, the closing lines of the
magnificant lyric will apply to the death of ABRAHAM LINCOLN:

> "As Christ died to make men holy, HE DIED to make men free,
> "While God is marching on."[2]

ANONYMOUS

The Great Crime—Abraham Lincoln's Place in History[†]

Abraham Lincoln, in the full fruition of his glorious work, has been
struck from the roll of living men by the pistol shot of an assassin. That is
the unwelcome news which has, for the last two days, filled every loyal
heart with sadness, horror and a burning thirst for retribution. That is
the news which has swept away from the public mind every sentiment of

1. Lewis Powell (1844–1865), a co-conspirator of Lincoln assassin John Wilkes Booth, on April
   14, 1865, attacked the bedridden Secretary of State William H. Seward, wounding him and
   several others present with a knife.
2. From "The Battle Hymn of the Republic" (1862), by Julia Ward Howe.
† *New York Herald*, April 17, 1865.

leniency or conciliation towards the conquered brigands of the South, and in whose lurid light, as by the phosphorescent flames recently enkindled in the crowded hotels of this city by men with rebel commissions in their pockets, we are again terribly reminded of the absolute barbarity and utter devilishness of the foemen we have now tightly clutched in our victorious grasp. The kindliest and purest nature, the bravest and most honest will, the temper of highest geniality, and the spirit of largest practical beneficence in our public life, has fallen a victim to the insane ferocity of a bad and mad vagabond, who had been educated up to this height of crime by the teachings of our "copperhead" oracles, and by the ambition of fulfilling those instructions which he received "from Richmond." Of him, however, and the bitter fruits to the South and to all Southern sympathizers which must follow his act as inevitably as the thunder storm follows the lightning flash, we do not care in this moment of benumbing regret and overwhelming excitement to allow ourselves to speak. The deliberations of justice must be held in some calmer hour; while, for the present, we can but throw out some few hurried reflections on the character of the giant who has been lost to our Israel, and the glorious place in history his name is destined to occupy.

Whatever judgment may have been formed by those who were opposed to him as to the calibre of our deceased Chief Magistrate, or the place he is destined to occupy in history, all men of undisturbed observation must have recognized in Mr. Lincoln a quaintness, originality, courage, honesty, magnanimity and popular force of character such as have never heretofore, in the annals of the human family, had the advantage of so eminent a stage for their display. He was essentially a mixed product of the agricultural, forensic and frontier life of this continent—as indigenous to our soil as the cranberry crop, and as American in his fibre as the granite foundations of the Apalachian range. He may not have been, and perhaps was not, our most perfect product in any one branch of mental or moral education; but, taking him for all in all, the very noblest impulses, peculiarities and aspirations of our whole people—what may be called our continental idiosyncracies—were more collectively and vividly reproduced in his genial and yet unswerving nature than in that of any other public man of whom our chronicles bear record. . . .

This estimate of the place inevitably to be occupied in the world's history by the great National Chief whose loss we mourn may not prove either a familiar or pleasant idea for the mere partisans of the present day to contemplate; but it will be found none the less a true and philosophical estimate. In the retrospective glance of history the "accidents," as they are called, of his elevation will all have faded out of sight; and the pen of the historian will only chronicle some such record as the following:—From the very humblest position in a family subsisting by agricultural labor, and himself toiling for daily bread in his early youth, this extraordinary man, by the gifts of self-education, absolute honesty of purpose, perfect sympathy with the popular heart and great natural endowments, first rose to eminence as a lawyer; then graduated in Congress; was next heard of as the powerful though unsuccessful rival for national Senatorial honors of the democratic candidate for the Presidency, over whom he subsequently triumphed in 1860; and four years later we find him, in the midst of overwhelming financial embarrassments, and during the uncertain progress of the bloodiest and most desolating civil war ever waged, so completely retaining the confidence of the American people as to be triumphantly re-elected to the first office in their gift. They will claim for him all the moral influences, which—acting through material forces and agencies—have led to the abolition of slavery, and the permanent enthroning of popular institutions on this continent; and, in their general summing up of this now unappreciated age in which we have our feverish being, and in their pictures of those events wherein the clamorous partisans of the past week were prone to urge that Mr. Lincoln had been but a passive instrument, his name and figure will be brought forward in glowing colors on their canvass, as the chief impelling power and central organizer of the vast results which cannot fail to follow our vindication of the popular form of government.

And surely some hundred years hence, when the staid and scholarly disciples of the historic Muse, bring their grave eyes to scan and their brief tapelines to measure the altitude and attitude, properties and proportions of our deceased Chief Magistrate, their surprise—taking them to be historians of the present type—will be intense beyond expression. It has been for centuries the tradition of their tribe to model every public character after the style of the heroic antique. Their nation-founders, warriors and lawmakers have been invariably clad in flowing togas, crowned with laurel or oak wreaths, and carrying papyrus rolls or the batons of empire in their out-stretched hands. How can men so educated—these poor, dwarfed ransackers of the past, who have always regarded greatness in this illusory aspect—ever be brought to comprehend the genius of a character so externally uncouth, so pathetically simple, so unfathomably penetrating, so irresolute and yet so irresistible, so bizarre, grotesque, droll, wise and perfectly beneficent in all its developments as was that of the great original thinker and statesman for whose death the whole land, even in the midst of victories unparalleled, is to-day draped in mourning? It will require an altogether new breed and school of historians to begin doing justice to this type-man of the world's last political evangel. No ponderously eloquent George Bancroft[1] can properly rehearse those inimitable stories by which, in the light form of allegory, our martyred President has so frequently and so wisely decided the knottiest controversies of his Cabinet; nor can even the genius of a Washington Irving[2] or Edward Everett in some future age elocutionize into the formal dignity of a Greek statue the kindly but powerful face of Mr. Lincoln, seamed in circles by humorous thoughts and furrowed crosswise by mighty anxieties. It will take a new school of historians to do justice to this eccentric addition to the world's gallery of heroes; for while other men as interesting and original may have held equal power previously in other countries, it is only in the present age of steam, telegraphs and prying newspaper reporters that a subject so eminent, both by genius and position, could have been placed under the eternal microscope of critical examination. . . .

While we all must mourn with sad and sickened hearts the success of the great crime which has removed our beloved and trusted President

---

1. A prominent Massachusetts statesman and historian (1800–1891).
2. American author (1783–1859), best known for his tales "Rip Van Winkle" and "The Legend of Sleepy Hollow." Everett: American educator, politician, and orator (1794–1865).

from the final scenes of the contest he had thus far conducted to a triumphant issue, let us not forget that by the circumstance of death the seal of immortality has been stamped upon his fame; nor is it any longer in the power of changing fortune to take away from him, as might have happened had he lived, one of the most solid, brilliant and stainless reputations of which in the world's annals any record can be found—its only peer existing in the memory of George Washington.

RALPH WALDO EMERSON

[He Is the History of the American People]†

We meet under the gloom of a calamity which darkens down over the minds of good men in all civil society, as the fearful tidings travel over sea, over land, from country to country, like the shadow of an uncalculated eclipse over the planet. Old as history is, and manifold as are its tragedies, I doubt if any death has caused so much pain to mankind as this has caused, or will cause, on its announcement; and this, not so much because nations are by modern arts brought so closely together, as because of the mysterious hopes and fears which, in the present day, are connected with the name and institutions of America.

In this country, on Saturday, every one was struck dumb, and saw at first only deep below deep, as he meditated on the ghastly blow. And perhaps, at this hour, when the coffin which contains the dust of the President sets forward on its long march through mourning States, on its way to his home in Illinois, we might well be silent, and suffer the awful voices of the time to thunder to us. Yes, but that first despair was brief: the man was not so to be mourned. He was the most active and hopeful of men; and his work had not perished: but acclamations of praise for the task he had accomplished burst out into a song of triumph, which even tears for his death cannot keep down.

The President stood before us as a man of the people. He was thoroughly American, had never crossed the sea, had never been spoiled by English insularity or French dissipation; a quite native, aboriginal man, as an acorn from the oak; no aping of foreigners, no frivolous accomplishments, Kentuckian born, working on a farm, a flatboatman, a captain in the Black Hawk war, a country lawyer, a representative in the rural Legislature of Illinois;—on such modest foundations the broad structure of his fame was laid. How slowly, and yet by happily prepared steps, he came to his place. All of us remember,—it is only a history of five or six years,—the surprise and the disappointment of the country at his first nomination by the Convention at Chicago. Mr. Seward, then in the culmination of his good fame, was the favorite of the Eastern States. And when the new and comparatively unknown name of Lincoln was announced, (notwithstanding the report of the acclamations of that Convention,) we heard the result coldly and sadly. It seemed too rash, on a purely local reputation, to build

† "Abraham Lincoln: Remarks at the Funeral Services Held in Concord, April 19, 1865," in *The Complete Works of Ralph Waldo Emerson* (New York: W. H. Wise, 1926), 11:337–38.

so grave a trust in such anxious times; and men naturally talked of the chances in politics as incalculable. But it turned out not to be chance. The profound good opinion which the people of Illinois and of the West had conceived of him, and which they had imparted to their colleagues that they also might justify themselves to their constituents at home, was not rash, though they did not begin to know the riches of his worth.

A plain man of the people, an extraordinary fortune attended him. He offered no shining qualities at the first encounter; he did not offend by superiority. He had a face and manner which disarmed suspicion, which inspired confidence, which confirmed good-will. He was a man without vices. He had a strong sense of duty, which it was very easy for him to obey. Then, he had what farmers call a long head; was excellent in working out the sum for himself; in arguing his case and convincing you fairly and firmly. Then, it turned out that he was a great worker; had prodigious faculty of performance; worked easily. A good worker is so rare; everybody has some disabling quality. In a host of young men that start together and promise so many brilliant leaders for the next age, each fails on trial; one by bad health, one by conceit, or by love of pleasure, or lethargy, or an ugly temper,—each has some disqualifying fault that throws him out of the career. But this man was sound to the core, cheerful, persistent, all right for labor, and liked nothing so well.

Then, he had a vast good-nature, which made him tolerant and accessible to all; fair-minded, leaning to the claim of the petitioner; affable, and not sensible to the affliction which the innumerable visits paid to him when President would have brought to any one else. And how this good-nature became a noble humanity, in many a tragic case which the events of the war brought to him, every one will remember; and with what increasing tenderness he dealt when a whole race was thrown on his compassion. The poor negro said of him, on an impressive occasion, "Massa Linkum am eberywhere."

Then his broad good-humor, running easily into jocular talk, in which he delighted and in which he excelled, was a rich gift to this wise man. It enabled him to keep his secret; to meet every kind of man and every rank in society; to take off the edge of the severest decisions; to mask his own purpose and sound his companion; and to catch with true instinct the temper of every company he addressed. And, more than all, it is to a man of severe labor, in anxious and exhausting crises, the natural restorative, good as sleep, and is the protection of the overdriven brain against rancor and insanity.

He is the author of a multitude of good sayings, so disguised as pleasantries that it is certain they had no reputation at first but as jests; and only later, by the very acceptance and adoption they find in the mouths of millions, turn out to be the wisdom of the hour. I am sure if this man had ruled in a period of less facility of printing, he would have become mythological in a very few years, like Æsop or Pilpay, or one of the Seven Wise Masters,[1] by his fables and proverbs. But the weight and penetration of many passages in his letters, messages and speeches, hidden now by the

---

1. An ancient story cycle of obscure origins. Aesop (620–564 B.C.E.), Greek storyteller credited with the volume *Aesop's Fables*. Pilpay is the reputed author of the 6th-century Sanskrit volume *Fables of Pilpay*.

very closeness of their application to the moment, are destined hereafter
to wide fame. What pregnant definitions; what unerring common sense;
what foresight; and, on great occasion, what lofty, and more than national,
what humane tone! His brief speech at Gettysburg will not easily be surpassed by words on any recorded occasion. This, and one other American
speech, that of John Brown to the court that tried him, and a part of Kossuth's speech[2] at Birmingham, can only be compared with each other,
and with no fourth.

His occupying the chair of State was a triumph of the good-sense of
mankind, and of the public conscience. This middleclass country had got
a middle-class President, at last. Yes, in manners and sympathies, but not
in powers, for his powers were superior. This man grew according to the
need. His mind mastered the problem of the day; and, as the problem
grew, so did his comprehension of it. Rarely was man so fitted to the event.
In the midst of fears and jealousies, in the Babel of counsels and parties,
this man wrought incessantly with all his might and all his honesty, laboring to find what the people wanted, and how to obtain that. It cannot be
said there is any exaggeration of his worth. If ever a man was fairly tested,
he was. There was no lack of resistance, nor of slander, nor of ridicule.
The times have allowed no state secrets; the nation has been in such fer-
ment, such multitudes had to be trusted, that no secret could be kept.
Every door was ajar, and we know all that befell.

Then, what an occasion was the whirlwind of the war. Here was place
for no holiday magistrate, no fair-weather sailor; the new pilot was hurried
to the helm in a tornado. In four years,—four years of battle-days,—his
endurance, his fertility of resources, his magnanimity, were sorely tried
and never found wanting. There, by his courage, his justice, his even temper, his fertile counsel, his humanity, he stood a heroic figure in the centre
of a heroic epoch. He is the true history of the American people in his
time. Step by step he walked before them; slow with their slowness, quick-
ening his march by theirs, the true representative of this continent; an
entirely public man; father of his country, the pulse of twenty millions
throbbing in his heart, the thought of their minds articulated by his tongue.

Adam Smith[3] remarks that the axe, which in Houbraken's portraits of
British kings and worthies is engraved under those who have suffered at
the block, adds a certain lofty charm to the picture. And who does not see,
even in this tragedy so recent, how fast the terror and rain of the massacre
are already burning into glory around the victim? Far happier this fate than
to have lived to be wished away; to have watched the decay of his own fac-
ulties; to have seen,—perhaps even he,—the proverbial ingratitude of
statesmen; to have seen mean men preferred. Had he not lived long enough
to keep the greatest promise that ever man made to his fellow-men,—the
practical abolition of slavery? He had seen Tennessee, Missouri and Maryland emancipate their slaves. He had seen Savannah, Charleston and
Richmond surrendered; had seen the main army of the rebellion lay down

2. Lajos Kossuth (1802–1894), Hungarian revolutionary, gave an eloquent endorsement of liberty
   in a speech in Birmingham, England, on November 12, 1851. Brown (1800–1859), abolitionist
   who, upon receiving the death sentence for his role in the raid on Harpers Ferry, Virginia, gave
   before the court an impromptu speech in which he forcefully presented his antislavery views.
3. Scottish philosopher and economist (1723–1790). Houbraken: Arnold Houbraken (1660–
   1719), Dutch artist.

its arms. He had conquered the public opinion of Canada, England and France. Only Washington can compare with him in fortune.

And what if it should turn out, in the unfolding of the web, that he had reached the term; that this heroic deliverer could no longer serve us; that the rebellion had touched its natural conclusion, and what remained to be done required new and uncommitted hands,—a new spirit born out of the ashes of the war; and that Heaven, wishing to show the world a completed benefactor, shall make him serve his country even more by his death than by his life? Nations, like kings, are not good by facility and complaisance. "The kindness of kings consists in justice and strength."[4] Easy goodnature has been the dangerous foible of the Republic, and it was necessary that its enemies should outrage it, and drive us to unwonted firmness, to secure the salvation of this country in the next ages.

The ancients believed in a serene and beautiful Genius which ruled in the affairs of nations; which, with a slow but stern justice, carried forward the fortunes of certain chosen houses, weeding out single offenders or offending families, and securing at last the firm prosperity of the favorites of Heaven. It was too narrow a view of the Eternal Nemesis. There is a serene Providence which rules the fate of nations, which makes little account of time, little of one generation or race, makes no account of disasters, conquers alike by what is called defeat or by what is called victory, thrusts aside enemy and obstruction, crushes everything immoral as inhuman, and obtains the ultimate triumph of the best race by the sacrifice of everything which resists the moral laws of the world. It makes its own instruments, creates the man for the time, trains him in poverty, inspires his genius, and arms him for his task. It has given every race its own talent, and ordains that only that race which combines perfectly with the virtues of all shall endure.

HENRY WARD BEECHER[1]

It Was As if He Had Died in Battle[†]

For myself, I cannot yet command that quietness of spirit needed for a just and temperate delineation of a man whom goodness has made great. Leaving that, if it please God, to some other occasion, I pass to some considerations, aside from the martyr President's character, which may be fit for this hour's instruction.

1. Let us not mourn that his departure was so sudden, nor fill our imagination with horror at its method. Men, long eluding and evading sorrow, when at last they are overtaken by it, seem enchanted, and seek to make their sorrow sorrowful to the very uttermost, and to bring out every drop of suffering which they possibly can. This is not Christian, though it may be natural. When good men pray for deliverance from sudden death, it is

---

4. A version of the following statement written by Napoleon Bonaparte (1769–1821) in an 1806 letter to his brother: "You must not forget that the kindness of kings consists in strength and in strict justice."
1. A Protestant clergyman (1813–1887), abolitionist, and brother of Harriet Beecher Stowe.
† From "Abraham Lincoln" (sermon preached in Brooklyn, April 23, 1865), in *Patriotic Addresses*, edited by John R. Howard (New York: Fords, Howard, & Hulbert, 1891), 701–10.

only that they may not be plunged without preparation, all disrobed, into the presence of their Judge. When one is ready to depart, suddenness of death is a blessing. It is a painful sight to see a tree overthrown by a tornado, wrenched from its foundations, and broken down like a weed; but it is yet more painful to see a vast and venerable tree lingering with vain strife against decay, which age and infirmity have marked for destruction. The process by which strength wastes, and the mind is obscured, and the tabernacle is taken down, is humiliating and painful; and it is good and grand when a man departs to his rest from out of the midst of duty, full-armed and strong, with pulse beating time. For such an one to go suddenly, if he be prepared to go, is but to terminate a most noble life in its most noble manner. Mark the words of the Master:

"Let your loins be girded about, and your lights burning; and ye yourselves like unto men that wait for their lord, when he will return from the wedding; that when he cometh and knocketh they may open unto him immediately. Blessed are those servants whom the lord when he cometh shall find watching."[2]

Not they that go in a stupor, but they that go with all their powers about them, and wide-awake, to meet their Master, as to a wedding, are blessed. He died watching. He died with his armor on. In the midst of hours of labors, in the very heart of patriotic consultations, just returned from camps and councils, he was stricken down. No fever dried his blood. No slow waste consumed him. All at once, in full strength and manhood, with his girdle tight about him, he departed, and walks with God.

Nor was the manner of his death more shocking, if we divest it of the malignity of the motives which caused it. The mere instrument itself is not one that we should shrink from contemplating. Have not thousands of soldiers fallen on the field of battle by the bullets of the enemy? Is being killed in battle counted to be a dreadful mode of dying? It was as if he had died in battle. Do not all soldiers that must fall ask to depart in the hour of battle and victory? He went in the hour of victory.

There has not been a poor drummer-boy in all this war that has fallen for whom the great heart of Lincoln would not have bled; there has not been one private soldier, without note or name, slain among thousands, and hid in the pit among hundreds without even the memorial of a separate burial, for whom the President would not have wept. He was a man from the common people that never forgot his kind. And now that he who might not bear the march, and toil, and battles with these humble citizens has been called to die by the bullet, as they were, do you not feel that there was a peculiar fitness to his nature and life, that he should in death be joined with them, in a final common experience, to whom he had been joined in all his sympathies.

For myself, when any event is susceptible of a higher and nobler garnishing, I know not what that disposition is that should seek to drag it down to the depths of gloom, and write it all over with the scrawls of horror or fear. I let the light of nobler thoughts fall upon his departure, and bless God that there is some argument of consolation in the matter and manner of his going, as there was in the matter and manner of his staying.

2. Luke 12:35–37.

2. This blow was but the expiring rebellion. As a miniature gives all the form and features of its subject, so, epitomized in this foul act, we find the whole nature and disposition of slavery. It begins in a wanton destruction of all human rights, and in a desecration of all the sanctities of heart and home; and it is the universal enemy of mankind, and of God, who made man. It can be maintained only at the sacrifice of every right and moral feeling in its abettors and upholders. I deride the man that points me to any man bred amid slavery, believing in it, and willingly practicing it, and tells me that he is a *man*. I shall find saints in perdition sooner than I shall find true manhood under the influences of so accursed a system as this. It is a two-edged sword, cutting both ways, violently destroying manhood in the oppressed, and insidiously destroying manhood in the oppressor. The problem is solved, the demonstration is completed, in our land. Slavery wastes its victims; and it destroys the masters. It destroys public morality, and the possibility of it. It corrupts manhood in its very centre and elements. Communities in which it exists are not to be trusted. They are rotten. Nor can you find timber grown in this accursed soil of iniquity that is fit to build our ship of state, or lay the foundation of our households. The patriotism that grows up under this blight, when put to proof, is selfish and brittle; and he that leans upon it shall be pierced. The honor that grows up in the midst of slavery is not honor, but a bastard quality that usurps the place of its better, only to disgrace the name of honor. And, as long as there is conscience, or reason, or Christianity, the honor that slavery begets will be a bye-word and a hissing. The whole moral nature of men reared to familiarity and connivance with slavery is death-smitten. The needless rebellion; the treachery of its leaders to oaths and solemn trusts; their violation of the commonest principles of fidelity, sitting in senates, in councils, in places of public confidence, only to betray and to destroy; the long, general, and unparalleled cruelty to prisoners, without provocation, and utterly without excuse: the unreasoning malignity and fierceness—these all mark the symptoms of that disease of slavery which is a deadly poison to soul and body.

1. I do not say that there are not single natures, here and there, scattered through the vast wilderness which is covered with this poisonous vine, who escape the poison. There are, but they are not to be found among the men that believe in it, and that have been moulded by it. They are the exceptions. Slavery is itself barbarity. That nation which cherishes it is barbarous; and no outward tinsel or glitter can redeem it from the charge of barbarism. And it was fit that its expiring blow should be such as to take away from men the last forbearance, the last pity, and fire the soul with an invincible determination that the breeding-ground of such mischiefs and monsters shall be utterly and forever destroyed.

2. We needed not that he should put on paper that he believed in slavery, who, with treason, with murder, with cruelty infernal, hovered around that majestic man to destroy his life. He was himself but the long sting with which slavery struck at liberty; and he carried the poison that belonged to slavery. And as long as this nation lasts, it will never be forgotten that we have had one martyred President—never! Never, while time lasts, while heaven lasts, while hell rocks and groans, will it be forgotten that slavery, by its minions, slew him, and, in slaying him, made manifest its whole nature and tendency.

3. This blow was aimed at the life of the Government and of the nation. Lincoln was slain; America was meant. The man was cast down; the Government was smitten at. The President was killed: it was national life, breathing freedom, and meaning beneficence, that was sought. He, the man of Illinois, the private man, divested of robes and the insignia of authority, representing nothing but his personal self, might have been hated; but it was not that that ever would have called forth the murderer's blow. It was because he stood in the place of government, representing government, and a government that represented right and liberty, that he was singled out.

This, then, is a crime against universal government. It is not a blow at the foundations of our government, more than at the foundations of the English Government, of the French Government, of every compacted and well-organized government. It was a crime against mankind. The whole world will repudiate and stigmatize it as a deed without a shade of redeeming light. For this was not the oppressed, goaded to extremity, turning on his oppressor. Not the shadow of a cloud, even, has rested on the South, of wrong; and they knew it right well.

*　*　*

4. The blow has signally failed. The cause is not stricken; it is strengthened. This nation has dissolved—but in tears only. It stands four-square, more solid, to-day, than any pyramid in Egypt. This people are neither wasted, nor daunted, nor disordered. Men hate slavery and love liberty with stronger hate and love to-day than ever before. The Government is not weakened, it is made stronger. *　*　*

*　*　*

5. Even he who now sleeps has, by this event, been clothed with new influence. Dead, he speaks to men who now willingly hear what before they refused to listen to. Now his simple and weighty words will be gathered like those of Washington, and your children, and your children's children, shall be taught to ponder the simplicity and deep wisdom of utterances which, in their time, passed, in party heat, as idle words. Men will receive a new impulse of patriotism for his sake, and will guard with zeal the whole country which he loved so well. I swear you, on the altar of his memory, to be more faithful to the country for which he has perished. [Applause.] They will, as they follow his hearse, swear a new hatred to that slavery against which he warred, and which in vanquishing him, has made him a martyr and a conqueror. I swear you, by the memory of this martyr, to hate slavery with an unappeasable hatred. [Applause.] They will admire and imitate the firmness of this man, his inflexible conscience for the right; and yet his gentleness, as tender as a woman's, his moderation of spirit, which not all the heat of party could inflame, nor all the jars and disturbances of this country shake out of its place. I swear you to an emulation of his justice, his moderation, and his mercy.

*　*　*

And now the martyr is moving in triumphal march, mightier than when alive. The nation rises up at every stage of his coming. Cities and states are his pall-bearers, and the cannon beats the hours with solemn progression. Dead, *dead*, DEAD, he yet speaketh! Is Washington dead? Is Hampden[3] dead? Is David dead? Is any man that ever was fit to live dead? Disenthralled of flesh, and risen in the unobstructed sphere where passion never comes, he begins his illimitable work. His life now is grafted upon the infinite, and will be fruitful as no earthly life can be. Pass on, thou that hast overcome! Your sorrows, oh people, are his peace! Your bells, and bands, and muffled drums, sound triumph in his ear. Wail and weep here; God makes it echo joy and triumph there. Pass on!

Four years ago, oh, Illinois, we took from your midst an untried man, and from among the people. We return him to you a mighty conqueror. Not thine any more, but the nation's; not ours, but the world's. Give him place, oh, ye prairies! In the midst of this great continent his dust shall rest, a sacred treasure to myriads who shall pilgrim to that shrine to kindle anew their zeal and patriotism. Ye winds that move over the mighty places of the West, chant his requiem! Ye people, behold a martyr whose blood, as so many articulate words, pleads for fidelity, for law, for liberty!

ANONYMOUS

[Lincoln's Death a Blow to the South][†]

Assassination of President Lincoln.—The heaviest blow which has ever fallen upon the people of the South has descended, Abraham Lincoln, the President of the United States, has been assassinated! The decease of the Chief Magistrate of the nation, at any period is an event which profoundly affects the public mind, but the time, manner, and circumstances of President Lincoln's death render it the most momentous, the most appalling, the most deplorable calamity which has ever befallen the people of the United States.

The thoughtless and vicious may effect to derive satisfaction from the sudden and tragic close of the President's career; but every reflecting person will deplore the awful event. Just as everything was happily conspiring to a restoration of tranquility, under the benignant and magnanimous policy of Mr. Lincoln, comes this terrible blow. God grant that it may not rekindle excitement or inflame passion again.

That a war, almost fratricidal, should give rise to bitter feelings and bloody deeds in the field was to be expected, but that the assassin's knife and bullet should follow the great and best loved of the nation in their daily walk, and reach them when surrounded by their friends, is an atrocity which will shock and appall every honorable man and woman in the land.

The secrecy with which the assassin or assassins pursued their victims indicates that there were but few accomplices in this inhuman crime. The abhorrence with which it is regarded on all sides will, it is hoped, deter insane and malignant men from the emulation of the infamy which attaches to this infernal deed.

We cannot pursue this subject further. We contemplate too deeply and painfully the terrible aspects of this calamity to comment upon it further.

3. John Hampden (ca. 1595–1643), a hero of the English Civil War.
† "The Death of the President," *Richmond Whig*, reprinted in the *Louisville* (Kentucky) *Journal*, April 27, 1865.

C. CHAUNCEY BURR

[Lincoln and John Brown]†

The pulpits generally, and a majority of Republican papers, now boastingly rejoice that *"the North has vindicated the cause of John Brown, and wiped out slavery."* Nor is this any foolish or unconsidered boast; it is strictly true. The policy of the Republican party, since it came into power, has been a faithful carrying out of the work begun by old John Brown. The administration of Abraham Lincoln was a John Brown raid on the grandest scale; and it was no more. That is the place it will occupy in history. The bloody business is done, and we do not write for the purpose of amending the great crime. We do not seek to raise the dead. We accept the *facts* as we find them; but it is our business to tell the truth about these facts. It is our business to strip off all these bandages of shams, hypocricies, and lies, and lay bare to the bone this monstrous carcass of frauds and despotism. The record of this party is in revolution and blood; in the revolution and blood inaugurated by John Brown. It has finished the raid which that prince of assassins and thieves, John Brown, began. * * *

It was the endorsement of the policy of this raider and murderer, by the North, that startled and aroused the South, and finally drove it into secession; for John Brown's raid *was* endorsed by the North. From almost every church and school-house, the voice of prayer and lamentation went up to Almighty God, canonizing his name, and endorsing his infamy. The whole Republican press lent its support to this abomination; and with entire consistency, when the New England soldiers marched through this city, they made it hideous as hell by singing and shouting *"John Brown's soul is marching on."*[1] So it is, we have little doubt, *marching on*, through seas of fire, in company with fiends, thieves and assassins, such as were his companions and abettors in this life. So it is *marching on* to the music of despotism, ignorance, revenge and lust, that swells up like a gorgon from the bottomless pit, out of the brazen throats of the negro-worshipping mobs! *Marching on*, as a pestilence or contagion, or a thing of horror and death marches on! Behind its march are the wails of widows, the screams of children, the vain implorations of defenseless old men, and the humiliation of manhood. Before it, the insane gibberish and fantastic dance of negroes, of both the white and black complexion, making night and day hideous with infernal delight. Marching on!—alas, poor country! alas, human nature! Why do we write these things now? Because we love, and would save our country. Because we would bring our countrymen of the North to their senses, by holding up the John Brown raid as a glass for them to see their faces in. We would remind them that there is both a *God* and *history*, and that justice and truth, sooner or later, will whip all of the shams and lies out of the records of human events. If the South has *follies* to repent of, we have *crimes*, crimes which will roll out of their graves and hunt us like demons through the world. Vainly do we seek to

† From "History of Old John Brown," *The Old Guard: A Monthly Journal Devoted to the Principles of 1776 and 1787*, July 1865.

1. From "John Brown's Song" (a.k.a. "John Brown's Body"), a popular Union marching song.

assure ourselves, by shutting our eyes and saying, *verily, what a good peo-*
ple are we! There is an eye that we cannot shut. There is an arm that we
cannot stay. Time is an inexorable avenger of all men's wrongs; and time
will strip us bare to the bone, and show what a carcass of frauds and
shams we are. We repeat again, the last four years of Republican rule have
been a stupendous John Brown raid. Logically, constitutionally, they have
been just that, and nothing more. What we dare to say is this, that John
Brown had as much Constitution and law for what he did, as the Republican administration had for what it has done. This is what we say, and no
leading Republican dare attempt to debate the merits of the question
with us before the people. They dare call names; but they dare not debate.
We love truth and respect justice above all things. We hold no opinion
which we will not gladly submit to the test of fair argument and debate;
but these *traitors* of the John Brown school dare not argue. They carry all
points by singing, shouting, and mobbing. Their throats are trumpets,
and their brains gongs and sounding-boards. In a late speech, Senator
Lowry, a prominent man in the Republican party of the State of Pennsylvania, said: "John Brown was the first martyr of this rebellion—Abraham
Lincoln the last. The names of Abraham Lincoln and John Brown will go
down in history together, as the first and lost martyr of this rebellion. The
war could not be averted. God Almighty is fighting this war for the right.
John Brown played his part, and Abraham Lincoln his."[2] Here the truth is
owned. The Republican administration is simply a John Brown raid. The
name of John Brown and of Abraham Lincoln will indeed *go down to pos-*
terity together; and the name of Seward, and Sumner, and Garrison,[3] and
such as they, will go with them—go with them into the abyss of infamy
and eternal shame. Over the most prosperous land, over the fairest civilization in the world, they have brought ruin, barbarism, and woe. If the
traitors of this school had never been born, the peace of our country had
never been broken. That is a truth that will stand as firmly as the word of
God, when the subterfuges and lies of this mad hour are swept away. The
record President Johnson has given of John Brown's character and his
raid[4] will stand the test of time. The historian will take it as the starting
point of the policy which has ruled us of the North since the accession of
the Abolition party to power. O, my countrymen! Have you abandoned
yourselves permanently to the shame, to the eternal infamy, of this policy?
The policy of a thief, a robber, and assassin! The name President Johnson
has given him is the one he must wear in history; and you who follow John
Brown's policy shall wear it also. Sing and shout, and dance while you
may! Time will last longer than your songs, and justice will one day throw
you under tie wheels of avenging retribution. If all history is not a liar, the
day of your shame is sure to come. O, you sneer! So have hundreds of
thousands of fools done before! If you did not sneer we should think we
had done you injustice. Sneer and mock as you will, for this is *your day.*
God's day, the day of justice, comes afterwards! It lasts forever!

2. Quotation from Pennsylvania abolitionist and politician Morrow B. Lowry (1813–1885), who
   visited the imprisoned John Brown in 1859.
3. Seward, Sumner, and William Lloyd Garrison (1805–1879), were prominent antislavery
   spokesmen.
4. In a speech before the Senate on December 12, 1859, Andrew Johnson of Tennessee described
   Brown as a murderous fanatic.

432

NOAH BROOKS[1]

[Lincoln's Temperament and His Tastes in Reading and Music][†]

Mr. Lincoln had not a hopeful temperament, and, though he looked at the bright side of things, was always prepared for disaster and defeat. With his wonderful faculty for discerning results he often saw success where others saw disaster, but oftener perceived a failure when others were elated with victory, or were temporarily deceived by appearances. Of a great cavalry raid, which filled the newspapers with glowing exultation, but failed to cut the communications which it had been designed to destroy, he briefly said: "That was good circus-riding; it will do to fill a column in the newspapers; but I don't see that it has brought any thing else to pass." He often said that the worst feature about newspapers was that they were so sure to be "ahead of the hounds," outrunning events, and exciting expectations which were sure to be disappointed. One of the worst effects of a victory, he said, was to lead people to expect that the war was about over in consequence of it; but he was never weary of commending the patience of the American people, which he thought something matchless and touching. I have seen him shed tears when speaking of the cheerful sacrifice of the light and strength of so many happy homes throughout the land. His own patience was marvelous; and never crushed at defeat or unduly excited by success, his demeanor under both was an example for all men. Once he said the keenest blow of all the war was at an early stage, when the disaster of Ball's Bluff and the death of his beloved Baker[2] smote upon him like a whirlwind from a desert.

* * *

The world will never hear the last of the "little stories" with which the President garnished or illustrated his conversation and his early stump speeches. He said, however, that as near as he could reckon, about one-sixth of those which were credited to him were old acquaintances; all of the rest were the productions of other and better story-tellers than himself. Said he: "I do generally remember a good story when I hear it, but I never did invent any thing original; I am only a retail dealer." His anecdotes were seldom told for the sake of the telling, but because they fitted in just where they came, and shed a light on the argument that nothing else could. He was not witty, but brimful of humor; and though he was quick to appreciate a good pun, I never knew of his making but one, which was on the Christian name of a friend, to whom he said: "You have yet to be elected to the place I hold; but Noah's *reign* was before Abraham." He thought that the chief characteristic of American humor was its grotesqueness and extravagance; and the story of the man who

1. A journalist (1830–1903) who befriended Lincoln in Illinois in the 1850s; the friendship deepened when he covered Lincoln's presidency in Washington D.C.
† From "Recollections of Abraham Lincoln," *Harper's New Monthly Magazine* 31 (July 1865): 222–30.
2. Edward Dickinson Baker (1811–1861), a colonel and senator and close friend of Lincoln's, was killed in the Battle of Ball's Bluff, Virginia, in October 1861.

was so tall that he was "laid out" in a rope-walk, the soprano voice so high that it had to be climbed over by a ladder, and the Dutchman's expression of "somebody tying his dog loose," all made a permanent lodgment in his mind.

His accuracy and memory were wonderful, and one illustration of the former quality may be given in the remarkable correspondence between the figures of the result of the last presidential election and the actual sum total. The President's figures, collected hastily, and partially based upon his own estimates, made up only four weeks after the election, have been found to be only one hundred and twenty-nine less in their grand total than that made up by Mr. M'Pherson, the Clerk of the House of Representatives, who has compiled a table from the returns furnished him from the official records of all the State capitals in the loyal States.

Latterly Mr. Lincoln's reading was with the humorous writers. He liked to repeat from memory whole chapters from these books; and on such occasions he always preserved his own gravity though his auditors might be convulsed with laughter. He said that he had a dread of people who could not appreciate the fun of such things; and he once instanced a member of his own Cabinet, of whom he quoted the saying of Sydney Smith,[3] "that it required a surgical operation to get a joke into his head." The light trifles spoken of diverted his mind, or, as he said of his theatre-going, gave him refuge from himself and his weariness. But he also was a lover of many philosophical books, and particularly liked Butler's Analogy of Religion, Stuart Mill on Liberty, and he always hoped to get at President Edwards on the Will.[4] These ponderous writers found a queer companionship in the chronicler of the Mackerel Brigade, Parson Nasby, and Private Miles O'Reilly.[5] The Bible was a very familiar study with the President, whole chapters of Isaiah, the New Testament, and the Psalms being fixed in his memory, and he would sometimes correct a misquotation of Scripture, giving generally the chapter and verse where it could be found. He liked the Old Testament best, and dwelt on the simple beauty of the historical books. Once, speaking of his own age and strength, he quoted with admiration that passage, "His eye was not dim, nor his natural force abated."[6] I do not know that he thought then how, like that Moses of old, he was to stand on Pisgah[7] and see a peaceful land which he was not to enter.

Of the poets the President appeared to prefer Hood and Holmes,[8] the mixture and pathos in their writings being attractive to him beyond any thing else which he read. Of the former author he liked best the last part of "Miss Kilmansegg and her Golden Leg," "Faithless Sally Brown," and one or two others not generally so popular as those which are called Hood's

---

3. British clergyman and humorist (1771–1845).
4. Jonathan Edwards, *The Freedom of the Will* (1754). Joseph Butler, *The Analogy of Religion* (1736). John Stuart Mill, *On Liberty* (1859).
5. Pseudonym of journalist Charles Graham Halpine (1829–1868). "Mackerel Brigade": a company of Tennessee juveniles that was the subject of humorous writings by journalist Robert Henry Newell (1836–1901), who wrote as Orpheus C. Kerr. The Reverend Petroleum V. Nasby was a comic figure in popular sketches by David Ross Locke (1833–1888).
6. Deuteronomy 34:7.
7. The mountain from which Moses saw the Promised Land (Deuteronomy 34:1).
8. Oliver Wendell Holmes, Sr. (1809–1894), American poet. Thomas Hood (1799–1849), British poet and humorist.

best poems. Holmes's "September Gale," "Last Leaf," "Chambered Nauti-
lus," and "Ballad of an Oysterman" were among his very few favorite poems.
Longfellow's "Psalm of Life" and "Birds of Killingworth" were the only productions of that author he ever mentioned with praise, the latter of which
he picked up somewhere in a newspaper, cut out, and carried in his vest
pocket until it was committed to memory. James Russell Lowell[9] he only
knew as "Hosea Biglow," every one of whose effusions he knew. He sometimes repeated, word for word, the whole of "John P. Robinson, he," giving
the unceasing refrain with great unction and enjoyment. He once said that
originality and daring impudence were sublimed in this stanza of Lowell's:

> "Ef you take a sword and dror it,
>   An' stick a feller creetur thru,
> Gov'ment hain't to answer for it,
>   God'll send the bill to you."

Mr. Lincoln's love of music was something passionate, but his tastes
were simple and uncultivated, his choice being old airs, songs, and bal-
lads, among which the plaintive Scotch songs were best liked. "Annie
Laurie," "Mary of Argyle," and especially "Auld Robin Gray," never lost
their charm for him; and all songs which had for their theme the rapid
flight of time, decay, the recollections of early days, were sure to make
a deep impression. The song which he liked best, above all others, was
one called "Twenty Years Ago"[1]—a simple air, the words to which are
supposed to be uttered by a man who revisits the play-ground of his
youth. He greatly desired to find music for his favorite poem, "Oh, why
should the spirit of mortal be proud?"[2] and said once, when told that
the newspapers had credited him with the authorship of the piece, "I
should not care much for the reputation of having written that, but
would be glad if I could compose music as fit to convey the sentiment as
the words now do."

He wrote slowly, and with the greatest deliberation, and liked to take
his time; yet some of his dispatches, written without any corrections, are
models of compactness and finish. His private correspondence was extensive, and he preferred writing his letters with his own hand, making copies himself frequently, and filing every thing away in a set of pigeon-holes
in his office. When asked why he did not have a letter-book and copying-
press, he said, "A letter-book might be easily carried off, but that stock of
filed letters would be a back-load." He conscientiously attended to his
enormous correspondence, and read every thing that appeared to demand
his own attention. He said that he read with great regularity the letters of
an old friend who lived on the Pacific coast until he received a letter of
seventy pages of letter paper, when he broke down, and never read another.

*   *   *

9. American poet (1819–1891). Henry Wadsworth Longfellow (1807–1882), American poet.
   Holmes, Longfellow, and Lowell were among the popular versifiers known as the Fireside
   Poets. The quotations here—"John P. Robinson, he," and "If you take a sword"—are from
   Lowell's vernacular poem collection *The Biglow Papers* (1848).
1. An anonymously written sentimental ballad.
2. Poem by the Scottish poet William Knox (1789–1825).

VICTOR HUGO[1]

From A Letter to President Andrew Johnson[†]

Two deaths killed slavery. The death of Lincoln completes what the death of John Brown began. These two murderers, Wysse in 1859, Booth in 1865,[2] one preparing the gallows, the other striking with a dagger, were unwitting liberators. They showed their principle, slavery erect and, as it were, sent to the pillory, between two assassinations.

October – November 1865

HERMAN MELVILLE[1]

The Martyr[†]

Good Friday was the day
  Of the prodigy and crime,
When they killed him in his pity,
  When they killed him in his prime
5 Of clemency and calm—
    When with yearning he was filled
    To redeem the evil-willed,
And, though conqueror, be kind;
  But they killed him in his kindness,
10   In their madness and their blindness,
And they killed him from behind.

      There is sobbing of the strong,
      And a pall upon the land;
      But the People in their weeping
15   Bare the iron hand:
      Beware the People weeping
      When they bare the iron hand.

He lieth in his blood—
  The father in his face;
20 They have killed him, the Forgiver—
  The Avenger takes his place,
The Avenger wisely stern,
    Who in righteousness shall do
    What the heavens call him to,

---

1. French poet and novelist (1802–1885) whose works include the novel *Les Misérables* (1862).
† From *Correspondance, 1849–1868*. Edition numérique (Paris: Arvensa Editions, n.d.). Translated by Suzanne Nalbantian for this edition.
2. John Wilkes Booth (1838–1865), the actor and Confederate sympathizer who assassinated Lincoln with a pistol (not a dagger) at Ford's Theatre on April 14, 1865. Wysse: Henry A. Wise (1806–1876), the governor of Virginia who signed the death warrant for John Brown in 1859.
1. Novelist, short story writer, and poet (1819–1891) whose works include *Moby-Dick* (1851), "Bartleby, the Scrivener" (1853), and "Benito Cereno" (1855).
† From *Battle-Pieces and Aspects of War* (New York: Harper & Brothers, 1866), 141–42.

25 And the parricides remand;
   For they killed him in his kindness,
   In their madness and their blindness,
   And his blood is on their hand.

      There is sobbing of the strong,
30   And a pall upon the land;
      But the People in their weeping
            Bare the iron hand:
      Beware the People weeping
         When they bare the iron hand.

FREDERICK DOUGLASS

[He Saved His Country]†

It must be admitted, truth compels me to admit even here in the presence of the monument we have erected to his memory, Abraham Lincoln was not, in the fullest sense of the word, either our man or our model. In his interests, in his associations, in his habits of thought, and in his prejudices, he was a white man. He was preeminently the white man's President, entirely devoted to the welfare of white men. He was ready and willing at any time during the last years of his administration to deny, postpone and sacrifice the rights of humanity in the colored people, to promote the welfare of the white people of his country. In all his education and feelings he was an American of the Americans.

He came into the Presidential chair upon one principle alone, namely, opposition to the extension of slavery. His arguments in furtherance of this policy had their motive and mainspring in his patriotic devotion to the interest of his own race. To protect, defend and perpetuate slavery in the States where it existed, Abraham Lincoln was not less ready than any other President to draw the sword of the nation. He was ready to execute all the supposed constitutional guarantees of the Constitution in favor of the slave system anywhere inside the Slave States. He was willing to pursue, recapture, and send back the fugitive slave to his master, and to suppress a slave rising for liberty, though his guilty masters were already in arms against the Government. The race to which we belong were not the special objects of his consideration. Knowing this, I concede to you, my white fellow-citizens, a pre-eminence in this worship at once full and supreme. First, midst and last you and yours were the object of his deepest affection and his most earnest solicitude.

You are the children of Abraham Lincoln. We are at best only his step-children, children by adoption, children by force of circumstances and necessity. To you it especially belongs to sound his praises, to preserve and perpetuate his memory, to multiply his statues, to hang his pictures on your walls, and commend his example, for to you he was a great and glorious friend and benefactor. * * *

---

† From "Oration in Memory of Abraham Lincoln," April 14, 1876, Washington, D.C., in *Frederick Douglass: Selected Speeches and Writings* (New York: Riverside Press, 1906).

Fellow-citizens: Ours is a new-born zeal and devotion, a thing of the hour. The name of Abraham Lincoln was near and dear to our hearts in the darkest and most perilous hours of the Republic. We were no more ashamed of him when shrouded in clouds of darkness, of doubt and defeat than when crowned with victory, honor and glory. Our faith in him was often taxed and strained to the uttermost, but it never failed. When he tarried long in the mountain; when he strangely told us that we were the cause of the war; when he still more strangely told us to leave the land in which we were born; when he refused to employ our arms in defense of the Union; when, after accepting our services as colored soldiers, he refused to retaliate when we were murdered as colored prisoners; when he told us he would save the Union if he could with slavery; when he revoked the proclamation of emancipation of General Frémont; when he refused to remove the commander of the Army of the Potomac,[1] who was more zealous in his efforts to protect slavery than suppress rebellion; when we saw this, and more, we were at times stunned, grieved and greatly bewildered; but our hearts believed while they ached and bled.

*   *   *

Can any colored man, or any white man friendly to the freedom of all men, ever forget the night which followed the first day of January, 1863? When the world was to see if Abraham Lincoln would prove to be as good as his word? I shall never forget that memorable night, when in a distant city I waited and watched at a public meeting, with three thousand others not less anxious than myself, for the word of deliverance which we have heard read to-day. Nor shall I ever forget the outburst of joy and thanksgiving that rent the air when the lightning brought to us the emancipation. In that happy hour we forgot all delay, and forgot all tardiness, forgot that the President had bribed the rebels to lay down their arms by a promise to withhold the bolt which would smite the slave system with destruction; and we were thenceforward willing to allow the President all the latitude of time, phraseology, and every honorable device that statesmanship might require for the achievement of a great and beneficent measure of liberty and progress.

Fellow-citizens, there is little necessity on this occasion to speak at length and critically of this great and good man, and of his high mission in the world. That ground has been fully occupied and completely covered both here and elsewhere. The whole field of fact and fancy has been gleaned and garnered. Any man can say things that are true of Abraham Lincoln, but no man can say anything new of Abraham Lincoln. His personal traits and public acts are better known to the American people than are those of any other man of his age. He was a mystery to no man who saw him and heard him. Though high in position, the humblest could approach him and feel at home in his presence. Though deep, he was transparent; though strong, he was gentle; though decided and pronounced in his convictions, he was tolerant towards those who differed from him, and patient under reproaches.

Even those who only knew him through his public utterances obtained a tolerably clear idea of his character and his personality. The image of

---

1. I.e., George McClellan (1826–1885).

the man went out with his words, and those who read him knew him. I
have said that President Lincoln was a white man, and shared the prejudices common to his countrymen towards the colored race. Looking back
to his times and to the condition of the country, this unfriendly feeling
on his part may safely be set down as one element of his wonderful success in organizing the loyal American people for the tremendous conflict
before them, and bringing them safely through that conflict. His great
mission was to accomplish two things; first, to save his country from dis-
memberment and ruin, and second, to free his country from the great
crime of slavery. To do one or the other, or both, he must have the earnest
sympathy and the powerful cooperation of his loyal fellow-countrymen.
Without this primary and essential condition to success, his efforts must
have been vain and utterly fruitless. Had he put the abolition of slavery
before the salvation of the Union, he would have inevitably driven from
him a powerful class of the American people, and rendered resistance to
rebellion impossible. Viewed from the genuine abolition ground, Mr. Lincoln seemed tardy, cold, dull, and indifferent: but measuring him by the
sentiment of his country, a sentiment he was bound as a statesman to
consult, he was swift, zealous, radical, and determined. Though Mr. Lincoln shared the prejudices of his white fellow-countrymen against the
negro, it is hardly necessary to say that in his heart of hearts he loathed
and hated slavery. He was willing while the South was loyal that it should
have its pound of flesh, because he thought it was so nominated in the
bond, but further than this no earthly power could make him go.

Fellow-citizens, whatever else in this world may be partial, unjust and
uncertain, *time! time!* is impartial, just and certain in its actions. In the
realm of mind, as well as in the realm of matter, it is a great worker, and
often works wonders. The honest and comprehensive statesman, clearly
discerning the needs of his country, and earnestly endeavoring to do his
whole duty, though covered and blistered with reproaches, may safely
leave his course to the silent judgment of time. Few great public men
have ever been the victims of fiercer denunciation than Abraham Lincoln was during his administration. He was often wounded in the house
of his friends. Reproaches came thick and fast upon him from within
and from without, and from opposite quarters. He was assailed by abolitionists; he was assailed by slaveholders; he was assailed by men who
were for peace at any price; he was assailed by those who were for a more
vigorous prosecution of the war; he was assailed for not making the war
an abolition war; and he was most bitterly assailed for making the war an
abolition war.

But now behold the change; the judgment of the present hour is, that
taking him for all in all, measuring the tremendous magnitude of the work
before him, considering the necessary means to ends, and surveying the
end from the beginning, infinite wisdom has seldom sent any man into
the world better fitted for his mission than was Abraham Lincoln.

※　※　※

WILLIAM H. HERNDON AND JESSE W. WEIK

[Lincoln the Orator]†

* * * Douglas was short,—something over five feet high,—heavy set, with a large head, broad shoulders, deep chest, and striking features. He was polite and affable, but fearless. He had that unique trait, magnetism, fully developed in his nature, and that attracted a host of friends and readily made him a popular idol. He had had extensive experience in debate, and had been trained by contact for years with the great minds and orators in Congress. * * *

Lincoln himself was constructed on an entirely different foundation. His base was plain common-sense, direct statement, and the inflexibility of logic. In physical make-up he was cold—at least not magnetic—and made no effort to dazzle people by his bearing. He cared nothing for a following, and though he had often before struggled for a political prize, yet in his efforts he never had strained his well-known spirit of fairness or open love of the truth. He analyzed everything, laid every statement bare, and by dint of his broad reasoning powers and manliness of admission inspired his hearers with deep conviction of his earnestness and honesty. Douglas may have electrified the crowds with his eloquence or charmed them with his majestic bearing and dexterity in debate, but as each man, after the meetings were over and the applause had died away, went to his home, his head rang with Lincoln's logic and appeal to manhood.

A brief description of Mr. Lincoln's appearance on the stump and of his manner when speaking may not be without interest. When standing erect he was six feet four inches high. He was lean in flesh and ungainly in figure. Aside from the sad, pained look due to habitual melancholy, his face had no characteristic or fixed expression. He was thin through the chest, and hence slightly stoop-shouldered. When he arose to address courts, juries, or crowds of people, his body inclined forward to a slight degree. At first he was very awkward, and it seemed a real labor to adjust himself to his surroundings. He struggled for a time under a feeling of apparent diffidence and sensitiveness, and these only added to his awkwardness. I have often seen and sympathized with Mr. Lincoln during these moments. When he began speaking, his voice was shrill, piping, and unpleasant. His manner, his attitude, his dark, yellow face, wrinkled and dry, his oddity of pose, his diffident movements—everything seemed to be against him, but only for a short time. After having arisen, he generally placed his hands behind him, the back of his left hand in the palm of his right, the thumb and fingers of his right hand clasped around the left arm at the wrist. For a few moments he played the combination of awkwardness, sensitiveness, and diffidence. As he proceeded he became somewhat animated, and to keep in harmony with his growing warmth his hands relaxed their grasp and fell to his side. Presently he clasped them in front of him, interlocking his fingers, one thumb meanwhile chasing another. His speech now requiring more emphatic utterance, his fingers unlocked and his hands

† From *Herndon's Lincoln: The True Story of a Great Life* (New York: Belford, Clarke & Company, 1889), 209–92.

fell apart. His left arm was thrown behind, the back of his hand resting against his body, his right hand seeking his side. By this time he had gained sufficient composure, and his real speech began. He did not gesticulate as much with his hands as with his head. He used the latter frequently, throwing it with vim this way and that. This movement was a significant one when he sought to enforce his statement. It sometimes came with a quick jerk, as if throwing off electric sparks into combustible material. He never sawed the air nor rent space into tatters and rags as some orators do. He never acted for stage effect. He was cool, considerate, reflective—in time self-possessed and self-reliant. His style was clear, terse, and compact. In argument he was logical, demonstrative, and fair. He was careless of his dress, and his clothes, instead of fitting neatly as did the garments of Douglas on the latter's well-rounded form, hung loosely on his giant frame. As he moved along in his speech he became freer and less uneasy in his movements; to that extent he was graceful. He had a perfect naturalness, a strong individuality; and to that extent he was dignified. He despised glitter, show, set forms, and shams. He spoke with effectiveness and to move the judgment as well as the emotions of men. There was a world of meaning and emphasis in the long, bony finger of his right hand as he dotted the ideas on the minds of his hearers. Sometimes, to express joy or pleasure, he would raise both hands at an angle of about fifty degrees, the palms upward, as if desirous of embracing the spirit of that which he loved. If the sentiment was one of detestation—denunciation of slavery, for example—both arms, thrown upward and fists clenched, swept through the air, and he expressed an execration that was truly sublime. This was one of his most effective gestures, and signified most vividly a fixed determination to drag down the object of his hatred and trample it in the dust. He always stood squarely on his feet, toe even with toe; that is, he never put one foot before the other. He neither touched nor leaned on anything for support. He made but few changes in his positions and attitudes. He never ranted, never walked backward and forward on the platform. To ease his arms he frequently caught hold, with his left hand, of the lapel of his coat, keeping his thumb upright and leaving his right hand free to gesticulate. The designer of the monument recently erected in Chicago has happily caught him in just this attitude. As he proceeded with his speech the exercise of his vocal organs altered somewhat the tone of his voice. It lost in a measure its former acute and shrilling pitch, and mellowed into a more harmonious and pleasant sound. His form expanded, and, notwithstanding the sunken breast, he rose up a splendid and imposing figure. In his defence of the Declaration of Independence—his greatest inspiration—he was "tremendous in the directness of his utterances; he rose to impassioned eloquence, unsurpassed by Patrick Henry, Mirabeau, or Vergniaud, as his soul was inspired with the thought of human right and Divine justice."[1] His little gray eyes flashed in a face aglow with the fire of his profound thoughts; and his uneasy movements and diffident manner sunk themselves beneath the wave of righteous indignation that came sweeping over him. Such was Lincoln the orator.

*   *   *

1. From journalist Horace White (1834–1916) in the *Chicago Tribune*, June 9, 1865. Patrick Henry (1736–1799), Virginia politician whose fiery speeches contributed to the American Revolution. Honoré Gabriel Riqueti, comte de Mirabeau (1749–1791) and Pierre Victurnien Vergniaud (1753–1793), eminent French statesmen during the French Revolution.

WALT WHITMAN[1]

Abraham Lincoln†

August 12th.—I see the President almost every day, as I happen to live where he passes to or from his lodgings out of town. He never sleeps at the White House during the hot season, but has quarters at a healthy location some three miles north of the city, the Soldiers' home, a United States military establishment. I saw him this morning about 8½ coming in to business, riding on Vermont avenue, near L street. He always has a company of twenty-five or thirty cavalry, with sabres drawn and held upright over their shoulders. They say this guard was against his personal wish, but he let his counselors have their way. The party makes no great show in uniform or horses. Mr. Lincoln on the saddle generally rides a good-sized, easy-going gray horse, is dress'd in plain black, somewhat rusty and dusty, wears a black stiff hat, and looks about as ordinary in attire, &c., as the commonest man. A lieutenant, with yellow straps, rides at his left, and following behind, two by two, come the cavalry men, in their yellow-striped jackets. They are generally going at a slow trot, as that is the pace set them by the one they wait upon. The sabres and accoutrements clank, and the entirely unornamental *cortège* as it trots towards Lafayette square arouses no sensation, only some curious stranger stops and gazes. I see very plainly ABRAHAM LINCOLN's dark brown face, with the deep-cut lines, the eyes, always to me with a deep latent sadness in the expression. We have got so that we exchange bows, and very cordial ones. Sometimes the President goes and comes in an open barouche.[2] The cavalry always accompany him, with drawn sabres. Often I notice as he goes out evenings—and sometimes in the morning, when he returns early—he turns off and halts at the large and handsome residence of the Secretary of War, on K street, and holds conference there. If in his barouche, I can see from my window he does not alight, but sits in his vehicle, and Mr. Stanton comes out to attend him. Sometimes one of his sons, a boy of ten or twelve, accompanies him, riding at his right on a pony. Earlier in the summer I occasionally saw the President and his wife, toward the latter part of the afternoon, out in a barouche, on a pleasure ride through the city. Mrs. Lincoln was dress'd in complete black, with a long crape veil. The equipage is of the plainest kind, only two horses, and they nothing

---

1. One of America's greatest poets (1819–1892) and the author of the innovative volume *Leaves of Grass*, first published in 1855. A Brooklynite, Whitman went to Washington, D.C. in 1862 and worked there as a volunteer nurse in the war hospitals for several years.
† From *Specimen Days* (1882), in *Prose Works* (Philadelphia: David McKay, 1892).
2. Carriage.

extra. They pass'd me once very close, and I saw the President in the face fully, as they were moving slowly, and his look, though abstracted, happen'd to be directed steadily in my eye. He bow'd and smiled, but far beneath his smile I noticed well the expression I have alluded to. None of the artists or pictures has caught the deep, though subtle and indirect expression of this man's face. There is something else there. One of the great portrait painters of two or three centuries ago is needed.

Abraham Lincoln[†]

Glad am I to give—were anything better lacking—even the most brief and shorn testimony of Abraham Lincoln. Everything I heard about him authentically, and every time I saw him (and it was my fortune through 1862 to '65 to see, or pass a word with, or watch him, personally, perhaps twenty or thirty times,) added to and anneal'd my respect and love at the moment. And as I dwell on what I myself heard or saw of the mighty Westerner, and blend it with the history and literature of my age, and of what I can get of all ages, and conclude it with his death, it seems like some tragic play, superior to all else I know—vaster and fierier and more convulsionary, for this America of ours, than Eschylus[1] or Shakspere ever drew for Athens or for England. And then the Moral permeating, underlying all! the Lesson that none so remote—none so illiterate—no age, no class—but may directly or indirectly read!

Abraham Lincoln's was really one of those characters, the best of which is the result of long trains of cause and effect—needing a certain spaciousness of time, and perhaps even remoteness, to properly enclose them—having unequal'd influence on the shaping of this Republic (and therefore the world) as to-day, and then far more important in the future. Thus the time has by no means yet come for a thorough measurement of him. Nevertheless, we who live in his era—who have seen him, and heard him, face to face, and are in the midst of, or just parting from, the strong and strange events which he and we have had to do with—can in some respects bear valuable, perhaps indispensable testimony concerning him.

I should first like to give a very fair and characteristic likeness of Lincoln, as I saw him and watch'd him one afternoon in Washington, for nearly half an hour, not long before his death. It was as he stood on the balcony of the National Hotel, Pennsylvania Avenue, making a short speech to the crowd in front, on the occasion either of a set of new colors presented to a famous Illinois regiment, or of the daring capture, by the Western men, of some flags from "the enemy," (which latter phrase, by the by, was not used by him at all in his remarks.) How the picture happen'd to be made I do not know, but I bought it a few days afterward in Washington, and it was endors'd by every one to whom I show'd it. Though hundreds of portraits have been made, by painters and photographers, (many to pass on, by copies, to future times,) I have never seen one yet that in my opinion deserv'd to be called a perfectly *good likeness*; nor do I believe there is really

---

† From *November Boughs* (1888), in *Prose Works* (Philadelphia: David McKay, 1892).
1. Ancient Greek tragedian (525–456 B.C.E.).

such a one in existence. May I not say too, that, as there is no entirely competent and emblematic likeness of Abraham Lincoln in picture or statue, there is not—perhaps cannot be—any fully appropriate literary statement or summing-up of him yet in existence?

The best way to estimate the value of Lincoln is to think what the condition of America would be to-day, if he had never lived—never been President. His nomination and first election were mainly accidents, experiments. Severely view'd, one cannot think very much of American Political Parties, from the beginning, after the Revolutionary War, down to the present time. Doubtless, while they have had their uses—have been and are "the grass on which the cow feeds"—and indispensable economies of growth—it is undeniable that under flippant names they have merely identified temporary passions, or freaks, or sometimes prejudice, ignorance, or hatred. The only thing like a great and worthy idea vitalizing a party, and making it heroic, was the enthusiasm in '64 for re-electing Abraham Lincoln, and the reason behind that enthusiasm.

How does this man compare with the acknowledg'd "Father of his country?" Washington was model'd on the best Saxon, and Franklin—of the age of the Stuarts (rooted in the Elizabethan period)—was essentially a noble Englishman, and just the kind needed for the occasions and the times of 1776–'83. Lincoln, underneath his practicality, was far less European, was quite thoroughly Western, original, essentially non-conventional, and had a certain sort of out-door or prairie stamp. One of the best of the late commentators on Shakspere, (Professor Dowden,)[2] makes the height and aggregate of his quality as a poet to be, that he thoroughly blended the ideal with the practical or realistic. If this be so, I should say that what Shakspere did in poetic expression, Abraham Lincoln essentially did in his personal and official life. I should say the invisible foundations and vertebra of his character, more than any man's in history, were mystical, abstract, moral and spiritual—while upon all of them was built, and out of all of them radiated, under the control of the average of circumstances, what the vulgar call *horse-sense*, and a life often bent by temporary but most urgent materialistic and political reasons.

He seems to have been a man of indomitable firmness (even obstinacy) on rare occasions, involving great points; but he was generally very easy, flexible, tolerant, almost slouchy, respecting minor matters. I note that even those reports and anecdotes intended to level him down, all leave the tinge of a favorable impression of him. As to his religious nature, it seems to me to have certainly been of the amplest, deepest-rooted, loftiest kind.

Already a new generation begins to tread the stage, since the persons and events of the Secession War. I have more than once fancied to myself the time when the present century has closed, and a new one open'd, and the men and deeds of that contest have become somewhat vague and mythical—fancied perhaps in some great Western city, or group collected together, or public festival, where the days of old, of 1863 and '4 and '5 are discuss'd—some ancient soldier sitting in the background as the talk goes on, and betraying himself by his emotion and moist eyes—like the

2. Edward Dowden (1843–1913), Irish critic whose works included *Shakespeare: His Mind and Art* (1875).

journeying Ithacan at the banquet of King Alcinoüs, when the bard sings the contending warriors and their battles on the plains of Troy:

> "So from the sluices of Ulysses' eyes
> Fast fell the tears, and sighs succeeded sighs."[3]

I have fancied, I say, some such venerable relic of this time of ours, preserv'd to the next or still the next generation of America. I have fancied, on such occasion, the young men gathering around; the awe, the eager questions: "What! have you seen Abraham Lincoln—and heard him speak—and touch'd his hand? Have you, with your own eyes, look'd on Grant, and Lee, and Sherman?"[4]

Dear to Democracy, to the very last! And among the paradoxes generated by America, not the least curious was that spectacle of all the kings and queens and emperors of the earth, many from remote distances, sending tributes of condolence and sorrow in memory of one rais'd through the commonest average of life—a rail-splitter and flat-boatman!

Consider'd from contemporary points of view—who knows what the future may decide?—and from the points of view of current Democracy and The Union, (the only thing like passion or infatuation in the man was the passion for the Union of These States,) Abraham Lincoln seems to me the grandest figure yet, on all the crowded canvas of the Nineteenth Century.

A Lincoln Reminiscence[†]

As is well known, story-telling was often with President Lincoln a weapon which he employ'd with great skill. Very often he could not give a point-blank reply or comment—and these indirections, (sometimes funny, but not always so,) were probably the best responses possible. In the gloomiest period of the war, he had a call from a large delegation of bank presidents. In the talk after business was settled, one of the big Dons[1] asked Mr. Lincoln if his confidence in the permanency of the Union was not beginning to be shaken—whereupon the homely President told a little story: "When I was a young man in Illinois," said he, "I boarded for a time with a deacon of the Presbyterian church. One night I was roused from my sleep by a rap at the door, and I heard the deacon's voice exclaiming, 'Arise, Abraham! the day of judgment has come!' I sprang from my bed and rushed to the window, and saw the stars falling in great showers; but looking back of them in the heavens I saw the grand old constellations, with which I was so well acquainted, fixed and true in their places. Gentlemen, the world did not come to an end then, nor will the Union now."

---

3. Homer's *The Odyssey*, Book 8, translated by Alexander Pope (1725–1726). Alicinoüs is king of Phaeacia in *The Odyssey*.
4. Union generals Ulysses S. Grant (1822–1885) and William T. Sherman (1820–1891); Confederate general Robert E. Lee (1807–1870).
† From *Notes Left Over* (1892), *Prose Works* (Philadelphia: David McKay, 1892).
1. Bosses.

A Soldier on Lincoln[†]

May 28.—As I sat by the bedside of a sick Michigan soldier in hospital to-day, a convalescent from the adjoining bed rose and came to me, and presently we began talking. He was a middle-aged man, belonged to the 2d Virginia regiment, but lived in Racine, Ohio, and had a family there. He spoke of President Lincoln, and said: "The war is over, and many are lost. And now we have lost the best, the fairest, the truest man in America. Take him altogether, he was the best man this country ever produced. It was quite a while I thought very different; but some time before the murder, that's the way I have seen it." There was deep earnestness in the soldier. (I found upon further talk he had known Mr. Lincoln personally, and quite closely, years before.) He was a veteran; was now in the fifth year of his service; was a cavalry man, and had been in a good deal of hard fighting.

Death of President Lincoln

April 16, '65.—I find in my notes of the time, this passage on the death of Abraham Lincoln: He leaves for America's history and biography, so far, not only its most dramatic reminiscence—he leaves, in my opinion, the greatest, best, most characteristic, artistic, moral personality. Not but that he had faults, and show'd them in the Presidency; but honesty, goodness, shrewdness, conscience, and (a new virtue, unknown to other lands, and hardly yet really known here, but the foundation and tie of all, as the future will grandly develop,) UNIONISM, in its truest and amplest sense, form'd the hard-pan of his character. These he seal'd with his life. The tragic splendor of his death, purging, illuminating all, throws round his form, his head, an aureole that will remain and will grow brighter through time, while history lives, and love of country lasts. By many has this Union been help'd; but if one name, one man, must be pick'd out, he, most of all, is the conservator of it, to the future. He was assassinated— but the Union is not assassinated—*ça ira!*[1] One falls, and another falls. The soldier drops, sinks like a wave—but the ranks of the ocean eternally press on. Death does its work, obliterates a hundred, a thousand— President, general, captain, private—but the Nation is immortal.

No Good Portrait of Lincoln

Probably the reader has seen physiognomies (often old farmers, sea-captains, and such) that, behind their homeliness, or even ugliness, held superior points so subtle, yet so palpable, making the real life of their faces almost as impossible to depict as a wild perfume or fruit-taste, or a passionate tone of the living voice—and such was Lincoln's face, the

---

† The three selections on this page are from *Specimen Days* (1882), in *Prose Works* (Philadelphia: David McKay, 1892).
1. It'll be fine (French).

peculiar color, the lines of it, the eyes, mouth, expression. Of technical beauty it had nothing—but to the eye of a great artist it furnished a rare study, a feast and fascination. The current portraits are all failures—most of them caricatures.

Death of Abraham Lincoln[†]

*Lecture deliver'd in New York, April 14, 1879—in
Philadelphia '80—in Boston, '81*

How often since that dark and dripping Saturday—that chilly April day, now fifteen years bygone—my heart has entertain'd the dream, the wish, to give of Abraham Lincoln's death, its own special thought and memorial. Yet now the sought-for opportunity offers, I find my notes incompetent, (why, for truly profound themes, is statement so idle? why does the right phrase never offer?) and the fit tribute I dream'd of, waits unprepared as ever. My talk here indeed is less because of itself or anything in it, and nearly altogether because I feel a desire, apart from any talk, to specify the day, the martyrdom. It is for this, my friends, I have call'd you together. Oft as the rolling years bring back this hour, let it again, however briefly, be dwelt upon. For my own part, I hope and desire, till my own dying day, whenever the 14th or 15th of April comes, to annually gather a few friends, and hold its tragic reminiscence. No narrow or sectional reminiscence. It belongs to these States in their entirety—not the North only, but the South—perhaps belongs most tenderly and devoutly to the South, of all; for there, really, this man's birth-stock. There and thence his antecedent stamp. Why should I not say that thence his manliest traits—his universality—his canny, easy ways and words upon the surface—his inflexible determination and courage at heart? Have you never realized it, my friends, that Lincoln, though grafted on the West, is essentially, in personnel and character, a Southern contribution?

And though by no means proposing to resume the Secession war tonight, I would briefly remind you of the public conditions preceding that contest. For twenty years, and especially during the four or five before the war actually began, the aspect of affairs in the United States, though without the flash of military excitement, presents more than the survey of a battle, or any extended campaign, or series, even of Nature's convulsions. The hot passions of the South—the strange mixture at the North of inertia, incredulity, and conscious power—the incendiarism of the abolitionists—the rascality and *grip* of the politicians, unparallel'd in any land, any age. To these I must not omit adding the honesty of the essential bulk of the people everywhere—yet with all the seething fury and contradiction of their natures more arous'd than the Atlantic's waves in wildest equinox. In politics, what can be more ominous, (though generally unappreciated then)—what more significant than the Presidentiads of Fillmore and Buchanan? proving conclusively that the weakness and wickedness of elected rulers are just as likely to afflict us here, as in the

---

[†] From *Collect* (1882), in *Prose Works* (Philadelphia: David McKay, 1892).

countries of the Old World, under their monarchies, emperors, and aristocracies. In that Old World were everywhere heard underground rumblings, that died out, only to again surely return. While in America the volcano, though civic yet, continued to grow more and more convulsive—more and more stormy and threatening.

In the height of all this excitement and chaos, hovering on the edge at first, and then merged in its very midst, and destined to play a leading part, appears a strange and awkward figure. I shall not easily forget the first time I ever saw Abraham Lincoln. It must have been about the 18th or 19th of February, 1861. It was rather a pleasant afternoon, in New York city, as he arrived there from the West, to remain a few hours, and then pass on to Washington, to prepare for his inauguration. I saw him in Broadway, near the site of the present Post-office. He came down, I think from Canal street, to stop at the Astor House.[1] The broad spaces, sidewalks, and street in the neighborhood, and for some distance, were crowded with solid masses of people, many thousands. The omnibuses and other vehicles had all been turn'd off, leaving an unusual hush in that busy part of the city. Presently two or three shabby hack barouches made their way with some difficulty through the crowd, and drew up at the Astor House entrance. A tall figure step'd out of the centre of these barouches, paus'd leisurely on the sidewalk, look'd up at the granite walls and looming architecture of the grand old hotel—then, after a relieving stretch of arms and legs, turn'd round for over a minute to slowly and good-humoredly scan the appearance of the vast and silent crowds. There were no speeches—no compliments—no welcome—as far as I could hear, not a word said. Still much anxiety was conceal'd in that quiet. Cautious persons had fear'd some mark'd insult or indignity to the President-elect—for he possess'd no personal popularity at all in New York city, and very little political. But it was evidently tacitly agreed that if the few political supporters of Mr. Lincoln present would entirely abstain from any demonstration on their side, the immense majority, who were any thing but supporters, would abstain on their side also. The result was a sulky, unbroken silence, such as certainly never before characterized so great a New York crowd.

Almost in the same neighborhood I distinctly remember'd seeing Lafayette[2] on his visit to America in 1825. I had also personally seen and heard, various years afterward, how Andrew Jackson, Clay, Webster, Hungarian Kossuth, Filibuster Walker, the Prince of Wales[3] on his visit, and other celebres, native and foreign, had been welcom'd there—all that indescribable human roar and magnetism, unlike any other sound in the universe—the glad exulting thunder-shouts of countless unloos'd throats of men! But on this occasion, not a voice—not a sound. From the top of an omnibus, (driven up one side, close by, and block'd by the curbstone and the crowds,) I had, I say, a capital view of it all, and especially of Mr. Lincoln, his look and gait—his perfect composure and coolness—his

---

1. A luxury hotel on Broadway between Vesey and Barclay Streets. Lincoln stayed there during his trip from Illinois to the inauguration in Washington, D.C.
2. Marquis de Lafayette (1757–1834), French general and American Revolutionary War hero.
3. Whitman here refers to other highly visible visits to New York. President Andrew Jackson (1767–1845). Henry Clay (1777–1852), senator. Daniel Webster (1782–1852), senator. Lajos Kossuth (1802–1894), Hungarian revolutionary. William Walker (1824–1860), a filibustering adventurer. Edward, Prince of Wales (1841–1910), later King Edward VII of Great Britain.

unusual and uncouth height, his dress of complete black, stovepipe hat push'd back on the head, dark-brown complexion, seam'd and wrinkled yet canny-looking face, black, bushy head of hair, disproportionately long neck, and his hands held behind as he stood observing the people. He look'd with curiosity upon that immense sea of faces, and the sea of faces return'd the look with similar curiosity. In both there was a dash of comedy, almost farce, such as Shakspere puts in his blackest tragedies. The crowd that hemm'd around consisted I should think of thirty to forty thousand men, not a single one his personal friend—while I have no doubt, (so frenzied were the ferments of the time,) many an assassin's knife and pistol lurk'd in hip or breast-pocket there, ready, soon as break and riot came.

But no break or riot came. The tall figure gave another relieving stretch or two of arms and legs; then with moderate pace, and accompanied by a few unknown looking persons, ascended the portico-steps of the Astor House, disappear'd through its broad entrance—and the dumb-show ended.

I saw Abraham Lincoln often the four years following that date. He changed rapidly and much during his Presidency—but this scene, and him in it, are indelibly stamped upon my recollection. As I sat on the top of my omnibus, and had a good view of him, the thought, dim and inchoate then, has since come out clear enough, that four sorts of genius, four mighty and primal hands, will be needed to the complete limning of this man's future portrait—the eyes and brains and finger-touch of Plutarch and Eschylus and Michel Angelo, assisted by Rabelais.[4]

And now—(Mr. Lincoln passing on from this scene to Washington, where he was inaugurated, amid armed cavalry, and sharpshooters at every point—the first instance of the kind in our history—and I hope it will be the last)—now the rapid succession of well-known events, (too well known—I believe, these days, we almost hate to hear them mention'd)—the national flag fired on at Sumter—the uprising of the North, in paroxysms of astonishment and rage—the chaos of divided councils—the call for troops—the first Bull Run—the stunning cast-down, shock, and dismay of the North—and so in full flood the Secession war. Four years of lurid, bleeding, murky, murderous war. Who paint those years, with all their scenes?—the hard-fought engagements—the defeats, plans, failures—the gloomy hours, days, when our Nationality seem'd hung in pall of doubt, perhaps death—the Mephistophelean sneers of foreign lands and attachés—the dreaded Scylla of European interference, and the Charybdis[5] of the tremendously dangerous latent strata of secession sympathizers throughout the free States, (far more numerous than is supposed)—the long marches in summer—the hot sweat, and many a sunstroke, as on the rush to Gettysburg in '63—the night battles in the woods, as under Hooker at Chancellorsville—the camps in winter—the military prisons—the hospitals—(alas! alas! the hospitals.)

The Secession war? Nay, let me call it the Union war. Though whatever call'd, it is even yet too near us—too vast and too closely overshadowing—its branches unform'd yet, (but certain,) shooting too far into the future—

4. François Rabelais (ca. 1494–1553), French Renaissance author of humorous, satirical works. Plutarch (ca. 46–120 C.E.), Greek historian. Aeschylus (ca. 525/524–ca. 456/455 B.C.E.), Greek tragedian. Michelangelo (1475–1564), Italian Renaissance sculptor and painter.
5. In Greek mythology, Scylla and Charybdis were sea monsters who imperiled passing sailors.

and the most indicative and mightiest of them yet ungrown. A great literature will yet arise out of the era of those four years, those scenes— era compressing centuries of native passion, first-class pictures, tempests of life and death—an inexhaustible mine for the histories, drama, romance, and even philosophy, of peoples to come—indeed the verteber of poetry and art, (of personal character too,) for all future America—far more grand, in my opinion, to the hands capable of it, than Homer's siege of Troy, or the French wars to Shakspere.

But I must leave these speculations, and come to the theme I have assign'd and limited myself to. Of the actual murder of President Lincoln, though so much has been written, probably the facts are yet very indefinite in most persons' minds. I read from my memoranda, written at the time, and revised frequently and finally since.

The day, April 14, 1865, seems to have been a pleasant one throughout the whole land—the moral atmosphere pleasant too—the long storm, so dark, so fratricidal, full of blood and doubt and gloom, over and ended at last by the sun-rise of such an absolute National victory, and utter breakdown of Secessionism—we almost doubted our own senses! Lee had capitulated beneath the apple-tree of Appomattox. The other armies, the flanges of the revolt, swiftly follow'd. And could it really be, then? Out of all the affairs of this world of woe and failure and disorder, was there really come the confirm'd, unerring sign of plan, like a shaft of pure light—of rightful rule—of God? So the day, as I say, was propitious. Early herbage, early flowers, were out. (I remember where I was stopping at the time, the season being advanced, there were many lilacs in full bloom. By one of those caprices that enter and give tinge to events without being at all a part of them, I find myself always reminded of the great tragedy of that day by the sight and odor of these blossoms. It never fails.)

But I must not dwell on accessories. The deed hastens. The popular afternoon paper of Washington, the little "Evening Star," had spatter'd all over its third page, divided among the advertisements in a sensational manner, in a hundred different places, *The President and his Lady will be at the Theatre this evening*. . . . (Lincoln was fond of the theatre. I have myself seen him there several times. I remember thinking how funny it was that he, in some respects the leading actor in the stormiest drama known to real history's stage through centuries, should sit there and be so completely interested and absorb'd in those human jack-straws, moving about with their silly little gestures, foreign spirit, and flatulent[6] text.)

On this occasion the theatre was crowded, many ladies in rich and gay costumes, officers in their uniforms, many well-known citizens, young folks, the usual clusters of gas-lights, the usual magnetism of so many people, cheerful, with perfumes, music of violins and flutes—(and over all, and saturating all, that vast, vague wonder, *Victory*, the nation's victory, the triumph of the Union, filling the air, the thought, the sense, with exhilaration more than all music and perfumes.)

The President came betimes, and, with his wife, witness'd the play from the large stage-boxes of the second tier, two thrown into one, and profusely draped with the national flag. The acts and scenes of the piece—one of

---

6. Pompous.

those singularly written compositions which have at least the merit of giving entire relief to an audience engaged in mental action or business excite-
ments and cares during the day, as it makes not the slightest call on either
the moral, emotional, esthetic, or spiritual nature—a piece, ("Our American Cousin,")[7] in which, among other characters, so call'd, a Yankee, certainly such a one as was never seen, or the least like it ever seen, in North
America, is introduced in England, with a varied fol-de-rol of talk, plot,
scenery, and such phantasmagoria as goes to make up a modern popular
drama—had progress'd through perhaps a couple of its acts, when in the
midst of this comedy, or non-such, or whatever it is to be call'd, and to
offset it, or finish it out, as if in Nature's and the great Muse's mockery of
those poor mimes, came interpolated that scene, not really or exactly to be
described at all, (for on the many hundreds who were there it seems to this
hour to have left a passing blur, a dream, a blotch)—and yet partially to be
described as I now proceed to give it. There is a scene in the play representing a modern parlor, in which two unprecedented English ladies are inform'd
by the impossible Yankee that he is not a man of fortune, and therefore undesirable for marriage-catching purposes; after which, the comments being
finish'd, the dramatic trio make exit, leaving the stage clear for a moment. At
this period came the murder of Abraham Lincoln. Great as all its manifold
train, circling round it, and stretching into the future for many a century,
in the politics, history, art, &c., of the New World, in point of fact the main
thing, the actual murder, transpired with the quiet and simplicity of any
commonest occurrence—the bursting of a bud or pod in the growth of veg-
etation, for instance. Through the general hum following the stage pause,
with the change of positions, came the muffled sound of a pistol-shot, which
not one-hundredth part of the audience heard at the time—and yet a
moment's hush—somehow, surely, a vague startled thrill—and then, through
the ornamented, draperied, starr'd and striped space-way of the President's
box, a sudden figure, a man, raises himself with hands and feet, stands a
moment on the railing, leaps below to the stage, (a distance of perhaps fourteen or fifteen feet,) falls out of position, catching his boot-heel in the copious drapery, (the American flag,) falls on one knee, quickly recovers himself,
rises as if nothing had happen'd, (he really sprains his ankle, but unfelt
then)—and so the figure, Booth, the murderer, dress'd in plain black broad-
cloth, bare-headed, with full, glossy, raven hair, and his eyes like some mad
animal's flashing with light and resolution, yet with a certain strange calmness, holds aloft in one hand a large knife—walks along not much back from
the footlights—turns fully toward the audience his face of statuesque beauty,
lit by those basilisk eyes, flashing with desperation, perhaps insanity—
launches out in a firm and steady voice the words *Sic semper tyrannis*[8]—and
then walks with neither slow nor very rapid pace diagonally across to the
back of the stage, and disappears. (Had not all this terrible scene—making
the mimic ones preposterous—had it not all been rehears'd, in blank, by
Booth, beforehand?)

A moment's hush—a scream—the cry of *murder*—Mrs. Lincoln leaning
out of the box, with ashy cheeks and lips, with involuntary cry, pointing to
the retreating figure, *He has kill'd the President.* And still a moment's

---

7. An 1858 comedy by the English playwright Tom Taylor.
8. Thus always to tyrants (Latin).

strange, incredulous suspense—and then the deluge!—then that mixture of horror, noises, uncertainty—(the sound, somewhere back, of a horse's hoofs clattering with speed)—the people burst through chairs and railings, and break them up—there is inextricable confusion and terror—women faint—quite feeble persons fall, and are trampled on—many cries of agony are heard—the broad stage suddenly fills to suffocation with a dense and motley crowd, like some horrible carnival—the audience rush generally upon it, at least the strong men do—the actors and actresses are all there in their play-costumes and painted faces, with mortal fright showing through the rouge—the screams and calls, confused talk—redoubled, trebled—two or three manage to pass up water from the stage to the President's box—others try to clamber up—&c., &c.

In the midst of all this, the soldiers of the President's guard, with others, suddenly drawn to the scene, burst in—(some two hundred altogether)—they storm the house, through all the tiers, especially the upper ones, inflamed with fury, literally charging the audience with fix'd bayonets, muskets and pistols, shouting *Clear out! clear out! you sons of——* . . . . . Such the wild scene, or a suggestion of it rather, inside the play-house that night.

Outside, too, in the atmosphere of shock and craze, crowds of people, fill'd with frenzy, ready to seize any outlet for it, come near committing murder several times on innocent individuals. One such case was especially exciting. The infuriated crowd, through some chance, got started against one man, either for words he utter'd, or perhaps without any cause at all, and were proceeding at once to actually hang him on a neighboring lamp-post, when he was rescued by a few heroic policemen, who placed him in their midst, and fought their way slowly and amid great peril toward the station house. It was a fitting episode of the whole affair. The crowd rushing and eddying to and fro—the night, the yells, the pale faces, many frighten'd people trying in vain to extricate themselves—the attack'd man, not yet freed from the jaws of death, looking like a corpse—the silent, resolute, half-dozen policemen, with no weapons but their little clubs, yet stern and steady through all those eddying swarms—made a fitting side-scene to the grand tragedy of the murder. They gain'd the station house with the protected man, whom they placed in security for the night, and discharged him in the morning.

And in the midst of that pandemonium, infuriated soldiers, the audience and the crowd, the stage, and all its actors and actresses, its paint-pots, spangles, and gas-lights—the life blood from those veins, the best and sweetest of the land, drips slowly down, and death's ooze already begins its little bubbles on the lips.

Thus the visible incidents and surroundings of Abraham Lincoln's murder, as they really occur'd. Thus ended the attempted secession of these States; thus the four years' war. But the main things come subtly and invisibly afterward, perhaps long afterward—neither military, political, nor (great as those are,) historical. I say, certain secondary and indirect results, out of the tragedy of this death, are, in my opinion, greatest. Not the event of the murder itself. Not that Mr. Lincoln strings the principal points and personages of the period, like beads, upon the single string of his career. Not that his idiosyncrasy, in its sudden appearance and disappearance, stamps this Republic with a stamp more mark'd and enduring than any yet given by any one man—(more even than

Washington's;)—but, join'd with these, the immeasurable value and meaning of that whole tragedy lies, to me, in senses finally dearest to a nation, (and here all our own)—the imaginative and artistic senses—the literary and dramatic ones. Not in any common or low meaning of those terms, but a meaning precious to the race, and to every age. A long and varied series of contradictory events arrives at last at its highest poetic, single, central, pictorial denouement. The whole involved, baffling, multiform whirl of the secession period comes to a head, and is gather'd in one brief flash of lightning-illumination—one simple, fierce deed. Its sharp culmination, and as it were solution, of so many bloody and angry problems, illustrates those climax-moments on the stage of universal Time, where the historic Muse at one entrance, and the tragic Muse at the other, suddenly ringing down the curtain, close an immense act in the long drama of creative thought, and give it radiation, tableau, stranger than fiction. Fit radiation—fit close! How the imagination—how the student loves these things! America, too, is to have them. For not in all great deaths, nor far or near—not Cæsar in the Roman senate-house, or Napoleon passing away in the wild night-storm at St. Helena—not Paleologus, falling, desperately fighting, piled over dozens deep with Grecian corpses—not calm old Socrates,[9] drinking the hemlock—outvies that terminus of the secession war, in one man's life, here in our midst, in our own time—that seal of the emancipation of three million slaves—that parturition and delivery of our at last really free Republic, born again, henceforth to commence its career of genuine homogeneous Union, compact, consistent with itself.

Nor will ever future American Patriots and Unionists, indifferently over the whole land, or North or South, find a better moral to their lesson. The final use of the greatest men of a Nation is, after all, not with reference to their deeds in themselves, or their direct bearing on their times or lands. The final use of a heroic-eminent life—especially of a heroic-eminent death—is its indirect filtering into the nation and the race, and to give, often at many removes, but unerringly, age after age, color and fibre to the personalism of the youth and maturity of that age, and of mankind. Then there is a cement to the whole people, subtler, more underlying, than any thing in written constitution, or courts or armies—namely, the cement of a death identified thoroughly with that people, at its head, and for its sake. Strange, (is it not?) that battles, martyrs, agonies, blood, even assassination, should so condense—perhaps only really, lastingly condense—a Nationality.

I repeat it—the grand deaths of the race—the dramatic deaths of every nationality—are its most important inheritance-value—in some respects beyond its literature and art—(as the hero is beyond his finest portrait, and the battle itself beyond its choicest song or epic.) Is not here indeed the point underlying all tragedy? the famous pieces of the Grecian masters—and all masters? Why, if the old Greeks had had this man, what trilogies of plays—what epics—would have been made out of him! How

9. Athenian philosopher (469–399 B.C.E.) who committed suicide while in prison. Julius Caesar (100–44 B.C.E.) was assassinated in the Roman senate. Napoleon Bonaparte (1769–1821) died in exile on the island of St. Helena, in the Atlantic Ocean off the southern coast of Africa. Palaeologus (1404–1453), a Byzantine emperor who died fighting alongside his troops (many of them Greek) while defending Constantinople against the Ottoman army.

the rhapsodes would have recited him! How quickly that quaint tall form would have enter'd into the region where men vitalize gods, and gods divinify men! But Lincoln, his times, his death—great as any any age—belong altogether to our own, and are autochthonic.[1] (Sometimes indeed I think our American days, our own stage—the actors we know and have shaken hands, or talk'd with—more fateful than any thing in Eschylus—more heroic than the fighters around Troy—afford kings of men for our Democracy prouder than Agamemnon—models of character cute and hardy as Ulysses—deaths more pitiful than Priam's.)[2]

When, centuries hence, (as it must, in my opinion, be centuries hence before the life of these States, or of Democracy, can be really written and illustrated,) the leading historians and dramatists seek for some personage, some special event, incisive enough to mark with deepest cut, and mnemonize, this turbulent Nineteenth century of ours, (not only these States, but all over the political and social world)—something, perhaps, to close that gorgeous procession of European feudalism, with all its pomp and caste-prejudices, (of whose long train we in America are yet so inextricably the heirs)—something to identify with terrible identification, by far the greatest revolutionary step in the history of the United States, (perhaps the greatest of the world, our century)—the absolute extirpation and erasure of slavery from the States—those historians will seek in vain for any point to serve more thoroughly their purpose, than Abraham Lincoln's death.

Dear to the Muse—thrice dear to Nationality—to the whole human race—precious to this Union—precious to Democracy—unspeakably and forever precious—their first great Martyr Chief.

From When Lilacs Last in the Dooryard Bloom'd[†]

I

When lilacs last in the dooryard bloom'd,
And the great star early droop'd in the western sky in the night,
I mourn'd, and yet shall mourn with ever-returning spring.

Ever-returning spring, trinity sure to me you bring,
5 Lilac blooming perennial and drooping star in the west,
And thought of him I love.

2

O powerful western fallen star!
O shades of night—O moody, tearful night!
O great star disappear'd—O the black murk that hides the star!
10 O cruel hands that hold me powerless—O helpless soul of me!
O harsh surrounding cloud that will not free my soul.

---

1. Native, indigenous.
2. Figures from ancient mythology: Agamemnon was a Greek king; Ulysses (Odysseus in Greek) was a hero of the Trojan War; Priam was the last king of Troy. cute: clever.
† First published in 1865–66, this poem later appeared in a cluster titled "Memories of President Lincoln" in the 1881 edition of Whitman's collection *Leaves of Grass*.

3

In the dooryard fronting an old farm-house hear the
    white-wash'd palings,
Stands the lilac-bush tall-growing with heart-shaped leaves
    of rich green,
With many a pointed blossom rising delicate, with the
    perfume strong I love,
15 With every leaf a miracle—and from this bush in the dooryard,
With delicate-color'd blossoms and heart-shaped leaves of
    rich green,
A sprig with its flower I break.

4

In the swamp in secluded recesses,
A shy and hidden bird is warbling a song.

20 Solitary the thrush,
The hermit withdrawn to himself, avoiding the settlements,
Sings by himself a song.
Song of the bleeding throat,
Death's outlet song of life, (for well dear brother I know,
25 If thou wast not granted to sing thou would'st surely die.)

5

Over the breast of the spring, the land, amid cities,
Amid lanes and through old woods, where lately the violets
    peep'd from the ground, spotting the gray debris,
Amid the grass in the fields each side of the lanes, passing
    the endless grass,
Passing the yellow-spear'd wheat, every grain from its
    shroud in the dark-brown fields uprisen,
30 Passing the apple-tree blows of white and pink in the orchards,
Carrying a corpse to where it shall rest in the grave,
Night and day journeys a coffin.[1]

6

Coffin that passes through lanes and streets,
Through day and night with the great cloud darkening the land,
35 With the pomp of the inloop'd flags with the cities draped in black,
With the show of the States themselves as of crape-veil'd
    women standing,
With processions long and winding and the flambeaus of the night,
With the countless torches lit, with the silent sea of faces
    and the unbared heads,

---

1. In a ceremonial procession, witnessed by thousands, Lincoln's coffin was carried 1,654 miles
by train for ten days from Washington, D.C., to Springfield, Illinois.

With the waiting depot, the arriving coffin, and the sombre faces,
40 With dirges through the night, with the thousand voices
        rising strong and solemn,
With all the mournful voices of the dirges pour'd around the
        coffin,
The dim-lit churches and the shuddering organs—where amid
        these you journey,
With the tolling tolling bells' perpetual clang,
Here, coffin that slowly passes,
45 I give you my sprig of lilac.

7

(Nor for you, for one alone,
Blossoms and branches green to coffins all I bring,
For fresh as the morning, thus would I chant a song for
        you O sane and sacred death.

All over bouquets of roses,
50 O death, I cover you over with roses and early lilies,
But mostly and now the lilac that blooms the first,
Copious I break, I break the sprigs from the bushes,
With loaded arms I come, pouring for you,
For you and the coffins all of you O death.)

8

55 O western orb sailing the heaven,
Now I know what you must have meant as a month since I
        walk'd,
As I walk'd in silence the transparent shadowy night,
As I saw you had something to tell as you bent to me night
        after night,
As you droop'd from the sky low down as if to my side,
        (while the other stars all look'd on,)
60 As we wander'd together the solemn night, (for something
        I know not what kept me from sleep,)
As the night advanced, and I saw on the rim of the west
        how full you were of woe,
As I stood on the rising ground in the breeze in the cool
        transparent night,
As I watch'd where you pass'd and was lost in the
        netherward black of the night,
As my soul in its trouble dissatisfied sank, as where you sad orb,
65 Concluded, dropt in the night, and was gone.

9

Sing on there in the swamp,
O singer bashful and tender, I hear your notes, I hear your call,
I hear, I come presently, I understand you,
But a moment I linger, for the lustrous star has detain'd me,
70 The star my departing comrade holds and detains me.

10

O how shall I warble myself for the dead one there I loved?
And how shall I deck my song for the large sweet soul that
        has gone?
And what shall my perfume be for the grave of him I love?

Sea-winds blown from east and west,
75 Blown from the Eastern sea and blown from the Western sea,
        till there on the prairies meeting,
These and with these and the breath of my chant,
I'll perfume the grave of him I love.

*   *   *

15

To the tally of my soul,
Loud and strong kept up the gray-brown bird,
80 With pure deliberate notes spreading filling the night.

Loud in the pines and cedars dim,
Clear in the freshness moist and the swamp-perfume,
And I with my comrades there in the night.

While my sight that was bound in my eyes unclosed,
85 As to long panoramas of visions.
And I saw askant the armies,
I saw as in noiseless dreams hundreds of battle-flags,
Borne through the smoke of the battles and pierc'd with
        missiles I saw them,
And carried hither and yon through the smoke, and torn and
        bloody,
90 And at last but a few shreds left on the staffs, (and all in silence,)
And the staffs all splinter'd and broken.

I saw battle-corpses, myriads of them,
And the white skeletons of young men, I saw them,
I saw the debris and debris of all the slain soldiers of the war,
95 But I saw they were not as was thought,
They themselves were fully at rest, they suffer'd not,
The living remain'd and suffer'd, the mother suffer'd,
And the wife and the child and the musing comrade suffer'd,
And the armies that remain'd suffer'd.

16

100 Passing the visions, passing the night,
Passing, unloosing the hold of my comrades' hands,
Passing the song of the hermit bird and the tallying song of
        my soul,
Victorious song, death's outlet song, yet varying ever-altering song,
As low and wailing, yet clear the notes, rising and falling,
        flooding the night,

105 Sadly sinking and fainting, as warning and warning, and
          yet again bursting with joy,
Covering the earth and filling the spread of the heaven,
As that powerful psalm in the night I heard from recesses,
Passing, I leave thee lilac with heart-shaped leaves,
I leave thee there in the door-yard, blooming, returning with
          spring.

110 I cease from my song for thee,
From my gaze on thee in the west, fronting the west,
          communing with thee,
O comrade lustrous with silver face in the night.
Yet each to keep and all, retrievements out of the night,
The song, the wondrous chant of the gray-brown bird,
115 And the tallying chant, the echo arous'd in my soul,
With the lustrous and drooping star with the countenance
          full of woe,
With the holders holding my hand nearing the call of the bird,
Comrades mine and I in the midst, and their memory ever
          to keep, for the dead I loved so well,
For the sweetest, wisest soul of all my days and lands—and
          this for his dear sake,
120 Lilac and star and bird twined with the chant of my soul,
There in the fragrant pines and the cedars dusk and dim.

O Captain! My Captain!†

O Captain! my Captain! our fearful trip is done,
The ship has weather'd every rack, the prize we sought is won,
The port is near, the bells I hear, the people all exulting,
While follow eyes the steady keel, the vessel grim and daring;
5   But O heart! heart! heart!
               O the bleeding drops of red,
                    Where on the deck my Captain lies,
                         Fallen cold and dead.

O Captain! my Captain! rise up and hear the bells;
10 Rise up—for you the flag is flung—for you the bugle trills,
For you bouquets and ribbon'd wreaths—for you the shores
          a-crowding,
For you they call, the swaying mass, their eager faces turning;
               Here Captain! dear father!
               This arm beneath your head!
15   It is some dream that on the deck,
                    You've fallen cold and dead.

† First published in 1865–66, this poem later appeared in a cluster titled "Memories of President
Lincoln" in the 1881 edition of Whitman's collection *Leaves of Grass*.

My Captain does not answer, his lips are pale and still,
My father does not feel my arm, he has no pulse nor will,
The ship is anchor'd safe and sound, its voyage closed and done,
20 From fearful trip the victor ship comes in with object won;
        Exult O shores, and ring O bells!
            But I with mournful tread,
                Walk the deck my Captain lies,
                    Fallen cold and dead.

MODERN VIEWS

CARL SANDBURG

From Abraham Lincoln: The Prairie Years[†]

During the year 1817, little Abe Lincoln, eight years old, going on nine, had an ax put in his hands and helped his father cut down trees and notch logs for the corners of their new cabin, forty yards from the pole-shed where the family was cooking, eating, and sleeping.

Wild turkey, ruffed grouse, partridge, coon, rabbit, were to be had for the shooting of them. Before each shot Tom Lincoln[1] took a rifle-ball out of a bag and held the ball in his left hand; then with his right hand holding the gunpowder horn he pulled the stopper with his teeth, slipped the powder into the barrel, followed with the ball; then he rammed the charge down the barrel with a hickory ramrod held in both hands, looked to his trigger, flint, and feather in the touch-hole—and he was ready to shoot—to kill for the home skillet.

Having loaded his rifle just that way several thousand times in his life, he could do it in the dark or with his eyes shut. Once Abe took the gun as a flock of wild turkeys came toward the new log cabin, and, standing inside, shot through a crack and killed one of the big birds; and after that, somehow, he never felt like pulling the trigger on game-birds. A mile from the cabin was a salt lick, where deer came; there the boy could have easily shot the animals, as they stood rubbing their tongues along the salty slabs or tasting of a saltish ooze. His father did the shooting; the deer killed gave them meat for Nancy's[2] skillet; and the skins were tanned, cut, and stitched into shirts, trousers, mitts, moccasins. They wore buckskin; their valley was called the Buckhorn Valley.

After months the cabin stood up, four walls fitted together with a roof, a one-room house eighteen feet square, for a family to live in. A stick chimney plastered with clay ran up outside. The floor was packed and smoothed dirt. A log-fire lighted the inside; no windows were cut in the walls. For a door there was a hole cut to stoop through. Bedsteads were cleated to the corners of the cabin; pegs stuck in the side of a wall made a ladder for young Abe to climb up in a loft to sleep on a hump of dry leaves; rain and snow came through chinks of the roof onto his bearskin cover. A table and three-legged stools had the top sides smoothed with an ax, and the bark-side under, in the style called "puncheon."

A few days of this year in which the cabin was building, Nancy told Abe to wash his face and hands extra clean; she combed his hair, held his face between her two hands, smacked him a kiss on the mouth, and sent him to school—nine miles and back—Abe and Sally[3] hand in hand hiking eighteen miles a day. Tom Lincoln used to say Abe was going to have "a real eddication," explaining, "You air a-goin' to larn readin', writin', and cipherin'."

† From *Abraham Lincoln: The Prairie Years and The War Years*. Copyright 1926, 1939 by Houghton Mifflin Harcourt Publishing Company. Copyright renewed 1953, 1966 by Carl Sandburg. Reprinted by permission of Houghton Mifflin Harcourt Publishing Company. The notes are the editor's.
1. Lincoln's father, Thomas Lincoln (1778–1851).
2. Lincoln's mother, Nancy Hanks Lincoln (1784–1815).
3. Lincoln's sister, Sarah Lincoln (1807–1828).

He learned to spell words he didn't know the meaning of, spelling the words before he used them in sentences. In a list of "words of eight syllables accented upon the sixth," was the word "incomprehensibility." He learned that first, and then such sentences as "Is he to go in?" and "Ann can spin flax."

Some neighbors said, "It's a pore make-out of a school," and Tom complained it was a waste of time to send the children nine miles just to sit with a lot of other children and read out loud all day in a "blab" school. But Nancy, as she cleaned Abe's ears in corners where he forgot to clean them, and as she combed out the tangles in his coarse, sandy black hair, used to say, "Abe, you go to school now, and larn all you kin." And he kissed her and said, "Yes, Mammy," and started with his sister on the nine-mile walk through timberland where bear, deer, coon, and wildcats ran wild.

Fall time came with its early frost and they were moved into the new cabin, when horses and a wagon came breaking into the clearing one day. It was Tom and Betsy Sparrow[4] and their seventeen-year-old boy, Dennis Hanks, who had come from Hodgenville, Kentucky, to cook and sleep in the pole-shed of the Lincoln family till they could locate land and settle. Hardly a year had passed, however, when both Tom and Betsy Sparrow were taken down with the "milk sick,"[5] beginning with a whitish coat on the tongue. Both died and were buried in October on a little hill in a clearing in the timbers near by.

Soon after, there came to Nancy Hanks Lincoln that white coating of the tongue; her vitals burned; the tongue turned brownish; her feet and hands grew cold and colder, her pulse slow and slower. She knew she was dying, called for her children, and spoke to them her last choking words. Sarah and Abe leaned over the bed. A bony hand of the struggling mother went out, putting its fingers into the boy's sandy black hair; her fluttering guttural words seemed to say he must grow up and be good to his sister and father.

So, on a bed of poles cleated to the corner of the cabin, the body of Nancy Hanks Lincoln lay, looking tired . . . tired . . . with a peace settling in the pinched corners of the sweet, weary mouth, silence slowly etching away the lines of pain and hunger drawn around the gray eyes where now the eyelids closed down in the fine pathos of unbroken rest, a sleep without interruption settling about the form of the stooped and wasted shoulder-bones, looking to the children who tiptoed in, stood still, cried their tears of want and longing, whispered "Mammy, Mammy," and heard only their own whispers answering, looking to these little ones of her brood as though new secrets had come to her in place of the old secrets given up with the breath of life.

And Tom Lincoln took a log left over from the building of the cabin, and he and Dennis Hanks whipsawed the log into planks, planed the planks smooth, and made them of a measure for a box to bury the dead wife and mother in. Little Abe, with a jackknife, whittled pine-wood pegs. And then, while Dennis and Abe held the planks, Tom bored holes and stuck the whittled pegs through the bored holes. This was the coffin,

---

4. Thomas and Elizabeth Hanks Sparrow, the childless aunt and uncle of Lincoln's mother, Nancy Hanks; they had raised Nancy and Dennis Hanks, Elizabeth's illegitimate nephew.
5. An illness caused by ingesting dairy products or meat from cattle that have eaten white snake root, a poisonous plant.

and they carried it the next day to the same little timber clearing near by, where a few weeks before they had buried Tom and Betsy Sparrow. It was in the way of the deer-run leading to the saltish water; light feet and shy hoofs ran over those early winter graves.

So the woman, Nancy Hanks, died, thirty-six years old, a pioneer sacrifice, with memories of monotonous, endless everyday chores, of mystic Bible verses read over and over for their promises, and with memories of blue wistful hills and a summer when the crab-apple blossoms flamed white and she carried a boy-child into the world.

She had looked out on fields of blue-blossoming flax and hummed "Hey, Betty Martin, tiptoe, tiptoe"; she had sung of bright kingdoms by and by and seen the early frost leaf its crystals on the stalks of buttonweed and redbud; she had sung:

> You may bury me in the east,
> You may bury me in the west,
> And we'll all rise together in that morning.[6]

ALLEN C. GUELZO

From Lincoln and Douglas: The Debates That Defined America[†]

At the deepest level, what Lincoln defended in the debates was the possibility that there could be a moral core to a democracy. The fundamental premise of Douglas's popular sovereignty was that democratic decision-making, in order to be free, has to be unencumbered by the weight of factors which are nonpolitical in nature, such as kinship, ethnic identity, or moral and religious obligations. The purpose of politics is not to lead "the good life" or to pursue what is good and true but to ensure fair play, toleration, and personal autonomy. As Theodore Parker wrote to Herndon after the election, Douglas did "not deal with *principles* which a man may spread abroad from the pulpit or by the press, but only with *measures* that require political place to carry out." In this way, no one particular path to virtue is laid out, no one morality is held against others as a standard, and the civil conflicts that emerge over differing standards of virtue and morality are held to a minimum. It creates a world, as T. S. Eliot once remarked, "of systems so perfect that no one will need to be good," where no one recognizes the right of anyone else in himself, where desire is the only reality and the only ends those we have chosen for ourselves. Solidarity becomes sentimentality; morality, a socially useless prejudice. Paul Berman, writing in *Terror and Liberalism*, speaks despairingly of the ways in which liberal democracy, at the moment of its greatest triumph with the fall of the Soviet empire, still managed "in its pure version . . . to seem mediocre, corrupt, tired, and aimless, a middling compromise, pale and unappealing—something to settle for, in spirit of resignation." He might as well have been talking about Douglas.

---

6. From the black spiritual "The Coming of John."
† *Lincoln and Douglas: The Debates That Defined America*. New York: Simon & Schuster, 2008. Copyright © 2008 by Allen C. Guelzo. Reprinted with permission of Simon & Schuster.

This was also the spirit Francis Fukuyama described in *The Last Man and the End of History* in 1992—with the fall of Soviet Communism, liberal democracy had triumphed, had at last freed humanity, and had removed any need to search further for a better politics. "There is no struggle or conflict over 'large' issues, and consequently no need for generals or statesmen," Fukuyama wrote in 1989, "what remains is primarily economic activity." But to what end? To sit at the end of the historical tracks, *free*, but free only to indulge one's personal preferences? Fukuyama's, and Berman's, nightmare was that the "last man" would turn out to be the "comfortable burgher, blinking stupidly and wondering about dinner . . . cowardly, greedy and self-absorbed," a society "with no ability or inclination to defend itself or anyone else." The assault on liberal democracy mounted by Islamic terrorism in the 1990s and culminating in 9/11, represented a judgment by Islamism that the West in general (and the United States in particular) was too fat, dumb, and happy to mount any effective response to its Islamized versions of fascism—just as Hitler and Stalin had judged the Western democracies in the 1930s and '40s as too morally vacuous to offer serious resistance to their aggressive and militarized ideologies.[1] Little in the response of those democracies after 9/11 suggests that the Islamists had been wrong.

The great exception to democratic stagnation, argues Berman, has been the United States, which in the 1850s "took the notion of a liberal society and, with a few earnest twists of the screwdriver, rendered the whole concept a little sturdier." Sturdier, in the sense that the United States turned the principles of self-government into a natural morality and then wedded those principles to a universalism, part Christian and part Enlightenment, which made them universally right—not merely convenient or useful but transcendently right. And among the possible candidates for chief turner of the screwdriver, Berman had only one worth talking about; "It was Lincoln who did this."[2]

We have been so content to take the Lincoln-Douglas debates as a purely historical event that we miss how much the great debates really are a defining moment in the development of a liberal democracy, and how much Lincoln is our greatest preceptor and Douglas our most tempting but disastrous alternative—for these are not the lessons modern liberal democracy wishes to hear. The "procedural republic" described by Michael Sandel treats its citizens strictly as independent individuals who have *rights*, which must always trump any appeal to morality, to responsibility, or to the general welfare of everyone else.[3] In 1858, in the midst of the deepening crisis over slavery in America, a commitment to the procedural republic pointed Stephen A. Douglas in the direction of arguing that slavery was a constitutionally guaranteed and morally neutral right, that it was no business of anyone in the free states to interfere with the free exercise of that right,

---

1. Parker, in Joseph Fort Newton, *Herndon and Lincoln* (Cedar Rapids, Ia., 1910), 239; Eliot, "Choruses from the Rock," in the *Complete Plays and Poems, 1909–1950* (New York, 1952), 106; Berman, *Terror and Liberalism* (New York, 2003), 164–65; Francis Fukuyama, "The End of History?" *The National Interest* 16 (Summer 1989): 3–18, and *The End of History and the Last Man* (New York, 1992), 4.
2. Berman, *Terror and Liberalism*, 169–71; David F. Ericson, *The Shaping of American Liberalism: The Debates Over Ratification, Nullification, and Slavery* (Chicago, 1993), 173.
3. Michael Sandel, *Democracy's Discontent: America in Search of a Public Philosophy* (Cambridge, Mass., 1996), 22–24.

and that the only way of dealing with slavery in the West was to leave to the people actually settling in the West the privilege of determining whether they wanted to legalize slavery or not.

Lincoln represented an entirely different perspective. For him, politics was not about helping people exercise rights apart from doing what was right; and slavery was so clearly a violation of the rights of black slaves that it was tantamount to a moral wrong. In the face of Douglas's belief that liberal democracy existed only to provide a procedural framework for exercising rights, Lincoln insisted that liberal democracy had a higher purpose, which was the realization of a morally right political order. No one managed to state this more clearly than Robert Todd Lincoln, speaking at the Galesburg celebration in 1896:

> Now, as then, there can be but one supreme issue, that between right and wrong. In our country there are no ruling classes. The right to direct public affairs according to his might and influence and conscience belongs to the humblest as well as to the greatest. . . . But it is times of danger, critical moments, which bring into action the high moral quality of the citizenship of America. The people are always true. They are always right, and I have an abiding faith they will remain so.[4]

And so Lincoln and Douglas pose anew a dilemma which has haunted Americans from the time of Plymouth Rock—what was the American experiment about? Finding space to be free, or finding an opportunity to do right? The Puritan Commonwealth or the Weimar Republic? A city on the hill or Sodom-by-the-Sea? Enlightened self-interest or beloved community? And was there a way to hold on to one without entirely losing a grip on the other? Although the Civil War eventually settled this question as it applied to slavery, it has continued to be a fundamental dilemma for American democracy and for liberal democracy everywhere else, even now, in the Age of Terror. The great debates in Illinois in 1858 turned out to be a more important victory than Lincoln could have imagined, for they pointed him to his national political debut in New York City in 1860, the Republican national convention, and finally his election as the sixteenth—and greatest—American president. And beyond even that, a beacon to us all.

JAMES OAKES

From Natural Rights, Citizenship Rights, States' Rights, and Black Rights: Another Look at Lincoln and Race[†]

Stephen Douglas was the first in a long line of observers frustrated by the inconsistent things Abraham Lincoln had to say about racial equality. In their fifth debate, at Galesburg, Illinois, on October 7, 1858, Douglas complained that when Lincoln went into the northern part of the state

4. *Speech of the Hon. Robert T. Lincoln Made at the Celebration of the Thirty-eighth Anniversary of the Lincoln-Douglas Debate, Galesburg, Ill., October 7, 1858* (Hancock, N.Y., 1921), 2.
† From *Our Lincoln: New Perspectives on Lincoln and His World,* edited by Eric Foner. Copyright © 2008 by James Oakes. Used by permission of W. W. Norton & Company, Inc.

"he stood up for negro equality" but that when he went into the southern counties Lincoln "discarded the doctrine and declared that there always must be a superior and inferior race."[1] Lincoln replied by demonstrating that he had said the same things about black inferiority in northern districts, including the district that had elected the abolitionist Owen Lovejoy to Congress, but Douglas was not persuaded. It was true, he said, that Lincoln was willing to endorse racial inequality everywhere in Illinois, but only in the northern parts of the state would Lincoln dare to assert the equality of blacks and whites. A few months earlier in Chicago, for example, Lincoln had asked his audience to "discard all this quibbling about this man and the other man—this race and that race and the other race being inferior, and unite as one people throughout this land, until we shall once more stand up declaring that all men are created equal."[2] Douglas denounced this "Chicago doctrine" as "a monstrous heresy" and condemned Lincoln for refusing to say such things in the southernmost parts of the state.[3]

Pinning Lincoln down on race has proved as difficult for historians as it was for Stephen Douglas. There's a simple reason for this: The evidence for Lincoln's views on the equality of blacks and whites is hopelessly contradictory. String together one set of quotations, and Lincoln comes off as a dyed-in-the-wool white supremacist. Compile a different body of evidence, and Lincoln reads like the purest of racial egalitarians. Compounding the confusion is the fact that so much of what Lincoln had to say about race was so ambiguous that it can be used to support either reading. The only thing Lincoln did make clear was that he disliked talking about race and resented the way Douglas kept forcing the issue.

Stephen Douglas was certain he knew what was going on: Lincoln was tailoring his views "for political effect," playing the race card in the southern counties where audiences expected it and parading his egalitarianism up north where abolitionism and antislavery were more popular. There is something to this, but only something. Like most politicians Lincoln emphasized those convictions most likely to appeal to the particular audience he was addressing. But he was not lying when he told listeners that he had never favored the social and political equality of blacks and whites, just as he was affirming his deepest convictions when he insisted that blacks and whites were equally entitled to the fundamental rights of life, liberty, and the pursuit of happiness. Give all due allowance to Lincoln's political motives and the contradiction is still there. Accordingly most historians have not been satisfied by Douglas's diagnosis. For some the temptation to simplify matters has been irresistible: Lincoln was little more than a mouthpiece for mid-nineteenth-century racism or, alternatively, he didn't have a racist bone in his body. Somewhat more satisfactory have been the efforts to parse Lincoln's various statements and to discern crucial distinctions—between the way he thought about race and the way he thought about slavery, for example, or between his egalitarian view of natural rights and his prejudicial view of social and political rights. This last distinction gets closer to the way Lincoln thought without quite getting there.

1. CW 3:214.
2. CW 2:501.
3. CW 3:216.

Here's a better explanation: Lincoln believed that race relations were regulated at three different levels. At the highest level, the natural rights guaranteed by the Constitution, Lincoln consistently favored the equality of blacks and whites. Below natural rights were the privileges and immunities of citizenship, sometimes called citizenship rights, and at this level Lincoln was cautiously egalitarian during the 1850s and unambiguously so during his presidency. Finally, there were aspects of race relations that fell solely within the purview of states—laws regulating marriage, voting, and jury duty, for example. These matters were determined by state legislatures elected by the people at large. Virtually every concession Lincoln made to racial prejudice concerned this third level.

Lincoln shared many, though by no means all, of the racial prejudices of his fellow Americans. He instinctively thought of the United States as a white man's country, agreed that the founders had imagined their new nation in the same way, believed the western territories existed for the benefit of whites, and said on various occasions that it would be best if blacks and whites were permanently separated. But when he bothered to justify these views Lincoln usually referred not to any notion of innate racial inequality but to the clearly expressed will of a racist white majority. Lincoln's democratic deference to popular opinion explains his perplexing inconsistencies at least as much as his own racial prejudices. He resisted the idea that either natural rights or the privileges and immunities of citizenship were subject to majority rule, and on those matters he was a racial egalitarian. But on issues that were distinctly the prerogative of elected officials in state legislatures Lincoln deferred. As was so often the case in antebellum America, Lincoln's prejudicial views had as much to do with democracy as with racism.

* * *

GILLIAN SILVERMAN

"The Best Circus in Town": Embodied Theatrics in the Lincoln-Douglas Debates[†]

During the seven senatorial debates of 1858, descriptions of Abraham Lincoln and Stephen Douglas repeatedly focus on the bodies and bodily functions of the two politicians. Newspapers, Democratic and Republican alike,[1] harped on Lincoln's "tall, angular form," his "lank proportions," his "nervous-excited manner," and his "face of grotesque ugliness."[2] To his critics, Lincoln's rangy body and unruly limbs came to stand as metaphors

---

[†] This article is a condensed and slightly revised version of Silverman's "The Best Circus in Town": Embodied Theatrics in the Lincoln-Douglas Debates," *American Literary History* 21 (2009): 757–87. Copyright © 2009 by Oxford University Press. Reprinted with permission of Oxford University Press.

1. In the 1850s, only 5 percent of the newspapers in circulation were independent, the vast majority being tools for various political interests. See Carl Bode, *The Anatomy of American Popular Culture, 1840–1861* (Berkeley, 1960), 250.

2. *The Lincoln-Douglas Debates of 1858*, edited by Edwin Earle Sparks (Springfield, IL, 1908), 12, 58, 67, 201. Except where otherwise noted, further references to newspaper accounts will be to this edition and will be cited parenthetically in the text.

for a general incompetence and lack of control unbefitting a would-be senator. Indeed, one extraordinary news account implied that Lincoln's loss of "natural powers" during the Freeport debate was so acute as to result in his incontinence (Sparks 190). Douglas, for his part, was continually lampooned for the contrast between his diminutive stature and his fierce combativeness. Reporters wrote patronizingly of the "towering ambition" of "Little Dug," describing the incumbent senator as "almost like a dwarf . . . but square-shouldered and broad-chested, a massive head upon a strong neck" (Sparks 129, 448). These depictions indicate the extent to which the political figure was interpreted in prodigious, even freakish terms. The Lincoln-Douglas debates offer an important moment in which the representative of the American body politic was imagined as a grotesque body.

This understanding of the politician's body is at odds not only with mainstream perceptions of Lincoln-Douglas (which tend to reference the debates in exalted terms) but also with modern scholarship on the eighteenth- and nineteenth-century public sphere. Drawing on the work of Jürgen Habermas and Hannah Arendt, much of this criticism tends to de-corporealize the civic realm, referring to white male political participation in abstract and disembodied terms.[3] In these accounts, embodiment and particularity are reserved for those subjects both disqualified from public life and marked by difference rather than by universality, that is, blacks and women. More recently, some scholars have revised this understanding by documenting the crucial role of performance, voice, and affect in the creation of the public sphere.[4] This study extends this latter scholarship by tying the Lincoln-Douglas contest to a debased and corporeal theatrics. Such spectacle functioned both as entertainment and as a tool for forging an American mass public. Thus, the debates indicate that national collectivity—usually thought to organize itself around the grotesque display of black visibility (either in the minstrel show or the lynching)—could be motivated by the fleshy figure of whiteness as well.[5]

Despite the intense summer heat and the absence of microphones or other amplification devices, as many as 20,000 people attended the first Lincoln-Douglas debate at Ottawa. This wide-scale immersion in Illinois public

3. See Michael Warner, "The Mass Public and the Mass Subject," *Habermas and the Public Sphere* edited by Craig Calhoun (Cambridge, MA, 1992), 377–401; Dana D. Nelson, *National Manhood: Capitalist Citizenship and the Imagined Fraternity of White Men* (Durham, NC, 1998); Robyn Wiegman, *American Anatomies: Theorizing Race and Gender* (Durham, NC, 1995); Anne Norton, *Reflections on Political Identity* (Baltimore, 1988); and Iris Marion Young, "Impartiality in the Civic Public," *Feminism as Critique*, edited by Seyla Benhabib and Drucilla Cornell (Minneapolis, 1987). On popular misconceptions of Lincoln-Douglas, see Michael Schudson, *The Good Citizen: A History of American Civic Life* (New York, 1998), 133–43; and Allen C. Guelzo, *Lincoln and Douglas: The Debates that Defined America* (New York, 2008), xi–xxi.
4. See Justus Nieland, *Feeling Modern: The Eccentricities of Public Life* (Urbana and Chicago, 2008); Sandra M. Gustafson, *Eloquence Is Power: Oratory and Performance in Early America* (Chapel Hill, 2000); Bruce Burgett, *Sentimental Bodies: Sex, Gender, and Citizenship in the Early Republic* (Princeton, 1998); Christopher Looby, *Voicing America: Language, Literary Form, and the Origins of the United States* (Chicago, 1996); and Jay Fliegelman, *Declaring Independence: Jefferson, Natural Language, and the Culture of Performance* (Palo Alto, 1993).
5. On the relation between the visibility of black bodies and the formation of white nationhood, see Michael Rogin, *Blackface, White Noise: Jewish Immigrants in the Hollywood Melting Pot* (Berkeley, 1996); and Mary Esteve, *The Aesthetics and Politics of the Crowd in American Literature* (New York, 2003).

life was no doubt a response to the growing polarization over slavery, which had intensified in the aftermath of Bloody Kansas and the Dred Scott decision.[6] But massive attendance at the Lincoln-Douglas contest was also a reflection of nineteenth-century popular folk culture. Taking place in markets and city squares, the debates were characterized by polyglot throngs, feasting and alcohol, processions, competitions, exuberant speech, and spectacle. They often began with elaborate parades in which noisy supporters marched through miles of dusty prairie land, carrying ornate banners, flags, and effigies.

The pageantry of these processions was usually self-conscious, executed in an attempt to highlight an aspect of a candidate's image or to parody his competitor. When Lincoln arrived in Freeport in an atypical display of elegance—a "splendid team of six enormous horses" drawing a "Conestoga wagon"—Douglas, recognizing the "burlesque" on his own equipage, canceled the elaborate entrance he had planned (Sparks 210–11). Both politicians appeared that day costumed—Douglas, foppishly in "plantation style," Lincoln, in a "coarse looking coat," cultivating a more modest demeanor (Sparks 207). Basking in their roles as performers, the two greeted the Freeport crowd "arm in arm" from the balcony of a hotel "and every time they bowed a bigger shout went up" (Sparks 206). On display here is what Michael McGerr has called "democratic theater," a ritualized acting out of political roles designed to evoke "an intense, enveloping partisan experience."[7]

The debates themselves were characterized by the same ethos of raucous performance and communal participation. The speeches of both orators were met with loud vocalizations from the crowd—"Stick it to him," "Don't spare him," "That's the doctrine."[8] Alcohol flowed liberally, and as crowds grew boisterous, they occasionally flung the remnants of their meals onto the floor of the raised podium. (The Chicago Times reported that at Freeport Douglas was pelted with a watermelon rind [Sparks 313].) Insults, too, were traded freely between candidates and crowd. When a spectator at Ottawa yelled to Lincoln "[Y]ou are a fool," Lincoln responded, "I guess there are two of us that are that way" (66). Newspapers printed the transcriptions of speeches along with audience commentary and partisan observations by reporters. As a result, printed accounts read almost as plays, complete with stage directions like, "Laughter and cheers. Mr. Lincoln greatly agitated, his face in his hands" (146) or "Lincoln chewing his nails in a rage in a back corner" (176).

6. At the time of the debates, America was embroiled in controversy over the slave-holding status of newly acquired territories, specifically Kansas and Nebraska. While Lincoln and the emergent Republican Party believed that Congress had the constitutional right to exclude slavery from these lands (at least until they acquired the requisite population to enter the union as states), Douglas and his followers insisted on the principle of "popular sovereignty," by which the residents of a territory could embrace or bar slavery as they saw fit. These disagreements erupted into a fierce battle in Kansas that would culminate in the Lecompton crisis. The Dred Scott decision of 1857 further divided the country by establishing (among other things) the inability of Congress to prohibit slavery in the territories. For more on the historical context of the debates, see David Zarefsky, Lincoln, Douglas, and Slavery: In the Crucible of Public Debate (Chicago, 1990); and Don E. Fehrenbacher, Prelude to Greatness: Lincoln in the 1850s (Stanford, 1962).

7. Michael E. McGerr, The Decline of Popular Politics (New York, 1986), 6, 23.

8. The Lincoln-Douglas Debates: The First Complete, Unexpurgated Text, edited by Harold Holzer (New York, 1993), 80, 270. Further references to the speeches of Lincoln and Douglas and the responses from their audience will be to this edition and will be cited parenthetically in the text.

This theatrical quality was intensified by the showcasing of Lincoln and Douglas's bodies, especially in uninhibited and debased form. Reporters commented relentlessly on Lincoln's "lank, ungainly body," "the uncouthness of his movement," and "his oddity of pose."[9] These pejorative assessments came from Lincoln's detractors but also, interestingly, from partisan supporters who worried that Lincoln might not have the *bon ton* to carry off the senatorship (and later the presidency).[1] Of particular fascination were Lincoln's height, which "caused him to tower, in appearance, a head and shoulders above those men who surrounded him," and his hyperbolically long limbs whose movements were described as "kinky and uncertain."[2]

Douglas's body was also the subject of unremitting commentary, but while Lincoln tended to be depicted as a freakish albeit harmless creature, the Senator was imagined as a savage beast. "He had a large head, surmounted by an abundant mane," reported one eyewitness at the Lincoln-Douglas contest, "which gave the appearance of a lion prepared to roar or crush his prey."[3] "[H]e could assume wild rage and defiance," wrote another. "He would shake his head with its mass of hair like a wild bull, and his admirers would cheer and cheer."[4] Still other accounts emphasized Douglas's canine-like qualities, accusing him of a "fierce bull-dog bark" and a consistent tendency to "foam at the mouth" (Sparks 129, 551). Indeed, even before the 1858 contest, Douglas's bestial reputation had been established. In an 1838 debate he was rumored to have bitten his opponent's thumb "almost in two" after the latter had forcibly attempted to remove Douglas from the stage for using offensive language.[5]

Douglas's foaming mouth was not the only reference to bodily fluids at the debates. As mentioned earlier, one news account at Freeport referenced a "leak" that came "from the roof or elsewhere" and which was "confined to the 'spot' where Lincoln stood," implying the politician's incontinence (Sparks 190).[6] Another reporter some months earlier suggested that Lincoln's pained expressions while speaking indicated that "he [was] suffering from an attack brought on by an imprudent indulgence in unripe fruit."[7] References to scatology, moreover, were not always abstract: A journalist revealed that between debates, Douglas's carriage was smeared with "loathsome dirt" or excrement.[8] Other bodily fluids, most notably sweat, also made their way into accounts of the two politicians. Remembering a speech of 1854, reporter Horace White described Lincoln's "mobile

---

9. Qtd. in *Lincoln as I Knew Him: Gossip, Tributes, and Revelations from His Best Friends and Worst Enemies*, edited by Harold Holzer (Chapel Hill, NC, 1999), 55, 167; HW 75.
1. For more on Eastern Republican assessments of Lincoln, see Harold Holzer, *Lincoln at Cooper Union: The Speech That Made Abraham Lincoln Famous* (New York, 2004). Holzer points out that Lincoln's body began to be read in more elevated terms only with the publication and wide-scale circulation of Matthew Brady's celebrated 1860 photograph.
2. Qtd. in Walter Stevens, *A Reporter's Lincoln*, edited by Michael Burlingame (Lincoln, 1998), 225; and *The Complete Lincoln-Douglas Debates of 1858*, edited by Paul M. Angle (Chicago, 1991), 97.
3. Horace White, *The Lincoln and Douglas Debates: An Address Before the Chicago Historical Society, February 17, 1914* (Chicago, 1914), 7.
4. Qtd. in Stevens, *A Reporter's Lincoln*, 82.
5. Qtd. in Zarefsky, *Lincoln, Douglas, and Slavery*, 30.
6. The reporter's particular emphasis on the word "spot" harkens back to a controversy surrounding Lincoln's position on the Mexican War.
7. Qtd. in *The Complete Lincoln-Douglas Debates of 1858*, Angle, 97.
8. Qtd. in Fehrenbacher, *Prelude to Greatness*, 103.

face wet with perspiration which he discharged in drops as he threw his head this way and that like a projectile."[9] White did similar justice to Douglas in 1861, describing "[t]he veins of his neck and forehead" as "swollen with passion" as the "perspiration ran down his face in streams."[1]

This emphasis not simply on the politician's body but on his bodily fluids and functions (biting teeth, foaming mouth, urine, feces, sweat, and so forth) speaks to the grotesque debasement that Mikhail Bakhtin describes as central to rituals of popular folk culture in early modern Europe. Here, the body's fecundity and materiality is emphasized as an antidote to the sterility of everyday life. In the degradation of the body, Bakhtin finds an affirmation of the life cycle, and it is for this reason that he celebrates carnival and its literary manifestations as "a mighty life-creating and transforming power, an indestructible vitality."[2] Bakhtin specifies that the life embraced at carnival is not individualized; it refers "not to the private, egoistic 'economic man,' but to the collective ancestral body of all the people."[3] In this context, the presence of protruding parts and teeming fluids is especially crucial, because it suggests a body that extends beyond itself, a body linked "to other bodies or to the world outside."[4]

And yet, to understand the Lincoln-Douglas contest only in terms of utopian communality and transgression of official life is problematic. After all, the debates reaffirmed the legality of slavery in certain parts of the US and contributed to the reputations of Lincoln and Douglas on the national stage. Their joint speeches, moreover, created a public *committed* to political organization, not "outside" of it. In this way, the debates, despite their pageantry and populism, do not adhere to the Bakhtinian understanding of carnival as "a second world . . . outside officialdom," one that is "never merged with the official culture of the ruling class."[5] The transgressive effects of Lincoln-Douglas were limited: The fluid border between speakers and audience at the debates and the showcasing of the politicians' grotesque bodies may have worked to invert hierarchical relations, but the largely white male attendance, participation and subsequent votes on election day served to legitimate the established political process. The result was a culture of American politics made stronger and more official through the widespread engagement of the masses who reveled in its nonhieratic forms.

If the Lincoln-Douglas debates were informed by a folk culture dating back to the early modern period, they were also more immediately shaped by the entertainment culture of their day, and in particular, by the wildly popular phenomenon of the Barnum museum. In 1858, the same year as the debates, P. T. Barnum was managing a string of successful international tours for his prize attraction, General Tom Thumb. Dubbed "General" by Barnum so as to emphasize the contrast between his size and his

9. Qtd. in HW, 91–92.
1. Qtd. in HW, 127.
2. Mikhail Bakhtin, *Problems of Dostoevsky's Poetics*, translated by Caryl Emerson (Minneapolis, 1984), 107.
3. Mikhail Bakhtin, *Rabelais and His World*, translated by Hélène Iswolsky (Bloomington, 1984), 19.
4. Bakhtin, *Rabelais*, 316–17.
5. Bakhtin, *Rabelais*, 6, 474.

pretensions to power, Tom Thumb (born Charles S. Stratton), would ride miniature ponies and perform mock battles in military uniform to the delight of thousands. Occasionally, Barnum would pair his exhibit with "giants" so as to emphasize the oddity of his diminutive sensation.[6]

Those who reported on the debates between Long Abe and Little Dug seemed to be borrowing Barnum's rhetoric of hyperbolic physical difference, confrontation, and spectacle. They contrasted Lincoln's "giant frame" with the "dwarf" features of Douglas, casting the two politicians as physically both anomalous and opposite.[7] The speakers themselves seemed willing to accommodate this Barnumesque narrative. As if to accentuate their physical differences, Lincoln, when debating, would "bend his knees and . . . then shoot up again with a vehemence that raised him to his tiptoes and made him look much taller than he really was," while Douglas "moved little when he spoke and seldom gestured."[8] Lincoln spoke in a "high-pitched tenor, almost a falsetto" that starkly contrasted "Douglas' heavy basso."[9] Occasionally the candidates even commented on their extreme physical differences, as when Lincoln compared Douglas's "round, jolly, fruitful face" to his own "poor, lean, lank" visage to gales of laughter in Springfield.[1]

Instances of grandstanding by the two politicians, but especially by the diminutive Douglas, added to the Barnumesque show. In the first debate at Ottawa, the Little Giant elicited cheers when he announced he would "trot [Lincoln] down to Egypt [the southwestern part of Illinois bordering slaveholding Missouri] . . . to make him answer there as well as here" (81). This announcement followed Douglas's promise to "bring [Lincoln] to his milk" (79), a threat that generated endless laughter and commentary, because it emasculated Lincoln, presumably by invoking lactation. (In this context, references to "Little Dug"—conjuring up a teat or nipple—may have had a similar unmanning effect.) Such bravado on the part of Douglas recalls the antics of Tom Thumb who would likewise mock the giants that accompanied him on stage. The media's response to the debates indicates that they, too, understood the contest in the register of entertainment. One Lincoln detractor suggested he "make arrangements . . . to include a speech" in one of the "very good circuses and menageries traveling through the State" (Sparks 56). Another reporter referred to a particularly theatrical incident in Alton as the "best circus . . . in town" (Sparks 503). The debates, then, were imagined by audience, speakers, and media alike as a form of popular amusement—part of a capacious entertainment industry that relied on theatrics and corporeal oddity to draw crowds.[2]

6. Neil Harris, *Humbug: The Art of P. T. Barnum* (Chicago, 1973), 155, 49–50, 93.

7. HW, 76; qtd. in *The Lincoln-Douglas Debates of 1858*, 448.

8. Qtd. in *The Lincoln-Douglas Debates of 1858*, 447; Forest L. Whan, "Stephen A. Douglas." *An Analysis of Lincoln and Douglas as Public Speakers and Debaters*, edited by Lionel Crocker (Springfield, 1968), 132.

9. Qtd. in HW, 124–25.

1. This comment was made during a speech shortly before the official start of the debates; see *The Complete Lincoln-Douglas Debates of 1858*, 68.

2. On the culture of entertainment in nineteenth-century America, see Leo Braudy, *The Frenzy of Renown: Fame and Its History* (New York, 1986), 462–506; Richard Brodhead, *Culture of Letters: Scenes of Reading and Writing in Nineteenth-Century America* (Chicago, 1993), 48–68; Thomas N. Baker, *Sentiment and Celebrity: Nathaniel Parker Willis and the Trials of Literary Fame* (New York, 1999); and Lawrence W. Levine, *Highbrow/Lowbrow: The Emergence of Cultural Hierarchy in America* (Cambridge, MA, 1988).

THE UNDECIDED POLITICAL PRIZE FIGHT.

"The Undecided Political Prize Fight." Cincinnati (1860).
Library of Congress Prints and Photographs Division.

If the debates highlight the influence of Barnum on antebellum political life, the events of the early 1860s further reveal the extent to which
Lincoln and Douglas were implicated in the culture of the great showman. In 1862, Barnum was traveling with his new diminutive sensation,
Commodore Nutt, when he received an invitation to the White House.
As Barnum describes it in his autobiography, despite the fact that the
country was in the throes of war, the president interrupted a cabinet
meeting to greet the two, and then "ben[ding] down his long, lank body,
and taking Nutt by the hand," he said:

> 'Commodore, permit me to give you a parting word of advice.
> When you are in command of your fleet, if you find yourself in dan-
> ger of being taken prisoner, I advise you to wade ashore.'
> The Commodore found the laugh was against him, but placing
> himself at the side of the President, and gradually raising his eyes up
> the whole length of Mr. Lincoln's very long legs, he replied:
> 'I guess Mr. President, you could do that better than I could.'[3]

The exchange is significant not simply because it showcases Lincoln's humor
but because it depicts him as accommodating Barnum's spectacle—playing
the "long, lank body" to the Commodore's tiny one, for an audience of
Lincoln's cabinet and ultimately for the wide readership of Barnum's
autobiography.

One year later, Lincoln would fulfill a similar role as "giant," this time
at a reception for General Tom Thumb and his bride Lavinia Warren, yet

3. P. T. Barnum, *Struggles and Triumphs* (Hartford, 1869), 572–73.

another of Barnum's diminutive marvels. The two had been married among much fanfare, and their honeymoon included a stop-over at the White House. According to reporter Grace Greenwood who attended the reception, "The pigmy 'General' . . . and his wife" advanced with "'pigeon-like stateliness' . . . almost to the feet of the President. . . . It was pleasant to see their tall host bend, and bend, to take their little hands in his great palm."[4] In an account written later, Greenwood would add, "Washington was the place to go to, if one would see extremes meet."[5] While Greenwood certainly meant to be facetious, her comment indicates how readily Washington politics could be translated into the discourse of bodily opposites and made into an object of specular fascination.

Significantly, Stephen Douglas was also perceived in the register of Barnum entertainment, partly through his own self-fashioning. His nickname, the "Little Giant," worked in the same oxymoronic manner as Barnum's sensations—General Tom Thumb, Commodore Nutt and later Admiral Dot and General Mite—to underscore the disparity between size and ambition. Perhaps more to the point, Douglas himself had a significant encounter with a member of the Barnum troupe—Lavinia Warren. Thirty-two inches tall and renowned for her beauty, Warren would later instigate a fierce rivalry between Commodore Nutt and General Tom Thumb, whom she would eventually marry. But these men, it seemed, were not the only competitors for her attention. According to her autobiography, Warren met Stephen Douglas in the fall of 1860 in Montgomery, Alabama when

> he made a formal call upon me. Shortly afterward we met again at Selma. . . . He expressed great pleasure at again seeing me, and, as I stood before him, he took my hand and, drawing me towards him, stooped to kiss me. I instinctively drew back, feeling my face suffused with blushes.[6]

Warren goes on to quote Douglas as commenting, "I am often called the 'Little Giant,' but if I am a giant, I am not necessarily an ogre and will not eat you, although you almost tempt me to do so."[7] This exchange is remarkable not least because here, Douglas helps to enact an entire scene worthy of a Barnum production, complete with a tiny damsel in distress, a "Little Giant"/"ogre," and a storyline at once fanciful and prurient. Warren's tale illustrates Douglas's immersion in and contribution to the popular culture of the day. In wooing Lavinia he assumes a role that would be repeated, on a more public stage, by Barnum's various dwarves, with whom he could not help but be compared. As with Lincoln, then, the people's perception of Douglas had everything to do with his self-conscious positioning of his body in relation to a popular culture deeply preoccupied with corporeal eccentricity and exhibition.

4. Qtd. in Philip B. Kunhardt Jr., Philip B. Kunhardt III, and Peter W. Kunhardt, *P. T. Barnum: America's Greatest Showman* (New York, 1995), 170.

5. Grace Greenwood, *Records of Five Years* (Boston, 1867), 160.

6. Lavinia Warren, "Mrs. Tom Thumb's Autobiography," *New York Tribune Sunday Magazine*, 16 September 1906, www.disabilitymuseum.org/lib/docs/1130.htm, accessed August 19, 2009, par. 20.

7. Ibid., par. 21.

In characterizing the debates as part of an emerging mass entertainment complex, I do not mean to minimize their civic function; indeed, these two aspects of the contest were always yoked together. The hyperbole so reminiscent of Barnum extended to the rhetorical arguments of Lincoln and Douglas, who pitched their political convictions in the language of extremes. Sometimes this could reinforce the prevailing racism of the day, as when Douglas declared "I care more for the great principle of self-government . . . than I do for all the niggers in Christendom" (367) or when Lincoln insisted that "anything that argues me into this idea of perfect, social, and political equality with the negro is but a specious and fantastic argument of words by which a man can prove a horse chestnut to be a chestnut horse" (284).[8]

But at other moments, rhetorical extravagance—or what David Reynolds has identified as "the –est factor" characteristic of antebellum popular culture—could work towards genuine progressive ends.[9] After all, Lincoln's insistence especially towards the end of the debates that blacks and whites were equal in respect to the guarantees of the Declaration was for many a deeply radical proposition. When Lincoln pronounced that "the entire records of the world . . . may be searched in vain for one single declaration from one single man, that the negro was not included in the Declaration of Independence" (252) or when he avers that "whoever teaches that the negro has no humble share in the Declaration of Independence . . . [is] blowing out the moral lights around us, and perverting the human soul" (265–66), he mobilizes a rhetoric of hyperbole in the name of a far-reaching democratic vision. The culture of Barnum could thrive within Lincoln-Douglas because several of its most salient features—exaggeration, caricature, populism, idealism—lent themselves to American political experimentation, especially as practiced in the West. Through the incorporation of the nascent entertainment industry, Lincoln-Douglas became an arena for the expression of convictions at the extremities of the political spectrum.

RICHARD N. CURRENT

From The Master Politician[†]

"If Abraham Lincoln was not a master politician, I am entirely ignorant of the qualities which make up such a character," Alexander K. McClure declared in 1892. And McClure was not entirely ignorant of politics, or of Lincoln either. But he may not have been altogether accurate in his analysis of the qualities that made Lincoln a master.

---

8. Lincoln's "chestnut horse" reference might have recalled for some listeners Barnum's famous "Woolly Horse," a fantastic creature (part "elephant, deer, horse, buffalo, camel and sheep") displayed in the American Museum and later revealed as a hoax. Lincoln himself had invoked this curiosity in an 1856 speech in which he commented that to keep the territories free of slavery he would "go for the woolly horse itself . . . with which . . . Barnum humbugged the public." Qtd. in Philip B. Kunhardt et al., *P. T. Barnum: America's Greatest Showman* (New York, 1995), 47, 186.
9. David S. Reynolds, *Waking Giant: America in the Age of Jackson* (New York, 2008), 277.
† From *The Best American History Essays on Lincoln*, edited by Sean Wilentz. Copyright © 2009, Organization of American Historians. Reprinted with permission of Palgrave Macmillan.

Lincoln had a "peculiar faculty," McClure said, "of holding antagonistic elements to his own support, and maintaining close and apparently confidential relations with each without offense to the other."

He had a way with politicians. "You know I never was a contriver," McClure heard him say in his quaint, disarming manner to a group of Pennsylvanians he had summoned to the White House; "I don't know much about how things are done in politics, but I think you gentlemen understand the situation in your State, and I want to learn what may be done to insure the success we all desire." He proceeded to interrogate each man minutely about the campaign then in progress, about the weak points of the party and the strong points of the opposition, about the tactics to be used in this locality or that. Generalities, mere enthusiasm, did not interest him. He wanted facts. And he got them, along with the wholehearted cooperation of the gentlemen from Pennsylvania.

He understood the voters. "He had abiding faith in the people, in their intelligence and their patriotism," McClure thought; "and he estimated political results by ascertaining, as far as possible, the bearing of every vital question that was likely to arise, and he formed his conclusions by his keen intuitive perception as to how the people would be likely to deal with the issues."

Above all, he harnessed and used political power to get things done. "He was not a politician as the term is now commonly applied and understood," McClure believed; "he knew nothing about the countless methods which are employed in the details of political effort; but no man knew better—indeed, I think no man knew as well as he did—how to summon and dispose of political ability to attain great political results; and this work he performed with unfailing wisdom and discretion in every contest for himself and for the country."

Now, McClure undoubtedly was right in saying that Lincoln possessed a remarkable ability for holding together antagonistic elements. Undoubtedly, too, he had a knack of appealing to fellow politicians and talking to them in their own language.

But it is a little hard to see the kind of mystic partnership between Lincoln and the people which McClure believed existed. Direct, popular appeal does not appear to have been one of the strong points of Lincoln the political master. Rather, his strengths seem to have been those of a politician's politician, a manager of the party machine, a wire puller—in short, such a "contriver" as he professed not to be. Especially he relied upon the spoils system, spending a large proportion of his waking hours, down to the very day of his death, in the disposal of government jobs. Instead of appealing to the public for support on specific issues—as Andrew Jackson or Franklin D. Roosevelt did—Lincoln avoided issues as much as possible. He had a gift of noncommittalism.

And the statement that Lincoln knew how to "attain great political results" raises a question as to the meaning and allure of success in politics. Presumably this consists in gaining power, as a means, and using it toward some public end. If so, real success requires more than the mere winning of elections or the mere holding of elective office. It requires also the achievement of a set of governmental aims.

Of course, Lincoln was elected and reelected to the Presidency, yet he received no such popular majorities as a number of others have done—

Dwight D. Eisenhower, Franklin D. Roosevelt, and Warren G. Harding, to name a few. In 1860 Lincoln was a minority winner, with only about 40 percent of the total popular vote. In 1864, though he got a seemingly comfortable majority, approximately 55 percent, the election was closer than that figure indicates. A shift of 2 percent, or a little more than 80,000 votes, in certain areas, would have resulted in his defeat.

As President, how well did he succeed in realizing a positive program of his own? If his aim was simply to save the Union, the answer would seem to be clear enough, for the war was won and the Union saved during his presidency. And the answer is enough to justify his high reputation for statesmanship.

He succeeded, then, in his great political objective. But to do this—to hold the party together, keep himself in power, and preserve the nation—he apparently had to sacrifice some of his lesser aims. At the start of the war he was, or at least he is supposed to have been, a conservative. Before the end of it he had many a fight with the Radicals of his party—the "Jacobins," as they were called by his secretary John Hay, who was familiar with the history of the French Revolution. These revolutionaries of the American Civil War sought to break up the social and political structure of the South. Lincoln presumably did not. Yet it seems that he gave in again and again to the Radicals.

"Against Lincoln and his conservative program the Jacobins waged a winning battle," T. Harry Williams contends. "The wily Lincoln surrendered to the conquering Jacobins in every controversy before they could publicly inflict upon him a damaging reverse. Like the fair Lucretia threatened with ravishment, he averted his fate by instant compliance."

And yet, perhaps, this seeming opposition between Lincoln and the Radicals did not really exist, or was in actuality much less sharp than it appears. Perhaps at heart he was a Radical himself in some respects, as earnest a friend of freedom as any of them. Perhaps he was only more understanding, more patient, more astute. Perhaps he only waited for the ideal moment when he could do most effectively what he had intended all along to do—that is, to free the slaves.

HAROLD HOLZER

From Lincoln at the Cooper Union: The Speech That Made Abraham Lincoln President[†]

Had Abraham Lincoln failed in New York, few would likely recognize his name or face today. We might not even recognize the country he went on to defend and rededicate. Without Cooper Union, Lincoln might have ended up, at best, as a historical footnote.

But Abraham Lincoln succeeded. He rose to the most arduous challenge of his career to that point. He delivered a speech that electrified an important audience that included two of the most prominent pro-Republican

† From *Lincoln at the Cooper Union: The Speech That Made Abraham Lincoln President*. New York: Simon and Schuster, 2004. Copyright © 2004 by Harold Holzer. Reprinted with permission of Simon & Schuster.

newspaper editors in the country, who made sure his words then reverberated in print until they reached tens of thousands of readers across the Northern states. Lincoln came to New York an aspiring politician who had endured more defeats than victories, and left politically reinvigorated, and ideally positioned for a political rebirth.

Cooper Union proved a unique confluence of political culture, rhetorical opportunity, technological innovation, and human genius, and it brought Abraham Lincoln to the center stage of American politics at precisely the right time and place, and with precisely the right message: that slavery was wrong, and ought to be confined to the areas where it already existed, and placed on the "course of ultimate extinction"; that the Union was sacred, and could never be rightfully destroyed by sectional discord.

A similar appearance, and a like message, merely a year earlier (thus before the introduction of mass-produced photography) could not have generated the same impact, could not have made Lincoln the principal icon of America's domestic altars. A year later (once the decisive 1860 election had been settled), Lincoln's visit either would not have occurred at all or would not have much mattered. Instead, time, place, and technology happily conspired to Lincoln's enormous benefit that winter—and it could only have happened in New York.

Still, it remains as crucial to understand what the Cooper Union address did *not* accomplish as it is to comprehend what it *did*. For generations, historians have given too much credit where it is not due, and paid insufficient attention where it *is*.

In the former category, the Cooper Union address did *not* make Abraham Lincoln a popular hero in New York City, nor translate into popularity among the city's voters, the majority of whom remained confirmed Democrats, eventually of the specifically anti-Lincoln variety.

Neither did the Cooper Union speech help the soon-active Lincoln presidential campaign to wrest New York delegates to their cause at the Republican National Convention that May.

Nor was Cooper Union just a happy accident—a chance meeting of man and audience yielding unexpected results. Rather, Lincoln's visit was a carefully staged act in a messy local political drama, organized to introduce New Yorkers to western Republicans in order to upstage and unhorse William H. Seward. Lincoln's was the last such address in the series, and turned out to be the most sensational, thanks to his meticulous preparation and riveting performance.

The Cooper Union address has been hailed—and in some instances criticized—by modern historians as a conservative speech, but it was not really conservative at all. This is yet another misconception. It was an ingenious attempt to make Republican principles *appear* unthreatening to moderate Northerners by identifying them with historical doctrine. But Lincoln's analysis did not make his message conservative; it merely invited conservatives to hew comfortably to his antislavery message.

Nor did the Cooper Union opportunity inspire from Lincoln a poetic masterpiece (at least until its peroration) on a rhetorical par with his great presidential addresses. This is precisely why the speech remains among the most frequently mentioned, yet least often quoted, of Lincoln's major pre-presidential addresses. For the most part, it was almost mordantly legalistic and historical, an appeal not to passion but to logic.

That is what the Cooper Union address was *not*. It did not win the hearts of New York City voters, New York State convention delegates, or students of great oratory. (Nor did New Yorkers brave a snowstorm to hear him.) And it was not a conservative speech.

Yet the Cooper Union address accomplished as much as any speech Abraham Lincoln ever delivered. Even though it barely created a ripple in New York City voting patterns, it unleashed a tidal wave of celebrity nationwide. And it did much more.

For one thing, it allowed Abraham Lincoln successfully to "campaign" for president of the United States on the North's most prestigious political stage, New York City, without violating mid-nineteenth-century taboos against personal campaigning. As a result, Lincoln there became a serious aspirant for the White House.

Cooper Union also gave Lincoln the chance to "debate" Stephen A. Douglas one last time, without facing the unsettling challenge of again meeting him face to face. Lincoln had never inspired as much press attention as he did in 1858 on the debate trail in Illinois. In New York he revived his long-standing public quarrel with Douglas on a far larger stage, shrewdly calculating that the approach would work even better in Douglas's absence, and earn the same outpouring of newspaper interest, as had the "joint meetings" for the Senate race.

In addition, Cooper Union gave Lincoln the opportunity to bury his lingering reputation as the radical doomsayer who had quoted the Bible in 1858 to warn that "a house divided against itself cannot stand," but then found himself on the defensive during the Lincoln-Douglas debates, repeatedly explaining and softening that position. In New York, Lincoln went on record, in the new political environment toxically charged by the recent John Brown raid at Harpers Ferry, as an unthreatening moderate (not a conservative), committed to accommodation with the evil of slavery, where it existed, if it would save the country. At the same time, he made it clear that he was unwilling to accept responsibility for the country's dissolution if Southern state rights radicals refused to listen to patriotic calls to reason. And he pointedly refused to call slavery right simply because Southern extremists demanded it.

And Cooper Union handed Lincoln, too, a powerful publicity tool with which to reach Republicans nationwide: the New York press. At Cooper Union, Lincoln managed to electrify the media in the media center of the nation.

The Cooper Union invitation also inspired Lincoln's most successful "standard" political speech—one that he successfully repeated and reiterated over the next few weeks with the same focus with which modern politicians take pains to stay "on message" during campaign news cycles.

Of equal significance, Cooper Union gave Lincoln the opportunity to prove his universal appeal beyond the confines of the western frontier that produced him. It demonstrated to the entire eastern region, through newspaper reprints and subsequent personal appearances, that he was a serious, learned, dignified public figure, far more civilized than the prairie-bred storyteller who had mesmerized rowdy crowds on the debate trail in 1858. Cooper Union helped cement Lincoln's reputation as a spellbinding orator while correcting the impression that he was merely a vulgar stump speaker and rustic comedian.

※　※　※

SEAN WILENTZ

From This Great Tribunal, the American People[†]

Lincoln departed Springfield for Washington on the same day, February 11, 1861, that Davis departed Mississippi for Montgomery. Northern majority opinion had already lined up solidly behind Lincoln's position (identical to Andrew Jackson's in 1832) that the Union was older than any of the states, that secession was anarchy, and that in this current crisis hung the fate of constitutional democracy. The foremost principle animating the Union, Lincoln would reflect, "is the necessity of proving that popular government is not an absurdity," and on this point, even the outgoing President James Buchanan seemed to agree. Although sharply critical of the North for starting the slavery agitation, Buchanan had startled his southern patrons by declaring, in his final annual message in early December, that secession over Lincoln's election was illegitimate and that the Union's dissolution "would be quoted as conclusive proof that man is unfit for self-government." Yet if the outgoing president opposed disunion, he also believed that, under the Constitution, he lacked any powers to prevent it. With Lincoln not due to take office until Match 4, 1861, and with members of the cabinet and the lame-duck Congress from the Deep South departing after their states seceded, the federal government was rudderless and adrift.[1]

Buchanan did offer a compromise of sorts in his final address, whereby the northerners would cease criticizing slavery, support a constitutional amendment protecting slavery in all territories, and approve of renewed efforts to secure Cuba. Republicans instantly saw through this as capitulation. Some pledged to break secession even if it meant reducing the South to rubble. At all events, the Republicans argued, the government had to enforce the laws of the United States, including the collection of customs duties in southern ports, and stand up to the rebels just as President Jackson had to the nullifiers. ("Oh, for one hour of Jackson!" the Springfield *Republican* exclaimed.) Other Republicans, including Horace Greeley, declared that if the Union could be saved only by surrendering Republican principles, it would be better simply to let the

[†] From *The Rise of American Democracy: Jefferson to Lincoln.* Copyright © 2005 by Sean Wilentz. Used by permission of W. W. Norton & Company, Inc.

1. Tyler E. Dennett, *Lincoln and the Civil War in the Diaries and Letters of John Hay* (New York, 1939), 19; James D. Richardson, *A Compilation of the Messages and Papers of the Presidents* (New York: Bureau of National Literature, 1897) 5: 3157–65, 3168 (quotation). On Lincoln and the details of the secession crisis, another topic with a voluminous scholarly literature, see above all David M. Potter, *Lincoln and His Party in the Secession Crisis* (Baton Rouge, 1942); Kenneth M. Stampp, *And the War Came: The North and the Secession Crisis* (Baton Rouge, 1950); Allan Nevins, The *Emergence of Lincoln* (New York, 1950), 2: 362–413, 436–71. For a judicious and more recent interpretation, see James M. McPherson, *Battle Cry of Freedom: The Civil War Era* (New York, 1988), 246–74.

South go and let it fester in its own backwardness. (Radical abolitionists, including William Lloyd Garrison and Frederick Douglass, agreed.)
Still others, fearful that bellicosity would provoke the upper South to
secede, tried to fashion a congressional compromise less one-sided than
Buchanan's.[2]

The most promising compromise plan emerged from the special Senate
Committee of Thirteen in early December, before any state had seceded.
Established to sift through the numerous compromises coming out of
Congress, the committee included some of the ablest and influential men
from all sides, among them William Henry Seward, Benjamin Wade,
Stephen Douglas, Jefferson Davis, and Robert Toombs. Chief credit for
crafting the committee's compromise proposal belonged to John Critten-
den of Kentucky, the aging ex-Whig and, lately, prominent Constitutional
Unionist. The plan called for a series of irrevocable amendments to the
Constitution, the most important of which would revive the old Missouri
Compromise line at 36°30', extend it all the way to the Pacific, ban slavery
in all territories to its North, and protect slavery in territories (including
any territories gained in the future) to its South. Although less offensive
to Republicans than Buchanan's suggestions, the so-called Crittenden
compromise was still one-sided. Yet some powerful Republican business
interests were worried that secession might touch off a financial panic far
worse than that of 1857, and they endorsed the idea. So did Thurlow Weed
and (in more muffled ways) William Henry Seward.[3]

In Springfield, President-elect Lincoln broke his determined silence in
order to help kill the plan. The ironies of the situation were large. Seward,
the supposed radical, was playing the conciliator, to the consternation
of Republican radicals like Joshua Giddings and Charles Sumner. ("God
damn you, Seward," one senator told him, "you've betrayed your principles and your party; we've followed your lead long enough.") It was left to
Lincoln the moderate, whose political fortunes the insurrectionist John
Brown had inadvertently improved, to stand by Republican principles.
The Crittenden plan, Lincoln wrote to a few influential Republicans—
most pointedly Seward and Weed—"would lose us everything we gained
in the election," reawaken the South's lust for Cuba, and put the nation

---

2. Richardson, 5: 3168–70; *Republican* (Springfield, IL, Dec. 17, 1860); *New-York Daily Tribune*
   (Nov. 9, 1860); Henry Mayer, *All on Fire: William Lloyd Garrison and the Abolition of Slavery*
   (New York, 1998), 516. The evocations of Jackson varied. While antislavery and some pro-
   Douglas editors alike pushed Lincoln to act more like the "vigorous and defiant" Jackson, some
   of the more conservative Democrats saw Jackson's legacy differently. "The sword of the old
   Hero of New Orleans might have leapt from its scabbard in this conflict," the *Daily Chicago
   Times* said, "but it would never have glittered in the ranks of the Abolitionists." For the first
   view, see *Cincinnati Daily Commercial* (Nov. 15, 1860) quotation; *Wisconsin Daily State Journal* (Madison, Nov. 17, 1860); *Sioux City Register* (Dec. 1, 1860); and for the second, *Circleville
   Watchman* (Ohio, Nov. 23, 1860); *Daily Chicago Times* (Dec. 7, 1860); *Cincinnati Daily
   Enquirer* (Dec. 27, 1860; Feb. 10, 1861), all in *Northern Editorials on Secession*, edited by Harold Cecil Perkins (New York, 1942), 1: 111, 169, 181, 216, 270, 429; 2: 991.
3. The text of the amendment compromise appears in *Congressional Globe*, "36th Congress, 2nd
   session," 114. See also Albert Dennis Kirwan, *John J. Crittenden: The Struggle for the Union*
   (Lexington, 1962), 391–421. Some southern sympathizers—notably New York's Fernando
   Wood, now the city's mayor—made noises about starting their own secession movement and
   turning Manhattan and some surrounding counties into an independent nation and free port,
   what an enthusiastic George Fitzhugh instantly dubbed "the Republic of New York." The plan
   died, although many of New York's pro-southern merchants and Irish Democrats would remain
   a thorn in the North's side for years to come. See Fitzhugh, "The Republic of New York," *De
   Bow's Review* 30 (1861): 181–87; more generally, William C. Wright, *The Secession Movement
   in the Middle Atlantic States* (Rutherford, NJ, 1973).

once again "on the high-road to a slave empire." More important, the plan repudiated the basic Republican proposition that slavery's expansion should be halted everywhere. At Lincoln's urging, all five Republicans on the committee voted against the compromise, and with Toombs and Davis also opposed, the measure failed. Crittenden brought the plan to the Senate floor anyway, but by the time it came to a vote in mid-January, senators from states that had seceded or were about to secede abstained, and the remaining Republican majority defeated it.[4]

Other compromise schemes made the rounds in January and early February—although with one Deep South state after another declaring secession, efforts at mediation increasingly looked like stalling maneuvers until Lincoln could formally take over. The House counterpart to the Senate's special committee offered two measures that avoided violating Republican fundamentals and gained Lincoln's passive support: a resolution in support of the Fugitive Slave Law (which eventually passed on February 27) and a constitutional amendment prohibiting federal interference with slavery in the states (which also passed, much more narrowly, the following day). Seward also supported a self-described "peace convention," called by the Virginia legislature, that met in Washington on the same day that the Confederate convention opened in Montgomery. Chaired by the seventy-one-year-old former president John Tyler, the assembly looked even more antique than the Constitutional Union Party. After three weeks of deliberations, it offered a revised version of the Crittenden compromise, limiting the extension of the Missouri Compromise to the existing territories, and requiring majority votes of senators from both the free and the slave states before adding any new territories. The idea got nowhere.[5]

Lincoln, while keeping tabs on these discussions and bolstering the Republican faith, applied all of his political skills to appointing his cabinet and preparing for his inauguration. Keeping his fractious Republican rivals in line—especially Seward, who believed that he should have been elected president—was extremely difficult. On the principle of keeping one's friends close and one's rivals even closer, Lincoln chose Seward as secretary of state, Edward Bates as attorney general, Simon Cameron as secretary of war, and Salmon Chase as secretary of the Treasury. When Seward objected to Chase's selection and threatened to withdraw, Lincoln persuaded him to stay. More unfortunate was Lincoln's decision to turn his journey to Washington into a twelve-day railroad tour of northern towns and cities. Not wanting to add fuel to the fire, Lincoln addressed the trackside crowds with platitudinous speeches which raised concerns that he really was the unexceptional provincial his critics had always claimed. As the train headed south, recurring reports about planned assassination attempts gained more credibility, compelling a sudden change of schedule that left the president-elect to arrive in Washington secretly and igno-

4. Glyndon VanDeusen, *William Henry Seward* (New York, 1967), 249; Abraham Lincoln, "To Thurlow Weed, Dec. 17, 1860" and "To William H. Seward, Feb. 1, 1861," CW 4:154, 183; *Congressional Globe*, "36th Congress, 2nd Session," 409.
5. On the peace convention, see Robert G. Gunderson, *Old Gentlemen's Convention: The Washington Peace Conference of 1861* (Madison, WI, 1961); Jesse L. Keene, *The Peace Convention of 1861* (Tuscaloosa, 1961). The Senate rejected the revised version of the Crittenden compromise by a vote of 28 to 7, while the House did not even bother to bring it up for final consideration. *Congressional Globe*, "36th Congress, 2nd Session," 1254–5.

miniously in the predawn hours of February 23—"like a thief in the night," he ruefully remarked.[6]

The situation in the capital was dismal. Since the election nearly four months earlier, almost half of the slaveholding states had seceded from the Union, formed their own country, and begun seizing federal property within their own borders. No clear policy had been established about the collection of customs duties in ports where the new Confederacy now claimed full authority, or about the disposition of what federal assets remained in Union hands—most auspiciously, Fort Sumter, perched on a man-made island in Charleston harbor. Yet Lincoln had some cause for hope. After buckling in the immediate aftermath of the presidential elections, Unionists had made a strong comeback in the Border South. Virginia and Missouri, as well as Arkansas, had elected Unionist majorities to their state conventions called to consider secession. Given the choice over calling a convention, voters in North Carolina (by a narrow margin) and Tennessee (by a four-to-one majority) rejected the idea. Lincoln's repudiation of the Crittenden compromise and the failure of the Virginia peace conference had somewhat undermined "conditional Unionist" sentiment in the upper South. Much like the conditional secessionists of the cotton states, large numbers of antisecessionists elsewhere would consider any armed intervention by the federal government an act of invasion. But short of taking any over military action against the South, Lincoln still had some room in which to operate, and he thought that his inaugural address could well determine the outcome. With input from Seward and from a close Illinois adviser, Orville Browning, Lincoln tried to compose a message that would help preserve the Union without abdicating his duty to assert federal authority. At the very last minute, he revised his text, on Seward's advice, to emphasize conciliation.[7]

March 4 dawned cold and gloomy in Washington, but a crowd estimated at twenty-five thousand turned up at the Capitol for the inauguration ceremonies, and bright sunshine broke through at noon, just as President Lincoln began his speech. Looking stately beneath a newly grown beard, Lincoln reversed the usual order and began the ceremonies by taking the oath of office from a man he considered an arch fiend (the feeling was mutual), Chief Justice Roger Brooke Taney. Then, with an eloquence that announced the lifting of the Pierce-Buchanan era's rhetorical fog, Lincoln developed a series of points and counterpoints about slavery and the Constitution, and defended the democracy that the southern disunionists had spurned and traduced.

As president, he said, he would refuse "directly or indirectly, to interfere with the institution of slavery in the States where it exists," but he would not countenance secession. He would enforce the constitutional obligation to return fugitive slaves, but he would also "hold, occupy, and

---

6. McPherson, *Battle Cry,* 260–2 (quotation on 262).
7. Daniel W. Crofts, *Reluctant Confederates: Upper Sound Unionists in the Secession Crisis,* (Chapel Hill, N.C., 1989), exhaustively studies the conflicts over secession in the Border South, focusing on Virginia, Tennessee, and North Carolina. The process of drafting and revising Lincoln's inaugural address, including Seward's and Browning's suggested revisions, can be tracked in the text and notes in CW 4: 249–62. Both advisers softened the language of Lincoln's first draft, adding much of the purposeful ambiguity and conciliatory language that appeared in the final speech.

possess the property and places belonging to the government, and . . . collect the duties and imposts." He would not deny "the very high respect and consideration" due Supreme Court rulings on constitutional questions (did Taney squirm at this obvious reference to *Dred Scott?*), but he would not allow "erroneous" decisions and their "evil effect" to fix irrevocably "the policy of the government upon vital questions, affecting the whole people." In a moving peroration, Lincoln pleaded with his native Border South and men of patriotic goodwill everywhere. "I am loth to close," he said. "We are not enemies, but friends. We must not be enemies. Though passion may have strained, it must not break our bonds of affection. The mystic chords of memory, stretching from every battle-field, and patriot grave, to every living heart and hearthstone, all over this broad land, will yet swell the chorus of the Union, when again touched, as surely they will be, by the better angels of our nature."[8]

The speech was a blend of political cunning and bedrock idealism, a style of leadership that Lincoln had been mastering since 1858. On the crucial matter of reasserting the government's authority over forts, customs houses, mints, and armories appropriated by the Confederates, he remained purposefully vague. Anything more specific could easily be regarded as a provocation, which would undermine his efforts to keep the Border South from seceding. A shrewd courtroom and political strategist thrown into a national crisis, Lincoln understood that what he needed above all else was time, time to get his White House in order, to persuade the persuadable of his moderation, and, if possible, to permit the secession fever finally to break. He made the point explicitly in his address: "Nothing valuable can be lost by taking time."

Yet Lincoln did not rely simply on temporizing and artful ambiguity. The speech's evocations of the Union and "the better angels of our nature" were as lofty an appeal to nationalist principles as any since the days of Webster and Jackson. And above and beyond the slavery issue, Lincoln unflinchingly defended certain basic ideals of freedom and democratic government, which he asserted he had been elected to vindicate. There was, he said, a single "substantial dispute" in the sectional crisis: "[o]ne section of our country believes slavery is *right*, and ought to be extended, while the other believes it is *wrong*, and ought not to be extended." There could be no doubt about where Lincoln stood, and where his administration would stand, on that fundamental moral question. But regardless of that, the only just and legitimate way to settle the matter, Lincoln insisted (with a direct echo of Thomas Jefferson's first inaugural address), was through a deliberate democratic decision by the nation's citizenry:

> Why should there not be a patient confidence in the ultimate justice of the people? Is there any better, or equal hope, in the world? In our present differences, is either party without faith of being in the right? If the Almighty Ruler of nations, with his eternal truth and justice, be on your side of the North, or on yours of the South, that truth, and that justice, will surely prevail, by the judgment of this great tribunal, the American people.

8. The final text of the address appears in CW 4: 262–71. On the scene at the inauguration, see *New York Herald* (March 5, 1861); *New-York Daily Tribune* (March 5, 1861); Nevins, *Emergence*, 2: 457–8.

The future of American democracy, the best hope in the world, would rise or fall on whether secession—"the essence of anarchy"—succeeded or failed.

Reactions to the address encouraged the new president. Not surprisingly, most Republicans applauded its mixture of moderation and adamancy, while Confederates and their supporters denounced it, either as an outright declaration of civil war—"couched in the cool, unimpassioned, deliberate language of the fanatic," the *Richmond Enquirer* claimed—or as a cleverly Delphic contrivance, "concealing dark designs, iniquitous and flagitious." But anxious Wall Street Republicans, and even some northern Democrats, who had pushed for conciliation found the speech reassuring. (One Wall Streeter named H. D. Faulkner reported to Lincoln that he heard almost unanimous praise from his friends, ranging from a Breckinridge Democrat who called the speech "first rate . . . and full of faith" to an old Silver Gray who thought it "splendid.") Moderates in the upper South worried over its lack of specifics, but hailed what the *Spectator* of Staunton, Virginia, called its "frank and conciliatory" tone. Contrary to the secessionists' diatribes, they insisted, Lincoln's speech was *"not a war message"* and was "not unfriendly to the South."[9]

More than Lincoln knew, however, time was running out. On inauguration day, Buchanan's departing secretary of war, Joseph Holt, received an alarming dispatch, dated February 28, from Major Robert Anderson, commander of the federal forces at Fort Sumter. Holt quietly put it aside for the incoming administration. Anderson reported it would take a force of at least twenty thousand troops to fight their way into Charleston harbor and relieve the weary garrison. The Union, it seemed, could evacuate Sumter—repudiating Lincoln's vows on the Capitol steps—or it could initiate a war with a massive and bloody show of force that was bound to unite the entire South and divide the North.[1]

The next morning, Lincoln walked into his White House office for his first full day's work as president and found Major Anderson's dispatch lying on his desk.

ERIC FONER

[Abraham Lincoln on Race]†

*   *   *

Efforts to assess Lincoln's own racial outlook run the danger of exaggerating the importance of race in his thinking. Race is our obsession, not Lincoln's. Other than in 1857–58, this was not a subject to which he devoted much attention before the Civil War. Many aspects of the slavery

9. *Richmond Enquirer* (March 5, 1861); T. W. MacMahon, *Cause and Contrast: An Essay on the American Crisis* (Richmond, 1862), 137; "Faulkner to Abraham Lincoln, Mar. 5,1861," *Abraham Lincoln Papers*, Library of Congress; *Staunton Spectator* (Virginia, March 5, 1861); *North Carolina Standard,* (March 9, 1861), *Nashville Republican Banner,* (March 14, 1861), qtd. in Croft, *Reluctant Confederates,* 260.
1. Nevins, *Emergence*, 2: 461–62.
† From Eric Foner, *The Fiery Trial: Abraham Lincoln and American Slavery* (New York: Norton, 2010). Copyright © 2010 by Eric Foner. Used by permission of W. W. Norton and Company, Inc.

controversy—the rights of free labor, domination of the federal government by the Slave Power, the way slavery violated basic American values—
were only marginally related to race. Although he carefully read proslavery
books and newspapers, Lincoln evinced no interest in his era's extensive
literature of racial theorizing, with its predictions about racial destinies
and debates over ethnography, separate genesis, and inborn racial difference. What was "political" or "strategic" in Lincoln's statements during
the 1858 campaign was not his disavowal of racial equality, but that he felt
the need to outline his views on race at all.[1]

Nonetheless, it is clear that while Lincoln had disengaged from many
aspects of frontier culture and was hardly unwilling to take unpopular
political positions—as his long career as a Whig stalwart demonstrated—he
shared many of the prejudices of the society in which he lived. Lincoln
used the word "nigger" privately and, occasionally, in public. He enjoyed
going to blackface minstrel shows, and his seemingly endless repertoire of
stories and jokes included overtly racist humor.[2] As we have seen, when
pressed by Douglas in the campaign of 1858, Lincoln disavowed belief in
black citizenship and civil and political equality. There is no reason to think
that Lincoln, at this point in the development of his ideas, was not sincere
in these statements. On the other hand, he consistently emphasized that
blacks were entitled to enjoy the natural rights of mankind, especially the
right to the fruits of their labor, a position that undoubtedly cost him votes
in parts of Illinois. His definition of equality as an aspirational principle
whose full accomplishment lay in the future could be taken to imply the
possibility of improvement in the black condition.

In some respects, what Lincoln did not say is as important as what he
did. He could turn racism into a political weapon, as he had done early in
his career against Van Buren and again in 1852 in a speech quoting a
sailor's sea chanty about a "bright Mullater" to criticize Franklin Pierce,
the Democratic presidential candidate, for seeking antislavery votes by
criticizing the Fugitive Slave Act. In the 1858 debates, Lincoln charged
that Douglas's policies, by promoting the spread of slavery, would also
encourage "amalgamation." But generally speaking, in the 1850s Lincoln's
comments on race came in response to Democratic charges of "Negro
equality." Unlike many contemporaries, he was not given to orations on
the glories of the Anglo-Saxon "race" and its supposed love of liberty. He
did not express contempt for free blacks, or refer to them as a vicious and
degraded group, descriptions ubiquitous among Democrats and hardly

1. For an introduction to the voluminous literature on Lincoln and race, see Benjamin Quarles,
   Lincoln and the Negro (New York, 1962); Arthur Zilversmit, "Lincoln and the Problem of Race:
   A Decade of Interpretations," *Papers of the Abraham Lincoln Association*, 2 (1980): 21–45;
   Lerone Bennett, *Forced into Glory: Abraham Lincoln's White Dream* (Chicago, 2000) (which
   claims, on p. 66, that "racism was the center and circumference of his being"); George M.
   Fredrickson, *'Big Enough to be Inconsistent': Slavery and Race in the Thought and Politics of
   Abraham Lincoln* (Cambridge, Mass., 2008); Henry Louis Gates Jr. and Donald Yacovone, eds.,
   Lincoln on Race and Slavery (Princeton, 2009); and James Oakes, "Natural Rights, Citizenship
   Rights, States' Rights, and Black Rights: Another Look at Lincoln and Race," in Eric Foner,
   ed., *Our Lincoln: New Perspectives on Lincoln and His World* (New York, 2008), 109–34.
   George M. Fredrickson discusses the burgeoning literature on race during the 1850s in *The
   Black Image in the White Mind: The Debate on Afro-American Character and Destiny, 1817–
   1914* (New York. 1971), 71–129.
2. *The Collected Works of Abraham Lincoln: First Supplement, 1832–1865* (New Brunswick, N.J.,
   1974), 3: 20, 28–29, 317; Bennett, *Forced into Glory*, 14, 90–100; David Mearns, *The Lincoln
   Papers* (2 vols.; Garden City, N.Y., 1948), 1: 169.

unknown among Republicans. In his 1852 eulogy for Henry Clay he spoke of the "troublesome presence of the free negroes." But later in the same paragraph, when he identified a "dangerous presence" in the United States, Lincoln referred not to free blacks, but to slavery itself. Lincoln justified discrimination on the basis not of innate racial inferiority but the will of the (white) majority in a political democracy. When speaking of black capacity his remarks were usually cautious and tentative. In his Springfield speech of July 1858, he said, "Certainly, the negro is not our equal in color—perhaps not in many other respects." Even in the debate at Charleston, when he said the two races could never coexist in the same country on the basis of equality, the reason he advanced was "physical," not moral or intellectual, difference.[3]

Lincoln's personal dealings with blacks did not reveal prejudice. Springfield when Lincoln lived there was a small city (its population had not reached 10,000) with a tiny black population (171 persons in 1850). Nonetheless, Lincoln could not have been unaware of the black presence. In the 1850s, more than twenty black men, women, and children lived within three blocks of his house. He and his wife employed at least four free black women to work as domestic servants at one time or another. Lincoln befriended and gave free legal assistance to William Florville, the city's most prosperous black resident, known as "Billy the Barber." In 1857, Lincoln and Herndon paid a fine incurred by John Shelby, a free black resident of Springfield who had been jailed in New Orleans while working on a Mississippi River steamboat, securing his release. W. J. Davis, a former slave who lived in Bloomington, Illinois, and claimed during the Civil War to have been "personally acquainted" with Lincoln since the mid-1850s, described him as "a kind-hearted, sociable kind of man."[4]

In 1860, the black community of Illinois numbered fewer than 8,000 in a population of over 1.7 million. How Lincoln in his heart of hearts viewed black people probably mattered less to this tiny group than his refusal to take a principled stand against racial inequality. He may not have fully embraced racism, but he did not condemn it. The most he would say, as at Peoria, was that in a democratic society, a "universal" prejudice could not be "safely disregarded," regardless of whether it accorded with "justice and sound judgment." This was an oddly agnostic position for a politician who repeatedly emphasized that the fundamental difference between Democrats and Republicans lay in the former's refusal to address the morality of slavery.

In at least some of his responses to the *Dred Scott* decision, Lincoln seemed to endorse the idea of free black citizenship. But, at a time when nearly all the rights of citizens derived from the states, Lincoln was not among the Illinois Republicans who spoke out against his state's oppressive Black Laws, nor did he assist the members of the legislature who

3. CW, 2: 132, 157, 520.
4. Richard E. Hart, "Springfield's African-Americans as a Part of the Lincoln Community," *Journal of the Abraham Lincoln Association* 20 (Winter 1999): 35–36, 45; Kenneth J. Winkle, *The Young Eagle: The Rise of Abraham Lincoln* (Dallas, 2001), 262–66; Kenneth J. Winkle, "'Paradox Though It May Seem': Lincoln on Antislavery, Race, and Union, 1837–1860," in Brian Dirck, ed., *Lincoln Emancipated: The President and the Politics of Race* (DeKalb, Ill., 2007), 19–20; Elmer Gertz, "The Black Codes of Illinois," *Journal of the Illinois State Historical Society* 56 (Autumn 1963): 493; *Christian Recorder*, March 21, 1863.

tried to have them modified. The black abolitionist H. Ford Douglas, a Virginia-born slave who escaped from bondage and moved to Chicago, claimed that in 1858 he asked both Lincoln and Trumbull to sign a petition for repeal of the Black Laws, whose provisions, Douglas observed, "would disgrace any Barbary State." Both, Douglas related, refused. Lincoln had not thought through how free blacks could enjoy the opportunity to rise if denied physical mobility, access to education, testifying in court, and serving on juries—essential attributes of free society. Was there really a difference, asked Henry L. Dawes, a prominent Massachusetts Republican, between discriminatory laws like those of Illinois and the idea that "the negro has *no* rights which the white man is bound to respect"?[5]

Abolitionists saw the fights against slavery and racism as symbiotically related. Racism, as Frederick Douglass put it, constituted "the greatest of all obstacles in the way of the anti-slavery cause," and he accused Republicans of betraying their own moral beliefs when they stood "opposed to Negro equality, to Negro advancement, to Negro suffrage, to Negro citizenship." Lincoln, by contrast, saw the question of "Negro equality" as a false one, an attempt to "divert the public mind from the real issue—the extension or non-extension of slavery." "Negro equality! Fudge!" Lincoln wrote in notes for a speech in 1858. "How long . . . shall there continue knaves to vend, and fools to gulp, so low a piece of demagoguism as this?"[6]

In an undated fragment written in the 1850s, Lincoln mused on the logical absurdity of proslavery arguments:

> If A. can prove, however conclusively, that he may, of right, enslave B.—why not may B. snatch the same argument, and prove equally that he may enslave A? You say A. is white, And B. is black. . . . Take care. By this rule, you are to be the slave to the first man you meet, with a fairer skin than your own.[7]

The same problem, he continued, existed if the right to enslave another were grounded in superior intelligence, or simply in self-interest. But Lincoln failed to acknowledge that precisely the same argument could be made against laws, like those of Illinois, in which the white majority imposed all sorts of disabilities on the free black population.

Lincoln challenged prevailing prejudices when it came to blacks' enjoyment of natural rights, but he would go no further. As was typical of Lincoln in the 1850s, his position occupied the middle ground of Republican opinion. In the context of the North as a whole, Lincoln's views on race fell far short of abolitionist egalitarianism, but differed substantially from the virulent and gratuitous racism of the Democrats, not to mention Chief Justice Taney's ruling in the case of *Dred Scott*. At this point in his career, Lincoln had not yet given serious thought to the role blacks might play in a post-slavery America. He distinguished between an entitlement to natural rights, which he always claimed for blacks, and membership in the American nation. "What I would most desire," he explained at Spring-

5. *Liberator*, July 13, 1860; Christopher R. Reed, *Black Chicago's First Century* (Columbia, Mo., 2005–), 1: 105; *New York Journal of Commerce*, October 11, 1859.
6. *North Star*, June 13, 1850; Foner, *Life and Writings of Frederick Douglass*, 2: 490; CW, 3: 399; 4: 504.
7. CW, 2: 222–23.

field in 1858, "would be the separation of the white and black races"—
that is, the colonization of blacks outside the United States.[8]

* * *

By 1858, Lincoln had emerged as a public spokesman for colonization.
His first extended discussion, as we have seen, came in 1852, in his eulogy
of Henry Clay. By the next year, Lincoln was closely enough identified
with the idea that when Reverend James Mitchell, a prominent colonization organizer from Indiana, traveled to Springfield seeking allies to
promote the cause, a local minister referred him to Lincoln. Lincoln
addressed the annual meeting of the Illinois Colonization Society in 1853
and again in January 1855, even as his first bid for election to the Senate
unfolded. No record has survived of the first speech and only a brief outline of the second. In 1858, when he ran for the Senate, Lincoln's was
the first name listed among the eleven members of the society's Board of
Managers. (The vice presidents included Chicago Republican editor
John L. Scripps and William Brown, at whose behest Lincoln compiled
his "book" on racial equality.) In his first debate with Douglas, Lincoln
read aloud the passage from his Peoria speech of 1854 in which he said
his "first impulse" in dealing with slavery would be to free the slaves and
send them to Africa.[9]

There is no reason to doubt the sincerity of Lincoln's advocacy of colonization or to explain it solely as a way of deflecting Douglas's accusation
that Republicans favored racial equality. When Lincoln made his first
extended remarks on the subject in 1852, he was not a candidate for office
and his political career appeared to have reached a dead end. Unlike
many other advocates of colonization, Lincoln never countenanced com-
pulsory deportation and expressed little interest in creating an American
empire in Central America or in the Christianization of Africa. Nonetheless, he believed that blacks would welcome the opportunity to depart for
a place where they could fully enjoy their natural rights. Lincoln seemed
to envision the bulk of the black population eventually emigrating. In his
Springfield speech of 1857, he cited biblical precedent: "The children of
Israel," in numbers comparable to American slaves, "went out of Egyptian bondage in a body."[1] For many white Americans, including Lincoln,
colonization was part of a plan for ending slavery that represented a middle ground between abolitionist radicalism and the prospect of the United
States existing forever half-slave and half-free.

Lincoln's thought seemed suspended between a civic conception of
American nationality, based on the universal principle of equality (and
thus open to immigrants with no historic roots in this country and, in
principle, to blacks), and a racial nationalism that saw blacks as in some
ways not truly American. He found it impossible to imagine the United
States as a biracial society. When he spoke of returning blacks to Africa,
their "own native land," Lincoln revealed that he did not consider them an
intrinsic part of American society. In fact, by the 1850s, the vast majority

---

8. CW, 2: 521; Dorothy Ross, "Lincoln and the Ethics of Emancipation: Universalism, Nationalism, Exceptionalism," *Journal of American History* 96 (September 2009): 391.
9. *St. Louis Globe-Democrat*, August 26, 1894; CW, 2: 131–32, 255–56, 298–99; 3:15; *African
Repository*, 34 (April 1858), 122.
1. CW, 2: 409.

of black Americans—a far higher percentage, indeed, than of the white population—had been born in the United States.

*   *   *

Lincoln's encounters with talented, politically active black men and women seemed to soften the prejudices with which he had grown up. To be sure, he never became a full-fledged racial egalitarian. In private, he continued to use words like "nigger" and "darky" and tell racially inflected stories. But not infrequently his humor used irony to undercut racism. One of his stories related how a Democratic orator in prewar Illinois had warned his audience that Republicans would extend political rights to blacks. Lincoln mimicked the speaker who related what would transpire: "Here comes forward a white man. . . . I will vote for [Stephen A.] Douglas. Next comes up a sleek pampered negro. Well Sambo, who do you vote for? I vote for Massa Lincoln. . . . What do you think of that?" Whereupon, Lincoln continued, a farmer shouted from the audience, "I think the darky showed a damd sight of more sense than the white man." Another instance of employing humor to express impatience with overt expressions of racism came in Lincoln's response to a telegram from Pennsylvania that bluntly stated, "Equal Rights & Justice to all white men in the United States forever—White men is in Class number one & black men is in Class number two & must be governed by white men forever." Lincoln drafted a reply to be sent by one of his secretaries:

> The President has received yours of yesterday, and is kindly paying attention to it. As it is my business to assist him whenever I can, I will thank you to inform me, for his use, whether you are either a white man or black one, because in either case, you can not be regarded as an entirely impartial judge. It may be that you belong to a third or fourth class of *yellow* or *red* men, in which case the impartiality of your judgment would be more apparent.[2]

When Lincoln moved to Washington to take up the presidency, William H. Johnson, a black resident of Springfield who had been working as his valet, accompanied him. Lincoln arranged for him to be placed on the Treasury Department payroll, describing him as a "colored boy" even though Johnson was a grown man. When Johnson died in 1864, Lincoln arranged for him to be buried at Arlington Cemetery, paid for a tombstone with Johnson's name on it, and chose a one-word inscription: "Citizen."[3]

Lincoln also abandoned the idea of colonization. When the Emancipation Proclamation was issued, the black abolitionist H. Ford Douglas predicted that the progress of the war would "educate Mr. Lincoln out of his idea of the deportation of the Negro."[4] The change Douglas predicted did come, but gradually. After January 1, 1863, Lincoln made no further public statements about colonization, perhaps realizing that such statements had failed both to persuade blacks to emigrate or to reconcile his critics in the northern and border states to emancipation. But later that month, after

2. CW, 7: 483, 506–8; John McMahon to Lincoln, August 5, 1864, ALP.
3. CW, 4: 277; James Oakes, "Natural Rights, Citizenship Rights, States' Rights, and Black Rights: Another Look at Lincoln and Race," in Eric Foner, ed., *Our Lincoln: New Perspectives on Lincoln and His World* (New York, 2008), 115–16.
4. *Douglass' Monthly* 5 (February 1863), 786.

meeting with an official of the Pennsylvania Colonization Society, Lincoln directed the Interior Department to advance money to a black minister who wanted to establish a settlement in Liberia. In February, Lincoln told Congressman William P. Cutler of Ohio that he was still "troubled to know what we should do with these people—Negroes—after peace came."

*   *   *

The continuing evolution of Lincoln's attitudes regarding blacks stands in stark contrast to the lack of change when it came to Native Americans. Lincoln's paternal grandfather, Abraham, after whom he was named, had been killed by an Indian while working on his Kentucky farm, an event witnessed by the seven-year-old Thomas Lincoln. Not surprisingly, this traumatic incident became part of family lore, "impressed upon my mind and memory," Lincoln later wrote. He mentioned it in the autobiographical sketches he produced for the 1860 campaign. But unlike many frontiersmen and military officers, Lincoln was never an Indian hater. He did not share the outlook, for example, of General John Pope, who wrote in August 1862 when he was dispatched to put down a Santee Sioux uprising in Minnesota, "It is my purpose utterly to exterminate the Sioux if I have the power to do so," or of the state's governor, Alexander Ramsey, who urged Lincoln to approve the execution of all 300 Indians condemned to death by courts-martial in the aftermath of that conflict. Lincoln carefully reviewed the trial records and commuted the sentences of all but thirty-eight. (Nevertheless, this still constituted the largest official execution in American history.) Lincoln subsequently signed a bill for the removal of the Sioux and Winnebago (who had nothing to do with the uprising) from their lands in Minnesota. Overall, not surprisingly, Lincoln devoted little attention to Indian policy during his presidency. He allowed army commanders free rein when it came to campaigns against Indians in the West, with the predictable result that the Civil War witnessed events like the 1864 Sand Creek Massacre in Colorado, where soldiers under the command of Colonel John Chivington attacked a village of Cheyenne and Arapaho Indians, killing perhaps 400 men, women, and children.[5]

Lincoln may not have had any special animus toward Indians but he shared the widespread conviction that they lacked civilization and constituted an obstacle to the economic development of the West. The influences that operated to change his views regarding blacks had no counterpart when it came to Native Americans. Blacks came to be identified with the fate of the Union, but key Indian tribes like the Cherokee, Choctaw, and Creek sided with the Confederacy, making them enemies of the nation's survival. Indeed, Indian claims to independent sovereignty, while guaranteed by treaty, increasingly seemed at odds with the unified nation-state that emerged from the war. Although some 5,000 Indian soldiers fought for the Union on the western frontier, their numbers were too small to raise the issue of postwar citizenship. Lincoln had virtually no contact with Native Americans either before or during his presidency. He spoke in 1862 with the Cherokee leader John Ross, but

5. David A. Nichols, *Lincoln and the Indians: Civil War Policy and Politics* (Columbia, Mo., 1978), 76–127, 175–83; OR, ser. 1, 13: 686; Alexander Ramsay to Lincoln, November 28, 1862, ALP; CW, 2: 217; 3: 511; 4: 61; 5: 493, 542–43; 6: 6–7.

nothing came of the encounter. In March 1863, he did hold a meeting at the White House with a group of fourteen western chiefs. His remarks were patronizing and illogical. He informed them that the world is round, as if they were unaware of this fact; urged them to take up farming; and ignoring the carnage going on around him, advised them to become less warlike and adopt the peaceful ways of white people. The Cheyenne chief, Lean Bear, pointed out that whites were responsible for most of the violence in the West. While many Americans recognized the need for reform of the notoriously corrupt Office of Indian Affairs (Lincoln mentioned this in his annual messages of 1862 and 1863), the future status of Native Americans was not the focus of a large social movement that pressured the White House for a change in national policy. Perhaps most important, the free-labor vision of the West, implemented in wartime measures such as the Pacific Railroad and Homestead Acts, meant continuing encroachment on Indian land. In his messages to Congress, Lincoln spoke of the need to extinguish the "possessory rights of the Indians to large and valuable tracts of land" and to encourage the exploitation of the West's land and mineral resources by whites, while providing for "the welfare of the Indian." He did not acknowledge that these aims were mutually contradictory.[6]

But if Lincoln's Indian policies are depressingly similar to those of virtually every nineteenth-century president, when it came to African-Americans, he began during the last two years of the war to imagine an interracial future for the United States.

*　*　*

Reconstruction now emerged as the foremost problem confronting the nation. On April 11, having returned to Washington, Lincoln delivered a speech on this subject to a large crowd that had gathered at the White House. According to one newspaper, he prepared it with "unusual care and deliberation." In part, it was a defense of the new government of Louisiana, to whose support Lincoln had devoted so much effort. In the past month, events in that state had taken an ominous turn. On the day of Lincoln's second inauguration, Governor Michael Hahn resigned after being elected to the Senate and was replaced by J. Madison Wells, a Unionist planter who had owned more than 100 slaves before the Civil War. Quickly taking stock of the political situation as the war neared its end, Wells realized that Confederates who took an oath of loyalty, thus restoring their right to vote, would soon vastly outnumber white supporters of his regime. He promptly began replacing Hahn's appointees in local and statewide offices with conservative Unionists and former rebels.[7]

In his speech, Lincoln acknowledged that the problem of Reconstruction was "fraught with great difficulty." Nonetheless, he again sought to bolster northern support for the Louisiana regime, while also trying to find common ground with his Republican critics. In fact, Lincoln had asked Charles Sumner to stand on the White House balcony while he delivered the address. Lincoln noted that when he issued his Ten Percent

6. CW, 5: 526; 6: 151–53; 7: 47–48; 8: 147; Nichols, *Lincoln and the Indians*, 27–41, 186–99.
7. *New York World*, April 13, 1865; Eric Foner, *Reconstruction: America's Unfinished Revolution, 1863–1877* (New York, 1988), 182; Philip S. Paludan, *The Presidency of Abraham Lincoln* (Lawrence, Kans., 1994), 305.

Plan, every member of the cabinet had approved it and he had received "many commendations . . . and not a single objection to it, from any professed emancipationist." (The next day, Chase wrote to Lincoln saying he had in fact objected to the exclusion of blacks from voting but admitted he had not done so strongly, not wanting to appear "pertinacious.") Lincoln praised Louisiana's accomplishments—the abolition of slavery, public education for both races, and the fact that abolition had been immediate, without an apprenticeship program of the kind he himself had once favored. However, he continued, it was "unsatisfactory to some that the elective franchise is not given to the colored men." For the first time, Lincoln acknowledged that "the colored man . . . desires" the right to vote. He now repeated the sentiment of his private letter to Governor Hahn in 1864: "I would myself prefer that [the vote] were now conferred on the very intelligent, and on those who serve our cause as soldiers." This was a remarkable statement. No American president had publicly endorsed even limited black suffrage. At this time only six northern states allowed black men to vote.[8]

What became known as his "last speech" (a description that, while factually accurate, suggests a finality scarcely anticipated when it was delivered) was in many ways typical of Lincoln. He urged Republicans to think of Reconstruction as a practical problem rather than a philosophical one. The question of whether the South was "in or out of the Union," he said, was not only "practically immaterial" but downright "mischievous," since all agreed that the seceded states were "out of their proper practical relation" to it. He insisted that the Louisiana regime should be supported, but denied being wedded to any "inflexible plan" for the other states. Even regarding Louisiana, he noted that "bad promises are better broken than kept," suggesting that the process he had set in motion there might have to be modified or even abandoned. Lincoln closed by telling his audience to expect a "new announcement" regarding Reconstruction.

It was significant that Lincoln spoke of "reconstruction" and not "restoration," as he had frequently done in the past. These terms carried very different implications. "Reconstruction," one Democratic party leader observed around this time, "is synonymous with radicalism, restoration conservatism." But if Lincoln expected the speech to quiet criticism of his course, he was disappointed. Lincoln, Sumner wrote to Chase, "had said some things better than any body else could have said them. But I fear his policy now." Other Radicals were even more critical. It would be "wicked and blasphemous," one wrote, "for us as a nation to allow any distinction of color whatever in the reconstructed states." Even the moderate New York Times wondered what would prevent the southern states, if restored with their traditional rights intact, from abusing blacks? "The government cannot, without the worst dishonor, permit the bondage of the black man to be continued in any form," it insisted.[9]

8. CW, 399–405; Peyton McCrary, *Abraham Lincoln and Reconstruction: The Louisiana Experiment* (Princeton, 1978), 5–7; CP, 5: 17.
9. Jerome Mushkat, *The Reconstruction of the New York Democracy, 1861–1874* (Rutherford, N.J., 1981), 65; Beverly W. Palmer, *Selected Letters of Charles Sumner* (Boston, 1990), 2: 283–85; R. F, Fuller to Charles Sumner, April 13, 1865, Charles Sumner Papers, Houghton Library, Harvard University; *New York Times*, April 13, 1865.

Many observers concluded from the speech that Lincoln remained undecided about Reconstruction. "Mr. Lincoln gropes . . . like a traveler in an unknown country without a map," were the unkind words of the *New York World*. In fact, as a Washington reporter noted, most Republicans at this point had not yet "made up their minds" about Reconstruction. Even the *Chicago Tribune*, which favored black suffrage, acknowledged that under the Constitution, states had the right to set their own voting qualifications. One member of the audience, however, thought he understood exactly what Lincoln intended. "That means nigger citizenship," the actor John Wilkes Booth is said to have remarked. Booth and a group of pro-Confederate conspirators had been plotting to kidnap the president and demand the release of southern prisoners of war. "Now, by God," Booth supposedly muttered, "I'll put him through."[1]

When the cabinet assembled on April 14, Lincoln noted that he had "perhaps been too fast in his desires for early reconstruction." Before the meeting, he showed Attorney General James Speed a letter he had received from Chase urging the enfranchisement of all "loyal citizens" regardless of race when new state governments were formed. Speed thought Lincoln was moving toward the Radical position. "He [never] seemed so near our views," Speed told Chase the next day. Lincoln now appeared to believe that the immediate problem was the prospect of anarchy in the South. He had directed Secretary of War Stanton to draw up a plan for interim military rule. Stanton presented to the cabinet a proposal to appoint a temporary military government for Virginia and North Carolina. Since his plan put off the establishment of civilian rule, he "left open" the question of whether blacks should vote. But Stanton's proposal clearly implied that reliance on white Unionists might not be enough to establish loyal, stable governments. Little discussion ensued, and Lincoln urged his colleagues to devote their attention to "the great question now before us," on which "we must soon begin to act." Stanton was directed to redraft his proposal for consideration at the next cabinet meeting.[2]

That night, April 14, 1865, John Wilkes Booth mortally wounded Lincoln while he sat at Ford's Theatre. He was carried to a house across the street, where his life slowly ebbed away. Before dawn, Secretary of the Navy Welles left Lincoln's bedside and went outside. Already, mourners thronged the streets of Washington. "The colored people," Welles wrote, "and there were at this time more of them perhaps than of whites, were painfully affected." A little after seven in the morning, Lincoln died. His passing inspired an unprecedented outpouring of grief, and the first national funeral in the country's history. Millions of men, women, and children viewed Lincoln's casket as his remains made their way on a circuitous 1,700-mile journey from Washington to Springfield, with stops in more than 100 cities. It essentially retraced the route Lincoln had taken in February 1861 on the way to his inauguration. Reading the accounts of his funeral journey, one senses that Americans recognized that Lincoln's experience during the war mirrored their own. For, as his bitter critic the

1. *New York World*, April 13, 1865; *Independent*, April 13, 1865; *Chicago Tribune*, April 8 and 14, 1865; Burlingame, *Abraham Lincoln: A Life*, 2: 803.
2. CP, 1: 528–30; 5: 15–16; Benjamin P. Thomas and Harold M. Hyman, *Stanton: The Life and Times of Lincoln's Secretary of War* (New York, 1962), 357–58; WD, 2: 281.

New York World noted after his death, "some have changed more rapidly, some more slowly than he; but there are few of his countrymen, who have not changed at all." Yet change was hardly total. When Lincoln's body reached New York, the city council sought to prevent blacks from marching in the procession, only to be overruled by the War Department.[3]

Coupled with the achievements of piloting the United States through its greatest crisis and presiding over the emancipation of the slaves, the manner of his death ensured Lincoln's place in the pantheon of the most revered American leaders. That the assassination occurred on Good Friday heightened the conviction that Lincoln had sacrificed himself to redeem a sinful nation. At the time of his death and for years thereafter, Lincoln was remembered primarily as the Great Emancipator. Not until the turn of the century, when the process of (white) reconciliation was far advanced, would Americans forget or suppress the centrality of slavery and emancipation to the war experience. Lincoln would then be transformed into a symbol of national unity, and the Gettysburg Address, which did not explicitly mention slavery, would, in popular memory, supplant the Emancipation Proclamation as the greatest embodiment of his ideas. More recently, we have returned to the insight Lincoln offered in the second inaugural: slavery was the war's cause and emancipation its most profound outcome. To which may be added that these questions were central to Lincoln's own rise to greatness.[4]

＊　＊　＊

MANISHA SINHA

From Allies for Emancipation? Lincoln and Black Abolitionists[†]

Even more than emancipation, it was in regard to black rights and citizenship that Lincoln "grew" during the war. Abandoning his antebellum position that blacks were entitled to no more than natural rights, he came to contemplate political and civil rights for them. The failure of colonization as well as black military service pushed Lincoln to reevaluate his position on African American rights. Moreover, strong African American, abolitionist, and Radical Republican demands for equality influenced Lincoln's evolution on this issue. More than any other factor, it was the contributions of African American soldiers to Union victory that made Lincoln amenable to the idea of black citizenship.

Black abolitionists had advocated the recruitment of black soldiers at the very start of the war. The antebellum exclusion of African American men from the state militias was symptomatic of their exclusion from the duties and rights of republican citizenship. Black abolitionists such as

3. *War Department*, 2: 298; Michael Burlingame, *Abraham Lincoln: A Life* (Baltimore, 2008), 2: 819–25; *New York World*, April 17, 1865.
4. *Independent*, April 20, 1865; Gabor S. Boritt, *The Gettysburg Gospel: The Lincoln Speech That Nobody Knows* (New York: Simon & Schuster, 2006), 173–87; David W. Blight, *Race and Reunion: The Civil War in American Memory* (Cambridge, Mass., 2001).
† From *Our Lincoln: New Perspectives on Lincoln and His World*. Edited by Eric Foner. Copyright © 2008 by Manisha Sinha. Used by permission of W. W. Norton & Company, Inc.

William Cooper Nell had pointed in vain to black military service during
the Revolutionary War and the War of 1812 in their efforts to combat
racial discrimination. With the onset of the Civil War, black abolitionists
were quick to realize that military service would allow African Americans
not only to strike a blow against slavery but also to demand citizenship
rights. As Douglass put it, "Once let the black man get upon his person
the brass letters, U.S.; let him get an eagle on his button, and a musket
on his shoulder and bullets in his pocket, and there is no power on earth
which can deny that he has earned the right to citizenship in the United
States."[1] The administration's policy of excluding black men from military service was thus particularly upsetting to African American leaders.
But once Lincoln decided to emancipate the slaves, his view of black
military service also changed. The exigencies of the war and the shortage
of manpower as the conflict dragged on led the Lincoln administration
and Congress to recruit African Americans, including slaves, and grant
freedom to those who served and their families.

The enlistment of black men, supported and led by abolitionists, raised
the question of racial equality. The all-black Fifty-fourth Massachusetts
was quickly recruited under the auspices of the abolitionist Governor
John Andrew. The wealthy manufacturer and abolitionist George L.
Stearns, a staunch advocate of black military service, hired prominent
black abolitionists such as Douglass, William Wells Brown, Charles
Lenox Remond, John Mercer Langston, Henry Highland Garnet, and
Martin Delany as recruiting agents. By the end of the war, about two hundred thousand African Americans had served in the Union army and navy.
Despite initial inequalities in pay and rank, black abolitionists supported
recruitment of black soldiers but demanded equal rights, including the
equalization of pay scales. In his broadside, "Men of Color, To Arms!"
Douglass argued that "action," rather than "criticism, is the plain duty of
the hour." But he added that he could not recruit more black men "with all
my heart" as long as inequalities persisted.[2]

Protests over racial inequalities in the Union army prepared African
Americans and abolitionists for the long fight for equality and citizenship
rights. Rock noted, "[T]he colored soldier has the destiny of the colored
race in his hands." The protest that inequality in pay sparked among African American soldiers was evident in the outpouring of letters they sent to
the *Christian Recorder*, a newspaper that was distributed widely among
black regiments during the Civil War. The editors reported that they were
"continually getting letters from our noble and brave colored soldiers" over
this issue. Black soldiers were paid ten dollars a month, from which three
dollars were deducted for their uniforms, while white soldiers were paid
thirteen dollars a month with an additional allowance of three dollars for
their uniforms. In protest, some black regiments refused their pay, caus-

1. James M. McPherson, *The Negro's Civil War: How American Negroes Felt and Acted During the War for the Union* (New York, 1955), 33; William C. Nell, *The Colored Patriots of the American Revolution, with Sketches of Several Distinguished Colored Persons: To Which Is Added a Brief Survey of the Condition and Prospects of Colored Americans* (Boston, 1855); Douglass is quoted by James M. McPherson, *Struggle for Equality: Abolitionists and the Negro in the Civil War and Reconstruction* (Princeton, NJ, 1964), 192.
2. *Freedom: A Documentary History of Emancipation 1861–1867 Series II The Black Military Experience*, edited by Ira Berlin et al. (New York, 1982); McPherson, *Struggle for Equality*, 204–07.

ing considerable hardship to themselves and their families. As one black soldier writing under the pseudonym Wolverine wrote, "It is not the money . . . that we are looking at! It is the principle; that one that made us men when we enlisted." Daniel Walker of the famous Fifty-fourth Massachusetts proudly asserted, "We have fulfilled all our agreements to the Government, and have done our duty wherever we have been, but thus far the government fails to fulfill their part of the contract, by not paying us." Black men should now be treated as equal citizens and soldiers, they argued.[3]

The federal government soon got wind of the storm brewing over inequality in pay. James Henry Gooding of the Fifty-fourth Massachusetts sent a letter to Lincoln asking for a soldier's pay for performing a soldier's duty. Black soldiers, the letter reminded the president, were poor, and their families could ill afford doing without their salaries. Seventy-four soldiers from the Fifty-fifth Massachusetts signed a letter to Lincoln warning of more "stringent measures" if their demands were not heeded. When asked to intervene, Lincoln felt that he could not act "upon grounds of moral right without regard to his Constitutional powers." Congress, where Sumner and his fellow senator from Massachusetts, Henry Wilson, led the fight for equal pay, passed an act equalizing pay scales retroactively from January 1, 1864, and to all those who had been free in April 1861 from the time of their recruitment. Abolitionist officers of black regiments soon got around the law by devising oaths for soldiers claiming that they had owed no man their labor since the time of their recruitment. Thomas Wentworth Higginson led a crusade for equal pay, deluging northern newspapers and politicians with letters until Congress passed a law in March 1865 granting retroactive pay to all black regiments from the time of their enrollment.[4]

Initially, African Americans were also barred from officer ranks. Douglass's desire for an officer's commission in the Union army came to naught. Ethio, for instance, asked for colored "chaplains, officers, sutlers, matrons, nurses, teachers, recruiters, contractors, traders, surgeons" and argued that blacks should not be confined to serving only as soldiers in the Union army. "All that we ask is to give us a chance, and a position higher than an orderly sergeant," wrote John H. W. N. Collins, a black orderly sergeant. In the last two years of the war, however, not only were pay scales equalized, but African Americans were also commissioned as officers. The most famous instance was the black abolitionist leader Martin Delany, commissioned as a major in the Union army. Another black abolitionist and Lincoln critic, H. Ford Douglas, received an officer's stripes. And Henry McNeal Turner, along with several dozen other African Americans, served as chaplains in the Union army. By the end of the war around a hundred African Americans had served as officers. A majority

---

3. "John S. Rock to the Soldiers of the Fifth United States Colored Heavy Artillery Regiment 30 May 1864," *The Black Abolitionist Papers*, edited by C. Peter Ripley et al. (Chapel Hill, NC, 1992), 5: 274; *Christian Recorder* (Jan. 2, 30, 1864); McPherson, *Negro's Civil War*, ch. 14.

4. *Freedom Series II The Black Military Experience*, Berlin, 362–68, 385–86, 401–2; Lincoln is quoted by Benjamin Quarles, *Lincoln and the Negro* (New York, 1962), 169–72; *Christian Recorder* (Aug. 20, 1864); McPherson, *Struggle for Equality*, 216–20; Thomas Wentworth Higginson, *Army Life in a Black Regiment and Other Writings*, with an Introduction and Notes by R. D. Madison (New York, 1997), Appendix D, *The Struggle for Pay*, 217–27.

of them however were with the Louisiana Native Guards, a militia composed of the state's free "gentlemen of color" that predated the war.[5]

Douglass's first meeting with Lincoln was about the issues of pay and
officer rank for African Americans as well as Confederate atrocities against
black Union soldiers. The president assured Douglass that he would sign
any commission for a black officer recommended by the secretary of war.
Lincoln would also issue a retaliatory order against the Confederate policy
of enslaving and killing black Union army soldiers, despite his misgivings
about punishing the innocent for the crimes of others and letting the war
descend into a brutal bloodletting on all sides. While the Lincoln administration did not retaliate for the Fort Pillow massacre of black Union troops,
it did suspend the exchange of prisoners with the enemy because of the
Confederacy's refusal to exchange black Union prisoners of war. For the
most part, Lincoln had decided that "having determined to use the Negro
as a soldier, there is no way but to give him all the protection given to any
other soldier."[6]

Black heroism at the battles of Fort Wagner, Milliken's Bend, and Port
Hudson impressed both the president and the northern public at large.
"T.S.W." of the First United States Colored Troops (USCT), wished "to
know, whether, after doing such daring exploits, we do not deserve the
rights and privileges of the United States of America." Lincoln, like his
military commanders, came to believe that "the emancipation policy, and
the use of colored troops, constitute the heaviest blow to the rebellion;
and that at least one of these important successes could not have been
achieved when it was, but for the aid of black soldiers." Indeed Lincoln
adopted nearly all the abolitionist arguments on the value and significance of black military service. When peace arrives, he wrote, "there will
be some black men who can remember that, with silent tongue, and
clenched teeth, and steady eye, and well-poised bayonet, they have helped
mankind onto this great consummation; while, I fear, there will be some
white ones, unable to forget that, with malignant heart, and deceitful
speech, they have strove to hinder it." Black Union army soldiers returned
the compliment. At its Christmas celebration in 1863, the Seventh Regiment of the Corps d'Afrique passed a resolution: "We cannot express in
words our love for the President of the United States, as language is too
weak to convey the estimation in which we hold him."[7] Not surprisingly,
black Union army veterans were the largest contributors to the Freedmen's Monument to Lincoln.

Lincoln soon came to sympathize with the idea that one could not deny
citizenship rights to black soldiers who had fought on behalf of the Union.
According to the precepts of republicanism, in which Lincoln, abolitionists, and the soldiers themselves were well versed, one deserved the rights
of citizenship after performing the duties of citizenship. In fact Lincoln
had suggested as early as the 1830s that even women, if they paid taxes or

5. *Christian Recorder* (Jan. 9, June 25, 1864); *Freedom Series II: The Black Military Experience*,
   Berlin, 302–12.
6. *Frederick Douglass Papers, Series 1, Speeches, Debates, and Interviews*, edited by John W. Blassingame (New Haven, 1995), 3: 607; *Christian Recorder* (Jan. 9, Apr. 30, 1864); McPherson,
   Negro's Civil War, ch. 5; Quarles, *Lincoln and the Negro*, 168 (Lincoln is quoted on 177–78).
7. *Christian Recorder* (Aug. 20, 1864); CW 6: 409–10; Quarles, *Lincoln and the Negro*, 182.

bore arms in defense of their country, should be given the right to vote. (While later suffragists used this remark to portray Lincoln as a champion of female suffrage, he was never involved in the women's rights movement, unlike black abolitionists such as Douglass.) The national black convention in Syracuse in October 1864, presided over by leading abolitionists like Douglass, Wells Brown, George T. Downing, Garnet, and John Mercer Langston, issued an "Address of the Colored National Convention to the People of the United States," demanding suffrage. It read in part, "Are we good enough to use bullets, and not good enough to use ballots? May we defend rights in time of war, and yet be denied the exercise of those rights in time of peace? Are we citizens when the nation is in peril, and aliens when the nation is in safety? May we shed our blood under the star spangled banner on the battlefield, and yet be debarred from marching under it at the ballot box?"[8]

Black soldiers themselves made the case for citizenship best. J. H. Hall of the Fifty-fourth Massachusetts asked why blacks were "not recognized as true and lawful citizens" after having "performed our duty as soldiers, and maintained our dignity and honour as citizens." As they had fought to "maintain a Republican government," he wrote, "we want Republican privileges." Hall concluded, "All we ask is the proper enjoyment of the rights of citizenship, and a free title and acknowledged share in our own noble birthplace, which we are ready and willing to defend while a single drop of blood courses through our veins." And R. M. Smith of the Third USCT reminded white Americans that "the black man has proved himself a patriot, a hero, and a man of courage. He is preparing by education, to be a true and worthy citizen of the United States." Thomas Webster of the Forty-third USCT thought that since black soldiers were "fighting as hard to restore the Union as the white man is," they should at least have "equal rights with a foreigner."[9]

The demands and protests of abolitionists and radicals also caused Lincoln to begin to come to terms with black suffrage. Throughout the war black and white abolitionists continued to fight for equality and against discrimination in the North. Over Garrison's opposition, the American Anti-Slavery Society under the leadership of Douglass and Phillips voted to continue the fight for equal rights in 1865. Douglass demanded "the most perfect civil and political equality," that black men should "enjoy all the rights, privileges and immunities enjoyed by any other members of the body politic." Abolitionists' work, he said, would not be done until "the colored man is admitted in good and regular standing into the American body politic." In a resolution written by Phillips, the Massachusetts Anti-Slavery Society declared that the black man had "an equal share with the white race in the management of the political institutions for which he is required to fight and bleed, and to which he is clearly entitled by every consideration of justice and democratic equality."

8. CW 1: 48; "Proceedings of the National Convention of Colored Men, Held in the City of Syracuse, NY, Oct. 4, 5, 6, and 7, 1864; With the Bill of Wrongs and Rights, and the Address to the American People" (Boston, 1864), in Howard Holman Bell, ed., *Minutes of the Proceedings of the National Negro Conventions 1830–1864* (New York, 1969), 58.
9. *Christian Recorder* (Aug. 27, Oct. 8, 1864, Jan. 7, 1865).

Abolitionist and black demands helped make African American citizenship a cornerstone of Radical Reconstruction.[1]

Lincoln came under increasing fire from African Americans, abolitionists, and Radical Republicans for not making black suffrage a precondition for the reconstruction of southern states. For Phillips, African American voters would form the foundation of a regenerated South. Sumner spent long hours with the president trying to convince him to act on black suffrage. These criticisms and conversations may have influenced Lincoln as black demands for the vote also made their way to the White House. As early as November 1863 New Orleans's politically active free blacks asked the military governor for the right to vote. In February 1864 they received an emissary from the Lincoln administration who asked that they inform the president of their demands. They replied that they wanted schools, the ballot, and equality before the law and expressed their "unbounded and heartfelt thanks to the President of the United States." By April they had drawn up a petition with a thousand signatures asking for the right to vote because they were free, owned property, and had served in the War of 1812 and in the Union army. Lincoln received their two representatives, Jean Baptiste Roudanez and Arnold Bertonneau, but is reported to have said, "I regret, gentlemen, that you are not able to secure all your rights and that circumstances will not permit the government to confer them upon you." The two delegates were feted by abolitionists in Boston, including Garrison and Douglass, and their visit must have made some impression on the president. Soon after, Lincoln penned his famous letter to Louisiana's governor, Michael Hahn, suggesting that "the very intelligent, and especially those who have fought gallantly in our ranks" be given the franchise. It would help, "in some trying time to come, to keep the jewel of liberty within the family of freedom." By this point he had enough interactions with black abolitionists to realize that African Americans did boast a "very intelligent," learned, and politically active leadership. A month later Lincoln received a delegation of black North Carolinians who asked him to "[g]rant unto your petitioners that greatest of privileges, when the State is reconstructed, to exercise the right of suffrage." According to the *Anglo-African*, he assured them "of his sympathy and earnest cooperation."[2]

Lincoln's wartime reconstruction plans were geared to end the war speedily and successfully. His 1863 Proclamation of Amnesty and Reconstruction called for the reunion of rebel states if at least 10 percent of the population swore loyalty to the government and accepted abolition. It did not include black suffrage, which Lincoln left to the discretion of the military-led state governments. Even radicals in Congress who proposed their own plan for reconstruction in the Wade-Davis bill of 1864 did not include black suffrage in their plans at this stage, though they granted African Americans specific legal protections and civil equality. In the year before his death Lincoln came to acknowledge that at least some black

1. Blassingame and McKivigan, eds., *Frederick Douglass Papers*, 4: 60–69; Blassingame, ed., *Frederick Douglass Papers*, 3: 572, 604; McPherson, *Struggle for Equality*, Douglass is quoted on 240, Phillips on 247, 287–307; *Christian Recorder* (May 21, 1864); Eric Foner, *Reconstruction: America's Unfinished Revolution, 1863–1877* (New York, 1989).
2. Quarles, *Lincoln and the Negro*, 226–30; CW 7: 243; McPherson, *Struggle for Equality*, 240–46.

Americans were entitled to the right to vote. He was assassinated before he could incorporate these beliefs in any permanent plan for reconstruction. In his last public speech, justifying his plans for the reconstruction of Louisiana under his 10 percent plan, Lincoln said he would "prefer" if suffrage was conferred on the "very intelligent" and "those who serve our cause as soldiers." The state's constitution, he argued, opened the public school system for blacks and whites and empowered the legislature "to confer the elective franchise on the colored man." He stated the same ideas informally from the balcony of the White House to a crowd gathered below on the eve of his assassination. In the audience was his assassin, John Wilkes Booth, the proslavery Confederate sympathizer and actor, who pledged to kill him for his championship of "nigger citizenship. That is the last speech he will ever make."[3]

African Americans mourned the death of the president as a genuine loss to the cause of black freedom and equality. For Douglass, Lincoln's death was "a personal as well as a national calamity; on account of the race to which I belong and the deep interest which that good man ever took in its elevation." The *Christian Recorder* noted: "Humanity has lost a friend, and the colored man one not easily replaced." Similarly, in an editorial for the *New Orleans Black Republican*, S. W. Rogers wrote, "The greatest earthly friend of the colored race has fallen by the same spirit that has so long oppressed and destroyed us. In giving us our liberty, he has lost his own life. Following the rule of the great and glorious in the world, he has paid the penalty of Apostleship. He has sealed with blood his Divine commission to be the liberator of a people." More than any other group, African Americans played a major role in anointing Lincoln with martyrdom for their cause. A freedmen's meeting on Hilton Head Island, South Carolina, resolved that in his "proclaiming *Liberty* to our race," Lincoln's career was crowned by "a blessed immortality, sealed by his blood, and embalmed him in the memory of future generations." Martin Delany, the father of black nationalism, mourned the death of "the humane, the benevolent, the philanthropic, the generous, the beloved, the able, the wise, great and good man, the President of the United States, ABRAHAM LINCOLN, the just." He recommended that "every individual of our race" contribute one penny each to build a monument to Lincoln as "a tribute from the black race."[4]

By the time of his death Lincoln's views on slavery and racial equality had evolved significantly, and black abolitionists had played no small part in pushing him along this path. If some men are born great, some acquire greatness, and others have greatness thrust upon them, Lincoln surely belonged to the second category. In his speech at the unveiling of the Freedmen's Monument, Douglass gave the best assessment of Lincoln's role as a bridge between abolitionism and public opinion, a corrective to the version of emancipation represented by the monument. "Viewed from genuine abolition ground, Mr. Lincoln seemed tardy, cold, dull, and indifferent;

3. CW 7: 53–56; 8: 403; LaWanda Cox, *Lincoln and Black Freedom: A Study in Presidential Leadership* (Columbia, MO, 1981); Herman Belz, *A New Birth of Freedom: The Republican Party and Freedmen's Rights, 1861–1866* (New York, 2000); David Donald, *Lincoln Reconsidered: Essays on the Civil War Era* (New York, 1961), 588.
4. *Frederick Douglass Papers, vol. 4* Blassingame et al., 4: 76; *Christian Recorder* (Apr. 22, May 20, 1865); "Editorial by W. W. Rogers, 22 April 1865," *Black Abolitionist Papers*, Ripley, 5: 315–16; McPherson, *Negro's Civil War*, 308.

but measuring him by the sentiment of his country, a sentiment he was bound as a statesman to consult, he was swift, zealous, radical and determined." Lincoln, Douglass pointed out, was preeminently "the white man's President." But "while Abraham Lincoln saved for you a country, he delivered us from bondage," he told his audience, and "in doing honor to the memory of our friend and liberator, we have been doing the highest honor to ourselves and those who come after us." For Douglass, Lincoln, as the author of the Emancipation Proclamation, was not just an ally for emancipation but at "the head of a great movement, and was in living and earnest sympathy with that movement."[5]

Abolitionists, especially black abolitionists, had played a crucial role in the coming of emancipation and in challenging Lincoln to abandon colonization and accept black rights. Their ideas on interracial democracy and equal citizenship, largely forgotten in the history of emancipation, forced both the president and the nation at large to accept the consequences of abolition and helped set the agenda for reconstruction. The radical egalitarianism of black and white abolitionists pushed Lincoln and the Republican Party, initially committed to only the nonextension of slavery, to adopt the twin abolitionist goals of immediate, uncompensated emancipation and black rights. Precisely because Lincoln had come around to these ideas during the war, his historical legacy would be inextricably bound with their struggle for freedom and the movement to abolish slavery. But it had been the pioneering efforts and ideas of black abolitionists crystallized in the broader interracial abolition movement that had helped initiate and shape the process of emancipation and introduced the idea of an interracial democracy under the presidency of Abraham Lincoln.

ROBERT A. FERGUSON

Lincoln and the Lawyer's Eloquence†

Half of the presidents of the United States have been lawyers. If Abraham Lincoln presents a special case among them as a speaker, it is because he spent more time in courtrooms than any of the others and honed his professional skills when oratorical delivery before a jury was the crucial ingredient of a successful practice.[1] Lincoln wrote himself about how important it was for a lawyer to learn to give a good speech, and he handled more than 5,000 cases across a legal career of 24 years, appearing before the Illinois Supreme Court some 333 times.[2] Steeped in courtroom advocacy, he adopted similar patterns of address in the White House—a point over-

---

5. *Frederick Douglass Papers*, Blassingame et al., 4: 431–36.

† This article is a condensed and slightly revised version of Ferguson's "Hearing Lincoln and the Making of Eloquence," *American Literary History* 21.4 (2009): 687–724. Copyright © 2009 by Oxford University Press. Reprinted with permission of Oxford University Press.

1. For Lincoln's adeptness and imagination before juries, see Brian Dirck, *Lincoln the Lawyer* (Urbana, 2007) 99–105.

2. Lincoln wrote that "extemporaneous speaking should be practiced and cultivated. . . . However able and faithful he may be in other respects, people are slow to bring him business if he cannot make a speech." CW 2: 81. For the statistics in Lincoln's legal career see Frank J. Williams, "Chapter 3: Abraham Lincoln: Commander in Chief or 'Attorney in Chief'?" *Judging Lincoln* (Carbondale and Edwardsville, 2002), 39. I rely on Williams's compilation from the Lincoln Legal Papers Project, Illinois State Historical Library in Springfield.

shadowed by his more obvious gift for language and the ability it gave him to refashion the presidential genres in which he spoke and wrote.[3]

The list of possibilities for analysis is long. Horace Greeley called "The First Inaugural" "worthy the charge of a Chief Justice to a jury, and containing more sound law than is often found in charges twenty times its length."[4] The first message to Congress on July 4, 1861, offers one of the best legal justifications of union ever written: "that form and substance of government, whose leading object is, to elevate the condition of men—to lift artificial weights from all shoulders—to clear the paths of laudable pursuit for all—to afford all, an unfettered start, and a fair chance, in the race of life."[5] "The Second Annual Message" of December 1, 1862, famously wrote out the country's legal obligation: "We shall nobly save, or meanly lose, the last best, hope of earth" (5:537).[6]

Reaching further, the Emancipation Proclamation of January 1, 1863 is most literally the work of a legal mind. Lincoln worried about his official right to emancipate against specific language supporting slavery in the Constitution, and the Proclamation is especially legalistic in consequence. Only the 13th amendment, in Lincoln's view, made emancipation "a King's cure for all the evils" (8:254).

But however rich each of these possibilities are in legal lore, the truest defense of the speaking lawyer in President Lincoln should rest on his most memorable words, and the subject of eloquence automatically privileges two late efforts. No two speeches in American history have been more frequently or closely interpreted than "The Gettysburg Address" on November 19, 1863, and "Second Inaugural" on March 4, 1865. Whole books have been written about the 271 words in the first speech and the 701 words in the second.[7]

The words themselves have been so widely accepted as the most expressive the nation has produced that all efforts to explain the studied intellectual dimensions in Lincoln's prose fall short. Nineteenth-century speeches tended to last several hours, and we have lost sight of the established forms of anticipation in oral performance on which they depended for reception. Lincoln never forgot these forms, even in his shortest and most concise efforts.

The myth of casual drafting by Lincoln, particularly over "The Gettysburg Address," has been completely exposed in recent scholarship. Everything Lincoln officially delivered as President was thoroughly, even minutely organized and crafted. Structure and rigor are crucial to Lincoln's style, and the oft-noted brevity of his "Address Delivered at the

---

3. Lincoln, among other things, is the first president to use heavy biblical imagery in his speeches and epistolary exchange in the newspapers in his own name.
4. Horace Greeley, *New York Tribune* (March 6, 1861), quoted in full in *Abraham Lincoln, A Press Portrait*, edited by Herbert Mitgang (Chicago, 1971), 238–39.
5. CW 4: 438. Lincoln's own words will be given parenthetically in the text from this definitive edition of his works.
6. The continuing gravity of Lincoln's fear that all might be lost in the fight for the Union is most graphically evident in the blind memorandum that he asked all cabinet members to sign on August 23, 1864, in which he bound them to continue working "to save the Union" if he failed of re-election in November. CW 7: 514. See, as well, Doris Kearns Goodwin, *Team of Rivals: The Political Genius of Abraham Lincoln* (New York, 2005), 648–49.
7. For good examples, see Garry Wills, *Lincoln at Gettysburg: The Words That Remade America* (New York, 1992), and Ronald C. White, Jr., *Lincoln's Greatest Speech: The Second Inaugural* (New York, 2002).

Dedication of the Cemetery at Gettysburg" gives perhaps the clearest view of these virtues.

Lincoln always spoke slowly. Even so, it took him less than three minutes to deliver his speech. Others have written of Lincoln's studied march through time sequences from the past (in the first paragraph), to the present (in the second paragraph), to the future (in the third), in "The Gettysburg Address" but no one has noticed how closely this projection follows the natural bent of courtroom oratory, where the task is to explain first what happened, then what it means in court, and finally, what should be done about it in the future through punishment, reward, or rectification.[8]

In another analogy to legal argument, the Address presents a dispute that must be dealt with through right proceeding, and the movement toward right proceeding is triggered, as in legal argument, through the interrogative mode. The primal or burning question raised at the outside is a close one in 1863. "Can" the nation "long endure" or will the horrors of civil war overwhelm it? Lincoln then adds a related one that applies more directly to his audience. Will those who fought at Gettysburg "have died in vain"? If so, if the Union is not to be saved, the responsibility for disaster becomes direct. The living who have not saved the Union will have committed a crime of omission against "these honored dead."

Lincoln obliquely recognizes an intolerable alternative in dedicating the cemetery of the war dead: the possibility of meaningless slaughter. He resists that prospect by tying the living to the dead through concepts of dedication and by insisting, through that exercise, that "this nation . . . shall not perish from the earth." The rhetorical shift from *testing* whether the nation "can long endure" to *resolving* that it "shall not perish" relies on the lawyer's oratorical device of redefining a key term through related iterations.

The speaker's first five uses of the word "dedication" move temporally from the original dedication of the country by the fathers of it, to continued dedication by intervening generations, to the dedication of those who fought at Gettysburg that the "nation might live," to the problem of dedication in the moment, to actual dedication at the battlefield. Lincoln uses the continuum to create a sequent progression.

His words then move inexorably toward a sixth and higher level of dedication to come, and the new level will be that "of the people" dedicated to "a new birth of freedom" for all Americans and not just, as it has been in the past, for some Americans. This new prospect of "increased devotion" is held in place through allegiance to the "honored dead" who "gave the last full measure of devotion." The six uses also march in pairs: from dedication to principle ("conceived and so dedicated), to dedication to the dead, to dedication to the unfinished work of the dead again in confirmation of the temporal progression of the whole address.

Scholars rightly suggest that these words work through Lincoln's ability to remove himself from the page while retaining the sincerity of voice

---

8. For insistence that Lincoln "built the Gettysburg Address upon a structure of past, present, and future time," see Ronald C. White, Jr., *The Eloquent President: A Portrait of Lincoln Through Words* (New York, 2005), 243.

and the embodiment of principle required.[9] Not coincidentally, the same tactic applies to courtroom advocacy. Every manual on the subject reminds lawyers that they are not the subject or even the object of debate, and the fact that Lincoln frequently adopted strategies of self-effacement in legal practice is a matter of record.[1] At Gettysburg, he followed suit. He kept his client, in this case the United States of America, as the focus of concern and resisted efforts to extract a more personal speech during his two days in and around the battlefield.

Many aspects of Lincoln's gift for language in the address, all found in the earlier lawyer, have been described: the measured tones, the biblical phraseology, the sixty-one repetitions, the parataxis of balanced terms, the grammatical inversions, the use of antithesis, the assignation of a turning point through self correction, the short sentences balanced against a long one, the frame of simple language (four of every five words are ones of one syllable) juxtaposed against a technical term like "proposition," and finally, the comprehensiveness that included both sides in the conflict without speaking down to either.[2] Despite the colossal bloodletting at Gettysburg, there are no enemies in Lincoln's speech. His use of "they" refers to "these honored dead" without differentiation.

There is, however, a driving argument beyond commemoration in Lincoln's speech. "The Gettysburg Address" is a meditation about how things have gone wrong for *all* parties, leading, in turn, to a closing directive that *all* must somehow answer that wrong. As in legal discourse, Lincoln's words move toward a solution, and his jury this time is the nation. Pronominal forms in the first-person plural, the emblem of national cohesion, steer this solution by incorporating every available listener. Expansive uses of "we," "our," and "us" receive constant reiteration—fifteen times in the three short paragraphs offered. Lincoln grasps, as theorists would later argue, that "the crucial question relating to national identity is how the national 'we' is constructed and what is meant by that construction."[3]

The move toward open-ended inclusiveness would have been natural as well as good policy. Courtroom orators in the nineteenth century reached for scope across concentric audiences from judge, to jury, to spectators, and on to the community at large. Lincoln speaks at Gettysburg but really beyond it. Notice, for example, that he never uses the name in the actual address. "Gettysburg," four months after the bloodiest battle of the war, stood for unexampled butchery. In just three days at the beginning of July in 1863, 50,000 men out of 170,000 engaged were lost in one way or another. Lincoln answers by turning to all Americans, North *and* South,

9. See Edwin Black, "The Ultimate Voice of Lincoln," *Rhetoric & Public Affairs* 3 (Spring 2000): 49 ff. "The 'single most important instance of rhetorical leadership by Lincoln during his presidency' was his disappearance . . . in the place of his vanished ego, he proposed a set of principles of which he became the personification."

1. Lincoln's parallel legal focus on clients over his own personal interests and personality in court is shown clearly in his penchant to settle cases wherever possible. CW 2:81. See, as well, Dirck, *Lincoln the Lawyer*, 67, 158, 160–61.

2. For perhaps the most thorough inventory of devices, see Wills, *Lincoln at Gettysburg*, 148–75, but see, as well, Michael Leff and Jean Goodwin, "Dialogic Figures and Dialectical Argument in Lincoln's Rhetoric," *Rhetoric & Public Affairs* 3 (Spring 2000): 59–69. Notably, each of these devices can also be found in the sections on "Rhetorick" and "Style" in Samuel Kirkham, *English Grammar in Familiar Lectures* (Rochester, NY, 1832), 219–20 ff., a work that Lincoln studied with great care while becoming a lawyer.

3. Michael Billig, "Imagining 'Us' as the National Community," *Banal Nationalism* (London, 1995), 70–73.

in the possibility of "a new birth," after so much death, out of the original birth in which all retain ideological stock. From the first sentence, every American is summoned through the figuratively mutual category of "our fathers," the forebears who "brought forth on this continent, a new nation" in which all continue to share.

Yet for all of its inclusiveness, "The Gettysburg Address" is not without distinguishing bite—a bite controlled by traditional structure in presentation. As innovative as the address appears, it relies on conventional notions of delivery to ease reception of a new idea. That new idea turns on the Declaration of Independence, which can no longer be said to favor slavery while also claiming that "all men are created equal." Lincoln at Gettysburg turns the Declaration into the fundamental document of foundation in order to correct the Constitution on slavery without overthrowing it.[4]

Lincoln himself had already privileged the Declaration in 1859 by declaring "all honor to Jefferson—to the man who, in the concrete pressure of a struggle for national independence of a single people, had the coolness, forecast, and capacity to introduce into a merely revolutionary document, an abstract truth, applicable to all men and all times, and so to embalm it there, that to-day, and in all coming days, it shall be a rebuke and a stumbling block to the very harbingers of re-appearing tyranny and oppression" (3:376).

These are the words of an accomplished wordsmith whose use and meaning of words reveal his own inclination and ability to transform a central document by filtering coolness, forecast, and capacity through the power to be found in abstract truth. The forgotten intricacy of Lincoln's effort at Gettysburg is all about the capacity to change thought through the way form, arrangement, and thematic projection point toward a better future.

The forgotten refinement of "The Gettysburg Address" is crucial in convincing nineteenth-century Americans of an idea that they would not have granted in cruder form. Although self-taught, Lincoln studied the form and use of language intensely, memorizing long sections of manuals on grammar and elocution as well as speeches of all kinds. Perhaps by instinct but also by long practice, he gave his words at Gettysburg the classical arrangement of oratory followed in Lincoln's time and popularized by copy after copy of Hugh Blair's *Lectures on Rhetoric and Belles Lettres* (1784).[5]

The six standard requirements of correct rhetorical arrangement guide Lincoln's thoughts to a receptive reader. They are, in order, *exordium* (catching the audience's attention), *narration* (setting forth the facts), *division* (distinguishing points stipulated from points to be contested),

4. Wills, *Lincoln at Gettysburg*, 100–101, 146–47.
5. Lincoln knew aspects of Samuel Kirkham's *English Grammar* (New York, 1832) and William Scott's *Lessons in Elocution; Or, a Selection of Pieces in Prose and Verse for the Improvement of Youth in Reading and Speaking* (Baltimore, 1806) by heart. See White, Jr., *The Eloquent President*, 103–04, and David Herbert Donald, *Lincoln* (New York, 1995), 48–49. See, as well, Wills, *Lincoln at Gettysburg*, 160–67. "Lincoln may have known [Hugh] Blair directly; he certainly knew his principles from derivative texts." The six parts that were said to compose "a regular formal oration" and that Lincoln employs are found in Hugh Blair, "Lecture 31," *Lectures on Rhetoric and Belles Lettres* (1783; Brooklyn, 1807) 2: 86–87. For Blair's profound impact on nineteenth-century American oratory, see *A History and Criticism of American Public Address*, edited by William Norwood Brigance (New York, 1943) 1: 21, 202–04, 330, 333, 485. The *Lectures* were particularly favored by nineteenth-century lawyers accustomed to long and colorful jury summations.

proof (supporting the case), *refutation* (confuting opposing arguments), and *peroration* (a summation that stirs the audience). As brief as it is, "The Gettysburg Address" follows the pattern in an era attuned to these rhythms in oratorical performance. Some contemporaries recognized as much by calling it "a model speech."[6]

Lincoln's *exordium*, the high-sounding opening sentence, gives us "a new nation, conceived in Liberty, and dedicated to the proposition that all men are created equal." The timing, "four score and seven years ago," reaches to the Declaration of Independence as the formative document rather than the Constitution as its primary guide, and in doing so, it legally demolishes the premise of secession by positing a *single* nation tied to the proposition of equality instead of a collection of separate states sharing limited powers and understandings. Lincoln underlines the point by setting this opening sentence off. It has its own paragraph. Patriotic phraseology—"our fathers brought forth on this continent"—diffuses protest over the deeper meaning.[7]

The *narration*, or statement of facts, is similarly brief, consuming the short second paragraph. Lincoln identifies the Civil War, the gathered meeting on a battlefield of that war, the reason for being there, the act of commemoration, and the propriety in doing so. Welded to these facts is the higher drama of another fact. Endangered by civil war, the Union is in a struggle for survival, "conceived," as it is, "in Liberty." A good lawyer uses the facts for more than context, and Lincoln doesn't miss the opportunity. Here, the "altogether fitting and proper" act of commemoration confirms the decorum of the occasion and echoes legal and constitutional import by deciding what can and cannot be done, while insisting that the struggle be continued so "that nation might live."[8]

Division follows immediately in the opening of the long third paragraph. Despite what has been just said, the gathering *cannot* dedicate, consecrate, or hallow ground already more profoundly consecrated by "the brave men, living and dead" who furthered the struggle for their country. Implicitly, the ceremonial gathering becomes a redundancy at this moment in Lincoln's argument, and the *division* becomes serious when he adds "the world will little note, nor long remember what we say here."

Proof, riding quickly to the rescue, answers this potential frustration by demonstrating that the living *do* have vital tasks to perform both here and elsewhere. On the present battlefield, the living must "highly resolve" that "these dead shall not have died in vain." Once resolved, they must prove their resolution on other battlefields in dedication to "the unfinished work" and "the great task remaining before us." Only the living can

---

6. The *Springfield Republican* came close to a realization of the structure of the address in its report of the event at Gettysburg when it observed, "Turn back and read it over, it will repay study as a model speech. Strong feelings and a large brain were its parents—a little painstaking its accoucher." Quoted in Earl Wellington Wiley, *Abraham Lincoln: Portrait of a Speaker* (New York, 1979), 538–39.

7. The bold reworking of the date of national formation did not go unchallenged at the time. The *Illinois State Register*, among others, in quoting the first sentence of the address announced, "Lincoln began his dedicatory address by the enumeration of the following political falsehood." See Wiley, *Abraham Lincoln: Portrait of a Speaker*, 537.

8. For the most obvious example of parallel legal language, look to the "necessary and proper" clause of the Federal Constitution [Article 1, Section 8, Number 18]. In legal argument, the phrase is often used to trigger what the speaker will do or not do in procedural terms. In this case, and again in "The Second Inaugural," Lincoln uses the device to show what *cannot* be done.

prove the validity of the founding fathers' original, but now challenged, "proposition," where "proposition" refers to Euclid's technical requirement of something in need of proof.[9] The living have not only a duty but an opportunity and a benefit when they guarantee that their still surviving nation, "so conceived and so dedicated," will endure.

In a subtle linguistic stroke, Lincoln allows a faint aura of *refutation* to hover over his last two sentences in the third paragraph; the device works through reiteration of the word "rather." "It is for us the living, *rather*, to be dedicated here to the unfinished work," and in a slight inversion," it is *rather* for us to be here dedicated to the great task remaining before us." The setting off of the first use with commas is quietly smoothed away in the second, which leads into the final long sentence of Lincoln's peroration, "that government of the people, by the people, for the people, shall not perish from the earth."

These last words are so moving and so memorable because they give the solution needed in celebrated affirmation. They give final assurance against the naked fear expressed earlier that the nation might not "long endure." The *narration* in the second paragraph of "The Gettysburg Address" could only state the danger in the dark days of 1863. Lincoln's *peroration* responds by reaching beyond time and overcoming all fear in the rolling reiteration of a *continuing* people's government. Not for the last time, the biblical intonations of Lincoln's words mask their deeper foundation in law. The musical rhythms in repetition invoke "We, the People of the United States" of timeless constitutional status (past, present, and future)—a resonance that carries the nation from a popular understanding of immortality through religion toward a separate but still comforting civil immortality in law.

Like all truly crafted narrative, "The Gettysburg Address" does more than resolve. It circles back on itself in its quest for thematic extension. It confirms, but it also ends on a new plane, a higher level of equilibrium, one that mirrors the way a closing argument in court would end with the decision required.[1] At the outset of the war, Lincoln told Congress "This is essentially a People's contest" (4:438). Now, in more confident phrasing, and without the qualifying adverb "essentially," he delivers not just his answer but the government itself into the hands of a people who have sacrificed for it and who, as a reward for their continuing sacrifice, will receive "a new birth of freedom."

Lincoln's "Second Inaugural Address," by way of contrast, has less to do with a people's freedom in its concentration on communal sin and penance. "The address sounded more like a sermon than a state paper," Frederick Douglass observed in Lincoln's audience on March 4, 1865, and

---

9. Lincoln was proud of having "studied and nearly mastered the Six-books of Euclid"—proud enough to mention the accomplishment in his autobiographical sketch for a campaign biography in 1860. He used the term "proposition" in its technical meaning, something to be proved. See CW 4: 62.

1. For these characteristics in narrative at its best, see Tzvetan Todorov, *The Poetics of Prose*, trans. Richard Howard (Ithaca, NY, 1977), 111. "An 'ideal' narrative begins with a stable situation which is disturbed by some power or force. There results a state of disequilibrium, by the action of a force directed in the opposite direction, the equilibrium is re-established; the second equilibrium is similar to the first, but the two are never identical." In Lincoln's hands, the founding of the nation is the stable first equilibrium, the Civil War is the disturbing power that threatens the founding, and the final articulation of the Union on terms of equality with a stronger government tied more directly to the people is the second but greater equilibrium.

there is plenty of evidence to support the claim.[2] Only one other president in the eighteen inaugural addresses delivered before Lincoln's had taken words directly from the Bible and even then the speaker, John Quincy Adams, used a single, more neutral passage.[3] Lincoln, breaking the mold again as a speaking president, quotes or paraphrases from four separate passages after naming the Bible directly. He invokes prayer three times and God fourteen times in the shortest inaugural but one by an American president.[4]

But if the religious orientation is clear, it has distracted attention from the lawyer who is speaking. Lincoln's "Second Inaugural" is a canny political document arranged against a legal crisis of unknown but serious dimensions. It is simultaneously the work of a man reaching for a an acceptable concept of judgment. Where is the justice in the astounding figure of 600,000 war dead and the related misery of millions more? Lincoln, burdened by his own role in producing those mountains of misery, needs a legal answer beyond himself, and he accomplishes this by translating his pain into general civic terms. He needs a commensurate theory of punishment and finds it in a sanitized version of the *lex talionis* or Mosaic law, "eye for eye, tooth for tooth, hand for hand, foot for foot."[5]

As before, a proper understanding of Lincoln's speech requires that we concentrate on the structure that Lincoln gave it in four tonally different paragraphs of unequal length. It is so much easier to understand what is at stake by knowing the structure and sound behind the words that Lincoln uses. It is too often quoted only in part when it should be read for all of its meaning, and you should begin by reading "Second Inaugural" aloud to yourself.

The seemingly perfunctory opening paragraph and the deliberately clumsy overall structure, with its immensely long third paragraph, are what a reader first notices when looking at the "Second Inaugural." Remarkably, the whole first paragraph dwells on what the speaker will *not* talk about ("little that is new could be presented") even as Lincoln typically removes himself as a persona from the scene of inauguration ("there is less occasion for an extended address than there was at the first"). And once again, the legal language of procedural notification, "fitting and proper," supplies the hook of arrangement.

The thing not to be dwelt upon because previous "public declarations have been constantly called forth on every point and phase" is euphemistically rendered as "the great contest." Lincoln can afford to talk in abstract terms because, despite the fact that "no prediction in regard to it

2. Frederick Douglass, *Autobiographies* (1893; rpt., New York, 1994), 802.

3. Ronald C. White, Jr., *Lincoln's Greatest Speech: The Second Inaugural*, 101, 114. John Quincy Adams quotes from Psalm 127:1. "Except the Lord keep the city, the watchman waketh but in vain."

4. George Washington's "Second Inaugural" was only 135 words long, but in terms of ceremonial implication, Lincoln's remains the shortest. Washington's cabinet debated whether his second taking of the oath of office should be a private or a public occasion. In a rare moment of agreement, both Alexander Hamilton and Thomas Jefferson wanted the ceremony to be private in the President's residence, but the opinion of other cabinet officials prevailed, and Washington took the oath in the Senate chamber. Given the controversy, however, and in keeping with the inclination of his most brilliant advisers, Washington minimized the public significance of the ceremony by speaking only about the nature of the taking of the oath with no comment at all on future policies. See *The Writings of George Washington*, edited by Jared Sparks (Boston, 1858), 10: 321–23.

5. Exodus 21:24.

is ventured," the conflict itself moves toward a successful conclusion. He signals that direction with the words "[t]he progress of our arms" has been "reasonably satisfactory and encouraging to all." Curiously, although never announced, this very success is the problem that the renewed presidency now faces. One of Lincoln's greatest talents is knowing what not to talk about. Once again, he follows his own earlier legal advice; "it is good policy to never plead what you need not, lest you oblige yourself to prove what you cannot."[6]

The second paragraph returns to the physical conflict, but now the voice is dramatic against the cooler opening. Lincoln's abstract "contest" metastasizes into an animated, driving, brutal force beyond human reckoning. The negative term withheld in the first paragraph is "war," and it comes wildly alive here in a litany of seven repetitions within five short sentences; what "All dreaded" and all continued to misunderstand has arrived. Enfolding dread in a monosyllabic closure of just four words, Lincoln ends this paragraph with the words "And the war came." Although no one wanted war, *still* it came and in horror. Words of fear and ruin dominate the paragraph: "anxiously," "impending," "dreaded," "avert," "insurgent," "*destroy*," "dissolve," "divide," "deprecated," "survive," and "perish."

Nor did anyone anticipate "the magnitude, or the duration" of war once it came. All Americans on every side expected "an easier triumph, and a result less fundamental and astounding." With universal misapprehension in play, the beginning of the long third paragraph takes up the failure of all to understand what war would do to *them*. This section is about the degeneration of everything and everyone in the face of war. Earlier, on October 5, 1863, Lincoln had written out his own view on the subject in a monody of disgust worth attention in this context:

> At once sincerity is questioned, and motives are assailed. Actual war coming, blood grows hot, and blood is spilled. Thought is forced from old channels into confusion. Deception breeds and thrives. Confidence dies, and universal suspicion reigns. Each man feels an impulse to kill his neighbor, lest he be first killed by him. Revenge and retaliation follow. But this is not all. Every foul bird comes abroad, and every dirty reptile rises up. These add crime to confusion. Strong measures, deemed indispensable but harsh at best, such men make worse by mal-administration (6:500).

The objective of Lincoln's "Second Inaugural" lies in answer to these ills. His words strive to prevent the insincerity, the malice, the confusion, the deception, the delusions, the revenge, the retaliation, the harshness, the crime, and the mal-administration of "this mighty scourge of war" from overflowing and polluting the peace that must follow. Lincoln's unstated problem as the first second-term President since Andrew Jackson is not the war, but the peace. It is a misnomer to think he speaks to pacify the South; he speaks to make the North relinquish the emotions and distortions of war when it becomes possible to restore the South to membership in the Union.

Congress had tried to wrest control of the war effort from Lincoln on several occasions, and now in further anger in 1865 it wanted "to take the

---

6. Allen D. A. Spiegel, *A. Lincoln, Esquire: A Shrewd, Sophisticated Lawyer in His Time* (Macon, GA, 2002), 45.

process of reconstruction out of the President's hands."[7] Lincoln's assassination would give his political enemies the means to maintain a warlike mentality against the vanquished. Even so, even if the words of the fallen President would come to mean nothing in the angers of Reconstruction, the words themselves were as cunning as anything Lincoln ever delivered, and his calculated touch contributes to their higher eloquence instead of detracting from it.

To see as much, we must first understand that slavery was always the second issue for Lincoln despite its prominence in the "Second Inaugural"; the unified constitutionally-protected destiny of the Union was his first concern. Early in the third paragraph, Lincoln makes all sides acknowledge that slavery "was, somehow, the cause of the war," but with emancipation accomplished he can add "Neither [side] anticipated the *cause* of the conflict might cease with, or even before, the conflict itself should cease." Accordingly, with slavery at an end, there is no need for the moral self-righteousness of further division, an aspect of delusion that is the very child of war.

Lincoln steadies this argument with two countervailing paraphrases from the Bible. Using Genesis 3:19, he wonders how Southerners "should dare to ask a just God's assistance in wringing their bread from the sweat of other men's faces," but he immediately counters with "let us judge not that we not be judged" from Matthew 7:1. The juxtaposition of biblical passages works to strip all sides of their pretensions to knowledge over the course of war that all have stumbled into while simultaneously leaving his normative onus in place.

There are two separate tactical moves at work in this strategy, one epistemological and legal; the other theological. In the first, Lincoln diminishes the anger-inducing and corrosive normative distance between North and South by forcing the recognition that opposing sides, whether on the battlefield or in a courtroom, will each believe in a right answer through separate understandings of justice. This insistence parallels Kant's influential notion of how legal positivism must work, but Lincoln undoubtedly came to the same conclusion by arguing legal cases where each side passionately held a different truth. If both sides can claim to be right while both can also be seen to be partly in the wrong, then accommodation requires thinking together about the problem in coordinate terms—terms that mirror how a court of law might proceed.[8]

In the second and more obvious theological move, Lincoln uses scripture to prepare the nation for a daring transition. Here he relies on what was still a Bible culture in 1865. For if humanity has been groping in the dark, Lincoln says "The Almighty has His own purposes," which are distinct and inscrutable but part of an overarching design. Once recognized, God's purposes dictate that meaningful anger must pass from human agency to Him. God exists as the only appropriate punisher of transgressions in which all have shared. "Woe unto the world because of offences!"

7. For treatment of congressional attempts to control the war effort and "to take the process of reconstruction out of the President's hands," see Donald, "Chapter Fourteen: A Pumpkin in Each End of My Bag," and "Chapter Twenty: With Charity for All," and "Chapter Twenty-One: I Will Take Care Of Myself," in *Lincoln*, 377–406, 558–64, and 589–92.
8. See Jeremy Waldron, "Kant's Legal Positivism," *Harvard Law Review*, 109 (1995–96): 1535–66, at 1566.

says God. Lincoln finds these word in Matthew 18:7, but he translates their implication into civic terms with another favorite literary text as a barely apparent rhetorical backdrop.

God enters as a mediating higher judge into the destiny of the Union in order to answer and punish communal-wide "offences" that have distorted the body politic and society. The humbling assertion is a daring stroke in the face of Union audiences flushed with the prospect of victory, and Lincoln may have been led to it by another source on "offences." Shakespeare's similarly disjointed society in *Hamlet, Prince of Denmark* contains a passage that Lincoln had memorized. In Act III of the play, King Claudius goes to his knees in recognition of the hollow success he has won by claiming the throne over the brother he has murdered.

Victory is not everything. Claudius, too, speaks of an "offence" that "smells to heaven." "[T]o confront the visage of offence" is to realize that "Offence's gilded hand" cannot escape divine justice whatever it might seem to accomplish "[i]n the corrupted currents of this world." The thrust, if not the result, of Claudius's speech, parallels the "Second Inaugural": God must punish, and it is right that He do so.[9]

With God in place, the longest sentence in the "Second Inaugural" follows. Its seventy-eight words fill more than ten percent of the whole document, and they form a question of the kind that lawyers frequently use in argument. Antiquity gave the device the name *hypophora*: asking the question posed in a way that allows you to answer the problem in the way you desire.[1] Lincoln uses this interrogative mode to reduce the national problem to manageable terms. To paraphrase, what American citizen could possibly question the divine attributes ascribed to the Living God for using the Civil War to punish the nation for the offence of slavery? In answer, "as was said three thousand years ago, so still it must be said 'the judgments of the Lord are true and righteous altogether.'"

The inner quotation in this fourth and last biblical reference comes from the 9th verse of the 19th Psalm, and the phrases just before it carry a dual message: "the commandment of the Lord *is* pure, enlightening the eyes" and "The fear of the Lord is clean." Only God's way can purify and enlighten the Republic. Only fear of Him can make us clean again, and the significant element in this cleansing design is God's presumed exactitude in punishment. Lincoln offers the plausibility that "every drop of blood drawn with the lash, shall be paid by another drawn with the sword." That is what "this mighty *scourge* of war" means. But if so, nothing will be left over. No further punishment by suddenly former combatants becomes necessary. So compelling is this distancing anger for absorbing the unclean blood of the Civil War that Lincoln proposes to his cabinet that an amendment be prepared to insert God into the Constitution.[2]

---

9. William Shakespeare, *Hamlet* 3.3., 36–71. Lincoln memorized the soliloquies in William Scott's *Lessons on Elocution*. This passage appears there, and Lincoln claimed Claudius's speech to be a personal favorite. See Scott, *Lessons on Elocution* (Wilmington, 1797), 343–44, and Donald, *Lincoln*, 15, 31, 337, 569.
1. See Richard A. Lanham, *A Handlist of Rhetorical Terms*, 2nd ed. (Berkeley, 1991), 184. To this day the first page of a lawyer's brief to the Supreme Court of the United States contains only the question an advocate wants answered phrased in the way that will give the answer desired.
2. Gideon Welles, *Diary of Gideon Welles, Secretary of the Navy Under Lincoln and Johnson* (Boston, 1909–11), 2: 190.

The "Second Inaugural" does not end here. It continues in Lincoln's peroration, the last and shortest paragraph of his speech, and it gives the normative words most memorably associated with his name: "With malice toward none; with charity for all, with firmness in the right, as God gives us to see the right." The immediate point to remember, however, is the structure that gives these final words their extraordinary power. Lincoln has siphoned off the anger, confusion, and hatred of war by giving it all to God, and that allows a return to humanity and ordains a new path for combatants miraculously robbed of their warlike traits.

Although the normative weight in this strategy of reconciliation is remarkable on its own, it has its mundane equivalent in the earlier lawyer. Lincoln "settled" wherever he could. "Discourage litigation," he advised. "Persuade your neighbors to compromise whenever you can. Point out to them how the nominal winner is often a real loser. . . . As a peacemaker the lawyer has a superior opportunity of being a good man" (2:81). The rhetorical strategy of *ethos*, establishing sincerity and credibility in performance as the "good man," was important to the practitioner known as "Honest Abe."[3] How the same "good man," now as President, secures his sincerity in the last words of this speech is as clever as it is moving.

A thousand questions were on the table in March of 1865. How were the Southern states to be reincorporated? What was to be done with the leaders of the Confederacy when captured? How far down the hierarchy of command would treason apply? Who was to rule now in Southern capitals? Lincoln wrote that "one eighth of the whole population were colored slaves." How was this huge, utterly impoverished, totally uneducated group to be cared for and habilitated as free citizens? Lincoln ignored all of these puzzles even though they were on the tip of every American's tongue.

Instead, the speaker devotes his last words to a framework of visible caring through the concept of biblical charity. This traditional language of care for the downtrodden is so abstracted and familiar that the personal becomes general. Lincoln offers only the solutions that were immediately possible and uncontroversial. Who could disagree with the need to "bind up the nation's wounds," or to care for the figure underneath that metaphor, the wounded or dying veteran, "his widow, and his orphan"? To a nation crying for it, Lincoln offered "a just and lasting peace." The mixture of abstract premise, synecdoche, and example works for Lincoln's time and every other, and Lincoln knew it.

The speaker's comment on his own performance came to the seasoned New York politician and journalist Thurlow Weed. Lincoln, by using this correspondent, offered sentiments he knew others would hear. He could assume that Weed would convey to the world "a truth which I thought needed to be told." "I expect [the Inaugural Address] to wear as well as—perhaps better than—any thing I have produced," Lincoln wrote, fully revealing the rhetorical protection that calling upon God had given him. "Men are not flattered by being shown that there is a difference of purpose between the Almighty and them," he explained. "To deny it, however, in this case, is to deny that there is a God governing the world" (8:356). The roles of accomplished orator, spiritual leader, shrewd politician, and conjurer of juries are all hived as one in "Second Inaugural,"

---

3. Mark E. Steiner, *An Honest Calling: The Law Practice of Abraham Lincoln* (DeKalb, 2006), 3.

and every one of them is recognized in these short sentences of explanation.

Abraham Lincoln is useful in approaches to the subject of eloquence not just because he is good at it. His innovative interest in concision from the platform while relying on established oratorical strategies is unusual in the nineteenth century. The combination of change and conventional acceptance allows us to see the planned movement in his speeches, and it also encourages a look forward in any judgment of what public speaking should be. The timeless appeal of his words helps, too. Lincoln seems almost as modern as he is traditional, and that is why he speaks to every generation.

GABOR S. BORITT

From The Gettysburg Gospel: The Lincoln Speech That Nobody Knows[†]

* * *

At the beginning of the day's program the audience seemed reluctant to applaud; indeed, the proceedings seemed in many ways like a church service.[1] After all, consecrating a burial ground has been a solemn occasion since time immemorial. When Lincoln arrived, he had been greeted with "perfect silence" and people uncovering their heads. When Everett was introduced, someone called out for three cheers for the orator, only to be greeted with silence. The reporter who signed his name "J.H." called the man "Mr. Idiot," someone who did not understand the occasion. After Everett finished, once again deeply respectful quiet greeted him. French's ode[2] changed the mood completely. Great applause greeted the glee club's performance and the lighter mood would continue for the rest of the day, broken momentarily only by the final dirge and benediction.

When the crowd quieted, Marshal Lamon[3] belted out, "Ladies and Gentleman, the President of the United States," and there he was, already standing. Everett had spoken from memory. Lincoln had on reading glasses and held his speech in his hands. The applause subsided. We will never know the exact words he used, but the minor variations that would come down to posterity did not change the substance of what he said—not for the people at the cemetery or for the host who would read his words in the newspapers:

[†] *The Gettysburg Gospel: The Lincoln Speech That Nobody Knows*. New York: Simon & Schuster, 2006. Copyright © 2006 by Gabor Boritt. Reprinted with permission of Simon & Schuster and the author.

1. The Consecration of the National Cemetery at Gettysburg, Pennsylvania, was held on November 19, 1863, to commemorate the thousands of soldiers who had died in the Battle of Gettysburg in early July. The event featured two main speeches—a two-hour oration by the Massachusetts politician Edward Everett (1794–1865) and Lincoln's speech, between two and three minutes long—as well as prayers, band music, and singing [editor's note].

2. Benjamin French's "Consecration Chant," set to music by Wilson G. Horner [editor's note].

3. Lincoln's friend and sometime bodyguard Ward Hill Lamon, marshal of the District of Columbia, whom Lincoln had selected to supervise the dedication ceremonies at Gettysburg [editor's note].

Four score and seven years ago our fathers brought forth upon this continent a new nation, conceived in Liberty, and dedicated to the proposition that all men are created equal.

The crowd applauded. He had been invited to make a few "remarks" that would console "the many widows and orphans" and also "kindle anew in the breasts of the Comrades of these brave dead" a confidence that their dead "are not forgotten."[4] Now he was trying to do that, and more. Some had urged on him the need to tell the people why they had to go on with this horrifying war, and his rarely erring sense told him that the need was there. Here he was giving the first prepared speech since his inauguration day, more than two and a half years earlier.[5]

Back in July of 1863 his instinctive reaction to the greatest of battles was to look back into history, to 1776, and to Jefferson's words. Facing the horrendous casualties, "the success" and "the want of success," he looked for the meaning of America with impromptu awkward words. "How long ago is it?—eighty odd years—since on the Fourth of July for the first time in the history of the world a nation by its representatives, assembled and declared as a self-evident truth that 'all men are created equal.'"[6]

As he found those words, his mind wandered back to another crucial moment of his life, the carefully crafted speech that he gave at Peoria, Illinois, in 1854, marking the start of his antislavery crusade. "Near eighty years ago we began by declaring that all men are created equal," he said then.[7] Even before the speech at Peoria, his eulogy for Henry Clay, his "beau ideal" of a politician, began: "On the fourth of July, 1776 . . ."[8]

The words of the Declaration of Independence had stayed on Lincoln's lips from the 1850s into his presidency. After he decided to go to Gettysburg, his thoughts returned to those lines. If he could not find time to put words on paper almost until he had to speak them, the thoughts he now expressed had churned in him for a long time. Even over the short run, as Nicolay would explain, "he probably followed his usual habit in such matters, using great deliberation in arranging his thoughts, and moulding his phrases mentally, waiting to reduce them to writing after they had taken satisfactory form."[9] His whole life prepared him for Gettysburg. Ideas, phrases, rattled around in his head, and the pressure of the occasion brought them forth.

July 4, 1776, had been much on the mind of Americans at least since the 1820s, Abolitionists appealed to the words in the Declaration of Independence and called for the end of slavery. The many moderates also exalted the words, giving them a different meaning. Perhaps for most Americans, "created equal" meant by the middle third of the century the God-given right to rise in life: equality of opportunity. But every Fourth of July resounded with words from '76. Lincoln's friend James C. Conkling, to whom the president had sent his August 1863 public letter defending

4. The invitation had come from the attorney David Wills, Lincoln's and Everett's host in Gettysburg; David Wills, "Wills to Lincoln, November 2, 1863," ALP.
5. Lincoln would give only three more prepared speeches: at the 1864 Baltimore Fair, the Second Inaugural Address, and his last speech before his assassination.
6. Response to Serenade, July 7, 1863, CW 6: 319–20.
7. Speech on the Kansas-Nebraska Act at Peoria, Illinois, October 16, 1854, CW 2: 275.
8. Eulogy on Henry Clay at Springfield, Illinois, CW 2: 121.
9. John G. Nicolay, "Lincoln's Gettysburg Address," *The Century Magazine* 47 (February 1894): 597.

Emancipation and the use of black troops, began a July speech in 1857: "Four score years have elapsed since that memorable Declaration of Independence. . . ."[1] Conkling, like countless others, easily mixed religious and classical references. July 4 was a day "as in Judea" when "its ancient tribes annually repaired to their magnificent temple . . . as in Rome. . . ."

Everett concluded his July 4, 1860, oration by declaring that "The question decided eighty-four years ago in Philadelphia *was* the greatest question ever decided in America; and the event has shown that greater, perhaps, never was nor ever will be decided among men. . . . The great Declaration, with its life-giving principles" had covered the continent, "crossed the land and the sea, and circled the globe."[2] Like so many of the best American minds, Everett, too, thought in universal terms. "If it is the will of Providence that the lands which now sit in darkness shall see the day," the world will be "regenerated" and even "the ancient and mysterious regions of the East, the cradle of mankind," old Mesopotamia, "shall receive back in these later days from the West the rich repayment of the early debt of civilization." "Constitutional freedom" would reign everywhere.

As Everett listened now, he may have understood Lincoln's words in such terms. Like Everett, Lincoln believed that the Civil War would save or destroy America, and with it constitutional democracy. But what Lincoln meant now by "democracy" went far.

He certainly meant to include immigrants or children of immigrants, who made up perhaps a quarter of the Union army. Lincoln hoped that the promise of the Declaration would embrace them, make them feel part of the American birthright. "They have a right to claim it as though they were blood of the blood, and flesh of the flesh of the men who wrote that Declaration," he had said at the start of his debates with Douglas in 1858, "and so they are."[3]

But quoting the Declaration of Independence in November 1863 cut much deeper: it defended the Emancipation Proclamation that had drastically changed the character of the war. It presented a strong message about liberty, without speaking of slavery outright and so alienating many. If Lincoln did not mention by name the great "evil," he knew that others would be explicit on the subject, as he had been on so many other occasions. Seward had already spoken the night before, and when he would receive congratulations on his words, Lincoln was immediately tied in: "God had exalted him for the very purpose" of freeing the slaves.[4] Everett, too, had mentioned emancipation, and so would later in the day another serious speaker, at the Presbyterian Church on Baltimore Street, with Lincoln present. But by speaking in broad philosophical terms, the president now reached beyond Seward and the others. The promise of the Declaration was to be attained as quickly and as far as the country would permit. "All men are created equal" left room for him to write less than four months later to the governor of Louisiana that at least some black

1. *Oration of Hon. James C. Conkling, Delivered in Springfield, Ill. July 4th, 1857* (Springfield, 1857), 1.
2. Edward Everett, *Oration Delivered Before the City Authorities of Boston, on the Fourth of July, 1860* (Boston, 1860), 47–48.
3. Speech at Chicago, Illinois, July 10, 1858, CW 2: 501–2.
4. Unknown to William H. Seward, November 24, 1863, copy, *The Papers of William H. Seward* (Woodbridge, Conn., 1981).

people there should have the right to vote. "They would probably help, in some trying time to come, to keep the jewel of liberty within the family of freedom."[5]

That Lincoln's whole being had been tied up with freedom, however many contradictions one may point to, is also clear. He believed that if history would remember him, it would be for his Emancipation Proclamation. As an ambitious young man, he had announced that "towering genius" could reach great renown in America by either "emancipating slaves, or enslaving freemen."[6] Soon after issuing the Proclamation, he invited the painter Edward Dalton Marchant, recommended by John Forney, to work in the White House for four months, during which Marchant created the presidential portrait with the broken chain.[7] He even ordered the painter's son to come from the army and help his father with the work. The painting was to go to Independence Hall in Philadelphia to keep company with the heroes of '76.

The president also invited another painter, Francis Carpenter, who would work at the White House for half a year. He recorded Lincoln saying that Emancipation was the "great event of the 19th century."[8] However accurate the words attributed to Lincoln, Carpenter painted the moment in the cabinet when the president announced that event. The huge oil painting, *The First Reading of the Emancipation Proclamation,* shows Lincoln with the document in his hand. When Lincoln's oldest friend, Joshua Speed, came to visit—so the trustworthy Speed recorded in 1866—they reminisced, and Lincoln recalled his youthful fear that his moment of life would be gone without a trace. Well, Lincoln had issued the Emancipation Proclamation. Now he would be remembered for doing something for "his fellow man." This was "what he desired to live for."[9]

Emancipation painters working at the White House, a confession to his oldest friend, and so much more, all make clear what Lincoln hoped for from history. But the Chief Mourner at Gettysburg wanted to avoid controversial words; a funeral was not a place to pronounce policy. Here he had to unite the people as best he could. And so he would rise for a moment above the squabbling of politics that he could be so good at. He would let his entire speech soar beyond the reach of the mundane world. He would not mention by name slavery, or Gettysburg, or the Confederacy, Lee's army or Meade's.

Yet being above politics itself was political. It allowed Lincoln not only the lofty presidential look, but also the ambiguity on the one hand to appeal to people desiring a quick radical route to equality, and on the other to keep in the fold those who did not care about the issue of slavery or were actively hostile to the idea of Emancipation. He knew that without a broad patriotic coalition the war would be lost, and with it the Union and Emancipation. Most of those who supported freedom for the enslaved would understand the meaning of "all men are created equal." Indeed, they could give it as broad a meaning as they wished. They would fully

5. To Michael Hahn, March 13 1864, CW 7: 243.
6. Address to the Young Men's Lyceum of Springfield, Illinois, CW 1: 114.
7. J. W. Forney to Lincoln, December 20, 1862, ALP.
8. Francis B. Carpenter, *Six Months at the White House with Abraham Lincoln* (New York, 1866), 90, 269.
9. Joshua Speed to William Herndon, February 1866, HI 197.

understand that "liberty," in which the United States was "conceived," applied to some; "freedom" that needed a "new birth," applied to all. As for angry opponents, Lincoln knew that they would lose no time in denouncing him for mixing the "negro" into the war and so desecrating the graves of Gettysburg.

But Lincoln needed the masses in the middle. Equating his use of Jefferson's words with the rights of black people was only one possible interpretation. Many did not understand the president's words in those terms. Equality could carry civil, economic, social, or racial connotations. To middle-of-the-road folk, the liberty he spoke about could be the white man's liberty. To think that way, they had to sidestep the full meaning of the Emancipation Proclamation; but people are always good at fuzzy thinking. They also had to bypass Lincoln's tendency, at his best, to think in terms of all humanity, to speak in universal terms.

Looking back to the Revolutionary War reminded people that the birth of America had cost great sacrifices. More specific, in appealing to Jefferson, Lincoln was certain that he appealed to the meaning the founders gave to the Declaration—though most scholars see this as historically inaccurate. Indeed, he did to Jefferson's words what future generations would do to his at Gettysburg. But in 1863 the meaning of the Declaration of Independence was much debated. And so how people understood Lincoln's words depended on what was in their heads. Lincoln understood that.

> Now we are engaged in a great civil war, testing whether that nation, or any nation so conceived and so dedicated, can long endure.

Lincoln's opening sentence led here with the phrase "dedicated to the proposition," the word "proposition" coming from his study of Euclid's geometry, something that had to be proven. He had said some of this from the start of the war. In his July 4, 1861, war message to Congress, he explained that "our popular government has often been called an experiment," and it remained to be seen whether it would succeed over the long run.[1] The Civil War was the test. But the implication at Gettysburg went further; it went from opposing the appeal from the "ballot to the bullet" to specifying that the rebel bullets aimed at the equality of all.

Yet, however much Emancipation cast its shadow over Lincoln's words, they reached beyond the American problem of slavery to the global problem of liberal democracy. Born in the optimism of the Enlightenment, democratic republicanism failed to triumph in Europe, much less anywhere else. Speaking to his countrymen, Lincoln's thoughts encompassed the world. The United States was, as he said in 1862, "the last best, hope of earth."[2] Would the vision of progress that most Americans shared fail?

The United States had a universal mission, but the focus now had to be on home. Here on a piece of "a great battle-field," Lincoln was helping to remember "those who here gave their lives that that nation might live." In the back of the minds of many in the crowd, Daniel Webster's unforget-

---

1. Message to Congress in Special Session, CW 4: 439.
2. Annual Message to Congress, December 1, 1862, CW 5: 537.

table words must have hovered: "Liberty and Union." "The brave men living and dead, who struggled here," Lincoln went on, already consecrated this land "far above our poor power to add or detract."

People applauded again, and the reporters struggled to take down the words. Not all of them would get the exact same expressions. Now some heard Lincoln say "poor" before "power"; others missed it. Though many of the reporters had a place on the platform, many others were scattered in the crowd. While some heard people responding repeatedly "Good, good," others did not, or did not note audience reaction at all. What was applause to some was "great applause" or "immense applause" to others. Sitting in different places with different vantage points, carrying various expectations and beliefs, the journalists, like Americans who would later read aloud to their families the Gettysburg reports, heard differing words and meanings.

> The world will little note nor long remember what we say here, but it can never forget what they did here.

No false humility in this. Everett had given his fine oration, touching hymns had been performed, Lincoln was saying a few words, and the newspapers would report them all. But he justly judged that the sacrifice of the soldiers should be and would be acclaimed. If he himself would be remembered, it would be for Emancipation. Nor was he considering Americans alone, but "The world."

As he spoke, a captain in the crowd with an empty sleeve buried his face in his good arm, shaking and sobbing aloud. Then he raised his eyes high and exclaimed in a low, solemn voice: "God Almighty bless Abraham Lincoln!" The reporter, noting the faces around the soldier, thought that people responded silently with "Amen."[3] And all the while the crowd applauded Lincoln again.

People had been roused. The next sentence, too, got applause:

> It is for us, the living, rather to be dedicated here to the unfinished work which they have thus far so nobly carried out.

Some of the best reporters would take down "refinished work," though this made no sense. Or perhaps the reporters did fine; the telegraph operators or typesetters fouled things up. The president had a voice that carried, but even those close to the platform could not take down everything accurately.

"The great task" remained before the country. All knew this meant carrying the war to victory; in the minds of some what victory would bring may have flashed for a moment. "We here highly resolve that these dead shall not have died in vain—" the crowd again interrupted with applause as Lincoln conjured up an image and words that had been hidden inside of so many since their childhood. "Their fall was not in vain," said the very popular Parson Weems's George Washington when he visited the graves of his soldiers.[4] The applause quieted so Lincoln could finish:

---

3. Isaac Jackson Allen in *Ohio State Journal*, November 23, 1863.
4. Mason Locke Weems, *The Life of Washington*, edited by Marcus Cunliffe (Cambridge, Mass., 1962), 124.

that the nation shall, under God, have a new birth of freedom; and that government of the people, by the people, for the people, shall not perish from the earth.

Silence—has the president finished?—then long, continued applause. Had Lincoln pronounced the universal "that government" as he spoke, departing from the written text of his second draft's "that this government," which referred only to the United States? He was a nationalist and could speak of Americans as an "almost chosen people."[5] In his "first draft," he used the universal; but as he wrote out his "second draft," he changed to the particular, to *the* one nation on the earth devoted to building equality in a democracy. Surely that's what many wanted to hear, and surely that is how some heard what Lincoln said.

But if he spoke from the "second draft," the likely possibility, he made two significant changes at the cemetery. Not only did he add "under God," but also turned his final sentence into a universal declaration. Nor would he vary from that as he prepared later versions of his speech. In like spirit, though newspaper reports sometimes capitalized both "Nation" and "Liberty" in his first sentence, he capitalized only "Liberty." Was Lincoln speaking to humankind?

Firm as Lincoln's voice was, it carried no touch of stridency or self-righteousness. Nor did he make any overt reference to Christianity. Though his official invitation asked that his "remarks" help set aside the ground for their "sacred use," it is not likely that Lincoln was familiar with the Christian rite of sanctifying a piece of the earth for the burial of the dead. He had been to funerals, even spoke at one as a young man, but now gave no indication of being aware of the religious aspect of the occasion, or perhaps if aware, considered it improper to participate. The evening before the ceremonies certainly provided no edification in this regard. Only after imbibing the atmosphere at the cemetery, the uncovered heads, prayer, and hymns, did he add, in the moment's inspiration, "under God." One can almost hear him coming in his speech to "that the nation shall," pausing for a second, then adding a little awkwardly "under God, have a new birth of freedom." Later he would revise the word order to make the sentence read better.

And yet, whatever expectations he may have taken to Gettysburg, however reluctant he was to make a personal profession of Christianity, much of what Lincoln said carried the rhythms of the Bible. This was the music of the ancient Hebrew and Greek turned into King James's English. This was the language he was raised on. "Four score and seven years ago." Psalm 90: "The days of our years are three score years and ten," one of the best-known sentences of the Book. "Brought forth" is not only the biblical way to announce a birth, including that of Mary's "first born son," but the phrase that describes the Israelites being "brought forth" from slavery in Egypt.

Birth, sacrificial death, rebirth. A born-again nation.[6] At a less than conscious level, Lincoln weaved together the biblical story and the American

---

5. Address to the New Jersey Senate at Trenton, New Jersey, February 21, 1861, CW 4: 235.
6. The phrase "born again," a synonym for "new birth," or the theological term "regeneration," had been in common use since the transatlantic evangelical awakenings of the eighteenth century. In contrast to being born as a babe, new birth—often a moment of sudden conversion—offered spiritual blessings here and now and eternal life in the future.

story: "Fathers." "Conceive." "Perish." "Consecrate." "Hallow." "Devotion."[7] The devout in the cemetery heard Lincoln speak an intimately familiar beloved language. His words pointing to rebirth went even deeper than the Christian message, if that was possible, reaching the primeval longing for a new birth that humankind has yearned for and celebrated with every spring since time immemorial.

Lincoln's words came from the heart. The bloodbath of the war, and the loss of his own second child, Willie, in 1862, had slowly changed his religious outlook. The secular fatalist of old began to turn into a religious fatalist. He jotted down for himself perhaps in 1862: "The will of God prevails."[8] Something of the Calvinism of his parents that he had rejected, even ridiculed, in his youth, started to reclaim him. He added "under God" to his remarks at Gettysburg. In his Second Inaugural Address in 1865, he would explain his course: "With malice toward none; with charity for all; with firmness in the right, as God gives us to see the right. . . ."[9] And God helped Lincoln "to see the right" of abolishing slavery and leading the country toward black citizenship.

If God loomed ever larger in Lincoln's thought as the war went on, if his words at Gettysburg spoke deeply to the devout, they spoke also to more secular people, for in some part he remained one of them. He would not join a church, could not embrace the Christian concept of sin and redemption, kept mostly silent about Jesus, and showed no inclination to build a personal relationship with God. The secularists could understand his Gettysburg speech largely on their own terms. Lincoln spoke from the heart to them, too.

A lesser person might have foundered on such bifurcation. Christians might have rejected him for not being sufficiently committed; the secular-minded for being too religious. Instead, the majorities embraced him as one of their own. His words at Gettysburg show how he did it. "Inauguration" is how Marshal Lamon described the ceremonies in the printed "Programme." In his own copy, Everett crossed out the word and replaced it with the religious "Consecration." As for Lincoln, "dedicate, consecrate"; he stayed in the middle, and so reached out to all—as many as he could reach.

His success depended in no small part on the beauty of his language. But with all the fresh graves around, the beautiful words would not hide the fact that the war had to go on. It had to go on indefinitely until victory came.

The rationalism of the Enlightenment combined with Protestant conscience. Lincoln's nine sentences had been welcomed by opening applause, interrupted by applause five times, and followed by applause. His perhaps two-and-a half-minute speech grew into something like three minutes. The people loved him. Lincoln had both voiced the beliefs of mainstream America and urged America on toward a "new birth." He reflected the oratory of the ancient Greeks, especially Pericles, whose speeches appeared in the McGuffey Readers that educated children. His conclusion echoed not only Weems's *Life of Washington*, but words memorized

---

7. Compare Lincoln's words with a Bible concordance—www.biblegate.com. "Four score," for example, appears thirty-five times.
8. Meditation on the Divine Will, ca. early September 1862, CW 5: 403.
9. Second Inaugural Address, March 4, 1865, CW 5: 333.

by generations of children from their readers—some of the best known words of American history, and of Lincoln's youth, the conclusion of Webster's 1830 reply to South Carolina's Robert Hayne in the Senate, denying that the U.S. government was a "creature" of the states. It was "the people's government," Webster had said, "made for the people, made by the people, and answerable to the people."[1] In the Bible, Lincoln had read many a time in the Book of Proverbs: "Where *there is* no vision, the people perish." He was providing a vision "for us, the living," not the dead.

Not that people listening to his words analyzed their meaning. There was now no time for that; for most people no inclination, either. They took in its poetry, understood its overall tone and message. To give a very short speech, especially after Everett's long oration delivered from memory, could have been a major error. Yet that many would not recall whether he had a sheet of paper before him suggests he got away with it. In any case, his audience did not mainly come from the people present, important though they were, but from the North as a whole, perhaps even beyond. The chief goal was to bind the nation together; to create a ritual that tied the past to the present and pointed to the future. Wire services carried the whole ceremony around the North, wherever the telegraph went, immersing "the people" in one fastening ritual, creating community. This was new, but Lincoln was good at understanding the new.

※　※　※

JAMES M. McPHERSON

From Lincoln and the Strategy of Unconditional Surrender[†]

It is ironic that one of the most oft-quoted passages from Lincoln's writings is the concluding paragraph of his second inaugural address. "With malice toward none," said Lincoln, "with charity for all," let us "bind up the nation's wounds" and strive to "achieve and cherish a just, and a lasting peace."[1] These words have helped shape Lincoln's image as a man of compassion and mercy who desired a magnanimous peace. This image is true enough; but it is only part of the truth. While Lincoln did want a soft peace, he had recognized long before 1865 that it could be achieved only by a hard war. And he insisted on the unconditional surrender of Confederate forces before he would even talk of peace.

The fact is, the overwhelming circumstance shaping Lincoln's presidency was war. He had been willing to risk war rather than let the nation perish. He was a war president. Indeed, he was the only president in our history whose entire administration was bounded by the parameters of

---

1. Daniel Webster, *The Papers of Daniel Webster: Speeches and Formal Writings*, edited by Charles Wiltse and Alan R. Berolzheimer (Dartmouth, NH, 1986), 1: 339–40. Herndon wrote that "Lincoln thought that Webster's great speech in reply to Haynes was the very best speech that was ever delivered"—William H. Herndon to Jesse W. Weik, January 1, 1886, *Herndon-Weik Collection* (Library of Congress).
† From *The Best American History Essays on Lincoln*. Edited by Sean Wilentz. Copyright © 2009, Organization of American Historians. Reprinted with permission of Palgrave Macmillan.
1. CW 8: 333.

war. The first official document that Lincoln saw as president—on the morning after the inaugural ball—was a letter from Major Robert Anderson at Fort Sumter stating that unless resupplied he could hold out only a few more weeks. This news, in effect struck the first blow of the Civil War; the fatal shot fired by John Wilkes Booth on April 14, 1865, struck virtually the last blow of the war. During the intervening one thousand, five hundred and three days there was scarcely one in which Lincoln was not preoccupied with the war. Military matters took up more of his time and attention than any other matter, as indicated by the activities chronicled in that fascinating volume, *Lincoln Day by Day*.[2] He spent more time in the War Department telegraph office than anywhere else except the White House itself. During times of crisis, Lincoln frequently stayed at the telegraph office all night reading dispatches from the front, sending dispatches of his own, holding emergency conferences with Secretary of War Stanton, General-in-Chief Halleck, and other officials. He wrote the first draft of the Emancipation Proclamation in this office while awaiting news from the army.[3] This was appropriate, for the legal justification of the proclamation was its "military necessity" as a war measure.

Lincoln took seriously his constitutional duty as commander in chief of the army and navy. He borrowed books on military strategy from the Library of Congress and burned the midnight oil reading them. No fewer than eleven times he left Washington to visit the Army of the Potomac at the fighting front in Virginia or Maryland, spending a total of forty-two days with that army. Some of the most dramatic events in Lincoln's presidency grew out of his direct intervention in strategic and command decisions. In May 1862, along with Secretary of War Stanton and Secretary of the Treasury Chase, he visited Union forces at Hampton Roads in Virginia and personally issued orders that led to the occupation of Norfolk. Later that same month, Lincoln haunted the War Department telegraph room almost around the clock for more than a week and fired off a total of fifty telegrams to half a dozen generals to coordinate an attempt to trap and crush Stonewall Jackson's army in the Shenandoah Valley—an attempt that failed partly because Jackson moved too fast but mainly because Union generals, much to Lincoln's disgust, moved too slowly. A couple of months later, Lincoln made the controversial decision to transfer the Army of the Potomac from the Virginia peninsula southeast of Richmond to northern Virginia covering Washington. And a couple of months later yet, Lincoln finally removed General George B. McClellan from command of this army because McClellan seemed reluctant to fight. A year later, in September 1863, Lincoln was roused from bed at his summer residence in a Maryland suburb of Washington for a dramatic midnight conference at the War Department where he decided to send four divisions from the Army of the Potomac to reinforce General William S. Rosecrans's besieged army in Chattanooga after it had lost the battle of Chickamauga.

Lincoln subsequently put Ulysses S. Grant in command at Chattanooga and then in the spring of 1864 brought him to Washington as the new general in chief. Thereafter, with a commander in charge who had

2. Abraham Lincoln, *Lincoln Day by Day: A Chronology 1809–1865*, vol. III: *1861–1865*, edited by C. Percy Powell and Earl Schenck Miers (Washington, 1960).
3. David Homer Bates, *Lincoln in the Telegraph Office* (New York, 1907).

Lincoln's full confidence, the president played a less direct role in command decisions than he had done before. Nevertheless, Lincoln continued to help shape crucial strategic plans and to sustain Grant against pressures from all sides during that dark summer of 1864. "It is the dogged pertinacity of Grant that wins," the president told his private secretary. Lincoln wired Grant in Virginia during the terrible fighting at Petersburg: "I begin to see it. You will succeed. God bless you all."[4] When Confederate General Jubal Early drove a small Union army out of the Shenandoah Valley in the summer of 1864, crossed the Potomac, and threatened Washington itself before being driven off, Lincoln went personally to Fort Stevens, part of the Washington defenses, to observe the fighting. It was on this occasion that a Union officer standing a few feet from Lincoln was hit by a Confederate bullet and that another officer—none other than Oliver Wendell Holmes, Jr.—noting without recognizing out of the corner of his eye this tall civilian standing on the parapet in the line of fire, said urgently: "Get down, you damn fool, before you get shot!" A chastened president got down.[5]

Grant subsequently sent several divisions from the Army of the Potomac with orders to go after Early's army in the Shenandoah Valley "and follow him to the death." When Lincoln saw these orders he telegraphed Grant: "This, I think, is exactly right." But "it will neither be done nor attempted unless you watch it every day, and hour, and force it."[6] In response to this telegram Grant came to Washington, conferred with Lincoln, and put his most trusted subordinate, Philip Sheridan, in command of the Union forces in the Shenandoah Valley where they did indeed follow Early to the death of his army. About the same time, Lincoln approved the plans for Sherman's march through Georgia. It was these three campaigns—Grant's chewing and choking of Lee's army at Petersburg, Sheridan's following of Early to the death in the Valley, and Sherman's march through Georgia and the Carolinas—that finally destroyed the Confederacy and brought about its unconditional surrender.

* * *

STEPHEN CUSHMAN

From Lincoln's Gettysburg Address and Second Inaugural Address[†]

* * *

In the case of the Gettysburg Address, those who intone with reverence its superbly crafted periods do not have to deny their reverence in order to bear in mind that by the time Lincoln delivered his address on the afternoon of Thursday, November 19, 1863, the victory at Gettysburg of

---

4. Abraham Lincoln, *Lincoln and the Civil War in the Diaries and Letters of John Hay*, edited by Tyler Dennett (New York, 1939), 180; CW 7: 393.
5. John Henry Cramer, *Lincoln Under Enemy Fire* (New York, 1948).
6. CW 7: 476.
† From *Cambridge Companion to Abraham Lincoln*. Edited by Shirley Samuels. Copyright © 2012 by Cambridge University Press. Reprinted with permission of Cambridge University Press.

the Army of the Potomac over the Army of Northern Virginia four months earlier had lost some of its luster, because, from Lincoln's point of view, Union General George Gordon Meade had squandered a precious opportunity to defeat the Confederate army of Robert E. Lee, allowing it to escape southward over the Potomac River. After a frustrating and inconclusive series of subsequent engagements in Virginia, Meade, under pressure from Lincoln, was about to launch the ill-fated Mine Run Campaign (November 27 to December 2, 1863). Meanwhile, in the west a decisive Confederate victory at the battle of Chickamauga, fought two months earlier in northwestern Georgia, had led to the penning up of United States forces in Chattanooga, Tennessee, and Ulysses S. Grant had not yet given Lincoln the crucial victories around that city that would convince the president to promote Grant and bring him east to face Lee in 1864, although those victories were only days away. In other words, when Lincoln delivered what many around the world now regard as the quintessential hymn to democracy in the United States, that democracy, precariously unstable, easily could have turned out a failed experiment, a quixotic delusion not worth hymning. Thirteen months after the Battle of Gettysburg, and nine months after the address there, Lincoln penned a private memorandum in which he anticipated losing the 1864 presidential election to Democratic rival George McClellan. If he had lost the election to McClellan and McClellan had concluded a peace with the Confederate States of America that recognized the independence of the latter, as he promised to do, it is questionable whether the Gettysburg Address would be read or remembered, whatever its intrinsic literary or stylistic merits.[1]

The high honor in which many hold those literary or stylistic merits is, to some extent then, an honor conferred retrospectively in light of later historical unfoldings, among them Union victory over the two major armies of the Confederacy in April 1865; the assassination of Lincoln the same month; the outpouring of Civil War memoirs and other writings in the last two decades of the nineteenth century, as many veterans' organizations began to hold local and national reunions; the development and dedication of the first national military park at Chickamauga; and the growing trend toward reconciliation, at least in public, of the white populations of North and South. If part of the rhetorical majesty of the Gettysburg Address comes from what now feels like its visionary prophetic force, that visionary prophetic force originated in November 1863, with Lee's defiant Army of Virginia dug in behind the Rapidan River in central Virginia, as a more limited exhortation in the optative mood, an exhortation on behalf of something uncertain and desired, not something inevitable and accomplished. It is important to acknowledge that in itself the Gettysburg Address made nothing happen. It did not, for example, inoculate citizens of the northern states against the extreme war-weariness of

---

1. Lincoln's artfulness appears in John G. Nicolay, "Lincoln's Literary Experiments," *Century Magazine* 47 (April 1894); Daniel Kilham Dodge, *Abraham Lincoln: Master of Words* (New York, 1924); Edmund Wilson, *Patriotic Gore: Studies in the Literature of the American Civil War* (New York, 1962), ch. 3; Don E. Fehrenbacher, "The Words of Lincoln," *Lincoln in Text and Context: Collected Essays* (Stanford, 1987); Ronald C. White, *Lincoln's Greatest Speech: The Second Inaugural* (New York, 2002); John Channing Briggs, *Lincoln's Speeches Reconsidered* (Baltimore, 2005); Douglas L. Wilson, *Lincoln's Sword: The Presidency and the Power of Words* (New York, 2006); and Fred Kaplan, *Lincoln: The Biography of a Writer* (New York, 2008).

the summer of 1864, which, as Lincoln well knew, could have cost him reelection if it had not been for William Tecumseh Sherman's capture of Atlanta in September of that year, a capture that inspired northern soldiers to vote overwhelmingly for Lincoln and reflected a strategic shift to total war, subsequently prosecuted by Sherman during his famous March to the Sea, which ended at Savannah in December 1864, after his army had deliberately and systematically reduced the abilities of southern civilians to support the Confederate war effort.

To acknowledge that the Gettysburg Address does not consist of magically efficacious words, which by themselves accomplished northern war aims and preserved the Union or by themselves adequately performed public rituals of mourning and consolation—with the unparalleled casualties of 1864 still to come (in one four-week period, from May 5 to June 3, Grant lost nearly 50,000 soldiers, killed, wounded, captured, or missing), no 1863 utterance could have been, adequate—in no way diminishes the distinct qualities of the address. If anything, such an acknowledgment clears the way for our realistic appraisal of the deliberate verbal means by which Lincoln achieved the distinct qualities that subsequent historical events and developments made so attractive to national retrospection and self-description.

These verbal means would not impress us so deeply in the present if a large shift in popular sensibility, taste, and expectation had not taken place since the Civil War, a shift both reflected in and furthered by changing norms in education. At Gettysburg, on November 19, 1863, Edward Everett's two-hour peroration fulfilled the expectations of educated taste and sensibility, whereas Lincoln's short speech did not attempt to. But for many reasons Everett's speech is unthinkable now, and Lincoln's, modest as it may have sounded in 1863 by comparison, now brims and resonates with sonorities that far exceed our expectations for speeches made by presidents.[2]

Consider the famous first sentence, as it appears in the Second Draft or Hay text, which recent scholarship identifies as the one Lincoln probably read: "Four score and seven years ago our fathers brought forth, upon this continent, a new nation, conceived in Liberty, and dedicated to the proposition that all men are created equal."[3] Sheer repetition of this nearly sacred sentence has made it almost impossible for us to imagine it any other way, but a comparison with translations into Romance and Germanic languages in Basler's collection, most of which open with some version of "eighty-seven years ago" (although the Italian speaks in terms of *lustri*, or five-year periods, and the German of "thirteen years" more until "it will be a century") vividly confirms Lincoln's artistry. If he had begun, "In 1776 our ancestors established a new government based on certain assumptions about individual freedom and on the principle that everyone has the same rights," he would have said much the same thing, but he would have forfeited two crucial features of the opening. The first is an

---

2. One early appreciation of the Gettysburg Address came from Ralph Waldo Emerson: "His brief speech at Gettysburg will not easily be surpassed by words on any recorded occasion." See "Abraham Lincoln," in *Miscellanies*, Riverside Edition of *Emerson's Complete Works* (Cambridge, 1895), 2: 311.

3. Gabor S. Boritt, *The Gettysburg Gospel: The Lincoln Speech That Nobody Knows* (New York, 2006), 272–75.

echo of Psalm 90, verse 10, in the King James Version: "The days of our years are threescore years and ten; and if by reason of strength they be fourscore years, yet is their strength labour and sorrow; for it is soon cut off, and we fly away." The Hebrew original does not include a literal equivalent of "fourscore," meaning four groups of twenty; this particular locution is a flourish of the King James translators, and it is a word Lincoln's audience would connect, either consciously or unconsciously, with this well-known biblical verse, a *memento mori* acknowledging the brevity of human life in a way wholly appropriate for a speech at a new rural cemetery, although, the echo carries with it some hard irony, too, because none of the soldiers interred at Gettysburg had managed to live seventy or eighty years.

The second sacrifice, which points beyond the first sentence to the entire address, as well as to the Second Inaugural, is sonority. The opening sentence bundles "Four," "score," "our," "fathers," "forth," "are" with varying degrees of rhyme, assonance, consonance, and alliteration, as it does "score," "continent," "dedicated," "created," and "equal." Since the literary modernism of the second and third decades of the twentieth century, fewer readers of English necessarily associate rhyme, or its subdivisions, with verse, let alone prose, but in fact the antecedents of Lincoln's rhyming prose include ancient Latin and Arabic precursors, although he would not have known it.[4] What he would have known, or felt, is what the writers of ancient rhyming prose knew and felt, that there are gradations and shadings on the spectrum leading from prose to verse, and certain occasions call for prose that is closer to verse. That Lincoln could also write prose wholly free of verse qualities should be immediately apparent to anyone reading through the Emancipation Proclamation. When he had to write like a lawyer and subordinate the resonating sonorities of language to more precise specifications, he certainly could do so. As the historian Richard Hofstadter commented wryly, "The Emancipation Proclamation of January 1, 1863 had all the moral grandeur of a bill of lading."[5]

Some may object at this point that to treat one of the preeminent scriptures of the United States as an aesthetic performance, without dwelling on the content of the speech, is as blasphemous as reading the Bible as literature. What about Lincoln's ignoring the Constitution, which is what legally "brought forth" the new nation and which did not dedicate the new nation to the proposition that all men are created equal, as the original version of Article 1, Section 2, which based representation and taxation on "the whole Number of free Persons" and "three-fifths of all other persons," makes perfectly clear? What about his not mentioning the South? What about his associating the war effort with bringing about "a new birth of freedom," thereby identifying emancipation as a primary war aim, although he never explicitly mentions slavery? What about the last sentence with its famous triad, "of the people, by the people, for the people" (Second Draft), which echoes, according to one dictionary of quotations, similar formulations by John Wycliffe, Daniel Webster, William Lloyd

---

4. See O. B. Hardison, Jr. and Roger M. A. Allen, "Rhyme-Prose," *Princeton Encyclopedia of Poetry and Poetics*, 4th ed., edited by Roland Greene, Stephen Cushman, et al. (Princeton, 2012).
5. Richard Hofstadter, *The American Political Tradition and the Men Who Made It* (New York, 1948), 131.

Garrison, and Theodore Parker, thereby linking Lincoln's speech with
antecedents in the Protestant Reformation, antebellum Whig Unionism,
abolitionism, and transcendentalism?[6]

To focus on Lincoln's verbal artistry is not to discount or dismiss any of
these questions or the significance of any of the issues they raise; it is to
point out that, significant as these issues were and still are, many, many
people wrote and spoke about them in writings and speeches we no longer know or read. It cannot be the issues alone that keep us reading and
reciting the Gettysburg Address or the Second Inaugural, and to admit
this conclusion enables us to raise another question, one that begins in
verbal artistry but rapidly ramifies in several directions: What is the political or social function of eloquence? Take, for example, the famous triad in
the last sentence of the Gettysburg Address. Yes, its antecedents may associate Lincoln's utterance with Protestantism, Unionism, abolitionism, and
transcendentalism, with all of which he had affinities of varying complex-
ity. But in addition to these considerations we must also recognize that Lincoln simply loved and used verbal triads throughout his writings and
speeches, and the verbal triad, as a schematic rhetorical archetype, especially effective as a device for closure, descended to Lincoln with the accumulated resonances and authority of the Bible ("the power, the kingdom,
and the glory"), the classical world (Caesar's *veni, vidi, vici*), Shakespeare
(the Second Apparition's "Be bloody, bold, and resolute," speaking to Macbeth), and earlier statesmen (Jefferson's "we mutually pledge to each other
our lives, our Fortunes, and our sacred Honor").

Many readers may want, quite understandably, to connect the verbal
form of the Gettysburg Address with the content of the speech, but there
is something naive about the insistence that, for example, Lincoln's careful auditory connections between and among words, phrases, clauses,
and sentences—another of his favorite rhetorical devices is syntactic par-
allelism, which, like rhyme, is a scheme of verbal repetition—somehow
reflect or represent or imitate or enact the binding together of the
wounded and disintegrating Union. Lincoln's favorite verbal patterns also
appear in writings composed before the Civil War, when binding together
a wounded and disintegrating Union would have been neither his chief
concern nor his chief responsibility. In his early Address to the Young
Men's Lyceum of Springfield, Illinois, delivered January 27, 1838, a quarter of a century before the Gettysburg Address, verbal triads abound,
along with anaphora (repetition of an initial word or phrase in successive
clauses or sentences), as in these two consecutive sentences from the pen-
ultimate paragraph: "Reason, cold, calculating, unimpassioned reason,
must furnish all the materials for our future support and defence. Let
those materials be moulded into *general intelligence, sound morality* and,
in particular, *a reverence for the constitution and laws*; and, that we
improved to the last; that we remained free to the last; that we revered
his name to the last; that, during his long sleep, we permitted no hostile
foot to pass over or desecrate his resting place; shall be that which to
learn the last trump shall awaken our WASHINGTON." What these two
sentences demonstrate is that by the time he was approaching his twenty-

6. John Bartlett, *Familiar Quotations*, 14th ed., edited by Emily Morrison Beck (Boston, 1969),
   639n.

ninth birthday, Lincoln had already developed his ability to organize his words into sonorous, eloquent patterns he could apply to many different subjects.

*   *   *

Built of four paragraphs, the fourth of which is the most famous and most often quoted, the Second Inaugural, in its second and long third paragraph, does what the Gettysburg Address does not do: It names the South, it names slavery, and it narrates the past, not the distant, storied past of 1776 and the Declaration of Independence, but the immediate past of 1854, the Kansas-Nebraska Act, and what followed as a result. What is both shrewd and tricky about Lincoln's account is that he ends up having it both ways, on the one hand, calling the country to rise above sectional partisanship as it moves toward Reconstruction, on the other, assigning a little more of the blame to the South. One does not have to be a Confederate sympathizer to wonder who is included in Lincoln's "us."

To appreciate the nature of Lincoln's narration, we can compare it productively with the point of view of two outsiders deeply interested by the American Civil War. Writing in November 1861 for *Die Presse*, one of the leading newspapers in Vienna, Karl Marx and Frederick Engels summarized the war this way for their Austrian readership: "The present struggle between the South and North is, therefore, nothing but a struggle between two social systems, between the system of slavery and the system of free labor. The struggle has broken out because the two systems can no longer live peacefully side by side on the North American continent.[7] Not all students of the Civil War will find this unidealized representation of the conflict palatable. It says nothing, for example, about democracy, the Constitution, or a theory of states' rights. But it does serve as an instructive contrast with Lincoln's representation of the same war in his Second Inaugural Address.

In his short second paragraph Lincoln adopts something of the detachment of Marx and Engels, describing the moment of "impending civil war" in March 1861 also by contrasting North and South, although Lincoln contrasts them not as competing social systems but as opposites with respect to the Union, one side committed to continuing the Union—Lincoln's word is "saving"—the other to ending the Union—his not quite neutral word is "destroying." Placing the genesis of the war solely in the context of Union, Lincoln appears to refrain from assigning responsibility for the outbreak of belligerence, acknowledging a basic likeness between North and South: "Both parties deprecated war." The series of parallel constructions, in which he lays out the opposition between North and South, culminates in one of Lincoln's great sentences, a four-word marvel of concision and understatement, which contrasts with the paragraph-long sentence at the end of the address and recalls the shortest verse in the King James Bible, "Jesus wept" (John 11:35): "And the war came." Known to students of rhetoric as parataxis, this use of the conjunction "and," reminiscent of the opening verses of Genesis, leaves unspecified the logical relationship of Lincoln's short sentence to what precedes

---

7. Karl Marx and Frederick Engels, *The Civil War in the United States*, vol. 30 of the Marxist Library, 2nd ed., edited by Richard Enmale (New York, 1940), 81.

it. It withholds the causal connection, as, for example, "So the war came" would not, and in withholding that connection appears to set aside a discussion of causality altogether.

But it does so only for a moment. Leading into the long third paragraph, this short sentence functions as the hinge on which Lincoln swings his account, now moving to join Marx and Engels in explicitly identifying slavery as cause—"All knew that this interest was, somehow, the cause of the war"—while diverging from them by framing his narrative according to a pattern of apostasy and retribution straight out of the Hebrew Bible, which despite the echo of Matthew 7:1 and a quotation of Matthew 18:7, drives both vision and rhetoric, as the quotation from Psalm 19, which closes the paragraph, confirms ("the judgments of the Lord are true, and righteous altogether"): Slavery is the offence, and the war is the compensation God exacts for it.

Two stylistic features of Lincoln's biblical account of the war and its causes are particularly noteworthy and revealing. The first appears in the first clause of the sentence containing the echo of Matthew 7:1: "It may seem strange that any men should dare to ask a just God's assistance in wringing their bread from the sweat of other men's faces; but let us judge not that we be not judged." Despite his appearances earlier as detached and somewhat objective, here the lawyer in Lincoln slyly works his audience by means of the rhetorical figure known as paralipsis, a Greek word meaning "passing by omission." In paralipsis, according to the *Oxford English Dictionary*, "the speaker emphasizes something by affecting to pass it by without notice." In this case, what he affects to pass but actually emphasizes is the strangeness—an understated synonym for something like "the indefensible hypocrisy"—of slaveholders who defend slavery while thinking of themselves as entitled by their faith to divine support and favor. The irony here is that in anticipation of Reconstruction, at a moment when he hopes to prevent continued acrimony between the warring sections, Lincoln should resort to such a pointed jab at the South, whereas in the Gettysburg Address, which focuses on northern war effort and losses, and in which such a jab would be more appropriate, he does no such thing. Although he quickly follows his semicolon with an injunction against judging, he has already judged, and the "us" in "let us not judge" clearly stands for those opposed to slaveholding. If Lincoln had truly wished to leave judgment out of the Second Inaugural, or at least the judgment of one section by another, as opposed to the divine judgment to which all must answer, he could and should have left this sentence out altogether.

The second feature appears four sentences later, immediately after the long question beginning, "If we shall suppose that American Slavery is one of those offences" and climbing steadily, through various right-branching segmentations, to the high plateau of sermonic fervor. We should not be surprised that Lincoln's prose makes pronounced use of rhyme at this moment, but what many who hear the rhyme may not realize is that the prose suddenly takes the metrical shape of a four-tine hymn stanza: "Fondly do we hope— / fervently do we pray— / that this mighty scourge of war / may speedily pass away." The model here is what a hymnal would identify as short meter, rhyming *xaya*, and Mary Stanley Bunce

Dana's 1840 Presbyterian hymn "Oh, Sing to Me of Heaven" typifies any number of hymns Lincoln and his hearers might have known and sung: "Oh, sing to me of heaven / When I am called to die, / Singing songs of holy ecstasy, / To waft my soul on high."[8] This breaking into song, and not just song but hymn, marks an extraordinary moment in the Second Inaugural and distinguishes it from Lincoln's other major speeches, including the Gettysburg Address, which from start to finish may be pitched closer to the verse end of the prose spectrum than the later speech, but which as a consequence does not have to travel as far to its heights as the Second Inaugural does.

Having reached this rhetorical and auditory high ground, the Second Inaugural does not descend again. By the time he concludes, Lincoln has sounded loudly the call to northern magnanimity and forgiveness, which we can only infer and imagine would have been the hallmarks of Reconstruction if he had lived to oversee it. The final vision here is not of democracy but of peace, and, unlike the vision of the Gettysburg Address, it has no place for the words "dead" or "died." With more than six hundred thousand deaths still accumulating a month from the end of the war, Lincoln resorts to periphrastic round-aboutness in the Second Inaugural, referring to the widow and the orphan of "him who shall have borne the battle," as well as to "every drop of blood drawn with the lash . . . paid by another drawn with the sword," a quaint archaism in the context of a war in which swords did a minute fraction of the killing. But nowhere bluntly does he name the dead as dead. Inaugurating a second presidency, in which war will end and rebuilding will begin, calls for different language from dedicating a cemetery while that war continues. At Gettysburg, Lincoln not only honored the dead, he also used them to strengthen northern resolve with a vision that attempted to put their deaths in a bearable perspective. On the platform in front of the Capitol, with northern resolve having nearly fulfilled its purpose, he needed to quiet the dead in order to quiet the living.

FAITH BARRETT

From Lincoln and Poetry[†]

*   *   *

The list of poets whom Lincoln admired is both long and varied, reflecting the extraordinary versatility of the genre of poetry in this era as well as the wide range of work being read by the American public. In addition to Shakespeare, Burns, Gray, and Holmes, Lincoln liked work by Fitz-Greene Halleck, Byron, Edgar Allan Poe, and John Greenleaf Whittier. As the inclusion of both Holmes and Halleck on this list makes clear, Lincoln enjoyed not only literary poetry but also lighter and wittier verse.

---

8. *American Hymns Old and New,* edited by Albert Christ-Janer, Charles W. Hughes, and Carleton Sprague Smith (New York, 1980), 557.

† From *Cambridge Companion to Abraham Lincoln.* Edited by Shirley Samuels. Copyright © 2012 by Cambridge University Press. Reprinted with permission of Cambridge University Press.

A witness to his own apotheosis in literature, he also read many of the poems written for and about him by both professional and amateur writers while he was in the White House. Hannibal Cox, an African-American soldier and a former slave, sent Lincoln a poem in praise of the flag of the Union in March of 1864, while Oliver Gibbs sent Lincoln a comic poem titled "The Presidential Cow" in May of that same year. We know that Lincoln read at least some of these pieces: When Frank Wells sent a poem in praise of Lincoln in June of 1864, Lincoln noted on the piece—perhaps with some self-mocking irony intended—that it was "pretty fair poetry." The many parodies and satires of Lincoln that appeared in the popular press in the form of both cartoons and jokes would have served as counterweight to the poetic effusions of his well-wishers and admirers. As these examples suggest, nineteenth-century American poetry was extraordinarily versatile both generically and rhetorically. The brevity of the genre and the lack of copyright protections meant that poems could be quickly read, recopied, and printed widely. Moreover, poetry also gave writers the possibility of combining different registers of diction and tone in one piece; the permeable boundary between poetry and popular song made poems highly portable and sped their circulation throughout the country. For example, while Julia Ward Howe's "Battle Hymn of the Republic" first appeared on the pages of the prestigious *Atlantic Monthly* in February of 1862, it soon became a favorite with Union troops and was widely sung in the North by both soldiers and civilians.

Like many Americans of his day, Lincoln wrote poems, both comic and serious, on several occasions throughout his life. Because of the cultural centrality of poetry both in educational settings and in print, many literate Americans tried their hand at writing poetry in the nineteenth century, penning Valentines for sweethearts or a few lines of verse for a friend's album. In this era, poetry was culturally ubiquitous: poems were widely printed in newspapers and magazines and also distributed in the form of broadsides and song sheets at campaign events, school programs, political rallies, and recruitment events for soldiers. Many Americans kept scrapbooks or albums of favorite poems, recopying them for inclusion in letters to family and friends. In his twenties and thirties, Lincoln wrote a number of poems, publishing at least one of them in a regional newspaper. As a political candidate in his fifties, he wrote souvenir verses in the autograph books of two young women he met while campaigning. And as president in the summer of 1863, Lincoln penned several lines of comic doggerel on Lee's defeat at Gettysburg, a seemingly improbable counterpoint to the gravity and dignity of the Gettysburg Address he would write in November of that same year.

Lincoln displayed remarkable range as a reader and writer over the course of his political career; in the genre of poetry he found a capaciousness and versatility of stance that would allow him to give voice to some of that extraordinary range of thought and feeling. Both his personal and his political life were shaped by his interest in poetry: Lincoln's relationship with Mary Todd was fueled in part by their shared love of poetry—Robert Burns was a favorite with both—and reminiscences about Lincoln's years in the White House return again and again to his reading aloud of poetry.[1] Lincoln would frequently open cabinet meetings with readings from humorous stories or verse, much to the irritation of some members, and during the war years, he read poetry both for diversion and for consolation.[2] Traveling by steamboat to visit Union troops in 1862, Lincoln read aloud from Fitz-Greene Halleck's "Marco Bozzaris," a contemporary poem that celebrated the heroism of a Greek soldier in the war against Turkey. Poetry's flexibility in adapting itself to both high literary and popular purposes would have only added to its appeal for Lincoln. Indeed the generic flexibility of poetry made it particularly well-suited to the American literary marketplace because poems could be multilayered and comic simultaneously, drawing in growing numbers of literate Americans as enthusiasts of the genre.

Two often-cited descriptions of Lincoln's style of thinking underline the reasons why poetry might have had such a strong appeal for him. Emerson writes: "He is the author of a multitude of good sayings, so disguised as pleasantries that it is certain they had no reputation at first but as jests; and only later by the very acceptance and adoption they find in the mouths of millions, turn out to be the wisdom of the hour."[3] The aphoristic compression and semantic polyvalence of poetry would certainly have attracted him. In his eulogy for Lincoln, Charles Sumner notes that his ideas "moved as the beasts entered Noah's ark, in pairs."[4] Poetry's focus on metaphor and analogical thinking would also have appealed to Lincoln's mind.

Moreover, Lincoln's literary tastes underline the relationship between the stances of the poetic speaker and the stances of political identity. Lincoln's fondness for the Scottish poets Knox and Burns likely resulted from the foregrounding of both class issues and nationalist pride in their work; Burns's commitment to writing in dialect would have appealed to Lincoln's interest in both rural and oral culture.[5] As an American reader of both European and American work, Lincoln found in poetry some of the freedoms of perspective that the Declaration of Independence promised in proposing that all Americans had the right not only to life and liberty but also to the pursuit of happiness. Praised for his talents at storytelling and mimicry, Lincoln loved poetry because poetry enabled him to inhabit imaginatively the lives and voices of other speakers. Civil War-era poems by northern writers often present Lincoln as a living saint, even as they also underline that his life trajectory—from rural poverty to the office of the presidency—is an archetypal American story. In view of its generic versatility, it is not surprising that poetry played a central role in conversations about American national identity during the Civil War era; poetic representations of the life of Abraham Lincoln were an important component of that dialogue.

* * *

1. See Doris Kearns Goodwin, *Team of Rivals: The Political Genius of Abraham Lincoln* (New York, 2008), and Peter Armenti, "Lincoln as Poetry Reader," in *Abraham Lincoln and Poetry*, February 9, 2011: www.loc.gov/rr/program/bib/lincolnpoetry/#reader.
2. See Joshua Wolf Shenk, *Lincoln's Melancholy: How Depression Changed a President and Fueled His Greatness* (Boston, 2005), 181–82.
3. Ralph Waldo Emerson, "Abraham Lincoln," *The Complete Works of Ralph Waldo Emerson* (Boston, 1911), 11: 333.
4. Charles Sumner, "Eulogy," *A Memorial of Abraham Lincoln* (Boston, 1865), 134.
5. For Lincoln's relationship to Burns, see Fred Kaplan, *Lincoln: The Biography of a Writer* (New York, 2008), 63–70, and also Ferenc Morton Szasz, *Abraham Lincoln and Robert Burns: Connected Lives and Legends* (Carbondale, 2008).

Lincoln's apotheosis in Civil War poetry happens with remarkable speed as northern poets seize on the image of Lincoln to represent the best and brightest aspirations of the American nation and the possibilities for upward mobility that America offers young men. Often invoked as the refrain in recruitment poems and calls to arms, Lincoln's name becomes a rallying cry for the Union Army, an incantation that underlines both Lincoln's powerful moral authority and his strong ties to the American land. In northern poems that celebrate Lincoln's rise to power—as in many poetic calls to arms—the solitary "I" of romanticism is often replaced by the celebratory nationalist "we" of the Union. In the recruitment poem "Three Hundred Thousand More," James Sloan Gibbons establishes the central image of Lincoln as the nation's moral patriarch: The "we" who speaks in the poem is the collective of newly recruited Union soldiers, soldiers who answer Lincoln's call, in July of 1862, for more troops. In its first stanza, the poem establishes Lincoln as a figure of biblical and prophetic authority:

> We are coming, Father Abraham, three hundred thousand more,
> From Mississippi's winding stream and from New England's shore;
> We leave our ploughs and workshops, our wives and children dear,
> With hearts too full for utterance, but with a silent tear;
> We dare not look behind us, but steadfastly before:
> We are coming, Father Abraham, three hundred thousand more![6]

Linking recruits from the West and the Northeast—and implicitly reminding its readers of Lincoln's western origins—Gibbons's poem converts the solitary stance of romantic mourning in poems like Lincoln's "My Childhood Home I See Again" into a collective nationalist "we." Whereas "My Childhood Home I See Again" expresses the private grief of the speaker's mourning—a mourning that is articulated by the madman's sorrowful song and assuaged by natures responsive tears—in "Three Hundred Thousand More," private grief is transformed into the collective and active response of the nation, a nation that is symbiotically reliant on the natural world. Paradoxically—and in keeping with romantic convention—the poem gives collective voice to the emotion that individual soldiers are unable to express. They shed "a silent tear" at parting with their families; their hearts are "too full for utterance."

Stanzas two and three of the poem foreground the idea that the new recruits spring bodily from a vital American landscape, underlying the close and redemptive relationship between the American people and an American natural world. Stanza two begins: "If you look all up our valleys where the growing harvests shine, / You may see our sturdy farmer boys fast forming into line."[7] The redemptive and cyclical work of agricultural labor—the labor that Lincoln himself performed as a young man—is thus allied with a redemptive cycle of fighting and dying on the battlefield. The fourth and final stanza makes clear that the "three hundred thousand" who speak in the poem are called to action by the "six hundred thousand" who have gone before them. In the first two lines of the last stanza, the soldiers' collective voice makes explicit that they are responding both to Lincoln's call and to the sacrifices of their predecessors: "You

6. James Sloan Gibbons, "Three Hundred Thousand More," Faith Barrett and Cristanne Miller, eds., *Words for the Hour: A New Anthology of American Civil War Poetry* (Amherst, 2005), 92.
7. Gibbons, "Three Hundred Thousand More," 92.

have called us and we're coming, by Richmond's bloody tide / To lay us down, for Freedom's sake, our brothers' bones beside."[8] The poem thus establishes as its central metaphor this symmetrical pattern; that soldiers will rise up from the land to replace those who have been buried in it, thereby redeeming the nation's destiny. Enlisting and fighting are likened to the natural cycles not only of agriculture but also of human birth, death, and regeneration; in the refrain that closes each stanza ("We are coming, Father Abraham, three hundred thousand more"), Abraham Lincoln is the father of the great interconnected family that springs from the American land. The figure of the solitary son who grieves in harmony with nature in "My Childhood Home I See Again" has in "Three Hundred Thousand More" been replaced by the figure of the inspiring and generative father who can call sons forth from the bountiful land itself.

It is a testament to Lincoln's extraordinary personal modesty that frequent paeans to him seem not to have turned his head or impaired his ability to function effectively as a leader. Gibbons's poem was first published anonymously in the *Saturday Evening Post* on July 16, 1862, two weeks after Lincoln's call for additional troops, and was widely circulated both as a poem and as a song—attributed to several different authors—throughout the war. Gibbons is reported to have sung the poem to Lincoln after the December 1862 battle at Fredericksburg; the piece is a typical example of the permeable boundary between popular song and poetry in the Civil War era. The close emotional relationship that Gibbons's poem imagines between Lincoln and the Union soldiers is of course confirmed by historians' accounts of the many visits Lincoln paid to Union soldiers and the many letters of condolence he wrote to grieving family members after soldiers' deaths. Elizabeth Keckley's portrait of Lincoln's profound grief at the death of his young son Willie is also implicitly a portrait of the father of the nation grieving for the metaphorical sons he has lost on the battlefield.

Moreover, Lincoln's own wartime poetry offers an alternative kind of evidence of his strong sense of connection to the Union troops. Following the battle at Gettysburg in July of 1863, Lincoln pens eight lines of comic doggerel that signal his relief that Lee's attempt at a northern incursion has been rebuffed:

Verse on Lee's Invasion of the North

Gen. Lees invasion of the North written by himself—

In eighteen sixty three, with pomp,
    and mighty swell,
Me and Jeff's Confederacy, went
    forth to sack Phil-del,

The Yankees they got arter us, and
    giv us particular hell,
And we skedaddled back again,
    And didn't sack Phil-del.

8. Gibbons, "Three Hundred Thousand More," 93.

Lincoln responds to the hero-making rhetoric of "We Are Coming, Father Abraham" with the rough humor that is characteristic of the poems written by amateur soldier-poets during the war years. Echoing the adolescent poems in which he jokingly boasted about his own literacy, Lincoln titles the poem with a phrase that insists comically on Lee's authorship and literacy ("written by himself") even as the brevity of the poem also mocks the brevity of Lee's northern incursion. In its two brisk stanzas, the poem uses working-class colloquialisms and dialect to demote Lee, a Virginia plantation owner and top graduate of West Point, to the ranks of his southern rural-born foot soldiers; in similar fashion, as the poem's speaker, Lee addresses the president of the Confederacy on a comically casual first-name basis. The poem's abundant use of commas and enjambment heightens the satire of its portrait of Lee, whose "pomp, / and mighty swell" are quickly deflated both by the military defeat at Gettysburg and by the poem's comic turns. The enjambment in particular suggests both the lurching swagger of a boastful leader and the quick reversals of fortune that can occur on the battlefield. The literary-military phrasing in the title and both stanzas ("invasion," "pomp, / and mighty swell"; "went / forth"; "sack") alternates with the comically compressed "Phil-del" and the rural and working-class phrases "they got arter us," "giv us particular hell," and "we skedaddled." In presenting a satirical version of Lee's voice, Lincoln's poem offers a cautionary tale about how easily military and political leaders can be corrupted by their own success; above all else, however, what the poem signals is Lincoln's powerful sense of identification with and affection for the Union troops, his ability to see the war imaginatively through the eyes of his own foot soldiers.

☆   ☆   ☆

DAVID S. REYNOLDS

My Captain: Lincoln and Walt Whitman[†]

In light of the almost mythic stature Whitman assigned to Lincoln, it is perhaps fitting that the relationship between the poet and the president was long the stuff of myth. In *Personal Reflections of Abraham Lincoln* (1916) Henry B. Rankin told of an incident in 1857 when Lincoln in his Springfield law office picked up a copy of Whitman's poetry volume *Leaves of Grass*, began reading it to himself, and was so entranced after half an hour that he started over again, reading it aloud to his colleagues. Another anecdote, originally contained in an 1865 letter by a Lincoln aide and repeated by Whitman's followers, had Lincoln gazing out a White House window, spotting the hale, bearded Whitman walking by, and exclaiming, "Well, *he* looks like a *man*."[1]

There is no way of confirming either of these stories; probably both are apocryphal. Lincoln's reaction to Whitman or his poetry, if any, is unclear.

† From *Walt Whitman's America: A Cultural Biography*. By David S. Reynolds. Copyright © 1995 by David S. Reynolds. Reprinted with permission of Alfred A. Knopf, an imprint of the Knopf Doubleday Publishing Group.
1. Horace Traubel, *With Walt Whitman in Camden* (New York, 1912), 3: 179.

But the kinship of spirits these stories suggest was very real, if we judge from Whitman's reaction to Lincoln. In Lincoln's life, Whitman saw the comprehensive, all-directing soul he had long been seeking. In Lincoln's death, he saw a grand tragedy that promised ultimate purgation and unification for America.

Whitman and Lincoln had much in common. Both rose to greatness from humble backgrounds, and both were largely self-taught. The cultural tastes of both ran the gamut from high to low. Like Whitman, Lincoln loved to recite Shakespeare and to hear grand arias but also had a weakness for minstrel shows and the songs of Stephen Foster. Whitman's favorite singing group, the Hutchinsons, helped elect Lincoln in 1860 by singing at Republican rallies, and during the war they entertained the Union troops. Both the president and the poet took delight in plays, even cheap melodramas and farces. There were temperamental similarities too: both were generally calm men given on occasion to explosions—of anger in Whitman's case, of laughter in Lincoln's. Both delighted in low humor and slang. Both had an amused curiosity about spiritualism: Whitman may have attended a séance given by the medium Charles H. Foster in the sixties, and Lincoln reportedly attended a séance in the White House ordered by his wife, Mary, after the death of their son Willie in 1862. Two of Whitman's favorite orators, Cassius Clay and John Hale, became part of Lincoln's administration, the former as minister to Russia, the latter as minister to Spain. Most importantly, both Whitman and Lincoln tried to cure America's problems through oratorical language. Whitman's quintessential work, *Leaves of Grass*, was a sprawling poetry collection that brought together cultural images in their variety and particularity. Lincoln's, the Gettysburg Address, was a terse, 262-word speech that soared beyond particulars into a transcendental realm of political abstractions. Both were written in the name of union, equality, and cultural retrieval.

Whitman saw Lincoln some twenty to thirty times in Washington. This was not unusual. Unlike today, when presidents are virtually inaccessible to average citizens except as images in the mass media, in those days they were available and visible in ordinary life. Even Lincoln, who had to be on guard because of death threats and the war situation, could be met personally by almost anyone, in the White House or at the Soldier's Home, his summer retreat three miles north of the city. Whitman didn't meet him, but he regularly saw him riding through Washington for business or pleasure. "I see the President almost every day," he wrote in the summer of 1863,[2] when he lived near where Lincoln passed by en route to and from the White House. Lincoln appeared to him ordinary but impressive, riding comfortably on an easygoing gray horse or in an open barouche, escorted by twenty or so cavalry in yellow-striped jackets with sabers poised on their shoulders. Some afternoons he caught sight of the president and his wife, both in black, riding in their plain two-horse carriage on unescorted pleasure jaunts. "We have got so that we exchange bows, and very cordial ones,"[3] Whitman wrote of Lincoln, who once gave him a long, direct stare that Whitman felt was friendly but inexpressibly sad. "He has a face like a hoosier Michel Angelo," Whitman wrote, "so awful

2. PW 1: 59.
3. PW 1: 60.

ugly it becomes beautiful, with its strange mouth, its deep cut, criss-cross lines, and its doughnut complexion."[4] Whitman continued to spot Lincoln, as in March 1864 when the war-weary president, his sallow face creased with deep wrinkles, rattled by in his carriage after enduring the tedious ceremonies of the Second Inaugural.

No other human being seemed as multifaceted to Whitman as Lincoln. There was hardly a quality he did not attribute to the president. Lincoln, he said, had "canny shrewdness" and "*horse-sense*," as seen in the down-home stories he told to drive home his points.[5] He seemed the average American, with his drab appearance and his humor, redolent of barnyards and barrooms. Whitman commented on the "somewhat rusty and dusty" appearance of Lincoln, who "looks about as ordinary in attire, etc., as the commonest man." He delighted in the ascendancy to power of one he called the embodiment of "the commonest average of life—a rail-splitter and a flat-boatsman!" He pointed to Lincoln's rural origins, which he thought made him totally American. His other cultural heroes paled in comparison. In contrast, Washington seemed "the first Saxon" and Franklin "an English nobleman," while Lincoln was "quite thoroughly Western," of the prairies and the outdoors.

Lincoln's homely, mysterious face, he thought, had never been captured by photographers or artists—indeed, could not be, since it was as ineffable as life itself. Funny and folksy, Lincoln nonetheless appeared basically sad; there was, Whitman wrote, "a deep latent sadness in the expression." He was both easygoing and tough: "generally very easy, flexible, tolerant, almost slouchy, respecting the minor matters" but capable of "indomitable firmness (even obstinacy) on rare occasions, involving great points," as when commanding his generals to win certain battles by any means. Lincoln was a family man—Whitman sometimes saw him with his wife or one of his children—but had an air of complete independence. "[H]e went his own lonely road," Whitman said, "disregarding all the usual ways—refusing the guides, accepting no warnings—just keeping his appointment with himself every time." He had tact and caution, Whitman emphasized, and his "composure was marvellous" in the face of unpopularity and the difficulties of war. Though grounded in everyday realities, he had what Whitman saw as a profoundly religious quality. His "invisible foundations" were "mystical, abstract, moral, and spiritual," his "religious nature" was "of the amplest, deepest-rooted, loftiest kind." Summing Lincoln up, Whitman called him "the greatest, best, most characteristic, artistic, moral personality" in American life.

In short, Lincoln, as Whitman saw him, was virtually the living embodiment of the "I" of *Leaves of Grass*. He was "one of the roughs" but also, for Whitman, "a kosmos," with the whole range of qualities that term implied. If *Leaves of Grass* and the Civil War were one, as Whitman once said, they particularly came together in Lincoln.

As impressive as Lincoln was in life, it was his death that represented for Whitman the transcendent, crucial moment in America's cultural life. John Wilkes Booth's murder of Lincoln in Washington's Ford Theatre on

---

4. Whitman, *The Correspondence*, edited by Edwin Haviland Miller (New York, 1961), 2: 82.
5. PW 2: 603. The remaining quotations in this paragraph, respectively, are on pp. 620, 604, and 603. The quotations in the next paragraph are in PW 2: 602–3.

April 14, 1865, was for Whitman a culminating moment in history. There was good reason Whitman would give his "Death of Abraham Lincoln" speech over and over again in the last dozen years of his life. He became fixated on what he called "the tragic splendor of [Lincoln's] death, purging, illuminating all."[6] The assassination, he declared, had unequaled influence on the shaping of the Republic.

Although Whitman was not in Washington at the time of the event, he had a vicarious presence at it. His close friend Peter Doyle was in Ford's Theatre the night of the assassination and gave him an intimate rendition of the tragedy. There were other associations too. John Wilkes Booth, the son of Whitman's favorite actor, Junius Brutus Booth, was a kind of inverse embodiment of many things Whitman had long held dear. A dashing actor with a large following, especially among starstruck women, Booth developed a melodramatic acting style that brought the emotional American style to a point of near frenzy. Whitman had seen Booth perform and thought he had moments of genius but lacked his father's subtlety. (He differed from Lincoln, who liked Booth's frenetic acting so much that he invited him to the White House; Booth did not accept the invitation.) A cocky man, Booth used as an advertising motto a line from Whitman's favorite play, *Richard III*—"I AM MYSELF ALONE"[7]—which had all the assertiveness and independence of Whitman's poetic boasts.

But in Booth, independence was fused with a Southern states'-rights viewpoint. The Maryland-bred Booth considered the Union an imposture, Lincoln a grasping tyrant, and slavery a positive good. He was an ardent white supremacist who believed in the inferiority of blacks. By a cruel irony Whitman was probably unaware of, Booth was secretly engaged to Lucy Hale, the daughter of Whitman's favorite political speaker, John Hale. Booth had dined with Lucy the evening of the murder, and after she heard of Booth's deed she remained loyal to him, saying she would die with him even at the foot of a scaffold.

These associations between Whitman and Booth, some explicit and some buried, made the events of Good Friday, 1865, especially poignant to the poet. But it was the cultural meanings of the assassination that he stressed in his many retellings of the event. If he saw Lincoln's death as "purging, illuminating all," it was largely because many of the social phenomena underlying his own poetry came to a spectacular culmination in that one moment. Many of America's social problems were reenacted and resolved, he believed, and many of its possibilities were guided toward fruition.

Among the social problems, the political crisis of the 1850s, as always, loomed largest in Whitman's mind. He began his Lincoln lecture by reviewing the difficult social conditions during the decade before his election. "The hot passions of the South," Whitman recalled, "—the strange mixture at the North of inertia, incredulity, and conscious power—the incendiarism of the abolitionists—the rascality and *grip* of the politicians, unparallel'd in any land, any age," with "the Presidentiads of Fillmore and Buchanan" proving "the weakness and wickedness of elected rulers."[8]

6. PW 1: 988.
7. Gene Smith, *American Gothic: The Story of America's Legendary Theatrical Family, Junius, Edwin, and John Wilkes Booth* (New York, 1992), 81.
8. PW 2: 498–99.

These were the social and political problems *Leaves of Grass* had been designed to correct, but Whitman believed that only the death of the Redeemer President truly resolved them. In Lincoln's murder, he declared, "A long and varied series of contradictory events arrives at last at its highest, poetic, single, central, pictorial denouement. The whole involved, baffling, multiform whirl of the secession period comes to a head, and is gather'd in one brief flash of lightning-illumination—one simple, fierce, deed."[9]

Far more than politics were involved, as Whitman told the story. Sensational news reportage, popular celebrations, acting and theater, music, audience involvement, mob violence—nearly all the cultural influences on *Leaves of Grass* were played out, in his retelling, the day of the murder. It had been a pleasant spring day in Washington. The city was in a festive mood in the aftermath of the Union's victory over the South. That afternoon, Whitman recalled, the popular Washington daily the *Evening Star* "had spatter'd all over its third page, divided among the advertisements in a sensational manner, in a hundred different places, *The President and his Lady will be at the Theatre this evening.*"[1] The whole event, then, was surrounded by the hype and sensationalism typical of nineteenth-century America. Also typical was the scene that evening at Ford's Theatre, with the usual noisy crowds, "the usual cluster of gas-lights, the usual magnetism of so many people, cheerful, with perfumes, music of violins and flutes," everyone joyful about "the triumph of the Union." This was Washington by gaslight, an urban spectacle of the sort described at length by many antebellum journalists, including Whitman. Also typically, the president had come to see a farce, Tom Taylor's *Our American Cousin,* about an American bumpkin who becomes heir to an English fortune. In the midst of this absurd play, Whitman said, occurred "the main thing, the actual murder" of "the leading actor in the stormiest drama known to real history's stage." A muffled shot rang out, a man leaped from the railing of the president's box, catching his heel on a draped flag and falling twelve feet to the stage, injuring a leg in the process. Then the raven-haired Booth, "his eyes like some mad animal's flashing with light and resolution, yet with a certain strange calmness," faced the crowd and firmly cried, "Sic semper tyrannis" ("Thus it shall always be for tyrants"). He walked offstage, and then bedlam broke loose. Mrs. Lincoln wailed loudly, and the crowd surged forward, splintering chairs and flooding chaotically onto the stage amid the terrified actors, as in "some horrid carnival." The president's guard finally cleared away the crowds. Outside the theater, frenzied mobs came close to murdering several innocent people, including a man who barely escaped lynching, when policemen intervened.

These were the details Whitman loved to dwell on. The entire scene, he said, was a "sharp culmination, and as it were the solution, of so many bloody and angry problems." "Fit radiation—fit close!" he exclaimed. "How the imagination—how the student loves these things!"

Whitman loved to meditate on the event because so many personal and cultural threads were tied up in it. His retelling of it in his Lincoln lec-

---

9. PW 2: 508.
1. PW 2: 503. The remaining quotations in this paragraph are on pp. 504–6. The quotations in the next paragraph are on p. 508.

tures was really an imaginative reshaping, for many of the details he mentioned had, at best, only a tangential relation to the murder. But because the fifties crisis, sensationalism, crowd participation at theaters, acting style, oratory, and mob violence had fascinated Whitman and had undergirded *Leaves of Grass*, he included them in his story. He stretched the truth a bit. He didn't mention, for instance, that the Ford's Theatre shooting was a kind of afterthought for Booth, whose original plan to kidnap Lincoln and throw the country into open revolution had been foiled. But it was important to Whitman that the assassination was a theatrical event whose protagonists and setting all related to the theater, for theater and crowds had been important parts of his own shaping. This was for him the ultimate violent American melodrama whose villain was a caricature of bad acting, whose victim was the hero of the nation's greatest drama, and whose effect was audience frenzy on a massive scale. For Whitman, the theatrical trappings, like every other aspect of the event, had an inevitability. "Had not all this terrible scene— . . . had it not all been rehears'd, in blank, by Booth, beforehand?"[2]

Many violent, contradictory cultural elements Whitman had tried to harness and redirect in *Leaves of Grass* found their outlet in the tragic event that he would always believe offered a model for social unification. In Lincoln's death, he declared, "there is a cement to the whole people, subtler, more underlying, than any thing in written constitution, or courts or armies."[3] The reminiscence of Lincoln's death, he noted, "belongs to these States in their entirety—not the North only, but the South— perhaps belongs most tenderly and devotedly to the South." Lincoln had been born in Kentucky, so that Whitman called him "a Southern contribution," and he had shown kindness to the South during the war— Whitman noted, for instance, that he avoided the word "enemy" in his speeches. Several of his generals, including Sherman and Grant, had ties to the South. In death Lincoln became the Martyr Chief, admired by many of his former foes.

Others at the time were also aware of the unifying effect of Lincoln's death. In a sermon nine days after the assassination, Henry Ward Beecher said, "[N]o monument will ever equal the universal, spontaneous, and sublime sorrow that in a moment swept down the lines and parties, and covered up animosities, and in an hour brought a divided people into unity of grief and indivisible fellowship of anguish."[4]

In life and death Lincoln had, in Whitman's view, accomplished the cleansing and unifying mission he had designed for *Leaves of Grass*. It is not surprising that Whitman's writings changed dramatically after the war. Never again would he write all-encompassing poems like "Song of Myself" or "The Sleepers," for he believed that all cultural materials had been encompassed by Lincoln and the war. Although fresh social problems after the war would impel him to insist continually on the poet's vital social role, never again would he himself produce poems reflecting this

2. PW 2: 505.
3. PW 2: 508. The remaining quotations in this paragraph are on p. 498.
4. Henry Ward Beecher, *Patriotic Addresses in America and England, from 1850 to 1885, on Slavery, the Civil War, and the Development of Civil Liberty in the United States* (New York, 1887), 705.

mission in a large-scale way. His poetic output decreased, and he left it to other "bards" to resolve the problems he saw.

Since many of his poetic voices were effectively silenced after the war, it is fitting that he often used images of silence to describe reactions to Lincoln's death. He was home in Brooklyn on a two-week break from his Interior Department job when news of the assassination came. His mother served the breakfast she had prepared, but nothing was eaten, and "not a word was spoken all day."[5] He later learned of a similar anecdote of silencing that he would incorporate into *Specimen Days*. Sherman's troops, returning from their victorious Georgia campaign, had been bellowing jubilantly during their homeward march until they heard of Lincoln's death, after which they were glumly silent for a week. "Hush'd Be the Camps To-day," one of Whitman's four poems on Lincoln, pictured the contemplative silence of grief-stricken soldiers.

In Whitman's best-known Lincoln poems, "O Captain! My Captain!" and "When Lilacs Last in the Dooryard Bloom'd," the silencing of his former poetic self is particularly noticeable. At first glance these poems seem to have little in common. "O Captain!" is a catchy, melodramatic poem, in conventional rhyme and meter, in which Lincoln is pictured as the fallen captain of the ship he has guided through the national storm. "Lilacs" is a free-flowing poem in which three images—the western star (Lincoln), the singing thrush (the poet), and the lilac (his poem offered in eulogy)—interweave with meditations on death and the war.

Despite their differences in style and tone, both poems signaled the passing of Whitman's poetry as it once was. Lincoln, as "My Captain" and the eternal western star, is the reified, autocratic self that Whitman's poetic "I" once embodied but was transferred to America's Martyr Chief, now the nation's main unifying symbol. Both poems concentrate on Lincoln and marginalize Whitman, presaging the poet's obsession with Lincoln in his later years. In "O Captain!" this fixation is visible in the image of the "I" staring relentlessly at Lincoln's bloody, pale corpse on the ship's deck amid celebrations heralding the ship's return to port. In "Lilacs," the poet calls himself "me powerless—O helpless soul of me" and marginalizes himself through the symbol of the "shy and hidden bird" singing of death with a "bleeding throat."[6] No longer does Whitman's brash "I" present himself as the Answerer or arouse readers with a "barbaric yawp." In the war and in Lincoln, many of the nation's most pressing problems had reached painful resolution, changing the poet's role from that of America's imaginary leader to that of eulogist of its actual leader.

Of the two poems, "Lilacs" resonates most powerfully with autobiographical voices, even as it reenacts the nation's central tragedy. A month before the assassination, on a March evening in Washington, Whitman had been struck by the singular beauty of Venus sinking on the western horizon. The lilacs that year bloomed early due to an unusually warm spring. The hermit thrush also had real-life reference, for it was a common bird on Whitman's native Long Island; Whitman learned much about the bird from his naturalist friend John Burroughs.

---

5. Walt Whitman, *Notebooks and Unpublished Prose Manuscripts*, edited by Edward F. Grier (New York, 1984), 2: 764.
6. Quotations from "Lilacs," are in Whitman, *Leaves of Grass, Comprehensive Reader's Edition*, edited by Harold Blodgett and Scully Bradley (New York, 1965), 328–37.

These kinds of topical or autobiographical images had always been common in Whitman's verse, but here they were subsumed to the eulogy of Lincoln, whose death provided a fixation point for the poet and the nation at large. Whitman announces in the third line that he "shall mourn with ever-returning spring"—an accurate prediction, for many years later he would say that every spring brought Lincoln alive in his mind. Describing the nation's fixation on the fallen chief, he gives a long poetic version of Lincoln's funeral train. The image was appropriate, for the funeral train was a public phenomenon unprecedented in American history. Lincoln's coffin was carried in a black-draped train of nine cars on a 1,662-mile journey from Washington to Springfield, passing through many American cities, including Baltimore, Philadelphia, New York, Albany, Cleveland, Indianapolis, and Chicago. It was viewed by more than seven million Americans as it wended slowly on its circuitous route; four and a half million more saw Lincoln's body when it lay in state in Springfield.

Whitman converted the mass witnessing of Lincoln's funeral train into an all-absorbing ritual, as momentous and eternal as nature itself:

Coffin that passes through lanes and streets,
Through day and night with the great cloud darkening the land,
With the pomp of the inloop'd flags with the cities draped in black,
With the show of the States themselves as of crape-veil'd women
     standing,
With processions long and winding and the flambeaus of the night,
With the countless torches lit, with the silent sea of faces and the
     unbared heads,
With the waiting depot, the arriving coffin, and the sombre faces,
     [. . .]
With the tolling bells' perpetual clang,
Here, coffin that slowly passes,
I give you my sprig of lilac.

The American masses, crisply drawn and individualized in Whitman's earlier poems, are here an undifferentiated "sea of faces" and "unbared heads," all turned silently toward Lincoln's funeral train. Whitman's poetry, once savage and omnivorous, is now a frail sprig of lilac thrown onto a president's coffin. Self-assertive individuality is transformed into self-effacing grief. The poem has an abstract, generalizing quality; even Lincoln is not named or described. The death of hundreds of thousands of Americans in the war and the murder of the nation's leader impel Whitman to contemplate death generally. "Not for you, for one alone," he writes, "Blossoms and branches green to coffins all I bring." He especially has in mind the war dead: "I saw battle-corpses, myriads of them, / And the white skeletons of young men, I saw them, / I saw the debris and debris of all the slain soldiers of the war."

In his prewar poems, thoughts of death had inspired some negative lines, as in "Out of the Cradle Endlessly Rocking," in which the sad bird's song makes the listener wonder whether life is only "chaos." Now, death and nature, while still mysterious, have clearer referents than before, for the war has clarified them. There is a simplicity and transparency about the poem's three central symbols, as though the war and its tragic climax have brought things into focus. "I understand you," he writes of the thrush, and of the western star. "Now I know what you must have meant as a month since I walk'd." Death and nature become unambiguous in light of those who have sacrificed themselves for the ideal of union. Death no longer threatens to make life seem "a suck and a sell," as it did in "Song of Myself." It has become, in the words of the thrush's song, "*lovely and soothing death*," a "*strong deliveress*" to be glorified above all else. The death of the soldiers and of Lincoln are to remain personal and cultural reference points, as perennial as nature's rhythms. Whitman ends by reaffirming Lincoln's centrality and by bringing together the three symbols in a proclamation of unity. He sings

> For the sweetest, wisest soul of all my days and lands—and this
>   for his dear sake,
> Lilac and star and bird twined with the chant of my soul,
> There in the fragrant pines and the cedars dusk and dim.

The unity that "Lilacs" affirmed is baldly stated in Whitman's fourth Lincoln poem, a simple statement of just four lines:

> This dust was once the man,
> Gentle, plain, just and resolute, under whose cautious hand,
> Against the foulest crime in history known in any land or age,
> Was saved the Union of these States.[7]

Salvation of "the Union of these States" by a plain person of varied qualities: this had been Whitman's original poetic goal, and it had been successfully accomplished by Lincoln.

*   *   *

RICHARD CARWARDINE AND JAY SEXTON

From The Global Lincoln[†]

That outside the United States Lincoln would become a protean symbol reflects in part the ambiguous and enigmatic elements of the man himself. This "most shut-mouthed" man, as his law partner William H. Herndon described him, revealed little of himself even to the closest of associates; his merited reputation for telling the truth did not mean he necessarily told the *whole* truth, and in political communication he commonly chose to leave much unsaid. Consequently Lincoln's contemporaries, and generations of biographers and historians since, have disputed the underlying motor of his politics and statecraft. Some see a reluctant emancipator "forced into glory," others a disguised radical, and yet others a gradualist reformer. Some identify a corporate railway lawyer, others a friend of the workingman and a hard-handed son of toil. Portraits of a pragmatic party political schemer contend with those of a principled statesman. Those who extol his nationalism for its liberal values have to

---

7. Whitman, "This Dust Was Once the Man," *Leaves of Grass*, 339.
† From *The Global Lincoln*. Edited by Richard Carwardine and Jay Sexton. Copyright © 2011 by Oxford University Press. Reprinted with permission of Oxford University Press.

confront those who damn its coercive practice. These antitheses are over-stated, and need not be mutually exclusive, but they highlight how hard it has been for Lincoln's American audiences to agree on his defining quali-ties.[1] Unsurprisingly, foreign assessments have been equally varied in what they have chosen to celebrate or revile.

Lincoln's international appeal reached its height during the last third of the nineteenth century and the early decades of the next, though he enjoyed further phases of visibility during the Cold War and in recent years, thanks in part to invocations of him by successive American presi-dents, George W. Bush and Barack Obama. During the heyday of his reputation, Lincoln's authority derived less from his role as emancipator than as the robust defender of the principles of liberal and democratic nationalism. Lincoln was widely cast as the heroic tribune of the people or democratic leading man whose defense of his nation's integrity was far removed from narrow chauvinism. Instead, he won the acclaim of radi-cals and nation-builders around the globe whose own lives were devoted to projects inspired by—and designed to advance—the same universal democratic principles. Lincoln cast American nationalism not in ethnic or racial terms but as a moral force for the improvement of humankind, a beacon of liberty to the world. This purposeful universalism or liberal nationalism spoke to a wide spectrum of political progressives abroad: socialists, radicals, and democrats, who combined nationalist aspirations with informal membership of a community dedicated to freeing the world from monarchical power, aristocratic privilege, and constrained popular rights. For them, the nation was not an end in itself, but the mechanism by which political freedom and individual rights might be universally achieved. Lincoln provided the model of how to transcend one's nation to become a symbol of the common people's universal struggle.

Thus in Spain, the *Progresistas* of the Revolutionary Sexennium of 1868–74 paid homage to Lincoln the democratic hero; Emilio Castelar, president of the First Spanish Republic, saw him as the apotheosis of a free political system that acted as "a school of liberty."[2] Garibaldi's Ital-ian democrats saw in the combined force of emancipation and assassina-tion Lincoln's potency as a champion of republican liberty. As a symbol of a new political order, he won admirers amongst German radicals and, following the Meiji restoration, Japanese modernizers. Cubans—above all the independence leader José Martí—extolled Lincoln as an uncorrupted natural man whose democratic wisdom derived from his authenticity as a man of the people; in Uruguay the commentator José Enrique Rodó like-wise deployed the president's "natural" qualities to press the case for the interlocking of democracy and meritocracy.[3] Several leading German social democrats and anti-Nazis of the Weimar Republic found an ideologi-cal anchor in Lincoln. He inspired influential figures amongst the Slavic minorities of the Austro-Hungarian Empire: during the 1880s and 1890s Tomáš Masaryk—self-made scholar, intellectual, and first pres-

---

1. For a recent overview of the vast scholarship on Lincoln, see Matthew Pinsker, "Lincoln Theme 2.0," *Journal of American History* 96 (September 2009): 417–40.
2. Carolyn P. Boyd, "Lincoln in Spain," *The Global Lincoln*, edited by Richard Carwardine and Jay Sexton (New York, 2011), ch. 11.
3. Emeterio S. Santovenia, ed., *Lincoln in Martí: A Cuban View of Abraham Lincoln*, trans. Don-ald F. Fogelquist (Chapel Hill, NC, 1953); see also Nicola Miller, "Images of Lincoln in Latin America," *The Global Lincoln*, ch. 12.

ident of Czechoslovakia—pressed for progressive reform and Czech autonomy within the empire, but after 1914 invoked Lincoln's and Woodrow
Wilson's democratic ideas in the pursuit of full independence, declaring
"that these principles have been and ever will be the policy of my government and my life."[4]

Successive British campaigns for suffrage extension enlisted him in the
cause. None was more eloquent than George Holyoake and fellow members of the Sheffield Secular Society. Holyoake—who had earlier informed
Lincoln that no president since Washington had "won the esteem of the
liberal portion of the English nation as you have"—deemed his assassination "a crime against . . . the liberties of the human race . . . [and] that
great doctrine of democracy which regards the whole people as entitled to
equal conditions of personal improvement of social prosperity and civil
equality." Lincoln, he wrote, "not only rose from the people, but he exalted
the people among whom he rose."[5] Lincoln's sublime exaltation of the
people, the Gettysburg Address, became the credo of both separatist and
consolidationist nationalists, each group invoking the democratic basis of
the cause. The versatility and utility of that address is no better exempli-
fied than in its adoption by both Irish Unionists and Irish republican
nationalists. "I believe fundamentally in the right of the Irish people to
govern themselves," republican Éamon de Valera declared in 1921. "I
believe fundamentally in government of the people by the people and, if I
may add the other part, for the people."[6] No less earnestly, Ulster Unionists
years later swore an oath en masse "that this nation under God shall have
a new birth of freedom, and that Government of the Ulster people, by the
Ulster people, for the Ulster people, within the United Kingdom shall not
perish from the earth."[7]

Indicative of the ecumenical applications of Lincoln's thought are the
many ways in which he was invoked to qualify or complicate a simple
celebration of the nation-state. His appropriation by exponents of pan-
Americanism exemplifies the attempt to separate Lincoln from the nation
and deploy him on behalf of an alternative, supranational structure that
would contain and control the ambitions of a powerful nation like the United
States. The co-option of Lincoln by British Liberals as part of a larger Anglo-
Saxonism revealed how Lincoln could be embraced in a racialized transnational way that sat awkwardly with his own concept of the nation. What may
have helped the perception of Lincoln as a generous internationalist or ecumenical nationalist was his relative silence on specific foreign issues, his
noninterventionist principles, and his elevating moral and political example
above military power.

Central to Lincoln's appeal abroad was his reputation as the archetypal self-made man. Audiences around the world have found inspiration in the story of his rise from obscure and humble origins, through

4. Thomas D. Matijasic, "In the Footsteps of Lincoln: Wilson, Masaryk & Czechoslovak Independence," *Lincoln Herald* 96 (Winter 1995): 133–39.
5. G. J. Holyoake to AL, September 4, 1864, ALP; *The Assassination of Abraham Lincoln and the
Attempted Assassination of William H. Seward, Secretary of State, and Frederick W. Seward,
Assistant Secretary, on the Evening of the 14th of April, 1865. Expressions of condolence and
sympathy inspired by these events* (Washington D.C., 1866), 445.
6. See Kevin Kenny, "Abraham Lincoln in Irish Political Discourse," *The Global Lincoln*, chapter 9.
7. The occasion was the huge 1962 commemorative celebration of the 1912 Ulster Covenant.
Belfast Telegraph, September 29, 1962.

self-education, enterprise, hard work, and the simple virtues of the natural man, in a fluid society whose political system nurtured "self-actualizing citizenship." The image of Lincoln the ax-wielding "rail-splitter" on the prairie is almost as widely encountered outside the United States as it is within. The self-made man theme harmonized with the democratic aspirations of many of Lincoln's foreign admirers. It also personified the miraculous economic growth of nineteenth-century America. What gave Lincoln special power was the way he served as an example of how the interests of the individual, self-improving laborer could be congruent with, indeed inseparable from, the larger development and modernization of a national economy. This view of Lincoln was most frequently articulated in places undergoing rapid economic development—late nineteenth century Argentina or Japan in the early twentieth century—where Lincoln served as hope or reassurance that the dislocating changes of economic modernization would benefit both the individual and the larger polity.

In the popular Lincoln narratives of this era, emancipation and racial liberation are more often than not a lesser theme, and in this they only mirrored the changes that had occurred in white Americans' own reading of their Civil War as Southern Reconstruction gave way to national reunification on the basis of Jim Crow.[8] During the war itself foreign radicals had questioned the president's approach to slavery. Lincoln's initiatives to colonize black Americans abroad rankled, his progress toward emancipation seemed sluggish, and when freedom was announced it looked limited in scope and effectiveness. Yet even the emancipationist Francis William Newman and other British critics—some of the sharpest of his detractors—recognized in Lincoln the best hope for the abolitionist cause, not least on account of his character and honesty of purpose.[9] After his death, Lincoln's presidential edict of emancipation meant he could be given the role of an anti-slavery champion—he would become an inspiration in South Asia to Dalit thinkers and activists engaged in the struggle to end caste slavery—but more often this aspect of his achievement served as an exemplary or symbolic element in the larger narrative of the hero of democratic freedom. When Irish separatists paid tribute to Lincoln for freeing the slaves it was to make a link with national liberation. German socialists, following the influential example of Karl Marx, tended to celebrate Lincoln, the slaves' liberator, for his emancipation of a class, not a race.[1]

The "Great Emancipator" view of Lincoln appears to have had the most purchase in Russia and Spain, which is not surprising given that both joined the United States in abolishing involuntary servitude in the second half of the nineteenth century. But even in these countries Lincoln's freeing of the slaves was viewed through the prism of political reform and economic modernization. Russian Emperor Alexander II—

8. David Blight, *Race and Reunion: The Civil War in American Memory* (Cambridge, 2001); Barry Schwartz, *Abraham Lincoln and the Forge of National Memory* (Chicago, 2000).
9. Stacy Pratt McDermott, *The Lincoln Editor: The Quarterly Newsletter of the Abraham Lincoln Papers* 9 (April–June 2009): 5–6.
1. Bettina Hofmann, "The Lincoln Image and the German Labor Movement, 1861–1914," unpublished conference paper, "A Humanitarian as Broad as the World: Abraham Lincoln's Legacy in International Context," German Historical Institute, 2007 [HBW].

liberator of the serfs in 1861 and loyal ally of the Union during the Civil War—held his fellow emancipator and "Great and Good Friend" in high esteem.[2] Yet Alexander's abolition of serfdom, which was part of a portfolio of reforms undertaken in Russia in the 1860s, was more an attempt to preserve an obsolete and rickety social and political system through unavoidable reform than it was a result of Lincolnian opposition to involuntary servitude.[3] In Spain, Lincoln was venerated by abolitionist Progresistas acutely aware of the stain of their country's being the only continental power still to tolerate slavery (in its colonies of Puerto Rico and Cuba, where emancipation would not triumph until, respectively, 1873 and 1886). In this instance, as well, anti-slavery was only one dimension of the liberal reformers' larger project of modernizing the nation and extending civil and political rights to all Spaniards. In Cuba itself, as in independent Brazil (where emancipation would not occur until 1888), Lincoln certainly featured in debates over abolition, but his predominant image there appears to have been that of the nation-builder, not the emancipator. That was certainly the case in Juárez's Mexico and in Argentina, where his influential biographer Domingo Sarmiento, drawing on firsthand experience of the power of entrenched local interests to obstruct centralizing liberals, praised Lincoln's tenacity in the face of Southern disunionists and his harnessing of abolitionist energies in the cause of unity.

Lincoln's emancipationist record took on particular significance for what it revealed about his humanitarianism, humility, moral code, and religion, elements which led early twentieth-century Japanese biographer Ōson Sakurai to deem him "the kindest man among the great men, and the greatest man among the kind men."[4] The theologian Albert Schweitzer saw him as a fount of "the ideas of truest and highest brotherhood"; Sigmund Freud wrote that he had widened "the limits of humanity."[5] Imperial Russian diplomats made much of Lincoln's humility, though for them it was not a sign of strength, unlike Soviet-era historians, who praised him for it.[6] That Lincoln never in fact made a declaration of Christian belief—and that his celebration of reason made him the hero of secularists—was no barrier to his widespread representation as a man of faith. In Britain in particular, Lincoln the foe of slavery (as well as the abstainer from alcohol and tobacco) won a place in the hearts and minds of pious, reform-driven, Protestant churchgoers. Those of the predominating nonconformist Protestant traditions in Wales, many of whom would have read and reread *Uncle Tom's Cabin* in their native tongue, saluted Lincoln for his religious devotion. This was a reading strengthened by the circumstances of his death. Assassination alone is no guarantee of enduring influence—

2. Tanis Lovercheck-Saunders, "Peculiar Moral Power: Russian Images of Lincoln," unpublished conference paper, HBW, 3. Alexander's admiration of Lincoln did not prevent him from later expressing his frustration that Lincoln's freeing of the American slaves received more global praise than his abolition of Russian serfdom.

3. For a comparative study of Russian serfdom and American slavery, see Peter Kolchin, *Unfree Labor: American Slavery and Russian Serfdom* (Cambridge, MA, 1987).

4. Ōson Sakurai, *Tales of Lincoln* [in Japanese] (Tokyo, 1913), quoted in De-min Tao, "A Standard of Our Thought and Action: Lincoln's Reception in East Asia," *The Global Lincoln*, chapter 13.

5. Albert Schweitzer, statement, November 22, 1937; S. Freud, statement, April 8, 1937, Lincoln Memorial University Archives, Abraham Lincoln Library and Museum, Harrogate, Tennessee.

6. Lovercheck-Saunders, "Peculiar Moral Power: Russian Images of Lincoln," 1–2.

witness James Garfield and William McKinley—but a deep and persisting religious sense of loss accompanied Lincoln's end. Booth's bullet created a sacrificial figure, a martyr who died to bring an end to the suffering of others, a composite of Moses and the redemptive Christ, whose Good Friday Passion he shared.

This interpretation of Lincoln enjoyed widespread and continuing influence throughout his reputational heyday. If Tolstoy really did call him "a Christ in miniature" in 1909, he was only echoing what men and women had been saying for nearly half a century since the torrent of eulogies and lamentation that followed his death. For Emilio Castelar he was a "new Moses" removed "in the very moment of his victory, like Christ, like Socrates, like all redeemers." Garibaldi described him as "the new Redeemer of man." French Masons regarded him as "the sublimest martyr . . . who came into the world, like Jesus of Bethlehem, to take away its sins."[7] As such, he spoke directly to the Christianized modernizers of Meiji Japan.

For many, the humanitarian Lincoln was entirely consistent with his alter ego, the forceful, resolute defender of constitutionalism, and the strong-willed, unyielding nationalist. He spoke to the strong moral, often profoundly religious, elements within the forces of aspiring nationalism. But to uphold justice and the democratic principle, a leader might have to overcome his natural inclination for peace and learn the arts of war. Argentineans, Germans, Irish, Italians, Slavs: all these, and more, found in Lincoln a supreme model of strength in defending the principle of national unity. Indomitable, manly, physically and morally strong, Lincoln evinced a firmness of purpose that took him to the edge of constitutional legitimacy, but whose natural prudence and wisdom would let him travel no further. Conscription, the suspension of the writ of habeas corpus, and the American Union's other war measures had not spilled over into despotism; popular opinion had been respected. Lincoln became the epitome of the firm, prudent, and moderate war leader. No one expressed this better than one of his greatest admirers, David Lloyd George, the British prime minister during the First World War and its aftermath. Lincoln, like himself, had dealt with troublesome generals and politicians, mastered military strategy, pursued unconditional surrender in the supreme crisis of the nation, and finally, in victory, worked for clemency and reconciliation. With the fate of democracy uncertain in postwar Europe, Lloyd George invoked the heroic Lincoln in what he called the "fight against the wave of autocracy that is sweeping over our continent. Russia, an autocracy; Italy for the moment a dictatorship; Germany, slipping into dictatorship—most of Europe having abandoned confidence in the people. It is the hour of Lincoln's doctrine to be preached in the countries of Europe."[8]

Lloyd George's embrace of Lincoln reflected a broader British impulse in the early part of the twentieth century to join with the United States

7. Boyd, "A Man for All Seasons: Lincoln in Spain," *The Global Lincoln*, chapter 11; Eugenio F. Biagini, "'The Principle of Humanity': Lincoln in Germany and Italy, 1859–1865," *The Global Lincoln* chapter 4; *The Assassination of Abraham Lincoln*, 104.
8. David Lloyd George, "Abraham Lincoln, the Inspirer of Democracy," October 18, 1923, *Building the Myth: Selected Speeches Memorializing Abraham Lincoln*, edited by Waldo W. Braden (Urbana, 1991), 206.

in exalting Anglo-Saxonism as the cure for the world's ills. The poet and playwright John Drinkwater cast Lincoln as the "World Emancipator," although the role he gave him—the exponent of the fundamental unity of America and Britain—was distinctly racialized and thus quite at odds with how Lincoln himself had seen his nation's mission.[9] Yet in emphasizing Lincoln's Anglo-Saxon qualities and his genealogical roots in rural Norfolk—"He belongs to the Race . . . as a man of pure English blood," claimed James Bryce in 1918—his English admirers constituted only one of many sets of claimants around the world.[1] In Wales he was called "our Welsh president," descended from medieval princes. Germans—finding a "Linkhorn" amongst his ancestors, and convinced that German immigrants played an essential role in securing the Republican party's electoral success in 1860—made him one of them; Friedrich Ebert, the first president of the Weimar Republic, became in death "the Abraham Lincoln of German history."[2] Latin Americans claimed him as a great *americanista* who counseled mutual respect in interstate relations, identified with the broad transnational interests of the region's modernizers, and sternly opposed the narrow self-interest of United States expansionists. Benito Juárez thus embraced the title of "the Mexican Lincoln." French Freemasons, erroneously convinced of his Masonic connections, claimed him as "one who had handled the hammer, the square, and compass, the living insignia of our immortal society," and saw in his life story a progression through degrees of Masonry.[3] In contemporary and near-contemporary graphic art his foreign portraits took on the social and ethnic features of the audiences for whom they were designed. At a later date, in Kenya, anti-colonial students said "I . . . Abraham Lincoln" when reciting the Emancipation Proclamation.[4] Such disparate appropriations reflect the universalist and adaptable dimensions of Lincoln's thought. They also reveal the perceived empowerment of claiming Lincoln's mantle.

Lincoln's impact on the world beyond his nation's borders would never again enjoy the range and force that it achieved during the half century or so after his death. Yet he would enjoy a new salience during the Second World War and the subsequent era of anti-colonialism and Cold War tensions. He took on renewed relevance in familiar settings: during the 1940s the British political class and wartime opinion-formers turned once more to his words, especially the Gettysburg Address, to give rhetorical and explicitly Anglo-American expression to the fight for democracy and humanity.[5] In Germany during the postwar era, West Berliners linked their cause to a narrative of United States history that deployed Lincoln as a symbol of anti-communism and self-determination. "The truths which Lincoln spoke . . . ," West Berlin Mayor Willy Brandt declared in 1959 of

9. John Drinkwater, *Abraham Lincoln* (London, 1919); Drinkwater, *Lincoln: The World Emancipator* (Boston, 1920).
1. Harry Brittain, *Happy Pilgrimage* (London, 1949), 289.
2. See Kenneth O. Morgan, "Kentucky's 'Cottage-Bred Man': Lincoln and Wales," *The Global Lincoln*, ch. 8; and Jörg Nagler, "National Unity and Liberty: Lincoln's Image and Reception in Germany, 1871–1989," *The Global Lincoln*, chapter 14.
3. *The Assassination of Abraham Lincoln*, 90, 92, 98–99, 103–4.
4. Kevin Gaines, "From Colonization to Anti-colonialism: Lincoln in Africa," *The Global Lincoln*, ch. 15.
5. Jake Campbell, "British Views of Abraham Lincoln" (M. St. dissertation, University of Oxford, 2009).

Lincoln's "house divided" speech a century before, "are perhaps even more applicable to the present situation of the German people than to the one which he faced."[6] He also came to be celebrated and deployed in parts of the globe where he had once been a less familiar presence. In the "new birth of freedom" that followed the fall of the Axis powers, the anti-colonialist movements to establish independent nations in Asia, Africa, and the Caribbean appropriated Lincoln as both an exemplar of freedom and a national unifier. In 1945, after the capitulation of Japan, the Indonesian leader Sukarno bedecked Jakarta with Lincoln's phrases to encourage Harry S. Truman's administration to oppose Dutch colonialism; in the 1960s, by contrast, he turned to Lincoln the national unifier to give consolidationist license for his ambitions in New Guinea, Borneo, and parts of the Malay peninsula. The ambiguities in the "real" Lincoln's historical actions, as both liberator and consolidator, allowed his deployment in these incongruent ways. Similarly, in the African transition from colonialism to independence, leaders of the freedom struggle might invoke both faces of Lincoln. Ghanaians were able to use him to legitimate liberation, yet the nation's first ruler, Kwame Nkrumah, would "read Lincoln's texts on national unity to those of his associates who worried about the massive force the new state used to defeat its internal enemies."[7]

This prompts a further reflection, on the authoritarian uses of the protean Lincoln. In the sixteenth president's energetic use of federal muscle—and his resort to what for the United States was unprecedented force to defend its constitution, laws, unity, and political continuity—ruling classes across the spectrum of the political right have discerned a valuable means of legitimating their own deployment of state power. From British conservatives' appreciation during the late Victorian and Edwardian ages of Lincoln's relevance as an instrument of stability, to the Japanese authorities' screening the democratic phrases of the Gettysburg Address from the public during the oligarchic period of Meiji rule, to President Pervez Musharraf's invocation of Lincoln in 2007 to defend the Pakistan government's iron fist, conservative-authoritarian forces have found a means of turning his popular appeal to their own advantage. The Lincoln story, as sponsored by the government of imperial Japan for the benefit of younger readers during the 1930s, not only sought to prepare the children for life within a military regime but also took the precaution of avoiding any allusion to the president's assassination.[8]

☆   ☆   ☆

The dissemination of Lincoln's story at times tells us as much about networks of communication, transnational movements, and geopolitics as it does about the man himself. The examination of Lincoln's international legacy also prompts an essential sense of perspective and a guard against a blinkered filio-piety. Far from being the only figure of his time to take on an iconic status, Lincoln became part of an international

---

6. Quoted in Thomas F. Schwartz, "Lincoln and the Cold War," *Abraham Lincoln Association Newsletter* 6.1 (Spring 2004).
7. "Interchange: The Global Lincoln," *Journal of American History* 96 (September 2009): 467, 493 (Arne Westad).
8. Michael Mogilevsky, "What Was Abe Lincoln Doing in Pre-War Japan?" *Lincoln Herald* 90 (Fall 1988): 87–90.

pantheon of great statesmen, most of whom were not Americans; they included Garibaldi, Simon Bolívar, Camillo di Cavour, Otto von Bismarck, and William E. Gladstone. Biographies of Lincoln were often part of a general series of eminent people.[9] An additional perspective comes from placing Lincoln in a historical line of American figures who have achieved high standing abroad. Benjamin Franklin (rather than George Washington) may be seen as the precursor of the self-made, enterprising, modernizing, and anti-slavery hero. If so, the international view of Lincoln draws, at least in part, from a more generic image of an ideal American forged earlier. Likewise Lincoln himself may have helped shape the image of his successors: Woodrow Wilson and, later, John F. Kennedy and Martin Luther King Jr. Since 2008, the inverse question can be put: how far do international observers now see Lincoln through the lens of Barack Obama?

The hunt for the international Lincoln prompts a further word of caution: his absences should be as much a spur to investigation as his presence. Why, for example, is Lincoln marginal to the Indian story of decolonization yet important to the experience of Ghana's independence? Absences may simply be a result of Lincoln's story not reaching indigenous populations in non-English speaking regions. But they may also indicate a measure of cultural or political choice. This appears to have been the case in France during the 1860s, when after his death Lincoln was an inspiring symbol, but then "disappeared" during the immediate prelude to the Paris Commune—a signal of progressives' disenchantment with the United States as the Johnson and Grant administrations acquiesced in the "counter-revolution" of Reconstruction policy in the American South. In post-1945 Britain, Lincoln lost some of his previous standing, perhaps because Winston Churchill could better fill the role.

Plotting Lincoln's reception around the globe remains a work in progress. He merits many more case studies than have been ventured here. The Swiss Confederation, a federal state established in 1848 and inspired by the constitutional example of the United States, witnessed an extraordinary outpouring of tributes to the assassinated president in 1865–66. Lincoln and the Union he represented clearly spoke to the condition of those Swiss unifiers and self-styled modernizers who had triumphed in the brief civil war against secessionist cantons in 1847 (the *Sonderbundskreig*), but the particular political and cultural nerve that he struck, and the duration of his influence, remain an untold story. When Norwegians gathered around Lincoln's statue in Oslo every July 4th during the Nazi occupation, on what collective understanding were they drawing? Why is there a Lincoln Foundation in Albania? How typical of the South Seas more generally is the Hawaiian reverence for Lincoln? What explains the continuing Korean appetite for his life story? How might the apparent Soviet embrace of Lincoln be reconciled with its Cold War anti-Americanism? The mapping of Lincoln images and sites remains in its infancy, as does the research on population censuses to track his name. The hundreds of foreign biographies cry out for an analysis of their contents and disparate emphases, as well as who published and read them.

9. "Interchange: The Global Lincoln," 479 (Caroline Boyd).

Despite these considerable lacunae, an overall picture is emerging. However difficult it is to move beyond a description of Lincoln's global reception to an assessment of his influence and significance, the evidence makes clear that he and his legacy have made a difference to the world beyond the United States. First, his intellectual and political example has inspired a range of political leaders and thinkers: Domingo Sarmiento, Karl Marx, David Lloyd George, José Martí, Emilio Castelar, Rafael María de Labra, Mohandas Gandhi, Bhimrao Ramji Ambedkar, Kwame Nkrumah, and Willy Brandt provide just some salient examples. Second, he has touched, often powerfully, countless ordinary lives. It is unlikely that many lived through anything to match the experience of a concentration camp internee, Henry Dubin, who described a visitation from a ghostly Lincoln whose words gave him the strength to survive his harrowing ordeal.[1] But the widespread use of "Lincoln" as a given name reveals at least a quiet influence on those who chose the name, those who bore it, and those whom they impressed. Third, invocations of Lincoln have had some hard, identifiable outcomes. For example, Lincoln's image at times mitigated Yankee-phobia in Latin America, and John Bigelow's appeals to French progressives in the name of the recently assassinated Lincoln helped to secure a remarkable coalition of the Second Empire's liberal and radical forces.

Above all, though Lincoln's influence on the larger global processes of the modern age cannot be precisely calibrated, he must be accorded a major inspirational role in the era of liberal and democratic nationalism. No historian of the United States would doubt that Lincoln is the central figure in the construction of the modern American nation, one premised not upon racial identity or state's rights, but upon a more inclusive idea of common peoples joined by democratic and civic principles. This, too, has constituted the core of his appeal abroad, combined as it has been with his standing as the premier self-made man of the age. Lincoln provided the perfect embodiment of the key features of "modernity": the entwined processes of economic development and self-improvement, signaled by the expansion of the capitalist market worldwide, the assault on ancestral privilege, and the widening of life-chances as individuals freed themselves from hierarchies of ascribed status. As a self-made man from humble origins, Lincoln stood for the dignity of labor; as statesman and war leader, he embraced the modernization of a national economy. Without these larger forces at work in the wider world it is doubtful that Lincoln would have had lasting impact beyond his own country. But America's interconnectedness with the broader currents of his time delivered that expansive arena of influence. In spare and memorable language fit for the modern age, he spoke directly during his own lifetime and beyond to those around the globe who saw themselves engaged in freeing the present from an ossified past and who looked, as Lincoln himself did, "to a vast future also."[2]

---

1. Andrew Ferguson, *Land of Lincoln: Adventures in Abe's America* (New York, 2007), 270–74.
2. CW 5:53.

Abraham Lincoln: A Chronology

1809 February 12: Abraham Lincoln born in a one-room log cabin on Nolin Creek, in Hardin (now Larue) County, Kentucky. Named Abraham after his paternal grandfather, he is the second child (sister is Sarah, b. 1807) of the farmer and carpenter Thomas Lincoln (b. 1778) and Nancy Hanks Lincoln (b. 1784).

1811 The Lincoln family moves to a 230-acre farm, largely uncleared, on Knob Creek, eleven miles northeast of present-day Hodgenville, Kentucky.

1812 Lincoln's brother, Thomas, dies in infancy.

1816 In the fall, attends school briefly with his sister. In December, the family moves across the Ohio River to southwestern Indiana and settles near Little Pigeon Creek in Perry (later Spencer) County.

1817 Helps father clear 80 acres of land for planting.

1818 In late winter, Lincoln is knocked unconscious when kicked in the head by a horse. October 5: His mother dies of milk sickness (a.k.a. tremotol vomiting) and is buried on a knoll a quarter mile from the family's cabin.

1819 December 2: His father marries Sarah Bush Johnson (b. 1788), a widow with three children, during a visit to Elizabethtown, Kentucky.

1820 Attends school briefly.

1822 Attends school for several months.

1824 Attends school during the fall and winter. Reads the Bible and borrowed books, including *Aesop's Fables*, Thomas Dilworth's *A New Guide to the English Tongue*, William Grimshaw's *History of the United States*, and books by John Bunyan, Daniel Defoe, and Mason Locke Weems.

1826 Works as a boatman and a farmhand. His sister, Sarah, marries Aaron Grigsby in Indiana.

1828 January 20: Lincoln's sister, Sarah, dies in childbirth at age twenty. April: Lincoln and Allen Gentry, on a flatboat loaded with farm produce, embark from Rockport, Indiana, on a trip to New Orleans; they return by steamboat.

1830 March: Moves with his family to Macon County, Illinois, settling on uncleared land southwest of Decatur. Makes his first known political speech, calling for improved navigation on the Sangamon River.

1831 Takes second trip to New Orleans on a flatboat carrying produce. Summer: moves to New Salem, Illinois, 20 miles northwest of Springfield in Sangamon County (his family now lives in Coles County). Meets Ann Rutledge, the daughter of a tavern keeper.

Works as a store clerk and part-time mill worker and does odd jobs. Joins local debating society.

1832   March: Becomes a candidate for Illinois General Assembly. April: Enlists in the Illinois militia when the Black Hawk War breaks out; serves as a company captain. Late May through June 10: re-enlists as a militia private and serves in northern Illinois but sees no action. August 6: Defeated soundly in the General Assembly election. Becomes a partner with William Berry in a village store in New Salem.

1833   The store fails and leaves the partners in debt. May: Lincoln is appointed postmaster of New Salem and serves until the post office moves to another town three years later. Studies surveying and in October is appointed deputy surveyor of Sangamon County.

1834   August 4: Elected to Illinois House of Representatives as a Whig. Starts to study law. December: Takes legislative seat at capital in Vandalia. Meets twenty-one-year-old lawyer and Democratic politician Stephen A. Douglas.

1835   January: His debt increases to around $1,100 when William Berry dies. Becomes a leader of the Whig Party in the Illinois legislature, voting with the majority for a charter for a state bank and a bill to build a canal between the Illinois River and Lake Michigan. August 25: Anne Rutledge dies from fever at twenty-two.

1836   August 1: Wins re-election to state legislature. September 9: Lincoln receives his law license. Starts to court twenty-eight-year-old Mary Owens, a Kentucky woman visiting New Salem. December: Experiences depression ("hypochondria").

1837   Along with other Whig politicians in Sangamon County, Lincoln brings about the relocation of the state capital from Vandalia to Springfield. April 15: Moves to Springfield (lives there until 1861). Rooms with store owner Joshua F. Speed, who becomes a close friend. Forms law partnership with John T. Stuart. For twenty-four years, handles various types of civil and criminal cases, occasionally as prosecutor but usually as defense attorney. His proposal to Mary Owens is declined, and their courtship ends in August.

1838   January 27: Delivers address on "The Perpetuation of Our Political Institutions" to the Springfield Young Men's Lyceum. August 6: Re-elected to the Illinois General Assembly.

1839   Travels as a lawyer on the Eight Judicial Circuit in Illinois, handling cases in nine counties. Debates Stephen Douglas on the issue of a national bank. December 3: Admitted to United States Circuit Court. Meets Mary Todd, the twenty-one-year-old daughter of a Kentucky banker, at a Christmas dance.

1840   While campaigning for the Whig presidential candidate William Henry Harrison, Lincolns debates Stephen Douglas and other Democrats. June: Lincoln presents his first case before the Illinois Supreme Court; he will argue cases before it over 240 times. August 3: Lincoln is re-elected to the Illinois General Assembly. Mary Todd accepts his proposal of marriage and the couple becomes engaged.

1841   January 1: Breaks off his engagement to Mary Todd. Suffers weeks of severe depression. March 1: Ends law partnership with Stuart and begins a new one with Stephen T. Logan. On a steamboat ride, sees twelve slaves that he likens to "so many fish upon a trot-line."

1842   February 22: Addresses a local temperance society. Summer: Resumes his courtship with Mary Todd. September: Challenged to a sword duel by Democratic state auditor James Shields over four anonymously published letters that ridiculed Shields. September 22: Duel averted when Lincoln assures Shields the letters were political, not personal, attacks. November 4: Marries Mary Todd. They will have four sons, the first of whom, Robert, will live to age eighty-two and will be minister to Great Britain, presidential candidate, and Secretary of War under President Garfield. The remaining sons will die young: Edward at age three, William ("Willie") at age eleven, and Thomas ("Tad") at age eighteen.

1843   Fails to get Whig nomination for U.S. Congress. August 1: Son Robert Todd Lincoln is born.

1844   The Lincolns move into home at Eighth and Jackson Streets in Springfield, where they will live until 1861. In the fall, visits his former home in Indiana. Dissolves his law partnership with Logan and starts his own practice, taking the twenty-six-year-old William H. Herndon as junior partner.

1845   Is earning around $1,500 annually as a lawyer.

1846   March 10: Second son, Edward Baker, is born. May 1: Wins Whig congressional nomination. August 3: Is elected to the U.S. House of Representatives, defeating Democrat Peter Cartwright, a Methodist preacher.

1847   The Lincoln family moves to a boarding house near the Capitol in Washington, D.C. December 6: Takes seat in the House of Representatives when the Thirtieth Congress convenes. December 22: Presents resolution asking President James Polk to inform Congress whether the "spot" where U.S. hostilities with Mexico began was or was not on Mexican soil.

1848   January 22: Gives a speech in the House against President Polk's war policy regarding Mexico. Early June: Attends national Whig convention in Philadelphia, where Zachary Taylor is chosen as the party's candidate. Campaigns for Taylor in Maryland and Massachusetts. Visits Niagara Falls. Returns to Illinois and campaigns until election. December 7: Returns to Washington for the reconvening of Congress. Endorses the principle behind the Wilmot Proviso, which would prevent the spread of slavery into territories acquired from Mexico.

1849   Does not speak during Congress's debates over slavery but votes for the abolition of the slave trade in the District of Columbia and for the exclusion of slavery from the western territories. March 31: Leaves politics to practice law in Springfield. When President Taylor offers to appoint him as secretary and then as governor of Oregon Territory, he declines.

1850   February 1: Second son, Edward Baker dies. Lincoln resumes his role in the Eighth Judicial Circuit, traveling 400 miles in twelve weeks through fourteen counties. July: Delivers eulogy of Zachary Taylor at a memorial meeting in Chicago. December 21: Third son, William Wallace (Willie), born.

1851   January 17: Father, Thomas Lincoln, dies in Coles County, Illinois at age seventy-three.

1852   July: Delivers eulogy of Henry Clay at a memorial in Springfield. Electioneers for Winfield Scott during presidential campaign.

1853   April 4: Fourth son, Thomas (Tad), born.

1854   May 22: Congress passes the Kansas-Nebraska Act, which repeals the Missouri Compromise and opens the western territories up for slavery. Lincoln gives speeches attacking the bill. Is elected to Illinois legislature but declines the seat in order to be eligible to run for the U.S. Senate.

1855   In the race for the Senate, Lincoln leads in early balloting, but support for him wanes, and he casts his influence behind anti-Nebraska Democrat Lyman Trumbull, who is elected on the tenth ballot. Lincoln is now earning some $5,000 a year as a lawyer.

1856   February 22: Attends Free-Soil political convention in Decatur. May 22: Participates in the founding of the Republican Party at convention in Bloomington, Illinois; inspires attendees with a speech that has not survived (known as the "Lost Speech"). June 19: Is nominated for vice president at Republican convention in Philadelphia but is not chosen by the party. In the fall, campaigns actively in Illinois for Republican presidential candidate John C. Frémont.

1857   June 26: Gives speech in Springfield against the *Dred Scott* decision, which denies U.S. citizenship to blacks. Late July: With wife, visits New York City, Niagara Falls, and Canada.

1858   June 16: Nominated as Republican senator from Illinois to run against Democrat Stephen A. Douglas. Holds seven debates with Douglas—on August 21, 27, September 15, 18, and October 7, 13, 15—in different locations in Illinois. Attendance at the debates averages between ten and fifteen thousand, ranging from some twelve hundred at Jonesboro (September 15) to perhaps around twenty thousand at Galesburg (October 7). In a close election, Lincoln does not win, but his performance in the debates makes him nationally famous as an opponent of the spread of slavery. He gathers clippings of the debates.

1859   January 5: Legislature re-elects Douglas to the Senate. August–October: Lincoln electioneers for Republican candidates in Ohio, Iowa, and Wisconsin. For the first time, he is mentioned as a possible future candidate for the presidency. Begins to arrange publication of his 1858 debates with Douglas.

1860   February 27: Delivers address on the founding fathers and slavery at the Cooper Institute in New York. May 9: On the third ballot at the Republican Party's national convention in Chicago, Lincoln is chosen over several rivals—notably Senator William H. Seward of New York, Senator Salmon P. Chase of Ohio, and Edward Bates of Missouri—as the party's presidential candidate. As was then the custom, Lincoln does not campaign for himself, but he keeps in close contact with several who electioneer for him. His debates with Douglas are published as a book. November 6: Lincoln is elected as sixteenth U.S. president, defeating his three opponents: Stephen A. Douglas (Northern Democratic), John Bell (Constitutional Union Party), and John C. Breckenridge (Southern Democratic). Wins a plurality of 40 percent of the popular vote and wins 180 of 303 electoral votes. December 20: In response to the election of an antislavery president, South Carolina secedes from the Union, followed over the next two months by Mississippi, Florida, Alabama, Georgia, Louisiana, and Texas.

1861   February 11: Leaves Springfield by train and makes brief appearances in five states. February 22–23: Warned of an alleged assassination conspiracy in Baltimore, he travels secretly by night from Philadelphia to Washington. March 4: Inaugurated sixteenth president of the United States. April 12: Attack on Fort Sumter in Charleston Harbor, South Carolina, by Confederates under General Pierre Beauregard marks the start of the Civil War. Lincoln calls up seventy-five thousand militia. April 17: Virginia secedes from the Union, followed by North Carolina, Tennessee, and Arkansas. The Confederate States of America consists of eleven states. April 19: Lincoln authorizes blockade of Southern ports. April 27: Suspends writ of habeas corpus in Maryland and in parts of the midwestern states. May 13: Directs the expansion of the regular army and navy. July 21: Hears of the defeat of the Union at Bull Run at the U.S. Telegraph Office, thereafter his base for receiving war news and sending orders. September 11: Revokes General John C. Frémont's proclamation of emancipation in Missouri, outraging antislavery advocates. October 24: Relieves Frémont of his command, replacing him with General David Hunter. November 1: Appoints General George B. McClellan commander of the Union Army.

1862   January 27: Issues General War Order No. 1, outlining the Union's military strategy. February 20: Third son, Willie, dies, probably from typhoid fever. Wife is devastated and is permanently affected by the death. April 16: Signs act abolishing slavery in the District of Columbia. June 19: Approves bill outlawing slavery in the territories. July 22: Reads draft of preliminary Emancipation Proclamation to his Cabinet. September 22: Issues preliminary Emancipation Proclamation, to take effect on January 1, 1863. September 24: Issues proclamation suspending habeas corpus for persons "guilty of any disloyal practice" against the Union. November 5: Replaces McClellan with General Ambrose Burnside as commander of the Army of the Potomac. December 1: In message to Congress, proposes a constitutional amendment mandating gradual, compensated emancipation. December 13: The Army of the Potomac suffers a crushing defeat at Fredericksburg.

1863   January 1: Signs Emancipation Proclamation, which frees enslaved people in Confederate-held territory. March 3: Signs bill introducing military conscription. May 1–4: The Union Army is defeated at Chancellorsville. July 1–4: Lincoln is heartened by Union victories at Gettysburg and Vicksburg. August 10: Confers with abolitionist Frederick Douglass in the White House about the participation of African American soldiers in the Union Army. September: After Union defeat at Chickamauga and the Confederate siege of Chattanooga, appoints General Ulysses S. Grant commander of the western theater. November 19: Gives dedicatory address at the Gettysburg Cemetery. December 8: Issues proclamation of amnesty and reconstruction, which offers pardon to rebels.

1864   March 12: Appoints Grant general-in-chief of the armies. June 8: At the National Union Convention, a coalition of Republicans and War Democrats, Lincoln is nominated for re-election by nearly unanimous vote. The convention nominates pro-Union Democrat Andrew Johnson of Tennessee for vice president and proposes a constitutional amendment abolishing slavery. June 30: Lincoln accepts Salmon P. Chase's resignation as secretary of the treasury and names Republican senator William P. Fessenden as his successor. July 4: Lincoln pocket vetoes the Wade-Davis Bill, a reconstruction plan he considers too harsh on the South. August 23: Writes in private memorandum that he expects not to be re-elected. September 2: General William Sherman captures Atlanta. October 9: General Phillip H. Sheridan defeats Lieutenant General Jubal Early at Cedar Creek in the Shenandoah Valley. Lincoln is buoyed by these Union victories. November 8: Re-elected as president, defeating Democratic candidate George B. McClellan by a large margin.

1865   Through political influence Lincoln helps win support in the House of Representatives for the Thirteenth Amendment, abolishing slavery; the amendment had been approved by the Senate in April 1864. January 31: By a three-vote margin, the House passes resolution to send the Thirteenth Amendment to the states for ratification. February 3: Meets with Confederate representatives at Hampton Roads, Virginia, in unsuccessful peace conference. March 3: Signs measure for the relief of freedmen and refugees. March 4: Inaugurated for second term. April 4: Visits Richmond, Virginia, after it has been evacuated by the Confederates. April 9: General Robert E. Lee surrenders to General Ulysses S. Grant at Appomattox Court House. April 11: Gives last public speech, focusing on Reconstruction. April 14, shortly after 10 P.M.: While attending a play at Ford's Theatre, Lincoln is shot by the actor John Wilkes Booth. April 15, 7:22 A.M.: Having never regained consciousness, Lincoln dies. April 19: Funeral service in White House. April 21: Funeral train leaves Washington and starts a 1,654-mile journey to Springfield, Illinois; the train, carrying Lincoln's casket and the remains of his son Willie, passes through seven states and 180 cities and is witnessed by thousands of grieving Americans. April 26: Booth slain while resisting arrest in Port Royal, Virginia. May 3: Funeral train reaches Springfield. May 4: Funeral in Springfield; Lincoln is buried in Oak Ridge Cemetery, outside Springfield.

1869   April 12: Stepmother Sarah dies at age eighty-one in Coles County, Illinois.

1871   July 15: Fourth son, Thomas (Tad), dies at age eighteen in Chicago, Illinois.

1882   July 16: Lincoln's widow, Mary, dies in Springfield, Illinois at age sixty-three.

1926   July 26: First son, Robert, dies at age eighty-two in Manchester, Vermont.

Selected Bibliography

Lincoln's Writings

Abraham Lincoln Papers at the Library of Congress, Manuscript Division. Washington, D.C.: American Memory Project, [2000–02]), http://memory.loc.gov/ammem/alhtml /malhome.html.

Basler, Roy P. et al., eds. *The Collected Works of Abraham Lincoln*. 9 vols. New Brunswick, NJ: Rutgers University Press, 1953.

Fehrenbacher, Don E., ed. *Abraham Lincoln: Speeches and Writings*. 2 vols. New York: Library of America, 1989.

Stowell, Daniel W., et al., eds. *The Papers of Abraham Lincoln: Legal Documents and Cases*. 4 vols. Charlottesville: University of Virginia Press, 2008.

Bibliographical Guides and Reference Works

Burkhimer, Michael. *One Hundred Essential Lincoln Books*. Nashville: Cumberland House, 2003.

Miers, Earl S., ed. *Lincoln Day by Day: A Chronology, 1809–1865*. 3 vols. Washington, D.C.: Lincoln Sesquicentennial Commission, 1960. Available online in a frequently updated version as *The Lincoln Log: A Daily Chronology of the Life of Abraham Lincoln*, at www.thelincolnlog.org.

Neely, Mark E., Jr. *Abraham Lincoln Encyclopedia*. 10 vols. 1982. Reprint. New York: Da Capo Press, 1984.

Biographical Studies

Burlingame, Michael. *Abraham Lincoln: A Life*. Baltimore: Johns Hopkins University Press, 2008.

———. *The Inner World of Abraham Lincoln*. Urbana: University of Illinois Press, 1994.

Carwardine, Richard. *Lincoln: A Life of Purpose and Power*. New York: Knopf, 2006.

Donald, David Herbert. *Lincoln*. New York: Simon & Schuster, 1995.

Foner, Eric. *The Fiery Trial: Abraham Lincoln and American Slavery*. New York: Norton, 2011.

Goodwin, Doris Kearns. *Team of Rivals: The Political Genius of Abraham Lincoln*. New York: Simon & Schuster, 2005.

Guelzo, Allen C. *Abraham Lincoln: Redeemer President*. Grand Rapids, MI: Eerdmans, 1999.

Herndon, William Henry, and Jesse William Weik. *Herndon's Lincoln*. Edited by Douglas L. Wilson and Rodney O. Davis Urbana: University of Illinois Press, 2006 [reissue of 1889 edition].

Lind, Michael. *What Lincoln Believed: The Values and Convictions of America's Greatest President*. New York: Doubleday, 2005.

McPherson, James M. *Abraham Lincoln*. New York: Oxford University Press, 2009.

Neely, Mark E. *The Last Best Hope of Earth: Abraham Lincoln and the Promise of America*. Cambridge, MA: Harvard University Press, 1993.

Nicolay, John George, and John Hay. *Abraham Lincoln: A History*. Edited by Paul M. Angle. Chicago: University of Chicago Press, 1966 [reissue of 1890 edition].

Oates, Stephen B. *With Malice Toward None: A Life of Abraham Lincoln*. New York: Harper & Row, 1977.

Shenk, Joshua Wolf. *Lincoln's Melancholy: How Depression Challenged a President and Fueled His Greatness*. Boston: Houghton Mifflin Co., 2005.

Wilson, Douglas L. *Honor's Voice: The Transformation of Abraham Lincoln*. New York: Knopf, 1998

Wilson, Douglas L., Rodney O. Davis, and Terry Wilson, eds. *Herndon's Informants: Letters, Interviews, and Statements about Abraham Lincoln*. Urbana: University of Illinois Press, 1998.

Essay Collections

Donald, David Herbert, ed. *Lincoln Reconsidered: Essays on the Civil War Era*. New York: Knopf, 1956.

Fehrenbacher, Don E., ed. *Lincoln in Text and Context: Collected Essays*. Stanford, CA: Stanford University Press, 1987.

Foner, Eric, ed. *Our Lincoln: New Perspectives on Lincoln and His World*. New York: Norton, 2008.

Samuels, Shirley, ed. *The Cambridge Companion to Abraham Lincoln*. New York: Cambridge University Press, 2012.

Wilentz, Sean, ed. *The Best American History Essays on Lincoln*. New York: Palgrave Macmillan, 2009.

Analyses of Lincoln's Writings, and Speeches

Boritt, Gabor S. *The Gettysburg Gospel: The Lincoln Speech That Nobody Knows*. New York: Simon & Schuster, 2006.

Franklin, John Hope. *The Emancipation Proclamation*. Wheeling, IL: Harlan Davidson, 1995.

Guelzo, Allen C. *Lincoln and Douglas: The Debates That Defined America*. New York: Simon & Schuster, 2008.

———. *Lincoln's Emancipation Proclamation: The End of Slavery in America*. Simon & Schuster, 2004.

Holzer, Harold. *Lincoln at Cooper Union: The Speech That Made Abraham Lincoln President*. New York: Simon & Schuster, 2006.

Kaplan, Fred. *Lincoln: A Literary Biography*. New York: HarperCollins, 2008.

Masur, Louis P. *Lincoln's Hundred Days: The Emancipation Proclamation and the War for the Union*. Cambridge, MA: Harvard University Press, 2012.

White, Ronald C. *Lincoln's Greatest Speech: The Second Inaugural*. New York: Simon & Schuster, 2002.

Wills, Garry. *Lincoln at Gettysburg: The Words That Remade America*. New York: Simon & Schuster, 1992.

Wilson, Douglas L. *Lincoln's Sword: The Presidency and the Power of Words*. New York: Knopf, 2006.

Zarefsky, David. *Lincoln, Douglas, and Slavery: In the Crucible of Public Debate*. Chicago: University of Chicago Press, 1990.

Lincoln As President

Bates, David Homer. *Lincoln in the Telegraph Office: Recollections of the United States Military Telegraph Corps during the Civil War*, 1907; rpt. Lincoln: University of Nebraska Press, 1995.

Belz, Herman. *Abraham Lincoln, Constitutionalism, and Equal Rights in the Civil War Era*. New York: Fordham University Press, 1997.

Boritt, Gabor S. *Lincoln and the Economics of the American Dream*. 1978; rpt., Urbana: University of Illinois Press, 1994.

———, ed. *Lincoln the War President*. New York: Oxford University Press, 1992.

Bruce, Robert V. *Lincoln and the Tools of War*. Indianapolis: Bobbs-Merrill, 1956.

Davis, William C. *Lincoln's Men: How President Lincoln Became Father to an Army and a Nation*. New York: Free Press, 1999.

Jones, Howard. *Abraham Lincoln and a New Birth of Freedom: The Union and Slavery in the Diplomacy of the Civil War*. Lincoln: University of Nebraska Press, 1999.

Klingamen, William K. *Abraham Lincoln and the Road to Emancipation, 1861–1865*. New York: Viking, 2001.

McPherson, James M. *Abraham Lincoln and the Second American Revolution*. New York: Oxford University Press, 1991

———. *Tried by War: Abraham Lincoln as Commander in Chief*. New York: Penguin, 2008.

Neely, Mark E. *The Fate of Liberty: Abraham Lincoln and Civil Liberties.* New York: Oxford University Press, 1991.

Oakes, James. *The Radical and the Republican: Frederick Douglass, Abraham Lincoln, and the Triumph of Antislavery Politics.* New York: Norton, 2007.

Paludan, Philip S. *The Presidency of Abraham Lincoln.* Lawrence: University Press of Kansas, 1994.

Winik, Jay. *April 1865: The Month That Saved America.* New York: HarperCollins, 2002.

Lincoln's America

Barrett, Faith. *To Fight Aloud Is Very Brave: American Poetry and the Civil War.* Amherst: University of Massachusetts Press, 2012.

Davis, David Brion. *Inhuman Bondage: The Rise and Fall of Slavery in the New World.* Oxford: Oxford University Press, 2006.

Faust, Drew Gilpin. *This Republic of Suffering: Death and the American Civil War.* New York: Knopf, 2008.

Foner, Eric. *Free Soil, Free Labor, Free Men: The Ideology of the Republican Party before the Civil War.* New York: Oxford University Press, 1970.

——. *Reconstruction: America's Unfinished Revolution, 1863–1877.* New York: Harper & Row, 1988.

Foreman, Amanda. *The World on Fire: Britain's Crucial Role in the American Civil War.* New York: Random House, 2011.

Foote, Shelby. *The Civil War: A Narrative.* 3 vols. New York: Random House, 1963.

Fuller, Randall. *From Battlefields Rising: How the Civil War Transformed American Literature.* New York: Oxford University Press, 2011.

Goldfield, David. *America Aflame: How the Civil War Created a Nation.* New York: Bloomsbury, 2011.

Goodheart, Adam. *1861: The Civil War Awakening.* New York: Knopf, 2011.

Guelzo, Allen C. *Fateful Lightning: A New History of the Civil War and Reconstruction.* New York: Oxford University Press, 2012.

Holzer, Harold. *Lincoln and the Power of the Press: The War for Public Opinion.* New York: Simon & Schuster, 2014.

Hutchison, Coleman. *Apples and Ashes: Literature, Nationalism, and the Confederate States of America.* Athens: University of Georgia Press, 2012.

McPherson, James M. *Battle Cry of Freedom: The Civil War Era.* New York: Oxford University Press, 1988.

——. *For Cause and Comrades: Why Men Fought in the Civil War.* New York: Oxford University Press, 1997.

Oakes, James. *Freedom National: The Destruction of Slavery in the United States, 1861–1865.* New York: Norton, 2012.

Reynolds, David S. *John Brown, Abolitionist: The Man Who Killed Slavery, Sparked the Civil War, and Seeded Civil Rights.* New York: Knopf, 2005.

——. *Mightier Than the Sword: Uncle Tom's Cabin and the Battle for America.* New York: Norton, 2011.

——. *Walt Whitman's America: A Cultural Biography.* New York: Knopf, 1995.

Samuels, Shirley. *Facing America: Iconography and the Civil War.* New York: Oxford University Press, 2004.

Stauffer, John. *GIANTS: The Parallel Lives of Frederick Douglass and Abraham Lincoln.* New York: Twelve, 2008.

——. *The Black Hearts of Men: Radical Abolitionists and the Transformation of Race.* Cambridge, MA.: Harvard University Press, 2001.

Stauffer, John, and Benjamin Soskis. *The Battle Hymn of the Republic A Biography of the Song That Marches On.* New York: Oxford University Press, 2013.

Stout, Harry S. *Upon the Altar of the Nation: A Moral History of the Civil War.* New York: Viking, 2006.

Wilentz, Sean. *The Rise of American Democracy: Jefferson to Lincoln.* New York: Norton, 2005.

Wilson, Edmund. *Patriotic Gore: Studies in the Literature of the American Civil War.* 1962; rpt., New York: Norton, 1994.

Wineapple, Brenda. *Ecstatic Nation: Confidence, Crisis, and Compromise, 1848–1877.* New York: HarperCollins, 2013.

Witt, John Fabian. *Lincoln's Code: The Laws of War in American History.* New York: Free Press, 2012.

Historiography and Memory

Blight, David W. *Race and Reunion: The Civil War in American Memory*. Cambridge, MA: Harvard University Press, 2001.

Carwardine, Richard, and Jay Sexton, eds. *The Global Lincoln*. New York: Oxford University Press, 2011.

Fehrenbacher, Don E. *The Changing Image of Lincoln in American Historiography*. Oxford: Clarendon Press, 1968.

Kunhardt, Philip B., and Peter W. Kunhardt. *Looking for Lincoln: The Making of an American Icon*. New York: Knopf, 2008.

Peterson, Merrill D. *Lincoln in American Memory*. New York: Oxford University Press, 1994.

Schwartz, Barry. *Abraham Lincoln and the Forge of National Memory*. Chicago: University of Chicago Press, 2000.

Steers, Edward, Jr. *Lincoln Legends: Myths, Hoaxes and Confabulations Associated with Our Greatest President*. Lexington: University Press of Kentucky, 2007.

Index

NOTE: 'A. L.' indicates Abraham Lincoln